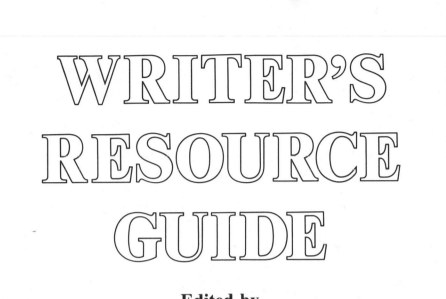

WRITER'S RESOURCE GUIDE

**Edited by
Bernadine Clark**

Cincinnati, Ohio

Acknowledgments

The editor wishes to acknowledge the valuable
assistance of the Reference Department staff
of the Ann Arbor Public Library, Ann Arbor,
Michigan, in reviewing the subject section
bibliographies in *Writer's Resource Guide*.

Writer's Resource Guide. © 1983 by F&W
Publishing Co., published by Writer's Digest
Books, 9933 Alliance Road, Cincinnati, Ohio
45242. Printed and bound in the United States
of America. All rights reserved. No part of
this book may be reproduced in any manner
whatsoever without written permission from
the publisher, except by reviewers who may
quote brief passages to be printed in a magazine or newspaper.

Library of Congress Cataloging
in Publication Data

Writer's resource guide.

    Bibliography: p.
    Includes indexes.
    1. Information services—United States—
Directories. 2. Associations, institutions,
etc.—United States—Directories. 3. Libraries—United States—Directories. 4. Museums—United States—Directories. I. Clark,
Bernadine.
Z674.5.U5W75 1983 027'.0025'73
82-25919
ISBN0-89879-102-2

Book Design by Charleen Catt

TABLE · OF · CONTENTS

INDEXES

The indexes are the winning combination for finding resources quickly. If you're looking for a specific organization or a reference to a particular topic, look in the indexes first. See page 2 for more information about the title and subject indexes.

BACKGROUND INFORMATION

RESEARCH: HOW-TO

SUBJECT SECTIONS

PREFACE

The office of a reference book is,
after all, to bring some sort of
order out of chaos . . .
—William Rose Benét

Writer's Resource Guide does that. It's a reference tool that brings a sense of order to the process of digging for facts. It's a research catalyst . . . your answer to dealing with the chaos of doing research amid a burgeoning information explosion.

Writer's Resource Guide is a book of contacts—connections, if you will—that can open research doors. The *Guide* identifies resources that let you fine tune your own discipline as a writer; it's the discipline that Rachel Carson described as learning to be still and listening to what your subject has to tell you.

But how do you hear the murmurings of your subject against the din of information you don't need? The key is knowing where to look for the information you *do* need. And *Writer's Resource Guide* gives you direction. It'll point the way to an opposing viewpoint to strengthen your article's argument; it'll put you on track to finding experts who can help you sort through the fluff and get to the heart of an issue.

Writer's Resource Guide is a road map of sorts. It's lined with information resources on a direct route to successful research.

But *Writer's Resource Guide* is not *just* a list of information sources. There's joy here, too. It's the joy of sparking an article idea after reading the entry for the Procrastinators' Club of America; of realizing that the background you need for that futures piece is probably in the archives of the Chicago Board of Trade; of discovering that a pesticide expert is just an area code away. It's the exhilaration of "running barefoot through a reference book," that Norman Cousins describes.

Whether you're in hot pursuit of facts or "on hold" between writing projects, take time to meander through the *Guide.* Go ahead and dog-ear the pages. Use it often. I guarantee you'll find something that raises your eyebrow, tugs at a soft spot or sets your mind's gears in motion. You'll probably learn something, too. And that's the joy you get to keep.
—*Bernadine Clark*

INTRODUCTION

Preparation for this Edition

This second edition of *Writer's Resource Guide* greatly expands the purpose of the 1979 edition—to provide writers a one-volume reference tool for locating information sources. This edition is completely revised and reorganized by subject. The subject orientation is beneficial for several reasons: 1) it streamlines and speeds up your search for needed resources; 2) it identifies related subject resources by grouping them in one section; 3) it includes a subject index to help you access additional relevant resources located in other sections of the book; 4) it expands your research horizons with bibliographies for each subject section.

Writer's Resource Guide reflects your need for quick, efficient research tools in the writing life. There are thirty broad subject categories that suggest the thousands of topics writers may need to research. These general divisions are umbrellas for resources in related subject areas.

More than nine hundred organizations from the first edition of *Writer's Resource Guide* were invited to update their original entries. In addition, some six thousand other organizations identified as possible information sources were sent questionnaires. The more than six-teen hundred entries in this edition (over 60 percent of which are first-time listings) represent those organizations which responded to these questionnaires.

Scope of this Edition

Potential resources solicited for the first time and those invited to update their listings from the first edition were selected on the basis of their national scope or interest, uniqueness or relevance and/or the special services they offer writers and other researchers. Libraries, museums, institutes, companies, associations, societies were contacted. Those who completed questionnaires were then linked by subject matter and grouped accordingly. Therefore, you will find national corporations next to one-of-a-kind societies, next to government agencies, next to volunteer groups—all in one subject section.

One of the unique features of *Writer's Resource Guide* is a unifying thread running through the listings: no matter what its subject or scope, each resource identifies itself as willing to share information. Every listing is a lead and a contact for other leads. If an organization can't answer your questions, in many cases it can refer you to other people/organizations who might.

WHAT THIS BOOK IS AND HOW TO USE IT

Upfront Articles

Before using the research leads in *Writer's Resource Guide*, be sure you have a handle on the research process. Six articles written by successful researchers shed valuable insight on the digging-for-information process. The first article looks at the process itself; it's an historical research overview with a bent toward looking at research today and in the future. The other pieces focus on the how-tos of research: using the library; using the government; researching fiction; finding experts; interviewing for information.

Resource Entries

Entries are arranged in numerical order throughout the book and alphabetically within each section. The entry numbers (not page numbers) are used in both the subject and title indexes.

Each listing has been written with information provided from the completed questionnaires, and in some cases, from follow-up telephone calls. Every entry includes a description of the organization and complete contact information, including a title of the person to whom inquiries should be addressed. The *Services* and *How to Contact* sections of the entry detail the kinds of information the organization provides and how and when it prefers to be contacted. Other helpful information includes: how soon you can expect a response; restrictions/stipulations imposed on researchers; costs charged; whether to include a self-addressed, stamped envelope (SASE), etc. In addition, many organizations have offered general research tips or suggestions for doing research in their subject area. Many of them responded to our call for a typical or recent information request. These sample questions will give you an idea of the kind of help you can anticipate, the depth or scope of the research facilities and the size of the operation. The information included in each listing

is intended to help you tap a resource to its full potential and your finely-tuned need.

Indexes

Two indexes are included to speed up your information search. In both indexes, entry numbers (not page numbers) refer you to the resource listings.

If you're looking for the entry number of a specific organization, check the title index, which is an alphabetical listing of all the entries in this edition of the *Guide*.

If you're looking for resources on a particular subject, check the subject index. Headings in this index reflect both popular terminology and those words/phrases organizations used to answer the "Our information covers . . ." question on the questionnaire. If a particular organization listed several areas of expertise, only the major topic areas were used in the index. As in using any subject index, be sure to check synonyms and related words in searching for resources on a specific topic.

Section Profiles

Another way to find resources on a particular subject is to use the Table of Contents. Turn to a category head you think may list a resource you could tap. Consult the brief section profile on the first page of the section. This will give you an idea of what's covered in that section—and what isn't. The profile offers suggestions on where else in the book you might look for a potential information source. Each section is introduced with a comment or reflection on the broad subject area covered therein. (The quotations are a reminder that people are the ultimate information sources.)

Bibliographies

Many representatives of the organizations in *Writer's Resource Guide* have stressed the need for writers to know enough about a subject to ask intelligent questions of the live resources they contact. To supplement and complement the listings in each section, a selected list of print resources is offered. These books can provide both ready reference and in-depth information. Whether the books are in your own collection or on a public or university library shelf, they are packed full of background material and answers.

The bibliographies have been compiled with input from my editorial colleagues, the readers of *Writer's Digest* magazine (who were invited to submit their most helpful reference books) and with the guidance of a knowledgeable public library reference staff. Brief annotations are included for those titles which benefit from a further description of their contents. Explanatory notes are included for such titles as the *ASCAP Biographical Dictionary* and the *Columbia Lippincott Gazetteer of the World*. Various subject periodical indexes such as the *Art Index*, *Humanities Index*, etc., (where you can find out about articles already written on your topic) are listed in the bibliographies and discussed in Alden Todd's article on library research (page 10). *Books in Print* is discussed both in Todd's piece and in John Feulner's article on finding experts (page 23).

Interviews with Writers

Eleven interviews provide glimpses of successful writers and other communicators who talk about their writing and research experiences. From them we learn what goes on behind the byline. The writers talk about the realities of putting pencil to paper; they offer tips, favorite reference books, a whiff of inspiration. Consult the Table of Contents for page numbers.

Comments and Suggestions

By its very aim, *Writer's Resource Guide* should never have a back cover or a final page. New organizations, resources and potential information gold mines are being born every minute. You, as a user of the *Guide*, are invited to submit for consideration in the next edition, the names and addresses of organizations you tap for information in your own research. Keep in mind that the resources should have potential national appeal or provide information/insight in an unusual subject area. Your comments and suggestions for the next edition of the *Guide* are also welcome. Write: *Writer's Resource Guide*, 9933 Alliance Rd., Cincinnati OH 45242.

Important

A listing in *Writer's Resource Guide* is **not** an endorsement of a particular organization.
Each is included for its subject orientation, resource potential and willingness to share information and expertise.

There are many reasons for not finding a particular reference: 1) the organization does not want to be listed as an information source for writers; 2) it does not have the staff and/or budget to handle questions or offer assistance; 3) it did not respond to the questionnaire; 4) it was not included because other entries already provided similar information and space limitations prohibited listing it; 5) its questionnaire arrived too late for this edition; 6) it was not solicited.

RESEARCH: AGE-OLD PROCESS WITH NEW-AGE TECHNIQUE

by Peter Fenner

"Hey, Mary, did you see my data pencil anywhere? I've just had a brainstorm about that oil and gas article I'm writing, and need to check some Petroleum Institute data we accessed yesterday."

"No, John, but your notebook computer is still attached to the communication wire at your kitchen chair. Maybe your data pencil is still in it."

Is this fanciful exchange closer than we realize? Could the time be near when our greatest research problem will be keeping track of where we've mislaid our data source? Or our personal computer? Is it science fiction to imagine a personal "biocomputer" or its significant components implanted under our skin?

Asking the Right Questions

If these questions add sweaty palms to the desperation of the blank page in your typewriter and the fear of refused manuscripts, perhaps a quick overview of the way writers have tackled research and managed information since recorded time will help better prepare you for what research means in the 80s and beyond. If we have a glimpse of how people "researched" in the past, we may be able to understand how we've evolved to now.

Remember that your researching experience as a writer is a matter of pulling information out of dusty recesses and tidy notebooks, then clarifying selectively, accurately, and significantly for your readers. It means knowing what to ask of whom. Technology may change the media, but not the process involved in getting the message.

You may remember CIA Director Casey's jest about an agent named Murphy. It was, the story went, imperative that Murphy personally be contacted at his station in a rural village in Ireland. The code words for recognition were to be, " 'Tis a fair day, but it'll be lovelier this evening."

The covert messenger, upon arriving at the only pub at the crossroads, began to inquire about Murphy.

"Well, if it's Murphy the farmer you'll be wanting," he was told, "he's two miles down the road north, on the east side. If it's Murphy the bootmaker, he's in the shop across the street. And, my name's Murphy, too."

Perplexed, the agent picked up his brew and tried: " 'Tis a fair day, but it'll be lovelier this evening."

"Oh," confided the bartender, "why didn't you say you were looking for Murphy the spy?"

In short, research—more than anything else—has always been a matter of first asking the right questions. To get into your subject you must launch into a series of associations that will result in a conceptual outline whose framework you wish to expand upon and fill in as you go. The entries in this framework will give you the key words, phrases, and ideas that are your basic working vocabulary.

To have a starting gate for the research race you'll run as a writer, you depend on what others have researched before you. You use an earlier systematization whereby data have been organized and new questions anticipated; you'll find sources that have answers and the potential to encourage investigation. The result of your research will be a concise, accurate account of what you learned in the process, filtered so as to be of use to your readers.

Peter Fenner is Executive Director of Education-Training-Communications, Ltd., offering consultation in the areas of higher education planning systems, management and communication. A former university professor and higher education administrator, he has written extensively in the field of geoscience. His recent book, co-authored with Martha Armstrong, is entitled, Research: A Practical Guide to Finding Information *(Los Altos CA: William Kaufmann, Inc.).*

Research Methods of the Past

There's nothing new about the notion that it's important to record information. But how did communicators long ago conduct their research? Civilization has long recognized documents' importance both for matters requiring current attention and for future research. Today we have examples of cultures that do not leave a written record. Aboriginal peoples pass along their "research" by word of mouth—an oral tradition that is mimicked by illiterates among us and by preschoolers in any society.

Surviving written records go back at least five thousand years. Those records have been studied by scholars; from them one can conclude that writing as an art form followed writing for administrative "research" purposes by centuries. Sumerian cuneiform tablets and cylinders preserved records of schools, social reforms, tax levies, political, social, and philosophical thinking. The library at Tello contained some thirty thousand such records.

Assurbanipal's Nineveh Library, about twenty-five hundred years ago, contained tens of thousands of clay tablets—these were, in turn, translated into Assyrian and copied by royal scribes. (Can you imagine entering a library with your own royal retinue and moist clay, and then spending some months taking notes from significant references?)

At the time of the Roman conquest, the world's greatest library must have been at Alexandria—it having then some seven hundred thousand rolls written in many languages. Explaining why that library, under Demetrius's care more than two millenia ago, had achieved such prominence, one writer noted:

> . . . that the sweet, little, old librarian . . . had not only maintained a quiet reading room, he had also operated a small overdue-book goon squad. . . . Travellers arriving in Alexandria were met at the quayside by a batch of illiterate, armed and hairy librarians looking for overdue books. Any book they found in baggage or on persons was automatically overdue at the library in Alexandria. . . .These books were copied; the originals were then cataloged and shelved in the library, and copies were returned to former owners without particular thanks.

The Growth of Libraries

Slowly, the systematizations I mentioned earlier began to take the shape of libraries as we know them. First there were the private libraries—status symbols in Rome. Perhaps those status symbols were one reason why the barbarian invasions later resulted in destruction of even the public libraries that had endured for five hundred years. (Obviously, these were not folks enamored of good research methodologies. They preferred action on the spot, then let others worry about it later.)

During the Dark Ages, monks helped some of the literature survive those barbarian onslaughts. Moslem libraries and Christian monasteries saved much of this record of Western culture. (How much, you might ask, of our concept of history and culture is due to this and later researchable literature? How might our world be different had the preserved written record been predominantly Oriental or African?)

Of a sudden, again, there were libraries. They were small, and manuscripts—some taking a year of painstaking manual labor to produce—were expensive. Research was difficult, because books were stored away from sight in cupboards or chests, and when used were chained to desks.

In pre-modern times, the responsibility for "higher" education (and "keeping the books") gradually was transferred from the monasteries to the cathedral schools, and on to the medieval university. It then became the local book dealer in order to guarantee the authenticity of the pre-Gutenberg books—which were copied by approved scribes and rented to students. The small library of the university still chained important works to desks, but now with chains long enough to permit students a seat at the table while studying. Ah, freedom.

The liberal arts tradition (or the "professional way of letters") evolved about 1700—the consequence of affordable paper, printing presses with moveable type, better inks, some standardization among books, and a resulting spread of writings in many languages. The presses both stimulated and broadcast the results of intellectual curiosity, and they set the research process heading on its way to modern times.

The university became a place in which to do research. The first American colleges all began as, or were founded in association with, gifts of books (although Yale with only forty volumes). By 1725, after nearly a hundred years, Harvard's collection had grown to three thousand volumes. Today's college library-hours dilemma might be looked on with less uproar if we recall that some of those early college libraries were open only one hour every two weeks.

The Information Explosion

That whirlwind trip through yesterday's and this morning's information research domain brings us to now. Some thirty-three hundred currently-accredited institutions of higher education in the United States probably average about seventy thousand volumes in their libraries. The list is topped by Harvard's ten-million-plus volumes and ninety-four thousand current serial titles. In the United States this collection is exceeded only by the nineteen million volumes and 76,500 current serials in the Library of Congress. New York City's Public Library is the next largest in the public domain, with six million volumes and 161,000 current serial titles (and from personal experience I can tell you it shouldn't be overlooked as an excellent resource for certain aspects of scholarly research). Years of systematization are the books on those shelves. And the opportunities for writers doing research have never been better.

The question is: How can we bring order to the information explosion at our disposal? A lot of our success in doing research in the 80s and beyond depends on our use of language. The way we use it may help explain some of the difficulties and simplifications inherent in research methods. Words become keywords for automated computer searches. The way we use and understand those words will lead us to articles, monographs and other resources in whatever field we are researching.

Think about all the information that's ours if we but know how to get at it. In the United States alone, military engineering drawings are numbered in the billions. Fingerprints, photographs, biochemical data on hospital patients, various insurance and ownership records, data transmission on securities, patent information, and myriad other kinds of data become bits of information with the potential of being readily and accurately accessible. All those facts and figures are waiting to be plucked by a know-ing writer who has the language skills and stamina to wade through the fluff and red tape. Researchers today are often bogged down by the cumbersomeness of dealing with such information; in fact, the government is searching for ways to preserve those records and all that information—to translate them via other media so they are easier to handle, to search, and to use for research.

The Computer as Research Tool

With the power of electronics technology, many of the world's significant modern data pools (the stuff of which books, magazines, newspapers and libraries are made) have been converted to electromagnetic impulses. This brings us to the notion of a data base. Should you be thinking of quivering at the sound of the phrase, don't. A data base is nothing more than what its manager makes it. It can be the total working text for your novel. It can be information on all known inhabitants of Atlantis. It can be the titles of the contents of all issues of the fifteen thousand journals that may contain articles about some aspect of geology. It could be all seats available on Transylvanian Airlines's schedules and charter flights through the year 1999.

But before you get carried away with dreams of data bases, there are several important considerations you must make when defining and designing your own method for doing research. For some, the obvious solution is to get a card for your local lending library and buy several packs of three-by-five index cards. For others, it would be foolhardy to do anything short of spending the $2,000 or $20,000 that a personal computer might cost, together with all you would need to turn it into an untiring, steady slave and research assistant (one, I might add, who will rarely need a beer and pizza break).

If you recognize that a computer system is just what you need to maximize your research process, you have several more considerations to make. What kind of system do you need? How much will it cost? How much will an individual information search cost in time, money, staff? What will be the system's total capacity? How many references can you keep track of? How reliable must the system be? How much can you afford to overlook? Can you afford errors of omission or commission in your research? How can you access the system? Is system security or confidentiality of records important to your research? How much access speed do you need?

Defining the right system for your needs will be easier if you have an idea how the data base concept works for writers seeking information that has been published by someone else. A few examples should illustrate its capabilities.

How the Data Base Concept Works

The *New York Times* keeps current an information bank of current events data, indexed from the newspaper and more than seventy other significant magazines and newspapers. Researchers can retrieve general information and citations for specific topics from a base of more than two million citations and abstracts.

The DIALOG Information Retrieval Service (with representatives in several major cities around the world, and with toll-free telephone information available throughout the continental United States) is only a decade old, and it continues to grow all the time. With more than 130 data bases now on the system, it is the most powerful online system of its type. Its data files include more than fifty million separate records that can be scanned usually within seconds or minutes for simple searches. Questions can be asked by computer terminal or teletype via telephone connections.

Here's an actual example. (This will be a simple one, without allowing for options—spelling variants; distinguishing among keywords selected from within a title and abstract, the text of a record on file or the descriptors for that work.) Seeking information about immigrant labor, we learn to query three data bases on the system. The computer terminal tells us that there are 5,639 entries about labor, and 20 about immigrant. If we expand that to request information about related words, we get this: 20 records about immigrants; 35 about immigrants, 126 about immigration, 147 including immigrant or immigrants or immigration (this number represents the likely overlap among the previous categories). If we next ask for records that include those 147 and labor, the new total is 67. We can then ask for a print-out of, say, the most recent 25 of those titles, completely cited, along with their abstracts. We could call for that to be printed out in one of several formats: for example, according to date pub-

lished, author's last name or the journal in which the article appeared. Cost for all of this information—print-outs included? Estimated $12.68; time elapsed, about four minutes.

Get the idea? There are other services that are less ambitious and less expensive. Some are marketed largely for the home computer user and serve entertainment information, stock market quotations, sporting event scores, movie reviews, restaurant critiques, and the like. Some operate on a flat subscription basis (like cable television); others charge on the basis of connect-time, or a combination of those. Within the larger systems (such as DIALOG), fees assessed will vary with the data base accessed. As with the telephone, some systems charge differentially according to the time of day or week when the system is addressed. The distinction previously made between the casual home user and the commercial user or library is now becoming less and less significant, and the means to communicate are becoming standardized.

Of course, there will always remain private systems. Should you elect to begin your own data base for your own research project (as undoubtedly you would), it becomes a privately-accessible file unless you elect to prepare it for sharing, put it on someone else's system, or add it to a larger file accumulated elsewhere. In the latter cases, some authority has the power to dip into your program/storage areas (which usually is the case when operating through a computer center at an institution).

Getting the Computer to Work for You

This quick review of computer capabilities should point out some obvious strengths and limitations of the computer searching process. How current is the "current event". . . ? Did it just miss being included? How carefully was the article you seek indexed or abstracted by a technician? Did you forget that significant variant spelling (e.g., colour, for color) which now precludes your title from being found? Was your Boolean statement (the "question" you ask the computer to get a reply) written with incorrect syntax to get a proper response? Are there too many or too few documents in the file being searched to give you a meaningful response? Is the movie review or article you seek not included in the files you are searching?

As we learn—sometimes through very frustrating experiences—more about managing our data bases and getting them to work for us, our results in working with them get better. Computers are, after all, very fast, but not real smart: they cannot be used (fortunately, I think) to make our subjective decisions. But we can program them with enough information to go through a decision-making process based on selected responses to a given set of inputs. Words matter.

What if you seek information about a plant, for example? You might as easily learn about Ford's Chicago Heights plant as about a hybrid tea rose found growing wild in Chicago Heights! Researchers have learned, after plenty of misdirected searches such as this, to inquire of the data base how many "hits" it contains before printing the responses. Researchers generally request a sample print-out or two before asking for all the information found to be displayed. This allows you an opportunity to go back and redefine your research question—with carefully-chosen words and logical syntax—to make it more accurate, more inclusive, or more exclusive.

Your computer can give you various kinds of information. It can display or print or magnetically store data for later use. It can manipulate statistical data, tabularized and graphic information, literature citations, abstracts or entire articles. As a researcher, your particular use will be easily tailored to your own needs. Today's small office computer comes with programs (sometimes as optional add-ons) that allow you to get directly to the business of writing (word processing); it also has pre-programmed electronic spread sheets (for accounting purposes), mailing list merger programs, inventory programs, etc. And no longer do you have to be able to do your own programming in order to be able to use your own terminal or computer—for that matter anyone else's either. Today it is possible to exchange information on data files among various systems with little difficulty. In some instances, a consulting programmer can tailor whatever modifications you require on a one-shot basis. This would be important were you to want special graphic capabilities (color, for example) or other odd applications. You need not be a very sophisticated user to discover relationships that likely would never have been spotted without a computer.

You, as a writer-researcher, will design your own uses for the equipment available to you. You can use the computer as a scratch pad. As a mailbox. As a filing system. As a memory aid. As an easy way to make systematic changes. (Halfway through writing your novel, you might want to alter the gender of a minor character introduced early on. Punching a few buttons changes Paul to Paula at every occurrence—without your having to locate every place where the name has been used.) For some writers, the most important use might be to prepare "original" letters for potential publishers or to produce "original" autobiographical sketches.

Another service available today uses the computer's power to let you know which authors have cited the work of which other writers. *Science Citation Index* uses this method to let the researcher have a rather direct way of "backing in" to the woof and warp of the networks that comprise scholars' invisible colleges and thousand-volume libraries. For example, say you've found a useful article by Jones on a subject of great interest to you. Jones refers to work by Smith that might be interesting. You'd like to know what else Smith has written—that's the standard search procedure. However, using this additional method, you can determine which other authors have cited Smith's work. That gets you to the other authors who might have more information that is likely to bear on the subject you have been researching. You might even want to check up exclusively on authors who have cited both Jones and Smith in one article—that would be important were there a serious controversy among the schools of thought those two authors represented.

Suffice it, then, to say that searches of literature are accomplished over a wider and wider array of data bases at a lower and lower cost. The doctoral literature searches of yesteryear that might have consumed six months at selected libraries may be accomplished today in six minutes and perhaps with far better results—and at a cost, say, under $100, or perhaps even under $10. Costs depend on the actual time required to search the data base, how many bases must be searched, how large the files are in each, flat service fees, how much information is viewed and how much is actually printed out.

The Future in Computer Research

Now you have the state-of-the-art in a nutshell . . . nut bowl. But to come full circle, what's the outlook ahead? My own guess is that we are just a few years or only months away from being able to market the computer-in-a-notebook that John and Mary opened our eyes to at the beginning of this article.

The PLATO system developed over the past few decades with millions of dollars in research at the University of Illinois is now commercially available and in use throughout the world. Its newest terminals use a technology that allows photographic slides to be projected on thin (plasma driven) screens outfitted with sensors that allow users direct touch interaction with whatever is displayed. You can touch the screen to answer a question or to modify a drawing. A horse might appear as a line drawing on the screen when you touch a printed word HORSE. Touch the drawing, and a voice might tell you its French or Russian name. We have already used liquid-crystal technology to produce experimental flat-screen displays (like the pocket electronic chess games). Commercial availability for a computer terminal screen using that technology is close enough to smell. Little discs, the size of old-fashioned 45 r.p.m. records can hold millions of bits of information; flexible ones not quite as much, but they are easier to handle than an audio cassette for your car's sound system.

Not too far from today, John could use one "cover" of his notebook computer to display his work. The other could be folded open to reveal a touch-sensitive, keyless, input surface. He could use the inside space of such a device to store his own data bases much more efficiently than on today's "floppy discs." Perhaps magnetic bubble technology would be used to put the equivalent into a pencil-shaped, data-base holder in this marvelous notebook computer. He could allow space to store several "pencils" in it. All the rest of his research needs could then be handled by plug connections for other necessary components, such as super-fast, low-energy-consuming print-out devices and telephone connections. Interconnecting devices for other systems would become totally standardized. At that point, John could handle all of his own work virtually anywhere he could balance this battery-driven or solar cell-powered electronic marvel on his lap. If only he could recall where he leaves his things, he could very easily complete that oil and gas article without leaving his kitchen.

Given that scenario, "biocomputers" may not be so far behind in the research world. What's been implanted under his skin will be hard for Johnnie to leave behind! The correct Murphy may be fairly easy to locate after we learn how best to inquire of his whereabouts—and after we learn how to interconnect with others' information banks.

Far from automated dullness, these new technologies are promising greater excitement and additional options for writers who, in doing research, are willing to accept the challenge.

THE LIBRARY: YOUR RESEARCH KEYSTONE

by Alden Todd

Anyone bold enough to be a writer should not be afraid of a library. Yet in sixteen years as a teacher of research techniques at New York University, UCLA and elsewhere, I have found a good many people, including college graduates, who have been overawed by a big library. Perhaps they hesitated to reveal their ignorance of reference books and research methods. Perhaps they feared that librarians would humiliate them in some way. Whatever the reason, these students within a few weeks overcame their hesitations and rejoiced in the new strength they gained from putting library collections to their own use. I believe that every writer should feel completely at home in the libraries within his or her reach, and take advantage of them.

All right, where do you start? It's easy to say, "Just go to the library and look it up." Not so easily done. "The library" may be of no help if the one you go to doesn't have what you need, or if you can't find in it what you are looking for.

Finding Special Libraries

Most of us live within reach of many more libraries than we know, and some of them can serve our needs much better than others. We are well aware of the city library and the nearby college and university libraries. But there are also many more special libraries, so called because they are collections on limited subjects usually run by private organizations for their own members or employees. In your own city there may be dozens, even hundreds, of special libraries run by corporations, law firms, hospitals, museums, social agencies or professional societies—to name a few. The trick is to find them and gain access to the ones that can help you with your writing.

A first step in surveying your local library resources is to ask an experienced professional librarian (NOT just anyone behind the checkout desk). The head librarian is usually a member of the American Library Association and therefore is in contact with his or her professional colleagues in the same city. A second step is to consult the *American Library Directory* (published by the R.R. Bowker Company). This massive book is usually kept in the librarian's office if it is not at the reference desk. It lists more than thirty thousand libraries in the United States and three thousand in Canada. Listings are arranged geographically by state and city, and each entry has enough detail to tell you whether it is worth your time to visit or telephone that library with a query. And there are other directories to libraries that you can discover by asking for them.

Most professional librarians in special libraries are members of the Special Libraries Association (SLA), and in many cities they have formed SLA chapters that have published lists of their members (both people and libraries). A notable example is the *Special Libraries Directory of Greater New York* which lists nearly twelve hundred special libraries in and near New York City. That number startles some of the most sophisticated writers in New York. The simple way to find out if there is such a directory or list in your city is to ask a member of the SLA. If there is such a list, it can often be found at the reference desk of a general library. It is usually kept out of sight, for the use of the staff, and not for readers like you and me. But if you ask, you can get it. In some places you can buy a copy and

Alden Todd is the author of Finding Facts Fast *(Berkeley CA: Ten Speed Press), a book of research methods. A news reporter, freelance book and magazine writer, and corporate publications director since 1946, he has also taught research techniques at New York University, UCLA and many writers' conferences.*

have it handy at your own desk.

In choosing a library for your research, remember that the total size of a library is less important to you than the strength of its collection in the subject field in which you are interested. For instance, a police academy library will have more material on law enforcement than will the city library, and the medical school library will have a better collection on surgery. Aside from the depth of its collections, the special library offers other advantages to the writer doing research. First, its experienced staff members know far more detail than you can usually expect from a reference librarian (who may not be a specialist) in a general library. Second, the special library staff usually has more time to help you because it has less traffic to deal with. Third, the special library is more likely to offer peace and quiet, plus easy access to duplicators.

Writers who would like to use a private special library (at a law firm, for example) may assume they would not be allowed in because, in principle, it is not open to the public. In a very few cases this may be so. But usually the librarian in charge of a special library will extend the courtesy of its use to an outsider, such as a writer, who gives evidence of a serious intent. I recommend an opener that I have often used:

"I am making a study of such-and-such, and I am told that you have the best collection in this field in the city. I certainly would appreciate coming in to see you." —In this way you are buttering up the librarian sincerely, and appealing to his or her pride. It works. I have used dozens of special libraries and have never been turned away.

Locating Books

Most of us are familiar with a library card catalog, and using the subject cards is a logical first step in finding the right books for your research. But the usefulness of that card catalog stops where that library's collection stops. So what about other books dealing with your subject that are not held by that library? You should ask the reference librarian (or a retail bookstore) for *Subject Guide to Books in Print*. This is an annual listing, broken down by subject, of all books offered for sale this year by all publishers in North America. Look up your subject—whether it is schizophrenia, or retirement living, or whatever—and you

can find the title, author, publisher, year of publication and price of all books in print indexed under that subject. Then you can search in libraries and bookstores for those particular books that interest you.

Two other quick tips on finding books for your research:

1. Look at the end of articles in *Encyclopaedia Britannica* and other good, general encyclopedias, and you will find a brief list of reference readings recommended by the scholar who wrote the encyclopedia article. These will be solid, established sources, not sensational or superficial works.

2. Buy your own copy of *Reference Books: A Brief Guide* (published by Enoch Pratt Free Library, 400 Cathedral St., Baltimore, Maryland 21201). This little paperbound book carries the most-useful and best-edited descriptions of reference books that I have found, and it costs only $3 including postage. New editions appear at intervals of four or five years. If you cannot find it in a bookstore, order it from Enoch Pratt Free Library. Then use it to speed up your use of reference books in the libraries where you do research for your writing.

Periodical Indexes

Back issues of two American newspapers, the *New York Times* and the *Wall Street Journal* are frequently on microfilm in many public libraries. Some large public and university libraries also have *The Times* of London. Published indexes to all three are also carried by many libraries. In addition, libraries throughout North America carry back issues of the local metropolitan dailies; in some cases there are indexes to their contents. So it is always worth your time to ask what newspapers the library keeps, and for which ones is there an index on hand.

The *New York Times Index* is particularly valuable as a way of pinning down the exact date of an event, which you can then look up under that date in any other newspaper (or in the magazines likely to have carried articles on the event). In this way, you can use the *New York Times Index* as a rough guide to news articles in all other papers. After that you are on your own in searching for follow-up articles, features and editorials on your subject.

Writers have relied for many years on the

Readers' Guide to Periodical Literature as the best single source for magazine and journal articles bearing on their subject. The *Readers' Guide* directs the researcher to articles in about 180 general-interest magazines, and it is fine as far as it goes. But writers often overlook several other valuable indexes issued by the same publisher (H.W. Wilson Company) that offer a far wider and deeper range of article references in specialized and technical magazines. For instance, law students become familiar with the *Index to Legal Periodicals*, which is usually found in law libraries, or in those of organizations concerned with the law. It indexes, by subject, the articles in some 430 law journals. Just think of the riches you can bring to an article on civil rights, or child custody, or any other subject that brings people to court, if you can quote the biting words of a judge, or give exact citations of cases. How much more impressive this can be than rewriting an article from *Time* magazine!

The same principle holds for using the *Business Periodicals Index*, which refers you to articles in 260 magazines concerned with business. Likewise, there is the *Applied Science & Technology Index*, covering articles in some 300 scientific and technical periodicals; the *Art Index* (200 periodicals); *Biological & Agricultural Index* (180 periodicals); *Education Index* (330 periodicals); *General Science Index* (90 periodicals); *Humanities Index* (250 periodicals); and *Social Sciences Index* (310 periodicals). You may have to search a bit for these indexes because most of them are carried by special libraries rather than by general libraries. But a cordial professional librarian can help you find them in your own town.

Once you have found the index you need and have used it to find references to the articles you want to read for your research, you next need the back issues of the magazines in which they appeared. Chances are that the most likely place to find them is in the library that carries the specialized index you used. Or else you can try another library in the same field—for instance, another law library, business library or medical library. Professional librarians are in a good position to help you find other nearby collections. Chances are, they've been referring readers back and forth between their respective collections for years.

If at first you do not find the index entries you want, ask yourself: What other term might an indexer have used in listing articles on this subject? In other words, try to think like an indexer. For example, you might have to look under "Vietnam War," or "student protest," "Kent State," "riots" or "Ohio National Guard" to find entries relating to the shooting of four Kent State University students during the period of protest over American participation in the war in Vietnam. You should not presume that the indexer has used the same terms that you might use if you had the indexing job.

Vertical Files

A great deal of research gold of value to writers is hidden in file cabinets in thousands of accessible places. Yet to find and use these files you must search in ways different from those you use to locate material in books and periodicals. Files contain just about anything on paper—pamphlets, brochures, and other publications too slim to be classified as books. They may hold publications having limited distribution, such as the news bulletin of an organization. These are not copyrighted, not sold anywhere, and not listed or cataloged anywhere. Mixed in with them may be tearsheets of magazine articles, pictorial material, leaflets, programs, unpublished manuscripts and mementos kept by an individual.

Librarians usually refer to their file collections (other than book collections, periodicals and manuscripts) as "vertical files," and express the extent of their holdings by the number of VFDs (verticle file drawers) on hand. When you consult a directory of special libraries, see how many VFDs a library lists so you can determine how much material it has. The critical question then becomes: How well are the files organized and indexed? A telephone inquiry may save you a trip. If you have a choice, it is the better-organized VFD collection, rather than the larger one, that is preferable for the first look. Although an interested professional librarian can sometimes help you, there is no substitute for examining the file drawers yourself. You know exactly what you are looking for and what interests you; other people don't.

Manuscript Research

There may come a time when you find there aren't printed materials on your subject, and you must look for information in original handwritten or typewritten notes, letters, diaries, logbooks and drafts. Librarians call such original papers "manuscripts." The first step in manuscript work is to find out whether there are any collections of papers which might be helpful in your research, and if so, where they are. You are in luck if the manuscripts you need are in one of the libraries within your reach. The most fruitful place to hunt for them is in research libraries, but they may also be found in the hands of private individuals or in the files of organizations.

An important part of the technique of manuscript research lies in thinking carefully about which people and which organizations would have been concerned with the subject of your research. Then look for their papers. For those papers that might be held by libraries or other repositories, consult the *National Union Catalog of Manuscript Collections* (NUCMC), a series of volumes published about once a year since 1962 by the Library of Congress. A one-volume directory entitled *A Guide to Archives and Manuscripts in the United States* (Yale University Press, 1961) may be helpful for earlier historical research.

Research in manuscript collections is always a challenge because you never know what you will find (or whether you will find anything) to use in your writing. But digging into unpublished manuscripts offers excitement that far exceeds material in print, because you have the sense of discovery—of being there first. In fact, this very excitement can lead you down fascinating paths and away from your subject. If you don't guard yourself against distraction you can lose sight of your original purpose. On the other hand, if the manuscripts interest you to that extent, you may find material for additional articles or stories. I recommend that every writer find some manuscript collection and explore it to see what lies inside. In my experience, everyone who does so comes away enriched and inspired.

Finding Specialists

Reading and libraries aside, you as a writer must also find the people who know your research field so you can interview them. They in turn can lead you to other readings and to other people. Here are two library sources to use in finding the right people for your research:

1. To find specialists in any community, consult the experienced reporters and editors of the daily newspaper, and ask them for the names of experts living nearby. To find the right person on a given newspaper, look at the *Editor & Publisher International Yearbook*, which is the annual directory of the newspaper industry of North America. It lists, for papers big enough to have them, the editors specializing in sports, science, business, gardening, art and other subjects. A phone call by name to one of these people at the newspaper can often put you in direct contact with someone who knows the whereabouts of the specialists in the city. In addition, reporters and editors have access to the newspaper's library with its files of clippings going back through the years. If you play your cards right, you may be allowed to look into the newspaper's clipping file yourself.

2. Another way of finding experts in your community is to determine the associations to which a source of information is likely to belong. Then find a library that carries the *Encyclopedia of Associations* (Gale Research Company) and look in that reference book to locate the headquarters of those organizations. Then write or call to find out the name and address of a member or local chapter president in your area. Though this way of finding experts takes some time, it can get you in direct contact with an expert on almost anything if your town is big enough—beekeepers, antique clock collectors, historians, amateur astronomers or any other recognized specialists. And frequently the expert or specialist whom you find and interview will have a great collection of books and periodicals in his or her private library that may go beyond anything you have found elsewhere. We are a nation of specialists and joiners. Often the best way to find specialists is through the associations they have joined.

To sum this all up, I remind you that our libraries are there to be used, and no one has a greater right to use them than writers. By learning how to put them to their highest use, namely in creating works that inform and inspire others, you carry on the greatest traditions of our civilization. Godspeed!

A WRITER'S ROUTE TO GOVERNMENT INFORMATION

by Leila Kight and Matthew Lesko

Where can you find a free expert on any topic? Where are there millions of published and unpublished market studies and statistical reports available for the asking? Where can one rummage through countless file drawers containing expert testimony about every imaginable issue? The answer can only be Washington, DC. And here's how we found out.

In the mid 70s we quit our jobs (Matthew as computer expert, Leila as higher education administrator), and set ourselves up as information consultants. We were entrepreneurs in search of an enterprise. It didn't take too long to discover that we were sitting on top of an information gold mine. We knew that business people needed information, and that the federal government produced unlimited quantities of it in the forms of people and paper. We knew, too, that business executives, corporate secretaries and management supervisors were busy people who didn't always have the know-how, patience or optimism required to ferret out the facts they needed from the morass of information the government produced. And the government has practically no budget for letting the public know what information is available. Recall that in 1982 the popular monthly *Selected US Government Publications* was replaced with the quarterly *New Books* publication.

We saw the dilemma (tons of information and few people who knew how to get at it) as an opportunity. With that, Washington Researchers was born. Our objective was to get and sell information to business clients who couldn't get it themselves. With little more than a desk and a telephone, we planned our strategy: Matthew would go out and "beat the bushes" for information; Leila would assemble the rough drafts and polish the reports for our clients.

But could we do it? Before we stuck our necks out too far, we had to test our skill. And would people pay to have their questions matched with Washington's resources? A friend of a friend was willing to test our research skills. He had nothing to lose; we only got paid if we produced. Matthew was put to the test. (He picks up the story from here.)

The test was this: To describe, in twenty-four hours, the basic supply and demand of Maine potatoes and explain why they were selling at double their normal price. (The only thing I knew about potatoes was that I liked french fried better than baked.)

Experts Galore

Convinced that there's a Washington expert on practically any topic, I did the most obvious thing. I called the general information number at the US Department of Agriculture and asked to speak with an expert on potatoes. Sure enough, there *was* one—his name was Charlie Porter.

The thought briefly crossed my mind that Charlie Porter might be the in-house code for handling crank calls, but the switchboard operator assured me that Charlie was a bona fide agricultural economist specializing in potatoes. I had found my man!

Now the problem was to get through to Charlie. I anticipated that the distance between him and me would be buffered by scores of self-important or, at least, disinterested receptionists, secretaries and the like. Much to my shock and pleasure, the telephone was an-

Leila Kight and Matthew Lesko are partners in Washington Researchers, an information broker- age firm which offers research services and provides analytical reports, etc., to the business community. Lesko is the author of several books on how and where to get information from gov- ernment sources. His newest book, Information USA, *is a guide to nearly every conceivable government program and bureau.*

swered by Charlie himself.

The next problem was to keep Charlie on the telephone long enough to help me—I was certain that he had more important things to do. Wrong again. I had barely begun my sob story about being a poor struggling entrepreneur in need of a helping hand, when I realized that it was all lost on Charlie. He did not have to be conned or courted. He was, of his own accord, kind and courteous and extraordinarily willing to aid the ignorant. The fact that I would be collecting a fee for the information he gave me was no deterrent. After spending an hour with me on the telephone he invited me to visit him in his office.

Charlie's office was a monument to the potato—it probably represented the most concentrated center of potato information in the history of civilization. For my every question, he pulled a book from the shelf and provided an immediate answer. But the information he possessed was not all historical. Across his desk was a strip of ticker tape showing the daily prices of potatoes from all over the country. In two hours, Charlie explained in microcosmic detail—and more importantly, in lay language—the supply and demand for Maine potatoes. He used overlaying computer print-outs to demonstrate the future demand for potatoes. He explained the misguided reasoning which caused the price of Maine potatoes to double in recent weeks. And finally, he convinced me that prices would soon fall back to their natural level. (If I could have convinced my client, he would be a much wealthier man today!)

Charlie was the answer to my prayers, but the story doesn't end there. Right across the hall from Charlie was a potato statistician, whose sole responsibility was to produce a monthly statistical report showing potato production and consumption in the United States. He even counted the number of potato chips consumed each month. (As I spoke with him, I couldn't help but recall that childhood rhyme,—"One potato, two potato, three potato, four . . .")

All in all, I spent half a day at the Department of Agriculture and got everything my client dreamed of and more. Do you begin to get the gist of the amount of government information out there? The problem is not one of getting enough information but, rather, of being inundated by too much. Once Charlie

started talking about potatoes, it was just about impossible to stop him. I sensed that Charlie had spent most of his life studying the supply and demand of potatoes and was pleased as punch that somebody *finally* cared.

Why all this about Charlie Porter when you don't care a hill of beans about potatoes? Well, the truth is that the federal government is chock full of Charlie Porters. And what we do as business at Washington Researchers, you can do for yourself as a writer in search of information. Granted, the quality and quantity of government experts vary considerably with different departments and agencies, but they are there, and they are available to you.

Our business success can be directly attributed to them and to the government sources they referred us to. Within four years, our business grew from a shoestring operation to an organization of more than forty employees. Today we serve the business community by providing research on any topic; we also train others (through publications and seminars) to find information for themselves. Using the government as a resource could be just the shot in the arm your research needs.

Now that you know there exists a qualified government expert in about any area of interest you could name, you have to know how to derive the greatest benefit from these experts.

Techniques for Winning the Hearts (and Expertise) of Federal Bureaucrats

Over the years, we've talked with a lot of people who have dealt with, or need to deal with, federal bureaucrats. These people sometimes have some very prevalent attitudes. They can generally be summarized as follows:
— I am a citizen and a taxpayer, so the government worker—my employee—is obligated to provide me with whatever I want, when I want it.
— The government worker is a substandard breed who is grossly underworked and not a little incompetent.

Let's replace these attitudes with some new observations:
— The government expert is likely to be a true professional, having spent many years studying a very narrow subject area. That experience *has* to be valuable to anyone interested in the same subject area.
— The government worker is employed by a

tremendous, impersonal bureaucracy where accomplishments often go unnoticed and unrewarded. Such an employee is especially responsive to outside praise and appreciation.

— Bureaucrats get the same paycheck whether they perform poorly or well. Consequently, their motivation to help you depends largely upon their personal sense of satisfaction—and upon you.

We've learned that bureaucrats can help you a lot or a little. Opting for "a lot" of assistance, we've developed a few techniques that can help you understand and motivate the federal expert. These techniques have made the difference in the quantity and quality of information we've passed on to clients over the years. There's a good chance they'll have the same effect for you. At first reading, they may seem like common sense. If you'll take the time to read them again, you may realize that you're not putting most of them into practice on a regular basis.

HOW TO SAY HELLO—The way you open the conversation will set the tone for the entire interview. Whatever the mood of the person on the other end of the line, it will be influenced by your opening comments. Make your voice work for you. Take the first few moments of conversation to show that you will be a bright spot in a bureaucrat's day. You must be pleasant—you must be special.

BE OPEN—You are asking the source to be open with you, so you must reciprocate. If you are deceitful or unnecessarily protective of your position, your source may be wary. If there are certain things you cannot reveal either because you don't know or you recognize that the material was given in confidence, explain these reasons. Most people will understand. If you're working on deadline or doing an article on speculation, say so. People tend to be accommodating if you're upfront with them. You should be as candid as possible so your source will want to be open and generous in return.

BE OPTIMISTIC—A positive, optimistic attitude will work wonders. If you display confidence that a particular source can help you, you'll be surprised how far he or she will stretch in order not to disappoint you. The quickest way to get a negative response is to begin with "You probably don't have any information on this, but . . ." This makes it

very easy for your source to say no, confirming what you already assumed. Try instead, "I have been looking all over for some information; I'm told you're just the person who can help me."

BE HUMBLE AND COURTEOUS—According to an old adage, you can catch more flies with honey than with vinegar. I have never been sure why anyone would want to catch more flies, but I do appreciate the application of the principle to information gathering. Treat your sources with respect, letting them know that you want to learn from them and benefit from their expertise. Such an approach is usually very successful. People in general, and experts in particular, love to tell others what they know, as long as their positions of authority are not questioned.

BE COMPLIMENTARY—This goes hand-in-hand with being humble. A well-placed compliment about the person's expertise or insight will come back to you a hundred times. Remember that, in your search for information, you are likely to talk to several individuals who may be colleagues of your source. It would be an ego boost to know that he or she is highly respected by colleagues.

DON'T BE A "GIMMIE"—A "gimmie" is someone who says "Give me this" or "Give me that," is generally demanding, and has no consideration for other people's feelings. Sure, you may have a legal right to certain information, but your attitude may make the difference in whether you get the *best* information *in time* to fill your need.

RETURN THE FAVOR—This will help you avoid appearing to be one of the "gimmies." You can always share with your source some bits of information or even gossip you may have learned from other contacts. When doing this, be certain not to betray the trust of another source. If you are at the beginning of your research and do not have any information to share with your source, be sure to call back when you are further along.

TALK ABOUT OTHER THINGS—The success of this technique greatly depends upon the personality of the source and his or her time availability when you call. However, you can often help break the ice by talking about things other than your information needs. Show your human side. Talk about the weather or the local sports team. If your source likes you, he or she will feel a greater responsibility to provide you with the information you need.

BE CAREFUL WHEN USING A LIST— When talking to sources, you should have a list of the main points you wish to cover. However, you must not go systematically down a list of questions. This technique results in a rigid and impersonal survey. Your conversation should appear to be free in format, while you are actually carefully noting answers to your questions and directing the discussion toward those items of interest yet to be covered.

LET YOUR SOURCE TALK—Too often, researchers and others in search of information miss golden opportunities by railroading the interview. They are so eager to ask their questions, that they fail to let the source talk. Often, the casual meanderings of a source will provide answers to questions which he or she would have refused to answer directly. Too, the source will experience greater satisfaction if able to provide some direction to the interview and to your overall research effort.

BE PERSISTENT—Last, but not least, be persistent and patient. You may find that industry experts in the government can't give you all the time you'd like to have. Or they may not be able to meet your schedule. Or government statistics may be painfully out of date. Don't despair—use the experts to pick up other government and non-government leads. Use the statistics as a base upon which to build other, more recent statistics. The information you want is almost certainly available, and persistence and patience will pay off. If you forget one or more of these techniques, there is a way to simplify your philosophy. Just remember to treat your information source as you wish to be treated; and don't give up, because the information you need will invariably be in the last place you look!

Starting Points

Now you're convinced that Washington has much to offer. You have the basics for a fine relationship with government employees. But how can you really know what's available? And how can you locate it?

Remember that there is something for everyone in terms of Washington information. Corporate America can find market studies and competitor data. Consumers can learn everything from how to grow better roses to how to trace their family tree. Writers can get insights into the workings of an Equal Employment Opportunity office or just how the National Weather Service tracks a hurricane. Often, you must stretch your mind to find the greatest value in the data, but there's no end to what's available.

Without question, Washington is the information capital of the world. Whether it is the source of endless frustration or surprising discovery is up to you and your creative bent.

Interested in where to begin? The most we can do in this short article is give you a few of the best places to start—then you're on your own.

One of the best buys in directories for Washington information is the *US Government Manual*. It is a must for anyone doing Washington research. Its purpose is to give in detail the organizations, activities and chief officers of the offices in all three branches of government. There are a host of other, more sophisticated publications, but this one is a great value at $9.50. Get it from the Superintendent of Documents, Government Printing Office, Washington DC 20402, (202)783-3238. Be sure to cite stock number 022-003-01082-3 when ordering.

In addition to the *Government Manual*, it's nice to have some ready addresses and phone numbers on your desk. Though it may be true that information is usually worth what you pay for it, there are exceptions to this rule. The following *free* sources can help you begin your research effort or answer a question along the way.

AGRICULTURAL REFERENCES
National Agricultural Library
US Department of Agriculture
10301 Baltimore Blvd.
Beltsville MD 20705
(301)344-3755
. . .Provides published material and research services in botany, zoology, chemistry, veterinary medicine, forestry, plant pathology, livestock, poultry, entomology and general agriculture.

AGRICULTURE AND FOOD STATISTICS
Secretary of the Crop Reporting Board
US Department of Agriculture
Room 5809, 14th & Independence Ave. SW
Washington DC 20250
(202)447-2122

AGRICULTURE INFORMATION CLEAR-
INGHOUSE
Information Office
Office of Public Affairs
US Department of Agriculture
Room 113-A Administration Bldg. SW
Washington DC 20250
(202)447-2791
. . .Provides specific answers or points you
to an expert who can help in most any agricul-
ture-related subject.

ARTS INFORMATION
Performing Arts Library
John F. Kennedy Center
Washington DC 20566
(202)287-6245
. . .Offers reference services in any subject
dealing with the performing arts.

BUSINESS INFORMATION
Library
US Department of Commerce
14th & Constitution Ave. NW
Washington DC 20230
(202)377-2161
. . .Provides reference services in commerce
and business.

CRIME STATISTICS
Uniform Crime Reporting Section
FBI
9th & Pennsylvania Ave. NW
Room 6212
Washington DC 20535
(202)324-5038

ECONOMIC AND DEMOGRAPHIC STA-
TISTICS
Customer Services
Data User Service Division
Bureau of the Census
Washington DC 20233
(301)763-4100

EDUCATION STATISTICS
National Center for Education Statistics
US Department of Education
Presidential Bldg., Room 1001
400 Maryland Ave. SW
Washington DC 20202
(301)436-7900

EMPLOYMENT, PRICES, LIVING CONDI-
TIONS, PRODUCTIVITY & OCCUPATION-
AL SAFETY AND HEALTH STATISTICS
Bureau of Labor Statistics
US Department of Labor
441 G St. NW
Washington DC 20212
(202)523-1239

ENERGY INFORMATION CLEARING-
HOUSE
National Energy Information Center
US Department of Energy
1F048 Forrestal Bldg.
100 Independence Ave. NW
Washington DC 20585
(202)252-8800
. . .Provides general reference services in all
aspects of energy.

ENERGY/TECHNICAL EXPERTISE
US Department of Energy
Technical Information Center
Box 62
Oak Ridge TN 37830
. . .Provides research and other information
services in all energy-related topics.

ENVIRONMENTAL INFORMATION
Environmental Science Information Center
NOAA
11400 Rockville Pike
Rockville Bldg.
Rockville MD 20852
(301)443-8137
. . .Provides information services in matters
relating to the environment.

EXPERT INFORMATION
National Referral Center
Library of Congress
Washington DC 20540
(202)287-5670
. . . Locates an organization that specializes
in providing free information in your area of
interest. See page 269.

GOVERNMENT ASSISTANCE NATION-
WIDE
a) Federal Information Center offices throughout the country. See page 184.
b) Local District Office of your Congressman
or Senator.

HEALTH AND WELFARE INFORMATION
Information
US Department of Health and Human Services
200 Independence Ave. SW, Room 118F
Washington DC 20201
(202)245-6296
. . .Directs you to an office in Health and
Human Services.

HEALTH INFORMATION CLEARING-
HOUSE
Information Office
Box 1133
Washington DC 20013
(800)336-4797
. . .Provides information referral and refer-
ence services in health-related topics.

HEALTH STATISTICS
National Center for Health Statistics
US Department of Health & Human Services
3700 East-West Highway, Room 1-57
Hyattsville MD 20782
(301)436-8500

HOUSING INFORMATION
Program Information Center
US Department of Housing and Urban Development
451 7th St. SW
Washington DC 20410
(202)755-6420
. . .Identifies a program which provides information on all aspects of housing.

INDUSTRY INFORMATION
Bureau of Industrial Economics
US Department of Commerce
Room 4878
Washington DC 20230
(202)377-1405
. . .Over 100 industry analysts supply or
guide you to information about companies and
industries.

INFORMATION FROM ASSOCIATIONS
Information Central
American Society of Association Executives
1575 Eye St. NW
Washington DC 20005
(202)626-2723
. . .Identifies an association that has informa-
tion on your subject.

LEGISLATIVE INFORMATION
Bill Status Office
US House of Representatives
House Annex # 2, Room 696
Washington DC 20515
(202)225-1772
. . .Determines if there is any specific legis-
lation active on a particular topic.

NATIONAL, REGIONAL AND INTERNA-
TIONAL ECONOMICS STATISTICS
Bureau of Economic Analysis
US Department of Commerce
Tower Bldg.
Washington DC 20230
(202)523-0777

SOLAR ENERGY INFORMATION
Conservation & Renewable Energy Inquiry &
Referral
Box 8900
Silver Spring MD 20907
(800)523-2929
(800)462-4983 in Pennsylvania
. . .Provides research, publications and other
information services in solar energy.

TECHNICAL INFORMATION
Science and Technology Division
Reference Section
Library of Congress
Washington DC 20540
(202)287-5639
. . . Offers both free and fee-based reference
and bibliographic services. See page 341.

US IMPORT AND EXPORT STATISTICS
Foreign Trade Reference Room
US Department of Commerce
Washington DC 20230
(202)377-2185

WORLD IMPORT AND EXPORT STATIS-
TICS
World Trade Statistics
US Department of Commerce
World Trade Reference Room
Washington DC 20230
(202)377-4855

RESEARCHING FICTION

by Patricia and Clayton Matthews

Many writers, as well as the general reading public, harbor a misconception about research and the writing of fiction. When we were in Tampa doing research for *Flames of Glory*, a young woman whom we met asked us what kind of books we wrote. When we told her that many of our novels were historicals, she shook her head.

"I love reading historicals," she said, "particularly historical romances, but isn't it awfully dull collecting all those facts and figures? Isn't it boring having to do all that research?"

It took us only a few minutes to change this young woman's mind concerning what researching fiction implies. But there are still many writers and readers out there who look upon research as merely the gathering of dry facts and impersonal dates.

Why Research Fiction

Literary research consists of collecting information of all kinds, and a good deal of it consists of reading everything you can find on the subject. Since writers presumably choose a topic, time and place that greatly interests them, such reading can be fascinating and fun.

One of the main purposes of research is to add the flavor and feeling of time and place to a novel, not only in the writing of historical fiction and family sagas, but in other types of novels as well. This is done by adding the details which describe the life of the period you are writing about. You include such things as details of furnishings, cooking utensils, clothing, manner of speech, political climate, social customs. Each era has its own social mores and morals which affect the actions of the characters who live in it. As a fiction writer, you aim to re-create that era in a novel's pages. Research helps you do it.

Another benefit of research is the enrichment of plot. Most of our books are sold from a brief plot outline, usually completed before any extensive research is done. When we get into the real research, a number of additional plot twists and characters are suggested by certain things that might have taken place during the time and place of the story.

In researching *Love, Forever More* which took place during the silver boom in Nevada, we found in the local library a book on San Francisco that told of an underground city existing beneath Chinatown prior to the great earthquake. Legends of the city exist to this day. We used this idea of an underground city to enrich the plot of our book. We found other books on Virginia City, for example, which told of the Chinese population in that town, and how the Chinese were abused. This information led to writing a subplot featuring a Chinese woman and her son who became important characters in the novel.

Our reading told us that Samuel Clemens was in Virginia City working at the *Enterprise* at the same time of the story. It was there that he first used the byline, Mark Twain. This so intrigued us that Clemens became a minor character in the book, thereby adding a sense of reality to the background. Using a real person present at the place and time we are writing about, as a minor character, is something we both like to do. We believe it adds interest for readers and helps them feel they are there, living the story with the characters.

Print Research

Much of the background material for your

Patricia Matthews, who began writing in 1959, has thirteen best-selling historical romances to her credit. Clayton Matthews, whose specialty is novels of power and passion, has been a full-time freelance writer since 1960. He has written more than a hundred books, fifty short stories and innumerable magazine articles. The two have recently collaborated on a suspense thriller.

novel is written somewhere. And a lot of information is as near as your local library. You will find books on the time, place or subject you are writing about, as well as magazines such as *National Geographic* and *Smithsonian*. These have wonderful photographs, and they seem to have published articles about every spot on the globe at one time or another.

Much historical research can be done close to home. A series of books that we have found particularly helpful is the *Time-Life* books. We have the series on the old West, and the series on ships and sailing. These books, with photos galore, are great for giving you a feeling for a particular time and place.

Other books we keep in our own library are: *Historic Dress in America 1607-1870* by Edith McClellan (Arno Press); *What People Wore* by Douglas Gorsline (Bonanza Books)—this is a visual survey of dress that covers over five thousand years of recorded history; *Domestic Life in England* by Norah Lofts (Doubleday and Company)—since many of America's early settlers were English, this is also useful in reference to our own country; *Seven Language Dictionary* edited by David Shumaker (Avenel Books). These basic books are valuable for documenting many periods and areas. In addition, we have collected books on the specific times and places we have written about. But the bulk of our research reading is done from books in our public library. If your local library is a small one, you can usually order books through interlibrary loan from a larger library.

Besides books, films (travel films in particular) can be very helpful in familiarizing you with locations. Some travel agencies show these to draw customers. And some films may be seen on television.

On-Site Research

Even with the most vivid re-creations that books, magazines and films provide, there's no better way to understand a place than to experience it. One of the most interesting aspects of research (one that we consider important) is visiting the site of the proposed book. Even if the story takes place a hundred or more years ago, it is important to get the feel of the location. The cities and the people may have changed over the years, but the terrain, in most instances, is pretty much the same. Without a visit, though, it's sometimes easy to

make a blunder. Take, for instance, our experience in researching *Love, Forever More*. Though we usually visit the site of a book before writing begins, time pressures prevented us from doing that with this book; the first chapter was written before we were able to visit Virginia City.

Although we had studied maps of the area, and had done some preliminary reading on Virginia City, it became clear, as we drove up the road leading to the old town, that the description of the area (done from imagination) was totally inaccurate. The first few pages had to be rewritten.

In addition to giving us a first-hand look at a place, visits to the sites of our novels usually produce books and pamphlets that cannot be found elsewhere. These are compiled by local historians and church groups; they are often sold in nearby souvenir shops and book stores. Local historical societies are also a gold mine of information for the researcher. They may have old diaries, newspapers and books; their facilities often come complete with copying machines so that you can make records of the material which interests you.

Being there can make a difference in the way you project a place. If you cannot visit the site of your novel, be careful to avoid writing descriptions of details you haven't verified. It is better to leave out such descriptions rather than portray a street, building or the terrain incorrectly.

Another advantage to visiting the site of your story is that you may well get ideas for other books or short stories. When we were doing research for *Love's Golden Destiny*, which takes place during the Klondike Gold Rush of 1898, we became so fascinated by Alaska that we conceived the idea for a contemporary novel concerning a powerful family whose empire had its beginning during that gold rush. Two years later we collaborated on the novel entitled *Empire*.

How-tos of Research

Of course, it may not always be possible for you to visit the area you wish to write about, particularly when you're starting out as a writer. But it's never too early to learn how to conduct on-site research—whether your site is just across the street or halfway around the world.

As far as the mechanics of travel for research go, we usually use the following procedure. We take notes with a micro-recorder, which is only about the size of your hand. It will fit easily into a handbag or pocket. The only disadvantage to using it is that strangers are apt to think you are a bit odd, talking to yourself in public places. The alternative, of course, is to have a good pad and pencil for taking notes. We also make extensive use of snapshots. We find these very helpful, for sometimes you can forget just how something looked. We have photographed locations, houses, public buildings, costumes and artifacts in museums—anything, in fact, that we think might be useful once we begin the book. We find the *Mobile Travel Guides* very useful in helping us decide what to see and where to go in an area. You can get them for every state in the Union.

Research Cautions

Occasionally we will find that our research causes problems. As mentioned earlier, our books are usually sold from outlines because deadlines in the field of paperback originals preclude our doing all the research ahead of time. Some difficulties are inevitable. We recall the problem with *Flames of Glory*. The story takes place against the background of the Tampa Bay Hotel, in Tampa, Florida, during the Spanish-American War. The outline called for one of the heroines to have an affair with a young lieutenant from Roosevelt's Rough Riders. When the in-depth research began, however, we discovered that this comic opera war only lasted "about five minutes." In point of fact, the war did last a few months, but the Rough Riders were in Tampa only a week or so. There was no way a 150,000-word story could be told in a few days of action. The dilemma was solved by having the hero sent to Cuba, get wounded and returned to Tampa. But vast changes had to be made in the outline because our research turned up facts that demanded attention.

There is another danger inherent in researching for a novel. It's easy to become so caught up in all the fascinating details discovered in a particular project that you make the mistake of trying to include all of this material in the book, thereby overloading the reader with information that interferes with the plot. Or you come across an item that really intrigues or amuses you, but you can't use it because it happened either before or after the time of your story. Some discretion must be used so that you do not bury the reader in detail or create confusion in the story's chronology. As we said before, a few well-chosen details, cleverly placed, will serve the purpose and will not slow down the story.

Research Reminders

As a writer you must be aware that research is necessary not only for a novel about historic times, but also for a novel as modern as today's newspaper headlines. We recently wrote a contemporary suspense novel, *Midnight Whispers*, which employed various European settings: London, Stonehenge, Old Sarum, Ireland, Frankfurt, Salzburg, and Zurich. We visited all of these places before writing the book, making ourselves familiar with the cities and sites. Some of this information would probably have been available in books and travel articles, but as in writing the historical novels, we felt it was important to feel the pulse of the places and witness the terrain.

Another point worth remembering about research and travel is that expenses incurred are generally legitimate income tax deductions. This is one of the pleasanter aspects of being a writer. You should keep a record of all costs you generate while doing your research: phone calls, photocopying, purchase of books, tapes, supplies, travel expenses—including food and lodging. Record accurately any expense legitimately charged while researching your novel or short story.

Researching fiction is fun. We thoroughly enjoy doing the research required for our books. We enjoy the reading, the travel, the discovery of new places and ideas. In fact, we believe that you can take almost any place in the world, dig back a few years or a hundred, and find the roots of a fascinating story waiting to be researched.

FINDING THE EXPERTS

by John A. Feulner

There are questions that come into a writer's life which no one but an expert can answer properly. Consider this one: You want to do a piece on the sinking of the *Titanic*. Family rumor has it that a distant uncle was a passenger on that ill-fated ocean liner. But how do you substantiate that Uncle Bill, the family black sheep who died a curious death many years ago in Nevada, was really a passenger? It would be so nice to add this extra little bit of human interest to your story. If only you could find someone who knew the passenger list. Hopeless? Not quite! There is a chance that the Titanic Society, a group of enthusiasts devoted to perpetuating the memory of the British ship that struck the iceberg, could help you.

Why an Expert

So, the question becomes: where and how does one find an expert? Before we entertain that problem, however, let us ask/determine who is an expert. Webster defines an expert as someone "having, involving, or displaying special skill or knowledge derived from experience or training." This definition is useful to keep in mind when you are looking for information; i.e., it is the expert's special skill or knowledge that you need to tap.

Some years ago we at the National Referral Center received the following request: "Dear Sirs: I have to do a science project. Would you please tell me what I should do? And please, when you research the topic and write the report, don't forget that it should be typed and double spaced. Thank you for your effort. Sincerely, Janet W.—P.S. I will need two copies of the report."

No, I am not joshing. This actually happened and I have tried to recount the letter as precisely as I can remember it. Needless to

say, we did not do the research nor write and type the report, double spaced. Politely, but firmly, we told the woman that no one could do this task as appropriately as she herself could. Even so, the story points out one cardinal sin committed by many writers—they want someone else to do their legwork for them. The result is that their requests turn off, rather than turn on, the intended resource.

An expert should be consulted only to provide specific information that cannot be found through regular channels (your library), or to comment or offer expert opinion on some point of controversy. If a writer becomes stumped at a critical point in the research process, that merits a call for assistance; but if a topic simply proves too difficult to handle, it should be simplified or changed.

Where to Find Experts

Before moving into the matter of how to deal with an expert or how best to seek his cooperation, let us first see how one goes about finding an expert. Generally, your search will begin in a library. If you already have the expert's name, then directories like *Who's Who in America*, *American Men and Women of Science*, *Faculty Directory*, etc., can be searched. If you do not have a name, consult the library's edition of *Books in Print*. The *Subject Guide to Books in Print* is an annual volume that lists in-print and forthcoming titles (except fiction, literature, poetry and drama) by one author under Library of Congress subject headings. Checking the 1983 edition under the heading for hitchhiking reveals that four authors have written books on the subject. Or, if an online data base is available in your library, check it to see what authors have already written on your topic. In many instances a reference will include the author's

John Feulner has been on the staff of the Library of Congress's National Referral Center since its beginning in 1962. He has directed its Referral Services Section for more than ten years.

affiliation, i.e., the company where he works, the university where he teaches and/or does research, etc.

Most experts belong to professional associations. This is especially true of scientists, but it is true of all disciplines. An excellent directory which lists these associations is the annual *Encyclopedia of Associations* published by the Gale Research Company. Most national organizations have some kind of mechanism through which they can put you in touch with an expert, be it through a local group, a membership directory (generally available for a fee), or a knowledgeable director or secretary. Another good source, from the same company, is the *Research Centers Directory* which lists university-related and other nonprofit organizations conducting ongoing research.

Colleges and universities in the United States are veritable meccas of experts. Many universities issue directories identifying faculty members and their particular expertise. Others maintain speakers' bureaus. Still others, Pennsylvania State University and Georgetown, for instance, offer yet another service for writers and the media. They issue regular bulletins highlighting faculty members who have been interviewed by writers in the university's public information office. *Story Ideas from Penn State* (issued quarterly) includes a summary of each faculty interview. Transcripts of the taped interviews are available; the public information office also offers assistance in arranging interviews. Consider contacting the information office of a college or university near you to find out how experts on campus are identified.

I do not know of a data base that lists all experts. The economics not only of establishing such a data base, but also of keeping it current would indeed be forbidding. Particularly in America, people are constantly on the move; very few remember or trouble themselves to keep a data base informed of changes in address, affiliation or telephone number.

Other sources of experts include museums, research institutes, regional government information centers, laboratories, offices, and, last but certainly not least, my own organization, the National Referral Center (NRC) of the Library of Congress, which is described in detail in the resource section of this book (page 269).

Expert Referrals at the NRC

The NRC can assist writers by putting them in touch, both efficiently and expeditiously, with organizations and agencies most closely related to their field of interest. To do this, NRC has compiled a data base of some thirteen thousand organizations—*not* individuals—which can either provide information themselves or are knowledgeable enough to be able to suggest appropriate experts.

What are some of the 'information resources' in the NRC data base, and why is this data base different from, let us say, the *Encyclopedia of Associations*? Candidates for inclusion in the NRC data base must possess relevant information, preferably specialized information. They may be libraries and information centers, data analysis centers, federal, state, or local government offices or laboratories, research institutes, university departments and research centers, committees of national or state academies, foundations, the headquarters of societies and associations, museums, herbaria, etc.

The second criterion an organization must meet to be eligible for inclusion in NRC's data base is that it must agree to make its information available to others. There indeed may be restrictions: a laboratory in the Department of Defense, for example, may provide information only to government contractors with an appropriate security clearance; the headquarters of an association may provide extensive services at no fee to its sponsoring members, but limit its services to the public in accordance with time and staff availability. Some organizations may charge a fee for their publications or services, especially if these latter involve computer time, laboratory work, etc. Not of interest to NRC, and therefore not registered in our data bank, are company-restricted information activities or companies providing information only on their products.

A typical search at NRC, using a recent request as an example, would go like this: A writer calls, stating that her interest is the history of saw mills in her region. She has read everything locally available, but can locate neither pictures nor any information concerning the relationship between the local timber industry and the US Forest Service. A search of the NRC data base discloses the existence of a major information center in her state capital. It is maintained by the state's historical society, and has extensive holdings of local newspapers, photographs, and records documenting the time frame in question. This information is transmitted to the writer immediately, who subsequently informs us that she did turn up much valuable, new material. As to her other question, that of industry-Forest Service relationships, NRC locates an expert in the Historical Office of the service. The expert is familiar with the geographical region and time frame and volunteers to get in touch with the writer directly.

Many questions directed to NRC can be answered simply by sending the requester a computer print-out of appropriate information resources, especially if the question is one of general or far-reaching interest, e.g., space flight, food and nutrition, psychological testing, scholarships and grants. A print-out may also be sent when our furnished list of appropriate organizations to contact is a long one. The majority of requests we receive, however, require special research. Consider this one: An advertising executive of a cosmetic company wanted information about a note that appeared in a national magazine. It was the announcement of an archaelogical find of a cosmetic box belonging to an unknown Egyptian princess who lived five thousand years ago. He felt that the old cosmetic box and its contents might be exploited to enhance the sale of some of his firm's products. One of the products he zeroed in on was henna, a red dye used even today in North Africa, the Near East and India to color fingertips, palms, toes and insteps at special occasions like a marriage. But the advertising executive wanted to know about the use of henna as a hair dye in ancient Egypt.

A search of the NRC data base produced only a society of cosmetic chemists. Calls to the society's library and to several members proved negative. However, there still remained the Egyptian angle. A talk with the curator of the Egyptian Department of New York's Metropolitan Museum elicited the information that in the 1930s a woman had written an authoritative book on ancient Egyptian cosmetics and as far as the curator knew, the author was still alive somewhere in New York. With the help of the telephone company and the post office, we did, indeed, locate and talk with her. No, she did not remember ever

having found a reference to the use of henna as a hair dye—fingers and feet, yes, but hair, no. However, if someone had access to the right papyri and could read hieroglyphs, she certainly could still direct that person where to look. We started with the University of Pennsylvania. The university had the correct copies, and for a fee one of the Egyptologists was willing to undertake the study. I do not know how the henna story ended, our task having been completed when we had produced the experts. But I never saw an advertisement for henna as a hair dye, based on the archaeological discovery of an old cosmetic box.

How to Enlist an Expert's Help

This example highlights several important aspects of searching. When you are looking for an expert, be patient. If your trail leads you to organizations the size of the Department of Defense, be prepared to make twenty phone calls before you find the correct agency and then twenty more before you get into the right office. It is not unusual to wind up in the same office where you started, after several hours of intense telephoning and being transferred.

Be ready to pursue the most unorthodox leads and always tell the truth about your ultimate goal—that you are writing a story. Talk to people about your project.

Once you have found your expert, how do you persuade him to help you? As already noted, tell him why you are contacting him and do not bother him with trivia or generalities. Be knowledgeable of what you are calling or writing about; your command of the subject will stimulate your expert to answer your questions. Tell him that you are keen to write your story, and that you want to "write it right."

Always give credit where credit is due. If you obtained your information from someone else, say so. Respect a person's right to intellectual property.

Report truthfully. Do not state as fact what someone else has reported as hypothesis. Do not write "this is" when someone else has said "this could be." Our libraries abound with untrue statements which get perpetuated from one generation of writers to the next. It is true that few of the general public will little know the difference—nor will they care— when you have misquoted an expert. But what of the serious student who may use your untrue statement; or the expert himself who, because of you, may lose face in the eyes of his peers? You can bet he will long hesitate before again helping a writer.

These observations may come through as sounding very didactic; but having been in the business of obtaining information for and out of people for more than twenty years, my observations are based in fact and derived from personal experience.

A Research Hint

When you have consulted the experts within your reach and still lack the information you seek, make a call to the NRC and let us pick up your investigation for additional experts. Do our methods work? When last surveyed, our audience gave NRC this vote of confidence: 85 percent of our requesters did receive assistance from the resources we suggested; of the other 15 percent, approximately half reported negatively; the others for some reason did not use the information we provided.

We know about experts and we exist to tell you about them. There remains a final bonus in contacting us: NRC's services are free for the asking to anyone—anywhere.

HOW TO CONDUCT THE INTERVIEW

by Dale Stevens

A moment with an actor in England sticks out in my mind when I think of interviewing over the years. He was calm and pleasant and in the course of the conversation he suddenly said, "You know, an actor never wins an interview." Years later I finally realized what he meant, and the revelation has colored my style since. I believe he meant that when the subject of an interview is asked a question, it creates thousands of little ramifications and shadings of ideas in his mind. You hear the answer. But you have no idea of the thousands of life experiences left unspoken which surrounded what the person was able to say. You get—by necessity—a piece of an answer, a fragment of a mind at work.

And there's more to it. A reporter, no matter how well intentioned, goes back to his typewriter or computer terminal and writes the story from his own point of view. And no matter how fair and accurate he or she might be, it will be subtly different from the story the interviewee would have written with the same questions and answers. So the actor, celebrity or expert can't really win the interview.

Does that mean only the reporter can? No, that would be a hollow victory. It's supposed to be the reader who wins.

No Two Are Alike

I love interviewing and if I have one tip for developing an interviewing technique, that would be it. Love interviewing. It is almost psychiatric, though psychological is the better word. A battle of wits. You against them. "Tell me who and what you are, whether you want to or not." An invasion of privacy into the most vulnerable place—the mind. So you

might as well understand going in—most people don't really want to be interviewed. Some do it because the ego overcomes all. Some are thrust into it by accident when a son, perhaps, is arrested on a murder charge. Most are using it for their own advantage—to promote a book or movie or recording.

I have interviewed people under those circumstances for newspapers or my own talk shows on television and radio: Burt Reynolds, Mick Jagger, Frank Sinatra, Lenny Bruce, Brooke Shields, Spencer Tracy, John Belushi, Marilyn Monroe, John Travolta, Dolly Parton, Robert Redford, the Beatles, Dudley Moore, Clark Gable, Kiss, Dizzy Gillespie, Elizabeth Taylor, Elvis, and on and on.

Burt was lightly arrogant. Jagger surprisingly friendly. Sinatra warm and helpful. Lenny brilliant. Brooke just a tot. Tracy guarded. Belushi effusive. Marilyn was seeking approval. Travolta seemed vulnerable. Dolly is maybe the easiest ever, both frank and funny. Redford can't be reached. The Beatles were bright and challenging . . . In other words, you need different techniques for everyone you interview.

Developing an Interview Style

I'm not going to bore you with the old awareness that establishing a quick rapport is the answer. By that time it might be too late. The answer is a personal style. It goes like this:

Research is half the game. Check the files (a library, a press kit, your memory) and know your subject. Make your first question as perceptive and interesting as possible. Don't give a damn whether they like you, but make them respect you.

That last bit of style reminds me of re-

Dale Stevens is an entertainment critic for the Cincinnati Post. *His pursuits in the communications field have included experience as reporter, magazine editor, sportswriter, disc jockey, television show host and comedy straight man. Stevens has interviewed movie stars on location around the world. He is currently writing two books—one on celebrities, one on jazz.*

searching actress Julie Harris. I found a quote in a *Time* magazine story in which she had said, "If I had boobs, I could rule the world." When I pitched that one at her, she turned to her husband and said, "Did I say that?" He assured her she had and the aura of a fine actress lacking only a Hollywood body became a good central theme.

On the other hand, there was Elvis Presley, who gave interviews only in his first flush of stardom. The problem with researching him was he would say only what his manager, Colonel Tom Parker, had programmed him to say: he ate only hamburgers; he wanted to be an actor like James Dean. Boring, and nothing would pull him out of it. That was twenty-five years ago, but it was an indication of things to come. Today, the toughest celebrity interview is any rock star. Most won't do interviews unless it's a rush job by long-distance telephone where they can hang up on a whim if they don't like your attitude. Barry Manilow would be a rare exception to that rule.

Words aren't the only answer, though. Any interview with another human is a revelation. You learn something about them no matter what they say or how they say it. If Burt Reynolds treats every serious question as a joke, it tells you he needs it as a defense mechanism. If Brooke Shields won't talk without a protective entourage, you quickly find out it's because she is so remarkably immature they need to be there to finish her sentences.

This is part of the thought that the subject of the interview can't win the interview. But the fact is, the writer has to supply the atmosphere, the background, the psychological setting and make a judgment on the person being interviewed. You don't have to call a bore, a bore. But if you can't bring the story alive with your own lively style, you'll be a bore, too.

Comedian/actor Jonathon Winters was aware of that. "Don't use your words," he quipped after the interview. "Just use mine." In that way, he might have won the interview.

Get Them Angry

Winning an interview is more than a minor tug of war. The person being interviewed has to say something interesting. The writer has to assemble it all and add a dimension, an awareness. Because simply, the reader must be intrigued or entertained.

Fortunately, there is a saving technique when you're up against the quiet subject, or a reluctant subject. But you should be aware of the possible consequences. The quiet subject usually is merely inarticulate. The reluctant one is protective. The trick with each is to get them angry. Goad them. Offend them, if necessary. This is not unfair. A certain amount of give and take is involved in any discussion between two professionals. Differences of opinion are healthy and productive. The quiet one probably isn't aware of that. I doubt if Elvis understood how boring he was. But the reluctant one understands perfectly. Robert Redford knows all the tricks. He knows when he's being manipulated. That's why he seldom gives interviews. Even getting him angry isn't easy. He knows what you're doing.

So how do you get them angry? Not with a dumb question, please. You can prime the pump by challenging their sincerity, their goals, their performances, their choice of material. The best comments I got from Dr. Albert Sabin, who perfected the polio immunization, came when I challenged the work of scientists when their achievements resulted in military weapons such as the atomic bomb and its radiation. Redford doesn't want to hear that any of his films were trivial. The Bee Gees rise angrily at the suggestion their singing style is accomplished by the engineer in the recording studio. Christopher Reeve, interestingly, resents any concentration upon his success as "Superman." Like Marilyn Monroe, he wishes to be taken seriously and he fights for it.

Where to Interview

One of the more difficult aspects of an interview is that the writer has virtually no control of the physical circumstances. Touring celebrities often want to do it over dinner in the city's most prestigious restaurant. Talking with a mouthful of escargot is difficult. So is putting down your fork after every sentence to write the quote. The plus side is, a restaurant setting usually guarantees you a couple of hours or more, and a good interview takes time.

However, I prefer to do the interview in the performer's hotel room where you both can be comfortable. It's worth turning down a lunch or dinner setting, though a few drinks over dinner can be wonderful for opening up a tough interview.

You might have to settle for taxi or limousine rides to or from an airport, jotting notes between potholes. Worse yet, you can be trapped in a press conference where a good angle seldom gets a follow-up because the next question veers in another direction. Telephone interviews are thankless because they usually connect an hour or two after the agreed time and end too quickly. The lack of eye contact can be fatal.

If you have good typewriter speed, it's great for keeping up with the quotes. Not many writers seem to use a typewriter during an interview. And only a telephone chat makes it possible. So the choice of techniques comes down to scribbling on paper or using a tape recorder. Some performers pointedly avoid a tape recorder, though their reasoning escapes me. It provides the most accurate quotes possible.

I have perfected a technique for the unique crowd interviews many movie companies use when they group five to ten reporters at several tables, with the star moving from table to table. I take two tape recorders. One I move from table to table with the star; the other I use at my own table when the director or secondary performers are there.

I've done a lot of dressing room interviews, in night clubs or theatres. Plenty, too, in the Hollywood movie studios. Talking to director Cecil B. DeMille and actor Charlton Heston in his Moses costume for *The Ten Commandments* seemed an awesome occasion at the time. And I've done interviews at faraway locations—with Julie Andrews in Salzburg, Austria, during *The Sound of Music*; Heston again, in the Sistine Chapel of the Vatican during *The Agony and the Ecstacy*.

Those kinds of moments are memorable, but valuable only for what they add to a story. I once stood in line for the lobby telephone at Romanoff's restaurant in Hollywood and the guy ahead of me who handed me the phone turned out to be Humphrey Bogart. I didn't say a word to him, but it gave me one of those flashes of insight I could use in later stories. It was the same kind of indelible accumulation I got one night in Cartagena, Colombia, when Marlon Brando, at the next table, asked me for a match and I lit his cigarette, again without saying a word. Observations, with or without words, are part of the story.

Today's Interviews

Times have changed in the thirty-six years I've been a journalist. Movie stars, nightclub comedians, Broadway actors, singers, and all their agents and managers once sought out the writers and made an interview an easy thing. Today only few celebrities—mostly young ones on the way up or old ones on the way down—seek interviews. It's better that way in the sense that we're not being "used" beyond our own awareness and willingness to be used. It's easier to conduct a tough interview now and skip the fluff.

Competitively speaking, the fearless interview is a must. Younger critics and reporters, spawned after Woodward and Bernstein uncovered Watergate and unseated a president, view their job as investigative, no matter who they're talking with. That's why technique is more important today; why you have to plan ahead, be probing, suggest the unexpected.

Today, a Dolly Parton (a wonderful interview subject) will talk about her love life and fantasies, even her physical ailments. These days, performers will argue with an interviewer. Challenge the writer's premise. Risk an unfavorable story. Today, an interviewer must be more skillful, more knowledgeable, more truthful. Being controversial is easy. Being fair within a controversial arena is the trick, and the public quickly separates the pros and the cons.

In recent months I've talked with Cleo Laine, Roger Moore, Sally Field, Harry James, George Carlin, plus movie directors, stuntmen, a Disney art director. The subjects have varied enormously. The technique hasn't. It might come down to the old "what are they like, really?" But it also comes down to maintaining the proper respectful distance, refusing to accept nonsense in place of an honest reply, showing a sincere curiosity and liking for the subject, and truly enjoying the conversation. It means actually listening to what they say instead of groping for a next question. And it means being able to go back to the office and place them within the correct context in their field. It means adding what I know about their business, as well as letting them talk.

You can do a hundred important interviews a day, but if you can't put it all together when the time comes to write, it's the reader who loses the interview.

SECTION · ONE

ANIMALS AND PLANTS

I think I could turn and live with animals,
they are so placid and self-contain'd . . .
                              —Walt Whitman

Our vegetable garden is coming along well,
with radishes and beans up, and we are less
worried about revolution than we used to be.
                              —E.B. White

Animal resources herein provide information
on pets, wildlife, endangered species, zoos

and the welfare of animals in general. Plant
resources offer information on horticulture,
botany, plant care, trees, hobby gardening, ar-
boretums and botanical gardens.

Additional listings related to plant and animal conservation are found in the Environ-
ment/The Earth section; information on the
use of animals and plants as food is available
in the Farming and Food category; references
to horses in racing sports are found in the
Sports section.

Bibliography

Bailey, Liberty H., ed. *Hortus Third: A Concise Dictionary of Plants Cultivated in the US &*
Canada. New York: Macmillan, 1976.

Burton, Maurice and Robert, eds. *The New International Wildlife Encyclopedia.* 21 vols.
Milwaukee: Purnell Reference Books, 1980.

Encyclopedia of Organic Gardening. Edited by Organic Gardening and Farming Magazine.
Emmaus, PA: Rodale Press, Inc., 1978.

Everett, T.H. *Encyclopedia of Horticulture.* 10 vols. New York: Garland Publishing, 1981.

Faust, Joan L. *New York Times Book of Flower Gardening.* New York: Times Books, 1982.

Faust, Joan L. *New York Times Book of Vegetable Gardening.* 1974. Reprint. New York:
Times Books, 1982.

Grzimek, Bernard, ed. *Grzimek's Animal Life Encyclopedia.* 13 vols. New York: Van Nostrand Reinhold, 1972-75.

Halpin, Anne M., ed. *Rodale's Encyclopedia of Indoor Gardening.* Emmaus, PA: Rodale
Press, Inc., 1980.

Kolisko, Eugen, ed. *Zoology For Everybody.* 2d ed. 4 vols. Spring Valley, NY: St. George
Book Service, 1977-80.

Manolsen, Frank, ed. *The Pet Encyclopedia.* Nashville, TN: Thomas Nelson Publishers,
1981.

1• ALL-AMERICA SELECTIONS
628 Executive Dr., Willowbrook IL 60521. (312)655-0010. Contact Person: Executive
Secretary. **Description:** "We test and evaluate flowers and vegetables for the home garden
conditions in the US and Canada." **Services:** Provides advisory and trade information. Offers
photos. **How to Contact:** Write. Responds to most inquiries within a month.

2• AMATEUR ENTOMOLOGISTS' SOCIETY
c/o 355 Hounslow Rd., Hanworth Feltham, Middlesex, England TW13 5JH. Contact Person:
General Editor. **Description:** Society for the furtherance of entomology for amateurs by
publications, field meetings and exhibitions. **Services:** Provides advisory, bibliographical,
how-to and referral information on entomology. "We have an advisory panel of experts on all
orders of insects." Offers brochures/pamphlets, publications. **How to Contact:** Responds to most
inquiries within a month. Services available only to members.

3• AMERICAN ASSOCIATION OF ZOOLOGICAL PARKS AND AQUARIUMS
Oglebay Park, Wheeling WV 26003. (304)242-2160. Contact Person: Executive
Director. **Description:** "Nonprofit association dedicated to the advancement of zoological parks
and aquariums for conservation, education, scientific studies and recreation." **Services:** Provides

advisory and referral information on the establishment of zoos and aquariums and federal wildlife laws. Offers brochures/pamphlets, informational newsletters and statistics. Publications include *Directory of Zoological Parks and Aquariums in the Americas*; annual and regional conference proceedings. **How to Contact:** Write. Responds to most inquiries within a week. Charges for some publications.

4• AMERICAN BONSAI SOCIETY, INC.
Box 358, Keene NH 03431. Contact Person: Executive Secretary. **Description:** "We are a nonprofit organization and educational corporation which promotes interest in and knowledge of bonsai." **Services:** Provides information on bonsai and how-to of growing, shaping and producing bonsai trees and landscapes. "Privileges include bonsai lending library, a question and answer service, tours, and film and slide rentals." Publications include a quarterly *Journal*; *ABStracts* pamphlet. **How to Contact:** Write. Responds to most inquiries within a week.

5• AMERICAN FARRIER'S ASSOCIATION
Box 695, Albuquerque NM 87103. Contact Person: President. **Description:** "The association is composed of professional horseshoers and other interested individuals brought together by several common needs: (1) to promote the science of and interest in the farrier, (2) to inform the horse-owner of the quality and standard of farrier service to which he and his horse are entitled, (3) to provide a means to develop and express policies of the profession to the public and private/public organizations, (4) to establish a medium for discussion of mutual problems, and (5) to assist in developing public understanding and appreciation of the horseshoer's role and contribution to the use and enjoyment of horses." **Services:** Provides advisory, analytical, referral and trade information on all phases of the horse industry: research and development of products and services, competition, performance, production, and merchandising. "Competency of the farrier is also our concern, as is the quality of education and training available to aspiring horseshoers." Offers aid in arranging interviews and brochures/pamphlets. Publications include member newsletter. **How to Contact:** Write. Responds to most inquiries within a week.

6• AMERICAN FEDERATION OF AVICULTURE
Box 1568, Redondo Beach CA 90278. (213)372-2988. Contact Person: Office Manager. **Description:** A.F.A is nonprofit organizaton whose purpose is "to help conserve the world's avian wildlife through education, research, and captive breeding." **Services:** Provides advisory, analytical, historical, how-to, referral, technical and trade information on all aspects of aviculture, keeping and breeding birds in captivity, avian medicine. Offers aid in arranging interviews, brochures/pamphlets, informational newsletter, photos and telephone reference services. "We have on file the most extensive collection of avicultural literature to be found. We have an excellent photo library and can refer writers to many experts in the field of conservation and aviculture." Publications include A.F.A. *Watchbird*; slide shows on lovebirds, cockatiels, finches; *Endangered Species Portfolio*; *Avian Medicine Seminar Proceedings*. **How to Contact:** Write or call. Responds to most inquiries within a month. "Some photos are available for fees ranging from $50-$100." **Tips:** Recent information requests: "How may bird-oriented people are there in Southern California?"; "How large is the advertising market and how can it be contacted?"

7• AMERICAN HORSE COUNCIL
1700 K St. NW, Suite 300, Washington DC 20006. (202)296-4031. Contact Person: Director of Publications. **Description:** "The purpose of our organization is to protect the horse and the horse industry through the legislative process." **Services:** Provides advisory, analytical, historical, how-to, referral and trade information on horses, racing, showing, trails, sport, statistics, etc., and legislation relating to those subjects. Offers brochures/pamphlets, informational newsletters, research assistance, statistics and telephone reference services. Publications include *The Horse Industry Directory*; *AHC Business Quarterly*; *Tax Tips for Horse Owners*; *The Horse Owners and Breeders Tax Manual*, and various pamphlets regarding the horse industry and aspects of the horse industry. **How to Contact:** Write or call. Responds to most inquiries within a week. Charges for materials to nonmenbers. Respect copyright and give credit to American Horse Council; "advertising exchanges may be arranged." **Tips:** "Be careful whom you quote, and don't take things out of context to suit a story. Give us a call; we'll do what we can—what we can't, we can most probably refer." Recent information requests: "What is the approximate number of horses in

each state?''; ''How much money is involved in the horse industry?''; ''What has the horse industry growth been in the last five years?''

8• AMERICAN HORSE PROTECTION ASSOCIATION
Box 53399, 1904 T St. NW, Washington DC 20099. (202)745-0611. Contact Person: President. **Description:** ''The Association is concerned with the welfare of horses, both wild and domestic.'' **Services:** Provides advisory and how-to information on horse abuse; federal legislation related to horse issues, i.e., wild horses, etc. Offers brochures/pamphlets, informational newsletters and photos. Publications include a quarterly newsletter. **How to Contact:** Write, call or visit. Responds to most inquiries immediately.

9• AMERICAN HORTICULTURAL SOCIETY
7931 East Boulevard Dr., Alexandria VA 22308. (703)768-5700. Contact Person: Publications Director. **Description:** ''Our organization educates individuals and organizations about horticulture and the horticultural field in the US.'' **Services:** Provides advisory, how-to, referral and technical information on horticulture. Offers informational newsletters, magazine, library facilities and research assistance. Preference given to AHS members. **How to Contact:** Write. Responds to most inquiries within a week. ''Credit the society when obtaining information from one of our publications.''

10• AMERICAN SOCIETY FOR THE PREVENTION OF CRUELTY TO ANIMALS
441 E. 92nd St., New York NY 10028. Contact Person: Head of Publications. **Description:** A nonprofit society dedicated to preventing cruelty to animals through humane law enforcement, humane education, and the distribution of informational materials to the media and public. Also maintains two NYC shelters open 24 hours a day, seven days a week; runs 4th largest veterinary hospital in America; has ambulance rescue service for stray and injured animals; and operates Animalport, pet boarding facility at Kennedy Airport. **Services:** Provides advisory and how-to information and news and feature articles about animal-related issues. Will arrange interviews; offers pamphlets and brochures (request ''Educational Resource List'' for complete list of available materials), *ASPCA Report* (newsletter), statistics, press releases. **How to Contact:** Write or call. Responds to most inquiries within a month. ''Some materials are free. Many are low-cost. For the use of photographs, we generally charge $30. The ASPCA should be given credit.'' **Tips:** ''Be specific in your request for information. Often, someone will ask for material on 'cruelty.' That could range from dogfighting to fur trapping to animal experimentation, and we have information on them all. Query first. Follow up with phone call if no response within 2 weeks.'' Recent information request: ''How many dogs are there in America?''

11• AMERICAN VETERINARY MEDICAL ASSOCIATION
930 N. Meacham Rd., Schaumburg IL 60196. (312)885-8070. Contact Person: National Media Coordinator. **Description:** The association works ''to advance the science and art of veterinary medicine, including its relationship to public health and agriculture.'' **Services:** Provides historical, how-to, interpretative, referral, technical and trade information on all aspects of veterinary medicine—canine, feline, equine, bovine, porcine, laboratory animal, public health, research, etc. Offers aid in arranging interviews, annual reports, biographies, brochures/pamphlets, library facilities, photos, placement on mailing lists, press kits and statistics. Publications include various brochures and reprints. **How to Contact:** Write, call or visit. Responds to most inquiries immediately. **Tips:** ''If you don't know where to start, contact us first and we'll do our best to help.'' Recent information requests: Questions on pet health insurance; canine parvovirus infection; veterinary careers; veterinary specialization; cancer in dogs.

12• ANIMAL BEHAVIOR SOCIETY
c/o Department of Zoology, Clemson University, Clemson SC 29631. Contact Person: Secretary or Newsletter Editor. **Description:** ''The Animal Behavior Society is a nonprofit, interdisciplinary, membership organization composed of scientists and other persons engaged in the study of animal behavior. It exists to promote a vehicle for cooperation among the many people who work in this field.'' **Services:** ''We have no salaried staff. As volunteer time is available, we will refer writers to experts on specific areas of animal behavior.'' Information covers (ethology, sociobiology, behavioral ecology, evolution of behavior, etc.). Offers brochures/pamphlets. Publications include *Animal Behavior* and *ABS Newsletter* (four times a year, for members);

Guidelines for Animal Care (a brief paper designed for scientists who use animals in research); *Graduate Programs in Animal Behavior* (send $1 for postage); a list of films in animal behavior; *Guidelines for the Use of Animals in Research*; a list of textbooks in the field; and *The Scope of Animal Behavior*, (an information sheet). **How to Contact:** Write. Responds to most inquiries within a week. "Postage for publications would be a help." For rental of the mailing list of ABS members, contact the Treasurer, Animal Behavior Society, Department of Zoology, Bartram Hall, University of Florida, Gainesville FL 32611. **Tips:** "The Animal Behavior Society holds an annual meeting where current research is presented. A press facility is available. Here a reporter can find out first-hand what scientists who study animal behavior are doing and why the study holds the interest of so many top researchers."

13• ARGUS ARCHIVES
228 E. 49th St., New York NY 10017. (212)355-6140. Contact Person: Research Associate. **Description:** Argus Archives is a foundation promoting the humane treatment of animals. "In its archives Argus maintains active files on over five hundred organizations in the U.S. and abroad. The files contain publications of these organizations dealing with animal suffering or conditions which affect the well-being of animals. There is a related collection of books, magazines, newspaper clippings and film reviews." **Services:** Provides information on attitudes towards animals, euthanasia, exhibitions (including zoos), fights, films, fishing, food and commercial uses (including furs, cosmetics, vaccines), humane education, hunting, legislation, performing animals, pets (including shelters), racing, research and testing, riding, science education, service animals, shows, transportation, trapping, veterinary medicine and wildlife. Offers library facilities and publications list. Publications include *Films for Humane Education* (manual of film and filmstrip reviews); *Alternatives to Pain in Experiments on Animals*; *Traps and Trapping—Furs and Fashion*; and *Unwanted Pets and the Animal Shelter—The Pet Population Problem in New York State*. **How to Contact:** Write. Responds to most inquiries within a week. "Writers, researchers and members of organizations engaged in humane work or conservation are welcome to consult the archives (by appointment)." Charges for books and publications and photocopies. **Tips:** "It's best to tell us area of interest before visiting—a time saver for all. The only questions *we* answer are organizational, but researchers have complete access to our resources."

14• ARNOLD ARBORETUM OF HARVARD UNIVERSITY
The Arborway, Jamaica Plain MA 02130. (617)524-1718. Contact Person: Public Relations Officer. **Description:** Arnold is both a 265-acre public park and university facility. "The arboretum is a public park and botanical collection of trees and shrubs. Faculty conduct botanical research on the living collections and staff provide a wide range of public programs and events." **Services:** Provides advisory, bibliographical, historical, how-to, interpretative, referral, technical and trade (horticulture) information about plants, history of the Arnold, general botanical and horticultural issues. "We have an extensive library and herbarium, and horticulturists and botanists on staff." Offers aid in arranging interviews, annual reports, brochures/pamphlets, computerized information searches (about plants at arboretum), informational newsletters, library facilities, photos, placement on mailing lists, press kits. "We do our best to put writers in touch with expert members on staff." Publications include *Arnoldia* (horticultural journal); *Journal of the Arnold Arboretum* (very technical); and *Plant Sciences* (newsletter). **How to Contact:** Write, call or visit. Responds to most inquiries within 2 weeks. Charges for journals; small cost for slides or photocopies. Library and herbarium use by appointment. **Tips:** "We have such vast resources about plants at Arnold; writers should have specific idea in mind so we can help set up interviews and get resource material together." Recent information request: "Who was Frederick Law Olmsted and why was he important to Boston?"

15• ASSOCIATION OF SYSTEMATICS COLLECTIONS
University of Kansas, Museum of Natural History, Lawrence KS 66045. (913)864-4867. Contact Person: Director of Operations. **Description:** "We are an organization of natural history museums and research biologists." **Services:** Provides advisory, historical, how-to, interpretative, referral, technical and trade information on biology, pest control, museum management and computer uses in museums. Offers aid in arranging interviews, annual reports, brochures/pamphlets, informational newsletters, placement on mailing lists and telephone reference services. Publications include *Controlled Wildlife*; *Pest Control in Museums*. **How to Contact:** Write. Responds to most inquiries within a week. Charges for extensive information. **Tips:** Recent information request: Current listing of endangered species.

16• BIDE-A-WEE HOME ASSOCIATION
410 E. 38th St., New York NY 10016. (212)532-6358. Contact Person: Director of Public Relations. **Description:** "We are a nonprofit animal welfare organization. Our main function is finding new homes for dogs and cats that can no longer be kept by their owners. Bide-A-Wee never destroys an animal unless incurably ill; once accepted into a Bide-A-Wee shelter an animal is kept until a suitable home is found. We also operate veterinary clinics and pet memorial parks and conduct a large number of community programs." **Services:** Provides advisory, how-to (pet care), referral and trade information on all phases of pet care, pet therapy, human/companion animal bond, humane education, veterinary care, volunteer activities, community involvement, and related programs. Offers aid in arranging interviews, brochures/pamphlets, informational newsletters and placement on mailing lists. Publications include Bide-A-Wee newsletter; also news releases and articles on various Bide-A-Wee programs, and information connected with the humane/animal welfare field. **How to Contact:** Write or call. Responds to most inquiries within a month. Give association "appropriate and significant credit in articles." **Tips:** "We're very understaffed and it's difficult to always fulfill last minute requests. Would like ample time to pull together information if necessary." Recent information request: "Query from a magazine writer about community involvement programs that could be recommended to other communities throughout the country.

17• THE CENTER FOR ACTION ON ENDANGERED SPECIES, INC.
175 W. Main St., Ayer MA 01432. (617)772-0445. Contact Person: Executive Director. **Description:** The Center provides public information, and is active in research and advocacy for endangered species of fauna and flora. **Services:** Provides advisory, analytical, bibliographical, historical, interpretative, referral, and technical information on endangered species and little-known or little-loved species such as bats, manatees, reptiles and amphibians, pangolins. Offers brochures/pamphlets, informational newsletters, library facilities, photos, placement on mailing lists, press kits, research assistance, statistics and telephone reference services. Publications include various monographs and fact sheets on endangered species. **How to Contact:** Write or call. Responds to most inquiries within a week. "Publications are low-priced. If we do a lot of work for and with writers, we encourage them to contribute a tax-deductible gift to the center for our work." **Tips:** "A phone call will let you know if we can help. Get the facts straight. Information on endangered species should be checked if it comes from general sources or any reference publication over two years old. We are especially concerned about writers who perpetuate myths about predators or such unpopular creatures as bats. We believe it is time to stop stereotyping animals as 'good' or 'bad,' and to get rid of the old-fashioned nonsense about Wise Owls and Sneaky Foxes." Recent information request: "When did the Indian Ocean become a whale sanctuary and what is its significance?"

18• CINCINNATI ZOO
3400 Vine St., Cincinnati OH 45220. (513)281-4703. Contact Person: Media Relations Manager. **Description:** The zoo's purposes are "conservation, recreation and education. We have the best educational department in the country, and offer a two-year high school alternative program with the Cincinnati Public Schools. We have the world record for successful gorilla births in captivity and in an outdoor display, and we're the only zoo with a whole building devoted to insects." **Services:** Provides historical and referral information on the Cincinnati Zoo specifically, the role of zoos, and specific animals and endangered species. Offers aid in arranging interviews, bibliographies, biographies, statistics, brochures/pamphlets, information searches, placement on mailing list, newsletter, photos, press kits, and data on breeding endangered species. Publications include a zoo brochure; *Cincinnati Zoo News*; a fact sheet; *Purpose of Zoos and Aquariums*; and *Zoo and Aquarium Careers*. **How to Contact:** Write or call. Responds to most inquiries within a week. **Tips:** "Don't use the Cincinnati Zoo as a reader for you. Most major libraries have animal encyclopedias which contain excellent information on many animal subjects. Use these first, if applicable." Recent information requests: Questions on the zoo's breeding success with white tigers; history of the Cincinnati Zoo; and highlighted exhibits.

19• DEER UNLIMITED OF AMERICA, INC.
Box 509, Clemson SC 29631. (803)654-6286. Contact Person: President. **Description:** "Deer Unlimited is a national conservation organization involved in wildlife management, legislative lobbying, seminars, publications. **Services:** Provides how-to information on deer hunting techniques, management of wildlife and habitat. Offers brochures/pamphlets, informational

newsletters and photos. Publications include *Deer Unlimited* magazine; newsletters; occasional research publications. **How to Contact:** Write. Responds to most inquiries within a week. "Must have permission to reprint." **Tips:** Recent information request: "What types of food do whitetail deer eat in Arizona?"

20• DESERT BOTANICAL GARDEN
1201 N. Galvin Parkway, Phoenix AZ 85008. (602)941-1217. Contact Person: Publications Director. **Description:** "DBG is a nonprofit, educational institution for the study and conservation of desert plants." **Services:** Provides advisory, bibliographical, historical, how-to, interpretive and technical information on arid regions of the world, cacti and succulents (our specialty), care and propagation of desert plants, ethnobotany, desert gardening and landscaping, poisonous and edible plants of western US. Offers brochures/pamphlets, informational newsletters, library facilities, photos, research assistance (limited), telephone reference services and herbarium facilities. Publications include monthly *Saguaroland Bulletin* (news, information on the garden, semi-scientific articles in the field of botany and biology related to deserts). **How to Contact:** Write, call or visit. Responds to most inquiries within a week. Charges 10¢/page for photocopies; 1½ times cost of duplication (which *includes* postage) for slide reproduction. "Contact garden ahead of time; credit line required on all photos; library materials must be used on site during library hours." **Tips:** "Writers interested in using our services should be prepared to be out of doors (except library work); try to schedule visits when plants are blooming (spring best); summer temperatures rise to 110-115° F." Recent information request: "What plants in the garden's collection are of economic importance?"

21• BOB EVANS NUTRITIONAL PET CENTER
c/o Morgan Communications, 20720 Ventura Blvd., Suite 260, Woodland Hills CA 91364. (213)702-0374. Contact Person: President, Morgan Communications. **Description:** "The center diagnoses and treats pet ailments caused by a variety of nutritional deficiencies." Also health foods store for animals; retail sales of pet foods, supplements, vitamins and grooming aids. **Services:** Provides advisory, analytical, bibliographical, historical, interpretive, referral and trade information on keeping pets healthy through diet and activity. Offers aid in arranging interviews, biographies, brochures/pamphlets, clipping services, informational newsletters, photos, placement on mailing lists, press kits and telephone reference services. **How to Contact:** Write. Responds to most inquiries within a week. **Tips:** "Do not attempt to learn all about pet nutrition in half an hour." Recent information request: "I have a low income but still want my pet to be healthy; how can I arrange this without spending too much money?"

22• FISH & WILDLIFE REFERENCE SERVICE
3840 York St., Unit J, Denver CO 80205. (800)525-3426. In Colorado (303)294-0917. Contact Person: Reference Specialist. **Description:** "Our purpose is to provide access to federally funded research in the field of fishery and wildlife management." **Services:** Provides bibliographical information: only research reports emanating from the Federal Aid in Fish and Wildlife Restoration Program. Offers computerized information searches, informational newsletters and library facilities. Publishes quarterly newsletter. **How to Contact:** Write, call or visit. Responds to most inquiries within a week. Charges 10¢/page for photocopy of reports; $30 for literature search; 50¢/fiche for microfiche of reports; no charge for newsletter. **Tips:** "Generally—limit requests to 'game type' or endangered species."

23• FRIENDS OF ANIMALS AND THE COMMITTEE FOR HUMANE LEGISLATION
11 W. 60th St., New York NY 10023. (212)247-8120. Contact Person: Vice President. **Description:** "Both Friends of Animals (FOA) and Committee for Humane Legislation (CHL) are engaged in protecting both domestic and wild animals from human exploitation. FOA is essentially a public information organization and CHL is a lobbying organization." **Services:** Provides information covering health/medicine, law, nature, science, self-help, technical data, humane education and wildlife. Offers aid in arranging interviews, statistics, brochures/pamphlets, information searches, placement on mailing list, photos and press kits. **How to Contact:** Write or call. Responds to most inquiries within a week. "We will be glad to accommodate any published writer who is researching work in relationships between the human and nonhuman species." **Tips:** Recent information request: "What federally-funded research is done at a particular university?"

24•   GARDENS FOR ALL
The National Association for Gardening, 180 Flynn Ave., Burlington VT 05401. (802)863-1308. Contact Person: Public Relations Director. **Description:** "We promote food gardening nationwide to save money and energy; gardening by young and old, handicapped, institutionalized (including prisoners). Our purpose is to help gardeners succeed, improve the state of the earth, air and water and use natural resources thriftily." **Services:** Provides how-to, technical and trade information on organizing community gardens and youth gardens; Gallup Survey on Gardening in the US (yearly, sponsored by GFA) "with statistics of all kinds relating to gardeners—who they are, where, why they garden, with what, what they seek to know, etc." Offers brochures/pamphlets, informational newsletters, library facilities and statistics. Publications include *Gardens for All News* (monthly); brochures and manuals; charts on pests, disease, planting, etc. **How to Contact:** Write. "We do not have enough staff to answer any but the briefest questions by phone. There is a charge for each of the publications named. No charge for answering simple questions, nor for library use by someone who comes to the office. Items culled from our *News* must be credited; if written for us by freelancers, freelancers must give permission." **Tips:** "We're glad to help anyone whose objective is to promote food gardening; we are not geared to assisting writers in particular, but some come to us for advice or use our publications and that's fine with us. Always send a written query ahead of you with a clear statement of what you need; if we can't provide the information, we can at least steer you to the right source." Recent information requests: Demographics on home community gardeners, their outside interests; how to reach community garden organizations; the search for open land; what tools and techniques are most popular; size of gardens, amount of yield nationwide, etc.

25•   THE HORTICULTURAL SOCIETY OF NEW YORK
128 W. 58th St., New York NY 10019. (212)757-0915. Contact Person: Librarian (or Public Relations Department). **Description:** "The Horticultural Society of New York is a nonprofit, membership organization dedicated to the knowledge and love of horticulture. The society operates a library and education department, a community garden program, flower shows and exhibitions, and a phone-in 'Plant Line.'" **Services:** Provides advisory, bibliographical, historical, how-to, referral, technical and trade information on horticulture and botany of a fairly current nature. "We provide secondary sources, not primary, in most cases." Offers brochures/pamphlets, clipping services, informational newsletters, library facilities, photos, statistics, telephone reference service ("Plant Line" 2-4 p.m., Monday-Friday) and on-site garden aid for community gardens. Publications include nursery catalogs, books, newsletters, slides, current clippings, bulletins. **How to Contact:** Visit. Responds to most inquiries within a week. "Must give credit to Horticultural Society of New York; library circulation (check out) for members only." **Tips:** "Writers and researchers should visit, rather than phoning in questions. We are better for garden writers than in-depth researchers because we have secondary sources, not primary sources." Recent information request: Books and references for article on ornamental grasses.

26•   THE HOYA SOCIETY INTERNATIONAL
Box 54271, Atlanta GA 30308. (404)223-5976. Contact Person: Bulletin Editor/Executive Secretary. **Description:** "Our society's purpose is to promote the wider growth of the genus Hoya; to disseminate knowledge of the genus; and to straighten out the horrible nomenclatural mess of this genus." **Services:** Provides advisory, bibliographical, historical, interpretative, referral, and technical information on "the entire Hoya genus (150 to 200 species and various varieties and cultivars)." Offers aid in arranging interviews, informational newsletters, photos, placement on mailing lists and research assistance. "Because of our low budget, non-profit status, we may have to charge for copy and postage if material is requested." Publications include quarterly bulletin, *The Hoyan*. "We also have photographic copies of almost all the known Hoya literature, including *all* of the original descriptions. Most has been translated, by us, into English." **How to Contact:** Call or write (include SASE). Responds to most inquiries within a month. "If we are quoted, we reserve the right to edit all copy before it is published." **Tips:** "Be patient. We operate entirely on volunteer help. Make sure your source is reliable. Many researchers are content to quote later works quoting and misquoting earlier works."

27•   THE HUMANE SOCIETY OF THE UNITED STATES
2100 L St. NW, Washington DC 20037. (202)452-1100. Contact Person: Director of Public Relations. **Description:** "The HSUS is a charitable, tax-exempt national animal welfare

organization dedicated to preventing cruelty to animals and spreading the humane ethic. We carry out our educational, legal, legislative, and investigative functions through our offices in Washington DC, seven regional offices and an education center in Connecticut. Also under our auspices is an Animal Control Academy in Alabama and a scientific institute in Washington DC." **Services:** Provides advisory, analytical, how-to, interpretative, referral and technical information on pets and pet care; wild animals (captive and free); livestock; marine mammals; horses; legal, legislative, and educational expertise on matters relating to animals. Offers aid in arranging interviews, annual reports, biographies, brochures/pamphlets, informational newsletters, library facilities, photos, press kits, research assistance, statistics and telephone reference services. Publications include *The Humane Society News* (quarterly membership magazine); *KIND* (youth magazine); *Humane Education* (teacher's magazine); *International Journal for the Study of Animal Problems* (scientific journal); quarterly issue reports. **How to Contact:** Write or call. Responds to most inquiries within a week. "Use of the library is by appointment only. No library materials may be taken from the premises." **Tips:** "The animal welfare field is more complex than most people imagine. Opinions on various issues vary widely and 'experts' frequently offer contradictory information. It's very important to check out a source's qualifications before you take what he or she says as gospel. We're glad to point writers to our own and outside sources. Simple questions and referrals to experts can usually be handled right away. Know what you want before you contact us." Recent information request: "How many dogs and cats are used every year for scientific research?; What types of experiments are they used for?"

28• INTERNATIONAL CRANE FOUNDATION
City View Rd., Baraboo WI 53913. (608)356-9462. Contact Person: Educational Coordinator. **Description:** Organization working "to save endangered species of cranes from extinction through research, habitat protection campaigns, captive breeding and public education. Although we are headquartered in Baraboo, the focus of our work lies in the politically polarized nations of central and northeast Asia." **Services:** Provides advisory, analytical, bibliographical, interpretative, referral and technical information covering endangered species, wetland conservation, international conservation programs, bird stories and captive breeding. Offers aid in arranging interviews, background information and photographs. "Our resources include an extensive photograph file, regular news releases and access to scientific contacts worldwide." **How to Contact:** Write, call or visit. Responds to most inquiries immediately. Charges minimal fee for publication of ICF-owned photographs. "On rare occasions we will request to review a manuscript to check facts. Make contact early—to allow time for several exchanges of information to complete a project." **Tips:** "We welcome new contacts from writers and can often suggest or advise on possible markets. We prefer a phone call or personal visit to a written list of questions. Use the phone to follow up on written inquiries; I can give a lot more information quickly verbally than I can in a letter. And conversation raises new questions and angles for a story. Don't be afraid to have your contact review a story before it goes to the editor."

29• KENDALL WHALING MUSEUM
Box 297, Sharon MA 02067. (617)784-5642. Contact Person: Director or Research Associate. **Description:** "The Kendall Whaling Museum collects, organizes and exhibits art, artifacts, books and manuscripts on whaling, whales, sealing and seals. **Services:** Provides historical, interpretative, referral and technical information covering worldwide whaling history, sealing, the natural history of whales and other marine animals. Offers brochure, whaling books, journals, paintings and prints in the KWM collection and publications such as *The Whale Is Ours*; *Creative Writing of American Whalemen*; and *Naked and a Prisoner: A Narrative of Shipwreck in Palau*. "The museum has an educational outreach program for schools and adult groups. A 4,500-volume research library is available to bona fide researchers by appointment." **How to Contact:** Write or call. Responds to most inquiries within a month "due to our small staff." Charges $7.50/b&w glossy print; $50/color transparency; other special fees "at discretion of Director. Make an appointment for on site research; some publication restrictions exist." **Tips:** "Select very specific topics—not 'the history of American whaling.' " Recent information request: "What contact did 19th century American whalemen have with the island of Madagascar?"

30• THE LEPIDOPTERISTS' SOCIETY
c/o Natural History Museum, 900 Exposition Blvd., Los Angeles CA 90007. (213)744-3364. Contact Person: Secretary. **Description:** The society "promotes the study, understanding, and

enjoyment of moths and butterflies by amateurs and professionals alike, throughout the world.'' **Services:** Provides referral information on all aspects of the study of Lepidoptera (Phylum Arthropoda, Class Insecta, Order Lepidoptera). Offers aid in arranging interviews and library facilities. Publications include quarterly *Journal* and bimonthly *News* (available through membership or subscription). **How to Contact:** Call. Responds to most inquiries within a week. **Tips:** ''Pose specific questions after having done enough background reading to be reasonably conversant in the field.'' Recent information requests: ''Where can I find a butterfly farmer to interview?''; ''How many insect zoos are there in the US?''; ''Can you suggest a local butterfly expert in the Lubbock, Texas area to be an advisor for a film we are shooting there?''; ''Where can I get information on the migration of butterflies.''

31• LONGWOOD GARDENS
Kennett Square PA 19348. (215)388-6741. Contact Person: Publicity Coordinator. **Description:** ''Longwood Gardens is a 1,000-acre horticultural showplace attracting 700,000 visitors yearly. Open every day of the year, the gardens have nearly four acres of heated conservatories, 14,000 types of plants, lavish fountain displays and an open air theatre.'' **Services:** Provides historical, how-to, interpretative and referral information. Offers aid in arranging interviews, brochures/pamphlets, placement on mailing list, publicity photos and press kits. Publications include a schedule of events, general informational brochure and *Food Gardening*, a booklet. **How to Contact:** Write or call. Responds to most inquiries within a week. ''We aid writers who are mostly researching Longwood Gardens or our contents, but please don't ask us to do all the work for you!'' **Tips:** Recent information request: ''Please send me information on the waterlily displays/collections at Longwood.''

32• MARINE LAND OF FLORIDA
Rt. 1, St. Augustine FL 32084. (904)471-1111. Contact: Public Relations Department. **Description:** ''The world's original marineland with the largest tropical fish display and 2 oceanariums.'' **Services:** Provides advisory, analytical, bibliographical, historical, interpretative, referral and technical information on nature and science. Offers aid in arranging interviews, annual reports, biographies, brochures/pamphlets, information searches, placement on mailing list, photos and press kits. **How to Contact:** Write or call. Responds to most inquiries within a month. Charges depend on use. Give credit to Marine Land of Florida. **Tips:** A marine research lab of the University of Florida is maintained on Marine Land property and may be used for information.

33• MEN'S GARDEN CLUBS OF AMERICA, INC.
5560 Merle Hay Rd., Des Moines IA 50323. (515)278-0295. Contact Person: Office Manager or Editor. **Description:** ''We provide educational and service programs on gardening through club activities in the community and the nation.'' **Services:** Provides advisory, how-to, interpretative and trade information on gardening and horticulture. Offers brochures/pamphlets, informational newsletters, library facilities and photos. Publications include *The Gardener* (bimonthly), subscriptions only. **How to Contact:** Write, call or visit. Responds to most inquiries within a week. Give credit to Men's Garden Clubs of America, Inc.

34• JULIE MOORE & ASSOCIATES
Box 5156, 6130 Camino Real, # 223, Riverside CA 92517. (714)685-5484. Contact Person: Bibliographer. **Description:** ''Our purpose is to identify and create a data base on wildlife, marine mammals, marine birds and bats; index all biological materials and publications within the fields of agriculture, forestry, ecology and ecosystems; provide literature searches. **Services:** Provides bibliographical and referral informaton on agriculture, forestry, botany, zoology, ecology, wildlife, ecosystems and marine fauna. Offers computerized information searches and indexing services. Recent publication: *The Updated Index to US Department of Agriculture Handbooks* # 1-540 (service aspect). **How to Contact:** Write or call. Responds to most inquiries immediately; data response within a month. Cost of each search is variable—average price is $50-80; hourly rate is $35. No resale of searches. **Tips:** ''Define topic of interest as specifically as possible. Set up 'keywords' for searching. Define your audiences, then the level of material you want. Our data bases are research-oriented but contain information needed for popular articles.'' Recent information requests: Search (1971-date) on oil pollution of marine birds and mammals (our files); indexing a book on Phytophthora (service aspect).

35• STERLING MORTON LIBRARY, THE MORTON ARBORETUM
Lisle IL 60532. (312)968-0074. Contact Person: Librarian. **Description:** The library supports the
work of the staff of the arboretum in collections, education and research; and provides a resource
for the general public in the Chicago area. **Services:** Provides bibliographical, historical, how-to,
interpretative and referral information on botany and horticulture of temperate zones, especially of
woody plants; landscape architecture; ecology and conservation, natural history. Offers
brochures/pamphlets, library facilities, photos, research assistance and telephone reference
services. **How to Contact:** Write, call or visit. Responds to most inquiries immediately. Charges
fee for photographing or photocopying services. Schedule available. **Tips:** Recent information
request: Two photographs of plants from our rare book collection to illustrate an article on herbal
collection.

36• MYSTIC MARINELIFE AQUARIUM
Coogan Blvd., Mystic CT 06355. (203)536-9631. Contact Person: Director of Public
Affairs. **Description:** Nonprofit organization dedicated to public education and research in animal
husbandry, water quality and breeding. Tourist attraction (open all year) with trained dolphins,
whales and sea lions, as well as 2,000 specimens of fish. Outdoor display of 5 types of seals and sea
lions. **Services:** Conducts educational programs and displays. Offers aid in arranging interviews,
statistics, brochures, newsletters, placement on mailing list and photos. Publications include
Seaword (members); *Schoolword* (children, kindergarten-6th grade); and *Marine Mammal
Bulletin* (grades 6-12). **How to Contact:** Write or call.

37• NATIONAL ARBORETUM
3501 New York Ave. NE, Washington DC 20002. (202)472-9279. Contact Person: Curator of
Education. **Description:** "The National Arboretum provides research and education on woody
landscape plants." **Services:** Provides how-to and referral information on horticulture. Offers aid
in arranging interviews, brochures/pamphlets, information searches, placement on mailing list and
photos. Publications include general brochures on the National Arboretum, *National Bonsai
Collection*; *Azaleas at the Arboretum*; *Camellias at the Arboretum*; *Hollies at the Arboretum*; *Fern
Valley at the Arboretum* and *National Herb Garden*. **How to Contact:** Write or call. Responds to
most inquiries within a week. "Staff time is limited." **Tips:** Include address and telephone number
in your inquiry. Recent information requests: Questions on plant propagation, hardiness, etc.;
educational programs at National Arboretum.

38• NATIONAL ARBORIST ASSOCIATION, INC.
3537 Stratford Rd., Wantagh NY 11793. (516)221-3082. Contact Person: Executive Vice
President. **Description:** The National Arborist Association is a national trade association of
commercial tree service firms. **Services:** Provides trade information on commercial tree service.
Offers informational newsletters and statistics. **How to Contact:** Write. Responds to most
inquiries within a month.

39• NATIONAL CHRISTMAS TREE ASSOCIATION, INC.
611 E. Wells St., Milwaukee WI 53202. (414)276-6410. Contact Person: Managing
Editor. **Description:** Organization designed to aid producers and individuals involved in the
Christmas tree industry; to provide information concerning natural Christmas trees and work in
conjunction with the 31 affiliated state associations. A biennial convention is sponsored and
includes technical sessions, farm tours and equipment and product demonstrations." **Services:**
Provides advisory, analytical, bibliographical, historical, how-to, interpretative, referral, technical and trade information pertaining to Christmas trees. Offers bibliographies, statistics, bro-
chures/pamphlets and press kits. Publications include *The American Christmas Tree Journal*
(quarterly trade magazine) and the *Christmas Merchandiser* (annual retail magazine). **How to
Contact:** Write or call. Responds to most inquiries within a week. Charges $2/copy for magazine.

40• NATIONAL GARDEN BUREAU
628 Executive Dr., Willowbrook IL 60521. (312)655-0010. Contact Person: Executive Secretary.
Description: "We provide educational materials to garden writers." **Services:** Provides how-to
and trade information on gardening. Offers photos. Mailings to garden writers approximately four
times a year. **How to Contact:** Write. Responds to most inquiries within a month.

41• NATIONAL MARINE FISHERIES SERVICE
National Oceanic and Atmospheric Administration, Department of Commerce, Washington DC 20235. (202)634-7281. Contact Person: Public Affairs Officer. **Description:** Biological and technical research administration and enforcement of the Marine Mammal Protection Act, the Endangered Species Act and the Fishery Conservation and Management Act; compiles statistical and technical facts on commercial fisheries and marine game fish; and conducts economic studies. **Services:** Provides advisory, analytical, bibliographical, historical, how-to, referral, technical and trade information on all aspects of commercial and recreational fishing, fish processing and marketing. **How to Contact:** Write or call. Responds to most inquiries immediately. No charge for information except for publications that must be ordered through the Government Printing Office. **Tips:** "Phone calls are more likely to get prompt attention; specific requests are better than general ones. If the writer is almost totally ignorant of just what he is looking for, a phone call (followed by a visit to the public affairs office) is usually a time saver. Specific, detailed requests, however, can generally be handled by mail." Recent information request: A question on the economic forecast for a sector of the fishing industry.

42• NATIONAL ZOOLOGICAL PARK
Smithsonian Institution, 3001 Connecticut Ave., Washington DC 20008. (202)673-4789. Contact: Office of Public Affairs. **Description:** "Our purpose is the advancement of science, instruction and recreation. The National Zoological Park is the official depository of animals donated by heads of state." **Services:** Provides information on history, nature, science, exotic animal science, medicine and zoo management. Offers aid in arranging interviews, annual reports, statistics, brochures/pamphlets, information searches, placement on miling list, newsletter, photos and press kits. **How to Contact:** Write or call. Responds to calls, press, etc. immediately; letters within a week. Charges for photos "depending on use." **Tips:** Recent information request: Question about giant pandas.

43• PONY OF THE AMERICAS CLUB, INC.
Box 1447, 1452 N. Federal, Mason City IA 50401. (515)424-1586. Contact Person: Administrative Assistant. **Description:** "We are a nonprofit organization involved with a breed of horses developed for youth. We put on horse shows and sales throughout the country. Our office registers horses and keeps their records up-to-date, puts out a monthly national publication, and keeps track of show points on all Pony of the Americas Club (POA) shows across the country for our several awards programs." **Services:** Provides historical information on the POA breed of pony. Offers brochures/pamphlets and photos. **How to Contact:** Write. Responds to most inquiries within a week. "There are no service charges unless more than 200 brochures are requested; we then charge 3¢ a piece after 200. We ask that a credit line be given on photos. As a youth organization, we are not in a position to reimburse writers who do stories for our magazine. They are given full credit for articles." **Tips:** "Tell us the deadline you need the material by, and send your requests in ample time (allowing several weeks extra if possible) for mailing material. We stress accuracy in using material provided by our association." Recent information request: "Does the POA Breed register every different pony there is?"

44• SAN DIEGO WILD ANIMAL PARK
Rt. 1, Box 725-E, Escondido CA 92025. (714)747-8702. Contact: Public Relations Department. **Description:** "A sprawling 1,800-acre sanctuary enabling animals to roam freely in settings similar to their native homelands. The park has gained worldwide recognition for its conservation efforts directed to the preservation of plants and animals." **Services:** Provides historical and interpretative information on anything regarding conservation and preservation of plants and animals. Offers brochures/pamphlets. Publications include *San Diego Wild Animal Park Wild World of Animals*. **How to Contact:** Write or call. Responds to most inquiries within a week. Charges $3/copy for *Wild World of Animals*; costs priced per job for researching. "All stories must be approved and coordinated through publications department. **Tips:** "Be as specific as possible about subject, and give plenty of advance notice." Recent information requests: Wild Animal Park history; endangered species research/breeding programs.

45• SAN DIEGO ZOO
Box 551, San Diego CA 92112. (714)231-1515. Contact: Public Relations Department. **Description:** "A zoo where animals are displayed year-round in outdoor settings that look like the animals' natural homes in the wild; a zoo with one of the world's best collections of rare animals; a

zoo where tropical plants cover the 100-acre grounds. Purposes of the zoo include recreation, education, conservation, and research in zoology, zoo medicine, zoo management and botany." **Services:** Offers brochures/pamphlets and photos. Publications include *San Diego Zoo*; *Zoonooz* (monthly); *Colorful World of Animals* and *Wild World of Animals*. **How to Contact:** Write or call. Responds to most inquiries within a week. For publications, address request to Public Services Department. For photos, address request to San Diego Zoo Photo Lab. Charges $1/copy for *Zoonooz*, $8/one-year subscription; $2/copy for books. Charges varying rates for photos, depending on use; also charges handling fee. "A credit line must be given on all photos. Permission to use photos is not authorized until full payment has been made." **Tips:** Recent information requests: "Many questions about the zoo's koala colony, and about our efforts to save endangered species."

46• SCIENTISTS' CENTER FOR ANIMAL WELFARE
Box 3755, Washington DC 20007. (301)468-2093..Contact Person: Administrator or President. **Description:** "The purpose of our organization is to address issues of a scientist's responsibilities toward the animals used in biomedical experimentation. We agree with animal experimentation but want to see that it is done humanely and that alternatives to animals are used whenever possible. The 9-member Board of Trustees consists of experimental medical scientists, physicians and veterinarians." **Services:** Provides advisory, historical, how-to and interpretative information on animal experimentation, guidelines for use of animals, federal and state laws on animal welfare and student use of animals in biology education. Offers aid in arranging interviews, annual reports and informational newsletters. Organizes workshops and conferences on animal welfare issues in biomedical experimentation. Publications include newsletter of the Scientists Center for Animal Welfare; *Scientific Perspectives on Animal Welfare*; reprints on many topics concerned with animal welfare as it impinges on scientists. **How to Contact:** Call. Responds to most inquiries immediately. "Writers/researchers using our services must write for responsible journals or publications—nothing of a sensational nature."

47• SOCIETY FOR ANIMAL RIGHTS, INC.
421 S. State St., Clarks Summit PA 18411. (717)586-2200. Contact Person: President. **Description:** "The society's purpose is to prevent the exploitation and abuse of animals and to promote the concept of animal rights. We collect, research and disseminate documentary material on the various forms of exploitation and abuse of animals and recommend appropriate action." **Services:** Offers bibliographies, brochures/pamphlets, information searches, placement on mailing list, statistics, newsletter and photos. "We maintain extensive subject files containing documentary material on animals. We also maintain a small but excellent library." **How to Contact:** Write or call. Responds to most inquiries within a week. "We are listed with the Library of Congress as an information resource and we in turn sometimes call upon the Library of Congress for information." **Tips:** Recent information request: Question on the use of monkeys by paraplegics.

48• THE TERRARIUM ASSOCIATION
57 Wolfpit Ave., Norwalk CT 06851. (203)847-7019. Contact Person: Editor/Founder. **Description:** "Founded in 1974 to promote continuing interest in terrarium gardening, the Terrarium Association is *not* a society with members that hold meetings. We provide printed information on the various aspects of terraria for individuals and groups." **Services:** Offers historical and how-to information: Wardian Case-Terrarium history and bibliography of terrarium publications dating from 1833; how to make and care for terrariums; sources of supply. Offers booklets, pamphlets, tracts and photos. Brochure listing publications and prices is available on request. **How to Contact:** Write. Responds to most inquiries within a month. "We appreciate a credit line whenever possible. We request that queries be accompanied by SASE." **Tips:** "Contact us well in advance of editorial deadline, allowing sufficient time to compile requested information. Be specific and make allowance for alternative related material or directives to other sources of information. Recent information requests: "Is terrarium gardening an American innovation that attained its greatest popularity during the 1970s?"; "When was the first terrarium exhibited publicly?"

49• UNITED HUMANITARIANS
16 E. Hatcher Rd., Phoenix AZ 85020. (602)997-6881. Contact Person: Executive Director. **Description:** "United Humanitarians is a nonprofit organization with 19 branches across the USA and over 17,000 members nationwide. The organization's purpose is the education of the general public in such areas as the mass spaying-neutering of dogs and cats; the elderly and

their pets in rental properties; program for the prevention of cruelty to animals; opposition to vivisection, etc." **Services:** Provides advisory, how-to and referral information. Offers brochures/pamphlets, informational newsgrams and telephone reference services. Publications include *How to Organize a Low-Cost Spaying-Neutering Program* manual; *Born to Be Killed* leaflet; *Who We Are* leaflet; *Please* leaflet (hot car warning); and *The National Humanitarians* quarterly magazine for members and other animal welfare agencies. **How to Contact:** Write. Responds to most inquiries within a week. Charges printing and shipping cost for leaflets; price list available; $2 for manual. **Tips:** Recent information request: "Where can I take my litter of dogs or cats that they won't be destroyed?"

50• URBAN WILDLIFE RESEARCH CENTER, INC.
10921 Trotting Ridge Way, Columbia MD 21044. (301)596-3311. Contact Person: Research Assistant. **Description:** "The center is a national scientific and educational organization dedicated to the conservation of wildlife and habitat in cities, suburbs, and developing areas." **Services:** Provides advisory, analytical, bibliographical, how-to, interpretative, referral and technical information on urban wildlife; urban vegetation; management of wildlife; fishes management in urban areas; wildlife in planned communities; strip mine rehabilitation for wildlife; highway-wildlife interactions; urban wetlands for stormwater control and wildlife enhancement. Offers brochures/pamphlets, informational newsletters, library facilities and research assistance. Publications include scientific reports; public informational leaflets on backyard wildlife; vegetation; quarterly newsletter, *Urban Wildlife News* and a publications list. **How to Contact:** Write or call. Responds to most inquiries within a month. Nominal charge for most publications; photocopying of library materials at cost; charges for extensive library research; no charge for most requests for information. "The library may be used by appointment only; non-circulating materials." **Tips:** "Request information well ahead of deadlines. Questions should be somewhat specific. Staff limitations require that extensive research must be charged for. We can suggest topics for articles concerning urban wildlife, as we are eager to educate the public to the potential benefits of urban conservation." Recent information request: "What case histories can you provide concerning homeowners who have challenged weed-control ordinances and allowed their lawns to go 'natural'?"

51• THE WHALE CENTER
3929 Piedmont Ave., Oakland CA 94611. (415)654-6621. Contact Person: Business Manager. **Description:** "The public purposes for which the corporation is organized include promoting the protection of whales, marine mammals, other wildlife, and their habitat through education, conservation, research and other activities." **Services:** Provides advisory, historical and technical information on the basic marine mammal in all areas, including biology, conservation problems (national and international), legal research, and information involving habitat. Offers brochures/pamphlets, informational newsletters, library facilities and statistics. **How to Contact:** Write, call or visit. Responds to most inquiries within a week. Charges are usually based on copy and mailing expense. Certain publications involve minor cost. **Tips:** "Be as specific as possible."

52• WORLD WILDLIFE FUND—UNITED STATES
1601 Connecticut Ave. NW, Washington DC 20009. (202)387-0800. Contact Person: Press Officer. **Description:** "WWF-US is a nonprofit, independent affiliate of World Wildlife Fund-International. WWF-US is the principal source of private US funding for the conservation of living resources worldwide. WWF funds scientific research programs aimed at international conservation." **Services:** Provides advisory, analytical and referral information on international conservation issues involving natural living resources: tropical forest, rainforest conservation; topics related to endangered or threatened species, or trade in endangered species. Offers aid in arranging interviews, annual reports, brochures/pamphlets, informational newsletters, library facilities, photos, placement on mailing lists, press kits, research assistance, statistics and telephone reference services. **How to Contact:** Write. Responds to most inquiries within a week. "We prefer to deal with specific questions and areas of interest. Limited staff means full-scale research in-house is impossible. As a matter of general policy, WWF does not fund writers." **Tips:** "WWF-US is the leading US group working in international conservation. Our projects list reads like a 'Who's Who' in international conservation research. We can provide referrals, confirm reports, numbers, etc." Recent information requests: "I am going to Nairobi in a few months, do you have any projects in that area that might make interesting stories?"; "What is

the elephant/rhino situation like in E. Africa?''; ''What are the problems facing the world's tropical rainforests?''

53•   WYE MARSH WILDLIFE INTERPRETATION CENTER
Box 100, Midland, Ontario, Canada L4R 4K6. (705)526-7809. Contact Person: Biologist-in-Charge. **Description:** ''Wye Marsh Wildlife Center is a nature interpretation facility operated by the Canadian Wildlife Service, Environment Canada. It is a place for public visitors to explore the natural environment of the Great Lakes Natural Region of Canada.'' **Services:** Provides interpretative information on nature. Offers brochures/pamphlets and photos. ''Writers are welcome to participate in the program of naturalist-led nature walks, talks, canoe trips and wildlife demonstrations, and to interview the interpretation biologists at Wye Marsh Wildlife Interpretation Center. Publications include *Hinterland Who's Who* (about wildlife); *Wye Marsh Bird Checklist*; Wye Marsh self-guiding trail booklets; and many handout fact sheets and identification booklets of plants and insects. **How to Contact:** ''Write or call to arrange a date for a visit or for more information. We suggest suitable attire for the outdoors if the writer plans a visit.'' Responds to most inquiries within a week. **Tips:** Write for information first; follow up with personal visit if required.'' Recent information requests: ''What variety of turtles are in the Wye Marsh area?''; ''Is turtle marking project ongoing?''

THE ARTS

Art teaches nothing, except the significance of life.

—Henry Miller

The Arts section includes resources on the performing and visual arts, including: music, drama, theatre, dance, art, craft, design (editorial and decorative), graphics, photography, architecture and sculpture, as well as more-specialized areas such as storytelling and puppetry.

Folk art and folk music listings are found in the Ethnic/Regional Heritage category. Resources in the entertainment arts (television, radio, film) are listed in the Communications/Entertainment division.

Bibliography

American Art Directory. Edited by Jaques Cattell Press, 49th ed. Biennial. New York: Bowker.

Art Index. 1929 to date, quarterly. New York: H.W. Wilson Co.

ASCAP Biographical Dictionary. 4th ed. New York: Bowker, 1980. (Biographies of 8,000 writing members of the American Society of Composers, Authors and Publishers)

Bell, Doris L. *Contemporary Art Trends, 1960-1980: A Guide to Sources*. Metuchen, NJ: Scarecrow Press, 1981.

Billboard International Buyer's Guide. Annual. Beverly Hills, CA: Billboard Publications, Inc. (Record companies, music publishers, sheet music, music services and supplies)

Chujay, Anatole and P.W. Manchester, comps. *The Dance Encyclopedia*. rev. and enl. New York: Simon and Schuster, 1967.

Fleming, John, Hugh Honour and Nikolaus Pevsner, eds. *The Penguin Dictionary of Architecture*. 3rd ed. New York: Penguin Books, 1980.

Hedgecoe, John. *Photographer's Handbook*. rev. ed. New York: State Mutual Book and Periodical Service, Ltd., 1982.

Mayer, Ralph. *Dictionary of Art Terms & Techniques*. New York: Barnes & Noble, 1981.

Popular Music, An Annotated Index of American Popular Songs. 6 vols. New York: Adrian Press, 1964-73.

Rachlin, Harvey. *The Encyclopedia of the Music Business*. New York: Harper & Row Publishers, 1981.

Sadie, Stanley, ed. *The New Grove Dictionary of Music & Musicians*. 20 vols. New York: Groves Dictionary of Music, Inc., 1980.

Slonimsky, Nicolas. *Baker's Biographical Dictionary of Musicians*. 6th ed. New York: Schirmer Books, 1978.

Smith, V. Babington. *Dictionary of Contemporary Artists*. American Bibliographical Center. Santa Barbara, CA: Clio Press, 1981.

Wasserman, Steven, ed. *The Lively Arts Information Directory*. Detroit: Gale Research Co., 1982. (Covers music, dance, theatre, film, radio, TV)

World Photography Sources. New York: Directories, 1982. (Catalog of picture sources)

54• ALLIANCE OF RESIDENT THEATRES/NEW YORK
325 Spring St., New York NY 10013. (212)989-5257. Contact Person: Director of Programs. **Description:** "Our purpose is to promote and foster nonprofit professional theatre in New York City through management consultations and seminars; collection and dissemination of statistics and other information; publishing of books and periodicals; and advocacy with government, the press and media." **Services:** Provides advisory, analytical, bibliographical, historical, how-to, referral, technical and trade information (geared mostly to New York City theatre) on accounting, advocacy, audience development, board development, Broadway transfers, cable TV, facilities management, film, fund-raising, insurance, legal assistance, loans, mailing lists, marketing, personnel referral, physical production, press, publications, public relations, television, touring and unions/leagues. "In addition, we conduct an annual fiscal/audience/production survey of New

York's nonprofit professional theatres, and compile statistics on the arena.'' Offers aid in arranging interviews, brochures/pamphlets, clipping services, informational newsletters, library facilities, photos, placement on mailing lists, press kits, research assistance, statistics and telephone reference services. Publications include *Theatre Times*. **How to Contact:** Write or call. Responds to most inquiries within a week. ''In general, our services are available to members at a cost of $30/ year for individuals ($25 for students), and $75-150 for institutions. Questions from the press answered gratis. Although assistance to our theatre members takes priority, we do our best to assist writers/researchers in their needs.'' **Tips:** Recent information request: ''How many people attend Off and Off-Off Broadway in a year?''

55• AMERICAN ACADEMY AND INSTITUTE OF ARTS AND LETTERS
633 W. 155th St., New York NY 10032. (212)368-5900. Contact Person: Researcher. **Description:** Artists, writers and composers (select membership of 250) dedicated to ''fostering, assisting and sustaining an interest in literature, music and the fine arts by giving awards, mounting exhibitions and purchasing paintings for distribution to museums, etc.'' **Services:** Provides bibliographical and historical information about living and deceased members (artists, writers and composers). Offers brochures/pamphlets, library facilities and photos. Publications include *Proceedings of the American Academy and Institute of Arts and Letters*, published annually and available for purchase. **How to Contact:** Write. Responds to most inquiries within a month. ''Persons using our library and archives must have written permission from the subject of their research or the estate.''

56• AMERICAN BALLET THEATRE
888 7th Ave., New York NY 10019. Contact Person: Director of Public Relations and Marketing. **Description:** Ballet company. **Services:** Offers aid in arranging interviews, brochures/pamphlets, biographies, information searches and photos. Publications include a souvenir book. **How to Contact:** Write. Responds to inquiries as soon as possible. ''It depends very much upon our touring commitments.'' Charges for photos. ''Be as specific as possible in your requests.''

57• AMERICAN COUNCIL FOR THE ARTS
570 7th Ave., New York NY 10018. (212)354-6655. Contact Person: Librarian or Director. **Description:** ''The American Council for the Arts is a national service organization for all the arts, open to all organizations and individuals interested in the arts. Its mission is to promote and strengthen cultural activities in the United States by helping to improve internal and external support systems through its work in the areas of management improvement and arts advocacy.'' **Services:** Provides analytical, bibliographical, how-to, referral and trade information on arts management, funding for the arts; government and arts; economic and social aspects of the arts; numerous books and other publications on arts management and related topics (catalog on request); mail and telephone information service; conferences and training seminars on arts management; current information and discussion of arts-related issues through the bi-monthly *American Arts* magazine and the monthly newsletter *Update*; a reference library open to the public at ACA headquarters; job listings in ''ACA Classifieds'' and ACA Jobline (212)944-8884; and a Washington office providing up-to-date information on federal activities. Publications include *Money Business*; *Grants and Awards to Creative Artists*. **How to Contact:** Write or call. Responds to most inquiries within a week. Charges 10¢/page for photocopying. **Tips:** ''State your inquiries as clearly and specifically as practical. We will respond either from our own files or by referrals to relevant service organizations.'' Recent information request: ''What was the amount of state arts funding for the last fiscal year?''

58• AMERICAN CRAFT COUNCIL
401 Park Ave. S, New York NY 10016. (212)696-0710. Contact Person: Librarian. **Description:** Association of craftworkers interested in supporting and encouraging craft and the works of American craftworkers. **Services:** Provides advisory and historical information on craftworkers and their work from 1945 to the present. Offers biographies, photos, press kits, research assistance and statistics. Publications include *American Craft* (bimonthly). **How to Contact:** Write or call. Responds to most inquiries within a month. Charges for extensive research assistance and publications. Most services to members only.

59• AMERICAN HARP SOCIETY, INC.
6331 Quebec Dr., Hollywood CA 90068. (213)463-0716. Contact Person: Executive Secretary. **Description:** "The society's purpose is to familiarize the public with the harp, stimulate composition for the harp, foster study of the harp and generally bring together all those who love the harp." **Services:** Provides advisory and referral information on availability of harp-related materials and supplies. Offers annual reports, biographies, informational newsletters and placement on mailing lists. Publications include *American Harp Journal* (biannual); regional newsletters; membership directory; and list of material included in the Repository at the Library of Congress. **How to Contact:** Write. Responds to most inquiries within a week. "Membership in the society is available to anyone interested for $15/year which includes the *Journal* and the membership directory and other national mailings during the year."

60• AMERICAN INSTITUTE OF ARCHITECTS
1735 New York Ave. NW, Washington DC 20006. (202)626-7300. Contact Person: Administrative Assistant, Public Relations Department. **Description:** "American Institute of Architects is a voluntary professional organization representing more than 38,000 registered architects. Its programs are addressed to improving professional competence, developing and supporting policies in the public interest on issues of national concern, and promoting public understanding of the architectural profession's role in shaping the built environment." **Services:** Offers aid in arranging interviews, annual reports, bibliographies, statistics, brochures/pamphlets, placement on mailing list, newsletter and press kits. **How to Contact:** Write. Responds to most inquiries within a week. Many publications available.

61• AMERICAN MUSIC CENTER, INC.
250 W. 54th St., Rm 300, New York NY 10019. (212)247-3121. Contact Person: Executive Director. **Description:** "AMC is a nonprofit membership corporation founded over 40 years ago to foster and encourage the creation, performance, publication, and recognition of American music. AMC Library contains over 18,000 scores of American musical compositions, available on loan for perusal." **Services:** Provides advisory, how-to and technical information. "AMC provides information on music publishing and recording; on performing groups and on how to obtain performances; on available grants and fellowships; on copyright; on funding available for the performance of new music. AMC cooperates with performers and performing ensembles to help them find repertoire." Offers biographies, informational newsletters, library facilities, research assistance and statistics. Publications include AMC brochure (describes AMC purposes and activities); AMC *Newsletter* (subscription quarterly); and AMC Library Catalogs: *Vol. I—Choral and Vocal Works, Vol. II—Chamber Music, Vol. III—Orchestra and Band Music* and *Vol. IV—Stage Works.* **How to Contact:** Write, call or visit. Responds to most inquiries within a week. **Tips:** Recent information requests: "Do you have (a particular score) in your library?"; "Do you have the birthdate of (a particular composer)?"

62• AMERICAN SOCIETY OF CINEMATOGRAPHERS
1782 North Orange Dr., Hollywood CA 90028. (213)876-5080. Contact Person: Secretary. **Description:** Educational and cultural organization of professionals in the motion picture and television photography field. **Services:** Provides historical, how-to, interpretative, technical and trade information on film and video. Publications include *American Cinematographer*; *American Cinematographer's Manual.* **How to Contact:** Write, call or visit. Responds to most inquiries within a month. Charges for publications. Membership in the society is by invitation only.

63• AMERICAN SOCIETY OF COMPOSERS, AUTHORS AND PUBLISHERS (ASCAP)
1 Lincoln Plaza, New York NY 10023. (212)595-3050. Contact: Public Relations Department. **Description:** ASCAP collects and distributes royalties for composers and publishers of music. **Services:** Offers aid in arranging interviews, annual reports, biographies, brochures/pamphlets, information searches, placement on mailing list and photos. Publications include pamphlets *How to Get Your Song Published* and *ASCAP—the Facts.* **How to Contact:** Write or call. Responds to most inquiries within a week.

64• AMERICAN SOCIETY OF MAGAZINE PHOTOGRAPHERS
205 Lexington Ave., New York NY 10016. (212)889-9144. Contact Person: Executive Director. **Description:** The society promotes and furthers the interests of professional

photographers in communications media such as journalism, corporate advertising, fashion and books. "We act as a clearinghouse for photographic information on markets, rates, and business practices of magazines, advertising agencies, publishers and electronic media. We work for copyright law revisions, and offer legal advice, through counsel, to members concerning questions of rights, ethics and payment." **Services:** Offers bibliographies, brochures/pamphlets, placement on mailing list, statistics and newsletter. Publications available. **How to Contact:** Write or call; prefers written requests. Responds to most inquiries within a week.

65• AMERICAN SOCIETY OF MUSIC ARRANGERS
Box 11, Hollywood CA 90028. Contact Person: Executive Secretary. **Description:** "Our purpose is to represent arrangers and orchestrators within the American Federation of Musicians; to educate the public as to the function of arrangers and orchestrators; to promote interaction between members by organizing social functions; to educate through workshops and teaching clinics; and to recognize outstanding achievement in the field with the presentation of the Golden Score award." (All ASMA activities are currently centered in the Los Angeles area.) **Services:** Provides analytical, how-to and trade information. Publications include a newsletter. **How to Contact:** Write. Responds to most inquiries within a month.

66• AMERICAN SOCIETY OF PICTURE PROFESSIONALS
Box 5283, Grand Central Station, New York NY 10163. (212)682-6626. Contact Person: President. **Description:** "The A.S.P.P. is the only professional organization that represents the interests of the nation's diverse photographic community. The society's six hundred members are all persons who work with still pictures: photographers, agents, designers, picture editors, researchers, librarians, curators and historians." **Services:** Provides trade information. Offers informational newsletters and placement on mailing lists. Publications include quarterly newsletter (for members); *Guide to Business Practices*. **How to Contact:** Write or call. Responds to most inquiries within a week. Charges membership fee.

67• AMERICAN THEATRE ASSOCIATION
1000 Vermont Ave. NW, Washington DC 20005. (202)628-4634. Contact Person: Administrative Assistant. **Description:** "The American Theatre Association is a nonprofit association that brings together individuals and organizations with an interest in and a concern for the growth and development of noncommercial theatre." **Services:** Provides advisory information covering theatre and theatre education. Offers aid in arranging interviews, brochures/pamphlets and newsletter. Publications include four magazines: *Theatre News*, *Theatre Journal*, *Children's Theatre Review* and *Secondary School Theatre Journal*. **How to Contact:** Write or call. Responds to most inquiries within a week. "We prefer written requests for detailed information." Charges only for publications. **Tips:** Recent information request: Listings of national community theatre groups.

68• ART DEALERS ASSOCIATION OF AMERICA, INC. (ADAA)
575 Madison Ave., New York NY 10022. (212)940-8590. Contact Person: Public Relations Director. **Description:** Founded in 1962, a nonprofit trade association of the nation's leading art dealers seeking to promote the interests of individuals and firms dealing in works of fine art (paintings, sculpture, drawings, graphics); to improve the stature and status of the fine arts business; and to enhance the confidence of the public in responsible fine arts dealers. **Services:** Provides fine arts information; art appraisals (for art works donated to nonprofit institutions); art theft archive (monthly notices listing stolen works of art); information on fakes and forgeries; authentication; evaluation of works of art; awards in art history; advice to buyers of fine art. Publications include handbook listing activities and membership; bimonthly newsletter. **How to Contact:** Write or call. Responds to most inquiries within a week.

69• ART INFORMATION CENTER
280 Broadway, Room 412, New York NY 10007. (212)227-0282. Contact Person: Director. **Description:** Clearinghouse of information on contempoary art and artists. Assists artists in finding outlets for their work. **Services:** Provides advisory, how-to and referral information about living artists and various types of contemporary art. Offers slides, research assistance and statistics. **How to Contact:** Call. Responds to most inquiries immediately.

70• ASSOCIATION OF CONCERT BANDS, INC.
19 Benton Circle, Utica NY 13501. (315)732-2737. Contact Person: Executive
Secretary. **Description:** "Our purpose is to promote interest in and provide information for the
adult band musician and to foster the growth of community and concert bands in America and
abroad." **Services:** Provides advisory, how-to, interpretative and referral information on adult
community and concert bands, the adult musician, band music, and organization and promotion of
concert bands. Offers annual reports, brochures/pamphlets and informational newsletters.
Publications include *Woodwind/Brass/Percussion Magazine* (8 issues/year). **How to Contact:**
Write. Responds to most inquiries within a week. Membership ($20) includes mailing list of mem-
bers and magazine.

71• BLACK MUSIC ASSOCIATION
1500 Locust St., Suite 1905, Philadelphia PA 19102. (215)545-8600. Contact Person: Executive
Director. **Description:** "Our purpose is to protect, preserve and perpetuate black
music." **Services:** Provides advisory, analytical, historical, referral and trade information on
communications, recording industry, performing arts and marketing and merchandising. Offers
annual reports, brochures/pamphlets, computerized information searches, informational
newsletters, placement on mailing lists, press kits and statistics. Publications include *Innervisions*
(inhouse newsletter). **How to Contact:** Write. Responds to most inquiries within a week. Services
for BMA membership only.

72• LOUIS BRAILLE FOUNDATION FOR BLIND MUSICIANS, INC.
215 Park Ave. S, New York NY 10003. (212)982-7290. Contact Person: Executive
Director. **Description:** The foundation provides services for and promotes blind musicians and
composers. **Services:** Provides trade information covering the music and entertainment industries
as they pertain to visually-impaired persons. Offers aid in arranging interviews and career guides.
How to Contact: Write or call. Responds to most inquiries within a month. "You must be visually
impaired, blind or otherwise physically handicapped to use our services. We will work with professional calibre visually impaired and blind published writers." **Tips:** "Please obtain medical or
state certificate of impairment prior to contacting us."

73• BROADCAST MUSIC, INC. (BMI)
320 W. 57th St., New York NY 10019. (212)586-2000. Contact: Public Relations
Department. **Description:** "Broadcast Music, Inc. (BMI) currently represents over 65,000
writers and publishers of music of all types in the licensing and collection of fees for the public
performance of their music by users of all kinds. Through reciprocal agreements, we also represent
writers and publishers associated with 39 similar societies all around the world. It is the largest
organization of its kind in the world." **Services:** Offers assistance to songwriters. Publications
include *Handbook for BMI Writers and Publishers, You and the Music You Use, BMI—The
World's Largest Licensing Organization* and *The Many Worlds of Music and You* (quarterly). **How
to Contact:** Write. Responds to most inquiries within a week.

74• BUTEN MUSEUM
246 N. Bowman Ave., Merion PA 19066. (215)664-6601. Contact Person: Assistant
Director. **Description:** The museum represents "the study, collection, exhibition and
preservation of Wedgwood ceramics and other English and continental ceramics and related
classical antiquities, decorative arts and literature. The museum houses over 10,000 examples of
Wedgwood from 1759 to the present." **Services:** Provides bibliographical, historical and referral
information on Wedgwood ceramics and the history of the Wedgwood company; continental
ceramics; classical antiques; decorative arts. Offers brochures/pamphlets, informational
newsletters, library facilities, photos and research assistance. Publications list available. **How to
Contact:** Write or call. Responds to most inquiries within a month. Charges for photographic
services and appraisals. Library use by appointment only. Credit to be given to museum where
appropriate, i.e. photo captions, etc. **Tips:** "Do as much research as possible at your own locale.
Be as specific as possible when inquiring for information via mail. If identification/dating of ceramics is needed, send clear photograph and list of all marks on the object." Recent information request: Question as to whether William Blake illustrated Wedgwood's 1817 sales catalog.

75• CALLERLAB, THE INTERNATIONAL ASSOCIATION OF SQUARE DANCE CALLERS
Box 679, McCauley Ave., Pocono Pines PA 18350. (717)646-8411. Contact Person: Executive Secretary. **Description:** "Our purpose is to assist the members both professionally and personally in all aspects of their involvement in the square dance activity." **Services:** Provides interpretative, referral and technical information on square dance calling. Offers brochures/pamphlets and telephone reference services. **How to Contact:** Write. Responds to most inquiries within a week. Include SASE, major city location and zip code area request. **Tips:** Recent information request: "Can you help me find a caller/club in my area?"

76• CANADIAN CONFERENCE OF THE ARTS
141 Laurier Ave. W, Suite 707, Ottawa, Ontario, Canada K1P 5J3. (613)238-3561. Contact Person: Membership Coordinator. **Description:** "The Canadian Conference of the Arts is a national non-governmental association linking together over 700 arts organizations and associations across Canada. Established in 1945, the CCA is the major advocate working on behalf of the arts, artists and the cultural industries at a national level, and is the major policy advisor for the collective interests of the arts, artists and the cultural industries on issues of national concern, particularly those which involve consultation with the federal government. Organizational memberships are available for $45, $85 and $120, depending on the annual operating budget of the organization. Individual memberships are also available for $20. **Services:** "We provide detailed information on what's happening in the arts and the cultural industries across Canada, and particularly we provide information on federal involvement in the arts and the cultural industries. Pertinent issues in the arts are examined from a national perspective." Offers brochures, policy papers, research studies and reports. Publications include *Arts Bulletin* (bimonthly), reports on a wide variety of subjects (arts and education, arts and municipalities, federal cultural policy, etc.); and a set of handbooks (*Who's Who*—government people in the arts, and *Who Does What*—national associations and unions in the arts). **How to Contact:** Write or call. Responds to most inquiries immediately. There is a charge for most publications. Telephone orders will be accepted with Visa card numbers. **Tips:** Recent information requests: Questions on taxation law as it applies to self-employed artists; federal support of book and magazine publishing; Canadian Content, etc.

77• CENTER FOR ARTS INFORMATION
625 Broadway, New York NY 10012. (212)677-7548. Contact Person: Executive Director. **Description:** Center "providing information about sources of services and funds so that artists can better manage their careers." **Services:** Provides advisory, bibliographical and referral information for all arts disciplines, including arts administration and management. Offers brochures/pamphlets, clipping services, informational newsletters, library facilities, placement on mailing lists, research assistance, statistics and telephone reference services. Publications list available. **How to Contact:** Write, call or visit. Responds to most inquiries immediately. Charges for some publications. "Use of our research facility is by appointment only." **Tips:** Recent information requests: How to plan an estate; questions on tax and legal problems of artists.

78• CENTER FOR BOOK ARTS
15 Bleecker St., New York NY 10012. (212)460-9768. Contact Person: President. **Description:** Nonprofit organization promoting the arts of the book through publications, exhibitions, classes. **Services:** Provides advisory, historical, how-to, referral, technical and trade information on papermaking, letterpress printing, hard bookbinding. Offers brochures/pamphlets and informational newsletters. **How to Contact:** Write or call. Charges tuition fees for classes.

79• CENTER FOR THE HISTORY OF AMERICAN NEEDLEWORK
Old Economy Village, 14th and Church Sts., Ambridge PA 15003. (412)266-6440. Contact Person: Director. **Description:** "We are a national study center for needlework and textiles offering information, research and referral services including library, photos and publications. **Services:** Provides bibliographical, historical, interpretative and referral information on textiles in American culture, history, labor and technology. Offers brochures/pamphlets, information searches, placement on mailing list, newsletter and photos. Publications available. **How to Contact:** Write or call. Responds to most inquiries immediately. "Our library includes some manuscript resources. We include not only general history in the needle arts, but also textiles, technology in the needlework industry, and sewing. We charge for exhibitions, search services,

photos (at cost), book publications and pattern portfolios. Bibliographies and many other publications are free for SASE." Give photo credit to the Center. **Tips:** "It's best to come here and use our library yourself." Recent information request: Name of 19th century crochet technique.

80• COLOR IN CONSTRUCTION NEWS BUREAU
6 E. 43rd St., Room 2000, New York NY 10017. (212)867-8896. Contact Person: News Director. **Description:** "The Color in Construction News Bureau is maintained by Mobay Chemical Corporation to provide information and photographs on the use of color in the construction of commercial, industrial and residential buildings. Current focus is on colored concrete products used to enhance office buildings, homes, parks, urban redevelopment. Photos of installations across the country are on file." **Services:** Provides advisory, interpretative, referral, technical and trade information on the architectural landscape, aesthetics, life cycle costing, psychology of color, energy conservation, fire safety, color through the ages. Offers aid in arranging interviews, informational newsletters, photos, placement on mailing lists and press kits. **How to Contact:** Write or call. Responds to most inquiries immediately.

81• COOPER-HEWITT MUSEUM
Smithsonian Institution, 2 E. 91st St., New York NY 10028. (212)860-6868. Contact Person: Public Information Officer. **Description:** "Cooper-Hewitt Museum is the Smithsonian Institution's national museum of design. It serves as a reference center for designers, scholars and students in all fields of design and the decorative arts." **Services:** Provides advisory, bibliographical, historical and referral information; comprehensive information about the decoratve arts collections in the Cooper-Hewitt Museum; history of the museum's home, the former Carnegie Mansion, now a national and city historic landmark; tangential information about decorative arts collections in the Smithsonian Museums. Offers placement on mailing list, photos and press kits. "We maintain a library of over 30,000 volumes and a picture reference library of over 1,500,000 illustrations relating to the arts and all aspects of design. In addition, there are archives of color, pattern, textiles, symbols and advertising." Publications include "folders describing the permanent collections of drawings, prints, textiles, wallpaper and all decorative arts; and information about the museum's home, the former Andrew Carnegie property." **How to Contact:** "Press information is obtained from the public information officer. Specific information about the museum's holdings is obtained by letter to the curator of the pertinent department. Anyone who wishes to use the museum's resources is asked to make an appointment in advance with the curator of the department in which he wishes to work, or with the librarian." Responds to most inquiries within a week. Permission to publish excerpted material and photographs is sometimes required. **Tips:** "Use the resources of public libraries and the like before requesting research assistance from specialized institutions and specialists. Do your general homework first. Make appointments in advance, by letter if possible, giving details about story requirements." Recent information requests: Background for feature stories on puppets, Belter furniture, silver tea services, Scandinavian modern design, and American suburbs.

82• COUNTRY MUSIC ASSOCIATION, INC.
7 Music Circle N., Nashville TN 37203. (615)244-2840. Contact Person: Editor. **Description:** "Country Music Association, Inc. (CMA) is a trade organization for the country music industry made up of approximately 7,000 members. We promote country music throughout the world and sponsor various activities, such as the annual CMA awards show, which is televised over national TV every October." **Services:** Provides information on country music business, country music celebrities, country entertainment and country music. Offers brochures/pamphlets, placement on mailing list, newsletter and press kits. "We also offer lists of country radio stations throughout the US, music publishing companies, record company personnel, artists and managers and booking agents, and publication lists. However, these are available to CMA members only." Publications include "two booklets (both are part of our press kit) which give statistical information about the country music industry, such as the dollar amount of country product sales in the US, the number of country radio stations, the number of hours country music is programmed, interesting facts about Nashville and the country music industry, etc." **How to Contact:** Write or call. Make appointment in advance of visit. Responds to most inquiries immediately. "We will, of course, help writers as much as we can. A freelance writer may get brochures or whatever information we have at CMA to help him. A writer assigned by a publication to do a story may get additional help from CMA in arranging interviews with celebrities, record company personnel, etc., depending upon the availability of CMA staff's time. In our busy seasons (May-June, September-October) we may

not be as able to help as at other times." **Tips:** "People wishing current information about country music in general should contact CMA first. People wishing historical information should contact the Country Music Foundaton, 4 Music Square E., Nashville TN 37203. The Country Music Foundation has a complete library and archives housing information about virtually all phases of country music. People wishing information about a specific artist should contact the artist's booking agent or record label."

83• COUNTRY MUSIC HALL OF FAME
Country Music Foundation, 4 Music Square E, Nashville TN 37203. (615)256-1639. Contact Person: Reference Librarian. **Description:** The purpose of the Country Music Hall of Fame is to preserve the history of country music. "We have a fully functioning museum and research facility with 85,000 recorded items." **Services:** Provides advisory, bibliographical, historical, referral, technical and trade information on country music and related areas (bluegrass, western, swing, Cajun, etc.); Anglo-American folksongs; music industry, etc. Offers aid in arranging interviews ("possibly"), clipping services, information searches, placement on mailing list, photos and press kits. Includes vertical file system with biographical sketches of country music artists. "We can provide basically any information—records, videotapes, clips and films." Publications include *Journal of Country Music*; *Bill Munroe: An Illustrated Discography*; *My Husband, Jimmy Rogers*; *Truth Is Stranger than Publicity*; and reprints of a 1921 Gibson Company catalog and a report of an 1890 Edison Phonograph Dealers convention proceedings. **How to Contact:** Write or call. Responds to most inquiries within a week. Charges for photos. "Library open by appointment only, Monday-Friday 9 a.m.-5 p.m., stack areas closed. Must write or call in advance for specific needs."

84• THE CRAYON, WATER COLOR AND CRAFT INSTITUTE, INC.
715 Boylston St., Boston MA 02116. Contact Person: Executive Vice President. **Description:** The institute provides referral and trade information on non-toxic, quality crayons and other art materials. Celebration of Youth Art Month in March each year. **Services:** Offers brochures/pamphlets. **How to Contact:** Write. Responds to most inquiries within a week. **Tips:** Recent information request: "What does the CP/AP seal on crayons, etc. mean?"

85• CROCHET ASSOCIATION INTERNATIONAL
Box 131, Dallas GA 30132. (404)445-7137. Contact Person: Executive Director. **Description:** Organization promoting interest in crochet as fiber art by introducing new stitches and methods for modern day crochet as well as offering information on the old methods. **Services:** Provides advisory, how-to, interpretative, technical and trade information on crochet, yarns, thread, crochet hooks of all types. Offers aid in arranging interviews. **How to Contact:** Write. Responds to most inquiries immediately. Charges for demonstrations.

86• THE SALVADOR DALI FOUNDATION, INC.
1000 3rd St. S., St. Petersburg FL 33701. (813)823-3767. Contact Person: Public Relations Director. **Description:** The foundation promotes the Salvador Dali Museum as a tourist and educational attraction. **Services:** Provides bibliographical (restricted) and historical information on Salvador Dali, surrealism and related movements; and interpretative information on the collection. Offers biographies (on the artist); brochures/pamphlets (limited); library facilities (restricted); photos (loans); press kits; research assistance (restricted); speakers and tours. Museum publications available. **How to contact:** Write. Responds to most inquiries within a week. "Limited assisted use of library and research materials." **Tips:** "Arrange to come to the museum and join a guided tour. It adds great insight into the collection."

87• DANCE CRITICS ASSOCIATION
Box 47, Planetarium Station, New York NY 10024. Contact Person: President. **Description:** "DCA is a professional organization of dance critics from the print and broadcast media, and others working in related fields. Its purpose is to encourage excellence in dance criticism through education, research and the exchange of ideas. We sponsor workshops and an annual conference." **Services:** Provides advisory and bibliographical information on dance criticism, and dance history and research. Offers brochures/pamphlets, informational newsletters and placement on mailing lists. Publications include a quarterly newsletter; pamphlets on copyright, research sources for dance writers, training opportunities for dance critics. **How to Contact:** Write. Responds to most inquiries within a month. Membership (voting: $35/year; associate: $25/year;

student: $10/year) includes newsletter and all publications; reduced registration fee at annual conferences. **Tips:** Recent information requests: "College students interested in dance and curious about what career opportunities exist in the field of dance criticism/journalism ask us how to learn more about the field."

88• DANCE NOTATION BUREAU, INC.
505 8th Ave., # 2301, New York NY 10018. (212)736-4350. Contact Person: Executive Director, Director of Education or Librarian. **Description:** The bureau incorporates the following: "recording of dance with the written system of symbols called Labanotation; reconstruction of those dances from the Labanotated scores; school for teaching the above two skills; and publisher and bookstore for text material on dance notation." **Services:** Provides advisory, interpretative, referral and technical information. Offers brochures/pamphlets, informational newsletters, library facilities, research assistance and statistics. **How to Contact:** Write, call or visit. Responds to most inquiries immediately. Research services and fees depend on amount of time involved. "Requests for information on bureau activities should be clearly worded with the assistance of people knowledgeable in the field of dance." **Tips:** Recent information requests: The future of dance notation and career opportunities in the field; the computerization of dance notation; developments in the field of choreography and copyright.

89• DRUM CORPS INTERNATIONAL, INC.
719 S. Main St., Lombard IL 60148. (312)495-9866. Contact Person: Publicity-Promotions Manager. **Description:** Drum Corps International is a nonprofit youth activity. "Our purpose is to promote the competition drum and bugle corps activity throughout the United States and Canada; and to promote competitive marching music as an entertainment format." **Services:** Provides advisory, historical, how-to, referral and trade information on drum and bugle corps, Drum Corps International, competition rules and procedures, and the basic judging process. Offers aid in arranging interviews, biographies, brochures/pamphlets, informational newsletters, photos, press kits and research assistance. Publications include *Annual Drum Corps International Yearbook*; and *Contest Guild*, bimonthly educational newsletter. **How to Contact:** Write or call. Responds to most inquiries within a month. "Because of severe staff limitations, requestees should exercise considerable patience. It is easier to service requests from September 1 through May 31. Use of any extracted information requires prior approval and inclusion of the appropriate credit line." **Tips:** "Clearly note, at all times, that a drum and bugle corps is a separate entity from a marching band." Recent information requests: "How many competition drum and bugle corps remain active in the US and Canada today?"; "How does a drum and bugle corps differ from a marching band?"

90• EDWARD-DEAN MUSEUM OF DECORATIVE ARTS
Riverside County Art & Culture Center, 9401 Oak Glen Rd., Cherry Valley CA 92223. (714)845-2626. Contact Person: Adminstrative Assistant. **Description:** "A collection of primarily European, Oriental and American furniture, porcelain, glass, textiles, jade, ivory, painting, sculpture, prints and watercolors from antiquity to the present with an emphasis on 17th, 18th and 19th century decorative arts." **Services:** Offers study environment and a library of the decorative arts. **How to Contact:** Write or call. Responds to most inquiries "for general information" immediately; all others are answered "as soon as possible." The library is available for serious research by appointment only." **Tips:** Recent information request: "What are some important things to look for in identifying an original?"

91• GALLERY OF PREHISTORIC PAINTINGS
220 5th Ave., Rm. 711, New York NY 10001. (212)689-7518. Contact Person: Director. **Description:** "We are specialists in prehistoric art. We make accurate silkscreened editions of cave art. We sell to France, Spain, Italy, North America and the United States." **Services:** Provides advisory, bibliographical, how-to, referral and technical information on worldwide cave and canyon art of prehistoric periods. Offers brochures/pamphlets, regular informational newsletter, photos (cave art), films, slides, and books. Publications include *Voices from the Stone Age* ($12.95). **How to Contact:** Write or call. Responds to most inquiries immediately. "We charge for slides, photographs and films."

92• THE GETZEN COMPANY, INC.
211 W. Centralia, Elkhorn WI 53121. (414)723-4221. Contact Person: Vice President of Sales. **Description:** "We manufacture brasswind musical instruments and publish educational

pamphlets on different phases of brasswind musical instrument playing.'' **Services:** Provides advisory, technical and trade information covering the manufacture of brasswind instruments. Offers brochures/pamphlets. **How to Contact:** Write. Responds to most inquiries immediately.

93• MARTHA GRAHAM DANCE COMPANY
316 E. 63rd St., New York NY 10021. Contact Person: Archivist or Publicity Coordinator. **Description:** ''We are involved in performing and organizing and training a performing group.'' **Services:** Provides advisory and historical information on the Martha Graham Dance Company and Miss Graham's works. Offers aid in arranging interviews, biographies, brochures/pamphlets, information searches, newsletter and photos. Publications include souvenir books and reviews. **How to Contact:** Write or call. Responds to most inquiries within a month, ''depending on the situation.'' Charges for use of materials or purchase of materials/publications. ''Due to fund raising time commitments and time limitations, not every request for information or service can be honored.'' **Tips:** ''Submit all requests in writing at least 1-2 months before information or materials are needed. Give a detailed explanation of purpose. You'll save time and effort if you use multiple resources and refer to major libraries or reference services before requesting information from the Martha Graham Dance Company.'' Recent information request: ''When did Miss Graham premiere her work *Appalachian Spring*?''

94• GRAPHIC ARTISTS GUILD
30 E. 20th St., New York NY 10003. (212)777-7353. Contact Person: Communications Director. **Description:** Union for graphic artists. **Services:** Provides referral, technical and trade information on pricing and industry standards, contracts, copyright. Offers aid in arranging interviews, brochures/pamphlets, informational newsletters and telephone reference services. Publications include *Pricing & Ethical Guidelines*; *Visual Artists Guide to the 1978 Copyright Law*. **How to Contact:** Write or call. Responds to most inquiries within a month. ''Any material excerpted from our publications must be cleared through us. Tell us what your goal in accumulating the information is.'' **Tips:** ''There isn't a lot of statistical information on graphic artists since so many are self-employed/freelance.'' Recent information requests: Trade practices; information on art contests; background on work-for-hire provision of the copyright law.

95• GRAPHIC ARTS TECHNICAL FOUNDATION
4615 Forbes Ave., Pittsburgh PA 15213. (412)621-6941. Contact Person: Communications Manager. **Description:** ''The Graphic Arts Technical Foundation is a member-supported, nonprofit, scientific, technical, and educational organization serving the international graphic communications industries. It is the oldest continuous organization of its kind. From its small beginnings in 1924 as the Lithographic Technical Foundation, this industry-inspired and member-directed Foundation has grown into one of the world's leading centers for graphic communications research and education. Today GATF programs cover major graphic arts processes and their applications. GATF has over 2,000 corporate members in 60 countries and a staff of over 80 people.'' **Services:** Provides advisory, analytical, bibliographical, how-to, referral, technical and trade information. Research activities include waste control, environmental studies, press and prepress research, quality control, and techno-economic forecasting. Among the many functions of GATF's Technical Services Department are the study of problems in the printing plant and consultation on technical problems related to the graphic arts. Educational activities include an outstanding library; an extensive publication program; career and curricular consultation for schools and universities; and seminars, workshops, and conferences for the graphic arts community. **How to Contact:** Call. Responds to most inquiries within a week. ''All services are priced. Rates are too many and varied to list. We will provide information on specific questions when they are received.'' **Tips:** ''Our E.H. Wadewitz Library is one of the most complete on graphic arts in existence.''

96• JOSE GRECO FOUNDATION FOR HISPANIC DANCE, INC.
866 United Nations Plaza, New York NY 10017. (212)355-7433. Contact Person: Executive Director. **Description:** ''The purpose of the foundation is to develop interest in Hispanic dance in the US and the world through performances, workshops and clinics.'' **Services:** Offers aid in arranging interviews, biographies, brochures/pamphlets, information searches, placement on mailing list, photos and press kits. Publications available. **How to Contact:** Write or call. Responds to most inquiries within a week. Prefers written requests, but will answer questions briefly by phone.

BEHIND THE BYLINE

Susan Stamberg
Writer and radio host

Susan Stamberg has the unique ability to communicate effectively in both broadcasting and print. She is co-host of National Public Radio's "All Things Considered" (ATC) program and author of *Every Night at Five: Susan Stamberg's "All Things Considered" Book*, which is a sampling of the show's highlights over the years.

"The weeks of research it takes to pull some stories together is translated into a few minutes on the air, and then it sort of disappears. *Every Night at Five* was a chance to freeze some of those moments, to revisit them and examine the work." Now that Stamberg has had a taste of putting words to paper, she finds an urge to write more.

"I've noticed that most of my life whenever I've had an experience, it was never really complete until I told it to someone. Now I'm finding that it's not complete for me until I write it down. That's really a change. But a novelist friend of mine tells me that's what it's all about. I guess an experience happens . . . it percolates and percolates and the pressure builds until it comes out and completes itself in writing.

"It's agony and ecstasy combined. When writing goes right, it's so marvelous. There's nothing so exhilarating except for a wonderful moment in the course of a radio interview."

But whether it's for broadcast or print, Stamberg says research is not as easy as it sounds. "Ugh, it's hard. It's a funny thing about research—we're raised to think of it as something horrible. The idea that you always have little three-by-five index cards, and it's always done in places that smell terrible and never have enough light; the stacks are narrow and people hunch over and they're very unfriendly. That's part of it, yes, but the best part of it is fastening on something that so intrigues and absorbs you that you want to learn more. That's when it becomes marvelous."

Stamberg's research for the book consisted of asking listeners, colleagues and member radio stations to recall memorable episodes in ATC's years of broadcasting. Much of what

was suggested became the spine for the book. Stamberg then went to the tape archives, transcribed the tapes, double checked facts and tracked down the spellings of people and places. "The most infuriating part of the research was the meticulous checking of spellings. Reporters keep notes, sure, but we don't really keep records. It's not important for us to know the spelling of a name on the air, just how to pronounce it. I had an editorial assistant who just sat on the phone and became best friends with every information operator in the world."

Stamberg's broadcasts call for daily research, and she lauds the assistance of the station's "indefatigable" librarian. But she likes to do her own in-depth research. "Other people can get dates and biographical stuff from a file; I'll read the same file and buried in the twelfth paragraph I'll find an observation that'll stick with me and tap around in my head. It can set off a million thoughts that I can play with in an interview or on the air. You have to trust your own curiosity."

In her book, Stamberg writes that ATC listens for America. "The program is really like a reference desk. We are not the experts; we find them and use them constantly. Part of the research is in being alert to possibilities. There are stories everywhere." She recalls talking to a listener from New Haven who mentioned the bluefish were running in the Connecticut River and he planned to take his son fishing for the first time.

"That's all I needed. I asked if I could call his son and see how it went. The listener's passing aside gave me a story people could connect with their own childhood memories of going fishing. Those are the life issues."

97• E. AZALIA HACKLEY COLLECTION
Detroit Public Library, 5201 Woodward Ave., Detroit MI 48202. (313)833-1000. Contact Person: Curator. **Description:** "The Hackley Collection seeks to document the achievements of blacks in the performing arts: music, dance, radio, TV, theater and moving pictures." **Services:** Provides advisory, bibliographical, historical and referral information covering blacks in the performing arts: music, dance, radio, TV, theater and movies. Offers bibliographies, biographies, brochures/pamphlets, records, sheet music, clipping services, information searches and photos. Publications include a brochure that provides descriptive information about the collection and services. **How to Contact:** Write or call. Responds to most inquiries within a week. "Materials do not circulate but many may be photocopied." Charges 10¢/photocopy plus 35¢ postage. Charges 50¢/photo plus 35¢ postage. "Special research rates are available on request. Extensive information searches are limited due to staffing limitations. If you will be visiting in person and need a tour or special assistance, call for an appointment. Identification is required for visits to do research in the collection." **Tips:** "Be persistent, specific, and thorough; valuable information can sometimes be located in sources which have not been analyzed or indexed." Recent information requests: "What do you have on black violinists?"; "Do you have any photos of Marian Anderson?"; "Send me information on the Hackley Concerts and how I can audition to perform."

98• HIRSHHORN MUSEUM AND SCULPTURE GARDEN
Smithsonian Institution, Washington DC 20560. (202)357-1618. Contact Person: Public Information Officer. **Description:** "The Hirshhorn Museum and Sculpture Garden is part of the Smithsonian Institution. A museum of contemporary art, the Hirshhorn houses one of the world's major collections of modern sculpture; the painting collection is primarily American." **Services:** Provides bibliographical, referral and museum-related information on 20th century art (sculpture, painting). Offers aid in arranging interviews, biographies, brochures/pamphlets, library facilities, photos, placement on mailing lists, press kits and research assistance. Publications include catalogs of exhibitions; museum shop also has selection of books/catalogs about modern artists/art movements. **How to Contact:** Write or call. Responds to most inquiries within a week. "Books and catalogs are billed through our Museum Shop. Photos and transparencies are billed through the museum's department of photography from which permission must be obtained for publication. Material is available to art historians; freelance writers should let us know where material will be published and when." **Tips:** "Staff limitations require that inquiries be about works in our own collection. We have a regular film program with a wide selection of films (noontime) about artists; we also have an evening program of films by artist filmmakers. The films are free and shown twice a week (no films in summer)." Recent information request: "Do you have a transparency and background material on Rodin's 'Burghers of Calais'?"

99• M. HOHNER, INC.
Box 15035, Richmond VA 23227. Contact Person: Director of Marketing Communications. **Description:** "Sole distributors of Hohner and Sonor products in the US. Product line includes harmonicas, keyboards, diatonic and piano accordions, recorders, melodicas, instruments for musical education and musical instrument accessories." **Services:** Provides historical and technical information. Offers brochures/pamphlets. "We have product literature on each of our musical instruments." **How to Contact:** Write or call. Responds to most inquiries within a week. "Single pieces of literature are supplied free of charge; forward SASE for quicker response. If quantities are requested, there may be a shipping and handling fee." **Tips:** Recent information request: Brochure on specific instrument.

100• IMC NEEDLECRAFT
55 Railroad Ave., Garnerville NY 10923. (914)429-2102. Contact Person: President. **Description:** IMC Needlecraft manufactures and markets needlecraft items. **Services:** Provides advisory, how-to and trade information on needlecraft. Offers brochures/pamphlets, informational newsletters, photos, press kits and telephone reference services. **How to Contact:** Call. Responds to most inquiries immediately. **Tips:** Recent information request: "What is the size of the needlecraft market?"

101• INDIAN ARTS AND CRAFTS BOARD
US Department of the Interior, Washington DC 20240. (202)343-2773. Contact Person: General Manager. **Description:** "The board encourages and promotes the development of traditional and

innovative native American arts and crafts—the creative work of American Indian, Eskimo and Aleut people—and related cultural concerns. The agency's general subject of expertise is contemporary native American arts." **Services:** Provides advisory, bibliographical, referral and trade information. Offers bibliographies, brochures/pamphlets and "referral to other appropriate sources of information about native American arts." Publications include *Source Directory of Native American Arts and Crafts Businesses*, *Bibliography on Native American Arts and Crafts* and *Fact Sheet: General Information about the Activities of the Indian Arts and Crafts Board*. A publications list is available. Only single copies of publications are provided. **How to Contact:** "Request by letter or phone." Responds to most inquiries within a month. **Tips:** "The board exists primarily to serve native American artists, craftsmen and organizations. Staff time devoted to others, including writers, is secondary and only provided as time permits. The more specific a writer can be about the information needed, the more effectively we can respond."

102• INSTITUTE OF OUTDOOR DRAMA
University of North Carolina, 052A, Chapel Hill NC 27514. (919)962-1328. Contact Person: Director. **Description:** "The Institute of Outdoor Drama is a service agency of the University of North Carolina at Chapel Hill. It serves as a communications link between operating dramas and as a resource for groups, agencies, or individuals concerned with the production of outdoor historical dramas or classics." **Services:** Provides advisory, analytical, bibliographical, historical, how-to, interpretative, referral, technical and trade information on techniques of outdoor drama organization, management, production, acting, writing, dance, music and other theatre arts. Offers aid in arranging interviews, brochures/pamphlets, informational newsletters, library facilities, placement on mailing lists, research assistance and statistics. Publications include *An Amphitheatre for Epic Drama*; *A Selected Bibliography on Outdoor Drama* and other books; a monthly newsletter; bulletins; also visual aids. Publications list available for SASE. **How to Contact:** Write or call. Responds to most inquiries within a week. Charges for publications. **Tips:** "See some of the major dramas. We will send a list on request (include SASE)."

103• INTERNATIONAL EDITORIAL DESIGN FORUM, INC.
131 W. 35th St., New York NY 10001. (212)868-1165. Contact Person: Producer/Director. **Description:** "Our purpose is to promote, sponsor and encourage the advancement of the field of editorial design, the public knowledge and appreciation of this area of graphic arts and to provide a service and communication network for the professionals engaged in this art." **Services:** Provides advisory, analytical, bibliographical, historical, how-to, interpretative, referral, technical and trade information on "graphic art as it applies to editorial design—magazines, books, annual reports and similar material. This includes technical subjects i.e., layout, typesetting, photography and illustration, printing and film separations; aesthetic subjects such as design with or without the grid." Offers research assistance and examples from our newly-formed archives. Plans "Best of Editorial Design" annual. **How to Contact:** Write or call. Responds to most inquiries immediately. "The organization must be given credit for any supplied information that is used. We also must receive a copy of the final product."

104• INTERNATIONAL FIRE PHOTOGRAPHERS ASSOCIATION
Box 201, Elmhurst IL 60126. (312)530-3097. Contact Person: President. **Description:** Individuals working "to improve the status of all aspects of photography, and specifically that of fire photography operations." **Services:** Provides advisory, how-to, referral, technical and trade information on how to use cameras; how to cover fires and arson scenes; how to process and print film; how to make public education programs. Offers brochures/pamphlets, informational newsletters, photos and research assistance. Publications include newsletter (quarterly). **How to Contact:** Write. Responds to most inquiries immediately. Charges for photos. "We require at least 2 months time to procure information requested." **Tips:** Recent information request: "How do you set up a photo service for a police or fire department?"

105• INTERNATIONAL FOUNDATION FOR ART RESEARCH, INC.
46 E. 70th St., New York NY 10021. Contact Person: Executive Director. **Description:** "We examine works of art to determine authenticity and maintain an index of stolen works and files on art forgeries." **Services:** Offers statistics, brochures/pamphlets, placement on mailing list; also "an archive of clippings and news items on the subjects we research. Our publications include an annual index of stolen art; a monthly newsletter, *Stolen Art Alert*; a detailed report on art theft; and

reports on the specific works we have examined." **How to Contact:** Write. Responds to most inquiries within a week. Charges for membership and subscription to monthly newsletter.

106• INTERNATIONAL JUGGLERS ASSOCIATION
Box 29, Kenmore NY 14217. (716)873-8193. Contact Person: Secretary/Treasurer. **Description:** "Our purpose is to enhance the art of juggling." **Services:** Provides advisory, bibliographical and historical information on juggling. Offers brochures/pamphlets, informational newsletters and placement on mailing lists. Publications include *Jugglers World Magazine.* **How to Contact:** Write. Responds to most inquiries immediately. Membership is $13 for a new member, $10 renewal.

107• INTERNATIONAL MUSEUM OF PHOTOGRAPHY
George Eastman House, 900 East Ave., Rochester NY 14607. Contact: Chief Archivist or Print Service. **Description:** Photo collection. Collection spans the history of photography from 1839 to present day. **Services:** Provides bibliographical, historical and technical information on the history and aesthetics of photography. "We do not do subject searches as a rule. Our collection is accessed by photographer's name, not subject." Offers photos. **How to Contact:** Write. Responds to most inquiries within a month. "Original prints do not leave the museum, except for approved traveling exhibitions. Photographic reproduction fees are charged; contact Print Service Department for details. Reproduction prints must be returned, and a credit line is required." **Tips:** "Do your homework. Consult published guides to collections so your questions can be as specific as possible to the particular collection." Recent information request: "What Civil War related material do you have by Brady and Barnard?"

108• THE INTERNATIONAL ROCK 'N' ROLL MUSIC ASSOCIATION, INC. (IRMA)
Box 50111, Nashville TN 37205. (615)352-1443, 297-9072. Contact Person: President. **Description:** "Our purpose is to preserve, promote and protect the interests of rock 'n' roll." **Services:** Provides bibliographical, historical, referral and trade information on rock 'n' roll music past and present. Offers brochures/pamphlets, informational newsletters, photos, placement on mailing lists and research assistance. **How to Contact:** Write. Responds to most inquiries within a week. Charges for memberships and publications, mailing lists and some services, depending on nature. **Tips:** Recent information request: "What influence did the Beatles have on modern day rock music?"

109• JOFFREY BALLET
130 W. 56th St., New York NY 10019. (212)265-7300. Contact Person: Press Representative. **Description:** "We are one of three major ballet companies in the country." **Services:** Offers aid in arranging interviews, biographies, brochures/pamphlets, information searches, placement on mailing list, photos and press kits. **How to Contact:** Write or call. Responds to inquiries "as soon as possible. Often press representative is on tour with the company and any correspondence has to wait until return."

110• JUILLIARD SCHOOL
Lincoln Center, New York NY 10023. (212)799-5000. Contact Person: Director of Public Relations. **Description:** A private, professional school of dance, music and drama. Has students from 36 foreign countries. **Services:** Offers brochures/pamphlets. Publications include school catalog. **How to Contact:** Write or call. Responds to most inquiries within a week.

111• LIBRARY OF CONGRESS, MUSIC DIVISION
Washington DC 20540. (202)287-5504. Contact Person: Head. **Description:** The Music Division "provides public reference service from our collections and proper custodial care for our collections." **Services:** Provides bibliographical, historical and referral information on music, musicians, musical instruments, etc. Offers biographies (very brief), brochures/pamphlets, computerized information searches, library facilities, research assistance and telephone reference services. Publications list available. **How to Contact:** Write, call or visit. Responds to most inquiries within a month. "Some donor restrictions on gift materials exist." **Tips:** "Any writer doing in-depth research would be well-advised to call first so our most knowledgeable staff person in that field can be ready to help. Give yourself time; more often than not, much more material will be found here than you expect to find." Recent information request: Historical background on a well-known song.

112• LIBRARY OF CONGRESS, PRINTS AND PHOTOGRAPHS DIVISION
Madison Building, Room LM 339, Washington DC 20540. (202)287-6394. Contact Person: Chief. **Description:** The Prints and Photographs Division of the Library of Congress provides visual materials. **Services:** Provides bibliographical and historical visual records of people, places, and events in America and throughout the world. Offers photos. **How to Contact:** Visit. Responds to most inquiries within a month. Charges for various photo reproduction services; copyright restrictions enforced.

113• LIZZADRO MUSEUM OF LAPIDARY ART
220 Cottage Hill Ave., Elmhurst IL 60126. (312)833-1616. Contact Person: Assistant to the Director. **Description:** Museum exhibiting lapidary art objects, primarily Chinese jade carvings; also minerals and fossils. **Services:** Provides advisory, how-to and referral information on lapidary art; earth sciences; minerals, fossils, gemstones and primarily jade. Offers aid in arranging interviews, brochures/pamphlets and library facilities. Semiannual publication. **How to Contact:** Write, call or visit. Responds to most inquiries immediately.

114• MARQUETRY SOCIETY OF AMERICA
32-34 153rd St., Flushing NY 11354. Contact Person: Trustee. **Description:** Individuals promoting the art/craft of marquetry. **Services:** Provides how-to and technical information. Offers informational newsletters. **How to Contact:** Write. Responds to most inquiries within a week.

115• THE METROPOLITAN MUSEUM OF ART
5th Ave. at 82nd St., New York NY 10028. (212)879-5500, ext. 3562, 3228. Contact: Photograph and Slide Library. **Description:** The Metropolitan Museum of Art has information covering the history of art from ancient times to the present. **Services:** Offers 4x5 and 8x10 b&w photos for sale; color transparencies for rent for publication only (mostly 8x10). These cover only objects in the museum's collections. Publications include *Color Transparencies for Rental.* **How to Contact:** Write or call. Responds to most inquiries within a month. Research must be done by the user. Charges $5-10/8x10 photo. Credit line required. Return required on color transparencies only; photographs made to special order are sold outright with one-time reproduction rights included. "Selections of specific items can be made from the various catalogs and *Bulletins* published by the museum and available in many libraries. The photograph files may be consulted by the public during departmental hours."

116• MUSEUM OF CARTOON ART
Comly Ave., Port Chester NY 10573. (914)939-0234. Contact Person: Director. **Description:** Research library which preserves and exhibits original artwork in all areas of cartooning. Animation library on video tape. **Services:** Provides analytical, historical, how-to, interpretive, referral and technical information on comic strips, comic books, editorial/political cartoons and animation. Offers library facilities and press kits. **How to Contact:** Write or call. Responds to most inquiries within a month. Charges $10/hour research fee. Make an appointment to use the library. **Tips:** Recent information requests: "What does Charlie Brown's father do for a living?"; "Who was the first comic strip character?"

117• MUSEUM OF MODERN ART
11 W. 53rd St., New York NY 10019. (212)708-9500. Contact Person: Director, Public Information Department. **Description:** "The museum was founded in 1929 to establish a permanent, public museum to acquire, from time to time, collections of the best works of modern art." **Services:** Provides advisory and historical information on the history of The Museum of Modern Art, and its past and ongoing exhibitions. Offers aid in arranging interviews, annual reports, bibliographies, biographies, statistics, brochures/pamphlets, information searches, newsletter, photos and press kits. Has reference library of articles written about the library, open by appointment. Publications include *Monthly Calendar.* **How to Contact:** Write or call. Responds to most inquiries immediately. Give credentials.

118• MUSEUM OF MODERN ART OF LATIN AMERICA
Organization of American States (OAS), 201 18th St. NW, Washington DC 20006. (201)789-6016. Contact Person: Director. **Description:** "We promote the visual arts of the Latin American countries in the hemisphere and elsewhere." **Services:** Provides advisory, bibliographical, interpretive, referral and technical information on Latin American art, emphasis

on modern art. Offers aid in arranging interviews, bibliographies, biographies, brochures/pamphlets and photos. Publications include exhibit catalogs. **How to Contact:** Write or visit. Responds to most inquiries within a month. Consultation on an appointment basis. Charges only to make copies of photographs or documents. "Material cannot be taken off the premises." Give credit to museum. **Tips:** "We own the most complete archive of all the periods of the visual arts of Latin America. Scholars, professors, lecturers and researchers in general are welcome." Research files divided by artist, country, and chronologically.

119• MUSEUM OF REPERTOIRE AMERICANA
Rt. 1, Mt. Pleasant IA 52641. (319)385-8937. Contact Person: Curator. **Description:** "The museum houses a collection of pictures, posters, programs and memorabilia from the repertory theatre companies that toured the opera house circuits or tent theatres throughout the United States. We have a great deal of material on an important yet overlooked phase of American theatre history." **Services:** Provides information on entertainment, history, music and old theatrical scripts. Offers aid in arranging interviews. Research library contains a variety of repertoire memorabilia including 1,000 play manuscripts and Chautauqua and Lyceum (1900-1930) memorabilia. **How to Contact:** Write or call. "Use of material must be cleared through head office of Midwest Old Threshers (parent organization)." Museum and library open by appointment only.

120• THE MUSICAL MUSEUM
S. Main St., Deansboro NY 13328. (315)841-8774. Contact Person: Curator. **Description:** "We have a large collection of early musical instruments and early complicated automatic musical instruments. We have a few photos on hand for purchase. We do not have a staff photographer, but welcome photographers, writers and recorders who may want to use our material as part of a story or for research. We will answer all letters and questions if return postage is provided." Also has antique oil lamps. **Services:** Offers brochures/pamphlets, information searches and photos. **How to Contact:** Write or call. Responds to most inquiries within a week. "Send good, clear questions, with payment for estimated time involved or we cannot answer." Charges $5/hour average. Postage must accompany request. **Tips:** "We expect credit to be given for the source of the information. We suggest a visit with a camera and recorder. We frequently send out packets of information about the museum to writers. A dollar for postage would be extremely helpful."

121• NATIONAL ACADEMY OF DESIGN
1083 Fifth Ave., New York NY 10028. (212)369-4880. Contact Person: Director. **Description:** The academy promotes American art through exhibitions, the school of fine arts, library and the archive of American art since 1825. **Services:** Provides historical information on 19th and 20th century American art. Offers photos and research assistance. Publications include exhibition catalogs. **How to Contact:** Write. Responds to most inquiries within a month. Charges for photographic services. "Call for an appointment." **Tips:** "Organize your queries by artist(s) rather than subject."

122• NATIONAL ASSEMBLY OF STATE ARTS AGENCIES
1010 Vermont Ave., NW, Suite 316, Washington DC 20005. (202)347-6352. Contact Person: Executive Director or Membership Services Coordinator. **Description:** "The NASAA is a nonprofit, membership organization of the state arts agencies in the 50 states and 6 special jurisdictions of the US. It exists to enhance the growth of the arts, to develop an informed membership, to represent the collective needs and concerns of the member agencies and to provide forums for the review and development of arts policy nationally." **Services:** Provides historical, referral and technical information on state arts agencies, national public policy and arts in general. Offers brochures/pamphlets, informational newsletters, library facilities, photos, placement on mailing lists, press kits, research assistance and statistics. Complete list of state arts agencies available on request. Publications include *NASAA News.* **How to Contact:** Write. Responds to most inquiries within a week. Requests review of article, etc. before publication. **Tips:** Recent information request: Question concerning the amount budgeted for legislative appropriations for the arts.

123• NATIONAL ASSOCIATION FOR REGIONAL BALLET
1860 Broadway, New York NY 10024. (212)757-8460. Contact Person: Executive Director. **Description:** "We are a service organization for decentralized, resident dance

companies." **Services:** Provides advisory, analytical, historical, how-to, interpretative, referral and technical information on dance: artistic and administrative. Offers annual reports, brochures/pamphlets, informational newsletters, photos, placement on mailing lists, press kits, research assistance, statistics and telephone reference services. Publications include: *Dance/America*; *Promo-Memo*; *Pro-Wing Bulletin*; *Directors' Bulletin*; and *United We Dance*. **How to Contact:** Write or call. Responds to most inquiries immediately. Include SASE with information request. Associate membership required for full publication schedule. **Tips:** Recent information request: "How many regional ballet companies are there in the country? How many ten years ago?"

124• NATIONAL ASSOCIATION FOR THE PRESERVATION AND PERPETUATION OF STORYTELLING (NAPPS)
Box 112, Slemons House Fox St., Jonesboro TN 37659. (615)753-2171. Contact Person: Administrative Assistant. **Description:** The association's purpose is to help preserve and perpetuate the art of storytelling. **Services:** Provides bibliograhical, how-to and referral information on storytelling: the art and technique, and resources. Offers biographies, brochures/pamphlets, informational newsletters, library facilities, photos, placement on mailing lists and research assistance. Library contains over 200 hours of audio and video recordings of storytelling material. Publications include *Yarnspinner*, a 10-page monthly newsletter on storytelling; *A National Directory of Storytellers*. **How to Contact:** Write or call. Responds to most inquiries immediately. Membership is open to anyone interested in storytelling. Annual membership dues are $15. **Tips:** Recent information request: "Can you tell me about the National Storytelling Festival?"

125• NATIONAL ASSOCIATION OF WOMEN ARTISTS
41 Union Square W., New York NY 10003. (212)675-1616. Contact Person: Secretary. **Description:** "The purpose of the association is to give professional women artists the opportunity to exhibit their works in creditable shows." **Services:** Provides information on art exhibitions for professional women artists. Offers brochures/pamphlets. Publications include synopsis of the organization's services and purpose. **How to Contact:** Write or call. Responds to most inquiries within a week.

126• NATIONAL CARTOONISTS SOCIETY
9 Ebony Court, Brooklyn NY 11229. (212)743-6510. Contact Person: Scribe. **Description:** "NCS, with a membership of about 500 of the world's foremost cartoonists, is neither guild nor union. It is a professional society whose main purpose is to further the interests of cartooning and of those individuals who work in the profession. It works to preserve high standards of artistic achievement and good taste in their relationship with the public and those agencies distributing cartoons for professionl use." **Services:** Publications include *The NCS Album*, containing history of the society, biographies, photos and art samples of members. **How to Contact:** Write. Responds to most inquiries within a week. Charges $16.75 for *The NCS Album*.

127• NATIONAL CARVERS MUSEUM
14960 Woodcarver Rd., Monument CO 80132. (303)481-2656. Contact Person: Administrator. **Description:** Museum which "fosters, cultivates, promotes, sponsors and develops the understanding of wood carving, past, present, and future." **Services:** Provides advisory, analytical, bibliographical, historical, how-to, interpretative, referral, technical and trade information on wood carving, inlay, power carving, whittling, sculpture, wood burning. Offers biographies, brochures/pamphlets, informational newsletters, library facilities, photos, research assistance and wood carving classes. Publications include *The Mallet Magazine* (monthly); other publications on wood carving. **How to Contact:** Write. Responds to most inquiries within a week. Recent information request: "What are the differences among whittling, wood carving and sculpture?"

128• NATIONAL ENDOWMENT FOR THE ARTS
2401 E St. NW, Washington DC 20506. (202)634-6033. Contact Person: Assistant Chairman, Press Office. **Description:** "Independent agency of the federal government set up in 1965 to encourage and assist national cultural progress." **Services:** Provides information in the areas of art, entertainment and music. Awards grants to individuals, arts agencies and nonprofit organizations representing the highest quality of art. Offers aid in arranging interviews. **How to**

Contact: Write or call the General Program and Publications Office (202)634-6369 for additional information and brochures/pamphlets on National Endowment for the Arts. Responds to most inquiries within a week.

129• NATIONAL GALLERY OF ART
Constitution Ave. at 6th St. NW, Washington DC 20565. (202)737-4215. Contact Person: Information Officer. **Description:** "The National Gallery contains one of the world's finest collections of western European painting, sculpture and graphic arts from the 13th century to the present, and American art from the colonial period to contemporary times. In addition to its permanent collections, the gallery also offers major international loan exhibitions. Regular activities include tours, films, lectures and concerts. The gallery's extension service runs free films and slide programs devoted to the collections and selected exhibitions to schools and civic groups throughout the nation." **Services.** Provides information on "the gallery as an institution, its permanent collections, special exhibitions and other activities." Offers aid in arranging interviews, annual reports, bibliographies, biographies, statistics, brochures/pamphlets, placement on mailing list, newsletter, photos and press kits. Publications include *Brief Guide to the National Gallery of Art, Invitation to the National Gallery of Art, A Profile of the National Gallery of Art*, and the annual report. Catalogs of color transparencies on special exhibitions available. **How to Contact:** Write or call; prefers written requests. Responds to most inquiries within a week. "Writers with assignments will be given priority. Please read all the literature the gallery distributes or is available on the gallery before conducting interviews. We're really glad to help anyone we can." Photographs of objects in the gallery's collection may be obtained from National Gallery of Art Photographic Services, Washington DC 20565. (202)737-4215. Charges for reproduction or rental of color transparencies, depending on use.

130• NATIONAL GUILD OF DECOUPEURS
807 Rivard Blvd., Grosse Pointe MI 48230. (313)882-0682. Contact Person: Executive Director. **Description:** The guild provides generalized and specialized education in the art form of decoupage and encourages quality in this art. **Services:** Provides advisory, how-to and referral information on all phases of decoupage: design, hand coloring, finishes, linings, under varnish, on and under glass, elevations, repousse, on a mirror, Mother of Pearl, illuminating, leafed ground, on fabric, Vue d'Optique, creative cutting. Offers aid in arranging interviews, brochures/pamphlets and informational newsletters (members only). Publications include *Digest*, 80-page how-to information; *Hand Coloring Lessons*. **How to Contact:** Write. Responds to most inquiries immediately. Charges for publications, and services "if extensive writing is involved. Visual Aid Programs are usually reserved for member-use only. Writer or researcher would have to view with member." **Tips:** "We are qualified to give full information on decoupage, its history and its techniques. Contact headquarters with particular interests; then persons can be suggested for interviews."

131• NATIONAL MUSEUM OF AFRICAN ART
Eliot Elisofon Archives, 318 A St. NE, Washington DC 20002. (202)287-3490. Contact Person: Archivist. **Description:** "The Elisofon Archives is a collection of photographs of African art and culture (modern and traditional) and of the African diaspora in the New World." **Services:** Photos represent all phases of African life. Offers 35,000 b&w and 45,000 color photos; "a portion of the total number of color photographs is in the form of film outtakes and work prints." Offers one-time rights, editorial rights, advertising rights or reproduction rights. Publications include a free informational brochure. **How to Contact:** Write or call. "Selection of photographs is best made in person; if this is impossible, we would be happy to make a selection for the writer. Permission is required for photo reproduction. Discounts are available for educational and other nonprofit institutions."

132• NATIONAL SCULPTURE SOCIETY
15 E. 26th St., New York NY 10011. (212)889-6960. Contact Person: Managing Editor. **Description:** The National Sculpture Society works to promote an appreciation of representational American sculpture. **Services:** Provides bibliographical and historical information on American sculpture (figurative). Offers biographies, library facilities and photos. **How to Contact:** Write. Responds to most inquiries within a week.

133•   NATIONAL STORY LEAGUE
5102 Evelyn Byrd Rd., Richmond VA 23225. (804)232-0520. Contact Person: President. **Description:** "The object of the National Story League shall be to encourage the appreciation of the good and beautiful in life and literature through the art of storytelling. We are a service organization composed of men and women interested in keeping the fine art of storytelling alive." **Services:** Provides information on storytelling. Publications include *The Story Art Magazine*. **How to Contact:** Write. Responds to most inquiries immediately.

134•   NATIONAL WOOD CARVERS ASSOCIATION
7424 Miami Ave., Cincinnati OH 45243. Contact Person: President. **Description:** "We further the aims of wood carvers and foster fellowship among members." **Services:** Provides advisory, historical, how-to, referral and trade information on wood carving in the round and bas-relief. Offers aid in arranging interviews, informational newsletters and telephone reference services. Publications include *Chip Chats* (bimonthly magazine). **How to Contact:** Write. Responds to most inquiries immediately. **Tips:** Recent information request: "Where can I find a carver to do a memorial plaque for our church?"

135•   NEW BRITAIN MUSEUM OF AMERICAN ART
56 Lexington St., New Britain CT 06052. (203)229-0257. Contact Person: Administrative Manager or Director. **Description:** "The New Britain Museum is a museum of American art dating from 1741 to the present. The collection numbers approximately 3,000 works of art, including paintings, sculpture and graphics. In addition to work from the colonial period by Copley, Smibert, Stuart, etc. the collection encompasses the Hudson River and Ashcan schools of art, murals by Thomas Hart Benton, and paintings by the Wyeth family." **Services:** Offers annual reports, brochures/pamphlets, placement on mailing list, newsletter and photos. Publications include several catalogs. **How to Contact:** Write. Responds to most inquiries immediately. "We charge for catalogs, and there is a reproduction fee for the use of photographs. Permission in writing must be given for the use of photos. Charges for information if it takes some time to research." **Tips:** Recent information request: Background material on an American artist.

136•   NEW YORK CITY BALLET
New York State Theatre, Lincoln Center, New York NY 10023. (212)870-5690. Contact Person: Press Representative. **Description:** "Our purpose is to have American dancers dancing American ballet. Our school was started in 1934 to train dancers." **Services:** Provides bibliographical, historical and referral information covering the New York City Ballet. Offers biographies, brochures/pamphlets, clipping services, information searches, placement on mailing list, photos and press kits. **How to Contact:** Write or call. Responds to most inquiries immediately. Prefers written request for lengthy or involved information. Restrictions exist on use of photos. **Tips:** "It helps if you write, but we can take phone requests, if you need the information urgently. Try to be specific about what you want to know. We are very busy, and it is hard to help people who don't or can't come to the point." Recent information requests: Dates ballets were choreographed; spelling of names and definition of ballet terms; names of music to which ballets are staged.

137•   ONTARIO PUPPETRY ASSOCIATION, THE PUPPET CENTRE
171 Avondale Ave., Willowdale, Ontario, Canada M2J 1B8. (416)222-9029. Contact Person: Administrator. **Description:** "We preserve and interpret an extensive collection of Ontario, Canadian and international puppets and related artifacts." **Services:** Provides historical, how-to, referral and trade information on puppetry, applied; Puppet Theatre. Offers library facilities, statistics, telephone reference services, access to archives and extensive museum. **How to Contact:** Write or visit. Responds to most inquiries within a week. "Library and Archives are non-circulating. Staff is limited for doing research for mail inquiries, so personal visit is best." **Tips:** Recent information requests: Uses of puppetry in education; research on career of noted Canadian puppeteer.

138•   PERCUSSIVE ARTS SOCIETY
Box 697, Urbana IL 61801. (217)367-4098. Contact Person: Administrative Manager. **Description:** The society's purpose is "to elevate the level of percussion performance and teaching; to expand understanding of the needs and responsibilities of the percussion student, teacher and performer; and to promote a greater communication among all areas of the percussion arts." **Services:** Provides advisory, bibliographical, historical, how-to, interpretative, referral,

technical and trade information on percussion music. Offers brochures/pamphlets, research digest and literature booklet. **How to Contact:** Write or call. Responds to most inquiries within a week.

139• THE PHILLIPS COLLECTION
Office of Public Affairs, 1600-1612 21st NW, Washington DC 20009. (202)387-2151. Contact Person: Public Information Officer or Librarian. **Description:** ''The Phillips Collection, the oldest museum of modern art in the United States, collects, exhibits and interprets works of art from the last quarter of the 19th century through the present. Included in the permanent collection are isolated examples of the work of such masters from the more distant past as El Greco and Giorgione. The correspondence of Duncan Phillips and all Phillips Collection correspondence is housed at the Archives of American Art—we have microfilm of the original materials.'' **Services:** Provides advisory, bibliographical, historical, referral and trade information and materials specific to the museum and its activities. ''The library, available to visitors and scholars by appointment, contains some 3,000 volumes (primarily monographs and catalogues) pertinent to the collection. Additional materials include periodicals and archival materials relevant to the museum.'' Offers aid in arranging interviews, bibliogrpahies, biographies, brochures/pamphlets, placement on mailing list, photos and press kits. Publications include an introductory handbook on the collection, the collection catalog, monographs, exhibition catalogs, checklists of individual exhibitions, and *Duncan Phillips and His Collection*. **How to Contact:** Write or call. Responds to most inquiries within a week. Charges photographic fee. ''Permission to reproduce Duncan Phillips's correspondence must be received in writing from Laughlin Phillips, Director of the museum. **Tips:** ''Calling or writing ahead for appointments also insures that we do indeed have the materials a writer might need.'' Recent information requests: Schedules of exhibitions, floor plans, history of museum or particular program—music or such past exhibitions.

140• PHOTO MARKETING ASSOCIATION
300 Picture Place, Jackson MI 49201. (517)788-8100. Contact Person: Associate Director of Communications. **Description:** ''Photo Marketing Association is an international trade association that caters to the needs of those businesses involved in selling, manufacturing and distributing photographic equipment for the consumer market, and to businesses engaged in the photofinishing industry.'' **Services:** Provides how-to, referral, technical and trade information on amateur photography and related photo industry. Offers biographies, statistics, brochures/pamphlets, information searches, placement on mailing list, newsletter, photos and press kits. Publications include *Photo Marketing* (monthly magazine with controlled circulation), six in-house newsletters and various reports on the photographic industry. **How to Contact:** Write or call. Responds to most inquiries within a month. Some services are available only to members of Photo Marketing Association. ''Rates for services vary. Most publications are free, and those with a fee are usually available only to members of the association.''

141• PHOTOGRAPHIC SOCIETY OF AMERICA
2005 Walnut St., Philadelphia PA 19103. (215)563-1663. Contact: Membership Services. **Description:** An organization existing to ''advance the art of photography among amateurs.'' **Services:** Provides referrals to experts in various areas of photography, such as color slide, motion picture, nature, photo-journalism, etc. Offers aid in arranging interviews, brochures/pamphlets and information on photo competition held in conjunction with annual international convention. **How to Contact:** Write. Responds to most inquiries within a week.

142• PROFESSIONAL PHOTOGRAPHERS OF AMERICA
1090 Executive Way, Des Plaines IL 60018. (312)299-8161. Contact Person: Membership Secretary, Public Relations Department. **Description:** ''We establish and maintain ethical standards as well as standards of performance. We try to expand the total market for pro photography.'' **Services:** Provides bibliographical, historical, how-to, referral, technical and trade informaton on professional photography: portrait, commercial, industrial, wedding, specialists. Offers aid in arranging interviews, annual reports, statistics, brochures/pamphlets, placement on mailing list, newsletter, and press kits. ''We also have a limited resource library.'' **How to Contact:** Write or call. Responds to most inquiries within a week. ''Books cannot be checked out. Information is copied and sent out or individual may research in building headquarters.'' **Tips:** ''Be specific as to requests.'' Recent information requests: Statistics on industry; career data; how to set up studio; pricing, technical data on photography; legal implications.

143•   REEL 3-D ENTERPRISES
Box 35, Dwarte CA 91010. (213)357-8345. Contact Person: President. **Description:** "We promote and further the interest, education and enjoyment of 3D photography and its many offshoots; we offer 3D photographic products which will aid in this goal." **Services:** Provides historical, how-to, referral and technical information on 3D photography; history of designs and designers of 3D equipment. Offers brochures/pamphlets, placement on mailing lists and telephone reference services. Publications include *Reel 3-D News*; *The World of 3-D*. **How to Contact:** Write. Responds to most inquiries within a week.

144•   RHYTHM AND BLUES ROCK 'N' ROLL SOCIETY, INC.
Box 1949, New Haven CT 06510. (203)735-2736. Contact Person: Director. **Description:** "The society's purpose is to sustain RnB and to educate the general public as to the 'Roots' of American rock 'n' roll." **Services:** Provides advisory, bibliographical and historical information on American black music. Offers biographies, informational newsletters, library facilities, photos, research assistance and statistics. Publications include *Big Beat Newsletter*. **How to Contact:** Write or call. Responds to most inquiries within a week. **Tips:** Recent information request: "Who created and developed American rock 'n' roll?"

145•   SCHOOL OF THE ART INSTITUTE OF CHICAGO
Columbus Dr. and Jackson Blvd., Chicago IL 60603. (312)443-3710. Contact Person: Director of Public Information. **Description:** Art school educating studio artists. Offers BFA, MFA, and post-MFA certificate programs; non-degree programs; video data bank; library and gallery; film center; poetry center. **Services:** Provides advisory, historical, interpretative and referral information on studio art and art education; health hazards and the arts; studio art areas including: ceramics, fashion design, fiber/fabric, visual communication, interior architecture, performance, painting and drawing, printmaking, photography, video, filmmaking, art and technology studies, sculpture, sound, art therapy, art history. Offers aid in arranging interviews, faculty/artist biographies, brochures/pamphlets, clipping services, informational newsletters, library facilities, photos, placement on mailing lists and telephone reference services. Publications include school catalog; newsletter; alumni/ae exhibit catalogs. **How to contact:** Write or call. Responds to most inquiries within a week. Give credit to the School of the Art Institute of Chicago. **Tips:** Recent information request: "What is the history of your pioneer art and technology program?"

146•   JUDITH SELKOWITZ FINE ARTS, INC.
c/o B.L. Ochman, 200 W. 57th St., Suite 1005, New York NY 10019. Contact Person: Public Relations Representative. **Description:** "Judith Selkowitz is a corporate art consultant, advising firms on the purchase of everything from posters to 'total art' for 50-story skyscrapers." **Services:** Provides advisory, analytical, how-to, interpretative, referral, technical and trade information on how to start an art collection; art fakes and forgeries; how to identify quality in art; collectibles for the 80s; American folk and modern art; why corporations support the arts. Offers brochures/pamphlets, photos, placement on mailing lists, press kits, research assistance and statistics. **How to Contact:** Write to address listed above. Responds to most inquiries immediately. Charges fee on hourly, daily or project fee rate. "Some clients cannot be named; all use of photos must be cleared with clients of JSFA." **Tips:** Recent information requests: "Why is there a trend for corporations to commission art works?"; "How do you start an art collection as a bride?"

147•   THE SHRINE TO MUSIC MUSEUM
USD Box 194, Vermillion SD 57069. (605)677-5306. Contact Person: Director. **Description:** "The collections of The Shrine to Music Museum consist of more than 3,000 musical instruments plus a large supporting library of music, books, sound recordings, photographs and related musical memorabilia." **Services:** Provides advisory, bibliographical, historical, interpretative, referral and technical information covering musical instruments and their use in all cultures and historical periods, as works of decorative art, as historical objects, and as cultural artifacts. Offers aid in arranging interviews, brochures/pamphlets, information searches and photos. **How to Contact:** Write. Responds to most inquiries within a week. No charge for routine inquiries, but charges for photos, reproductions of printed material and extensive research searches. Permission of Director required for on-site use of research facilities. **Tips:** "Write as far in advance as possible and make requests for information specific." Recent information requests: Photos of musical instruments; information about now obsolete instruments and their makers.

148• THE SOCIETY FOR THEATRE RESEARCH
77 Kinnerton St., London, England SW1X 8ED. Contact Persons: Joint Hon. Secretaries. **Description:** "The purpose of the society is to provide a meeting point for all those—scholars, research workers, actors, producers and theatre-goers—who are interested in the history and technique of the theatre. It encourages further research, and through its world-wide membership and journals acts as a clearing house for historical and technical information." **Services:** Provides advisory, bibliographical, historical, referral and technical information on the history and technique of the theatre in Great Britain and allied performing arts, such as pantomime, circus, juvenile theatre and the staging of ballet and opera. Offers annual reports, brochures/pamphlets, advice on research and lectures. Publications (for members) include *Theatre Notebook* (index, published three times each year); annual publications, hard or soft bound. Past publications are available. **How to Contact:** Write. Responds to most inquiries within a month. "We expect enquirers to have exhausted the normal sources of information available to the general public, such as public libraries and readily obtainable reference resources, before coming to us for specialized help with problems. Then, if writing, explain clearly and briefly the nature of the problem and the sources already tried." **Tips:** Recent information request: Sources of information for a history of entertainment in Boltor (Lancs).

149• STUDIO SUPPLIERS ASSOCIATION, INC.
548 Goffle Rd., Hawthorne NJ 07506. (201)427-9384. Contact Person: Executive Secretary. **Description:** Trade association for suppliers to professional photographers. **Services:** Provides analytical, referral and trade information on professional photography. Offers statistics. Publications include photographic trade magazines. **How to Contact:** Write. Responds to most inquiries within a week. Charges for photocopying and postage. "Any statistics used must contain proper credit." **Tips:** Recent information request: "How big is the professional portrait market?"

150• SUZUKI ASSOCIATION OF THE AMERICAS, INC.
Box 354, Muscatine IA 52761. (319)263-3071. Contact Person: Executive Director. **Description:** SAA is the "singular extension of Talent Education for the teachings of Dr. Suzuki in the Northern, Central, and Southern Americas. It is a nonprofit, professional association of teachers and parents in the Americas dedicated to meeting the needs of all those interested in Talent Education, or the 'mother tongue' approach to music education. SAA provides an opportunity for music educators and parents to join together in an exciting adventure of nurturing and realizing the potential of each child." **Services:** Provides how-to, referral and technical information on music-education: violin, viola, cello, flute, piano; and pre-school education. Offers brochures/pamphlets, computerized information searches, informational newsletters, placement on mailing lists, research assistance and telephone reference services. Publications include *American Suzuki Journal.* **How to Contact:** Write. Responds to most inquiries within a week. Active membership $32; subscribing membership $16. **Tips:** Recent information requests: Location of Suzuki teachers; bibliography of Talent Education.

151• THEATRE COMMUNICATIONS GROUP, INC. (TCG)
355 Lexington Ave., New York NY 10017. (212)697-5230. Contact Person: Director. **Description:** "Theatre Communications Group, the national service organization for the nonprofit professional theatre, was founded in 1961 to provide a national forum and communications network for the then-emerging nonprofit theatres, and to respond to the needs of both theatres and theatre artists for centralized services. Today, TCG is a unique national arts organization, creatively combining the activities of both service organization and national professional association by addressing artistic and management concerns, serving artists and institutions, and acting as advocate and provider of services for a field diverse in its aesthetic aims and located in every part of this country. TCG's almost 200 Constituent and Associate theatres, as well as thousands of individual artists, participate in more than 25 programs and services. TCG encompasses artistic and managing directors, actors, playwrights, directors, designers, literary managers, trustees and administrative personnel. TCG's goals are to foster cross-fertilization and interaction among different types of organizations and individuals that comprise the profession; to improve the artistic and administrative capabilities of their field; to enhance the visibility and demonstrate the achievements of the American theatre by increasing the public's awareness of theatre's role in society; and to encourage a nationwide network of professional theatre companies and individuals that collectively represent our 'national theatre.' " **Services:** Provides advisory, analytical, bibliographical, historical, how-to, interpretative and referral information on theatre

and the performing arts; casting for actors; job referrals for artists, administrators, technicians; *ArtSEARCH* employment bulletin for performing arts; play publishing; opportunities for playwrights; annual survey of finances and productivity of theatres nationwide; computer software program for performing arts institutions; how-to books for performing arts administrators; national advocacy for theatre; advice and consultation; conferences and seminars; travel grants; classified advertising. Publications include monthly magazine *Theatre Communications*; resource book on theatres *Theatre Profiles*; *Theatre Directory*; and others. **How to Contact:** Write or call. Responds to most inquiries within a week. Most information is free; charges for some services and for purchase of publications. **Tips:** "Be very specific with questions asked and prepare well in advance. TCG does not supply information on the commercial theatre or avocational theatre." Recent information request: "Interpretation of the economic conditions of theatres nationwide."

152• THE HENRY FRANCIS DU PONT WINTERTHUR MUSEUM
Winterthur DE 19735. (302)656-8591. Contact Person: Head of Public Relations. **Description:** "Museum, gardens and research library in American decorative arts to early 20th century and their European antecedents. The museum of American decorative arts covers the period from 1650 to 1850, displayed in more than 200 rooms and small area settings. Graduate education programs in connoisseurship and conservation of decorative and fine arts are offered in conjunction with the University of Delaware." **Services:** Provides analytical, bibliographical, historical, interpretative, referral and some technical information on American decorative arts and their European antecedents to 1914, history of Winterthur estate, now-closed Winterthur farm, history of Winterthur gardens, art conservation. Offers annual reports, bibliographies, brochures/pamphlets, information searches, placement on mailing list, newsletter, photos and press kits. Offers b&w photos and color transparencies of furniture, silver, ceramics, prints, paintings, textiles, and other decorative art objects made or used in America from 1640 to 1840. Winterthur's libraries are open to the public. Publications available. **How to Contact:** Write or call. Responds to most inquiries within a month. Charges vary for photography and filmmaking, and may include overtime and utility costs. Articles should be written for a specific publication with a commitment from that publication. Submit the request in writing, but make the initial inquiry by telephone. Selection of photos should be made from Winterthur publications or from photo files in registrar's office at the museum. Charges $10/b&w print (which includes print and one-time use). Credit line required. Charges for document reproduction, photocopying, microfilm. Advance appointment required; some restrictions for publication. Must credit Winterthur; other restrictions and regulations available on request. **Tips:** "Do thorough research in printed works before using original documents." Recent information requests: "Do you have any correspondence between H.F. duPont and Sotheby Parke-Bernet?"; "Do you have any drawings for the Winterthur gardens?"; "Can you identify the mark in this picture of a piece of pewter?"

153• WORLD PRINT COUNCIL
Fort Mason Center, San Francisco CA 94123. (415)776-9200. Contact Person: Director. **Description:** "World Print Council is a nonprofit organization supporting international contemporary printmaking. Activities include major traveling exhibitions, monthly gallery exhibits, educational symposia, books, slide referral service, resource center." **Services:** Provides advisory, bibliographical and referral information on printmaking technique and resources; catalogs of international print exhibitions; papermaking techniques and resources. Offers informational newsletters, library facilities and research assistance. Publications include *PrintNews*, bimonthly journal of contemporary trends, techniques, critical issues, resources, book reviews. **How to Contact:** Write or call. Responds to most inquiries within a month. **Tips:** "We do not have a librarian or staff researcher. Our resource center has developed as a result of our magazine archive materials. Writers should be as specific as possible with their questions, as we are not able to devote staff time to helping people define their subjects. We are probably best able to act as a referral service, unless the writer can come to our offices and use our archives." Recent information request: Polish artists to illustrate a volume of Polish poems.

154• FRANK LLOYD WRIGHT ASSOCIATION
Box 2100, Oak Park IL 60303. (312)383-1310. Contact Person: Editor. **Description:** Individuals interested in adding to the body of knowledge on Frank Lloyd Wright by collecting and disseminating information about him and his work. **Services:** Provides advisory, analytical, bibliographical, historical, interpretative and technical information on art, architecture, building technology, furniture, stained glass, solar design, sociology. Offers aid in arranging interviews,

biographies, informational newsletters, library facilities, photos, research assistance and telephone reference services. Publications include *Frank Lloyd Wright Newsletter*. **How to Contact:** Write. Responds to most inquiries within a week. Charges for newsletter ($24/year) and extensive research "by arrangement." **Tips:** "Look at available literature in libraries first." Recent information request: "What year did the Robie House begin construction?"

155• THE WRITERS THEATRE

Box 810, Times Square Station, New York NY 10108. Contact Person: Administrative/Artistic Director. **Description:** "The Writers Theatre's ultimate commitment is to enriching the quality of language on the living stage through the discovery, development and performance of new plays, adaptations and poetry performances. We strive to encourage the literary talents of our time, be they poets, novelists, essayists or playwrights; to conceive new, original plays; and to adapt masterworks from our literary heritage for the stage." **Services:** Provides a development period, through workshops and play readings "for writers to work on their scripts in collaboration with professional actors and directors." **How to Contact:** Write. Responds to most inquiries within a month.

SECTION · THREE

BUSINESS

Business is a combination of war and sport.
—André Maurois

The Business category lists resources providing information on general business activities, as well as advertising, banking, finance, insurance, investment, money management, credit and taxes.

Personnel resources are located in the Workplace section. Specific companies/corporations are categorized according to their major concerns (e.g., Cardinal Industries, in House and Home; IBM, in Science, Engineering, Technology, etc.). Others are found in the Products and Services section.

Bibliography

Brownstone, David M. & Irene M. Franck. *The VNR Investor's Dictionary*. New York: Van Nostrand Reinhold, 1981.

Business Periodicals Index. 1958 to date, monthly. New York: H.W. Wilson Co.

Daniells, Lorna. *Business Information Sources*. Berkeley, CA: University of California Press, 1976.

Federal Tax Handbook. Annual. Englewood Cliffs, NJ: Prentice-Hall.

Greenwald, Douglas, ed. *Encyclopedia of Economics*. New York: McGraw-Hill, 1982.

How to Find Information About Companies. 2d ed. Washington DC: Washington Researchers, 1981.

Kruzas, Anthony T. and Robert C. Thomas, eds. *Business Organizations and Agencies Directory*. Detroit: Gale Research Co., 1980.

Moskowitz, Milton, Michael Katz and Robert Levering, eds. *Everybody's Business: An Almanac (The Irreverent Guide to Corporate America)*. San Francisco: Harper & Row Publishers, 1980.

Munn, Glenn G. *Encyclopedia of Banking & Finance*. Edited by F.L. Garcia. 7th rev. ed. Boston: Banker's Publishing Co., 1973.

Small Business Sourcebook. Detroit: Gale Research Co., 1982.

Standard & Poor's Corporations. 3 vols. Annual. New York: Standard & Poor's Corporation. (Directory of corporations and their officers and products arranged alphabetically, geographically and by SIC code)

Wasserman, Paul, et. al., eds. *Encyclopedia of Business Information Sources*. 4th ed. Detroit: Gale Research Co., 1980. (Resources of interest to business managerial personnel)

156• THE ADVERTISING COUNCIL, INC.
825 Third Ave., New York NY 10022. Contact Person: Director of Public Affairs. **Description:** "The Advertising Council was founded in 1942 to produce public service advertising campaigns for the war effort. Since the end of World War II, it has continued its good work, now producing 30 public service campaigns annually in all media—TV, radio, press, magazines, business press, transit and outdoor advertising." **Services:** Provides advisory, historical, and referral information about the Advertising Council itself and public service advertising in general. Offers annual reports, brochures/pamphlets, placement on mailing list, newsletter, photos and press kits. **How to Contact:** Write. Responds to most inquiries within a week. **Tips:** "Keep your requests brief and to the point. We cannot do research due to limited staff." Recent information request: Historical background on the Advertising Council and its campaigns.

157• ALLIED CAPITAL CORPORATION
1625 I St. NW, Washington DC 20006. (202)331-1112. Contact Person: Executive Vice President. **Description:** "We invest in small businesses in the United States." **Services:** Provides advisory, analytical and trade information on "our investments in small growing businesses, our knowledge of venture capital in the USA." Offers annual reports and research assistance.

Publications include annual report and brochures on venture capital and small business loans. **How to Contact:** Write or call. Responds to most inquiries immediately. **Tips:** Recent information requests: "What is your opinion of what's happening to small businesses?"; "What type of venture capital investments are you making?"

158• AMERICAN ADVERTISING FEDERATION

1225 Connecticut Ave. NW, Washington DC 20036. Contact Person: Director/Educational Services. **Description:** "We are the only organization in the United States that relates to all aspects of the advertising community and seeks to improve advertising and the climate in which it functions through constructive programs in areas of government and public information, education, public service and self-regulation. Our headquarters are in Washington, but we also maintain a western regional office in San Francisco." **Services:** Provides trade information on advertising (general career and industry). Offers brochures/pamphlets. **How to Contact:** Write. Responds to most inquiries within a week. "Free" literature for SASE. Charges for publications.

159• AMERICAN BANKERS ASSOCIATION

1120 Connecticut Ave. NW, Washington DC 20036. (202)467-4273. Contact Person: Director of Public Relations. **Description:** "American Bankers Association (ABA) is the national trade association for America's full-service commercial banks. ABA's membership comprises 13,254 banks, 92% of the nation's total. ABA manages the largest private adult education program in the world and represents the banking industry on the federal government level. Information on all aspects of banking is available from the ABA Public Relations Division." **Services:** Offers aid in arranging interviews, annual reports, biographies, statistics, brochures/pamphlets, information searches, placement on mailing list, photos, press kits and a wide variety of information and publications. **How to Contact:** Call. Responds as promptly as possible. "If you are writing about banking, call us. We may very well have more current information, good interview contacts and, possibly, another point of view not yet considered. It doesn't matter if the questions are extremely specific or very general. If we have an answer, it's yours. If we don't know, we'll tell you that. If we know a better place to get the information we'll refer you to it." **Tips:** "Narrow the topic as much as possible." Recent information requests: "What impact have farm banks had on the US banking industry?"; question about bank legislative history.

160• AMERICAN COUNCIL OF LIFE INSURANCE

1850 K St. NW, Washington DC 20006. (202)862-4064. New York Office: 1270 Avenue of the Americas, New York NY 10020. (212)245-4198. Contact: Press and Editorial Services. **Description:** "The public relations division of the council provides the public with information about the purpose of life insurance and pensions, maintains research facilities to record the performance of the business and measures attitudes of the public on issues relevant to the business." **Services:** Provides information and statistics on life and health insurance and health care costs. Offers aid in arranging interviews, statistics and brochures/pamphlets. "We can provide helpful booklets to meet appropriate requests." **How to Contact:** Write or call the appropriate regional office. Responds to most inquiries "within a week to 10 days."

161• AMERICAN FEDERATION OF SMALL BUSINESS

407 S. Dearborn St., Chicago IL 60605. (312)427-0206. Contact Person: Assistant Secretary-Treasurer. **Description:** "The federation's purpose is to promote and preserve small business enterprises in the US and the world as the mainstay of economic freedom, competitive growth, social progress, political liberty and world peace." **Services:** Provides advisory, analytical, bibliographical, historical, how-to, interpretive, referral, technical and trade information on economics; labor-management relations; government: executive, legislative and judicial; demography; international relations; natural resource development; defense of the free world; and the Marxist threat. Offers aid in arranging interviews, brochures/pamphlets, informational newsletters, library facilities, placement on mailing lists, press kits, research assistance, statistics, and telephone reference services. Publications include *The Moral Basis of a Free Society*; *Twelve Articles of Economic Wisdom*; *Solzhenitsyn on Communism*; *The Case for a Return to the Gold Standard*; *Labor Union Monopoly: A Clear and Present Danger*; and *The U.S. Must Take the High Ground in Space*. **How to Contact:** Write or call. Responds to most inquiries immediately. **Tips:** Recent information request: A statistical breakdown of the 20 million small businesses in the US.

162• AMERICAN INSTITUTE OF CERTIFIED PUBLIC ACCOUNTANTS
1211 Avenue of the Americas, New York NY 10036. (212)575-3878. Contact Person: Manager, Press Relations. **Description:** The purpose of the institute is "to organize the body of accounting knowledge; to conduct research; to enforce the profession's technical and ethical standards; to guide the profession's overall development along lines serving the broadest public interest; to encourage cooperation between CPAs and professional accountants in other countries." **Services:** Provides advisory, analytical, bibliographical, historical, how-to, interpretative, referral and technical information on accounting and auditing. Offers aid in arranging interviews, annual reports, biographies, statistics, brochures/pamphlets, information searches, placement on mailing list and press kits. "We have the most comprehensive US library of published materials on accounting and related subjects." Numerous publications available. **How to Contact:** Write, call or visit. Prefers written request. Responds to most inquiries immediately. "We can set a writer up to do research in our library."

163• AMERICAN STOCK EXCHANGE
86 Trinity Place, New York NY 10006. (212)938-6000. Contact Person: Assistant Vice President, Press Relations. **Description:** "We provide a market-place for trading securities, options, equities, etc.; arrange conferences (national/international) sponsored by Amex; provide media exposure for newly listed companies, as well as companies previously listed (i.e., press releases, radio and TV coverage, etc.)." **Services:** Provides historical, how-to and technical information including how to become listed on the Amex, i.e., qualifications and paperwork required; preparing a press release on the company about to commence trading and filming live on the trading floor an interview with CEO of listed company; market activity; trading information; compliance with securities laws; options market and gold coin trading. Offers aid in arranging interviews, brochures/pamphlets, computerized information searches, photos, press kits, research assistance and statistics. **How to Contact:** Write. Responds to most inquiries immediately.

164• ASSOCIATION FOR SYSTEMS MANAGEMENT
24587 Bagley Rd., Cleveland OH 44138. Contact Person: Director of Publications. **Description:** "We are the one professional association serving the business systems field, i.e., office and paperwork management." **Services:** Provides advisory and referral information covering systems management and information resource management. Offers statistics and information searches. Publications include a monthly journal and 35 publications in the field. **How to Contact:** Write. Responds to most inquiries within a week. Charges according to "extent of research. We will not rewrite or conduct *extensive* research."

165• ASSOCIATION OF NATIONAL ADVERTISERS
155 E. 44th St., New York NY 10017. (212)697-5950. Contact Person: Director of Press Relations. **Description:** "The Association of National Advertisers (ANA) is a nonprofit organization founded in 1910. We represent the interests of over 400 companies that use advertising regionally or nationally to provide information on their products and services to the public. Through workshops, surveys, reports and books, ANA has developed an extensive library which includes material on all aspects of advertising and other forms of marketing communications (audiovisuals, trade shows, etc.). It does not provide industry statistics other than in areas of management practice in which members have been surveyed." **Services:** Provides information on anything to do with advertising and marketing communications. Offers assistance in developing accurate information on advertising and promotional activities: their management, execution and evaluation. Publications include a publications list. **How to Contact:** Write or call. Responds to most inquiries immediately. Charges for some publications. "An appointment to visit the ANA library for research may be arranged. We are willing to work with writers and researchers whenever called upon. (We prefer them to be from member companies.)" **Tips:** "Be specific as possible in requesting information. We serve well as a point-of-view spokesman for the industry." Recent information request: Questions on trends in advertising.

166• BUREAU OF INDUSTRIAL ECONOMICS
US Department of Commerce, Room 4321, Washington DC 20230. (202)377-2250. Contact Person: Industry Economist. **Description:** Government agency engaging in economic research and forecasts of the US industrial economy. **Services:** Provides analytical, interpretative, technical and trade information on all domestic consumer goods and services industries. Offers research assistance and statistics. Publications include *US Industrial Outlook.* **How to Contact:**

Write or call. Responds to most inquiries within a week. "No access to confidential data." **Tips:** "Obtain a copy of *The Outlook*; read relevant section and then inquire." Recent information request: "Describe factors in the demand for evaporated and condensed milk."

167• THE CANADIAN INSTITUTE OF CHARTERED ACCOUNTANTS
150 Bloor St. W, Toronto, Ontario CN M5S 2Y2. (416)962-1242. Contact Person: Director of Information. **Description:** "The Canadian Institute of Chartered Accountants (CICA) is a professional organization to which all of Canada's chartered accountants belong. CICA's research department and committees issue generally accepted accounting principles and auditing standards for Canadian business. CICA also produces professional development courses for chartered accountants, a monthly professional magazine, and keeps records of the membership." **Services:** Provides advisory, historical and technical information on accounting and auditing research and standards, policies and activities of the chartered accounting profession in Canada. Offers aid in explaining accounting and auditing matters. **How to Contact:** Write. Responds to most inquiries within a week. **Tips:** Submit clearly written requests. Recent information request: "What is the profession's view of the Federal Budget?"

168• THE CHASE MANHATTAN BANK
1 Chase Manhattan Plaza, New York NY 10081. (212)552-4505. Contact Person: Vice President, Public Relations. **Description:** "The Chase Manhattan Bank is a commercial bank, headquartered in New York City, with branches throughout New York State and the world. The public relations division can handle any questions dealing with the bank's business; its subsidiaries, affiliates and associate banks; and, through the archives, inquiries about the bank's history and development." **Services:** Offers aid in arranging interviews, annual reports, biographies, statistics, brochures/pamphlets, limited information searches, placement on mailing list and photos. Publications include the speeches of the chairman, president and others; historical pamphlets on the bank; miscellaneous publications on energy, finance and business; and quarterly reports. **How to Contact:** "Inquiries made by mail are more desirable than telephone inquiries." Responds to most inquiries within a week. "We generally don't extend ourselves to freelance writers working on speculation." **Tips:** Recent information requests: Economic data on a particular country; brief history of the bank; speeches; and articles by top management.

169• CHICAGO BOARD OF TRADE
141 W. Jackson, Chicago IL 60604. (312)435-3620. Contact Person: Director of Public Relations. **Description:** "A commodity futures exchange. The CBT is an open auction market of over 2,000 full and associate members who buy and sell commodity futures contracts for customers and for themselves. Listed contracts cover the following areas: agriculture (grains and soybeans), financial instruments (treasury bonds and other rate-related contracts), precious metals (silver and gold), forest products and energy (unleaded gasoline). Founded in 1848, the CBT is the world's oldest and largest commodity futures exchange." **Services:** Offers aid in arranging interviews, annual reports, bibliographies, biographies, brochures/pamphlets, information searches, placement on mailing list, library facilities, tours, newsletter, photos and press kits. Publications include pamphlets on commodity futures trading in general; specific futures in wheat, corn, oats, soybeans, soybean oil, soybean meal, plywood, silver, US Treasury bonds, 10-year treasury and 2-year treasury notes, commercial papers and government-backed mortgage certificates. Current and historical statistics are available in exchange's market information department (312)435-3637. University of Illinois (Chicago campus) has a special collection—the CBT Archives (312)996-2742. **How to Contact:** Write, call or visit. Responds to most inquiries within 2 weeks.

170• COLONIAL PENN GROUP
5 Penn Center, Philadelphia PA 19181. (215)988-8000. Contact Person: Director of Communications. **Description:** "Our company offers insurance, primarily for persons aged 50 and over." **Services:** Provides advisory, referral and trade information on insurance, gerontology, travel, temporary employment, direct-response marketing. Offers aid in arranging interviews, annual reports, brochures/pamphlets, informational newsletters, photos and publications on Medicare supplement insurance. **How to Contact:** Write. **Tips:** Recent information request: "What should people be aware of when purchasing Medicare supplementary insurance?"

171• COMMITTEE FOR ECONOMIC DEVELOPMENT
477 Madison Ave., New York NY 10022. (212)688-2063. Contact Person: Associate Director of Information. **Description:** "Founded in 1942, CED is an independent, nonprofit, nonpolitical public policy research group. CED's trustees, who are top business leaders or university presidents, develop proposals and speak out on economic and social policy. CED trustees join their practical experience with the objective research of top economists and social scientists who work with them to formulate recommendations on pressing issues of national and international scope." **Services:** Provides advisory, interpretative and referral information. "CED puts out studies on important economic and social issues such as energy, urban economies, technology, Third World development, unemployment, productivity, industrial strategy and trade, education, and the federal budget process." Offers aid in arranging interviews, annual reports, brochures/pamphlets, informational newsletters, placement on mailing lists and press kits. Publications include: Statements on National Policy, which contain policy recommendations authorized by CED's Research and Policy Committee; Supplementary Papers, which contain background studies from a policy statement; Program Statements, which update previous policy statements; and miscellaneous publications. **How to Contact:** Write. Responds to most inquiries within a week. "CED publications cost anywhere from $1-$19.95. CED also offers audio-visual aids for sale and rental. CED publications can be purchased by subscription; the basic rate is $15/year." **Tips:** "Write or call for free catalog and brochures to learn about CED's activities and goals. Check your college or local library to see if they carry CED publications." Recent information requests: CED's views and quotes of CED trustees on the issue of US retirement policies; background about CED's scope, activities and personnel.

172• CONSUMER CREDIT INSURANCE CORPORATION
307 N. Michigan Ave., Chicago IL 60601. Contact Person: Director of Communications. **Description:** "A credit insurance trade group representing 140 insurers which sell credit insurance. We provide information to our member companies regarding legislative and regulatory activities in the states regarding credit insurance. We also sponsor two yearly meetings. PR activities include publicizing favorable studies regarding the credit insurance product. We are not a credit rating bureau, and our dealings with credit itself are minimal. We are involved with credit insurance, credit life and credit auto and home insurance, as well as credit property insurance and its regulation." **Services:** Provides advisory and trade information. Offers statistics, brochures/pamphlets and newsletter. Publications include various studies on the credit insurance field, as well as *Proceedings*, covering annual meetings and fall executive planning conferences. **How to Contact:** "Write the association on letterhead stationery. Please have specific questions in mind." Responds to most inquiries within a week.

173• THE CONSUMER FINANCIAL INSTITUTE
430 Lexington St., Newton MA 02166. (617)969-2632. Contact Person: Executive Director and Co-Founder. **Description:** The institute provides unbiased personal financial techniques to middle income individuals and families. "We are the largest such organization in the US and Canada; we are interested in assisting in any way to increase the knowledge of personal finance nationally." **Services:** Provides advisory, analytical, how-to, technical and trends information on personal finance, corporations, benefits programs; bank, brokerage and financial service company trends and marketing. Offers brochures/pamphlets, computerized information searches, informational newsletters and research assistance. **How to Contact:** Write or call. Responds to most inquiries within a week. "We prefer a 'CFI, Newton MA' reference or ideally our address." **Tips:** Recent information requests: "Where should someone go who has only $10-30,000 to invest?"; "How can the average person plan better and reduce taxes?"

174• THE COOPERATIVE LEAGUE OF THE USA
Suite 1100, 1828 L St. NW, Washington DC 20036. (202)872-0550. Contact Person: Vice President for Communications. **Description:** "The league is a national federation of all types of customer-owned businesses. It is the US member of International Cooperative Alliance." **Services:** Offers cooperative news service for co-op publications. Publications list available. **How to Contact:** Write. Responds to most inquiries within a month. Charges for some publications. **Tips:** Recent information requests: Inquiry from a writer for article entitled "How to Live on Half Your Income"; also, frequent requests for consumer information.

175• COUNCIL OF BETTER BUSINESS BUREAUS
1515 Wilson Blvd., Arlington VA 22209. (703)276-0100. Contact Person: Director, Public Information. **Description:** "The council's purpose is to inform, educate consumers; assist business. **Services:** Provides advisory, interpretative and referral information on mediation-arbitration, charitable solicitations, advertising, industry standards, general consumer information. Offers annual reports, brochures/pamphlets, informational newsletters and statistics. Publications list available. **How to Contact:** Write. Responds to most inquiries within a month. "Write for reprint permission."

176• CREDIT UNION NATIONAL ASSOCIATION
Suite 810, 1730 Rhode Island Ave. NW, Washington DC 20036. (202)828-4500. Contact Person: Director of Washington Public Relations. **Description:** "Credit Union National Association (CUNA) is a trade association that represents more than 90% of the nation's 20,000 federal and state chartered credit unions. Working through the 50 state credit union leagues and the leagues in the District of Columbia and Puerto Rico, CUNA provides legislative, public relations, research, educational and development support for the National Credit Union Movement." **Services:** Provides advisory, how-to, and trade information on consumer borrowing and lending. Offers aid in arranging interviews, annual reports, brochures/pamphlets, placement on mailing lists, press kits and statistics. **How to Contact:** Call. Responds to most inquiries immediately.

177• DEPARTMENT OF COMMERCE
14th St. & Constitution Ave. NW, Washington DC 20230. (202)377-4901. Contact Person: Chief of News Room. **Description:** "The department was established by Congress to foster, serve and develop the economic development and technological advancement of the United States." **Services:** Offers aid in arranging interviews, annual reports, bibliographies, biographies, statistics, brochures/pamphlets, photos and press kits. Publications available. **How to Contact:** Write. Responds to most inquiries immediately. Charges for some publications. "We do no research but can put you in touch with the proper official. We also have a 4-page subject directory which lists the agency, the official, address and phone number that would cover a particular topic." **Tips:** "Call the information officer for the area you're interested in. If you don't get any satisfaction there, give us a call."

178• DEPARTMENT OF THE TREASURY
15th St. and Pennsylvania Ave. NW, Washington DC 20220. (202)566-2041. Contact Person: Public Information Officer. **Description:** The Department of the Treasury "raises revenues for the United States government." **Services:** Offers annual reports, biographies, placement on mailing list and news releases. **How to Contact:** Write or call. Responds to most inquiries immediately. **Tips:** Recent information requests: Many questions on bills pending in Congress.

179• DIRECT MARKETING ASSOCIATION
6 E. 43rd St., New York NY 10017. (212)689-4977. Contact Person: Director of Communications. **Description:** "The DMA represents companies involved in any aspect of direct marketing from direct mail to telemarketing." **Services:** Provides how-to, referral, technical and trade information in all areas of direct marketing: creative direct response, direct mail catalogs, telemarketing, DRTV, samples of successful mail campaigns, statistics, growth, etc. Offers aid in arranging interviews, library facilities, placement on mailing lists, press kits, research assistance and statistics. **How to Contact:** Write or call. Responds to most inquiries within a week. "Call to make an appointment to use the facilities." **Tips:** "Most of our research is geared to our membership. We are not able to provide lengthy research assistance to nonmembers. Recent information requests: "What effect does color and texture of paper have on the rate of response to a direct mail program?"; "Is the catalog industry growing?"

180• DIRECT SELLING ASSOCIATION
1730 M St. NW, Suite 610, Washington DC 20036. (202)293-5760. Contact Person: Director of Communications. **Description:** "We are a national trade association representing approximately 100 firms which manufacture and distribute goods and services directly to the consumer. The association acts as liaison between the direct selling industry and all levels of government. DSA works to help the public better understand the direct selling industry and form of retailing. Internationally, the association keeps in close contact with direct selling associations around the world." **Services:** Provides facts and figures on the direct selling industry. Offers aid in arranging

interviews, bibliographies, statistics, brochures/pamphlets, placement on mailing list and press kits (available through the Direct Selling Educational Foundation, at the same address). Publications available. **How to Contact:** "We prefer that writers contact us through the mail." Responds to most inquiries within a week. "Give the association as much lead time as possible." **Tips:** "Please be as specific as possible."

181• DISCOUNT AMERICA
51 E. 42nd St., Rm. 417, New York NY 10017. (212)580-0541. Contact Person: Editor. **Description:** "We disseminate information on discount mail order shopping to consumers. To this end, we publish *Discount America Guide*, a directory of discount mail order companies." **Services:** Provides how-to, referral and trade information on mail order shopping, discount shopping in general, and discount mail order shopping. Offers aid in arranging interviews, press kits, research assistance and telephone reference services. **How to Contact:** Write or call. Responds to most inquiries within a week. **Tips:** Give credit to Discount America. Recent information request: "How can a company sell at such low prices?"

182• FEDERAL TRADE COMMISSION
Public Reference Branch, 6th and Pennsylvania Ave. NW, Washington DC 20580. (202)523-3600. Contact Person: Secretary. **Description:** The commission is a law enforcement agency whose mission is to protect the public (consumers and businessmen) against abuses caused by unfair competition and unfair and deceptive business practices; to guide and counsel businessmen, consumers, and federal, state and local officials. **Services:** Offers reprints, copies of speeches, or other pertinent documents. Publications include *News Summary*, a weekly. **How to Contact:** Write or call. Responds to most inquiries within a week. **Tips:** "Be specific in your requests. Include a telephone number." Recent information requests: "Do you have any free publications on consumer credit?"; "Do you have any information on the funeral business?"

183• FUTURES INDUSTRY ASSOCIATION
1825 Eye St. NW, Suite 1040, Washington DC 20006. (202)466-5460. Contact Person: Public Relations Vice President. **Description:** "FIA membership is comprised of 88 of the nation's leading commodity futures brokerage firms which effect an estimated 80% of all futures contracts traded on US exchanges on behalf of the public. In addition, FIA has 104 associate members including all of the US futures exchanges, several banks, law and accounting firms, commerical users of futures, major farm organizations and others interested in futures trading. FIA has established the following objectives: to provide a forum for discussion of industry concerns and proper means for their solution; to protect and preserve free and competitive commodity markets; to preserve and promote a high standard of ethics and financial integrity; to build public awareness of the economic role of futures trading; to publish accurate and reliable market information and statistical data; to make available at reasonable cost the finest industry educational programs; and to review and critique all proposed regulatory legislation." **Services:** Provides advisory, analytical, historical, technical and trade information. Offers clipping services, informational newsletters, statistics and educational material regarding futures trading, and educational programs in the form of lecture courses, correspondence courses, seminars, and other activities. Publications include *Commodity Futures Trading Course*; *Financial Futures Trading Course*; *Clearing Directory and Handbook*; *Introduction to the Futures Markets*; *Weekly Bulletins*; *Congressional Report*; and *CFTC Report*. **How to Contact:** Write, call or visit. Responds to most inquiries immediately. Charges membership and tuition fees. **Tips:** "Some publications are strictly for members only."

184• HEALTH INSURANCE ASSOCIATION OF AMERICA
1850 K St. NW, Washington DC 20006. (202)862-4063. Contact: Press and Editorial Services. **Description:** "The institute is maintained by the nation's insurance companies as a central source of information for the public on health insurance." **Services:** Provides information on health care costs and health insurance. Offers aid in arranging interviews, statistics and brochures/pamphlets. **How to Contact:** "If possible, write a letter to the institute, detailing needs. Allow sufficient time if request is detailed." Responds to most inquiries within a week to 10 days.

185• HOUSEHOLD INTERNATIONAL
Money Management Institute, 2700 Sanders Rd., Prospect Heights IL 60070. (312)564-6291. Contact Person: Director. **Description:** Financial corporation. **Services:** Provides how-to and

trade information on basic money management, basic financial planning, credit, savings and investments, children and money management; buying clothing, home furnishings, housing, equipment, and automobiles; recreation and shopping. Offers brochures/pamphlets, placement on mailing list and semiannual newsletter. **How to Contact:** Write. Responds to most inquiries immediately. "To order booklets, the fee of postage and handling is charged, but generally not to writers. All material is copyrighted and, therefore, credit lines must be used and permission must be granted." **Tips:** "Contact the Money Management Institute and state your objectives." Recent information request: A syndicated writer called regarding an article on parent awareness in the area of teaching children how to handle money management.

186• INA ARCHIVES
1600 Arch St., Philadelphia PA 19101 (215)241-3293 or 241-4894. Contact Person: Archivist. **Description:** "INA, now part of CIGNA Corporation, is one of the nation's largest diversified financial institutions, with major interests in insurance and insurance-related services, health maintenance organizations and financial services. The archive's collection is composed primarily of documents generated by the Insurance Company of North America, founded in 1792 to write marine, fire and life insurance. Documents relating to the history of INA and INA subsidiaries are also held by the archives." **Services:** Provides historical, interpretive and trade information on the business and history of Insurance Company of North America, INA Corporation and INA subsidiaries. Offers answers to questions. "The archives staff will research specific questions or make available material for the researcher to use in the archives." Publications include company histories, *Biography of a Business*; and *Perils: Named and Unnamed*; *Perils* may be requested when visiting the archives. "These volumes are available at many libraries. A guide to the materials in the archives is also available upon request." **How to Contact:** "The writer may telephone or address written inquiries to the archivists. An appointment is needed to visit the archives, and materials must be used according to our instructions." Responds to most inquiries within a week. "We may charge for a significant amount of photocopying and for prints of photos in our collection." All historical materials are open to the public. **Tips:** "Plan to talk to the archivist before scheduling a trip—we have only company materials and can accommodate only one or two researchers at a time." Recent information request: Appointment for a scholar researching the routes and cargos of ships we insured between 1794 and 1821 sailing to the West Indies.

187• INSTITUTE FOR MONETARY RESEARCH, INC.
1200 15th St. NW, Washington DC 20005. (202)223-9050. Contact Person: Executive Director. **Description:** Established in 1960, this nonprofit organization is concerned with research on monetary questions and the need for monetary reform. **Services:** Provides information on monetary issues including business, economics, research and politics. **How to Contact:** Write or call. Responds to most inquiries within a week.

188• INSURANCE INFORMATION INSTITUTE
110 William St., New York NY 10038. (212)669-9200. Contact: Press Relations Division. **Description:** "A public relations and educational organization for all lines of insurance except life and health insurance. It is sponsored by several hundred insurance companies, and provides services on a fee basis to major industry organizations. The institute has 12 field offices across the US. The headquarters in New York houses a Media Relations Division, a Publications Division and a Planning and Issues Division (which contains the following departments: Education, Research, Consumer Affairs and our library)." **Services:** Offers aid in arranging interviews, statistics, brochures/pamphlets, information searches, press kits, and films related to property and casualty insurance. **How to Contact:** Write or call. "We're happy to answer questions about basic areas of insurance. We have an extensive list of publications. Most of our publications are free in single copies. Due to a limited staff, the institute will not conduct research projects for college and high school students. We will, however, be glad to provide any relevant data that has been requested. Also, the institute may be able to refer the person to the proper source of information." **Tips:** "We're most eager to work with writers." Recent information requests: How to save money on insurance; what kinds of discounts are available.

189• INTERNATIONAL ASSOCIATION OF BUSINESS COMMUNICATORS
870 Market St., Suite 940, San Francisco CA 94102. (415)433-3400. Contact Person: Director of Research. **Description:** Organization designed "to provide information about communication and

to help members do their jobs and advance in their fields. Members include more than 9,500 communication managers, publication editors and writers, audiovisual specialists and others in the communication field." **Services:** Provides advisory, bibliographical, interpretative (of our own research), referral and trade information covering the communication areas including organizational issues, publications, skills, audiovisuals, work, feedback, other media, etc. Offers annual reports, bibliographies, statistics, brochures/pamphlets, information searches and a newsletter. Also has placement service, awards program and extensive reference library. Publications include membership directory; *Communication World* (tabloid); and *Journal of Communication Management* (magazine). Books include *Excellence in Communication* (1981, 1982); *Without Bias*; *Inside Organizational Communication*. **How to Contact:** Write. Responds to most inquiries immediately or within a week "depending on the nature of the inquiry. We will be charging for the loan of materials from the library; we do not charge for referrals or other types of services. In-house use of materials is also free. Service is primarily member-oriented; $80/year membership. We limit nonmember access to materials. Some publications are restricted to member use. Applicants for membership must be connected in some way with the field." **Tips:** "A visit to the library would probably be most beneficial since much material is cross filed in a number of places. Have a fairly good idea of what it is you're looking for. Resources of the IABC include profit and not-for-profit communicators as well as journalism and communication educators. A major part of the time in our library is spent consulting with writers and other communicators on specific topics of special concern. Our library maintains information (and tapes) on some 300 topics." Recent information requests: "How do you explain benefits package to employees?"; "What are current trends in organizational publications?"

190• INTERNATIONAL EXECUTIVES ASSOCIATION
122 E. 42nd St., Suite 1014, New York NY 10168. (212)661-4610. Contact Person: Office Manager. **Description:** An organization of international executives of American firms. **Services:** Offers aid in arranging interviews, statistics, brochures/pamphlets and press releases for special events. Publications include *Sale Executive*. **How to Contact:** "Written request from editor or writer. Interviews must be reviewed before being granted." Responds to inquiries as soon as possible. Charges $15/year for nonmembers and $5/year for members for *Sale Executive*.

191• INTERNATIONAL TRADE COMMISSION
701 E St. NW, Washington DC 20436 (202)523-0161. Contact Person: Public Affairs Officer. **Description:** "We are a government agency." **Services:** Provides analytical and trade information covering trade data, economic issues concerning imports, reports in response to legal disputes involving imports and their impact on US economy. Offers aid in arranging interviews, annual reports, biographies, brochures/pamphlets, information searches, placement on mailing list, newsletter and press kits. Publications include an annual report and investigation reports that are issued periodically. **How to Contact:** Write or call. Responds to most inquiries within a week. Charges for photocopying; current rate: 10¢/page. "Some data is classified 'business confidential' and cannot be released to the general public." **Tips:** "There are many advantages in doing research *on site* at the commission, including a library open to the public." Recent information request: Facts surrounding a number of ITC investigations involving selected South American countries.

192• MANUFACTURERS HANOVER CORPORATION
350 Park Ave., New York NY 10022. (212)350-5254. Contact Person: Press Relations Director. **Description:** "Manufacturers Hanover Corporation is a multi-bank holding company whose flagship bank, Manufacturers Hanover Trust Company, is the fourth largest in the US. It serves domestic and international customers through banks and bank-related subsidiaries in mortgage banking, factoring, leasing, consumer finance and merchant banking." **Services:** Offers annual reports, bibliographies, biographies, statistics, brochures/pamphlets, placement on mailing list, newsletter, photos and press kits. **How to Contact:** Write or call. Responds to most inquiries immediately. Recent information requests: Questions dealing with banking and our operations.

193• MUTUAL OF OMAHA
Mutual of Omaha Plaza, Omaha NE 68175. (402)342-7600. Contact: Media Relations Department. **Description:** "As a leader in the insurance field, Mutual of Omaha offers a wide range of insurance coverages (health, life, auto, home, credit) as well as mutual funds. The Media Relations staff is available to answer any questions relating to these products and services or to the

insurance industry in general. In addition, information is also provided on the company's unique, energy-efficient, three-level underground building." **Services:** Provides advisory, analytical, bibliographical, historical, how-to, interpretative, referral, technical and trade information on insurance products (health, life, auto, home, credit), financial services (mutual funds), and on company's underground building/energy savings. Offers aid in arranging interviews, annual reports, biographies, brochures/pamphlets, photos, placement on mailing lists, press kits, research assistance and statistics. Publications include brochures on various products, fact sheets and photos of underground building, annual reports, company histories, histories of life and health insurance, insurance informational booklets. **How to Contact:** Write or call. Responds to most inquiries immediately. **Tips:** "Give us a call or drop us a note. We want to be of service." Recent information request: "What benefits are provided under Mutual of Omaha's major medical/catastrophic health plan?"

194• NATIONAL ASSOCIATION OF INCOME TAX PRACTITIONERS
6628 212th St. SW, Lynnwood WA 98036. (206)771-5988. Contact Person: Executive Director. **Description:** Individuals who prepare tax returns for others. The association "provides opportunities for growth for the tax practitioner through education; provides communication between the tax practitioner and government; establishes an awareness by the public, government and by the professional community of the importance of the tax practitioner to the community." **Services:** Provides advisory, analytical, bibliographical, historical, how-to, interpretative, referral, technical and trade information on income tax and tax planning. Offers brochures/pamphlets, informational newsletters, placement on mailing lists, research assistance and telephone reference services. Publications include newsletter. **How to Contact:** Write, call or visit. Responds to most inquiries immediately. **Tips:** Recent information request: "Does the new tax law really help the average taxpayer?"

195• NATIONAL ASSOCIATION OF LIFE UNDERWRITERS
1922 F St. NW, Washington DC 20006. (202)331-6030. Contact Person: Public Relations Director. **Description:** "Professional organization of individuals engaged in the broad range of life underwriting." **Services:** Provides information on life and health insurance and other financial vehicles. "We are a reference and resource body on life and health insurance sales and service. We'd be glad to make referrals to other organizations that may be able to help." Offers bibliographies, biographies, brochures/pamphlets, information searches, newsletter and magazines, photos and press kits. Publications include *NALU*; *Your Life Insurance Agent and You*; *You and Your Life Insurance Agent*; and *Why the Life Insurance You Already Own May Be Your Best Buy*. **How to Contact:** Write or call. Responds to most inquiries immediately. "We're not in the business of giving ratings of individual companies or products." **Tips:** "Life insurance industry is undergoing significant changes in marketing and products." Recent information request: "In view of inflation, what developments have taken place in life insurance to make it viable and healthy?"

196• NATIONAL ASSOCIATION OF PROFESSIONAL INSURANCE AGENTS (PIA)
400 N. Washington St., Alexandria VA 22314. (703)836-9340. Contact Person: Manager, Media Relations. **Description:** "The PIA represents independent insurance agents specializing in property/casualty insurance." **Services:** Provides advisory, technical and trade information on any area affecting independent insurance agents—rating, distribution, etc. Offers aid in arranging interviews, annual reports, brochures/pamphlets, photos, press kits and research assistance. Publications include: *Consumers Guide to Effective Arson Control*; *Homeowners and Renters Insurance and Inventory Guide*; and *A Parents' Guide to Child Safety*. **How to Contact:** Write or call. Responds to most inquiries within a week. **Tips:** Recent information request: "How can consumers save on homeowners' insurance?"

197• NATIONAL FOUNDATION FOR CONSUMER CREDIT, INC.
8701 Georgia Ave., #601, Silver Spring MD 20910. (301)589-5600. Contact Person: Receptionist. **Description:** The National Foundation for Consumer Credit is a nonprofit organization. "We have over 200 affiliated consumer credit counseling agencies across the US and Canada to help persons who have over-extended themselves with credit. They offer budget counseling and debt management programs. We do no counseling in this office." **Services:** Provides historical, how-to and referral information on credit and credit card users, how to estab-lish and maintain good credit; provides referral to affiliated nonprofit credit counseling services.

Offers brochures/pamphlets, informational newsletters, placement on mailing lists, statistics and telephone reference services. Publications include *Consumer Credit*; *The Forms of Credit We Use*; *Establishing Good Credit*; *The Emergency Problem—What to Do about It*; *Measuring Credit Capacity*; along with various financial counseling modules and several other pamphlets. **How to Contact:** Write or call. Responds to most inquiries immediately. "We generally send sample copies of pamphlets free of charge; however, if a quantity is desired, we do charge a small fee."

198• NATIONAL PLANNING ASSOCIATION
1606 New Hampshire Ave. NW, Washington DC 20009. (202)265-7685. Contact Person: Director, Public Affairs. **Description:** NPA is an independent, private, nonprofit, nonpolitical organization that carries on research of economic policy issues, both domestic and international. **Services:** Provides analytical, interpretative, technical and trade information. Offers brochures/pamphlets, informational newsletters and statistics. Publications list available. **How to Contact:** Write. Responds to most inquiries within a month. "Publications are available at a cost ranging from $1-$10; the projections series are available for $850-$1,400/year (approx.). See publications list." Give appropriate attribution/citation. **Tips:** Call or write for a publications list. Recent information request: "What are employment and population prospects for Texas in year 2000?"

199• NATIONAL SMALL BUSINESS ASSOCIATION
1604 K St. NW, Washington DC 20006. (202)296-7400. Contact Person: Communications Director. **Description:** "Our purpose is to communicate with the federal government on issues affecting small business and to advance and protect small businesses." **Services:** Offers aid in arranging interviews, statistics, placement on mailing list, newsletter and photos. **How to Contact:** Write or call. Responds to most inquiries immediately. **Tips:** "A specific question always gets a better answer." Recent information request: "How does the 1982 tax bill change the status of independent contractors?"

200• NATIONAL TAX ASSOCIATION—TAX INSTITUTE OF AMERICA
21 E. State St., Columbus OH 43215. (614)224-8352. Contact Person: Executive Assistant. **Description:** "The purpose of the National Tax Association is to educate and benefit our members and to interest and inform the general public in areas concerning taxation and public finance." **Services:** Provides analytical, interpretative and technical information on taxation and public finance. The association holds an Annual Conference on Taxation every fall; an annual Symposium on a specific subject of taxation in the spring; co-sponsors Public Utility Workshop with Wichita State University every summer; and has study committees on various types of taxation. Publications include *National Tax Journal* (quarterly); *Proceedings of the Annual Conference*. **How to Contact:** Write. Responds to most inquiries immediately. Charges for membership and subscription to the *Journal*.

201• OFFICE OF BUSINESS LIAISON
Roadmap Program, US Department of Commerce, Washington DC 20230. (202)377-3176. Contact Person: Associate Director. **Description:** "We provide technical assistance and referral program on a wide range of government/business information to business firms, individuals, trade associations and others. The program is especially useful to small business." **Services:** Provides referral and trade information on general business and international trade, including trade, taxes, funding, product standards, business licensing, franchising, Department of Commerce and Administration programs and policies. Offers aid in arranging interviews, research assistance, statistics and telephone reference services. **How to Contact:** Write, call or visit. Responds to most inquiries within a week. **Tips:** "We do not prepare research studies but can provide information and identify other reference sources. Indicate intended use of requested information. Sometimes alternate routes or sources can be suggested." Recent information request: "What is the duty rate on a product imported into the US from a specific country?"

202• OTC INFORMATION BUREAU
120 Broadway, New York NY 10271. (212)964-5940. Contact Person: Manager. **Description:** "Our purpose is to inform and educate the investing and general public and the media about the over-the-counter stock market." **Services:** Provides analytical, historical, interpretative and trade information on parent organization, National Security Traders Association; NASDAQ (the computerized stock quotation system); and the OTC market and changes taking place in the securities

industry. Offers aid in arranging interviews, biographies, brochures/pamphlets, informational newsletters, photos, placement on mailing lists, statistics and telephone reference services. Publications include NASD publications; bimonthly newsletter for corporate bureau members. **How to Contact:** Write or call. Responds to most inquiries immediately. **Tips:** "Make a list of specific areas in which you feel we might help before contacting us." Recent information request: "What effect will the current changes that are taking place in the securities industry have on the OTC market?"

203• PACKAGE DESIGNERS COUNCIL
Box 3753, Grand Central Station, New York NY 10017. (212)682-1980. Contact Person: President. **Description:** "We are a nonprofit, professional and international organization of design consultants and members who specialize in package design as well as other forms of visual communications." **Services:** Provides advisory, historical, how-to and trade information on packaging and marketing specifically related to visual communications. Offers information on package design, services, and holding exhibits and seminars. **How to Contact:** Write or call. Responds to most inquiries within a week. Charges for surveys that have been conducted and that are available to the public.

204• SAVINGS BONDS DIVISION
Department of the Treasury, Washington DC 20226. (202)634-5377. Contact Person: Director of Public Information. **Description:** "We promote the sale of bonds. The office of public information provides information on savings bonds—their sales, redemption, relationship to the treasury's debt management, purposes and qualities of the bonds. We also provide information on changes in the bond program, the division's personnel and so on." **Services:** Offers aid in arranging interviews, statistics, brochures/pamphlets, photos and press kits. Publications include several different brochures describing Series EE and HH US savings bonds; a booklet on legal aspects of savings bonds; a booklet for bond tellers on cashing and selling bonds; various booklets for bond canvassers in companies and organizations; a history of the bond program; monthly sales releases on bond sales; other news releases as necessary; and questions and answers on specific bond questions. **How to Contact:** Write or call. Responds to most inquiries within a month. **Tips:** "Any information you can give on the date and series of the bonds is helpful." Recent information request: Tax questions on savings bonds.

205• SECURITIES AND EXCHANGE COMMISSION
450 5th St. NW, Washington DC 20549. Contact: Office of Public Affairs. For documents filed with SEC: Public Reference Department, (202)272-7462; Referral for legal interpretations: Public Affairs Department, 272-2650; Historical and reference: Library, 272-2618. **Description:** "The SEC's purpose is to administer the securities laws, which have two basic objectives; to provide investors with financial material and other information on securities and to prohibit fraud in the sale of securities." **Services:** Provides information filed by corporations or individuals who must register with SEC, and information on securities laws. Offers biographies of commissioners. Quarterly and annual reports, registration statements, proxy material and other reports filed by corporations, mutual funds or broker-dealers are available for inspection in the Public Reference Room. Some reports and statements also available at regional offices. **How to Contact:** Write for publications list. Response time depends on complexity of inquiry. "There is a copying charge for documents; varies with the type of service—10¢/page ($5 minimum)." **Tips:** "Be as specific as possible as to information desired—company names, dates, types of filings, etc." Recent information requests: Questions on reports required to be filed with SEC by corporations, broker-dealers or others who must register with SEC.

206• SECURITIES INDUSTRY ASSOCIATION
120 Broadway, New York NY 10005. (212)425-2700. Contact Person: Director of Public Information. **Description:** "The Securities Industry Association is the trade association of brokerage firms and investment banks." **Services:** Provides referral and trade information on the stock market, brokerage firms, investment banking and the securities industry. Offers aid in arranging interviews, informational newsletters, press kits and research assistance. **How to Contact:** Write or call. Responds to most inquiries within a week.

207• SERVICE CORPS OF RETIRED EXECUTIVES ASSOCIATION
822 15th St. NW, Washington DC 20416. (202)653-6279. Contact Person: Director of Public

Relations. **Description:** "SCORE is an organization of more than 8,200 business executive volunteers who offer free business management counseling to the American small business community. SCORE is sponsored by the Small Business Administration. SCORE also offers pre-business workshops and problem clinics covering the major fundamental aspects of business—marketing and advertising, planning, merchandising, accounting, legal considerations, business insurance and taxes." **Services:** Offers aid in arranging interviews, statistics and brochures/pamphlets. Publications include "free publications on nearly every subject of business management and operation." **How to Contact:** "Contact the SCORE organization in your local area, or write the Washington office. SCORE can't undertake any research projects, but will endeavor to supply answers to specific questions." Responds to most inquiries immediately.

208• SOCIETY OF ACTUARIES
208 S. LaSalle St., Chicago IL 60604. (312)236-3833. Contact Person: Director of Communications. **Description:** "The Society of Actuaries is a professional membership association for actuaries in life and health insurance and pensions." **Services:** Provides analytical, interpretative, referral, technical and trade information on insurance, pensions, employee benefits, mortality statistics, body build and blood pressure statistics. Offers aid in arranging interviews, brochures/pamphlets, library facilities, placement on mailing lists, press kits and statistics. Publications are technically oriented. Information to the general public is distributed mostly through press kits. Publications for sale only. **How to Contact:** Write or call. Responds to most inquiries within a week. "Writers must cite the Society of Actuaries as a source of information." **Tips:** Recent information request: "What is the average weight of a woman, 5'5''?"

209• STANDARD & POOR'S CORPORATION LIBRARY
25 Broadway, New York NY 10004. (212)248-7911. Contact: Central Inquiry Unit. **Description:** "The corporation is involved in financial publishing and debt rating." **Services:** Provides "on demand, for a fee" analytical, historical, referral, technical and trade information on corporations, industries, finance and economics. Offers computerized information searches, informational newsletter, research assistance, statistics and telephone reference services. **How to Contact:** Call between 9 a.m. and 4 p.m. Services and fees schedule available. Minimum monthly billing $15. "Sample copies of current S&P publications are available for inspection and evaluation in the library between 9 a.m. and 4:30 p.m. weekdays. We have limited capability for servicing visitors; please call first. Access to the library's reference collection is not available except by special arrangement." **Tips:** Recent information requests: Stock quotes; financial data.

210• TRANSIT ADVERTISING ASSOCIATION, INC.
60 E. 42nd St., Suite 1027, New York NY 10165. (212)599-2352. Contact Person: Executive Director. **Description:** "We serve as a central information bureau for the transit advertising industry." **Services:** Provides historical and trade information. Offers photos and statistics. **How to Contact:** Write. Responds to most inquiries within a week. **Tips:** Recent information request: "How widespread is the transit advertising industry and how long has it been in existence?"

211• UNITED STATES CHAMBER OF COMMERCE
1615 H St. NW, Washington DC 20062. (202)463-5682. Contact Person: News Director. **Description:** "National federation of business organizations and companies. Membership includes 4,000 chambers of commerce and associations, and more than 200,000 business firms. US Chamber determines and makes known to the government the recommendations of the business community on national issues and problems affecting the economy and the future of the country; works to advance human progress through an economic, political and social system based on individual freedom and initiative; informs, trains, equips and encourages members to participate in policy-making decisions at federal, state and local levels and in legislative and political action at the national level. Produces weekly, nationally televised program, "It's Your Business," and radio program, "What's the Issue," and operates the American Business Network (BizNet)." **Services:** Provides advisory and analytical information on all subject areas in which business deals with government: antitrust, trade policy, regulation, fiscal matters, the economy, economic education, resources and environment, transfer payments, etc. Offers aid in arranging interviews, annual reports, brochures/pamphlets, informational newsletters and statistics. Conducts continuing education programs for business executives. Publications include: *US Chamber Annual Report*; US Chamber staff specialists, consumer and

business confidence surveys; economic outlook reports; newsletters on international affairs and business-government affairs; special reports, studies and research papers. **How to Contact:** Write, call or visit. Responds to most inquiries immediately. **Tips:** Recent information requests: "Does business favor cuts in the growth of Social Security benefits?"; "How have employee 'perks' (benefits) grown over the past 20 years?"; "What steps are necessary to increase US productivity rates?"

212• UNITED STATES CHOICE IN CURRENCY COMMISSION
325 Pennsylvania Ave. SE, Washington DC 20003. (202)745-1020. Contact Person: Executive Director. **Description:** "The US Choice in Currency Commission is a foundation for research in monetary policy and alternatives to centralized management of money supply." **Services:** Provides advisory, analytical, bibliographical, historical, interpretative, referral and technical information on monetary policy, banking and bank-deregulation, gold and the proposals for a gold standard, interest rates, Federal Reserve System, foreign exchange rates, I.M.F., and international finance. Offers brochures/pamphlets, informational newsletters, press kits, research assistance, telephone reference services and free consulting on economic theories affecting policy. Publications include: *Currency Competition* newsletter; research reports. **How to Contact:** Write, call or visit. Responds to most inquiries within a week. "We like to receive favorable mention as a resource, but this is not a requirement." **Tips:** "Since there are several prevailing theories of economics that may be used to explain important events, we offer a service to sort out the theories and their underlying assumptions, so that the writer can provide an objective, balanced analysis for readers." Recent information requests: "How is monetary policy formulated?"; "What role can gold play in international finance?"; "What's the distinction between monetary price rules and quantity rules?"; "Is money tight or loose today?"

SECTION·FOUR

COMMUNICATIONS/ENTERTAINMENT

Good communication is stimulating as black coffee, and just as hard to sleep after.
            —Anne Morrow Lindbergh

Culture relates to objects and is a phenomenon of the world; entertainment relates to people and is a phenomenon of life.
            —Hannah Arendt

This section identifies information sources in the areas of communications technology, journalism, broadcast and print media, audio-visual programming and production (records, tapes, film) and human communications (public speaking, handwriting, consulting). Also listed are resources in the field of the communicative arts, including motion pictures, radio and television.

Additional sources of entertainment information (games, amusement parks, toys) are found in the Hobby and Leisure section. The lively arts such as music, theatre and dance are listed in The Arts category.

Bibliography

Ayer Directory of Publications. rev. ed. Bala Cynwyd, PA: Ayer Press, 1981. (The equivalent of a *Books in Print* for newspapers)

Blum, Eleanor, ed. *Basic Books in the Mass Media.* 2d ed. Urbana, IL: University of Illinois Press, 1980.

Broadcasting Yearbook. Annual. Washington DC: Broadcasting Publications, Inc. (Current information on the broadcast business)

Brooks, Tim and Earl Marsh. *Complete Directory to Prime Time Network TV Shows, 1946-Present.* New York: Ballantine Books, 1981.

The Contact Book. Annual. New York: Celebrity Service, Inc. (Directory of contacts in print and broadcast media, entertainment and sports in celebrity cities around the world)

Editor & Publisher International Yearbook. Annual. New York: Editor & Publisher Co., Inc.

Frost, Jens. *World Radio TV Handbook.* New York: Watson-Guptill, 1983.

Halliwell, Leslie. *Halliwell's Film Guide.* New York: Scribner, 1982.

Halliwell, Leslie. *Halliwell's Filmgoer's Companion.* New York: Scribner, 1980.

The Home Video Yearbook. Annual. White Plains, NY: Knowledge Industry Publications.

Kurian, George Thomas, ed. *World Press Encyclopedia.* New York: Facts on File, 1982.

Literary Market Place. Annual. New York: Bowker. (Directory-type information on the publishing industry)

O'Dwyer, Jack, ed. *O'Dwyer's Directory of Public Relations Firms.* Annual. New York: J.R. O'Dwyer Co.

Terrace, Vincent, ed. *Radio's Golden Years: The Encyclopedia of Radio Programs 1930-1960.* San Diego: A.S. Barnes, 1981.

Toll Free Digest. Toll Free Digest Co., Inc., Box 800, Claverack NY 12513. (Directory of "800" numbers issued by AT&T)

Ulrich's International Periodicals Directory. 21st ed. New York: Bowker, 1982.

US Book Publishing Yearbook & Directory. Annual. White Plains, NY: Knowledge Industry Publications.

213• A&M RECORDS, INC.
1416 N. LaBrea Ave., Hollywood CA 90028. (213)469-2411. Contact Person: Director of Publicity. **Description:** Company manufacturers and distributes records and promotes recording artists. **Services:** Provides bibliographical and trade information on artists' careers, entertainment and music. Offers aid in arranging interviews, clipping services, biographies, newsletter and press kits. **How to Contact:** Write or call. Responds to most inquiries within a week. Charges for services. "We deal with active freelance, staff or trade journalists writing about music. Send a cover letter with clips if it is a first request." **Tips:**Recent information request: "How many albums have the rock group, The Police, put out?"

214• ACADEMY OF MOTION PICTURE ARTS AND SCIENCES: NATIONAL FILM
INFORMATION SERVICE
8949 Wilshire Blvd., Beverly Hills CA 90211. (213)278-8990. Contact Person: Coordinator,
National Film Information Service. **Description:** National film information service. **Services:**
Provides bibliographical and historical information covering film history and people in the film in-
dustry. "We also have general files on certain broad topics, e.g., censorship, communism, etc."
Offers film stills filed by personality and by film title. **How to Contact:** Write or call. Responds to
most inquiries within a week. Charges $10/8x10 still. Larger sizes available on special order.
Charges 50¢/page for photocopying. "For large orders a research fee will be added. No catalog of
the collection is available, but we will answer all research requests. We do not have information on
TV; we do not own the rights to stills in our holdings." **Tips:** "Be as specific as possible in your requests for information. Use your local library, first." Recent information request: Photocopies of
an actor's clipping file, reviews of his films and stills.

215• ACCURACY IN MEDIA
1341 G St. NW, Suite 312, Washington DC 20005. (202)783-4406. Contact Person: Chairman.
Description: "Accuracy in Media is a media watchdog organization which conducts research into
inaccurate and biased reporting." **Services:** Provides analytical and research reports on news and
information coverage in all media. Offers informational newsletters, library facilities and research
assistance. Publications include *AIM Report*, (a bimonthly newsletter). **How to Contact:** Write or
call. Responds to most inquiries immediately. "There is no charge for assisting writers and researchers on specific projects; however, there is a charge for our newsletter of $15/year by Third
Class Mail and $30/year by First Class Mail. We request writers/researchers to give us credit for
any quotes from our materials and for any reprints." **Tips:** "We do not provide a service per se to
writers, but we do have reference materials that can assist them in their research, and knowledgeable writers who can provide them with information on many subjects." Recent information requests: "Have you done any research on the Jim Johnson-Guyana incident?"; "What information
do you have on the media's coverage of Watergate?"

216• ACTION FOR CHILDREN'S TELEVISION
46 Austin St., Newtonville MA 02160. (617)527-7870. Contact Person: Editorial
Director. **Description:** "Action for Children's Television is a nonprofit consumer organization
which works to increase diversity and eliminate commercial abuses for children's
television." **Services:** Provides advisory, analytical, bibliographical, how-to, interpretative,
referral and trade information covering children's TV, FCC and FTC regulation, TV technology,
parental and educational guides, health and nutrition, programming and advertising practices, and
viewing statistics. Membership available. Publications include news magazine, brochures, books,
pamphlets. **How to Contact:** Write or call. Responds to most inquiries within a week. Charges $1
for basic information package; $3 for news magazine. "Send self-addressed stamped envelope
with request for informational packet (enclose check). ACT library is not open to the
public." **Tips:** "Give credit to ACT when quoting materials." Recent information requests: child
viewing statistics; "What does ACT think about TV violence?"

217• ADULT FILM ASSOCIATION OF AMERICA
c/o Morgan Communications, 20720 Ventura Blvd., Suite 260, Woodland Hills CA 91364.
(213)702-0374. Contact Person: President, Morgan Communications. **Description:** Association
of adult film industry people who support and defend the industry socially, legally, and
economically. Activities include the Annual Erotica Awards. **Services:** Provides analytical,
historical, interpretative, referral and trade information on the history of the adult film industry;
where it has been and where it is going. Offers aid in arranging interviews, biographies, clipping
services, informational newsletters, photos, placement on mailing lists, press kits and telephone
reference services. **How to Contact:** Write or call. Responds to most inquiries within a week.
Requests writers have a "positive or non-biased opinion about the adult film industry." **Tips:**
"Familiarize yourself with the association through the use of AFAA press kits." Recent information request: "How has the adult film industry changed over the years since the AFAA evolved?"

218• AMERICAN COUNCIL FOR BETTER BROADCASTS
120 E. Wilson St., Madison WI 53703. (608)257-7712. Contact Person: Executive
Director. **Description:** "We promote quality programming in broadcasting via educational means
to help the teaching of critical viewing." **Services:** Provides advisory information on

telecommunications/consumer participation, media literacy (electronic media). Offers brochures/pamphlets and newsletter. "We also sponsor annual look-listen opinion polls." Publications available. **How to Contact:** Write or call. Responds to most inquiries within a month. Charges for some publications. "Members of ACBB receive certain services free; nonmembers pay for *Look Listen Opinion Report.*" **Tips:** "Students should not expect ACBB to write their term papers for them. However, we can often suggest resources where the needed material can be found and can supply addresses." Recent information request: Help with materials on media literacy; selected bibliography on children and television; requirements for participation in Look Listen Opinion Poll; KIDS-4 children's channel (interactive TV by kids for kids).

219• AMERICAN SOCIETY OF PROFESSIONAL CONSULTANTS
2 Hamilton Ave., New Rochelle NY 10801. (914)632-0610. Contact Person: Editor, *The Consultant.* **Description:** "The American Society of Professional Consultants is a nonprofit association dedicated to furthering professionalism among the nation's consultants, no matter what their field of specialty. Through the delivery of a complete range of support services, the association guides consultants in how to enhance the quality of services they provide their clients and at the same time, to increase the profitability of their consulting practice." **Services:** Provides how-to, referral, and trade information. Offers informational newsletters, placement on mailing lists, research assistance, statistics, telephone reference services, seminars, conferences and conventions. Publications include: *The Consultants Library*; *The Consultants Kit*; *The Consultant* (newsletter); and *The Professional Papers.* **How to Contact:** Write. Responds to most inquiries within a week. Charges $85 personal membership, $175 corporate membership. **Tips:** Recent information requests: What kind of contract to write; how to structure a fee.

220• ARBITRON RATINGS COMPANY
1350 Avenue of the Americas, Suite 1105, New York NY 10019. (212)887-1402/1420. Contact Person: Assistant to the Director, Communications. **Description:** Activities include "radio, television, cable audience measurement and research." **Services:** Provides historical, how-to and trade information on broadcast audience measurement and research. Offers brochures/pamphlets, library facilities and statistics. Publications include *Description of Methodology—Radio & Television*; *How to Read and Use Broadcast Estimates*; *Radio & Television Local Market Reports* for reference purposes. **How to Contact:** Write or call. Responds to most inquiries within a week. "Some information is copyrighted and we must give permission for printing of it." **Tips:** "Be as specific as possible. It is hard to help if the writer doesn't know what information he needs." Recent information requests: "What are the top five radio stations in New York City?"; "How do you do your surveys?"

221• ASSOCIATED TELEPHONE ANSWERING EXCHANGES
320 King St., Suite 320, Alexandria VA 22304. (703)684-0016. Contact Person: Director of Communications. **Description:** "We are a trade association for telephone answering bureaus, international in scope. Information provided members includes new technology, conversion, regulation, marketing, related services, etc." **Services:** Provides referral and trade information on operator training, conversion, accounting, new technology, regulation, related services, management, financial analyses and association activities. Offers aid in arranging interviews, brochures/pamphlets, informational newsletters, press kits and telephone reference services. Publications include *Answer Magazine.* **How to Contact:** Write or call. Responds to most inquiries within a week. Charges for magazine and mailing. "Apply for permission to reprint or use copyrighted material." **Tips:** "Ask specific questions. General information available in press kit." Recent information requests: "Where do telephone answering bureaus fit into the telecommunications revolution?"

222• ASSOCIATION OF INDEPENDENT VIDEO & FILMMAKERS
625 Broadway, 9th Floor, New York NY 10012. (212)473-3400. Contact Person: Media Coordinator. **Description:** "As a national trade association for independent film and videomakers, we represent independent producers' interests through advocacy and lobbying to government, industry and the general public. As a nonprofit service organization dedicated to the promotion of independent video and film, we provide services to independent producers and enhance and support the growth and public awareness of independent media in this country. Such services include: a health plan, screenings and seminars, a monthly magazine, publications, an international festival bureau, consultation and referral services, information clearinghouse

services, a national membership directory, etc.'' **Services:** Provides how-to, referral and technical information on film and video. Offers clipping services, placement on mailing lists, research assistance and telephone reference services; in-house files on independent producers, their tapes/films, their distributors, other service organizations and media facilities, and materials on film/video legislation and policies related both to government and industry; phone and in-person referral services; monthly magazine, *The Independent*, concerning practical advice, opportunities and information on independent film/video production; series of special publications and pamphlets dealing with aspects of independent production; comprehensive national mailing list of independent film/video producers. **How to Contact:** Write, call or visit. Responds to most inquiries within a week. **Tips:** ''Call first with your inquiry.''

223• BONNEVILLE INTERNATIONAL CORPORATION
c/o WRFM Radio, 485 Madison Ave., New York NY 10022. (212)752-3322. Contact Person: Special Assistant to the President. **Description:** ''Bonneville International Corp. covers Latin American involvement in radio and television, representing US broadcasters to the Inter-American Association of Broadcasters; consultants to UNESCO on communications policies, etc.'' **Services:** Provides information covering entertainment, music, news dissemination, communications, journalist training, etc. Offers statistics. Publications include *Doctrine for Public Broadcasting in the Americas*; *Statement of Ethics for Broadcasters throughout the Americas* and *Bases for Legislation throughout the Americas*. **How to Contact:** Write or call. Responds to most inquiries within a week, ''but it depends on the complexity of the requested data.''

224• BROADCAST PIONEERS LIBRARY
1771 N St. NW, Washington DC 20036. (202)223-0088. Contact Person: Director. **Description:** ''A research library dedicated to the history of broadcasting. The library contains photos, oral histories and runs of old broadcasting journals, as well as books, pamphlets and vertical file holdings.'' **Services:** Provides advisory, analytical, bibliographical, historical, how-to, interpretative, referral, technical and trade information covering broadcasting history. Offers ''limited'' information searches. **How to Contact:** ''Make an appointment to use the library; write or phone information requests. Be specific as to what you want.'' Responds to most inquiries within a week. ''Fees are cited upon request. An appointment is required for a visit.''

225• BURLINGTON LIARS CLUB, INC.
Burlington WI 53105. (414)763-3341. Contact Person: Vice President. **Description:** ''The organization was founded in 1929 to name a World's Champion liar each year. It was disbanded in 1980 and reformed in 1981. Persons may send in 'tall tales' in the annual contest, and persons may become honorary members of the club by sending in a lie and $1.'' **Services:** Provides advisory information, interviews with news media and others in regard to lies submitted by club members and others. News release each January 1 names the world's champion liar. *50 Years of Championship Lies* available for $2.50. **How to Contact:** Write, call or visit. Responds to most inquiries within a month. **Tips:** ''We are anxious to hear from writers and others in regard to the history and the championship lies of the club.'' Recent information requests: ''During a hot weather spell in New York, a radio station in NYC called and wanted some 'hot weather lies.' Also personal interviews by electronic and print media were arranged.''

226• CELEBRITY SERVICE, INC.
171 W. 57th St., New York NY 10019. (212)757-7979. Contact Person: Manager. **Description:** Celebrity Service provides information and research on celebrities. ''We have on file approximately 500,000 names.'' Central offices are located in New York, Hollywood, London, Paris and Rome. **Services:** Celebrity Service subscribers ''have access to the addresses (both permanent and temporary), affiliations, agents and other contacts, biographies and current activities of celebrities all over the world in every field.'' Offers biographies, informational newsletters, photos, research assistance and telephone reference services. Publications include *The Celebrity Bulletin*, *The Theatrical Calendar* and *Contact Book*. **How to Contact:** Write. Responds to most inquiries within a week. Services available by subscription primarily (rate sheet available), or $10/individual inquiry. **Tips:** Recent information request: ''How do I get in touch with Robert Redford?''

227• THE CENTER FOR THE BOOK
Library of Congress, Washington DC 20540. (202)287-5221. Contact Person: Executive Director. **Description:** ''Established by Act of Congress in 1977, the Center exists 'to keep the book flour-

ishing' through a stimulating program of projects, lectures, symposia and publications.'' **Services:** Provides information on books, publishing, literacy, libraries—most anything to do with the dissemination of the printed word. Offers placement on mailing list. The Center for the Book coordinates the CBS/Library of Congress book project called ''Read More About It.'' The project uses network TV and well-known TV stars to promote books and reading. **How to Contact:** Write or call. Responds to most inquiries immediately.

228•   CHILDREN'S BOOK COUNCIL
67 Irving Place, New York NY 10003. (212)254-2666. Contact Person: Publications Director. **Description:** ''Our purpose is to encourage interest in children's books; in using and enjoying children's books; and the promotion of children's books in a general way.'' **Services:** Offers bibliographies, informational brochures and informational sheets. Publications available. **How to Contact:** Write or call (no collect calls). Responds to most inquiries within six weeks. Charges for publications. **Tips:** ''The council does not evaluate or publish children's books. We do have two very helpful brochures for people wanting to become either writers or illustrators of children's books.''

229•   CNB-TV (CENTER FOR NON-BROADCAST TELEVISION)
49 E. 68th St., New York NY 10021. (212)794-3271. Contact Person: Executive Director. **Description:** CNB-TV is a nonprofit developmental television corporation whose activities include experimental and developmental television production and distribution, and domestic and international transmission. **Services:** Provides advisory, how-to, referral and trade information on television and new technology, satellite communications, cable TV, and national ad hoc or permanent networking. Offers aid in arranging interviews on tape, annual reports by video and research assistance. **How to Contact:** Write or call. Responds to most inquiries within a week. **Tips:** ''Be wary of published information and statistics on cable TV industry.'' Recent information request: Uses of electronic media for dissemination of public affairs information for preparation of a handbook.

230•   COMICS MAGAZINE ASSOCIATION OF AMERICA, INC.
60 E. 42nd St., New York NY 10165. (212)682-8142. Contact Person: Executive Secretary. **Description:** ''We are a trade association for the comics magazine industry; operate a comics library; and, chiefly, enforce a code of decency for editorial and advertising matter published in comic books.'' **Services:** Provides historical, technical and trade information covering comic books. Publications include *Code of the Comics Magazine Association of America* and *Americana in Four Colors*, a paperback of comic books and code enforcement. ''We also have articles, newspaper clippings and books about comics in our library.'' **How to Contact:** Write. Responds to most inquiries immediately. ''Visits to our office must be by appointment. We do not allow our reference material to be taken from our office.'' **Tips:** Recent information request: The name of the originator of a comic character.

231•   COMMUNICATIONS WORKERS OF AMERICA
1925 K St. NW, Washington DC 20006. (202)785-6740. Contact Person: Director of Public Affairs. **Description:** Labor organization. **Services:** Information covers telephone work and workers, communicators and technology from workers' point of view. Offers placement on mailing list. Publications available. **How to Contact:** Write. Responds to most inquiries within a week. ''Written requests must state what the information will be used for.''

232•   CORPORATION FOR PUBLIC BROADCASTING
1111 16th St. NW, Washington DC 20036. (202)293-6160. Contact: Office of Corporate Communications. **Description:** ''Corporation for Public Broadcasting is a private, nonprofit corporation. We provide funding support to public radio and public television stations for programs and production.'' **Services:** Provides technical and trade information on public broadcasting in America. Offers aid in arranging interviews, annual reports, biographies, brochures/pamphlets, informational newsletters and press kits. **How to Contact:** Write, call or visit. Responds to most inquiries within a week. Give credit to Corporation for Public Broadcasting. **Tips:** ''Do as much reading/research as possible about your subject before you ask questions or request data.'' Recent information request: Amount of financial support given to a specific station.

233• COUNCIL OF GRAPHOLOGICAL SOCIETIES
635 N. Merrill, Park Ridge IL 60068. (312)823-8196. Contact Person: Co-Director. **Description:** "Our purposes are to establish professional standards in graphology; exchange information among the graphological community; and promote public understanding and recognition of the profession through the dissemination of information, education and research." **Services:** Provides referral information on handwriting analysis, member organizations and individual instructors. Publica tions include *Journal of the Council of Graphological Societies*. **How to Contact:** Write to 575 E. Remington, 22-D, Sunnyvale CA 94087.

234• DALY ASSOCIATES, INC.
702 World Center Bldg., Washington DC 20006. (202)659-2925. Contact Person: Assistant Vice President. **Description:** "We are communications consultants providing professional counsel to firms and groups who need specific help in the areas of our expertise. We also conduct seminars and workshops." **Services:** Provides analytical, and how-to information. Offers brochures/pamphlets for modest fees. Publications include: Free catalog of "Communications Tipsheets" covering topics such as managing and promoting meetings, developing public relations or publicity programs, using direct-mail marketing principles, saving on postal procedures and speeding mail delivery, advancing your career, managing time, speaking effectively in public, becoming a consultant or working with them (enclose self-addressed double-stamped # 10 envelope, long size); "$ixty $ix $ugge$tion$ About $aving Money on Po$tage" (send $5 and a triple-stamped return-addressed # 10 long envelope). **How to Contact:** Write. Responds to most inquiries within a week. "No charge for catalog or informal, brief coun- sel but we do charge for professional services. We usually request that writers/reseachers cite us as source and, if possible, note our full address so we can respond to readers." **Tips:** Be specific; state your question concisely, send queries in writing; note realistic deadline. Recent information re- quests: "What are some ways to 'mail smarter'?"; "What six tips do you have to offer for 'time management'?"; "What are some tips about speaking?"; "Who in Washington DC can I contact to. . . ?"

235• EDUCATIONAL FILM LIBRARY ASSOCIATION
Research Library, 43 W. 61st St., New York NY 10023. (212)246-4533. Contact Person: Director of Reference Service. **Description:** "Among its many activities, the Educational Film Library Association (EFLA) maintains a research library containing over 1,200 books, 150 periodicals, film distributors' catalogs, subject files and other reference materials. As a national information center for nontheatrical film, EFLA provides reference and advisory services to members by mail or phone. The staff is prepared to assist film users to locate sources of films, suggest films for particular needs, supply information about film library administration, advise about film distribution and assist researchers with special projects." **Services:** Provides advisory, referral and trade information on film (documentaries, shorts, features), video, TV. Offers bibliographies, brochures/pamphlets, information searches, placement on mailing list and newsletter. Publications include a quarterly magazine, *Sightlines*, and a quarterly newsletter, *EFLA Bulletin*. "We also publish and sell specialized pamphlets and books on the 16mm nontheatrical field. A publications list is available on request." **How to Contact:** "Make an appointment with our reference libarian to use our library, which is open to the public Monday through Friday, 9 a.m. to 5 p.m. Materials may not be removed from the premises. EFLA publications may be purchased by mail or at the office. EFLA is a membership organization; membership is preferred for intensive searches and preferred treatment, and especially important if phoning for reference aid. Materials not published by EFLA do not leave the library. We have a full library of books and periodicals and files on film and video, but they may not be removed from the library." Responds to most inquiries within a week. **Tips:** "Do not expect librarians to do your research for you. Our librarian will guide you to all the resources; you'll have to do the work of compiling the information that will best help your project."

236• EXANIMO PRESS
Box 18, Segundo CO 81070. Contact Person: Manager. **Description:** "We publish 'how-to-do-it' books in the adventure field and at the same time give experienced advice to authors outside of this field on how to get their books published." **Services:** Provides how-to, technical and trade information on typesetting, advertising, distribution, bad checks and debts, paste-up, shipping and mailing, and anything pertaining to the small publisher. Offers placement on mailing lists, research assistance and general informational aid to the self-publisher. **How to Contact:** Write.

Responds to most inquiries within a month. "There is no charge for our assistance because we are originally self-publishers and proud of the help we have given first-book authors." **Tips:** "List your questions numerically and then allow space between each question for an ample answer. Don't waste our time with questions that are easily and simply answered in your nearest public library." Recent information requests: "How can I get good reviews for a book on child training?"; "How do I get ISBN and L/C Catalog Card numbers?"; "Where can I get low-cost typesetting for my historical book relating to Death Valley?"

237• FAMILY COMMUNICATIONS, INC.
4802 Fifth Ave., Pittsburgh PA 15213. (412)687-2990. Contact Person: Director of Public Relations. **Description:** Children's television programming designed to help children and families grow emotionally. "We produce a children's television program for PBS entitled *Mister Rogers' Neighborhood*. It is designed for the preschooler. We take care to develop each *Neighborhood* program around a single theme suited to the every day growing experience of children." **Services:** Provides bibliographical and historical information on Fred Rogers and *Mister Rogers' Neighborhood*, the longest running children's program on PBS. Offers aid in arranging interviews, biographies, photos, press kits and research assistance. **How to Contact:** Write or call. Responds to most inquiries within a month. **Tips:** Recent information request: "How does Mr. Rogers feel about the use of puppets?"; questions on children's television and the impact of TV and electronic games on children and families.

238• FEDERAL COMMUNICATIONS COMMISSION
1919 M St. NW, Washington DC 20554. (202)254-7674. Contact: Office of Consumer Assistance. **Description:** The FCC regulates all forms of telecommunications, broadcasting, cable, common carrier (telephone, telegraph, satellite), CB, safety or special radio. **Services:** All material, except for certain special information (trade secrets, etc.), is available for public inspection. Does not do research for writers. Detailed material is available in Federal Communications Commission (FCC) public reference rooms. **How to Contact:** Write. Responds to most inquiries within a week.

239• FILM ADVISORY BOARD
1727 N. Sycamore, Hollywood CA 90028. (213)874-3644. Contact Person: President. **Description:** "FAB's purpose is to promote better family films and TV programs. We present Award of Excellence plaques, technical awards and awards to young newcomers." **Services:** Provides information on ratings of motion pictures; how to qualify for our awards. Offers aid in arranging interviews, informational newsletters, placement on mailing lists and telephone reference services. Publications include *FAB Monthly Filmlist*. **How to Contact:** Write. Responds to most inquiries within a week. Charges for phone calls and mailings; $20 yearly dues. **Tips:** Recent information requests: Ratings of films.

240• FREEDOM OF INFORMATION CENTER
Box 858, Columbia MO 65201. (314)882-4856. Contact Person: Media Assistant. **Description:** "Nonprofit organization tied to a university journalism school. Serves as clearinghouse and research center on First Amendment, access and censorship issues." **Services:** Provides historical, how-to, interpretative, referral and trade information on "everything from international access issues, the Freedom of Information and Privacy Acts to cable TV and advertising." Offers brochures/pamphlets, clipping services, informational newsletters and research assistance. Publications include *The Freedom of Information Center Report* (bimonthly); *The Freedom of Information Center Digest* (access issues in the 50 states). **How to Contact:** Write, call or visit. Responds to most inquiries within a week. Charges for publications and 10¢/page for photocopying. **Tips:** "We are not a litigation service, nor do we make Freedom of Information requests for others. Call with questions. It's best to come to the University of Missouri, School of Journalism to peruse our files." Recent information request: Material on nonprofit hospitals open meetings law.

241• THE FUND FOR INVESTIGATIVE JOURNALISM
1346 Connecticut Ave. NW, Washington DC 20036. (202) 462-1844. Contact Person: Executive Director. **Description:** Organization dedicated "to increasing the public knowledge about the concealed, obscure or complex aspects of matters significantly affecting the public." **Services:** Offers brochures/pamphlets and grants. **How to Contact:** Write or call. Responds to most inquiries within a week.

242• HANDWRITING ANALYSIS RESEARCH LIBRARY
91 Washington St., Greenfield MA 01301. (413)774-4667. Contact Person: Curator. **Description:** "Our purpose is to make available, for on-the-spot use, a reference and research collection of over 60,000 items dealing with graphology, handwriting, handwriting analysis, penmanship and questioned documents. We are *not* a lending library. Inquirers must come here, by appointment, or write us." **Services:** Provides advisory, analytical, bibliographical, historical, referral and technical information on graphology, handwriting, handwriting analysis, penmanship, questioned documents. Offers brochures/pamphlets, library facilities and research assistance. Publications include *Needles in Haystacks*, our research report and case study on intensive literature searching ($40). **How to Contact:** Write or visit. Responds to most inquiries within a week. "We ask a donation of $4/inquiry to help meet our costs of shelf search and reply. Credit line must be given to H.A.R.L. for information, as well as to authors whom we cite." **Tips:** "Most inquirers seem to want bibliographic citations in English. We can also furnish citations in French, German, Italian and Spanish. We occasionally conduct seminars and workshops on literature searching methods and techniques."

243• HANNA-BARBERA PRODUCTIONS
3400 Cahuenga Blvd., Hollywood CA 90068. (213)851-5000. Contact Person: Vice President of Communications. **Description:** "We are a production studio involved in animated and live-action series, specials, telemovies and full-length features. We are also connected with amusement parks across the country and produce educational, industrial and commercial films. Merchandising for shows and characters is another important dimension of the company." **Services:** Provides information on celebrities, entertainment and recreation. Offers aid in arranging interviews, annual reports, biographies, brochures/pamphlets, information searches, photos and press kits. Publications include "press releases and artwork available on all shows produced here, the celebrities involved, and historical information on the studio and animation process." **How to Contact:** Write, "specifying materials needed and intended use. Send requests well in advance." Responds to most inquiries within a week. "Artwork must be credited with copyright. If the material requested (especially artwork) is needed for a book, the writer must go through a licensing procedure." **Tips:** "We answer many trivia-type questions about our shows and cartoon characters."

244• HOME BOX OFFICE, INC.
Time & Life Bldg., Rockefeller Center, New York NY 10020. (212)484-1461. Contact Person: Public Relations Director. **Description:** "We are the nation's largest pay television network, serving over 3,600 cable affiliates in 50 states with approximately 9½ million American homes subscribing to the service. Home Box Office provides 24-hour programming: motion pictures, entertainment specials, children's programs. We provide advertising, marketing, technical and administrative support to affiliated systems. The Home Box Office is primarily delivered via satellite." **Services:** Offers aid in arranging interviews, bibliographies, statistics, brochures/pamphlets, photos and press kits. **How to Contact:** Write or call. Responds to most inquiries within a month.

245• INTERNATIONAL TAPE/DISC ASSOCIATION
10 Columbus Circle, # 2270, New York NY 10019. (212)956-7110. Contact Person: Executive Vice President. **Description:** "ITA is the largest international trade association in the audio/video field." **Services:** Provides interpretative and trade information covering sales statistics for audio and video. Offers informational newsletters and statistics. Publications include *ITA News Digest* (bimonthly publication); *ITA Source Directory* (annual). **How to Contact:** Write. Responds to most inquiries within a week.

246• INTERNATIONAL TELECOMMUNICATIONS SATELLITE ORGANIZATION
490 L'Enfant Plaza SW, Washington DC 20024. Contact Person: Public Information Officer. **Description:** "INTELSAT is the 106-member country organization that owns and operates the global system of communications satellites that supplies most of the world's overseas telecommunications services and all overseas television." **Services:** Provides advisory, historical, technical and trade information on communications satellites, INTELSAT launch arrangements, international organization set-up and administration, history of communications satellites. Offers annual reports, brochures/pamphlets, informational newsletters, library facilities, photos, placement on mailing lists, press kits and 30-minute audio visual presentation at INTELSAT headquarters. Pub-

BEHIND THE BYLINE

P.J. Bednarski
TV critic

"Everything that happens in life is in some way reflected on TV. It's a terrific platform for everything that's going on—from news documentaries to social issues in sit-coms; you find it on TV in some form. And cable is expanding the turf. Newspapers have, in the last decade or so, become more aware of the importance of TV coverage."

P.J. Bednarski, one of two TV critics writing for the national newspaper, *USA Today*, takes his job seriously. "I think of the column as more sociology than entertainment. The classic quote is that a TV critic is one critic at a newspaper who is presumed to hate the thing he covers. But I like TV. I'm more interested in the whole process than I am in the individual programs. I'm interested in what it means that forty million people across the country sit down and watch something at the same time."

Bednarski says watching TV is a big part of his job. "It's one of the major parts of research. When a TV critic doesn't watch television because he's at work writing about it, it can be a destructive thing. You can end up missing the tone of TV that way."

In addition to watching, Bednarski does a lot of reading for his columns. "The fact is, you get a lot of the tone of your column from the tone of other things being written. Trade material—*Variety, Hollywood Reporter, Broadcasting* magazine, as well as *Advertising Age* and the general circulation papers: *New York Times, Washington Post, Wall Street Journal, Los Angeles Times.* You also get mail from the networks and PR agencies.

"Being a TV critic is an incredibly PR-intensive business. You get a lot of people pitching you ideas. You hear and read about a lot of trends. A big part of writing a column is thinking about all those things."

There's also the quick research involved in writing a TV column. "I've never been very good at trivia," he says. So to pinpoint facts, check spellings and refresh his memory about

the last episode of *The Mary Tyler Moore Show*, he relies on reference books like the *New York Times Encyclopedia of Television*, *The TV Book*, and for addresses and phone numbers, the annual *Broadcasting Yearbook*. "It's crucial to get the facts straight," Bednarski says, "because you're still a reporter.

"Reporting is about 40 percent of your job. And almost all of that is subjective reporting where you start with a bias and talk to people on both sides. You sort things together and come up with an idea of what might be the truth. The rest is criticism and analysis. You have to have a reporting instinct, though, and not be so critic-oriented that you can't write an objective story, or understand when there's a news story there."

Bednarski recognizes a responsibility to his readers. "I want people to know, especially when something bad happens on TV, that this is really very thin, either dramatically or philosophically. You have to be skeptical of the networks' intentions and be aware that there are very few good TV shows that come out in a year. You try to be fair, but not necessarily objective. You have to come up with a point of view.

"Some critics never say anything," he continues. The result is that people will probably not react to their columns. "You know a piece works when you get a reaction. Getting a rise out of people is important."

lications include *INTELSAT is . . .* ; *The INTELSAT System*; annual reports; INTELSAT System Map; satellite posters; launch vehicle posters. **How to Contact:** Write. Responds to most inquiries within a week. "INTELSAT's publications are available upon request; visits to INTELSAT can be arranged. Use of the library is by appointment only." **Tips:** "Begin by reading our publications, then contact us with questions or for further information."

247• INTERNATIONAL TELEPHONE AND TELEGRAPH
320 Park Ave., New York NY 10022. (212)940-1265. Contact Person: Manager of Media Information. **Description:** "We have five areas of business: telecommunications and electronics, consumer products and services, insurance and finance, engineered products and natural resources." **Services:** Offers annual reports, brochures/pamphlets, statistics, photos and press kits. **How to Contact:** Write or call. "We prefer written requests." Responds to most inquiries within a week.

248• INTERNATIONAL TELEVISION ASSOCIATION
136 Sherman Ave., Berkeley Heights NJ 07922. (201)464-6747. Contact: Public Relations/Publications. **Description:** "The International Television Association serves the professional development of over 6,000 video specialists in the educational and industrial (non-broadcast) industry." **Services:** Provides how-to, referral, technical and trade information in all areas of video production for in-house production or use, i.e. technical, managerial, production techniques, etc. Offers aid in arranging interviews; conferences, workshops and seminars on video related subjects. Publications include: a quarterly journal on video related topics; the ITVA also publishes a yearly *Salary Survey*, and is the sole US distributor of *Private Communications* ($29.95 members/$39.95 non-members) and *Video Production Techniques* ($125/$40 annual update service). **How to Contact:** Write or call. Responds to most inquiries immediately. Membership $60/year. "You should be very specific about what you are using the information for." **Tips:** "Being a professional organization, we can refer you to experts. Please do not call expecting more than a referral." Recent information request: "What is telenetting?"; "Who can I talk to for information on teleconferencing?"

249• INVESTIGATIVE REPORTERS & EDITORS, INC.
Box 838, Columbia MO 65205. (314)882-2042. Contact Person: Executive Director. **Description:** "IRE is an educational, not-for-profit group that teaches journalists how to do a better job of researching their articles and how to do investigative journalism." **Services:** Provides advisory, bibliographical, how-to and referral information. "The Paul Williams Memorial Resource Center has more than 1,200 newspaper, magazine and television citations of an investigative or public affairs nature. We counsel writers on backgrounding problems." Offers brochures/pamphlets, clipping services, informational newsletters, library facilities and research assistance. Publications include *The IRE Journal* (quarterly 24-page tabloid; examines successful investigations and analyzes or reports on sources of information for writers and reporters; $15 annually); and *On the Record* (St. Martin's Press, New York). **How to Contact:** Write or call. Responds to most inquiries within a week. Charges $10 search fee for nonmembers when researching IRE resource center or finding reporters with a particular expertise; mailing and photocopying costs; search fee waived for members. **Tips:** "Telephone first with specific query." Recent information requests: "How do I background an individual?"; "What records are available for backgrounding a business?"; "Where do I look for information about a not-for-profit organization?"

250• LAUBACH LITERACY INTERNATIONAL
Box 131, Syracuse NY 13210. (315)422-9121. Contact: Public Communications. **Description:** "We serve illiterate adults by providing volunteer training and technical assistance to 560 community-based literacy groups; we also publish instructional materials for adult learners. We give financial support and technical assistance to literacy programs in 5 other countries." **Services:** Provides bibliographical, historical, how-to and interpretative information on current Laubach program activities in the US and abroad; nature and extent of the illiteracy problem in the US. Offers aid in arranging interviews, annual reports, brochures/pamphlets, informational newsletters, library facilities, placement on mailing lists and statistics (bibliographical). Publications include *Interpretation of US Illiteracy Statistics*; *Clipping File of US Programs*. **How to Contact:** Write or call. Responds to most inquiries within a week. Charges $2 each for *Interpretation of US Illiteracy Statistics* and *Clipping File of US Programs*. Other materials (pamphlets, annual reports, etc.) are free. **Tips:** "Adult illiteracy is a complex and, until recently, a highly invisible problem. An inter-

view with a volunteer tutor who knows the daily struggle of the illiterate adult helps make an article more concrete, and we would be happy to refer writers to our local affiliates for this information." Recent information request: "How many illiterate adults are there in the United States? What is your program doing about it?"

251• LIBRARY OF CONGRESS, MOTION PICTURE, BROADCASTING & RECORDED SOUND DIVISION
Washington, DC 20540. (202)287-5840. Contact Person: Reference Librarian. **Description:** This division of the Library of Congress "acquires and preserves selected films, videotapes and sound recordings that reflect the diversity of American life and culture." **Services:** Provides bibliographical, historical and referral information. Offers library facilities, research assistance and telephone reference services. Publications include brochures describing the collections. **How to Contact:** Write, call or visit. Responds to most inquiries within a month. **Tips:** "Viewing and listening facilities are available.at no charge to serious researchers by advance appointment."

252• LOUIS B. MAYER LIBRARY, THE AMERICAN FILM INSTITUTE
Box 27999, 2021 N. Western Ave., Los Angeles CA 90027. (213)856-7655, 856-7656. Contact: Reference Desk. **Description:** Reading, reference and research library "primarily devoted to motion pictures, televison and video. Seeks to provide documentation and information covering such topics as history, aesthetics, biography, production and business aspects." **Services:** Provides advisory, bibliographical, historical, how-to, technical and trade information. Offers library facilities and telephone reference services. Library collection includes 5,500 books on all aspects of motion pictures, TV and video as well as selected titles on photography, theatre, costume design, stage plays and short stories. Other reference materials include clipping files on the entertainment industry; film festival files; screenplays and TV scripts; oral history transcripts. Publications include *Checklist of Books on Scriptwriting* (free); *Script Checklist* ($23). **How to Contact:** Write or visit. Call "if necessary." Responds to inquiries as soon as possible. "All materials must be used in the library proper." **Tips:** Recent information requests: "Who wrote *Raiders of the Lost Ark*?"; "What does a treatment look like?"; "Where can I find an agent?"

253• MEDIA ALLIANCE
Bldg. D, Fort Mason Center, San Francisco CA 94123. (415)441-2557. **Description:** "Media Alliance (MA) is a 2,000-member organization made up of writers, editors and broadcast workers working for newspapers, radio and television stations, magazines and as freelancers. We assist members in honing professional skills and protecting professional rights. We have developed a social network which enables members to overcome the isolation which is characteristic of much media work. Underlying all activity is the recognition that media workers play a pivotal role in shaping society: consequently we are active in defense of the First Amendment, developing media access for groups which have traditionally been deprived of such access and building awareness of the responsibilities of media workers." **Services:** Provides how-to, referral, technical and trade information. Offers a job file, a network/referral service, a skill sharing program (for members), continuing education classes. Publications include: "Media How-To Notebook"; "People Behind the News"; and *MediaFile*, a monthly newspaper. **How to Contact:** Write, call or visit. Responds to most inquiries immediately. Annual membership dues $40/full membership, $20/low-income membership. "Media workers must be members to have access to our services."

254• MEDIA CENTER FOR CHILDREN
3 West 29th St., New York NY 10001. (212)679-9620. Contact Person: Executive Director. **Description:** "Media Center for Children is a nonprofit information resource. Our goal is to improve the quality of children's media and to make it more child-oriented. Through our ongoing media evaluation program, MCC staff, consultants, and interns go directly to children to find out what children like or dislike, understand or are confused by in media, and why. We make inexpensive, practical and child-centered information available to people who make or use film, video, and develop media formats with children under the age of thirteen." **Services:** Provides advisory, analytical, how-to, interpretative, referral and trade information on children's media. Offers brochures/pamphlets, informational magazine, placement on mailing lists, press kits, research assistance, telephone reference services, workshops, conferences, courses, film programming and exhibition, books, museum and hospital consultation. Publications include: *Films Kids Like*; *More Films Kids Like*; *What To Do When the Lights Go On*; *On the Nature of Motion Pictures for Children*; *Young Viewers* magazine. **How to Contact:** Write. Responds to

most inquiries within a month. "Extensive consultations may involve a fee." **Tips:** "MCC has a small staff who will answer specific questions or offer reference. We cannot do individual research. Be as specific as possible when defining the information needed."

255• MOVIE STAR NEWS
212 E. 14th St., New York NY 10003. (212)777-5564. Contact Person: Owner. **Description:** "We do photo research and provide photos of show business people (theatre, movies, TV) to writers, editors, etc." **Services:** Offers photos of silent film personalities and today's stars. **How to Contact:** Write, call or visit. Responds to most inquiries immediately. Charges $25 research fee.

256• MUSEUM OF INDEPENDENT TELEPHONY
412 S. Campbell, Abilene KS 67410. (913)263-2681. Contact Person: Curator. **Description:** The museum includes a research library of telephony-related books and publications dating from 1880s to present. **Services:** Provides bibliographical, historical and technical information related to telephony. Offers biographies, brochures/pamphlets, library facilities, photos, press kits and research assistance. **How to Contact:** Write, call or visit. Responds to most inquiries within a week. "Small research requests no charge. Any large project must pay for time. Our research library is open for all researchers here in the museum. Books cannot be sent out." **Tips:** "Know your subject well enough so that you can ask specific questions." Recent information requests: Telephone identification; history of particular independent company; where to find parts for old telephones.

257• MUSEUM OF MODERN ART
Film Stills Archive, 11 W. 53rd St., New York NY 10019. (212)956-4209. Contact Person: Film Stills Archivist. **Description:** A research archive of movie photographs. **Services:** Provides advisory information on film history. Offers approximately 3,000,000 b&w stills on foreign and American productions, film personalities and directors. Duplicates of original stills are sold at a cost of $10/still. Credit line required. "Publication rights are not inclusive and copyright should be cleared with the film studios." **How to Contact:** Write or call. Responds to most inquiries within a week.

258• NATIONAL ACADEMY OF TELEVISION ARTS & SCIENCES, INC.
110 W. 57th St., New York NY 10019. **Description:** The purpose of the NATAS is to advance television arts and science by fostering creative leadership in the industry and recognizing outstanding television achievements through annual Emmy Awards. **Services:** "Questions concerning the activities of the National Academy should be addressed to our public relations firm: Barbara Hendra, c/o Barbara Hendra, Inc., Empire State Building, 350 Fifth Ave., New York NY 10118. Questions that deal with official office matters should be directed to our New York headquarters."

259• NATIONAL ASSOCIATION OF BROADCASTERS
1771 N St. NW, Washington DC 20036. (202)293-3579. Contact Person: Librarian. **Description:** The association works "to foster and promote the development of the arts of aural and visual broadcasting in all their forms; to uphold the American system of broadcasting, free from government censorship; to encourage and promote customs and practices which will strengthen and maintain the broadcasting industry to the end that it may best serve the public." **Services:** Provides bibliographical, referral and trade information on radio and television broadcasting. **How to Contact:** Write or call. Responds to most inquiries within a month. **Tips:** "We can devote up to 30 minutes to a question; persons are then referred to other sources or urged to carry on the search themselves. We cannot do research, and we cannot photocopy. We're a natural place to start for those who are researching broadcasting. Make an appointment to use our extensive library which is open *by appointment* Tuesday-Friday, 10-5."

260• NATIONAL CITIZENS COMMITTEE FOR BROADCASTING
Box 12038, Washington DC 20005. (202)462-2520. Contact Person: Office Manager. **Description:** The purpose of the National Citizens Committee for Broadcasting is "media reform, especially broadcasting and telecommunications." Represents consumers in the electronic media. **Services:** Provides advisory, analytical, historical, how-to, interpretative, referral and technical information on telephone, television, cable TV, radio, LPTV, direct broadcasting satellites, media access, media reform, FCC, NAB and media concentration. Offers

aid in arranging interviews, brochures/pamphlets, placement on mailing lists, statistics and newsletter. **How to Contact:** Write or call. Responds to most inquiries immediately. Publications price list available. **Tips:** "Write us—if we can help, we will; if we can't, we'll say so." Recent information requests: Many inquiries about cable TV, citizen access, etc.

261• NATIONAL FEDERATION OF LOCAL CABLE PROGRAMMERS
906 Pennsylvania Ave., Washington DC 20003. (202)544-7272. Contact Person: Executive Director. **Description:** "Our purpose is to foster and encourage public access to telecommunications." **Services:** Provides advisory, how-to, referral and trade information on video production, public access, cable TV legislation, franchising for cable TV and renegotiation for franchise agreements. Offers brochures/pamphlets, informational newsletters and library facilities. **How to Contact:** Write. Responds to most inquiries within a month. Charges for publications. "First priority for our services is given to our members." **Tips:** "Be specific about your needs; do some background research before writing to us." Recent information request: "What communities are receiving part of franchise fee for community access use?"

262• NATIONAL PUBLIC RADIO
2025 M St. NW, Washington DC 20036. (202)822-2060. Contact Person: Librarian. **Description:** National Public Radio produces and distributes public radio programs. **Services:** Provides analytical and historical information on music, arts, public affairs, science and technology in the forms of live recording, reporting, interviewing "and so forth, as they are in the NPR programs." Offers brochures/pamphlets and library facilities. "All of our programs are recorded on tape; brochures/pamphlets are in printed form." **How to Contact:** Write or call. Responds to most inquiries within a week. "Service charge is only applied on in-depth research and on requests for making copies of our programs if the rights permit. Being precise about what you want would save a lot of our and your time and money." **Tips:** "Call or write to us about your purpose for our materials before you come to us." Recent information request: "Do you have a copy of Nixon's resignation speech?"

263• NATIONAL SHORTHAND REPORTERS ASSOCIATION
118 Park St. SE, Vienna VA 22180. (703)281-4677. Contact Person: Communications Director. **Description:** "Our purpose is to promote understanding regarding the special competency, importance, and value of shorthand reporters to the judicial system, business, unions, and others with a need for accurate, verbatim records of proceedings." **Services:** Provides advisory, analytical, bibliographical, historical, how-to, interpretative, referral, technical and trade information on transcript production, computer-aided transcripts, role of the reporter in the judicial system, shorthand theory and training. Offers aid in arranging interviews, brochures/pamphlets, informational newsletters, press kits and statistics. Publications include: *National Shorthand Reporter*; *Making the Record* (how-to for attorneys); career pamphlets; technical monographs, studies, etc. **How to Contact:** Write or call. Responds to most inquiries within a week. Charges for some publications; photocopying at cost as applicable. "We need to know use to which information will be put." **Tips:** "Staff time is limited, so please prepare and be specific." Recent information requests: Number of reporters in US; "How do computers apply to shorthand reporting?"; "How do live reporters' transcripts stack up against electronic recording?"

264• NORTH AMERICAN RADIO ARCHIVES, LTD.
4418 Irvington Ave., Fremont CA 94538. (415)656-6436. Contact Person: President. **Description:** "The purpose of NARA is the study, preservation and enjoyment of old time radio." **Services:** Provides bibliographical, historical and trade information on old time radio. Offers library facilities: printed materials including books, scripts, magazines, newspaper articles, logs, photos and slides; tape recordings of radio programs. Publications include *NARA News*, a quarterly magazine of radio history. **How to Contact:** Write. Responds to most inquiries within a week. "A $14 membership fee is required to gain access to lending libraries. *NARA News* is $2/issue without membership." **Tips:** "Know specifically (as much as possible) what it is you are looking for."

265• OLD TIME WESTERN FILM CLUB
Box 142, Siler City NC 27344. Contact Person: President. **Description:** "Our purpose is to preserve the history of old time movies and radio (westerns, etc.). Hundreds of us meet regularly and travel hundreds of miles to our film festivals." **Services:** Provides advisory, historical,

referral and technical information. Offers aid in arranging interviews, biographies, informational newsletters, library facilities and photos. Publishes newsletters. **How to Contact:** Write or visit. Responds to most inquiries immediately. **Tips:** "Talk to as many film collectors and historians as possible and get ideas from all." Recent information requests: Name of a star's horse; "When was first western movie made?"

266•   RADIO FREE EUROPE/RADIO LIBERTY, INC. (RFE/RL)
1201 Connecticut Ave. NW, Washington DC 20036. (202)457-6900. Contact Person: Assistant Secretary to the Corporation. **Description:** "Radio Free Europe/Radio Liberty, Inc. (RFE/RL) is a nonprofit, private corporation, funded by congressional appropriations, broadcasting news and information in 21 languages to Eastern Europe and the Soviet Union." **Services:** Offers research subscription program. Publications include research reports and brochure listing all research reports. **How to Contact:** Write. Responds to most inquiries within a week. **Tips:** "Be as specific as possible. Don't write us with such a broad request as 'all of our information on Eastern Europe.' "

267•   RCA RECORDS, NASHVILLE
30 Music Square W., Nashville TN 37203. (615)244-9880. Contact Person: Manager, Press and Publicity. **Description:** RCA Records, Nashville is concerned with "the promotion and development of careers of artists signed to RCA Records, Nashville Operations." **Services:** Offers aid in arranging interviews, biographies, placement on mailing list, newsletter, photos and press kits. **How to Contact:** Write or call.

268•   WILL ROGERS MEMORIAL
Box 157, Claremore OK 74017. (918)341-0719. Contact Person: Director or Curator. **Description:** "We exist to preserve the memory and promote the spirit of Will Rogers." **Services:** Provides advisory, analytical, bibliographical, historical, how-to (some), interpretative and referral information on Will Rogers and related material. Publications include *Roping Will Rogers Ancestors*, $15; a biographical brochure; and a list of books in print and those available from the Will Rogers Memorial. "We are adding quite a bit of genealogical material, especially Cherokee-white related; also adding early newspapers of Rogers County, Oklahoma plus some early Cherokee papers on microfilm. Our new library at the Will Rogers Memorial opened August 15, 1982. We have no more staff at present, but much more space for research and quite a bit of new material (more books on wild west shows, vaudeville, early aviation, ranching, California, films—both silent and early talkies, etc.). Also, we are gradually getting all the personal papers of Will Rogers on microfilm—business correspondence and contracts, personal correspondence and papers, etc." **How to Contact:** "Write or call for an appointment." Responds to most inquiries immediately; "harder ones take a little time. We have half a million tourists a year here, and we cannot be of service to drop-ins who wish to do serious research without some notice. The staff is limited and we must make arrangements for someone to work with the researcher. No charge is made for academic research and most other serious research unless it costs us extra money. For example, pictures that have to be copied, etc. We are not a lending library, and it is necessary for a serious student or researcher to come here to see the massive amount of material on Will Rogers. We can answer brief questions by mail or phone. We are open every day of the year, 8 a.m. to 5 p.m." **Tips:** "Just let us know what you're looking for and what you want to do with the material, etc. We help any person with respectable, reasonable request." Recent information requests: Background on Will Rogers's Indian ancestry; the number and type of films he made; his radio broadcasts. "Be cautious about using secondary sources for information about Will Rogers. Much of it is untrue; he is misquoted in many books. Also, since Will Rogers was a Cherokee, he qualifies as a 'minority' person in textbooks, etc. There is a real need for more books for young people on this Indian-Cowboy."

269•   SOCIETY FOR PRIVATE AND COMMERCIAL EARTH STATIONS (SPACE)
1920 N St. NW, Suite 510, Washington DC 20036. (202)887-0605. Contact Person: Counsel or Vice President. **Description:** "SPACE is the trade association representing the manufacturers, dealers and users of satellite earth station equipment." **Services:** Provides trade information on the satellite earth station industry. Offers brochures/pamphlets, informational newsletters, placement on mailing lists and press kits. Publications include newsletters; interviews; background information on the industry. **How to Contact:** Write. Responds to most inquiries within a week. **Tips:** Recent information request: "What are the laws affecting or restricting the satellite earth station industry?"

270• SONS OF THE DESERT
Box 8341, Universal City CA 91608. (213)985-2713. Contact Person: Grand Vizier. **Description:** "The purpose of our organization is to keep alive the comedic genius of Laurel and Hardy and those who worked with them. Sons of the Desert is an international organization of over 70 chapters that show films and collect knowledge and memorabilia pertaining to Laurel and Hardy." **Services:** Provides advisory, analytical, bibliographical, historical, interpretative and referral information. "Most facts pertain to the life and times of Laurel and Hardy, their films, personal lives, and those who worked with them. We refer interested parties to local chapters, and disperse convention information." Offers aid in arranging interviews, biographies, brochures/pamphlets, informational newsletters, photos, placement on mailing lists, research assistance, statistics and telephone reference services. Publications include *Intra Tent Journal*, quarterly of club information and activities; *Pratfall*, irregular publication devoted to the life and times of Laurel and Hardy. **How to Contact:** Write or call. Responds to most inquiries within a week. "SASE, please." **Tips:** Recent information request: "What were the names of Stan Laurel's wives?"

271• TELEVISION INFORMATION OFFICE
Research Services Department, 745 Fifth Ave., New York NY 10022. (212)759-6800. Contact Person: Manager, Research Services. **Description:** The Television Information Office (TIO) was established in October 1959 to provide "a 2-way bridge of understanding between the television industry and its many publics." The Research Services Department collects and distributes information from all sources relating to TIO's areas of interest. "We are supported by the 3 major televison networks (ABC, CBS, NBC), individual commercial stations and groups, public television stations and the National Association of Broadcasters." **Services:** Provides bibliographical, referral and trade information on social and cultural and programming aspects of television. Offers biographies, brochures/pamphlets, library facilities, statistics and telephone reference services. Publications list available. **How to Contact:** Write or call. Responds to most inquiries within a week. "Informational services are free, but there is a charge for some publications." **Tips:** "Make requests as specific as possible; don't wait until you have an imminent deadline as we are often backlogged. We cannot mail copies of reports and articles copyrighted by others. Our research staff is unable to undertake specific research projects for writers, but we accommodate them by opening up our research facilities to them and by referring them to helpful organizations or publications."

272• TELOCATOR NETWORK OF AMERICA
2301 E St., NW, Washington DC 20036. (202)659-6446. Contact Person: Executive Director or Editor. **Description:** "The Telelocator Network of America is the national association of Radio Common Carriers (RCCs). RCCs provide radiotelephone (car), portable telephone and pager (beeper) service to hundreds of thousands of individuals and companies across the country. Telocator promotes land mobile communications through its *Telocator* magazine, news *Bulletin*, and *Filings & Grants* license fact sheet. We sponsor one mid-year meeting and one national convention every year where hundreds of people interested in communications gather for seminars and exhibits." **Services:** Provides bibliographical, interpretative, referral and trade information covering radio paging (beeper) and car telephone service, as well as FCC regulations and communications information. Offers research reports, biographies, statistics, clippings, brochures/pamphlets, bibliographies, placement on mailing list, magazine and newsletter, and a free general information package on the association and the paging and car telephone industry. Publications available. **How to Contact:** Write or call. Responds to most inquiries within a week. Charges for membership and some publications. "There are no restrictions; however, the researcher usually visits our offices to obtain the information since our function is not primarily as a research organization. Give credit for all information." **Tips:** "Read as much pertinent material as possible before asking questions." Recent information request: Background on "cellular" car/portable telephone service.

273• THEATER ARTS LIBRARY
University of California at Los Angeles, Room 22478, Research Library, Los Angeles CA 90024. (213)825-4880. Contact Person: Librarian. **Description:** A research and reference collection serving the Department of Theater Arts, the university community and the entertainment industry. **Services:** Offers materials primarily devoted to motion pictures and television. In addition to books, reference works, and periodicals, the collection includes such specialized

materials as screenplays, television scripts, production stills, portraits of personalities, clipping files, film festival programs, motion picture programs, art work, the 20th Century Fox Collection, and the *Star Trek* papers. **How to Contact:** Write or visit. Responds to most inquiries immediately. Charges 5¢ for photocopies. "During exam periods or other periods of high demand, use of this library may be restricted."

274• TOASTMASTERS INTERNATIONAL
2200 N. Grand Ave., Santa Ana CA 92711. (714)542-6793. Contact Person: Manager of Public Relations. **Description:** "Toastmasters International is the world's largest organization devoted to training individuals in public speaking, communication and leadership skills. The organization has 4,600 Toastmasters clubs in the US, Canada and 46 other countries. Founded in 1924, Toastmasters is one of the oldest self-help organizations in existence. Major emphasis today is on corporate public speaking programs through in-house Toastmasters clubs." **Services:** Offers aid in arranging interviews, bibliographies, brochures/pamphlets, information searches, placement on mailing list and press kits. "Anyone preparing a story. on public speaking, corporate communications, speech seminars, etc., should start by contacting Toastmasters." Publications include *All About Toastmasters*; *Communication—Your Success Depends On It!*; *The Toastmaster* (monthly); and *Annual Directory of Toastmaster Clubs.* **How to Contact:** "Call or write the membership, club extension and public relations departments. We can then put writers in touch with local Toastmaster volunteer leaders." Responds to most inquiries within a week. **Tips:** "*Book of Lists* ranked speaking in public as the number one fear of most Americans (it outranked the fear of death by a two to one margin!)." Recent information request: Women in our organization.

275• VANDERBILT TELEVISION NEWS ARCHIVE
Vanderbilt University Library, Nashville TN 37203. (615)322-2927. Contact Person: Administrator. **Description:** The Television News Archive contains "videotape collection, network evening news broadcasts and related specials, from August 5, 1968, to the present. Purpose: for reference, research and study. Tapes may be viewed at the archive, or borrowed to use for study or instruction elsewhere." **Services:** Offers "source material for research. We publish a monthly index to network evening news broadcasts titled *Television News Index and Abstracts.* In short, it is a videotape collection of the network evening newscasts for use for the same purposes newspaper collections are used." **How to Contact:** Write or call. Responds to most inquiries immediately. "Users borrrowing tapes from the archive have the responsibility of using them in accord with copyright law. Contact archive for list of charges." **Tips:** "Research in television news generally is more time-consuming than comparable research in print media. Tailor research as specifically as possible. Questions are as varied as the news itself."

276• WARNER CABLE TV/QUBE CABLE
c/o Goodwin, Dannenbaum, Littman & Wingfield, Inc., Box 770100, Houston TX 77215. (713)977-7676. Contact Person: Account Supervisor. Or contact Qube Cable (713)895-2628. **Description:** Cable television system. "Two-way, interactive cable system, permitting actual viewer involvement with programming; produces original programming." **Services:** Provides advisory, analytical, bibliographical, historical, how-to, interpretive, referral, technical and trade information on cable TV economics, technology, advertising, new media, videotex, marketing, community access, public service, programming, relations with standard media. Offers aid in arranging interviews, annual reports, brochures/pamphlets, clipping services, computerized information searches, informational newsletters, photos, placement on mailing lists, press kits, research assistance, statistics and telephone reference services. "Reporters and writers preparing pieces for major media may be invited to participate in live interactive program to put questions directly to QUBE cable audience, get their answers tallied instantly, experience the medium." Publications include newsletter; special reports as available. **How to Contact:** Write or call. Responds to most inquiries immediately. "May charge for unusual and expensive request." Give credit to Warner Cable TV. Requests advance look at draft. **Tips:** "Because of rapid change in technology and economics and programming in the industry, there is little in print which remains accurate for long. Best bet is to use individuals as original sources." Recent information requests: "How can the Social Security Administration gain access to cable systems in various communities; what can the systems offer them; how can they best use cable TV?"

277• WARNER RESEARCH, BURBANK PUBLIC LIBRARY
110 N. Glenoaks Blvd., Burbank CA 91501. (213)847-9743. Contact Person: Research
Librarian. **Description:** The library "provides research to the entertainment industry's creative
people: writers, art directors, set designers, etc. Our library allows us to provide visual (in the form
of photographs, diagrams and magazine articles) and written documentation in a variety of areas
and time periods. Our collection strengths include excellent period information on all subjects;
architecture; costume; transportation; all major wars; and United States military information. We
have numerous catalogs and regulation manuals on all subjects." **Services:** Provides advisory,
analytical, bibliographical, historical, how-to, interpretative, referral and technical information on
art, entertainment, food, health/medicine, history, industry, politics, recreation, sports and travel.
Offers bibliographics, clipping services and information searches. **How to Contact:** Call for an
appointment. "At this time, state the research needed; we will then prepare the request in advance
of the appointment, and the material will be ready. Service fee: $20/hour; $10/half hour minimum.
This is charged for the amount of time it takes us to compile the information. Charges are also assessed for long distance calls placed on your behalf, photocopies, etc." **Tips:** "Call us whether
or not you are certain that we have what you need. We are a good sounding board and can provide
you with lots of ideas on how to proceed. There is no charge for initial consultations on any project.
There are several basic types of questions we answer for writers: these include story idea and
development; we provide text and pictures on a variety of subjects—limited only by the writers'
needs or imagination; basically the who, what, when, where and why of any subject required."

278• WOMEN IN COMMUNICATIONS, INC.
Box 9561, Austin TX 78766. (512)345-8922. Contact Person: Executive Director. **Description:**
"WICI (founded in 1909) unites members for the purpose of promoting the advancement of wom-
en in all fields of communications; works for the First Amendment rights and responsibilities of
communicators; recognizes distinguished professional achievements; and promotes high professional standards througout the communications industry. **Services:** Provides historical, how-to
and trade information on the communications industry. Offers brochures/pamphlets, placement on
mailing list, newsletter and press kits. Publications include professional papers, job and salary survey, careers booklet, and PRO/COMM, The Professional Communicator, a national magapaper
for members and subscribers ($12/year). **How to Contact:** Write. Responds to most inquiries
within a month. Charges cost plus postage for publications. **Tips:** Recent information request:
Background about communications careers.

279• YESTERYEAR MUSEUM
20 Harriet Dr., Whippany NJ 07981-1906. Contact Person: Director. **Description:** "We
specialize in history of mechanical and automatic music in all fields: music boxes, nickelodeons,
player pianos, phonographs, records and ragtime, especially Edison and Victor. The shop offers
items related to these fields." **Services:** Provides advisory, bibliographical, historical, referral
and technical information covering celebrities, entertainment, history, music industry, etc. Offers
photos. **How to Contact:** Write or call. Responds to most inquiries within a week. Charges
according to services and costs incurred. No charge for referrals. Give credit to Yesteryear
Museum.

SECTION·FIVE

EDUCATION

Education is not a product: mark, diploma, job, money—in that order; it is a process, a never-ending one.

—Bel Kaufman

This section identifies resources offering information on the participants of education: students, teachers, administrators, counselors. It includes information sources for educational alternatives, methods, services and research, as well as creativity, evaluation and the educational process itself. Also listed are writing and correspondence programs.

Bibliography

Altbach, Philip G., Gail P. Kelly and David H. Kelly. *International Bibliography of Comparative Education*. New York: Praeger, 1981.

Barron's Profiles of American Colleges. 2 vols. rev. ed. Woodbury, NY: Barron's Educational Series, Inc., 1982.

Current Index to Journals in Education. Annual Cumulation. New York: Macmillan Information.

Education Index. 1929 to date, monthly. New York: H.W. Wilson Co.

Educational Media Yearbook. Annual. Littleton, CO: Libraries Unlimited.

Elliot, Norman F. and Douglas C. Moody, eds. *Patterson's American Education*. Annual. Mt. Pleasant, IL: Educational Directories, Inc. (Lists public and private school systems in the US)

Encyclopedia of Education. 10 vols. New York: Macmillan, 1971.

Learner, Craig Allen. *The Grants Register*. Biennial. New York: St. Martin's Press. (Up-to-date information on scholarships, fellowships, grants, awards, competitions, etc. available for graduate study, research, creative work or training of an educational nature)

The National Faculty Directory. Annual. Detroit: Gale Research Co.

Page, G. Terry and J.B. Thomas, eds. *International Dictionary of Education*. New York: Nichols Publishing Co., 1977.

Resources in Education. Annual Cumulation. Phoenix, AZ: Oryx Press.

Sedlak, Michael W. and Timothy Walch, eds. *American Educational History: A Guide to Information Sources*. Detroit: Gale Research Co., 1981.

Wasserman, Paul, James Sanders and Elizabeth Talbot Sanders, eds. *Learning Independently*. 2d ed. Detroit: Gale Research Co., 1981. (Directory of self-teaching materials and services)

280• AGENCY FOR INSTRUCTIONAL TELEVISION
Box A, Bloomington IN 47402. (812)339-2203. Contact Person: Communications Associate. **Description:** "Our purpose is to strengthen education through television and other technologies. AIT develops joint program projects involving state and provincial agencies, and acquires and distributes a wide variety of television and related printed materials. Many of the television materials are available in audiovisual formats. Established in 1973 as a nonprofit American-Canadian organization, the predecessor organization was National Instructional Television, founded in 1962." **Services:** Provides advisory, how-to and trade information on instructional television and instructional media. Offers brochures/pamphlets, informational newsletters, photos, placement on mailing lists for press materials and informational pieces. Publications include *AIT Newsletter*. **How to Contact:** Write. Responds to most inquiries within a month. Give Agency for Instructional Television appropriate credit. **Tips:** "Please know what you want and be specific."

281• AMERICAN ASSOCIATION FOR ADULT AND CONTINUING EDUCATION
1201 16th St. NW, Suite 301, Washington DC 20036. (202)822-7866. Contact Person: Executive Director. **Description:** "Our purpose is to provide leadership in advancing education as a lifelong

learning process by: serving as a central forum for a wide variety of adult and continuing education special interest groups; advocating for the field of adult and continuing education; encouraging the use of research, and assisting in the development of human resources." **Services:** Provides advisory, analytical, bibliographical, historical, how-to, interpretative, referral, technical and trade information. Offers annual reports, brochures/pamphlets and informational newsletters. Publications include: *Lifelong Learnings: An Omnibus of Theory & Practice*; newsletters. **How to Contact:** Write. Responds to most inquiries within a month. Members only receive services.

282• AMERICAN MONTESSORI SOCIETY
150 5th Ave., New York NY 10011. (212)924-3209. Contact Person: National Director. **Description:** "A national, nonprofit, nondiscriminatory, tax-exempt organization dedicated to promoting better education for all children through teaching strategies consistent with the Montessori system, and the incorporation of the Montessori approach into the framework of education." **Services:** Provides advisory, bibliographical and historical information covering the Montessori method; early childhood education (birth to 12 years of age). Offers aid in arranging interviews, annual reports, bibliographies, biographies, statistics, brochures/pamphlets, information searches and photos. Publications include *Montessori Education; Montessori Philosophy; Basic Characteristics of a Montessori Program*; "The Montessori Infant," reprint from *American Baby Magazine*; "What is the Montessori Method," reprint from *Town and Country*; and "Make Mine Montessori" and "Big on Promises, Short on Delivery," reprints from *Parents Magazine*. **How to Contact:** Write or call. Responds to most inquiries within a week. "Give specifics on the nature of the kind of writing you do. Written requests should be accompanied by a 6x9 envelope and $2 to cover mailing costs. Costs of photostating any additional materials must be paid. We should like to check for accuracy any articles for which we have supplied data and assistance. Credit must be given to AMS as a resource." **Tips:** "Allow time for an appointment." Recent information request: Number of AMS-affiliated schools and their enrollments.

283• ASSOCIATED WRITING PROGRAMS
Old Dominion University, Norfolk VA 23508. (804)440-3839. Contact Person: Executive Director. **Description:** "Support group for creative writers and college and university creative writing programs. Active in literary arts advocacy and writer job placement." **Services:** Provides advisory, analytical and bibliographical information on writing programs, publication possibilities, writing contests, books by members, writing colonies, special events. Offers aid in arranging interviews, brochures/pamphlets, informational newsletters, research assistance, statistics and publication assistance. Publications include newsletter; *Intro* (poetry and fiction annual); AWP catalog of writing programs; job list. **How to Contact:** Write or call. Responds to most inquiries immediately. Charges for membership and newsletter.

284• ASSOCIATION FOR CHILDREN & ADULTS WITH LEARNING DISABILITIES
4156 Library Rd., Pittsburgh PA 15234. (412)341-1515. Contact Person: National Executive Director. **Description:** "Our purpose is to encourage research, increase public awareness of L.D., disseminate information, serve as advocate and improve special education." **Services:** Provides advisory, bibliographical, how-to and referral information on learning disabilities. Offers annual reports, biographies, brochures/pamphlets, informational newsletters, library facilities and research assistance. **How to Contact:** Write.

285• ASSOCIATION FOR COMMUNITY BASED EDUCATION
1806 Vernon St. NW, Washington DC 20009. (202)462-6333. Contact Person: Publications Director. **Description:** "We are a membership organization, providing publications and technical assistance to community-based groups, free-standing alternative colleges that offer educational opportunities to adults at the post-secondary level." **Services:** Provides how-to and technical information. Offers annual reports, informational newsletters, research assistance and technical assistance bulletins on public relations, other subjects. Publications include *T/A Bulletin # 1: Promotion and Public Relations*; file of community-based education practices. Write for publications list. **How to Contact:** Write or call. Responds to most inquiries within a week.

286• ASSOCIATION FOR EXPERIENTIAL EDUCATION (AEE)
7200 E. Dry Creek Rd., Suite F203, Englewood CO 80112. (309)779-0519. Contact Person: Executive Officer. **Description:** "AEE is exclusively not for profit, educational, and public

service oriented. It is united in a commitment to the process of learning through direct experience.'' **Services:** Provides advisory, historical, how-to and referral information on experiential education, outdoor education, service learning, cooperative education, internships, apprenticeships, adventure alternatives, special populations. Offers brochures/pamphlets, informational newsletters, library facilities (limited), placement on mailing list, research assistance and networking resources. Publications include *Jobs Clearing House* (lists openings in experiential education); *Journal of Experiential Education* (philosophy and theory); various others. List available. **How to Contact:** Write, call or visit. Responds to most inquiries within a week. Charges for publications, or they can be reviewed in office. Appreciates credit to AEE as resource. **Tips:** Recent information requests: ''Are there any adventure/outdoor programs for handicapped populations?''; ''Is certification required of outdoor educators?''

287•   THE ASSOCIATION FOR THE GIFTED
1920 Association Dr., Reston VA 22091. (703)620-3660. Contact Person: Division Secretary. **Description:** Division of the Council for Exceptional Children (same address; see listing 297). ''Our purpose is to encourage educational programs for the gifted and talented.'' **Services:** Provides advisory, bibliographical and referral information. Offers aid in arranging interviews, brochures/pamphlets and informational newsletters. Publications include *Journal for the Education of the Gifted*; *TAG Update*. **How to Contact:** Write. Responds to most inquiries within a month. *Journal* is $2.50/issue. ''We do not have unlimited services as we are primarily volunteer.'' **Tips:** ''Do library research *before* calling or writing. Specific questions are most productive.'' Recent information requests: Existing program options; discussion of argument for meeting the needs of the gifted.

288•   ASSOCIATION OF COLLEGE HONOR SOCIETIES
1411 Lafayette Pkwy., Williamsport PA 17701. (717)323-7641. Contact Person: Secretary-Treasurer. **Description:** Coordinating agency for college and university honor societies. Provides facilities for the consideration of matters of mutual interest, defines honor societies and classifies existing societies and assists college administrators in maintaining standards and useful functions. **Services:** Provides interpretative and referral information covering honor societies in ACHS, including descriptions of member societies and minimum requirements for members. Offers brochures/pamphlets. Publications include *ACHS Booklet of Information*. **How to Contact:** Write. Responds to most inquiries immediately.

289•   COLLEGE AND UNIVERSITY PERSONNEL ASSOCIATION
11 Dupont Circle, Suite 120, Washington DC 20036. (202)462-1038. Contact Person: Assistant Executive Director/General Counsel. **Description:** Professional organization for human resources management in colleges and universities. **Services:** Provides how-to, interpretative, referral, technical and trade information in all areas related to higher education personnel administration (e.g., AA/EEO, labor relations, benefits, wage and salary, training and development, management information systems). Offers statistics (salary and wages), newsletter (weekly), and a host of publications on issues ranging from interviewing techniques to guidance on employing aliens. **How to Contact:** Write or call. Responds to most inquiries within a week. Charges for photocopying. ''Member institutions get first priority for our services; we will respond to nonmember requests as time permits.'' **Tips:** ''Requests/inquiries by phone are easier for us to respond to than written inquiries because of our small support staff.''

290•   CONVENTION OF AMERICAN INSTRUCTORS OF THE DEAF
814 Thayer Ave., Silver Spring MD 20910. (301)585-4363. Contact Person: Membership Secretary. **Description:** ''We offer updated information regarding the education of the deaf to teachers, parents and professionals who work in the field of deaf education.'' **Services:** Provides how-to and referral information—research in the field of education of the deaf (as opposed to technological advancements). ''We offer information on different schools, classes, training programs and summer camps for the deaf and hard of hearing in the US and Canada.'' Offers annual reports, brochures/pamphlets, computerized information searches, informational newsletters, placement on mailing lists and statistics. Publications include *American Annals of the Deaf*; April reference issue of the *Annals* (directory of schools and classes). **How to Contact:** Write. Responds to most inquiries within a week. Services for members only; membership $30. ''To be a member of the Convention of American Instructors of the Deaf one must be involved with deaf education somehow, or show reason enough for wanting to become a member. Anyone may

contact us by mail or phone for a newsletter/brochure and an application." **Tips:** Recent information request: Question about locations of schools for the deaf in the US and Canada.

291• COUNCIL FOR BASIC EDUCATION
725 15th St. NW, Washington DC 20005. (202)347-4171. Contact Person: Deputy Director. **Description:** "CBE is a nonprofit organization which promotes better basic education for primary and secondary schools. 'Basics' include English (reading, writing, speech, literature), social studies, geography, mathematics, science, government, foreign languages, history and arts." **Services:** Provides advisory, analytical, how-to, interpretative and referral information on most subjects in the realm of *education* (K-12), e.g., bilingual education, testing, textbooks, curriculum, private schools, moral education, etc. Offers annual reports, brochures/pamphlets, informational newsletters, press kits, research assistance and telephone reference services. Publications include *The American High School: Time for Reform* by Bruce Boston; *Basic Education*, monthly journal published September-June. **How to Contact:** Write, call or visit. Responds to most inquiries within a week. Give credit to Council for Basic Education. **Tips:** Recent information requests: "What is happening concerning high school reform?"; "Name some specific alternative, fundamental schools in a given area."; "What are the advantages of minimum competency tests?"

292• CREATIVE EDUCATION FOUNDATION
1300 Elmwood Ave., Buffalo NY 14222. (716)878-6221. Contact Person: Executive Director. **Description:** The foundation's purpose is "to help people reach a higher level of thought, imagination, and action" through increased creativity and problem-solving ability. **Services:** Provides information on CEF activities and Creative Problem-Solving Institute. Offers brochures/catalog and placement on mailing lists. Publications include *Journal of Creative Behavior*; series of mini-books on creativity and problem solving and *Classic Series*. **How to Contact:** Write. Responds to most inquiries within 2 weeks.

293• END VIOLENCE AGAINST THE NEXT GENERATION, INC.
977 Keeler Ave., Berkeley CA 94708. (415)527-0454. Contact Person: Executive Director. **Description:** "Our purpose is to abolish corporal punishment in schools and institutions that educate or care for children. Our newsletter covers legal cases, local regulations, protests of parents, opinion, attitude surveys, nostalgia, book reviews, etc. concerning physical punishments in schools and suggests local actions that can mitigate the damage." **Services:** Provides information on corporal punishment in schools and institutions and child abuse. Offers bibliographies, statistics, brochures/pamphlets and newsletter. **How to Contact:** Write or call. Responds to most inquiries immediately. **Tips:** "Ask specific questions." Recent information request: "Who can we get as a speaker?"

294• ERIC CLEARINGHOUSE ON COUNSELING AND PERSONNEL SERVICES (CAPS)
2108 School of Education, University of Michigan, Ann Arbor MI 48109. (313)764-9492. Contact Person: LRC Coordinator. **Description:** "ERIC (Educational Resources Information Center) is a national information system which obtains and makes available hard-to-find, often unpublished information in all areas of education." **Services:** Provides analytical, bibliographical, how-to, referral and technical information covering counseling and guidance—including the preparation, practice and supervision of counselors at all educational levels and in all settings. Offers aid in arranging interviews, bibliographies, statistics, brochures/pamphlets, information searches, placement on mailing list and newsletter. Publications include the counselor renewal series, the new vistas in counseling series, monographs and publications list. **How to Contact:** Write, call or visit. Responds to most inquiries immediately. Charges for computer searches only. **Tips:** "Define your topic as precisely as possible." Recent information request: Reports on computer literacy in counseling services.

295• ERIC CLEARINGHOUSE ON EDUCATIONAL MANAGEMENT (EA)
University of Oregon, Eugene OR 97403. (503)686-5043. Contact Person: Director. **Description:** "ERIC (Educational Resources Information Center) is a national information system which obtains and makes available hard-to-find, often unpublished information in all areas of education." This clearinghouse monitors, acquires and processes information on educational management. **Services:** Provides information on all aspects of administration of private and public educational facilities at elementary and secondary levels.

Offers annual reports, bibliographies, statistics, brochures/pamphlets, information searches, placement on mailing list, newsletter, and reproduction on microfiche or paper of most reports. Publications include thesaurus; *Best of ERIC* (monthly); *School Management Digest*; *Resources in Education* (monthly); and *Current Index to Journals in Education.* **How to Contact:** Write, call or visit. Responds to most inquiries within a week. Charges for information search and for some publications. **Tips:** ''Be specific in your request.'' Recent information request: ''What would be the impact on budgetary decision-making in the face of declining enrollments?''

296• ERIC CLEARINGHOUSE ON ELEMENTARY AND EARLY CHILDHOOD EDUCATION(EECE)
College of Education, University of Illinois, 805 W. Pennsylvania Ave., Urbana IL 61801-4897. (217)333-1386. Contact Person: Coordinator of User Services. **Description:** ''ERIC (Educational Resources Information Center) is a national information system which obtains and makes available hard-to-find, often unpublished information in all areas of education.'' Collects documents relating to all aspects of the development and education of children to 12 years of age, excluding special elementary school curriculum areas. **Services:** Provides information on prenatal and infant development and care; preschool and day care programs; child development through age 12; related community services at the local, state and federal levels. Offers bibliographies, statistics, brochures/pamphlets, information searches, newsletter, resource lists, microfiche abstracts, indexes and library (no lending). Publications include a bibliography on fathering, research reviews and the *ERIC/EECE Newsletter.* **How to Contact:** Write, call or visit. ''Requests must be very specific. Call or write ahead as far as possible.'' Responds to most inquiries within a week. Charges for information searches; $5/year for newsletter subscription.

297• ERIC CLEARINGHOUSE ON HANDICAPPED AND GIFTED CHILDREN (EC)
CEC Dept. of Information Services, Council for Exceptional Children, 1920 Association Dr., Reston VA 22091. (703)620-3660. Contact Person: Information Specialist. **Description:** ''ERIC (Educational Resources Information Center) is a national information system which obtains and makes available hard-to-find, often unpublished information in all areas of education.'' The Clearinghouse processes information and conducts computer searches ''on the education of children and youth deemed exceptional.'' **Services:** Provides bibliographical, how-to and referral information on education of handicapped and gifted children. Offers bibliographies, brochures/pamphlets and information searches. Will refer researchers to other ERIC clearinghouses or agencies if needed. Library and microfiche collection are available for use. Publications include fact sheets, computer search reprints, and monographs. **How to Contact:** Write, call or visit. Responds to most inquiries within a week. ''Publications range from free fact sheets to more extensive publications (range of $2-20). Custom computer searches start at $27.50. Computer search reprints $10.'' Library is open to public but materials are not loaned. **Tips:** Recent information request: ''How can handicapped children be motivated to participate in playground activities?''

298• ERIC CLEARINGHOUSE ON HIGHER EDUCATION (HE)
George Washington University, Suite 630, 1 Dupont Circle, Washinton DC 20036. (202)296-2597. Contact Person: User Services Specialist. **Description:** ''ERIC (Educational Resources Information Center) is a national information system which obtains and makes available hard-to-find, often unpublished information in all areas of education.'' **Services:** Provides bibliographical and some referral information covering all aspects of higher education including professional education, graduate study, students, faculty, etc. Offers information searches. **How to Contact:** Write, call or visit. Responds to most inquiries immediately. ''Most question-answering is free. We charge a $30 fee ($15 for students) for developing individualized computer-generated bibliographies, $7.50 for on-file bibliographies.'' **Tips:** ''ERIC is basically a bibliographic system.'' Recent information request: College and university experiences with developing and evaluating basic skills programs.

299• ERIC CLEARINGHOUSE ON INFORMATION RESOURCES(IR)
Syracuse University School of Education, 150 Marshall St., Syracuse NY 13210. (315)423-3640. Contact Person: User Services Coordinator. **Description:** ''ERIC (Educational Resources Information Center) is a national information system which obtains and makes available hard-to-find, often unpublished information in all areas of education.'' **Services:** Provides information on educational technology and library and information science. Information covers

libraries, learning centers, instructional design, development and evaluation systems, analysis, instructional media, the delivery of information and instruction through the media. Offers bibliographies, fact sheets, information searches, placement on mailing list and newsletter. Will answer reference questions in scope areas. Publications include *ERIC/IR Update* (newsletter); *Current Index to Journals in Education*; and *Resources in Education*. **How to Contact:** Write, call or visit. Responds to most inquiries within a month. "Computerized literature searches cost $20 for the first 50 citations with abstracts, and 10¢ for each additional citation, in the ERIC database. No charge for the mini-bibliographies, fact sheets or newsletter. Publications also available for sale from the clearinghouse." **Tips:** "State request completely and be as specific as possible when requesting information. Keep in mind that the ERIC database deals with the field of education, and includes unpublished materials and periodical citations." Recent information requests: "How can I evaluate software for my microcomputer?"; "What has been done with foreign language teaching and computer-assisted instruction?"; "Are there curriculum materials for library science courses in ERIC?"

300• ERIC CLEARINGHOUSE ON JUNIOR COLLEGES (JC)
University of California-Los Angeles, Room 96, Powell Library, 405 Hilgard Ave., Los Angeles CA 90024. (213)825-3931. Contact Person: Associate Director. **Description:** "ERIC (Educational Resources Information Center) is a national information system which obtains and makes available hard-to-find, often unpublished information in all areas of education." Holdings include over 700,000 documents on all aspects of education at all levels. **Services:** Provides bibliographical and interpretive information covering all aspects of two-year college education. Offers annotated bibliographies, information searches, placement on mailing list and newsletter. Conducts computer searches on "the development, administration and evaluation of public and private community and junior colleges." Will refer researchers to other ERIC clearinghouses or agencies if needed.Publications include information packets, state of the art papers, and a publications list. **How to Contact:** Write, call or visit. Responds to most inquiries within a week. "All services are free, including publications. The only item costing the user is the computer search ($20 for up to 50 citations) for which we recover the computer time costs. We will usually provide only one copy of a publication. Since we hold no copyright, the publications may be duplicated freely. Writers may use reference materials on the premises free of charge." **Tips:** "Be specific in your research; define your goals not to support an idea but to support the reality of the research. Know your audience." Recent information request: "Do you have any information on staff development programs at community colleges?"

301• ERIC CLEARINGHOUSE ON READING AND COMMUNICATION SKILLS (RCS)
National Council of Teachers of English, 1111 Kenyon Rd., Urbana IL 61801. (217)328-3870. Contact Person: Coordinator of Research Services. **Description:** "The ERIC/RCS provides information on teaching communication skills." It has special relationships with professional associations including the International Reading Association and the Speech Communication Association. **Services:** Provides information related to education in reading, English, journalism, theatre, and speech. Offers annotated bibliographies, state-of-the-art studies, interpretative reports, monographs, informal literature searches, abstracts of documents, reprints of ERIC/RCS Reports from professional association journals, fact sheets on topics of current interest, names of organizations and institutions with ERIC collections, and locations of ERIC computer search services. Publications include *ERIC/RCS News Bulletin* (semiannual newsletter); *TRIP* (Theory and Research Into Practice) series of booklets based on concrete education needs; *Resources in Education* (monthly abstracts of published documents worldwide); and *Current Index to Journals in Education* (annotated index of over 700 periodicals). Publications brochure and list of no-cost items available. **How to Contact:** Write, call or visit 8 a.m.—5 p.m. Monday—Friday. Responds to most inquiries within a week. Charges for computer searches and some publications.

302• ERIC CLEARINGHOUSE ON RURAL EDUCATION AND SMALL SCHOOLS (RC)
New Mexico State University, Box 3AP, Las Cruces NM 88003. (505)646-2623. Contact Person: User Services Specialist. **Description:** "ERIC (Educational Resources Information Center) is a national information system which obtains and makes available hard-to-find, often unpublished information in all areas of education." **Services:** Answers questions pertaining to American Indian, Mexican American, migrant, and outdoor education or pertaining to rural education and/or small schools. Performs computer searches ($25 for up to 50 complete citations); provides workshops (when expenses are provided). Free materials: fact sheets, news bulletins, publications

lists, ERIC microfiche locations lists. Publications: Monograph Series (write for publications list). **How to Contact:** Write or call with questions on above educational topics. Responds to most inquiries as soon as possible but within a month. Monographs priced individually. "Questions must pertain to education in the aforementioned areas."

303• ERIC CLEARINGHOUSE ON TESTS, MEASUREMENT AND EVALUATION(TM)
Educational Testing Service, Princeton NJ 08541. (609)734-5181. Contact Person: User Services Coordinator. **Description:** "ERIC (Educational Resources Information Center) is a national information system which obtains and makes available hard-to-find, often unpublished information in all areas of education." Collects and disseminates materials on testing and measurement devices, programs, procedures and techniques. **Services:** Provides bibliographical and referral information on educational testing, measurement and evaluation; research methodology; and background and quotable sources to education writers. Offers brochures/pamphlets, information searches and placement on mailing list. Will provide sources for statistical information. **How to Contact:** Write, call or visit by appointment. Responds to most inquiries within a week. Open Monday through Friday, 8:30 a.m. to 4:45 p.m. Charges $25 initial fee for computerized search; 10¢/citation. Publications price list available. **Tips:** Recent information request: "Who is doing research on methods for identifying gifted children?"

304• ERIC CLEARINGHOUSE ON URBAN EDUCATION (UD)
Box 40, Teachers College, Columbia University, New York NY 10027. (212)678-3015. Contact Person: Director. **Description:** "ERIC (Educational Resources Information Center) is a national information system which obtains and makes available hard-to-find, often unpublished information in all areas of education." Collects and disseminates information and research on urban young people, from third grade through college entrance. Information covers Puerto Rican, black, Asian/American and other minority groups in urban and suburban schools. (Native Americans and Mexicans are not included). Conducts computer research and will refer to other ERIC clearinghouses or agencies if needed. **Services:** Offers bibliographies, *In Fact Sheets*, brochure/pamphlets, information searches, placement on mailing list and newsletter. Publications include information packets, information bulletin and monographs in the urban diversity series. Backlist available, $5/publication; prices for new monographs will vary. **How to Contact:** Write, call or visit. Make appointment in advance of visit. Charges reprint fee for microfiche information and for information searches.

305• ERIC, EDUCATIONAL RESOURCES INFORMATION CENTER
ERIC Central, National Institute of Education, 1200 19th St. NW, Washington DC 20208. Contact Person: Chief. **Description:** "ERIC is a network funded by the US Department of Education with clearinghouses operated by associations, institutions of higher learning and affiliations with private businesses. ERIC is designed to provide users with ready access to primarily the English-language literature dealing with education. It does this through a variety of products and services, e.g., data bases, abstract journals, microfiche, computer searches, online access, document reproductions." **Services:** Provides analytical, bibliographical, historical, interpretative, referral and technical information on practically every facet of information related to education, e.g., reading, writing, counseling, special education, urban education, teacher education, tests, etc. Offers brochures/pamphlets, computerized information searches, informational newsletters and research assistance. Publications include *Resources in Education*, a monthly publication; and commercially published *Current Index to Journals in Education*. **How to Contact:** "We prefer that writers contact any one of the sixteen clearinghouses covering a specific facet of education. Responds to most inquiries within a month. "Some services do have a fee, such as computerized searches and large publications. Many publications are free." **Tips:** "Before doing any research in education-related topics check with the pertinent ERIC clearinghouse." *Editor's Note:* ERIC Clearinghouse on Languages and Linguistics is in the Language and Literature section; ERIC Clearinghouse on Science, Mathematics and Environmental Education is in the Science, Engineering, Technology section; ERIC Clearinghouse on Social Studies/Social Science Education is in the Society and Culture section. ERIC clearinghouses not listed in this book are: ERIC Clearinghouse on Career Education, Ohio State University, Center for Vocational Education, 1960 Kenny Rd., Columbus OH 43212. (614) 486-3655; ERIC Clearinghouse on Teacher Education, American Association of Colleges for Teacher Education, 1 Dupont Circle NW, Sute 610, Washington DC 20036. (202)293-2450.

306• GALLAUDET COLLEGE
7th St. and Florida Ave. NE, Washington DC 20002. (202)651-5100. Contact Person: Director of Media and Campus Relations. **Description:** "Gallaudet serves deaf individuals internationally in a variety of ways. For example, educationally the college offers demonstration programs on the elementary and secondary school levels, a liberal arts college, a graduate school, and a network of continuing education programs. The library houses one of the largest collections of material on deafness. The National Center for Law and the Deaf and the International and National Information Center on Deafness are located at Gallaudet, and research related to deafness is being conducted at the college." **Services:** Provides information on research, education, communications methods, sign language, linguistics and deaf people in different areas of work. Offers aid in arranging interviews, annual reports, statistics, brochures/pamphlets, photos and "individual assistance as requested." Publications include *Preview* and *Perspective*, magazines focusing on deaf education; *Directions*, a research journal. **How to Contact:** Write or call. Make appointment in advance of visit. **Tips:** "If writers have special needs for individual interviews, detailed information, etc., allow as much time as possible. We have a small office working extensively with radio, television, film, newspaper, magazine and other media personnel."

307• HEATH RESOURCE CENTER
One Dupont Circle, Suite 20, Washington DC 20036. (202)833-4707 (voice and telecommunication for the deaf). Contact Person: Director. **Description:** "We are a national clearinghouse on post-secondary education for disabled people. We select, create, and disseminate information and answer inquiries so that disabled people can pursue a higher education if they choose." **Services:** Provides advisory, bibliographical, how-to, interpretative, referral and technical information on the handicapped/disabled student, financial aid, advising/counseling, types of post-secondary institutions, learning disabilities, hearing impairment, conference planning, audio-visual materials, student organizations, architectural access, long range institutional planning, disabled educators, disabled scientists. Offers telephone reference services; telephone and mail inquiry response; conference planning; information dissemination about the topic of higher education and the handicapped (HEATH). Publications include *1982-83 HEATH Higher Education and the Handicapped Resource Directory*; *Information from HEATH* (thrice yearly newsletter); and fact sheets. **How to Contact:** Write or call. Responds to most inquiries within a week. "Our material is in the public domain. Writers are encouraged to give us credit, but no 'permission' is necessary to use our materials." **Tips:** "Writers interested in the rights and opportunities of disabled people in colleges, technical institutes and universities, both students and staff, should know about the HEATH Resource Center and what materials have already been developed in this fairly new field. If you are not quite sure what you want, call and we can help you clarify your ideas. If you have specific questions or want to review some of our material first and then talk, write for our newsletter and *Resource Directory*." Recent information request: "What opportunities exist for people with learning disabilities who want to go to college?"

308• INSTITUTE FOR RESEARCH ON TEACHING
Michigan State University, E. Lansing MI 48824. Contact Person: Editor. **Description:** "IRT is a government-funded institute that is part of the university. We serve as a center for research on teaching, with studies emphasizing teacher decision making; a forum for communication among researchers, teachers, teacher educators, and policy makers; and a training program for researchers (doctoral studies—5 interns per year). **Services:** Provides analytical, interpretative and technical information through a series of research reports. Offers informational newsletter and placement on mailing list to receive the newsletter. Publications include *Communication Quarterly* and many research reports. **How to Contact:** Write. Responds to most inquiries within a week. "We charge for publications to cover printing and mailing costs only; the newsletter is free." **Tips:** "We would appreciate that any writer allow the researcher whose work she or he writes about to look over the article before it is published to prevent misinterpretation of the research."

309• INSTITUTE FOR THE ADVANCEMENT OF PHILOSOPHY FOR CHILDREN
Montclair State College, Upper Montclair NJ 07043. (201)893-4277. Contact Person: Director. **Description:** "The institute conducts research in reasoning and inquiry skill education for children; produces curricula and trains teachers and professors." **Services:** Provides advisory, analytical, bibliographical, historical, how-to, interpretative, referral and technical information on education; philosophy; child development; cognition. Offers brochures/pamphlets, informational newsletters, research assistance and statistics. Publications include *Thinking: The Journal of*

Philosophy for Children (quarterly). **How to Contact:** Write. Responds to most inquiries within a week. "Writers/researchers using our services should be qualified and have serious, specific projects (such as writing an article for publication, or doing a thesis or dissertation)." **Tips:** Recent information request: "What is 'philosophy for children'?"

310• INSTITUTE OF INTERNATIONAL EDUCATION (IIE)
809 United Nations Plaza, New York NY 10017. Contact Person: Manager, Communications Division. **Description:** "IIE is the largest educational exchange agency in the United States. It is best known for its work on the US International Communication Agency's Fulbright Program." **Services:** Provides advisory and referral information primarily on higher education, international education and exchange, 'clearinghouse' on information of programs of study in the United States and abroad. Offers annual reports, brochures/pamphlets, informational newsletters, library facilities (limited by appointment), and telephone reference services. Publications include *Learning Traveler* books (basic guides to study abroad); an extensive group of guides and handbooks for the foreign student; a magazine, *World Higher Education Communiqué*; and *Open Doors*, a compilation of statistical data on educational exchange. **How to Contact:** Write (preferred) or call. Responds to most inquiries within a week. **Tips:** "Write and be as specific as possible about your project." Recent information requests: statistical analysis of the number and types of foreign students in the United States; overview of the field of study abroad for US students.

311• INTERNATIONAL READING ASSOCIATION
Box 8139, 800 Barksdale Rd., Newark DE 19711. (302)731-1600. Contact Person: Public Information Officer. **Description:** "The International Reading Association has three general goals: to improve the quality of reading instruction through the study of the reading process and teaching techniques; to promote the lifetime reading habit and an awareness among all people of the impact of reading; and to promote the development of every reader's proficiency to the highest possible level." **Services:** Provides information on reading and education. Offers aid in arranging interviews, annual reports, statistics, brochures/pamphlets, placement on mailing list, newsletter and press kits. **How to Contact:** Write or call. Responds to most inquiries within a week.

312• JUNIOR ACHIEVEMENT (JA)
550 Summer St., Stamford CT 06901. (203)359-2970. Contact: Public Relations Department. **Description:** The purpose of JA is to provide students and the general public the opportunity "to further their understanding of the workings of the American business system." Conducts economic education and applied management programs in junior high and high schools, and economic awareness programs among 5th and 6th graders. **Services:** Offers aid in arranging interviews, annual reports, bibliographies, biographies, statistics, brochures/pamphlets, information searches, placement on mailing list, photos, press kits and speakers bureau. Also maintains hall of fame for US business leaders. Publications include *The Achiever* (monthly). **How to Contact:** Write or call. Responds to most inquiries within 10 business days. **Tips:** "Be as specific as possible." Recent information request: "How can I obtain photos of kids and business leaders?"

313• NATIONAL ASSOCIATION FOR CREATIVE CHILDREN AND ADULTS
8080 Springvalley Dr., Cincinnati OH 45236. (513)631-1777. Contact Person: Editor. **Description:** "We are dedicated to helping us become the best we can be through understanding and applying the research on creativity. When constructively expressed, this enables individuals and groups to achieve more with less time and energy and on higher levels." **Services:** Provides advisory, analytical and how-to information covering art, writing, music, daily innovative problem solving and applying research on creativity. Offers biographies, brochures/pamphlets and newsletter. Also offers programs, projects, workshops, conferences, publications, in-service training, books and question and answer service for members. Publications include *The Creative Child*; *Adult Quarterly*; and *Common Sense Creativity*. **How to Contact:** Write. Responds to most inquiries within a month. Enclose SASE and 50¢ for more information about membership, association projects, inservice workshop, etc.

314• NATIONAL ASSOCIATION FOR INDUSTRY-EDUCATION COOPERATION
235 Hendricks Blvd., Buffalo NY 14226. (716)278-5726. Contact Person: President. **Description:** "National organization for representatives of business, industry, education, government and labor designed to promote increased levels of cooperation; to identify areas of mutual interest; to formulate programs and procedures which meet acceptable standards;

and to communicate with any group concerned with education about cooperative programs and projects.'' **Services:** Provides advisory, analytical, how-to, interpretative and referral information covering industry-education cooperation. Offers brochures/pamphlets and newsletter. Publications include handbooks on industry education councils and community resources workshops. **How to Contact:** Write. Responds to most inquiries immediately.

315• NATIONAL ASSOCIATION OF INDEPENDENT SCHOOLS (NAIS)
18 Tremont St., Boston MA 02108. (617)723-6900. Contact Person: Director of Public Information. **Description:** ''The National Association of Independent Schools is a nonprofit, tax-exempt, voluntary membership organization which serves over 900 independent schools in the United States and abroad, as well as some 65 local, state, regional and special-purpose associations of independent schools.'' **Services:** Provides advisory, analytical, bibliographical, historical, interpretative and referral information on education and independent schools. Offers aid in arranging interviews, annual reports, bibliographies, biographies, statistics, brochures/pamphlets, information searches, suggestions for feature articles and trend stories, placement on mailing list and regular NAIS publications. **How to Contact:** Call or write. Responds to most inquiries immediately. **Tips:** ''We can usually direct writers/researchers to appropriate sources of information or to the right people if we cannot answer the question ourselves. We have excellent ideas and sources for feature articles as there are all sorts of interesting and unusual schools in our membership.'' Recent information requests: Enrollment trends in private schools; trends in parents' organizations.

316• NATIONAL CENTER FOR EDUCATIONAL BROKERING
c/o AHP, 325 9th St., 3rd Floor, San Francisco CA 94103. (415)626-2375. Contact Person: Director. **Description:** ''The National Center for Educational Brokering was established in January 1976 to foster the expansion and improvement of impartial educational and career counseling services for people no longer in school or college. The Washington-based center is a unit of the National Institute for Work and Learning.'' **Services:** ''The NCEB provides information, technical assistance and public respresentation for over 465 counseling programs with 680 service sites in 49 states. They all offer the six basic functions that are generally described as educational brokering services: *outreach* to disadvantaged people; *information* on occupational and educational opportunities; *counseling* on plans for working and learning; *assessment* for occupational and educational choices; *referrals* to sources of information, human services, and education; and *advocacy* for people who encounter red tape and other institutional barriers.'' Offers informational newsletters and telephone reference services. ''The center also organizes conferences and workshops to improve the linkages and competencies of people at the state and local levels concerned with the collection, dissemination and counseling use of career and educational information.'' Publications include *Bulletin* (10 times/year); *Directory of Educational and Career Information Services for Adults* (annual); *Educational Brokering: A New Service for Adult Learners*; *Educational and Career Services for Adults*. **How to Contact:** Write or call. Responds to most inquiries within a week. *Bulletin* subscription $14/year.

317• NATIONAL CENTER FOR THE STUDY OF CORPORAL PUNISHMENT AND ALTERNATIVES IN THE SCHOOLS
Temple University, Philadelphia PA 19122. (215)787-6091. Contact Person: Center Director. **Description:** ''The center is dedicated to the study of school discipline, research, training, advocacy and dissemination of information in the area of corporal punishment and alternatives.'' **Services:** Provides advisory, analytical, bibliographical, historical, interpretative and referral information on corporal punishment, discipline in home and school, child abuse. Offers aid in arranging interviews, annual reports, brochures/pamphlets, clipping services, computerized information searches, informational newsletters, library facilities, research assistance and statistics. ''The collection of articles in the center's library regarding discipline is one of the most extensive in the world. In addition to the library, the center maintains an up-to-date file on corporal punishment in the schools derived from a national press clipping service. These resources are used by writers, journalists and researchers from all over the country.'' **How to Contact:** Write or visit.

318• NATIONAL COMMITTEE FOR CITIZENS IN EDUCATION
410 Wilde Lake Village Green, Columbia MD 21044. (301)997-9300. Contact Person: Associate for Public Information. **Description:** ''Our purpose is to improve the education of children by

mobilizing and assisting citizens—including parents—to strengthen public schools. NCCE is an advocate for citizens and helps them gain and use information and skills to influence the quality of public education.'' **Services:** Provides advisory, analytical, how-to and referral information on the involvement of citizens in public school decision-making. Offers annual reports, brochures/pamphlets, computerized information searches, informational newsletters and placement on mailing lists. Publications include *The Rights of Parents in the Education of Their Children*; *Network, the Paper for Parents*; *School Closings and Declining Enrollment*; *Parents Can Understand Testing*; *The School Budget: It's Your Money*; *It's Your Business*. **How to Contact:** Write or call. Responds to most inquiries within a week. Charges for publications. **Tips:** ''We respond to inquiries involving research on a time-available basis. Make sure inquiry is related to our field of expertise, citizen involvement in public schools. Make use of Periodical Indexes available at library and for education research, access the ERIC system.'' Recent information request: ''What local citizen groups have successfully challenged a school policy?''

319• NATIONAL EXTENSION HOMEMAKERS COUNCIL, INC.
Route 2, Box 3070. Vale OR 97918. (503)473-2619. Contact Person: President. **Description:** ''Nonprofit, volunteer, educational organization of homemakers working to strengthen, develop, coordinate and extend adult education to improve the quality of living. We help members and families recognize their interests and needs by developing and implementing education programs to meet those needs. We promote programs relative to preservation of the American home.'' **Services:** Provides historical, how-to and referral information on citizenship and community outreach; cultural arts; textiles and cloth; family relationships and child development; family resource management; international interests; health, food and nutrition; housing, energy and environment; safety and emergency preparedness; consumer concerns. Offers annual reports, placement on mailing lists, press kits, research assistance and statistics. Publications include *NEHC Fact Sheet*; *The Homemaker* magazine. **How to Contact:** Write or call. Responds to most inquiries within a week.

320• NATIONAL FORUM OF CATHOLIC PARENT ORGANIZATIONS/NCEA
1077 30th St., NW, A100, Washington DC 20007. (202)293-5954. Contact Person: Executive Director. **Description:** Commission of the National Catholic Educational Association founded in 1976 ''to support and promote the role of parents as primary educators of their children.'' **Services:** Provides advisory, analytical, how-to, interpretative and referral information and resources for Catholic parent organizations (PTA's, PTO's, Parent Clubs, home, school). Offers newsletters. Publications include *Parentcator* (newsletter); *Catholic Parent Organizations Handbook* and *Catholic Parent Organizations Program Guide*. **How to Contact:** Write ''or call and follow up with a letter.'' Responds to most inquiries within a week ''if possible.'' Services free to members; charges nonmembers for photocopying services. **Tips:** Serious writers ''are welcome to come in and consult our Resource File on their own. Many times a backlog can delay services.'' Recent information requests: ''Who can I talk to about tuition tax credits?''; ''How do I start a home-school association?''; ''Who can I contact about cults?''

321• NATIONAL HOME STUDY COUNCIL
1601 18th St. NW, Washington DC 20009. (202)234-5100. Contact Person: Director of Publications. **Description:** ''NHSC, a nonprofit educational association, serves as a clearinghouse of information about the home study/correspondence field, and sponsors a nationally recognized accrediting agency.'' **Services:** Provides trade information on correspondence education, home study education. Offers brochures/pamphlets, informational newsletters, placement on mailing lists and research assistance. Publications include *NHSC Directory of Accredited Home Study Schools*; *NHSC News* (semiannual magazine); and a variety of literature. **How to Contact:** Write. Responds to most inquiries within a week. **Tips:** Recent information requests: ''How many people study by correspondence education?''; ''Can you get a degree by home study education?''

322• NATIONAL SCHOOL BOARDS ASSOCIATION
1055 Thomas Jefferson St. NW, Washington DC 20007. (202)337-7666. Contact Person: Public Information Director. **Description:** ''NSBA represents the nation's 95,000 local school board members who serve as policy makers for the elementary and secondary public schools. It conducts training workshops for both board members and school administrators; produces a variety of consulting services; publishes two national monthly magazines (*The American School Board*

Journal and *The Executive Educator* and a biweekly newspaper, *School Board News*); represents school board interests on Capitol Hill; and conducts an annual convention each April." **Services:** Provides advisory, historical, interpretative and referral information on public school finance, policies, operations, trends, federal regulations, legislation, court decisions and statistics covering major issues in public education. Offers aid in arranging interviews, statistics and placement on mailing list. **How to Contact:** Write or call. Responds to most inquiries immediately "or within 24 hours." Credit official NSBA publications when such are source of information used. **Tips:** "To help us provide appropriate information, be specific in indicating types of information requested, including intended purpose or use."

323• OUTWARD BOUND, INC.
384 Field Point Rd., Greenwich CT 06830. (800)243-8520. In Connecticut (203)661-0797. Contact Person: Information Coordinator. **Description:** "Outward Bound is an intense wilderness adventure in which newly acquired skills are applied to progressively more difficult situations. A deliberately structured and demanding educational experience. We are a nonprofit outdoor education organization where you learn by doing." **Services:** Provides information on Outward Bound programs in 5 locations around the country (program for the handicapped in Minnesota and 4 others: Hurricane Island—off the coast of Maine, North Carolina, Colorado and Oregon). Programs cover survival skills, stress management (applying what is learned in the wilderness to everyday life), self-respect and going beyond one's own limits. Offers annual reports, brochures/pamphlets, informational newsletters (only to alumni of the program), placement on mailing lists, statistics, and a speakers bureau. Publications include *Outward Bound: A Reference Volume* (provides access to the research literature on Outward Bound, through 1977, $37); *Outward Bound: Schools of the Possible* (representative experiences at US Outward Bound schools, with many photographs, $10.95); *Outward Bound U.S.A.: Learning Through Experience in Adventure-Based Education* (a history of Outward Bound in the United States, $8.95); *Outward Bound Adaptive Programs for Independent Schools* (a how-to manual for starting an Outward Bound program in your school, $7.50). **How to Contact:** Write or call. Responds to most inquiries immediately.

324• P.A.R.E.N.T.S.
6706 3rd Ave., Kenosha WI 53140; Rt. 4, Emerald Dr., Watertown WI 53094. (414)654-6867 (Kenosha), (414)699-3780 (Watertown). Contact Person: Co-Chairman. **Description:** "Our purpose is to support parental rights and traditional academic education for private and public schools." **Services:** Provides advisory, analytical, historical and how-to information on parent's rights, drug education, sex education, values education, secular humanism, parenting and traditional education. Offers brocures/pamphlets, informational newsletters and research assistance. **How to Contact:** Write. Responds to most inquiries immediately. **Tips:** "Do your own research and do it well." Recent information request: "What is values clarification?; How is it used?; How can you deal with it?; Oppose it?"

325• PARENT COOPERATIVE PRESCHOOLS, INTERNATIONAL
Box 31335, Phoenix AZ 85046. Canadian office: 481 Queens Ave., London, Ontario, Canada N6B 1Y3. Contact Person: Executive Secretary. **Description:** "Parent Cooperative Preschools (PCPI) is a service organization for member co-op preschools, teachers and parents." **Services:** Provides advisory, bibliographical, how-to and referral information covering cooperative preschools and parent participation preschools. Offers aid in arranging interviews, bibliographies, brochures/pamphlets and regular informational journal. **How to Contact:** Write. Responds to most inquiries within a month. Publication list available on request. "Members get first priority, except in processing orders of pamphlets, reprints and journals." Charges for mailing. **Tips:** "Don't address letters to our organizations as 'Dear Sir'!"

326• PARENTS RIGHTS IN EDUCATION
12571 Northwinds Dr., St. Louis MO 63141. (314)434-4171. Contact Person: President. **Description:** "Our purpose is to disseminate information and research material in support of the parents' natural, human right to direct and control the education of their own children. Our special interest is to reform the present government controlled monopoly in education, in order to allow parents a free choice of schools and the type of education they desire for their own children. Such solutions as a tuition voucher, tax credits and exemption from public school taxation have been researched. Reform of compulsory attendance laws and minimum

school standards are considered.'' **Services:** Provides advisory, analytical, historical, how-to, interpretative and referral information on parents' rights in education. Offers statistics, brochures/pamphlets, information searches and newsletter. Publications include *Parents Rights* (newsletter); *Legal Brief in Support of Parents Rights in Education*; *A Case for Liberty and Justice*; *Freedom in Education*; *Family Choice in Education*; *Secular Humanism and the Schools*; *How to Start Your Own School*; and *Educational Freedom*. **How to Contact:** Write (include SASE) or call. Responds to most inquiries within a month. "There is a charge for the material we send. Prices are listed. To be placed on our mailing list, we require at least a $5 yearly donation." Membership/subscription $10/year. Give credit to Parents Rights in Education. **Tips:** Recent information request: Inquiry on "a school where secular humanism is not taught as in the public schools."

327• SEX INFORMATION AND EDUCATION COUNCIL OF THE UNITED STATES (SIECUS)
80 5th Ave., Suite 801, New York NY 10011. (212)929-2300. Contact Person: Executive Director. **Description:** "Our aim is to establish human sexuality as a health entity. Through our publications, our own programs (and those cosponsored as part of our affiliation with the department of health education, school of education, health, nursing, and arts professions of New York University), we try to serve as a clearinghouse for information on all aspects of human sexuality, with special emphasis on sex education." **Services:** Offers bibliography, biographies, brochures/pamphlets and newsletter. Publications include *Winning the Battle for Sex Education*; specific bibliographies on adolescent pregnancy, religion and sexuality, alcoholics and sexuality, illness/disability/aging and sexuality, etc. **How to Contact:** Write or call.

328• TEACHERS & WRITERS COLLABORATIVE
84 Fifth Ave., New York NY 10011. (212)691-6590. Contact Person: Director. **Description:** "The Teachers & Writers Collaborative conducts long-term classroom residencies in poetry, prose, visual arts, dance or theater, and publishes and distributes literature resulting from the residencies in order to aid others elsewhere in successfully conducting writing and other art programs in the schools." **Services:** Provides advisory, how-to and interpretative information on teaching writing, learning to write, devising curricula. Offers informational magazine and books. Publications include *Teachers & Writers Magazine*. **How to Contact:** Write or call. Responds to most inquiries within a week. **Tips:** "We employ writers and artists, but do not give out grants. Writers who want to apply for the program should call or write for an application."

329• UNITED STATES STUDENT ASSOCIATION
2000 P St. NW, Washington DC 20036. (202)775-8943. Contact Person: Vice President. **Description:** "The United States Student Association (USSA) is the nationally recognized representative of college and university students in the US. Representing students in all 50 states through more than 300 student government members, we lobby on issues such as federal financial aid, department of education, affirmative action and abortion rights, on Capitol Hill and at the White House. Our information service collects data on 100 subjects from collective bargaining to drug abuse and student fees.'' **Services:** Offers annual reports, statistics, brochures/pamphlets, information searches, placement on mailing list, newsletter, photos, press kits, press releases, "legislative alerts," mailing lists, conferences and conventions and manuals. Publications include a variety of manuals dealing with important campus issues, affirmative action, fund raising, Title 9, financial aid, etc. **How to Contact:** Write, call or visit. Call in advance of visit. Charges for publications, mailing lists, conference registration, copying costs and postage. "We prefer that freelance writers tell us where stories are going to be published. Our archives material on 32 years of student association history is restricted and requires USSA permission for reporters or researchers to look at documents." **Tips:** "We always have a million potential leads and stories for interested reporters on subjects as varied as South Africa and financial aid."

330• WORLD RESEARCH INCORPORATED
11722 Sorrento Valley Rd., San Diego CA 92121. (714)755-9761. Contact Person: Director of Program. **Description:** "World Research is a nonprofit, educational organization. We create and distribute materials which stimulate discussion on current national topics within a classroom setting. Materials (including brochures, a book, and several films) are created primarily for colleges, universities, high schools, and business educational programs. Several film productions

have appeared on television nationwide.'' **Services:** Provides analytical information on national issues, including: government regulation, inflation, pollution, energy, poverty, eminent domain, and labor-management relations. Offers brochures/pamphlets and library facilities. ''Our library is open for use by writers on a loan basis.'' Publications include: topical, educational brochures (one copy at no charge); *The Incredible Bread Machine* ($3.95); specific study guides ($7.95 each). **How to Contact:** Write. Responds to most inquiries within a month. ''Contact us by mail well in advance of dealine. We are primarily involved in the creation of our own programs, and supply information on a courtesy basis only. If a writer and/or publication wishes to quote directly from a WRI publication, permission and credit line are required.'' **Tips:** ''Be persistent in questioning sources. Just because a fact has been spoken or printed does not mean it is valid. As much as possible, utilize only primary sources. It is remarkable how much liberty is taken with original facts by secondary sources.'' Recent information request: ''Describe the process by which inflation occurs.''

331• WRITER'S DIGEST SCHOOL
9933 Alliance Rd., Cincinnati OH 45242. Contact Person: Director. **Description:** Home study courses in fiction and nonfiction writing. **Services:** Provides information on writing and publishing stories and articles in national magazines. Offers brochures/pamphlets. Publications include *Getting Started in Writing*. **How to Contact:** Write. Responds to most inquiries within 2 weeks. **Tips:** ''If you have a complex topic to research, use the children's department of the library as your first step in understanding the subject before going on to more detailed adult books, data bases, etc.'' Recent information request: ''I have been writing a personal journal and poetry for 5 years . . . What are the chances of a possible future in writing emerging from this kind of writing?''

332• WRITERS INSTITUTE
112 W. Boston Post Rd., Mamaroneck NY 10543. Contact Person: Director. **Description:** The institute teaches a correspondence course in writing. **Services:** Provides historical and interpretative information on the school and its courses. **How to Contact:** Write. Responds to most inquiries within a week.

SECTION · SIX

ENVIRONMENT/THE EARTH

*We have changed our environment more
quickly than we know how to change ourselves.*

—Walter Lippman

The resources listed here cover environmental
concerns (pollution, hazardous waste, energy);
conservation of wildlife and natural resources;
weather and earth sciences; geography and
oceanography and natural history.

Additional listings on animal wildlife conservation are found in the Animals and Plants
category. Further information on citizens'
groups concerned with other environmental/
earth issues (such as nuclear power and the
arms race) is available in the Public Affairs
category.

Bibliography

Bartholomew, John C., ed. *New York Times Atlas of the World*. rev. ed. New York: Times
  Books, 1980.
Bryant, Jeannette, ed. *Conservation Directory*. Vienna, VA: National Wildlife Federation,
  1981.
Buenker, John D., Gerald M. Greenfield and William J. Murin, eds. *Urban History: A Guide
  to Information Sources*. Detroit: Gale Research Co., 1981.
Fairbridge, R., ed. *Encyclopedia of Oceanography*. Encyclopedia of Earth Sciences Series,
  vol. 1. New York: Academic Press, 1966.
Glunt, Donald F., ed. *New Dinosaur Dictionary*. Seacaucus, NJ: Citadel Press, 1982. (Al-
  phabetical listing of every known genus of dinosaur; illustrations)
Harder, Kelsie B., comp. *Dictionary of Place Names, US & Canada*. New York: Van Nos-
  trand Reinhold, 1976.
Palmer, Lawrence, ed. *Fieldbook of Natural History*. rev. ed. Edited by Seymour Fowler.
  New York: McGraw-Hill, 1975.
Parker, Sybil P., ed. *McGraw-Hill Encyclopedia of Energy*. 2d ed. New York: McGraw-
  Hill, 1981.
Ridgeway, James. *Who Owns the Earth*. New York: Macmillan, 1980. (Descriptions of natu-
  ral resources and places where minerals, water and energy resources are located)
Ruffner, James and Frank Bair, eds. *The Weather Almanac*. Detroit: Gale Research Co.,
  1981.
Seltzer, Leon, ed. *Columbia Lippincott Gazetteer of the World with 1961 Supplement*. New
  York: Columbia University Press, 1952. (A voluminous geographical dictionary citing
  pronunciation, location, area, physical description, population and historical data on
  countries, cities, mountains, rivers, etc.)
Weather of US Cities. 2 vols. Detroit: Gale Research Co., 1981.
Webster's New Geographical Dictionary. Springfield, MA: G&C Merriam Co., 1980. (Similar to the *Columbia Lippincott Gazetteer*).

333• AMERICAN ASSOCIATION OF PETROLEUM GEOLOGISTS
1444 S. Boulder, Tulsa OK 74119. Contact Person: Executive Director. **Description:** A
professional society of geologists engaged in research and teaching. **Services:** Provides trade and
statistical information relating to petroleum, energy and mineral resources. "The bulletin of the
American Association of Petroleum Geologists (AAPG) and other special publications include
scientific information relating to the geology of petroleum resources worldwide." Publications
include a monthly bulletin—the November issue is an annual membership directory; the October
issue (World Energy Development issue) contains North American and overseas drilling activity
reports; a monthly newspaper, *Explorer*. **How to Contact:** Write. Responds to most inquiries
immediately. "We have a publications catalog that gives prices." **Tips:** Recent information
requests: Many questions on drilling statistics.

334• AMERICAN FOREST INSTITUTE
1619 Massachusetts Ave. NW, Washington DC 20036. (202)797-4500. Contact Person: Vice President, Communications. **Description:** "We are a communications organization serving the forest products industry." **Services:** Provides analytical, interpretative, referral and trade information on forest products industry and forest management. Offers aid in arranging interviews, statistics, brochures/pamphlets, photos, press kits, forest tours and briefings. Publications include *American Tree Farmer* (issued four times/year); *Forest Facts and Figures*; *Managing The Great American Forest*; and Green Papers on wildlife, forest management, industry facts, herbicides and clear-cut harvest. **How to Contact:** Write or call. Responds to most inquiries within a week. **Tips:** Recent information request: "Who owns most of the nation's forests?"

335• AMERICAN GEOLOGICAL INSTITUTE
5205 Leesburg Pike, Falls Church VA 22041. (703)379-2480. Contact Person: Executive Director. **Description:** "Our association encourages public understanding of the geological sciences." **Services:** Provides bibliographical and referral information on geological sciences (geology, geochemistry and solid-earth geophysics) Offers computerized information searches (operates GeoRef, a computer-based reference file of worldwide geological literature) and placement on mailing lists. Publications include bibliographies; and *Directory of Departments*. **How to Contact:** Write, call or visit. Responds to most inquiries within a week. Charges for services when the response requires an unusual amount of time. Give credit to Institute. **Tips:** "Writers should familiarize themselves with the nature of our organization." Recent information requests: Salaries of geology faculty; enrollments of geology departments.

336• AMERICAN MUSEUM OF NATURAL HISTORY LIBRARY
Photographic Collection, Central Park W. at 79th St., New York NY 10024. (212)873-1300, ext. 346. Contact Persons: Photographic Collection Librarians. **Description:** "The photographic collection, which has been growing since the museum's opening in 1869, now consists of about 800,000 images. Many of these images are from museum expeditions to locations previously unseen through the lens of a camera. Examples of human beings, scenery, animals, plants, and minerals from all over the world are to be found in the files, as well as visual documentation of scientific phenomena." **Services:** Photos cover art, health/medicine and nature including anthropology, archaeology, botany, geology, mineralogy, paleontology, zoology and astronomy. **How to Contact:** Write or call. Responds to most inquiries within a month. "Open Monday through Friday, 11 a.m. to 4 p.m. No appointment is needed, and guidance with files is provided. Prints may be ordered on a prepayment basis. Transparencies may be rented for preview or purchased for personal use." Charges for prints and transparencies and permissions. Request an information sheet for specific policies. **Tips:** Recent photo request: Prehistoric art involving human hand prints.

337• AMERICAN MUSEUM OF SCIENCE & ENERGY
300 S. Tulane Ave., Oak Ridge TN 37830. (615)576-3218. Contact Person: Information Officer. **Description:** Exhibitions in science and energy alternative areas. "The American Museum of Science & Energy is operated for the United States Department of Energy (DOE) by Science Applications, Inc." **Services:** Provides advisory, historical and interpretative information. Photos also available. Free catalog or brochure to writer on request. **How to Contact:** Write or call. Responds to most inquiries within a week. "Some of the photographs will require a credit line for the photographer." **Tips:** "Visit the museum first if at all possible as the city of Oak Ridge provides history to background writers on the museum." Recent information requests: "What makes the American Museum of Science and Energy unique?"; "Who does your museum exhibition appeal to?"; "Does your museum offer educational programs for teachers or classroom activities for youngsters?"

338• AMERICAN PETROLEUM INSTITUTE
2101 L St. NW, Washington DC 20037. Contact Person: Manager, Print Media. **Description:** "We are the best source of statistical information about current issues in the petroleum industry." **Services:** Provides analytical, bibliographical, historical, referral, technical and trade information covering energy, particularly petroleum. Offers b&w glossy photos pertaining to petroleum for noncommercial, nonadvertising use *only*. **How to Contact:** Write. Responds to most inquiries immediately. The American Petroleum Institute must be given a credit line. **Tips:** "Always check with original sources such as API. In many instances writers have accepted information from

sources which have interpreted data to suit their own ideological preferences." Recent information request: "Are gasoline supplies adequate for the summer driving season?"

339• AMERICAN PLANNING ASSOCIATION
Public Information Department, 1776 Massachusetts Ave. NW, 704, Washington DC 20036. (202) 872-0611. Library and Bookstore: 1313 E. 60th St., Chicago IL 60637. (312)947-2560. Contact Person: Director of Public Information, Washington. **Description:** "The American Planning Association is a nonprofit organization whose membership is open to anyone. APA represents over 20,000 practicing planners, local officials, architects, engineers, students, educators and other citizens dedicated to developing and maintaining well-planned urban and rural communities. AICP, the American Institute of Certified Planners, functions within the association and fosters the professional development of APA members. It administers the certification exam for planners. Two offices, one in Chicago and the other in Washington, D.C. house administrative, research, public information, publications, planning policy and chapter and division member services departments." **Services:** Provides advisory, analytical, bibliographical, historical, interpretative, referral, technical and trade information. Offers reports, surveys pertaining to planning and related issues, aid in arranging interviews, brochures/pamphlets, clipping services, informational newsletters, current and back issues of APA publications, library facilities, placement on mailing lists, research assistance and statistics. Publications include *Planning and Advisory Service (PAS) Reports*; *Journal of the American Planning Association*; *Planning Magazine*; *APA News*; Planners Bookstore publications: *The Citizen's Guide to Planning*; *Growth and Settlement in the U.S.: Past Trends and Future Issues*; *Zoning for City Housing Markets*. **How to Contact:** Write or call. Responds to most inquiries immediately (unless further research is required). *PAS Reports* available for a nominal fee; books must be purchased through the Planners Bookstore, Chicago. Price lists are available from Public Information Department. "Most of the materials cannot be removed from the library." **Tips:** "Most requests come from members or subscribers to *PAS*, therefore the research center is geared toward a specialized audience rather than the general public. General requests should be directed to the Public Information Department in the Washington office."

340• AMERICAN SOLAR ENERGY SOCIETY, INC.
110 W. 34th St., New York NY 10001. (212)736-8727. Contact Person: Director of Publications. **Description:** "We promote the wide use of solar energy through science and technology, education, basic and applied research, and dissemination of information about solar energy." **Services:** Provides advisory, bibliographical, referral and technical information. Offers annual reports, informational newsletters and placement on mailing lists. "We offer published materials which provide technical details of ongoing research and development in every aspect of solar energy; conferences present technical materials and provide industry with an opportunity to expose new developments and viable products." Publications include: *Membership Directory* ($45; includes names, addresses, telephone numbers of leading researchers, manufacturers, consultants, etc.). **How to Contact:** Write or call. Responds to most inquiries within a week. Charges for publications, conference registration, mailing lists. **Tips:** "Wide background reading is invaluable for a good beginning. Attend conferences and meet leading researchers in solar energy R&D."

341• AMERICAN UNDERGROUND-SPACE ASSOCIATION
University of Minnesota, 221 Church St. SE, Minneapolis MN 55455. (612)376-5580. Contact Person: Executive Director. **Description:** "We promote recognition of the potential of earth sheltered and deep underground space use; provide forum for exchange of information among the many different disciplines involved; further analysis, research and distribution of information on technical, environmental, legal, economic, social and political aspects of underground space use; provide recognition to persons and organizations with a professional interest in the field." **Services:** Provides advisory, analytical, bibliographical, historical, how-to, interpretative, referral, technical and trade information on all aspects of underground space use. Offers aid in arranging interviews, brochures/pamphlets, computerized information searches, informational newsletters, placement on mailing lists, research assistance, telephone reference services, publications, conferences, seminars, and design competitions. Publications include *Underground Space* (bimonthly journal); newsletter; books; technical notes; reprints—such as proceedings of conferences, outstanding examples from design competitions and results of research by members; publications list. **How to Contact:** Write, call or visit. Responds to most

inquiries immediately. Charges for publications, conferences, seminars, computer printouts, mailing labels. "Give proper credit to us and keep us informed of results." **Tips:** "Take advantage of information already developed by others. Write or phone us to obtain our brochures and publication lists, or to get help on specific information needs." Recent information requests: Advantage of underground storage facility compared with surface facility; extent of use of earth sheltered housing in China; source of information on earth sheltered construction in writer's local area.

342• AMERICAN WATER RESOURCES ASSOCIATION
5410 Grosvenor Lane, Bethesda MD 20814. Contact Person: Executive Director. **Description:** "The American Water Resources Association is a nonprofit scientific organization devoted to the advancement of water resources research, planning, development, management and education. Additionally, the association presents annual meeting forums for persons in the field of water resources and disseminates ideas and information in the field of water resources science and technology through the publications of the association." **Services:** Provides technical information on all aspects of water resources. Offers aid in arranging interviews, brochures/pamphlets and placement on mailing list. Publications include membership brochures and news releases. **How to Contact:** Write or call. Responds to most inquiries immediately. Charges "if extensive time is required of staff personnel for assistance; however, we would attempt to provide information and limited services on a gratis basis if at all possible. Writers are restricted from using any copyrighted material without permission of the organization. Additionally, services requested should be outlined in detail in order to keep assistance time to a minimum."

343• AMERICAN WIND ENERGY ASSOCIATION
2010 Massachusetts Ave. NW, Washington DC 20036. (202)775-8910. Contact Person: Executive Director. **Description:** "AWEA is the trade association for the wind energy industry." **Services:** Provides referral and trade information on wind energy. Offers brochures/pamphlets, informational newsletters (samples), photos (limited number) and research assistance. **How to Contact:** Write or call. Reponds to most inquiries within a week. Charges for general information brochures ($2); copying costs if extensive. **Tips:** "AWEA has a limited staff; information services basically limited to referrals to expert sources within the industry. Be specific with inquiries; explain purpose of article." Recent information requests: Comments on future of wind energy industry; sources for statistics on the market.

344• AMERICANS FOR ENERGY INDEPENDENCE
1629 K Street NW, # 1201, Washington DC 20006. (202)466-2105. Contact Person: Executive Director. **Description:** "AFEI is a nonprofit energy policy organization working to educate policymakers and the general public about the need to decrease our dependence on foreign oil." **Services:** Provides advisory, historical, interpretative and referral information on all aspects of energy policy both domestic and international. Offers aid in arranging interviews, brochures/pamphlets, informational newsletters, placement on mailing lists and telephone reference services. **How to Contact:** Write or call. Responds to most inquiries immediately. Give credit to AFEI. **Tips:** "Be sure to get all sides and opinions on a subject or issue." Recent information request: "What do trends in oil usage mean to the future of OPEC?"

345• AQUATIC RESEARCH INSTITUTE LIBRARY
2242 Davis Ct., Hayward CA 94545. Contact Person: Librarian. **Description:** Library includes information on marine biology, fish and fisheries, aquaculture, limnology and related subjects; also archival materials. **Services:** Provides information on all phases of aquaculture, aquaristic matters, marine biology, water research and limnology—natural science subjects related to the freshwater and marine environment. **How to Contact:** Write or visit. Responds to most inquiries within a week. "No journals or reprints can be issued out of the library, all material utilized within the library (except photocopies)."

346• ASHLAND OIL, INC.
1401 Winchester Ave., Ashland KY 41101. Contact Person: Director, Public Relations. **Description:** "Ashland Oil, Inc. is the 35th largest corporation in the United States. Major operating divisions include Ashland Petroleum Company which transports crude oil and refined products and markets petroleum products; Valvoline Oil company which markets broad lines of automotive lubricants, chemicals and filters; Ashland Chemical Company which manufacturers and distrib-

utes a variety of specialty chemicals including foundry products, industrial chemicals and solvents, carbon black, resins, plastics, and petrochemicals. Through wholly owned and affiliated companies, Ashland Oil has become the fifth largest coal producer in the United States with mines in southwestern Illinois, Wyoming, Alabama and Appalachia." **Services:** Provides advisory, analytical, bibliographical, historical, how-to, interpretative, referral, technical and trade information. Offers aid in arranging interviews, annual reports, biographies, statistics, brochures/pamphlets, placement on mailing list, newsletter, photos, press conferences and background information to news editors/directors. **How to Contact:** Write or call. Responds to most inquiries immediately.

347• ASSOCIATION FOR CONSERVATION INFORMATION (ACI)
458 Lowell Blvd. Denver CO 80204. (303)934-6734. Contact Person: Editor. **Description:** "We are an organization which deals in keeping information and education personnel in state and provincial conservation agencies (mainly hunting, fishing and parks) informed on ways and means of keeping the public informed on the latest developments in hunting, fishing, and other forms of outdoor activities (including hiking, backpacking, camping, bird-watching, nature hikes and studies, etc.). The ACI itself does not distribute this information to the public. The member agencies keep each other informed through our publication, *The Balance Wheel*, on what we are doing in the form of publications or electronic media to keep the general public informed and educated." **Services:** Offers information on where to get information. "As an organization, we have no leaflets, pamphlets, booklets or any other form of information. But our member states and provinces have informational material on a wide variety of subjects in the outdoor recreational field and the conservation of our wildlife resources. Interested parties can get information more quickly by contacting state or federal conservation (mainly hunting, fishing and parks) departments directly." **How to Contact:** Write or call. Responds to most inquiries immediately. **Tips:** Recent information request: Inquiry about various conservation publications.

348• BUREAU OF LAND MANAGEMENT
Office of Public Affairs, Department of the Interior, Washington DC 20240. Contact Person: Director of Public Affairs. **Description:** The bureau is responsible for the management of public lands, including resources management and the sale of public lands. **Services:** Offers information and photos on the management of 473 million acres of national resource lands (public domain) mostly in 10 western states and Alaska; on forest, range, water, wildlife and recreation resources; on resource uses, including camping, hunting, fishing, hiking, rock hunting and off-road vehicle use; and on primitive, historic, natural and scenic areas. **How to Contact:** Write or call. Responds to most inquiries immediately. **Tips:** "Written inquiries are helpful. Be specific." Recent information requests: "Many questions on oil and gas leasing, and the sale of public lands."

349• BUREAU OF MINES
Department of the Interior, 2401 E St. NW, Washington DC 20241. (202)634-1004. Contact Person: Chief, Office of Technical Information. **Description:** "The Bureau of Mines is a research and statistics agency. We conduct scientific and engineering research in metallurgy and mining, compile and analyze statistical information on nonfuel mineral supply and demand, and investigate mineral potential of federal lands proposed for preservation as parks, refuges and other special purposes. Because of a series of US government reorganizations, several important functions historically associated with the Bureau of Mines have been transferred out of the bureau and reassigned to newly-established federal agencies. Mine safety regulations and inspections are now the responsibility of the Labor Department's Mine Safety and Health Administration, although mine safety and health research is still the responsibility of the Bureau of Mines. All Bureau of Mines programs directly concerned with energy (fuel statistics, technology of oil, coal and natural gas production and use) have been transferred to the Department of Energy." **Services:** Provides advisory, analytical, interpretative, referral and technical information on mineral resources, mining, mine health and safety research, mineral economics, mineral statistics, explosives, recycling, mine reclamation research, metallurgy and mineral extraction research. Offers aid in arranging interviews, annual reports, statistics, brochures/pamphlets, placement on mailing list, informational motion pictures on mineral subjects, and free subscriptions to a monthly list of new Bureau of Mines technical publications. Publications include "popular-style descriptive booklets on the bureau and its programs"; *Mineral Commodity Summaries*, (free on request from Bureau of Mines); and other material available through the Government Printing Office, including *Dictionary of Mining, Mineral and Related Terms* and *Mineral Facts and Problems*. **How to**

Contact: Write or call. Responds to most inquiries within a week. "We basically provide information and access to subject-matter experts. We do not perform research for inquirers, and cannot (except in unusual circumstances) provide photographs. Many reports are distributed by the bureau without charge, and many university and federal depository libraries keep a complete file of Bureau of Mines publications. Other bureau reports are issued on a sales basis by the Government Printing Office. Reprints and papers or microfiche copies of unpublished 'open file reports' are sold by the Commerce Department's National Technical Information Service, Springfield VA 22161." **Tips:** "Be as specific as possible about what you need to know. Formulate your questions as clearly as possible, and then be persistent in pursuing answers." Recent information request: Inquiry about milling and smelting operations in Nevada.

350• BUREAU OF RECLAMATION
Department of the Interior, Public Affairs Center, Denver Federal Center, Bldg. 67, Denver CO 80225. (303)234-6260. Contact Person: Media Relations Officer. **Description:** "The Bureau of Reclamation is the primary water resource development agency of the federal government operating in the 17 western states. We construct dams and other water conveyances. Our reservoirs are used for numerous kinds of recreation, such as boating, fishing, water skiing, camping and sightseeing. We are conducting research in new sources of energy, such as solar, wind and geothermal." **Services:** Provides historical, interpretative, referral, technical and trade information; literature on most bureau dams (descriptions, features). Offers aid in arranging interviews, annual reports, biographies, statistics, brochures/pamphlets, limited information searches, placement on mailing list, newsletter, photos and press kits. **How to Contact:** Write or call. Responds to most inquiries immediately. **Tips:** "We are eager to assist. If we know the publication/media involved, we can tailor material to its needs and provide art/illustrations to complement the text." Recent information request: One-page status reports on seven projects currently under construction.

351• CAREIRS: CONSERVATION AND RENEWABLE ENERGY INQUIRY AND REFERRAL SERVICE
Box 8900, Silver Spring MD 20907. (800)523-2929, U.S., including Virgin Islands, Puerto Rico; (800)462-4983, Pennsylvania. Contact Person: Information Analyst. **Description:** "CAREIRS is operated for the Department of Energy by the Franklin Research Center. It is a clearinghouse for information on energy conservation and renewable energy." **Services:** Provides bibliographical, how-to and referral information on energy conservation and renewable technologies, such as solar, photovoltaics, wind, wood, bioconversion, solar thermal, geothermal, ocean energy, alcohol fuels, and small scale hydropower. Offers brochures/pamphlets and press kits. Publications include fact sheets, bibliographies and brochures. **How to Contact:** Write or call. Responds to most inquiries within a week. "CAREIRS cannot make political comments (i.e., DOE budget, etc.)." **Tips:** "Try to avoid calling on deadline." Recent information requests: Federal tax credits; general data on renewable energy.

352• CARNEGIE INSTITUTE: MUSEUM OF ART, CARNEGIE MUSEUM OF NATURAL HISTORY
4400 Forbes Ave., Pittsburgh PA 15213. (412)622-3328. Contact Person: Communications Coordinator. **Description:** "The museum collects and exhibits art and natural history objects for the general public. We are noted worldwide for our dinosaur collection." **Services:** Provides referral and trade information covering art, health/medicine, history, nature, science and technical data. Offers aid in arranging interviews, annual reports, biographies, brochures/pamphlets, placement on mailing list, statistics, newsletter, photo and press kits. **How to Contact:** Write. Responds to most inquiries within a week. **Tips:** Recent information request: "What ongoing research is being carried out by curatorial staffs at the Carnegie Institute?"

353• CENTRAL ABSTRACTING & INDEXING SERVICE
American Petroleum Institute, 156 William St., New York NY 10038. (212)587-9660. Contact Person: Assistant Manager. **Description:** "Our department monitors technical journals and business news publications of importance to the petroleum industry to call attention to pertinent new developments, and to create an archival index to the information in these publications." **Services:** Provides bibliographical and trade information covering petroleum and alternative energy technolgy and petroleum-related business news. Offers information searches. **How to Contact:** Write. Responds to most inquiries immediately. Charges $195 for

literature information search. **Tips:** Recent information request: Locate recent literature related to exhaust emissions from diesel engines.

354• CITIZENS' ENERGY PROJECT
1110 6th St. NW, 3rd Floor, Washington DC 20001. (202)289-4999. Contact Person: Coordinator. **Description:** "Citizens' Energy project is a nonprofit research group that conducts research in the areas of energy policy (primarily pro-solar and anti-nuclear), environmental protection and consumer safety, and appropriate technologies. We are also an advocacy and organizing group working to promote alternative energy technologies and to help localities to become energy self-reliant through the development of indigenous renewable resources." **Services:** Provides advisory, bibliographical, how-to, referral and technical information on energy policy in general, more specifically solar energy with an emphasis on passive solar energy technologies and policies. Offers bibliographies, brochures/pamphlets, placement on mailing list and newsletter. **How to Contact:** Write. Responds to most inquiries within a week. "Consulting is free if limited, charged for if extensive; the rate depends on the task." **Tips:** "Know your subject well and be critical of any information received; always be prepared to be a gadfly or to play devil's advocate." Recent information request: Inquiry on sources of information on a specific aspect of solar energy policy.

355• CITIZENS FOR A BETTER ENVIRONMENT
59 E. Van Buren, Chicago IL 60605. (312)939-1530. Contact Person: Director, Environmental Reference Center. **Description:** "We research environmental problems; provide citizens with the technical assistance they need to solve these problems; interact with government agencies working to protect the environment." **Services:** Provides advisory, referral and technical information on hazardous wastes, pesticides, air pollution, water pollution, toxic substances, energy policy. Offers informational newsletters and research assistance. Publications include *CBE Environmental Review*; CBE Comments; *CBE Research Reports*. **How to Contact:** Write, call or visit. Responds to most inquiries within a week. Charges for postage if information is mailed; and/or photocopying. *CBE Environmental Review*, $15/year subscription. "We will not do a writer's research for him/her; we will provide information and advice." **Tips:** "Be specific; carefully define the parameters of your question." Recent information request: "Pesticide X has just been sprayed in our community. What can you tell me about its hazards?"

356• CONCERN, INC.
1794 Columbia Rd. NW, Washington DC 20009. (202)328-8160. Contact Person: Office Manager. **Description:** "Our purpose is to promote public awareness of environmental issues and to recommend appropriate citizen action. Guides called eco-tips cover drinking water, land use, toxic substances, hazardous waste, acid rain, protection of wetlands and oceans." **Services:** Offers brochures/pamphlets, information searches and newsletters. Write for publication price list. Publications include pamphlet on air and water. **How to Contact:** Write. Responds to most inquiries within 2 weeks. "All material is copyrighted and a credit line is required." **Tips:** "Be very specific in requesting information." Recent information request: Questions about hazardous waste landfills.

357• CONSERVATION AND RESEARCH FOUNDATION, INC.
Box 1445, Connecticut College, New London CT 06320. (203)873-8514. Contact Person: President. **Description:** The Foundation works "to promote conservation of the earth's natural resources, to encourage research in the biological sciences, and to deepen understanding of the entire relationship between man and the environment that supports him. We make research and facilitating grants." **Services:** Offers brochures/pamphlets. **How to Contact:** Write or call. Responds to most inquiries within a week. **Tips:** "We have a very small staff and are basically a fund-granting organization."

358• THE CONSERVATION FOUNDATION
1717 Massachusetts Ave. NW, Washington DC 20036. (202)797-4300. Contact Person: Librarian. **Description:** "Since its founding in 1948, the Conservation Foundation has attempted to provide intellectual leadership in the cause of wise management of the earth's resources—its land, air, water and energy." **Services:** Offers annual reports, placement on mailing list and newsletter. Maintaines a library of 7,000 volumes. "The Conservation Foundation regularly publishes books and issues reports on a number of environmental subjects." Publications include

The Conservation Foundation Newsletter (monthly) and *Resolve* (quarterly). **How to Contact:** Write or call. Reponse time "depends on the seriousness of the request. If it's a phone call we try to take care of it immediately. We will try to put writers in touch with the foundation staff members who can respond to their questions, or who would be available for interviews." Charges for books and the newsletter. **Tips:** "The Conservation Foundation might be most useful to writers who are looking for a reaction, or expert response, to some environmental issue of the day. The foundation may not know the specifics of the issue—unless it has conducted research in that area—but may have helpful observations to make regarding the general issue involved."

359• DEPARTMENT OF ENERGY
Office of Public Affairs, 1000 Independence Ave. SW, Washington DC 20585. (202)252-5568. Contact: Information Branch. **Description:** "We answer public and private inquiries and help educate the public about energy topics; we don't provide statistical data as that is available from the National Energy Information Center (202)252-8800. We provide walk-in service for Department of Energy publications and this office is a clearinghouse for policy statements issued by the department's offices." **Services:** Offers information of a general nature related to energy matters. **How to Contact:** Write or call; prefers written requests. Responds to most inquiries within a month. **Tips:** Recent information requests: Background on the new fusion program, geothermal energy, the nuclear program, etc.

360• DEPARTMENT OF THE INTERIOR
Interior Bldg., Washington DC 20240. (202)343-7220. Contact Person: Director of Public Affairs. **Description:** The nation's principal conservation agency, with responsibilities for energy, water, fish, wildlife, mineral, land, park, and recreational resources, and Indian and territorial affairs. **Services:** Provides advisory, bibliographical, historical, interpretative and referral information covering all concerns of the Department of the Interior. **How to Contact:** Requests for information should be directed to the office most concerned with specific subjects of interest. Responds to most inquiries within a week. Work done for writers is handled on a "time available basis." **Tips:** "Individual bureaus in the department are the best source of specifics." These include: National Park Service; US Fish & Wildlife Service; Bureau of Land Management; Bureau of Reclamation; Office of Water Research & Technology; Geological Survey; Bureau of Mines; Office of Surface Mining; Bureau of Indian Affairs; Office of Territories & International Affairs. "Do basic research in the library before asking us questions." Recent information request: "What is the department's policy on snowmobiling in national parks?"

361• EARTHSCAN/INTERNATIONAL INSTITUTE FOR ENVIRONMENT AND DEVELOPMENT
1319 F St. NW, Suite 800, Washington DC 20004. (202)462-0900. Contact Person: Washington Bureau Chief. **Description:** News and information service on development and environment issues. **Services:** Provides analytical and interpretative information on Third World development and environment issues. Offers informational newsletters, photos, placement on mailing lists and press kits. "We provide journalists with briefing documents on environment and development issues." **How to Contact:** Write or call. Responds to most inquiries within a week. Charges for services to individuals, not journalists. "Our primary interest is to specialist journalists on environment and development issues." **Tips:** Recent information request: Material on the destruction of tropical forests.

362• EARTHWATCH: FIELD RESEARCH CORPS
10 JuniperRd., Box 127, Belmont MA 02178. (617)489-3030. Contact Person: Director of Communications. **Description:** "We are a nonprofit organization offering members of the public the chance to join noted university and museum professionals on field research expeditions in archaeology, marine biology, geology, zoology, etc. worldwide. Our purpose is both to facilitate and fund research and to promote public understanding of basic research." **Services:** Provides advisory, bibliographical, historical, interpretative and referral information. "We have sponsored over 450 expeditions in the earth, life, marine sciences and the humanities, and receive some 300 proposals a year from experts who seek Earthwatch volunteer help. About 85 projects each year are sponsored in 30 countries and 20 states. We can supply myriad story ideas as well as photographs." Offers aid in arranging interviews, brochures/pamphlets, photos, placement on mailing lists, press kits, research assistance (if it's research we've sponsored), and telephone reference services. Publications include our quarterly magazine, *Earthwatch News*, which

describes each of the projects we're recruiting people to help on each year, with articles by scientists and team members on progress in the field, discoveries, etc; also past field reports, and "Expedition Briefings" (50-60 pages) on each project. **How to Contact:** Write or call. Responds to most inquiries immediately. "We charge for use of photos if the story is not about our efforts." Complimentary issues of *Earthwatch News* are available upon request ($2 first class postage). **Tips:** "It's probably best to telephone, then we can tell you very quickly what sort of information we have before either of us goes to a lot of work." Recent information requests: "A freelancer wanted businessmen who were avid amateur archaeologists to interview. Another wanted to interview scientists doing research on barrier island migration. And we have some 6,000 veterans of research teams throughout the U.S. who make great candidates for 'unusual vacation' type local stories. Past scientists and team members are computerized for easy retrieval by interest or discipline."

363• ENVIRONMENTAL ACTION COALITION
417 Lafayette St., New York NY 10003. (212)677-1601. Contact Person: Executive Director. **Description:** "Environmental Action Coalition is concerned with environmental self-help and education." **Services:** Provides interpretative, referral and technical information on a wide variety of environmental topics. "In terms of staff expertise, most information centers around solid waste and hazardous/toxic wastes, urban forestry, water-related issues. Information on teaching environmental topics a specialty." Offers aid in arranging interviews, statistics, brochures/pamphlets, placement on mailing list, newsletter and press releases as needed. Publications include *Cycle*, membership newsletter; and *Echo*, children's newsletter. **How to Contact:** Write or call. "Detailed information requires written request." Responds to most inquiries within a week. **Tips:** "Be as specific in your needs for service as possible." Recent information request: "How many tons per day of solid waste is generated in (location)? How much of that is recyclable? How much *is* recycled? How is that done, physically and technically?"

364• ENVIRONMENTAL ACTION FOUNDATION
724 Dupont Circle Bldg., Washington DC 20036. Contact Person: Administrative Coordinator. **Description:** "EAF is a national, nonprofit public interest organization providing technical and organizing expertise to local activists tackling energy and pollution issues. Founded by organizers of Earth Day 1970." **Services:** Provides advisory, analytical, how-to, referral, technical and trade information on toxic substances, recycling, solid waste management, electric utility issues, nuclear power, solar energy, worker health and safety. Offers brochures/pamphlets, computerized information searches, informational newsletters, research assistance and telephone reference services. Publications include *Powerline* (energy issues, monthly, $15/year); and *Exposure* (pollution issues, monthly, $15/year). **How to Contact:** Write or call. Charges for publications. **Tips:** Recent information request: "Are the power lines in my backyard dangerous to my family's safety?"

365• ENVIRONMENTAL ACTION, INC.
1346 Connecticut Ave. NW, # 731, Washington DC 20036. (202)833-1845. Contact Person: Membership Coordinator. **Description:** "EA is a nonprofit, national environmental lobbying organization that seeks to improve the environment through political and social change. We educate our 25,000 members through *Environmental Action* magazine and legislative alerts, hold training workshops and conferences on our issues around the country, and provide a full range of consulting advice to groups and individuals." **Services:** Provides advisory, analytical, bibliographical, historical, how-to, interpretative, referral, technical and trade information on "pollution and energy issues as well as a full range of other environmental issues like housing, military spending and the nuclear freeze; what's happening in the environmental movement; what our members can do as citizen activists." Offers annual reports, brochures/pamphlets, computerized information searches, informational newsletters, placement on mailing lists, press kits and research assistance. Publications include *Environmental Action* magazine. **How to Contact:** Write. Responds to most inquiries within a week. Preferably writer/researcher using services should be a member/subscriber to magazine. "We will work with the media for pro-environmental coverage of issues." **Tips:** "Don't just ask one source for the information. Attack several sources at once, both to get a balanced viewpoint and also ensure getting the information. We appreciate recognition for our help—membership, positive quote in publication, etc. We have a listing of all groups in D.C. and around the country that have a national emphasis on the environment as a starting point. It can be purchased from us for 50¢. In trying to obtain

governmental information, it is probably better to start with a citizens' group (national). We've all been there before—probably.'' Recent information requests: "What was the worst oil spill in history and when did it take place?''; cities with departments of environmental protection.

366• ENVIRONMENTAL DEFENSE FUND
444 Park Ave. S., 9th Floor, New York NY 10016. (212)686-4191. Contact Person: Public Information Associate. **Description:** "We are a nonprofit national membership organization staffed by scientists, economists and attorneys whose purpose is to protect environmental quality and public health. EDF concentrates its efforts in these four areas: energy, toxic chemicals, water resources, wildlife." **Services:** Provides advisory, analytical, interpretative, referral, technical and trade information on ecology, water quality, air pollution, health effects of toxic chemicals, species extinction and protection, utility company investment analyses (alternative energy sources), etc. Offers aid in arranging interviews, annual reports, brochures/pamphlets, informational newsletters and press kits. Publications include *EDF Letter*, newsletter which describes EDF activities; numerous publications on toxic chemicals, utility and investment studies. **How to Contact:** Write or call. Responds to most inquiries immediately. **Tips:** Recent information requests: "What are you doing about acid rain, toxic dumpsites, endangered species, water pollution?''

367• ENVIRONMENTAL PROTECTION AGENCY
401 M St. NW, Rm 2404, Headquarters Library, Washington DC 20460. (202)755-0707. Contact: Public Information Center (PM 211B). **Description:** The US EPA "is engaged in pollution abatement and control and the protection and enhancement of the environment involving such programs as those for air, water, noise, pesticides, toxic substances, solid waste-resource recovery—hazardous waste disposal, and radiation." **Services:** Offers pamphlets/brochures; maintains library. Publications include popular booklets and leaflets on water and air pollution, solid waste management, radiation and pesticides control and noise abatement and control. **How to Contact:** Write. Responds to most inquiries within a week. **Tips:** "You need to be very precise on the information you want. For example, if you want information on ocean dumping, don't ask for information on water."

368• EXXON RESEARCH & ENGINEERING COMPANY
Public Affairs Division, 180 Park Ave., Florham Park NJ 07932. (201)765-2567. Contact Person: Media Relations Coordinator. **Description:** "ER&E is a wholly-owned subsidiary of Exxon Corp. with responsibility for conducting research, development and engineering activities in energy and chemical-related areas." **Services:** Provides technical information on petroleum products and processing; coal science; synthetic fuels; engineering planning, design, start-up and management; photovoltaics; combustion science; surface science; solid state physics; catalysis; metallurgy; laser science and the bio-sciences. Offers aid in arranging interviews, photos, placement on mailing lists and technical papers/presentations. **How to Contact:** Write. Responds to most inquiries within a week. **Tips:** "Questions should be as specific as possible." Recent information request: "What is Exxon doing in the area of coal characterization?''

369• FEDERAL ENERGY REGULATORY COMMISSION
825 N. Capitol St. NE, Washington DC 20426. Contact Person: Director of Public Information. **Description:** The commission regulates interstate aspects of natural gas and electric power industries, and licenses nonfederal hydroelectric power projects. **Services:** Offers lists of publications and special reports, and general information on regulatory activities. Media representatives may also receive, upon request, a complimentary copy of nonsubscription items on the publications list. **How to Contact:** Write. Responds to most inquiries within a week. **Tips:** Recent information requests: Names of commissioners; "What does the Commission do?''

370• FIELD MUSEUM OF NATURAL HISTORY
Roosevelt Rd. at Lake Shore Dr., Chicago IL 60605. (312)922-9410. Contact Person: Public Relations Manager. **Description:** "One of America's finest natural history museums; Field Museum presents public exhibits and sponsors research in the fields of anthropology, botany, geology and zoology." **Services:** Provies advisory and referral information on anthropology, botany, geology and zoology. Offers aid in arranging interviews, brochures/pamphlets, library facilities, photos and press kits. **How to Contact:** Write. Responds to most inquiries within a

month. Charges for photos and transparencies. **Tips:** "Library is available for reference use; public exhibits are available for photographing with available light upon request."

371• FOREST HISTORY SOCIETY, INC.
109 Coral St., Santa Cruz CA 95060. Contact Person: Librarian. **Description:** "We collect, interpret, publish and promote North American forest and conservation history." **Services:** Provides advisory, bibliographical, historical and referral information covering North American forest and conservation history. Offers bibliographies and newsletter. **How to Contact:** Write or call. Responds to most inquiries within a week. Charges for photocopying, photo duplication and extended use of staff time.

372• FOREST SERVICE
US Department of Agriculture, Box 2417, Washington, DC 20013. (202)447-4211. Contact Person: Press Officer. **Description:** "The Forest Service is dedicated to the principles of multiple-use management of the nation's forest resources for sustained yields of water, forage, wildlife, wood and recreation. Through management of the national forests and national grasslands, cooperation with states and private forest owners and forestry research, it strives, as directed by Congress, to provide increasingly greater service to a growing nation." **Services:** Provides advisory, factual, historical and referral information on forestry, forest resources and national forests. Offers reference services, reference information and news releases. **How to Contact:** Write or call. Responds to most inquiries within a week. **Tips:** "Be as specific as possible with your request." Recent information request: "I'm interested in writing about national forests in the state of —. Where can I get specific information?"

373• FREEPORT-MCMORAN, INC.
200 Park Ave., New York NY 10166. (212)578-9200. Contact Person: Public Relations Director. **Description:** "Freeport-McMoran, Inc., is engaged in the production of sulphur, phosphate rock, phosphoric acid, kaolin, copper, gold, silver, oil and gas, nickel, cobalt and uranium oxide." **Services:** Provides advisory, bibliographical, historical, how-to, interpretative, technical and trade information covering mining, natural resources and energy. Offers annual reports, biographies, statistics, brochures/pamphlets and photos. Publications include "general booklets on sulphur, phosphoric acid and kaolin and numerous reprints on Indonesian copper, offshore sulphur mining, etc. as well as films on sulphur and Indonesian copper." **How to Contact:** Write or call. Responds to most inquiries immediately. **Tips:** Recent information request: "How much energy is required to produce a ton of sulphur?"

374• GEOLOGICAL SURVEY
Department of the Interior, Information Office, National Center, Reston VA 22092. (703)860-7444. Contact Person: Information Officer. **Description:** "Major federal earth science research agency. Through field and lab studies and investigations, obtains fundamental data and makes assessments of the nation's mineral, energy, and water resources. Programs include resource estimates, mapping, studies of surface and ground water, studies of geologic hazards (earthquakes, volcanoes, landslides, subsidence and glaciers)." **Services:** Offers "news media services: press releases, backgrounders, news photos, arranges interviews, etc." Publications include a variety of nontechnical leaflets, and writers may request press release mailings. **How to Contact:** Write or call. Responds to most inquiries immediately. "We would be pleased to receive inquiries from any writer on general earth science subjects, including natural resources and environmental monitoring." **Tips:** "Be specific about what you want."

375• INDEPENDENT PETROLEUM ASSOCIATION OF AMERICA
1101 16th St. NW, Washington DC 20036. (202)857-4722. Contact Person: Director of Communications. **Description:** "The Independent Petroleum Association of America (IPAA) is a Washington-based association representing 7,000 independent producers of domestic crude oil and natural gas. IPAA is dedicated to the advancement of an aggressive, competitive domestic petroleum industry to assure increased production of oil and gas for an expanding economy and national security. Its functions include congressional relations, federal departmental and agency liaison, and public information. It is a non-profit organization." **Services:** Provides trade information on crude oil and natural gas—economics, industry and energy. Offers aid in arranging interviews, statistics and brochures/pamphlets. Publications include *Petroleum Independent* (bimonthly magazine) and *The Oil Producing Industry in Your State*. **How to Contact:** "For

statistical information, call (202)857-4760. For booklets and press information, call (202)857-4770.'' Responds to most inquiries within a week.

376• INTERNATIONAL OCEANOGRAPHIC FOUNDATION (IOF)
3979 Rickenbacker Causeway, Virginia Key, Miami FL 33149. (305)361-5786. Contact Person: *Sea Secrets* Editor. **Description:** IOF is a nonprofit foundation that educates the public concerning the marine sciences through publication of the periodicals *Sea Frontiers* and *Sea Secrets*, membership information service, film rentals, book discounts, etc., and the educational exposition Planet Ocean. **Services:** Provides advisory, bibliographical and referral information covering marine sciences. **How to Contact:** Write or call. Responds to most inquiries within a month, ''depending on the type of inquiry.'' Services free to members of the foundation. Current US membership $15/person. ''Answers to members' questions are primarily reference lists, but specific questions are answered, if possible.'' **Tips:** ''Be specific in wording your inquiry. Send only *duplicate* transparencies for identification; send only *preserved* marine specimens for identification. SASE for reply. Recent information requests (answered in *Sea Secrets* May-June 1982): ''Has anyone succeeded in cloning fishes?''; ''If I find a piece of ambergris on the beach, who would buy it?''

377• KEEP AMERICA BEAUTIFUL, INC.
99 Park Ave., New York NY 10016. (212)682-4564. Contact Person: Public Information Coordinator. **Description:** ''We are a national nonprofit, nonpartisan, service organization founded in 1953 to work with civic groups, government agencies, private industry and academic institutions, to stimulate individual involvement in community improvement. We are meeting our objectives through the Clean Community System, the behavioral approach to waste handling now being implemented in more than 270 cities and counties in America.'' **Services:** Provides advisory, how-to, interpretative and referral information covering litter, recycling, solid waste management, community improvement. Offers aid in arranging interviews, annual reports, brochures/pamphlets, placement on mailing list, statistics, newsletter, photos and press kits. **How to Contact:** Write or call. Responds to most inquiries within a week. Charges for materials only. Requires credit be given to Keep America Beautiful, Inc. **Tips:** Recent information request: background on successful community improvement programs.

378• LIBRARY OF CONGRESS, GEOGRAPHY AND MAP DIVISION
10 1st St. SE, (LM B-01), Washington DC 20540. (202)287-6277. Contact Person: Librarian. **Description:** The Geography and Map Division ''offers library services for a comprehensive cartographic and geographic collection; and contributes to scholarship in the above fields through a publication program.'' **Services:** Provides bibliographical and referral information on geography, cartography and historical cartography and geography. Offers brochures/pamphlets, journal and newspaper clipping file, library facilities, telephone reference services and photoduplication services. Publications list available. **How to Contact:** Write, call or visit. Responds to most inquiries within a month. Researchers/writers must be 18 years of age or older to use the division's services.

379• MARINE TECHNOLOGY SOCIETY
1730 M St. NW, Suite 412, Washington DC 20036. (202)659-3251. Contact Person: Executive Director. **Description:** ''The society's purpose is the dissemination of marine science and technical information. MTS is concerned with the application of science and technology to the exploration and utilization of the oceans.'' **Services:** Provides advisory, referral and technical information on buoy technology, cables and connectors, coastal zone management, diving, education, geology and geophysics, marine biology, marine fisheries, marine food and drug resources, marine geodesy, marine law and policy, marine materials, marine mineral resources, marine power systems, marine salvage and towing, ocean economic potential, ocean energy, oceanographic instrumentation, oceanographic ships, offshore structures, satellite and aircraft remote sensing, seafloor engineering, technology exchange, undersea vehicles, undersea physics, underwater photography and sensing, water quality. Offers aid in arranging interviews, library facilities (limited), placement on mailing lists, research assistance and telephone reference services. Publications include *Marine Technology Society Journal* (quarterly); articles from proceedings of conferences and workshops. **How to Contact:** Write, call or visit. Responds to most inquiries within a week. No charge for services unless inquiry is overly time consuming. Preference is given to members. **Tips:** ''Requests for information should be of a specific nature.'' Recent information request: ''Where can I find information on deep-sea mining?''

380• MOBIL CORPORATION
150 E. 42nd St., New York NY 10017. (212)883-4408. Contact Person: Press Relations Coordinator. **Description:** "We are the second largest energy company in the United States. Mobil Corporation (formed July 1, 1976) owns Mobil Oil Corp. (including worldwide energy interests and growth-oriented chemical interests), Montgomery Ward (one of the largest retailers) and Container Corp. of America (the leading United States manufacturer of paperboard packaging)." **Services:** Offers aid in arranging interviews (Mobil Oil only), annual reports (all companies), brochures/pamphlets (Mobil Oil only), statistics (all companies) and press kits. **How to Contact:** Write.

381• MUSEUM OF GEOLOGY
South Dakota School of Mining & Technology, Rapid City SD 57701. (605)394-2467. Contact Person: Director. **Description:** "We collect, preserve and interpret the geologic diversity of the past." **Services:** Provides advisory, how-to, interpretative, referral and technical information. Offers library facilities, photos and research assistance. **How to Contact:** Write. "If the request is directly related to museum collections and activities there is no charge. Background information of a more general nature will be charged at a negotiated rate per hour or per job." **Tips:** "Have more than one authority check facts and interpretations." Recent information request: "What dinosaurs lived in North America?"

382• NATIONAL ASSOCIATION OF NOISE CONTROL OFFICIALS (NANCO)
Box 2618, Ft. Walton Beach FL 32549. (904)243-8129. Contact Person: Director of Information Services. For publications, contact: Executive Director. **Description:** "NANCO is a nonprofit association dedicated to environmental noise control. It provides a mechanism for free exchange of information; promotes laws to control noise pollution and the most effective methods for noise measurement and analysis; cooperates with industry and the scientific community." **Services:** Provides bibliographical, referral and technical information on environmental noise and methods to control it; and health effects of noise. Offers brochures/pamphlets, informational newsletters, and center collection of documents. Publications include *Noise Effects Handbook/A Desk Reference to Health and Welfare Effects of Noise*; *Vibrations* (monthly). **How to Contact:** Write. Responds to most inquiries immediately. Charges for photocopying, postage and handling. **Tips:** "Only specific questions can be answered or referred, because of staff limitations. No research assistance."

383• NATIONAL AUDUBON SOCIETY
950 3rd Ave., New York NY 10022. (212)832-3200. Contact: Information Services Department. **Description:** Individuals interested in conservation of the environment, ecology and restoration of natural resources. **Services:** Provides historical, interpretative, referral, and technical information on endangered species, land preservation, pollution, natural history. Offers brochures/pamphlets, library facilities, placement on mailing lists. Publications include *From Outrage to Action* (history); *Selling the Bugs Out* (wise use of pesticides); fact sheets. **How to Contact:** Write (preferred) or call. Responds to most inquiries within a week. Charges for library services and some science books.

384• NATIONAL COAL ASSOCIATION
1130 17th St. NW, Washington DC 20036. (202)463-2641. Contact Person: Director of Media Relations. **Description:** Offers 2,000 photos, "mostly b&w shots of bituminous coal production, transportation and use, and reclamation of mined land. Some color transparencies of coal production, many showing land reclamation. Most are modern—no historical pix." **How to Contact:** Write or call. Responds to most inquiries within a month. Charges $15/photo for commercial use. Credit line required.

385• NATIONAL ENERGY INFORMATION CENTER
EI 20, 1000 Independence Ave. SW, Room 1F-048, Forrestal Bldg., Washington DC 20585. (202)252-8800. **Description:** The NEIC provides ready reference information related to energy concerns. **Services:** Provides bibliographical and referral information on Energy Information Administration (EIA) publications covering "energy production, consumption, prices and resource availability, as well as projections of energy supply and demand." Offers computerized information searches, publications directories, information directories and Energy Fact Sheets. **How to Contact:** Write, call or visit. Charges for publications. "Reference copies of EIA

publications are available for research use in the NEIC reading room.'' **Tips:** ''The NEIC maintains a reference center housing a variety of reference works, trade journals, newsletters, reports and vertical file materials useful in responding to statistical and general inquiries. Vertical file materials include pamphlets, policy statements, testimony and articles filed by subject. DATALINE supplies key energy data from upcoming EIA publications. Messages are recorded each week and average 2-3 minutes in length. Dial (202)252-NEIC.''

386• NATIONAL MAP COLLECTION AND NATIONAL ARCHITECTURAL ARCHIVES
Public Archives of Canada, 395 Wellington St., Ottawa, Ontario, Canada K1A 0N3. (613)995-1077. Contact Person: Director. **Description:** Canadian Archives whose purposes are the acquisition of, custody of, and provision of reference service to Canada's cartographical and architectural records, both public and private. The National Map Collection has holdings of approximately 1 million items. **Services:** Provides bibliographical, historical and interpretative information on the history of cartography, Canadian cartography and Canadian architecture. Offers library facilities, photos, research assistance and telephone reference services. Publications list available. **How to Contact:** Write, call or visit. Responds to most inquiries within a month. Charges for photos, photocopying and some publications. ''Restrictions may apply to the use/copying of material which may be in poor physical condition; which have restrictions placed by donors, or which are in current production.'' **Tips:** ''Please contact us by letter or phone prior to your arrival. Large parts of our holdings are stored in other buildings, so there may be delays in providing material for your use.'' Recent information requests: The contribution of the Amerindians to mapping of North America; location of prisoner of war camps in Canada during World War II; plans of ships used during the War of 1812.

387• NATIONAL MUSEUM OF NATURAL HISTORY
Smithsonian Institution, 10th St. & Constitution Ave. NW, Washington DC 20560. (202)357-2458. Contact Person: Public Information Officer. **Description:** ''The Museum's public areas house permanent and special exhibitions of natural history and anthropology. Behind-the-scenes, a staff of more than 100 scientists manage and conduct research on the Museum's national collections, made up of over 60 million plants, animals, rocks and minerals, fossils, and man's cultural artifacts.'' **Services:** Provides advisory and referral information on all museum activities. ''Offers aid to media in obtaining museum press releases and photographs relating to exhibitions and scientific work. Advises media on museum activities and publications and helps arrange interviews with museum administrators, exhibit and scientific experts.'' **How to Contact:** Write or call. Responds to most inquiries immediately.

388• NATIONAL OCEANIC AND ATMOSPHERIC ADMINISTRATION
11400 Rockville Pike, Rockville MD 20852. (301)443-8243. Contact: Headquarters Public Affairs. **Description:** ''This is a major civilian agency in the provision of scientific services and research in oceanography and marine and atmospheric sciences.'' Components include the National Weather Service, National Ocean Survey, National Marine Fisheries Service, National Environmental Satellite Service, Environmental Data and Information Service, Office of Coastal and Ocean Management, Office of Sea Grant, and the National Oceanic and Atmospheric Administration (NOAA) Corps. **Services:** Offers aid in arranging interviews, biographies, statistics, brochures/pamphlets, placement on mailing list, and photos. ''Brochures are available on all forms of severe weather (tornadoes, hurricanes, etc.), commercial fisheries, scientific research in the ocean and atmospheric sciences.'' **How to Contact:** ''Write or call for a NOAA brochure describing the agency's range of activities. Responds to most inquiries immediately. If face-to-face interviews are needed, arrangements can be made.'' **Tips:** ''Recent information request: Statistics on US fisheries.

389• NATIONAL PARKS AND CONSERVATION ASSOCIATION
1701 18th St. NW, Washington DC 20009. (202)265-2717. Contact Person: Public Information Officer. **Description:** The National Parks and Conservation Association is concerned with the ''preservation of national parks, wildlife, and the history of general conservation issues.'' **Services:** Provides historical, how-to and interpretative information on the National Park System and related areas including nature, recreation, appreciation pieces, issue pieces (threats to parks), proposed park units. Offers occasional reports. **How to Contact:** Write and include SASE. Responds to most inquiries within 2 weeks. Charges $3/copy of magazine.

390• NATIONAL PETROLEUM COUNCIL
1625 K St. NW, Washington DC 20006. (202)393-6100. Contact Person: Director of Information. **Description:** "The National Petroleum Council advises, informs and makes recommendations to the Secretary of the Interior on any matter relating to petroleum or the petroleum industry. Members of the National Petroleum Council are appointed by the Secretary of the Interior and represent all segments of petroleum interests." **Services:** Provides information covering economics, industry and technical data. Offers placement on mailing list and publications. Publications include *US Arctic Oil and Gas*; *Environmental Conservation* and others. **How to Contact:** Write. Charges for publications. **Tips:** "The council does not maintain any statistics on an ongoing basis. Several of the council's reports are statistically oriented, however."

391• NATIONAL SPELEOLOGICAL SOCIETY, INC.
2813 Cave Ave., Huntsville AL 35810. (205)852-1300. Contact Person: Public Relations Chairman. (214)742-3447 or 814-2965. **Description:** "The National Speleological Society is an organization dedicated to the study, exploration and conservation of caves. Our activities are as diverse as our membership. Membership is made up of cave scientists, conservationists, cave owners and cave explorers." Works to prevent exploitation of caves. **Services:** Provides advisory and historical information on caves and related phenomena. Offers brochures/pamphlets. Maintains library of 24,000 volumes on geology, biology, mineralogy and related subjects. **How to Contact:** Write or call. Responds to most inquiries within a week.

392• NATIONAL WEATHER SERVICE
National Oceanic and Atmospheric Administration, Department of Commerce, 8060 13th St., Silver Spring MD 20910. Contact Person: Public Affairs Officer. **Description:** The Weather Service reports the weather of the US and its possessions; provides weather forecasts to the general public; and issues warnings against tornadoes, hurricanes, floods, and other weather hazards. **Services:** Offers specialized information which supports the needs of agricultural, aeronautical, maritime and space operations. Some 300 weather service offices in cities across the land maintain close contact with the general public to ensure prompt and useful dissemination of weather information. **How to Contact:** Write. Responds to most inquiries within a month. Agency publications may be purchased from Superintendent of Documents, Government Printing Office, Washington DC 20402.

393• NATIONAL WILDLIFE FEDERATION
1412 16th St. NW, Washington DC 20036. Contact Person: Director of Public Affairs. **Description:** "A nonprofit, conservation education organization, dedicated to encouraging public awareness of the wise use, proper management and conservation of the natural resources upon which all life depend: air, water, soil, minerals, forest, plant life and wildlife." **Services:** Provides analytical, bibliographical, how-to, interpretative, referral (to in-house experts) and technical information covering natural resource issues, analysis of government agencies (EPA, Interior, US Forest Service), wildlife, pollution (air and water). Offers aid in arranging interviews, bibliographies, statistics, brochures/pamphlets, placement on mailing list and several newsletters on different subjects. **How to Contact:** Write or call. "To get listing of materials, write for bibliography." Responds to most inquiries immediately. "Minimal charges for some publications; most are free to working journalists. We sometimes ask to check quotes/material for accuracy." **Tips:** "Try not to come to us on a tight deadline. Research the subject *before* you ask to speak to the experts." Recent information request: Explain the history of 1982 as The Year of The Eagle.

394• OCCIDENTAL PETROLEUM
10889 Wilshire Blvd., Los Angeles CA 90024. (213)879-1700. Contact Person: Vice President of Public Relations. **Description:** Diversified company involved in oil and gas, chemicals, coal, beef, cattle, research and development. **Services:** Provides historical, referral, technical and trade information covering Occidental matters described above. Offers aid in arranging interviews, annual reports, bibliographies, biographies, statistics, brochures/pamphlets, information searches, photos, press kits and progress reports. **How to Contact:** Write or call. Responds to most inquiries within a week. Requests for literature should be in writing, addressed to the Publications Department. **Tips:** Recent information requests: Oxy's number of employees; oil and gas output/position in Libya, etc.

BEHIND THE BYLINE

Madeleine L'Engle
Writer

"If it's not good enough for an adult, then it's not worth offering to a child," Madeleine L'Engle tells writers on her trips around the country. "You don't write for children; you write for yourselves. I am an adult, and what I write about and do research in are subjects that have caught my interest and excite me."

L'Engle is very interested in the post-Newtonian sciences, for example. "I find them easier to understand because they deal with ideas; whereas the pre-Newtonian sciences are much more pragmatic. When I'm doing research, say, in quantum mechanics, the books I read deal with subjects a lot of people wouldn't turn to—like the nature of being, for instance." Contrary to what some people may say about the appropriateness of this and similar mystical concepts for children, L'Engle feels young people are open to grasping new ideas. "All adolescents ask cosmic questions: 'What am I about?'; 'Why am I here?'; 'What is time?' And storytellers go on asking these same questions, and some of it requires research. I think we owe the kids the absolute best we can possibly offer, so you research as much as you need to know."

L'Engle has published over thirty books; only four of which are nonfiction. Her genre preference is clear. "In the imaginary world we discover reality. When I'm writing, I'm not conscious that I'm writing fiction. I do an awful lot of thinking and research (one of the best things I learned in college was how to do research) before I write. I always learn something in the process of writing. For *A Wind in the Door*, I had to give myself a crash course in cellular biology, because there was no cellular biology when I was in school."

A big part of research for L'Engle is being in touch with her world. "Where I am in my own life and what I'm doing—it all goes together into the slow cooker and bubbles away quietly." Years ago, she and her family were camping under "undimmed stars." About that same time, L'Engle was reading books on cosmology and astrophysics. The idea for her Newberry Award-winning book, *A Wrinkle in Time* came out of those life experiences. "I can't separate myself as writer, woman, wife, mother. It all comes together in a wholeness."

Much of it also comes together in the journal she keeps (and has kept since she was nine). "It's a big garbage can, and I dump everything in it." The journal is a resource for her fiction. She recalls an episode in *Meet the Austins* that was an actual dinner table conversation. "I set it down in my journal and there it was when I needed it. It's not always that direct, but when something delicious comes out, I have it to remember."

L'Engle believes keeping a journal is a good tool for any writer. "People forget their experiences, and if you're going to write fiction, you have to write out of your own experience. You don't lose yourself if you've written it all down in your journal."

But keeping a journal is not all a writer needs to be successful. "Being a writer necessitates discipline. Some people think you go to a typewriter and punch out a book. They don't realize it takes so much time. If you have to have special time to write, you won't do it; you grab time and make time. And you revise and revise. For every page I keep, I may throw away nine or ten. I'm very lucky, though, because I can write anywhere—in airports, on airplanes, in waiting rooms. I can move right into concentration. I think the earlier you learn that, the easier it is."

L'Engle has no particular audience in mind when she writes. "All I have in mind when I'm doing a book is the book. What I hope my books will *be* comes when I'm not writing. That's when I hope that they will give people courage—courage to be creative; courage to be willing to change; courage to be vulnerable and open; courage to love."

395• PEABODY COAL COMPANY

301 N. Memorial Dr., St. Louis MO 63102. (314)342-3400. Contact Person: Director of Public Affairs. **Description:** "Peabody Coal Company is in the coal mining industry exclusively." **Services:** Provides historical, interpretative, technical and trade information covering coal mining and marketing. Offers aid in arranging interviews, bibliographies, biographies, statistics, brochures/pamphlets, information searches, placement on mailing list, newsletter and photos. **How to Contact:** Write or call. Responds to most inquiries immediately. **Tips:** "Requests must pertain to coal production and use."

396• PEABODY MUSEUM OF NATURAL HISTORY

Yale University, 170 Whitney Ave, New Haven CT 06520. (203)436-0850. Contact Person: Public Education Officer. **Description:** "The Peabody Museum of Natural History is one of the oldest of its kind in the United States and is known throughout the world. It serves as a valuable research facility for scholars and as an educational resource for area schools. Approximately 165,000 people visit the museum each year to study the dinosaur hall, the outstanding anthropological exhibits, the third-floor dioramas, the bird hall and the many other fascinating and informative displays. The museum also mounts several temporary exhibits each year." **Services:** Provides bibliographical and referral information on anthropology, meteorites, botany, paleobotany, invertebrate paleontology, mineralogy, oceanography, vertebrate paleontology, invertebrate zoology, vertebrate zoology, scientific instruments. Offers bibliographies, brochures/pamphlets, placement on mailing list, photos and press kits. Publications include "a guidebook and succinct brochure. The museum also publishes *Discovery*, a magazine which presents museum and natural scientific activities in layman's terms. Some special exhibitions will include catalogs. The curators of various departments of the museum can individually provide bibliographies of their publications." **How to Contact:** Write to Public Education Officer or Editor, Publications Office. Responds to most inquiries within a week. Charges for *Discovery* and museum bulletins.

397• PHILLIPS PETROLEUM

c/o Gross & Associates, 592 Fifth Ave., New York NY 10036. (212)221-2267. Contact Person: Executive Vice President. **Description:** Phillips Petroleum is engaged in energy and alternate energy research and development. **Services:** Provides advisory, interpretative, referral, technical and trade information on oil, coal, geothermal, shale, gas, offshore drilling, chemicals and plastics. Offers aid in arranging interviews, annual reports, biographies, brochures/pamphlets and photos. **How to Contact:** Write or call Gross & Associates or Phillips Petroleum, Phillips Building, Bartlesville OK 74004. Responds to most inquiries immediately.

398• RESOURCE POLICY INSTITUTE

1346 Connecticut Ave. NW, # 217, Washington DC 20036. (202)466-2954. Contact Person: Director. **Description:** "We are a research and education group which develops and disseminates information on resource policy issues." **Services:** Provides advisory, how-to, referral and technical information on energy, environment, materials technology and policy, including hazardous waste, conservation, etc. Offers research assistance. Publications include *The Waste Watchers*; *Toxic Substances: Decisions and Values*; and a variety of others. **How to Contact:** Write. Responds to most inquiries within a month. Charges for research time on hourly or daily basis, and for publications. **Tips:** "Before you start research, make a list of all the sources that might be of help. Then make a calculation as to time and money that tapping these sources will require. Writers interested in using our services should outline specific needs and maximum budget allocations for services." Recent information requests: Publications on toxic substances subjects; an association that can answer a specific question on, e.g., mine tailings disposal or solar energy.

399• RESOURCES FOR THE FUTURE

1755 Massachusetts Ave. NW, Washington DC 20036. (202)328-5000. Contact Person: Associate Director of Public Affairs. **Description:** "Our institution does research and analysis of social science public policy issues concerning natural resources, energy, and environmental quality." **Services:** Provides analytical and technical information on the economics of natural resources. Offers aid in arranging interviews, annual reports, brochures/pamphlets and placement on mailing lists. Publications include *Resources* (a free quarterly magazine); and 200 + books, individually priced. **How to Contact:** Write. Responds to most inquiries within a week.

400• SEA GRANT MARINE ADVISORY PROGRAM
Agricultural Communications Extension, Oregon State Univeristy, Corvallis OR 97331.
(503)754-3311. Contact Person: Exterior Communication Specialist. **Description:**"The Sea
Grant Marine Advisory Program is chartered to provide information and education on the uses of
marine resources. It is the statewide educational arm of the state's Sea Grant college. As such, it
conducts workshops and short courses on the management of marine resources, interprets applied
research for marine resource users, and publishes educational materials relating to vocational and
recreational uses of marine resources. Its information resources cover the Pacific Northwest,
Columbia River and Oregon natural resources and their uses." **Services:** Provides how-to,
interpretative, referral, technical and trade information on marine science, oceanography,
commerical fisheries, marine economics, coastal resource management, maritime industry,
marine education, vessel and crew safety, recreation, law, food and agriculture. Offers aid in
arranging interviews, brochures/pamphlets and photos. "The program maintains more than 50
educational publications." **How to Contact:** Write or call. Responds to most inquiries within a
week. Charges for copies of publications, b&w prints and slide duplication. "We appreciate
receiving credit as source of information." **Tips:** Recent information request: "What is the
economic outlook for Oregon's commerical fishing industry for the coming year?"; "How can a
small fishing boat be adapted for use in more than one fishery?"

401• SHELL OIL COMPANY
Box 2463, Houston TX 77001. (713)241-4544. Contact Person: Manager, Media Relations.
Description: Shell Oil is a petrochemical company. **Services:** Provides advisory, analytical, historical, how-to, interpretative, referral, technical and trade information covering Shell Oil Company and energy in general. Offers aid in arranging interviews, annual reports, brochures/pamphlets
and placement on mailing list. **How to Contact:** Write or call. Responds to most inquiries within a
month. "Shell publishes a variety of position papers on energy issues. We prefer to review your
material prior to publication." **Tips:** "Allow adequate lead time. Be specific about what you
want." Recent information request: "How do you make gasoline?"

402• SIERRA CLUB
530 Bush St., San Francisco CA 94108. Contact Person: Information Services Coordinator.
Description: "The purpose of the Sierra Club is to explore, enjoy and preserve the nation's forests, water, wildlife and wilderness." **Services:** Provides referrals to issue experts within the club;
printed material on club history, policy and programs. Publications include *Sierra* (bimonthly) and
National News Report (35 issues/year). **How to Contact:** Write. Responds to most inquiries within a week. Charges for printed material, $8/year for *Sierra*, $12/year for *National News Report*.
Tips: Recent information request: "What was the club's involvement in the passage of the Alaska
National Interest Lands Act?"

403• SOIL CONSERVATION SERVICE
Information Division, Department of Agriculture, Box 2890, Washington DC 20013.
(202)447-4543. Contact Person: Director, Information Division. **Description:** "Our purpose is to
help landowners and operators control soil erosion and manage water efficiently. We assist local
groups with flood, drought, excessive sedimentation or other water problems. Information covers
soil, water, plant and wildlife conservation; flood prevention; better use of water by individuals
and communities; and improvement of rural communities through better use of natural resources,
and preservation of prime farmland. In addition to material of interest to the agricultural and
outdoor media, our work in urban and educational fields offers article possibilities." **Services:**
Offers "background materials on all phases of our work," aid in arranging interviews, and photos.
"We can also help arrange field trips and find locations for shooting films. We publish a variety of
general and technical publications on practically all aspects of our programs and on soil and water
conservation." **How to Contact:** Write. Responds to most inquiries within a week. Single copies
of publications are available from the Publications Unit.

404• SOUTHWEST RESEARCH AND INFORMATION CENTER
Box 4524, Albuquerque NM 87106. (505)262-1862. Contact Person: Publications
Coordinator. **Description:** A public information and education center producing information on a
wide variety of environmental subjects. "One of our main goals is to provide information on the
'alternative' side of issues." **Services:** Provides advisory, analytical, bibliographical, historical,
how-to, interpretative, referral, technical and trade information on uranium mining and milling,

health and radiation, water quality, radioactive waste management. Offers brochures/pamphlets, expert testimonies, library facilities, research assistance (minimal) and seminars and conferences on environmental issues and how-to of publishing; courses on radiation and health and the teaching of organization skills. Publications include *The Workbook*; *The Self-Reliance Journal*; *Mine Talk*; *Radioactive Waste News*. **How to Contact:** Write. Responds to most inquiries within a week. Charges for publications, photocopying, mailing and phone expenses; library available at no cost. "Give credit to the Southwest Research and Information Center for all materials used."

405• TECHNICAL INFORMATION PROJECT, INC.
1346 Connecticut Ave. NW, Washington DC 20036. (202)466-2954. Contact Person: Director. **Description:** "We generate and disseminate information on resource, environmental, and energy policy issues." **Services:** Provides advisory, analytical, bibliographical, how-to, interpretative, referral and technical information on hazardous and non-hazardous waste management, energy conservation, recycling, technology assessment, emergency planning, and other related energy/environment fields. Offers brochures/pamphlets, placement on mailing lists, research assistance and telephone reference services. Various publications. **How to Contact:** Write. Responds to most inquiries within a month. Charges for information search and assembling, $25/hour. "References to our materials must be cited." **Tips:** "Always keep an open mind about information sources—don't get hung up on certain books, periodicals, or persons as the only credible places to look." Recent information requests: Sources of listings on national waste carriers; emergency planning procedures; energy conservation technologies.

406• TENNECO, INC.
Box 2511, Houston TX 77001. (713)757-3430. Contact Person: Director of Public Relations. **Description:** "We are the corporate public relations office for Tenneco, Inc., a diversified company with major business interests in oil, natural gas pipelines, construction and farm equipment, automotive components, chemicals, shipbuilding, packaging and agriculture/land management." **Services:** Provides trade information covering subjects related to the company's business activities. Offers aid in arranging interviews, annual reports, biographies, statistics, brochures/pamphlets, placement on mailing list and photos. **How to Contact:** Write or call. Reponse time dependes on the nature of the news medium and the inquiry. "At certain times we will provide information for background purposes only." **Tips:** "We deal primarily with daily and weekly press."

407• TENNESSEE VALLEY AUTHORITY
400 Summit Hill Dr., Knoxville TN 37902. (615)632-3257. Contact Person: Director of Information. **Description:** The Tennessee Valley Authority (TVA) is an independent federal agency created by Congress in 1933 to develop the resources of the Tennessee Valley region. This comprehensive effort involves a broad range of activities that includes flood control, navigation development, electric power, environmental protection, energy research, agricultural and fertilizer development, forestry, fisheries and wildlife, land-use planning, regional and community development, outdoor recreation and related fields. **Services:** Provides bibliographical, historical, interpretative, referral and technical information covering agriculture, economics, health/medicine, law, nature, recreation and technical data. Offers aid in arranging interviews with staff, annual reports, bibliographies, research aid, statistics, brochures/pamphlets and photos. Publications include maps and navigation charts and various publications in the subject areas listed above. **How to Contact:** For maps, write to: Map Service, 101 Haney Building, Chattanooga TN 37401, or Map Sales, WPA3, 400 Summitt Hill Dr., Knoxville, TN 37902. For other information, publications and assistance, write to the main address above. Responds to most inquiries within a month. Charges for photo prints, photocopying and similar services. **Tips:** "Write before visiting." Recent information request: "Does TVA have photographs of the structures removed from the reservoir area of Fontana Dam in western North Carolina?"

408• UNION CAMP CORPORATION
1600 Valley Rd., Wayne NJ 07470. (201)628-9000. Contact Person: Director of Public Relations. **Description:** "Union Camp's major national resource base is 1.7 million acres of woodlands in the Southeast. Its activities—concentrated in the eastern third of the United States but extending to Colorado and Texas with sales activity on the West Coast—include paper manufacture, packaging, school supplies and stationery, printing papers, building products,

chemicals, minerals exploration and mining, development of residential communities, and the retailing of building products and home improvement materials.'' **Services:** Information covers business, industry, new product information, environmental protection and woodlands management. Offers aid in arranging interviews, annual reports, biographies, brochures/pamphlets, placement on mailing list, newsletter, photos and press kits. **How to Contact:** Write or call. Prefers to work with writers on assignment.

409• URBAN LAND INSTITUTE
1090 Vermont Ave. NW, Washington DC 20005. (202)289-8500. Contact Person: Director, Marketing and Public Affairs. **Description:** ''A nonprofit educational and research organization of over 6,000 developers, builders, owners, financial officers, architects, planners, brokers, and public officials committed to advancing the quality of development and land use.'' **Services:** Provides bibliographical, historical, interpretative, referral, technical and trade information on residential, urban, recreational, office, industrial, mixed use, and commercial and retail development; regulations; and environmental protection. Offers aid in arranging interviews, brochures/ pamphlets, informational newsletters, library facilities, photos, research assistance, statistics and telephone reference services. Publications (available to members only) include *Urban Land* (monthly magazine); *Land Use Digest* (newsletter style periodical); *Project Reference File* (quarterly); many books and reports in the development field; and publications catalog. **How to Contact:** Call. Responds to most inquiries immediately. Charges for publications.

410• UTAH FIELD HOUSE OF NATURAL HISTORY AND DINOSAUR GARDENS
235 E. Main, Vernal UT 84078. (801)789-3799. Contact Person: Superintendent. **Description:** Museum and Dinosaur Garden exhibiting geological and natural history of the Uinta Basin, northeastern Utah. Exterior exhibit of 14 life-sized fiberglass dinosaur models. **Services:** Provides historical and interpretative information on geology and natural history of the Uinta Basin, Utah, and dinosaur and travel information. Offers library facilities. **How to Contact:** Write, call or visit. Responds to most inquiries within a week (in winter); within a month (in summer).

411• IZAAK WALTON LEAGUE OF AMERICA, INC.
1800 N. Kent St., Suite 806, Arlington VA 22209. (703)528-1818. Contact Person: Media Coordinator. **Description:** Organization which ''promotes the wise use and conservation of America's natural resources and helps educate the public to effect these goals.'' **Services:** Provides analytical and interpretative information covering public lands, air and water pollution, acid rain, wetlands, soil conservation, wildlife management. Offers publications and interviews with staff experts on major conservation issues. **How to Contact:** Write or call. Responds to most inquiries within a month. ''We do not provide information to students working on papers; writers must be bona fide freelancers or journalists working for publication.'' **Tips:** ''Narrow your topic; make questions as specific as possible.'' Recent information requests: Identify innovative conservation activities/projects being carried out in communities across the country; offer statements/interviews on the problem of acid rain, public land sales.

412• WEYERHAUSER COMPANY
Tacoma WA 98477. (206)924-2345. Contact Person: Director of External Communications, Manager of Corporate Information or Manager of Business Communications. **Description:** ''We are a forestry manufacturer and research company.'' **Services:** Provides information on the forestry industry, new products, politics (forestry issues), business and economics. Offers aid in arranging interviews, annual reports, biographies, statistics, brochures/pamphlets, placement on mailing list, photos and press kits. **How to Contact:** Write or call. Responds to most inquiries immediately. **Tips:** Recent information request: The economic aspects of forestry and trade.

413• WILDERNESS SOCIETY
1901 Pennsylvania Ave. NW, Washington DC 20006. (202)828-6600. Contact Person: Director of Education. **Description:** ''National nonprofit citizens' organization maintaining contact with Congress to work with public on issues concerning wilderness and the public lands.'' **Services:** Provides advisory, analytical and technical information on ''any issues dealing with the public lands (national forests, national parks, Alaska, wildlife refuges, etc.), particularly congressionally-designated wilderness or potential wilderness areas.'' Offers aid in arranging interviews, annual reports, statistics and brochures/pamphlets. Publications include *Wilderness* (quarterly) and special mailing alerts. **How to Contact:** Write or call detailing information needed. Responds to press

inquiries for news stories immediately; other inquiries, within a week. **Tips:** "Call us. If we can't help, we will refer you to another organization that might be able to."

414• WORLD INFORMATION SERVICE ON ENERGY (WISE)
1346 Connecticut Ave. NW, Rm 533, Washington DC 20036. (202)429-9556. Contact Person: National Coordinator. **Description:** WISE is an international news service which provides information and networking to grassroots anti-nuclear and safe energy groups around the world. **Services:** Provides information on nuclear energy, appropriate energy, uranium mining and movement tactics. Offers brochures/pamphlets, informational newsletters and placement on mailing lists. Publications include *News Communiqué* (weekly); *Bulletin* (monthly); and *Keep It in the Ground* (newsletters). **How to Contact:** Write. Responds to most inquiries immediately. Charges for publications (subscription).

SECTION·SEVEN

ETHNIC/REGIONAL HERITAGE

*To forget one's ancestors is to be a brook
without a source, a tree without a root.*
                                    —*Chinese proverb*

Herein is a sample of the many and varied information sources in the areas of genealogy;
ethnic, racial and nationality affairs; regional

history and folklife.

Consult the entry for American Association
for State and Local History in the History section for information on the hundreds of historical societies in the country. Additional information on nationalities may be found in the
Embassies section of the World Scope category.

Bibliography

Bernardo, Stephanie. *The Ethnic Almanac*. New York: Dolphin Books, Doubleday, 1981.
Ethnic Information Sources of the United States. 2d ed. Detroit: Gale Research Co., 1983.
   (Organizations and print sources of information about 89 identifiable ethnic groups)
Felt, Thomas E. *Researching, Writing & Publishing Local History*. Nashville, TN: Ameri-
   can Association for State and Local History, 1976.
Grimal, Pierre, ed. *Larousse World Mythology*. New York: Excalibur Books, 1981. (An en-
   cyclopedia of articles highlighting the mythology of various regions of the world; illustra-
   tions, subject index)
Leach, Maria, ed. *Funk & Wagnall's Standard Dictionary of Folklore, Mythology & Legend*.
   New York: Funk & Wagnall's Publishing Co., 1972.
McDonald, Donna, ed. *Directory of Historical Societies & Agencies in the US & Canada*.
   Nashville, TN. American Association for State and Local History, 1978.
Thernstrom, Stephan, ed. *The Harvard Encyclopedia of American Ethnic Groups*. Cam-
   bridge, MA: Harvard University Press, 1980.
Yantis, Netti Schreiner-, comp. *Genealogical & Local History Books in Print*. 3d ed. Spring-
   field, VA: Genealogical Books in Print, 1981.

415• ALASKA STATE MUSEUM
Pouch FM, Juneau AK 99811. (907)465-2901. Contact Person: Curator of Collections.
Description: The museum's purpose is "preservation, collection and conservation. We have a
unique collection of Northwest Coast Indian art and Alaskan native art." **Services:** Provides historical, referral and technical information on Alaska native art and artifacts, contemporary Alaskan
artists. Offers brochures/pamphlets, information searches and placement on mailing list. Publications include pamphlet on the museum, newsletter, catalogs. **How to Contact:** Write. Responds to
most inquiries within a month. Open Monday through Friday, 9 a.m. to 5 p.m.; Saturday and Sunday, 1 p.m. to 5 p.m. Charges for copies of photographs, extensive copying work. Policy on photographs, credits and educational use. **Tips:** "Be specific on initial inquiry. Know what you need;
make personal contacts prior to visit; make appointments: don't just 'drop in' and expect to do research." Writers might also wish to contact the Alaska Historical Library, State Office Blvd., Juneau 99811. Recent information request: "What native tribe in Alaska used birch bark for
baskets?"; "When did Rockwell Kent visit Alaska?"

416• AMERICAN-CANADIAN GENEALOGICAL SOCIETY
Box 668, Manchester NH 03105. (603)623-1781. Contact Person: Librarian. **Description:** The
American-Canadian Genealogical Society serves genealogists interested in ancestries of Canadian
origin. "The chief aim of the society is to serve as a resource center for the gathering, preservation,
and dissemination of American-Canadian genealogical information." **Services:** Provides
advisory, analytical, bibliographical, historical, how-to, interpretative, referral and technical
information on genealogy and local history. Offers aid in arranging interviews, biographies,
brochures/pamphlets, computerized information searches, informational newsletters, library

facilities, placement on mailing list, research assistance and statistics. The Acadian Genealogical & Historical Association of New England, at same address, offers similar services and information on Acadian genealogy and local history. Contact Person: President, (603)356-3009. Publications include *The Genealogist* (semiannual). **How to Contact:** Write. Responds to most inquiries within a month. Charges for postage, copying and handling. **Tips:** Recent information request: "I would like to trace my Canadian ancestry; can you help me?"

417• AMERICAN JEWISH HISTORICAL SOCIETY
2 Thornton Rd., Waltham MA 02154. (617)891-8110. Contact Person: Director. **Description:** The American Jewish Historical Society "collects, preserves, and disseminates information on the history of the American Jewish experience." **Services:** Provides advisory, bibliographical, historical, interpretative and referral information on all phases of the American Jewish experience. Offers aid in arranging interviews, biographies, brochures/pamphlets, library facilities, photos, research assistance and telephone reference services. The society maintains a specialized library of 66,000 volumes and a collection of 4 million pages of manuscripts, photos, miniatures and other items related to Jewish history in America. Publications include *American Jewish History*; and miscellaneous publications. **How to Contact:** Write. Responds to most inquiries within a week. Charges for extensive research. Give proper citation/identification. **Tips:** Do "homework" before contacting the society. Recent information requests: Genealogy, biographical data.

418• ARIZONA STATE MUSEUM
Photographic Collections, University of Arizona, Tucson AZ 85721. (602)626-2445. Contact Person: Associate Curator. **Description:** "The photographic collections are open for research purposes. Primary subject matter includes prehistoric and historic southwestern archaeology, ethnology of the Indians of the American Southwest and Mexico, museum artifacts, specimens, displays, exhibits and additional materials. The collections consist of approximately 150,000 negatives, glassplates, 35mm (and larger) color transparencies, lantern slides, photographic prints, photogravures, and mounted photographic displays covering a timespan from the late 19th century to the present." **Services:** Provides advisory, analytical, bibliographical, historical, interpretative, referral and technical information covering anthropology, archaeology (of the American Southwest), ethnology (of Indians of the American Southwest), environment, agriculture, history, natural history, art, architecture, artifacts, museums, exhibits and education. Offers information searches and photos of artifacts/specimens in the museum's collections. **How to Contact:** Write or call for information on fees, availability of specific subject areas for research and appointments to view the collections. Responds to "easy requests within a week, complex requests within a month. Charges for nonprofit and commercial use of photographs. Write for "terms and conditions" sheet. Credit must be given to Arizona State Museum, Univeristy of Arizona and photographer. **Tips:** "BE SPECIFIC. Requests for materials and information on 'Everything you wanted to know about . . . .' go to the bottom of the pile. Research takes time. Most institutions with scholarly or esoteric material have extremely limited staffs. Give plenty of lead time on difficult requests and telephone occasionally to check the status of the research. Quoted deadlines change often in nonprofit institutions." Recent information requests: Research and photographic material for a book on Native American Indian architecture; a journal article on southwestern landscape architecture.

419• ASSOCIATION FOR THE STUDY OF AFRO AMERICAN LIFE AND HISTORY
1401 14th St. NW, Washington DC 20005. (202)667-2822. Contact Person: Managing Director. **Description:** An organization of historians and others interested in the research and study of black people. Collects manuscripts and materials relating to black people throughout the world. **Services:** Provides bibliographical, historical and referral information on the African presence. Offers biographies, computerized information searches, informational newsletters, photos, press kits, and media festival. Publishes books, pamphlets, volumes, kits, photos on the African presence in the world. **How to Contact:** Write. Responds to most inquiries within a week. Charges for research on the African presence ($10/hour). Extra charges will be coordinated with individuals before final commitment. All copyrighted materials are to be cleared with owner before use in any publication. **Tips:** "Check all information thoroughly. Many mistakes are passed on year after year after year." Recent information request: "Who succeeded Congressman Oscar DePriest? By what means?"

420• ASSOCIATION OF PROFESSIONAL GENEALOGISTS
Box 11601, Salt Lake City UT 84147. (801)532-3327. Location: 19 W. South Temple, Salt Lake City UT 84101. Contact Person: President or Editor. **Description:** The association works "to better the genealogy profession." **Services:** Provides advisory, bibliographical, business and how-to information on genealogy and history. Offers trade access to genealogy interviews, annual reports, brochures/pamphlets, informational newsletters, placement on mailing lists and professional research assistance. Publications include *APG Newsletter*; *Directory of Professional Genealogists and Related Services*; *APG Green Sheet*; various pamphlets. **How to Contact:** Write, call or visit. Responds to most inquiries within a week. Charges for publications.

421• BALCH INSTITUTE FOR ETHNIC STUDIES
18 S. 7th St., Philadelphia PA 19106. (215)925-8090. Contact Person: Director of Development. **Description:** "The Balch Institute for Ethnic Studies documents and interprets America's multicultural heritage through the activities of its library, museum and educational programs." **Services:** Provides information related to ethnicity and immigration history in America. Offers bibliographies, educational programs and museum and library facilities. "Library collections are indexed by ethnic group as well as by author, title and subject. The library collections include 50,000 books, 5,000 reels of microfilm, 1,200 linear feet of manuscripts and other materials, including photographs, posters, other graphics, phonograph and tape recordings, and sheet music." The library and museum are open to the public. "The educational programs consist of seminars for scholars, forums for the general public and instruction for secondary and elementary school students." Publications include bibliographies on ethnicity and immigration history for 25 different ethnic groups in America. **How to Contact:** Visit.

422• BALZEKAS MUSEUM OF LITHUANIAN CULTURE
4012 S. Archer Ave., Chicago IL 60632. (312)847-2441. Contact Person: President. **Description:** "The museum presents an outstanding and diverse collection of Lithuanian antiquities, artifacts, memorabilia and literature spanning 800 years in the history of Lithuania. Our information includes exhibits, classes, lectures and slide programs." **Services:** Offers publications including *Lithuanian Museum Review* (bimonthly). **How to Contact:** Write or call. Responds to most inquiries within a week. "Contact us for placement on our mailing list." Charges $1 general admission fee. **Tips:** "We have a fine archive and library and would be happy to assist writers in their searches. We recently helped the Chicago Historical Society find various ethnic musical groups."

423• BERNICE PAUAHI BISHOP MUSEUM
Box 19000-A, Honolulu HI 96819. (808)847-3511. Contact Person: Communications Coordinator. **Description:** "Bishop Museum is a nonprofit museum and research organization founded in 1889 to preserve and research objects of cultural and natural history in Hawaii and the Pacific. Research, exhibition, education and publication are our primary goals." **Services:** Provides historical/scientific and interpretative information on Pacific anthropology, ethnology and history, entomology, botany, zoology (vertebrate, invertebrate, ichthyology, malacology). Historical photographs (mainly Hawaii) and historical manuscripts are also collected. Offers annual reports, brochures/pamphlets, informational newsletters, library facilities, photos and press kits. Publications include general information on museum; annual reports; newsletters; and press releases. Bishop Museum Press has over 1,000 titles on specific data; catalog available. **How to Contact:** Write or call. Responds to most inquiries within a month. Charges for reprints of historic photos, publications, use of curatorial time and collections; costs vary as to situation. "All usage of materials in collections restricted for security purposes, but special arrangements can be made for researchers. Use is determined by department chairman. Request permission as per copyright laws for publications; credit line requested on usage of photos." **Tips:** "If you are interested in any subject within our realm, contact us; if we don't have the answer we can generally direct you to who would. The more detail you can give us on your subject, the more we can help." Recent information requests: "What can visitors to the Museum expect?"; background on Hawaiian culture/history; information on flora/fauna.

424• CANADIAN ASSOCIATION IN SUPPORT OF THE NATIVE PEOPLES
16 Spadina Rd., Toronto, Ontario, Canada M5R 2S7. (416)964-0169. Contact Person: National Coordinator. **Description:** "Our purpose is the education of the non-native public toward native

Canadian issues and concerns; and alliance with native organizations in their struggle for self-determination, justice and respect as a unique cultural entity within the Canadian framework. **Services:** Provides advisory, analytical, bibliographical and historical information on native political organizations and policies, native child welfare, education, housing, native people in prison, native women, culture, history, land claims, treaties, aboriginal rights and the Canadian constitution. Offers annual reports, brochures/pamphlets, informational newsletters, placement on mailing lists, research assistance and sale of publications. **How to Contact:** Write.

425• CANADIAN FOLK MUSIC SOCIETY
1314 Shelbourne St. SW, Calgary, Alberta, Canada T3C 2K8. Contact Person: President. **Description:** "Our purpose is the promotion of Canadian folk music." **Services:** Provides advisory, bibliographical, historical, how-to and referral information. Offers brochures/pamphlets and informational newsletters. Publications include *Bulletin* (quarterly); and *Canadian Folk Music Journal* (annually). **How to Contact:** Write. Responds to most inquiries within a month. Services for members only. **Tips:** Recent information request: Author looking for Canadian children's games and songs to include in a short story.

426• CENTER FOR SOUTHERN FOLKLORE ARCHIVES
Box 40105, 1216 Peabody Ave., Memphis TN 38104. (901)726-4205. Contact Person: Director of Research or Administrative Director. **Description:** The center distributes information and educational material of the South. **Services:** Provides analytical, historical, interpretative and referral information on traditional culture, music, crafts, films and the ways of life in the South. Offers brochures/pamphlets, photos, placement on mailing lists, press kits and documentary film. Publications include *American Folklore* (film, videotapes and index) 2 volumes. **How to Contact:** Write. Responds to most inquiries within a month. Charges for film; other charges "depend on service." **Tips:** Recent information request: Materials on Southern blues artists.

427• CHEROKEE NATIONAL HISTORICAL SOCIETY, INC.
Box 515, TSA-LA-GI, Tahlequah OK 74464. (918)456-6007. Contact Person: Chief Executive Officer. **Description:** "We are dedicated to the preservation of the Cherokee heritage and culture; education of members of the tribe in their own history; education of the general public about Cherokee history and culture. We own and operate the TSA-LA-GI, which includes the Cherokee National Museum; the Cherokee National Archives and Library (currently in the process of accumulating material); the Theatre at TSA-LA-GI which presents each summer the historial drama 'Trail of Tears'; the Ancient Museum Village at TSA-LA-GI (living museum circa 1650-1700 AD). Our collection of several hundred original newspapers dating back to 1762 and containing articles about the Cherokees is a fruitful source of interesting historical material. Our collection is particularly strong covering the late 18th and 19th centuries through the Civil War. Our archival collection includes, among others, the personal papers of W.W. Keeler, the former chief of the Cherokees for 26 years, amounting to approximately 35 linear feet." **Services:** Provides advisory, bibliographical, historical, interpretative, referral and technical information covering Cherokee culture and heritage and the art and history of the period up through the Civil War. Offers aid in arranging interviews, bibliographies, biographies, brochures/pamphlets, placement on mailing list, photos and press kits. Also available are promotional material concerning TSA-LA-GI and limited genealogical service relating to Cherokee families. Publications include brochures/pamphlets on TSA-LA-GI (the Cherokee Cultural Center); short history of TSA-LA-GI and the Cherokee National Historical Society, the Cherokee tribe (incorporated in a souvenir program covering the 'Trail of Tears,' an outdoor symphonic drama presented in the outdoor theater at TSA-LA-GI); and bibliography of books and pamphlets about the Cherokees. **How to Contact:** Write or call ahead. Responds to most inquiries within a month. Research material may not be removed from the archives and library. Charges $5/name for genealogical requests.

428• CHICKASAW COUNCIL HOUSE HISTORIC SITE AND MUSEUM
Court House Square, Tishomingo OK 73460. (405)371-3351. Contact Person: Site Director. **Description:** "The purpose of the organization is to display and promote the high culture of the Chickasaw Indians. We do research on various Indian families and assist many people to establish their quantum of Indian blood. The Chickasaws are one of the Five Civilized Tribes. Tishomingo was their capital during the days of the Indian Territory." **Services:** Offers biographies, brochures/pamphlets, information searches and photos. "We do have a small library. The majority of the material we have is about the state of Oklahoma, the Indian Territory and the

Chickasaws. We have brochures on the various historical sites of Oklahoma (one on the council house), and maps and other items of information about our state.'' **How to Contact:** Write or call the office, visit the museum, or make an appointment with a member of the staff for help. Responds to most inquiries within a week. "We are not open on Monday. Saturday and Sunday, the hours are 2 to 5 p.m., and during the remainder of the week we're open 9 a.m. to 5 p.m.'' **Tips:** "Remember that we're not a large facility. We're glad to do what we can. Recent information requests: Biographical sketches.

429• CSA FRATERNAL LIFE
2701 S. Harlem Ave., Berwyn IL 60402. (312)795-5800. Contact Person: Vice President or Museum Curator and Librarian. **Description:** "We provide fraternal life insurance; perpetuate the language and ethnic heritage of the Czech and Slovak people.'' **Services:** Provides bibliographical, historical and referral information on "anything dealing with the Czech migration, etc., fraternals, schools, institutions, etc.; minutes of the fraternal societies in all mergers; program books of anniversary years, etc.; histories of various Czech institutions and some political references. Offers aid in arranging interviews, biographies, informational newsletters, library facilities, photos and research assistance. Also some information available on Slovak migration, etc. "Our library contains many first editions of world classics in the Czech language and classics of the Czech literature; first Czech publications which were published in the US; many fraternal publications beginning with 1891. **How to Contact:** Write. Responds to most inquiries within a week. Research must be done in-house. **Tips:** "Put requests in writing and always phone ahead for appointments. Bring your own 'tools', i.e., paper, pencils, magnifying glass, etc.'' Recent information request: Names of persons who served in the Civil War who were of Czech or Slovak descent.

430• THE DANISH BROTHERHOOD IN AMERICA
Box 31748, 3717 Harney St., Omaha NE 68131. Contact Person: Director of Fraternal Services. **Description:** "We provide life insurance benefits, fraternal benefits, and perpetuate the culture and heritage of Denmark.'' **Services:** Provides historical, referral and trade information on the "history of The Danish Brotherhood in America, and as much as possible, the history of Denmark and its culture; referral to other Scandinavian scholars; information concerning our products or other contacts.'' Offers brochures/pamphlets, press kits and research assistance (within our archives only). Publications include *Centennial* brochure (a condensed history); *The American Dane*; monthly, $1/issue, $6/year, $8/foreign. **How to Contact:** Write. Responds to most inquiries within a month. "Access to specific archival materials determined by individual requests.'' **Tips:** "Determine in advance the information needed and state requests clearly.''

431• ETHNIC MATERIALS INFORMATION EXCHANGE TASK FORCE
68-71 Bell Blvd., Bayside NY 11364. (212)229-1510, 520-7194. Contact Person: Coordinator. **Description:** Organization dedicated to the positive treatment of all minority groups. Assists in developing ethnic heritage programs and promoting library materials and services for ethnic groups in the country with a multi-ethnic thrust. **Services:** Provides bibliographical, interpretative and referral information on the multi-ethnic problems of prejudice, discrimination and stereotype. Offers names of ethnic authors, research assistance and telephone reference services. Publications include *Directory of Ethnic Publishers and Other Resource Organizations*; *Multi-Ethnic Media: Bibliographies Currently Available*. Both available from American Library Association in Chicago. **How to Contact:** Write or call. Responds to most inquiries within a week.

432• FEDERATION OF FRANCO-AMERICAN GENEALOGICAL & HISTORICAL SOCIETIES
Box 3558, Manchester NH 03105. (603)356-3009. Contact Person: President. **Description:** The federation is a nonprofit organization which "serves as a united voice for organizations in the United States who specialize in genealogical and historical research of French origins and their mutual concerns.'' Activities include help in organizing new societies and reactivating and supporting existing ones; establishing and maintaining communication among members societies; "cooperating with public agencies and private groups in an effort to obtain, exchange, reproduce and conserve all objects and documentation of a genealogical and historical nature; developing, encouraging and popularizing genealogical and historical research and its publication; and acting as a watchdog to insure that all resolutions, commitments, and agreements made by governmental

agencies in the field of genealogy and local history are met and maintained." **Services:** Provides advisory, analytical, historical, how-to, interpretative and referral information on Americans doing French-Canadian and Acadian genealogical research. Offers aid in arranging interviews, brochures/pamphlets, informational newsletters and placement on mailing lists. Publications include *Gen Histo-Gram* (quarterly). **How to Contact:** Write. Responds to most inquiries within a month. Charges for postage, copying and handling. **Tips:** Recent information request: "Can you put me in touch with a group doing this type of genealogical research?"

433• FLICKINGER FOUNDATION FOR AMERICAN STUDIES, INC.
300 St. Dunstan's Rd., Baltimore MD 21212. (301)323-6284. Contact Person: President. **Description:** "The foundation's purposes are cultural and educational with emphasis on research and programs relating to the culture of the Chesapeake-Allegheny-Potomac region as a phase of American Studies (especially the Colonial and Revoluntionary period). We are inter-disciplinary." **Services:** Provides advisory, analytical, bibliographical, historical and interpretative information on the culture of the Chesapeake-Allegheny-Potomac region. Offers aid in arranging interviews, brochures/pamphlets and research assistance. "We are working on publications, especially new editions of writers long out of print." **How to Contact:** Write or call. Responds to most inquiries within a week. Charges for services "depending on time and effort involved." **Tips:** "Writers/researchers should have their problems in focus. We can help them by suggesting new approaches." Recent information requests: The inter-relationship of the various cultural components of communities and the region as a whole; inter-relationships with other regions, especially the West Indies.

434• FRENCH INSTITUTE/ALLIANCE FRANCAISE
22 E. 60th St., New York NY 10022. (212)355-6100. Contact Person: Librarian. **Description:** "The French Institute/Alliance Française is a nonprofit privately-supported organization whose purpose is to encourage the study of the French language and culture and to foster friendly relations between the French and American peoples." **Services:** Provides advisory, bibliographical, historical and referral information on the French language, literature, history, art, civilization. Offers library facilities, research assistance and telephone reference services. Publications include *French XX Bibliography* (annual), critical and biographical references for French literature since 1885, including references to all types of literature, theatre, cinema, etc. **How to Contact:** Write, call or visit. Responds to most inquiries within a week. Charges for copying costs; $20 annual fee for borrowing library materials. "We cannot handle in-depth research; we can guide writers/researchers to sources and answer specific questions. Almost all materials in the collection are in French and we cannot provide extensive translation services." **Tips:** "Questions should be specific enough to permit searching." Recent information request: "A writer compiling information for a work on gastronomy asked us to locate the founding date of Harry's New York Bar in Paris."

435• GREAT PLAINS BLACK MUSEUM/ARCHIVES & INTERPRETIVE CENTER
2213 Lake St., Omaha NE 68110. (402)344-0350. Contact Person: Director. **Description:** "Our museum is the only black history museum in the Great Plains area which serves Nebraska, Iowa, South Dakota, North Dakota, Wyoming, Kansas, Missouri, Wyoming, Montana and Colorado. We are interested in documenting old information and seeking new information on the history of blacks in this area. Our original research has led us to new information on the Underground Railroad, the black settlers-homesteaders, the black cowboy and other people who came early to the Great Plains area. We also have a collection of old, rare books, photographs and artifacts relating to the Great Plains area. Much of the history of blacks in the Great Plains area has been lost, but our museum continues to find new materials such as magazines, letters, diaries and photographs that would excite anyone looking for new sources and new information pertaining to blacks from the end of the Civil War to the present time." **Services:** Offers informtion searches and photos. "The information available to writers would pertain more to original artifacts, letters and other information about blacks that would make interesting material for stories, scripts and plays. Our museum does not do genealogy, but will work with writers interested in locating and/or tracing specific individuals. Would prefer that researchers visit the site because of limited staff." **How to Contact:** Write or visit. Responds to most inquiries within a month. "Charges depend on the amount of work we have to do and/or the reproduction of photographs and other work, i.e., both rare and out-of-print and original manuscripts that could lead to more information. All original research done at the museum should be credited. If photographs are from a private collection, arrangements should be made to pay a fee and credit the collection." **Tips:** "Suggest

that writers using our services be familiar with black history, and have a working knowledge of the black homesteaders, Malcolm X and others who lived in the Great Plains area. A limited amount of material is available; much needs to be catalogued, but is in good usable condition if the persons know what they need and want for their particular project." Recent information request: "Do you have photographs of Nat Love, the black cowboy?"

436• GYPSY LORE SOCIETY
North American Chapter, Department of Social/Behavioral Sciences, Centenary College, Hackettstown NJ 07840. Contact Person: Editor. **Description:** The society's purpose is the "promotion of the study of the Gypsy peoples and analogous groups; dissemination of information aimed at increasing understanding of Gypsy culture in its diverse forms; establishment of closer contact among scholars and others interested in Gypsy Studies." **Services:** Provides bibliographical and referral information.Offers informational newsletters, library facilities (limited) and research assistance. Publications include *Newsletter of the Gypsy Lore Society, North American Chapter* (quarterly); proceedings of meetings sponsored by the chapter; and membership directory (available to members only). **How to Contact:** Write. Responds to most inquiries within a week. "The chapter is not an ethnic organization of Gypsies, nor does it claim to speak for Gypsies. It cannot arrange interviews with Gypsies." **Tips:** "Writers are advised to do their own first-hand research. Priority in informational inquiries is given to members. Staff is entirely volunteer and lacks time for complex replies. Most inquiries are answered with bibliographical information."

437• IMMIGRATION HISTORY SOCIETY
690 Cedar St., St. Paul, MN 55101. Contact Person: Editor-Treasurer. **Description:** The society provides a bibliographical and informational service. **Services:** Provides bibliographical, historical and referral information on ethnic history; immigration. Offers newsletter and journal. **How to Contact:** Write. Responds to most inquiries within a week. **Tips:** Recent information request: Letter seeking bibliographical advice on thesis.

438• INSTITUTE OF AMERICAN INDIAN ARTS MUSEUM
Cerrillos Rd., Santa Fe NM 87501. (505)988-6281. Contact Person: Museum Director. **Description:** "We are a museum (under the auspices of the US Department of Interior) but also offer the Native American Videotape Archives for research. This is comprised of some 350 ½-inch b&w tapes, 50 1-inch edited master tapes and 100 ¾-inch color cassettes on various aspects of native American culture." **Services:** Provides advisory, historical, how-to, interpretative, technical and trade information on native American Indian arts and crafts subjects; museum training and museum problem solving information; and Indian history and cultural studies. Offers annual reports, brochures/pamphlets and placement on mailing list. Publication available. **How to Contact:** Write. "Arrangements for visits to museum collections and requests for information, videotapes and duplication of slide files must be made in advance because of the small staff and available space limitations." Responds to most inquiries within a week. "Must credit the Institute of American Indian Arts." **Tips:** Recent information request: Object list of available baskets from Indian tribes in Arizona.

439• LA SOCIETE HISTORIQUE ACADIENNE
C.P. 2363, Station A, Moncton, New Brunswick, Canada E1C 8J3. (506)388-3045. Contact Person: Secretary. **Description:** "The society's purpose is to organize all of those interested in Acadian history. Our first objective is appropriation, discovery, collection and the publication of all of those who have contributed to the teaching and the love of Acadian history." **Services:** Provides historical information. Referral service only. Offers publications, including *Les Cahiers*, quarterly. Vol. 9, Nos. 2 and 3 contain an index of the last 15 years. **How to Contact:** Write. Responds to most inquiries within a week. Charges for photocopies only—10¢/copy.

440• LIBRARY OF CONGRESS, AMERICAN FOLKLIFE CENTER
Washington DC 20003. (202)287-6590. Contact Person: Director. **Description:** "The American Folklife Center preserves and presents all aspects of American folklife through public programs, consultation, publications, exhibits, field projects and coordination within the field." **Services:** Provides advisory, bibliographical, how-to, interpretative, referral and technical information on American folk culture, historical and contemporary. Offers annual reports, biographies, brochures/pamphlets, informational newsletters, photos and placement on mailing lists. Publications

include *Folklife and the Library of Congress*, a directory to the folklife resources of the library. **How to Contact:** Write or visit. Responds to most inquiries within a week. **Tips:** "We respond to specific inquiries but recommend that general inquiries and broader research questions be handled by the individual writer/researcher."

441• LIBRARY OF CONGRESS, LOCAL HISTORY & GENEALOGY READING ROOM
Jefferson Building # 244, Washington DC 20540. (202)287-5537. Contact Person: Head, Local History and Genealogy Reading Room. **Description:** The reading room offers public access to printed sources of genealogical and historical information. **Services:** Provides advisory, bibliographical, historical and referral information on genealogy and local history. Offers library facilities and reference assistance (very limited) and telephone reference services. **How to Contact:** Write, call or visit. Responds to most written and telephone inquiries within 2 weeks. **Tips:** "Writers and researchers do not receive any special services not also available to the general public. The staff of the Library of Congress cannot undertake research in family history or heraldry. This assistance may be obtained by contacting the Executive Secretary, Board for Certification of Genealogists, 1307 New Hampshire Ave. NW, Washington DC 20036. For $2 the Board will send a list of certified genealogists and record searchers who undertake, for a fee, this kind of research in the Library of Congress, the National Archives, and other information centers in the Washington area as well as in local record repositories throughout the nation. Enclose SASE and 37¢ postage."

442• MOORLAND-SPINGARN RESEARCH CENTER
Howard University, 500 Howard Pl. NW, Washington DC 20059. Contact Person: Director. **Description:** "The Research Center is a research library on Afro-American, African, Caribbean and Afro-Hispanic subjects. In addition to a large library, it includes a Manuscript Division, a museum and the Howard University Archives." **Services:** Provides bibliographical, historical and referral information. Offers biographies, library facilities, photos, research assistance and telephone reference services. The Library Division includes works of Afro-American and African scholars, statesmen, poets and novelists; a collection of black newspapers and magazines from early 19th century to present; and the world's only copy of *Negro Patentees of the United States 1834-1890*. The Manuscript Division includes departments of prints and photographs, black music, and oral history, which contains the Ralph J. Bunche Oral History collection. **How to Contact:** Write, call or visit. Responds to most inquiries immediately. Charges for photoduplication, photography and micrographics. Some collections are restricted by their donors. **Tips:** "It is wise to call in advance to discuss a project with a reference librarian."

443• MUSEUM OF AFRO AMERICAN HISTORY
Smith Court, Box 5, Boston MA 02119. Contact Person: President. **Description:** "The museum is concerned with the research and exhibition of Afro-American history in New England, including photography and film collections, historic preservation and walking tours." **Services:** Provides advisory, analytical, bibliographical, historical, interpretative, referral and technical (historic archaeology, historic preservation, including consultations) information on Afro-American history in New England; Roxbury (Boston) history; historic archaeology; and historic preservation. Offers aid in arranging interviews and brochures/pamphlets, information searches and photos. "We also have tours of black communities, historic and present, in New England." **How to Contact:** Write or call. Responds to most inquiries within a week. Charges for tours. Charges $10-20/hr. for extensive searches and research. "Some stipulations exist for review of collections with donor restrictions." **Tips:** Recent information requests: Afro-American biographies of 19th century black abolitionists; verification of Underground Railroad sites; histories of black churches; Roxbury Revolutionary War histories; industrial (breweries, organ manufacturers, etc.) histories; histories of houses and neighborhoods.

444• NATIONAL GENEALOGICAL SOCIETY
1921 Sunderland Pl. NW, Washington DC 20036. (202)785-2123. Contact Person: Executive Director. **Description:** "We promote interest and scholarly research nationwide in genealogy." **Services:** Provides information on genealogy and local history. Offers library facilities. Publications include *NGS Quarterly* and *NGS Newsletter*. **How to Contact:** Visit. "Our members may borrow library materials by mail for a registration fee of $15 and a service fee per order thereafter." Services are available only to NGS members in good standing. Dues $25/year ($20 for those over 65 after the first year).

445• THE NEW YORK GENEALOGICAL AND BIOGRAPHICAL SOCIETY
122 E. 58th St., New York NY 10022. Contact Person: Associate Librarian or Executive Secretary. **Description:** "The society's purpose is to discover, procure, preserve and perpetuate whatever may relate to genealogy and biography and family history; to maintain a library and to cause to be written, copied, printed and published accounts and records of genealogy, biography and family history; and primarily to carry on the work of education." **Services:** Provides referral information relating primarily to New York City, state and surrounding areas. Offers library facilities. Publications include *The New York Genealogical and Biographical Record* (quarterly, $20/year); and publications list. Back issues of *Record* available for sale from NYG&BS office. **How to Contact:** Write or visit. Responds to most inquiries within a month. Charges for research service: $10 fee/item "for search on a specific, clear question if within our province. We have a very limited staff and cannot undertake any extensive research. List of qualified researchers in the area provided upon request to the office for assistance with genealogical questions." Give credit to NYG&BS. **Tips:** "Visit the library and use the facilities; staff available for help. Suggested donation of $2/day from non-members. No material circulates and none available on inter-library loan."

446• NORTHWEST TERRITORY FRENCH & CANADIAN HERITAGE INSTITUTE
Box 26372, St. Louis Park MN 55426. Contact Person: Treasurer. **Description:** The institute's purpose is educational. "We collect information on all known families of French-Canadian descent who have settled in the area which was roughly the original Northwest Territory." **Services:** Provides historical and how-to information on family histories. Offers biographies, brochures/pamphlets, informational newsletters and research assistance. Publications include *Cousins et Cousines* (quarterly newsletter); and an 8-volume set of books *French-Canadian Families of the North Central States.* **How to Contact:** Write. Responds to most inquiries immediately.

447• ORIENTAL LIBRARY
University of California at Los Angeles, Room 21617, Research Library, Los Angeles CA 90024. Contact Person: Acting Librarian. **Description:** "The Oriental Library is primarily a research facility." **Services:** Offers information in archaeology, art, Buddhism, premodern history, and the literature of China and Japan. The collection is mainly in Chinese and Japanese languages, with some Korean. **How to Contact:** Write or call. Responds to most inquiries within a week. Nonstudents must pay $24/year to remove books from the library. **Tips:** "We do our best to help with any kind of question. If *we* can't help, we'll try to recommend another information source."

448• PENNSYLVANIA DUTCH FOLK CULTURE SOCIETY, INC.
Lenhartsville PA 19534. (215)562-4803. Contact Person: President. **Description:** "Our purpose is to preserve the history, lore, culture, and dialect of the Pennsylvania German people." **Services:** Provides historical information: folklore, all areas; and genealogy, mostly Berks, Lehigh and Northampton counties. Offers biographies, brochures/pamphlets, clippings, informational newsletters, library facilities and photos. **How to Contact:** Write.

449• THE POLISH INSTITUTE OF ARTS & SCIENCES OF AMERICA
59 E. 66th St., New York NY 10021. (212)988-4338. Contact Person: Deputy Director. **Description:** "The PIASA is an American learned society founded in 1942 to advance Polish studies and culture in America. The Institute is composed of approximately 700 scholars, scientists, artists and writers, mostly, but not exclusively, of Polish origin." **Services:** Provides advisory, historical and referral information on "all matters connected with Poland, its history, culture, present and past political situation, political ideas, parties, etc." Offers annual reports, brochures/pamphlets, informational newsletters, library facilities and "unique archives of political documents," and research assistance (limited). "We have a highly specialized library of some 15,000 volumes, in the areas of the humanities and social sciences, a valuable collection (about 400 titles) of periodicals relating to Poland, her history and culture." Publications include *The Polish Review* (scholarly quarterly). **How to Contact:** Write or call. Responds to most inquiries within a week. "Our materials, books, documents, etc. can only be perused on the premises. Permission must be obtained for making photocopies (on the premises)." **Tips:** "Call or write in advance for appointment with staff member."

450• SCHOMBURG CENTER FOR RESEARCH IN BLACK CULTURE
New York Public Library, 515 Lenox Ave., New York NY 10037. (212)862-4000, 4001. Contact
Person: Chief. **Description:** Research library in black culture. **Services:** Provides
bibliographical, historical and referral information. Offers biographies, clipping services,
informational newsletters, library facilities, photos, placement on mailing lists, research
assistance and telephone reference services. **How to Contact:** Write, call or visit. Responds to
most inquiries within a month. Charges for photocopies and postage. All material must be used on
the premises. **Tips:** Recent information requests: Birth, death dates; bibliographic information;
holdings of a particular author.

451• SOCIETY FOR AMERICAN INDIAN STUDIES & RESEARCH
Box 443, Hurst TX 76053. (817)281-3784. Contact Person: Director. **Description:** "A nonprofit
consortium of individuals and institutions with no bond holders, mortgagees or other security
holders, created to promote the discovery, collection, preservation and publication of materials in
anthropology, history and literature, as they relate to Indians in North and Middle America."
Services: Offers *S.A.I.S.& R. Reviews*, a quarterly publication which contains book reviews and
notes. **How to Contact:** "Become a dues-paying member of the society." Responds to inquiries
"sometimes in a matter of weeks, when we're out in the field; other times, it's only a few days."
Tips: "If a request for information involves bibliographical information, we ask that the writer include return postage." Recent information request: Question regarding the purchase of Manhattan
Island.

452• SOCIETY FOR ETHNOMUSICOLOGY
Box 2984, Ann Arbor MI 48106. (313)663-1947. Contact Person: Office Director. **Description:**
"The object of the Society for Ethnomusicology shall be the advancement of research and study in
the music of the world's peoples and its place in world cultures." **Services:** Provides advisory,
bibliographical and referral information on music, anthropology, theatre and dance. Publications
include *Journal* (3 a year); *Newsletter* (3 a year); and *Special Series* (studies, discographies, source
lists). **How to Contact:** Write. Responds to most inquiries within a week. "Quotes from printed
materials must be cleared with the author and reprint fees are applied."

453• SOUTHWEST COLLECTION
Texas Tech University, Box 4090, Tech Station, Lubbock TX 79409. (806)742-3749. Contact
Person: University Archivist. **Description:** "Our purpose is to locate, collect and preserve
historical materials pertaining to West Texas and the near American Southwest from the late 19th
century to the present." **Services:** Provides historical information on ranching, land colonization,
evolution of agriculture, petroleum industry, mining industry, urban development, education,
politics and pioneer settlement in West Texas. Offers library facilities, photos and telephone
reference services. **How to Contact:** Visit. "We do answer mail and telephone inquiries; the
amount of research we will do is limited due to manpower, time and funds." Responds to most
inquiries within a week. Charges for involved research that is required by mail or phone inquiries;
photocopies and photograph reproductions. "Some materials may be restricted by the donors.
Give credit to the Southwest Collection." **Tips:** "Be prepared to spend time doing your research.
Do not expect to look at one source that will provide all the information you need. Contact us
before coming to do research so that we may better serve you."

454• SPERTUS MUSEUM OF JUDAICA
618 S. Michigan Ave., Chicago IL 60605. Contact Person: Curator. **Description:** "The museum
houses a collection of Judaica from many parts of the world, containing ceremonial objects, a
pertinent collection of sculpture, paintings, and graphic arts, and ethnographic materials spanning
centuries of Jewish experience." **Services:** Provides historical and interpretative information on
Jewish art and Jewish cultural heritage. Offers biographies and photos. Publications include
catalogs and price list. **How to Contact:** Write or call. Responds to most inquiries within a week.
"We charge for photographic reproduction. Appropriate credit must be given." **Tips:** Recent
information request: Verification of types of Jewish customs and ceremonies in various parts of the
world in different periods.

455• THE WELSH SOCIETY
Box 190, Darby PA 19023. (609)964-0891. Contact Person: Secretary. **Description:** "The
society's purposes are educational, benevolent, social—to maintain our Welsh cultural identity

and heritage." **Services:** Provides advisory, bibliographical, historical and referral information on Welsh customs, history and current Welsh-American activities. Offers brochures/pamphlets, informational newsletters and placement on mailing lists. Publications include *The History of the Welsh Society*. **How to Contact:** Write or call. Responds to most inquiries within a month. **Tips:** "Generally we refer writers/researchers to one of the two Welsh monthly newspapers in circulation in the US." Recent information requests: Questions mainly related to genealogy, scholarship loans or current activities.

456• WESTERN JEWISH HISTORY CENTER
2911 Russell St., Berkeley CA 94705. (415)849-2710. Contact Person: Archivist. **Description:** "We are a manuscript and archival research library concentrating on the contributions of Jews and their institutions to the American West. The center is on the top floor of the Judah L. Magnes Memorial Museum, and includes the Jesse C. Colman Libary and the Jacob H. Voorsanger Archive Room." **Services:** Provides bibliographical, historical, how-to and referral information on the contributions of Jewish people and their institutions to the American West, including some Canadian and Mexican material. "We have a publishing program and an extensive oral history program along with our archives and library." Offers bibliographies, biographies, brochures/pamphlets and information searches. **How to Contact:** Write. Responds to most inquiries within a week. "We charge off-premises researchers (correspondence, telephone requests) $7/hour after thirty minutes free time. No fee for on-premises researchers. We charge for photocopying, a fee that will probably be raised to 25¢/page to cover staff time. Right to publication of unpublished manuscripts is subject to the approval of the Board. Photographic and reproduction policy currently under revision. In all cases, credit must be given to the center. Case study forms required for some collections where names may not be used." **Tips:** "Have in mind the questions you really want to ask and be specific. We need data to answer genealogical questions and we need to know the focus of a work in order to be of assistance." Recent information requests: "What was the reaction to Hitler in the San Francisco Bay Area Jewish press, 1933-38?"; "What information is available on Jewish farming communities in the western states, and particularly in Petaluma CA?"

SECTION · EIGHT

FAMILY

No matter how many communes anybody invents, the family always creeps back.

—Margaret Mead

Family information sources cover the areas of marriage and divorce; birth and adoption; children and day care; parents' groups and parenting.

Additional resources related to family life (death, runaways, alcoholism, drug abuse) are listed in the Human Services section. Sources on human behavior are found in the Society and Culture category.

Bibliography

Auerback, Stevanne. *The Whole Child: A Sourcebook*. New York: G.P. Putnam, 1981.

Catalyst Career and Family Center. *Two-Career Families: An Annotated Bibliography of Relevant Readings*. Princeton, NJ: Peterson's Guides, Inc., 1981.

Friedman, James T. *The Divorce Handbook: Your Basic Guide to Divorce*. New York: Random House, 1982.

Milden, James W. *The Family in Past Time: A Guide to the Literature*. New York: Garland Publishing, Inc., 1977.

Olson, David H. and Roxanne Markoff, eds. *Inventory of Marriage and Family Literature*. Beverly Hills, CA: Sage Publications, 1982.

Peck, Theodore P. *The Troubled Family: Sources of Information*. Jefferson, NC: McFarland & Co., 1982.

457• AMERICAN DIVORCE ASSOCIATION FOR MEN (ADAM)
1008 White Oak St., Arlington Heights IL 60005. (312)394-1040. Contact Person: Executive Director. **Description:** "A men's rights group in domestic relations area effecting attitudinal and legal changes. Members' dues ($70/year) support the movement, and in return, they receive individualized legal and nonlegal counseling, as well as referral to competent attorneys, investigators and other professional services. We work mainly in the areas of pre- and post-divorce issues." **Services:** Provides advisory, analytical, how-to, interpretative and referral information covering economics, law and self-help. Offers brochures/pamphlets and information searches. "We will cooperate with writers or researchers for mutual considerations." **How to Contact:** Write or call. Responds to most inquiries within a week. "We will be glad to share our insights and knowledge for honorable ventures."

458• AMERICAN INSTITUTE OF FAMILY RELATIONS
4942 Vineland Ave., North Hollywood CA 91601. (213)763-7285. Contact Person: Executive Director. **Description:** The institute provides counseling services to engaged and married couples, single, widowed and divorced adults, adolescents and families. **Services:** Provides advisory, bibliographical, how-to and interpretative information on family life, parenting and sexuality. Offers childbirth teacher-training program. M.A. degree in Pastoral Psychotherapy Counseling and M.S. degree in Marriage and Family Counseling. **How to Contact:** Write or call. Responds to most inquiries within a month. Give credit to institute.

459• AMERICAN SOCIETY OF DIVORCED MEN, INC.
575 Keep St., Elgin IL 60120. (312)695-2200. Contact Person: President. **Description:** The society is an international membership organization concerned with equality and justice in divorce courts. **Services:** Provides information in all areas of pre- and post-divorce problems. Offers aid in arranging interviews, brochures/pamphlets and informational newsletters. **How to Contact:** Write, call or visit. Responds to most inquiries immediately.

460• ASSOCIATION FOR BIRTH PSYCHOLOGY
444 E. 82nd St., New York NY 10028. (212)988-6617. Contact Person: Executive Director. **Description:** "Our purpose is to establish birth psychology as an autonomous behavioral science and to stimulate research and communication among professionals." **Services:** Provides advisory, analytical, bibliographical and referral information on childbirth, psychology, psychotherapy, obstetrics, psychiatry. Offers brochures/pamphlets, informational newsletters, placement on mailing lists, research assistance, telephone reference services, journal, conferences, etc. Publications include *Birth Psychology Bulletin* ($6/issue). **How to Contact:** Write or call. Responds to most inquiries within a week. Charges for some services; "depending upon time involved." Include SASE with information requests. **Tips:** Recent information requests: Listing of resources; names and referral to professionals.

461• ASSOCIATION FOR VOLUNTARY STERILIZATION, INC.
122 E. 42nd St., New York NY 10168. (212)573-8350. Contact Person: Public Information Director. **Description:** "The Association for Voluntary Sterilization, Inc. (AVS) is a voluntary, nonprofit organization that seeks to make permanent contraception available to all adults on a voluntary basis. AVS works toward this end in the United States and overseas by undertaking or supporting programs in education, service and research." **Services:** Provides analytical, bibliographical, referral and technical information on medical, biomedical, surgical, psychological aspects of sterilization and its reversal. Offers annual reports, brochures/pamphlets, informational newsletters, library facilities, press kits, statistics and telephone reference services. **How to Contact:** Write or call. Responds to most inquiries within a week. "We request manuscripts be submitted to us to check for medical accuracy of information." **Tips:** Recent information request: "What are the long-range immunologic implications in the development of sperm antibodies among some men who have had a vasectomy?"

462• CANDLELIGHTERS FOUNDATION
2025 Eye St. NW, Washington DC 20006. (202)659-5136, 544-1696. Contact Person: Director of Policy, Planning and Publications. **Description:** "An international organization of parents groups (our children have or have had cancer). We have postal parent-to-parent and group-to-group buddy systems, parent-to-parent phone lines, a speakers bureau, promotion of quality educational materials, surveys of patient and family needs, and placement of parents on federal and state social services advisory." **Services:** Provides bibliographical and referral information on childhood cancer. Offers bibliographies, brochures/pamphlets, placement on mailing list, and newsletter. Publications available. **How to Contact:** Write or call. Responds to most inquiries within a week. "Information from our materials can be reprinted only with specific permission for each reprint. It cannot be sold for profit. Credit must be given." **Tips:** "We have information from most materials written on pediatric cancer, or we have the actual materials in our library. We are eager to cooperate with writers who wish to spread information on pediatric/adolescent cancer and its effects on families." Recent information requests: How to seek second opinions; knowing your rights.

463• CHILD WELFARE LEAGUE OF AMERICA, INC.
Informational Resource Services, 67 Irving Place, New York NY 10003. (212)254-7410. Contact: Informational Resource Services. **Description:** The purpose of the league, a national membership-based organization, is to promote the well-being of all children and their families, in particular to give priority to the unmet needs of children lacking physical, emotional and intellectual care and nurturing. The goals of the Child Welfare League of America are to strengthen delivery of services to children and families; to formulate, promote and advocate public policies that benefit all children and their families; to develop and promote sound policies and standards for child welfare services; to seek and disseminate knowledge concerning those conditions of life that affect the development of children and their families; and to broaden and deepen public awareness of and commitment to society's responsibility for responding to the needs of children and their families. CWLA conducts research; administers special projects such as the Permanent Families for Children Project; publishes a journal and other professional literature; sponsors annual training conferences; provides consultation; maintains a library and information service in the New York office and a public affairs office in Washington DC. **Services:** Provides information on all aspects of child welfare services. Copies of CWLA's publications list, audio-visual catalog, brochures and pamphlets are free upon request. **How to Contact:** Write or call. Responds to most non-member inquiries within a month. Charges for services.

464• CHILDBIRTH EDUCATION ASSOCIATION
5636 W. Burleigh, Milwaukee WI 53210. (414)445-7470. Contact Person: Director of Outreach. **Description:** "We provide comprehensive preparation for pregnancy and childbirth. Classes for childbirth with a teaching staff of 50 instructors." **Services:** Provides advisory, analytical, bibliographical, historical, how-to, interpretative, referral and technical information on pregnancy, childbirth, breastfeeding, cesarean birth, early parenting, postpartum, grieving a loss, nutrition, consumer awareness, labor support, training childbirth educators, relaxation and breathing techniques. Offers aid in arranging interviews, annual reports, bibliographies, brochures/pamphlets, information searches, placement on mailing list, statistics and newsletter. **How to Contact:** Write, or call 9:30 a.m.-4:00 p.m. weekdays. Responds to most inquiries within a month. Charges for classes, film rights, newsletter, some books and membership. **Tips:** Recent information requests: "What options for giving birth are available?"; "Why the increase in cesarean birth . . . is the trend reversing?"; "What effects does nutrition education have on outcome of teenage pregnancies?"

465• EDNA MCCONNELL CLARK FOUNDATION
250 Park Ave., New York NY 10017. (212)986-7050. Contact Person: Director of Communications. **Description:** "The Clark Foundation funds organizations whose goals are consistent with the following four program areas: the Program for Children seeks to assure that children now in foster and institutional care are provided permanent families; the Program in Jobs for the Disadvantaged seeks to improve the school-to-work transition of urban disadvantaged youth; the Program for Justice is involved with improving prison conditions and alternatives to incarceration; and the Program in Tropical Disease seeks the reduction of schistosomiasis." **Services:** "One of the functions of the Communications Department is to publish booklets, pamphlets and brochures that extend the work of our grantees. We would be willing to distribute these publications to interested writers." **How to Contact:** Call or write. Responds to most inquiries within a week.

466• CUSTODY ACTION FOR LESBIAN MOTHERS (CALM)
Box 281, Narberth PA 19072. (215)667-7508. Contact Person: Coordinator. **Description:** Litigation support service for lesbian mothers. "We provide free litigation in the Delaware Valley and free consultation nationally to lesbian mothers seeking child custody or visitation." **Services:** Provides advisory, how-to, interpretative, referral, technical and legal information, and psychological studies. Offers aid in arranging interviews, brochures/pamphlets, research assistance, telephone reference services and aid in litigation. **How to Contact:** Write or call. Responds to most inquiries within a week.

467• DAY CARE & CHILD DEVELOPMENT COUNCIL OF AMERICA
1602 17th St. NW, Washington DC 20009. (202)638-2316. Contact Person: Executive Director. **Description:** "Our purpose is to foster the improvement and expansion of child care services in the United States—providing information and assistance to organizations and individuals professionally caring for children—and informing the general public on needs and issues relevant to day care and child development." **Services:** Offers brochures/pamphlets, statistics and journal. **How to Contact:** Write or call. Responds to most inquiries within a week. Charges for publications. "As a small organization, the council can best respond to specific requests for information and can offer on-site use of a resource library in the central office in Washington."

468• FAMILIES ADOPTING CHILDREN EVERYWHERE (FACE)
Box 102, Belair MD 21014. Contact Person: Co-President. **Description:** "We are an adoptive parent support group. Our purpose is to disseminate information on adoption." Provides course "Family Building through Adoption." **Services:** Provides advisory, how-to and referral information on adoption, infertility, foster care and child advocacy. Offers informational newsletters. Publications include *Face Facts* (monthly newsletter). **How to Contact:** Write. Responds to most inquiries within a week. Membership dues $10 includes newsletter and all activities; associate member $8, newsletter only. **Tips:** "We have all up-to-date information on adoption sources around the world. Contact us for specific information." Recent information request: "An infertile couple inquired about adoption after being told by local social service agencies 'there are no kids.' "

469• FAMILY SERVICE ASSOCIATION OF AMERICA, INC.
44 E. 23rd St., New York NY 10010. Contact Person: Director of Public Relations. **Description:** "Our purpose is to build a network of strong local organizations able to help families in trouble and to influence policies nationally to help strengthen family life." **Services:** Provides advisory, analytical, bibliographical, historical, interpretative and referral information on marriage, divorce, parent-child relations, family violence, unemployment, family stress, debt counseling, bereavement, teenage pregnancy, remarried families and single parent families. Offers aid in arranging interviews, annual reports, informational newsletters, library facilities and statistics. **How to Contact:** Write. Responds to most inquiries within a week. **Tips:** "Writers should first check their local libraries, local human service organizations, narrowing their interest in a subject to one, two, or three specific questions or emphases." Recent information request: Referral to experts in debt counseling.

470• THE FATHERHOOD PROJECT, BANK STREET COLLEGE
610 W. 112th St., New York NY 10025. (212)663-7200. Contact Person: Director. **Description:** "We encourage the development of new options for male involvement in child-rearing and serve as a national clearinghouse for father-participation programs." **Services:** Provides analytical, bibliographical, historical, interpretative and referral information on all aspects of male parenthood in the areas of law, employment, health, education, social services and religion. Offers aid in arranging interviews, brochures/pamphlets, computerized program searches and limited research assistance. **How to Contact:** Write; include SASE. Responds to most inquiries within a week. Charges for computerized referrals. **Tips:** "Arrangements for interviews and other assistance should be made well in advance—we have a limited staff and many requests for help! We must reserve the right to select those requests for assistance that will provide us with needed media exposure." Recent information request: "What's happening to support the changing role of the father in the US today?"

471• FATHER'S DAY/MOTHER'S DAY COUNCILS
Father's Day Council, Inc., 47 W. 34th St., New York NY 10001. (212)594-5977. Mother's Day Council, Inc., 1328 Broadway, New York NY 10001. Contact Person: Executive Director. **Description:** "Our purpose is to create awareness of the family and community values of Mother's Day and Father's Day, through non-commercial activities in all media." **Services:** Provides advisory, historical and trade information, including background history; importance of holidays; family activities on Mother's Day and Father's Day; gift preferences, etc. Offers aid in arranging interviews, photos, press kits and statistics. **How to Contact:** Write, call or visit. Responds to most inquiries within a week.

472• THE ALAN GUTTMACHER INSTITUTE
360 Park Ave. S., New York NY 10010. (212)685-5858. Contact Person: Director of Communications and Development. **Description:** "Our purpose is to foster sound public policies on voluntary fertility control and population problems and to develop adequate family planning programs through research, policy analysis and public education." **Services:** Provides analytical, referral and technical information on family planning and abortion services, teenage pregnancy and other issues related to the family planning/population field. Offers annual reports, informational newsletters, placement on mailing lists, press kits, research assistance and statistics. Publications include *Family Planning Perspectives* (bimonthly); and *Washington Memo* (22 times a year). **How to Contact:** Write or call. Responds to most inquiries immediately.

473• HOLT INTERNATIONAL CHILDREN'S SERVICES
Box 2880, Eugene OR 97402. (503)687-2202. Contact Person: Information Coordinator. **Description:** "We facilitate adoption of children, mostly from other countries; raise funds and develop child welfare programs overseas." **Services:** Provides bibliographical, historical and technical information on intercountry adoption and foreign child welfare. Offers aid in arranging interviews, annual reports, biographies, brochures/pamphlets, informational newsletters and statistics. Publications include newsletter; *HI Families*; *Adoption: A Family Affair*. **How to Contact:** Write or call. Responds to most inquiries within a month. "Must have permission of family before releasing names and addresses of adoptive families." **Tips:** Recent information request: "How long must a family wait before receiving an adoptive child?"

474• INFORMED HOMEBIRTH
Box 788, Boulder CO 80306. (303)449-4181. Contact Person: National Director or Assistant Director. **Description:** "We provide education and support for those who are looking for alternative care in the birth experience. We certify childbirth educators, provide midwifery skills workshops, sell books and tapes, publish a newsletter, and network those in the birthing field." **Services:** Provides how-to, interpretative and referral information on childbirth education, midwifery skills, homebirth management, referrals to homebirth teachers, and political issues in midwifery. Offers brochures/pamphlets, informational newsletters, placement on mailing lists, telephone reference services and workshops and classes. Publications include *Special Delivery* (quarterly newsletter); *Special Delivery* (book); *Suturing for Midwives*; *Complications of Labor and Delivery*; *Herbs for Women* and *Prenatal Lab Book for Midwives*. **How to Contact:** Write. Responds to most inquiries within a week. Charges for tapes and books; brochures, pamphlets and referrals are free. "We are a resource/referral service—we won't be the end of the line." **Tips:** Recent information request: Information on the recent passing of a lay midwifery bill in New Hampshire.

475• INSTITUTE FOR FAMILY RESEARCH AND EDUCATION
760 Ostrom Ave., Syracuse NY 13210. (315)423-4584. Contact Person: Director. **Description:** "The institute's main purpose is to support parents as primary sexuality educators of their children; to prevent some unwanted side effects of premature sexual activity such as adolescent pregnancy and venereal disease; and to promote some of the fundamental ideals on which this country is based: the worth and dignity of each person, for example." **Services:** Provides bibliographical, how-to, interpretative and referral information on adolescent sexuality, sex education at home and in school, adolescent pregnancy, venereal disease, parenting, the politics of human sexuality, freedom of speech. Offers aid in arranging interviews, brochures/pamphlets, informational newsletters, photos, placement on mailing lists, press kits and speaker's bureau. Publications include *Impact* ($1). **How to Contact:** Write or call. Responds to most inquiries immediately. Charges for publications; fee for speaker's bureau. **Tips:** Recent information request: "What do you think about the Health and Human Services regulations requiring parental notification when contraceptives are prescribed for adolescents?"

476• JOINT CUSTODY ASSOCIATION
10606 Wilkins Ave., Los Angeles CA 90024. (213)475-5352. Contact Person: President. **Description:** "A nonprofit association concerned with the joint custody of children and related issues of divorce, including research, information dissemination, and legal and counseling practices." **Services:** Provides advisory, analytical, bibliographical, historical, how-to, interpretative, referral and technical information on statutes, case results, guidance in achieving joint custody, monitoring of results, guiding legislative action, developing local support groups, public appearances, seminars, research aid. Offers aid in arranging interviews, biographies, brochures/pamphlets, clipping services, informational newsletters, library facilities, placement on mailing lists, press kits, research assistance, statistics and telephone reference services. Publications include a number of individual publications created to answer particular questions and demands. **How to Contact:** Write, call or visit. Responds to most inquiries within a week. Charges for photocopying.

477• LA LECHE LEAGUE INTERNATIONAL, INC.
9616 Minneapolis, Franklin Park IL 60131. Contact Person: Reference Librarian. **Description:** "We give help and encouragement primarily through personal instruction to those mothers who want to nurse their babies. We believe breastfeeding is the ideal way to initiate good mother-child relationships and strengthen family ties. The international office reaches out to mothers through 4,225 groups in which certified league leaders meet with women who want to know about the womanly art of breastfeeding. There are more than 11,000 league leaders who volunteer their time to help other mothers." **Services:** Offers annual reports, brochures/pamphlets, newsletter and press kits. Publications available. **How to Contact:** Write. Responds to most inquiries within a month. Charges for publications.

478• LESBIAN MOTHERS NATIONAL DEFENSE FUND
Box 21567, Seattle WA 98111. (206)325-2643. Contact Person: Director. **Description:** "We assist lesbian women and their attorneys with information, financial assistance and emotional support in child custody cases. We have legal and expert referrals covering 47 states." **Services:**

Provides advisory, bibliographical, referral and technical information on all aspects of lesbian child custody. Offers aid in arranging interviews, pamphlets, informational newsletters. "We provide legal briefs from actual cases." Publications include briefs, papers, articles, etc., dealing with lesbian child custody; and a quarterly newsletter. Materials list available. **How to Contact:** Write or call. Responds to most inquiries within 2 weeks. Charges for printing costs of materials; postage requested.

479• METRO-HELP/NATIONAL RUNAWAY SWITCHBOARD
2210 N. Halsted, Chicago IL 60614. (312)929-5854. Contact Person: Executive Director. **Description:** "We provide information, referral and crisis intervention to 200,000 teens and families per year." **Services:** Provides advisory, analytical, bibliographical (sometimes) and interpretative information in all youth-related areas: runaways, drugs, family problems, alcoholism, suicide, abuse, volunteers, etc. Offers aid in arranging interviews, annual reports, brochures/pamphlets, photos and statistics. **How to Contact:** Write or call. Responds to most inquiries within 3 days. **Tips:** "Please don't call at the very last second before deadline." Recent information requests: "How many children are missing in the US?"; "Why do children leave home?"; "Do social services help?"

480• NATIONAL ASSOCIATION FOR WIDOWED PEOPLE, INC.
Box 3564, Springfield IL 62708. (217)522-4300. Contact Person: President. **Description:** "The National Association for Widowed People, Inc. is a nonprofit organization that serves all widowed men and women everywhere. NAWP is supported by membership and donations." **Services:** Provides advisory, analytical, how-to, interpretative and referral information on first person experiences, taxes, recreation, research and development, case studies, health, etc. Offers aid in arranging interviews, brochures/pamphlets, informational newsletters, library facilities, photos, press kits, research assistance, statistics, telephone reference services and persons for interviews and talk shows. **How to Contact:** Write (preferred) or call. Responds to most inquiries within a month. Charges for any detailed research/information and studies/speaker's bureau. Give credit to the association and send proof before publication. **Tips:** "It is our feeling that too many writers are not getting the real facts on being a widowed person."

481• NATIONAL CENTER FOR FAMILY STUDIES
Clearinghouse on Family Policy & Programs/Clearinghouse on Family Ministries, The Catholic University of America, Washington DC 20064. (202)635-6087. Contact Person: Information Director. **Description:** Clearinghouse and referral center "providing information on family matters: people, policy and programs; provides a contact point where those working in family problems can obtain information about other programs and people that will help them provide better service to families." **Services:** Provides bibliographical, how-to and referral information on family-related subjects. Offers brochures/pamphlets, informational newsletters, research assistance and statistics. Publications include *American Family: National Action Overview*; *American Catholic Family: The Newsletter of National, Diocesan and Parish Family Ministries*. **How to Contact:** Write. Responds to most inquiries within a week. Charges for searches on specific subjects, collation of materials and photocopying. Cost is $25/hour plus postage and cost of reproduction. "We reserve the right to reject requests for information." **Tips:** "Please be as specific as possible about what you want and the purpose for which you want it." Recent information request: Programs and literature on marriage enrichment; comparison of the status of the father now and 20 years ago.

482• NATIONAL ORGANIZATION OF MOTHERS OF TWINS CLUBS, INC.
5402 Amberwood Lane, Rockville MD 20853. (301)460-9108. Contact Person: Executive Secretary. **Description:** "The purpose of NOMOTC is to help parents of multiples and educate the public." **Services:** Provides bibliographical information on multiple birth and rearing children. Offers brochures/pamphlets and informational newsletters. Publications include *Your Twins and You (30¢)* and *MOTC's Notebook* (quarterly newspaper, $5/year). **How to Contact:** Write. Responds to most inquiries within a week.

483• NORTH AMERICAN COUNCIL ON ADOPTABLE CHILDREN, INC.
1346 Connecticut Ave. NW, Suite 229, Washington DC 20036. (202)466-7570. Contact Person: Executive Director. **Description:** "We promote permanent families for children without parents. We provide information, education, training and publications on adoption and related issues. We

advocate for children at the national and state level through a network of over 500 volunteer groups." **Services:** Provides advisory, analytical, historical, how-to and interpretative information on adoption policy and practice, parenting special needs children, role of volunteers in child advocacy, foster care system reforms, legal implications of adoption. Offers aid in arranging interviews, brochures/pamphlets, informational newsletters, photos, placement on mailing lists and statistics. Publications include *Adoptalk* (newsletter); *Adoption Help Directory*; brochures; and *Directory of Adoptive Parent Group Resources*. **How to Contact:** Write or call. Responds to most inquiries within a week. Charges for publications, usually less than $5. Give credit to NACAC; submit direct quotations for review and approval; respect confidentiality. **Tips:** "You cannot adequately cover adoption and foster care issues unless you speak to the parents. We can provide many contacts in adoption and foster care." Recent information requests: "Why is it so hard to adopt?"; "What are the major issues in parent/child bonding?"; "What is wrong with foster care and what is happening to children in the child welfare system?"

484• ORPHAN VOYAGE
2141 Road 2300, Cedaredge CO 81413. (303)856-3937. Contact Person: Coordinator. **Description:** Organization serving the adoption population. "Life history of members of the adoption population, particularly adopted individuals who desire to find kindred; as well as birth parents of adopted people wishing reunion." **Services:** Provides advisory, bibliographical, historical, interpretative and referral information about the world of adoption. Offers aid in arranging interviews, annual reports, bibliographies, brochures/pamphlets, placement on mailing list and newsletter. Publications available. **How to Contact:** Write and enclose SASE. Reponds to most inquiries within a week. Charges for publications, or, if in-depth assistance with research is needed, charges will be worked out individually. "We are busy here, and have to be motivated. Our focus is on giving service to members of the adoption population." **Tips:** "When it comes to human affliction, statistics are not all that important. Each individual bears the truth within him. When repeated, it becomes very persuasive. But the language of the social orphan, one who has lost parents by a social decision, is difficult to hear. The meaning of our words is different from the meanings of words of standard people. Approaching any afflicted population should imply some sensitivity and sympathy."

485• PARENTS AND CHILDREN'S EQUALITY, INC.
4977 87th Ave. N., Pinellas Park FL 33565. (813)544-8286. Contact Person: Public Relations Director. **Description:** "Our purpose is to promote the interests of children in divorce, child custody, child abuse, child snatching, and other situations of legal disadvantage to children." **Services:** Provides advisory, analytical, bibliographical, how-to, interpretative and referral information on child abuse, child custody, parental abduction of children, paternity, and divorce-related issues affecting children's rights. Offers aid in arranging interviews, brochures/pamphlets, research assistance, statistics and telephone reference services. Publications include *Men's National Newsletter* c/o M.E.N. International, Box 189, Forest Lake MN 55025 ($15/year). **How to Contact:** Call. Responds to most inquiries immediately. Charges for some services. Scale depends on purpose, agency requesting, and service being requested. Quotation on request. **Tips:** Recent information requests: Demographic incidence of child abuse by gender and relationship to child; most frequent allegations by female parents against male parent to prevent male custody.

486• PARENTS OF LESBIANS & GAY MEN, INC.
Box 553, Lenox Hill Station, New York NY 10021. (914)793-5198. Contact Person: Executive Director. **Description:** "Our purpose is to help parents to understand and support their homosexual children; to educate society about homosexuality; and to work for civil rights for our children." **Services:** Provides advisory, analytical and interpretative information on homosexuality and family relationships. Offers aid in arranging interviews, brochures/pamphlets and informational newsletters. **How to Contact:** Write or call. Responds to most inquiries within a month.

487• PARENTS OF PUNKERS
Box 4830, Long Beach CA 90804. (213)493-5081. Contact Person: Director. **Description:** "Our purpose is to provide support to parents whose children are involved in the punk rock movement and to help their children who are involved in the punk rock scene." **Services:** Provides advisory, analytical, interpretative and referral information on punk rock. **How to Contact:** Write or call.

BEHIND THE BYLINE

Ellen Goodman
Syndicated columnist

In the introduction to *Close to Home*, a collection of her columns, Ellen Goodman observes that you need three things to write a column: the egocentric confidence that your view of the world is important enough to be read; the pacing of a long-distance runner; and (in her case) two opinions a week. Her syndicated column appears in more than three hundred newspapers across the country; she calls herself an expert on only one subject—the ambivalence of life.

"I don't give sermons from the mount; that's not my style. I'm more of a fellow traveler. Like my readers, I'm going through the world. I write about what I see and feel along the way."

In addition to her columns and books, her writing has appeared in magazines such as *McCalls*, *The Village Voice* and *Harper's Bazaar*. Headquartered at the *Boston Globe*, she says, "Research is a general word, but for me it means news reporting—calling people up, getting facts and figures straight. It means knowing where to look. Before I was a columnist, I was a street reporter for ten years; I found out where to look for things. You can't run on empty for long. I'm notorious as an over researcher. I over research so that I have the solidity from which to write. I may end up spending four days talking to twelve people and using none of it, but it's part of feeling solid enough to write about something. I'm not a 'wing it' person. You could probably do that for awhile, but you wouldn't last long in this business.

"Research also encompasses everything you do in your daily life. It means observing, being aware and being able to translate that awareness."

How does she prepare daily to transform awareness into print? "I have to read a certain number of words before I can write. I have to read all the papers, and then I try to get a certain number of lines down before lunch. I also use a CRT or VDT or whatever you want to call it; using one of those machines changes your writing style. For example, I'm an unbelievable rewrite person. With the machine it's not really rewriting—it's a constant fiddling with words."

Goodman's column ideas come from different places. "It's a morphous process," she says. "I might read something and say, 'Oh, yuk' and then I'll try to figure out 'why yuk?'. Or I sense that everyone's talking about something, and I ask, 'What's going on here to cause people to be interested?'. Other times I have a strong reaction to legislation or a court case."

Goodman writes about universal themes, family and society. And she routinely tackles emotional issues (abortion, equal rights, values clarification) while managing to keep an objective distance. "I'm just not a very maudlin person, so it's unlikely that I would write goop. But if I border on it, I read it and say, 'Goop—blechhkt!' " Though she can detect when her writing doesn't work, she admits that she's not always her own best critic.

The realities of the newspaper business are the reason. "Sometimes things get into the paper that I'm not happy with, because I'm working on deadline and that's what's real. Until they've done it, people don't understand the constraints of this business; that you're working with 750 words and *on deadline*. There are times when you write something that you're not thrilled with, but you've got to get it in.

"After awhile, that word limit becomes the context in which you write. And writing to space becomes part of what you write whether you are figuring out a perspective on some legislation or looking at the why of human behavior."

Responds to most inquiries within a month. Charges for some services depending on nature of the particular situation.

488• PARENTS WITHOUT PARTNERS, INC.
7910 Woodmont Ave., Bethesda MD 20814. (301)654-8850. Contact Person: Information Center Director. **Description:** "We are a volunteer national and international organization of single parents—the widowed, divorced, separated or never-married—who are bringing up children alone, or who, through not having custody, are still parents and concerned with the upbringing of their children. Chapters in the US and Canada plan and conduct programs of help, with general guidelines and material provided by PWP, Inc. PWP, with over 210,000 members, is tax-exempt under federal law as a nonprofit educational organization." **Services:** Provides advisory, bibliographical, how-to, interpretative and referral information on custody, divorce, single fathers, child support, widowhood, children, raising children alone and childcare. Offers bibliographies, brochures/pamphlets, statistics; 700 + volume reference library on premises. **How to Contact:** Write. Responds to most inquiries within a week. Charges for cost of materials plus postage/handling. **Tips:** Recent information request: "How many single parents are there?"

489• PLANNED PARENTHOOD FEDERATION OF AMERICA, INC.
810 7th Ave., New York NY 10025. (212)541-7800. Contact Person: Public Information Coordinator. **Description:** "PPFA is the oldest and largest voluntary family planning agency in the US. We are dedicated to the principle that every individual has the fundamental right to choose when or whether to have children. We provide medical, educational, and counseling services." **Services:** Provides historical and interpretative information on family planning, individual rights and family planning, contraception, sexuality education and abortion. Offers aid in arranging interviews, annual reports, brochures/pamphlets, library facilities, placement on mailing lists, research assistance and statistics. Publications include *Planned Parenthood Review*, $4/yr. (quarterly). **How to Contact:** Write. Responds to most inquiries within a week.

490• SOLO CENTER
6514 35th Ave. NE, Seattle WA 98115. (206)522-7656. Contact Person: Director. **Description:** "We serve as a resource, information and referral program and growth center for adults (and their families) in transition by reason of separation, divorce, widowing or never having married. We offer a social/emotional support system during crisis caused by loss of marital or relationship partner. Programs are scheduled 365 evenings of the year, a monthly newspaper/program is published and distributed, and special programs and brochures are provided." **Services:** Provides advisory, how-to and referral information on self-help and guidance during separation and divorce and to singles new in town; also social resources. Offers programs, annual reports, brochures/pamphlets, placement on mailing list, information and referral services and a "listening ear. We are neither a social club nor a mental health center." Publications include a monthly newsletter, various brochures and reprints. **How to Contact:** Write or call. Responds to most inquiries immediately. "Small entry/use fee of $3/person/attendance includes drop-in socializing and/or regular nightly programs. Writers/researchers obtain permission in advance for story and identities and give appropriate attribution." **Tips:** Recent information requests: "What is unique about Solo Center?"; "Why do people seek its services?"

491• STEPFAMILY FOUNDATION, INC.
333 West End, New York NY 10023. (212)877-3244. Contact Person: Assistant to the Director. **Description:** "We serve stepfamilies and those who live in step relationships through information and educational counseling. We also provide training seminars for professionals and lecturers." **Services:** Offers aid in arranging interviews, brochures/pamphlets, clipping services, informational newsletters, press kits and research assistance. Publications include digest of "step" articles; *Living in Step* ($8); Introductory Information Packet ($4); and Complete Information Packet ($20, includes *Living in Step*, pamphlets and selected articles). **How to Contact:** Write or call. Responds to most inquiries within a week.

492• SURROGATE PARENT FOUNDATION, INC.
c/o Harris & Associates, 1745 W. Katella, Suite E, Orange CA 92667. (714)532-6825. Contact Person: Information Officer. **Description:** The foundation "provides information on the new area of surrogate parenting and developments in related fields; sponsors informational clinics and symposium. We are currently establishing a library of all known articles, papers and taped

interviews." **Services:** Provides advisory and referral information on surrogate parenting: definition, principles involved, ethical practitioners in the field, legal aspects, medical aspects, sociological and psychological aspects. Offers aid in arranging interviews, biographies, brochures/pamphlets, informational newsletters, library facilities and placement on mailing lists. Publications include studies; interviews with professionals; journal and consumer publications. **How to Contact:** Write or call. Responds to most inquiries within a week. Charges for multiple copies and cassette duplicates. **Tips:** "Writers must respect anonymity of surrogates or couples when interviewed, if requested. Freelance writers must indicate where the stories will be published and verification of assignment. We can provide an initial reading list—preliminary research may help them develop better story angles."

493• WOMEN IN TRANSITION
112 S. 16th St., 7th Floor, Philadelphia PA 19102. (215)563-9984. Contact Person: Executive Director. **Description:** "Women in Transition is a nonprofit organization which provides counseling, training, community education and advocacy to women and their families who are experiencing difficulties during any life transition." **Services:** Provides information on abused women, displaced homemakers, separation and divorce, widowhood, midlife transition, remarriage, marital counseling, career readiness skills, group process skills, single parenting, singlehood, infertility. Publications include *A Facilitator's Guide to Working with Separated and Divorced Women*; and *Stepping Out to Work*, a career readiness curriculum for low-income women. **How to Contact:** Write or call. Responds to most inquiries within a week. "Writers/researchers must be willing to attribute material to Women in Transition; all issues of confidentiality must be maintained. We prefer that we see our 'quotes' to verify accuracy prior to publication." **Tips:** "Do some preliminary research, as much as possible, to see what else has been written so that you are very clear about what is the best use you can make of a primary source." Recent information request: "What are the specific issues facing the career women in their thirties who have never married?"

494• YESTERDAY'S CHILDREN
Box 1554, Evanston IL 60204. (312)475-1700. Contact Person: President. **Description:** "Yesterday's Children is a nonprofit national organization of adults dedicated to the proposition that every adult has a right to knowledge of his own historical past. The majority of members are persons who have been separated from their biological families through foster care or adoption, divorce or death of parents. We propose to work to amend state laws to recognize the right of the adult to the information that concerns him; we propose to speak out in behalf of children currently growing up in adoption or foster care; and we propose to offer counsel and assistance to adults seeking their own historical roots." **Services:** Provides advisory and referral information. Publications include *National Adoption Registry*. **How to Contact:** Write or call. Charges for publication and membership.

SECTION · NINE

FARMING AND FOOD

Farming looks mighty easy when your plow is a pencil, and you're a thousand miles from a corn field.
—*Dwight D. Eisenhower*

It's odd how large a part food plays in memories of childhood. There are grown men and women who still shudder at the sight of spinach, or turn away with loathing from stewed prunes and tapioca . . . Luckily, however,

it's the good tastes one remembers best.
—*Caroline Lejeune*

This category includes resources in agriculture; farming technology and research; food and drink; nutrition and dietetics; food services and food processing.

Home and flower gardening is covered in the Animals and Plants section.

Bibliography

Bibliography of Agriculture. Annual Cumulation. Phoenix: Oryx Press.

Biological and Agricultural Index. 1964 to date, monthly. New York: H.W. Wilson Co.

Culinary Arts Institute. *Nutrition Cookbook*. New York: Delair Publishing Co., 1978.

Farm and Garden Index. Edited by Minnesota Scholarly Press. Mankato, MN: Minnesota Scholarly Press, 1980.

Food and Agriculture Organization. *Traditional and Nontraditional Foods*. Food & Nutrition Series No. 2. New York: Unipub, 1981.

McGraw-Hill Encyclopedia of Food, Agriculture and Nutrition. New York: McGraw-Hill, 1977.

Scarpa, Ioannis, et. al., eds. *Sourcebook of Food and Nutrition*. 2d ed. Chicago: Marquis Who's Who, 1980.

Simon, Andre Louis. *A Concise Encyclopedia of Gastronomy*. Woodstock, NY: Overlook Press, 1981.

US Department of Agriculture. *Agricultural Statistics*. Annual. Washington DC.

US Department of Agriculture. *Composition of Foods*. Handbook No. 8. Washington DC: Government Printing Office, 1980.

US Department of Agriculture. *Nutritive Value of American Foods in Common Units*. Edited by Catherine F. Adams. Agricultural Handbook # 456. Washington DC: Agricultural Research Service, 1975.

Winburne, J.N., ed. *Dictionary of Agricultural & Allied Technology*. Lansing, MI: Michigan State University Press, 1962.

495• AGRICULTURAL COOPERATIVE DEVELOPMENT INTERNATIONAL
1012 14th St. NW, Suite 201, Washington DC 20005. (202)638-4661. Contact Person: Director of Publications and Editor. **Description:** ACDI is a nonprofit, educational, consulting and management assistance organization created by the leading agricultural cooperative and farmer organizations of the United States. Its purpose is to respond to the needs of agricultural cooperatives, farm credit systems and supporting government agencies in the developing countries by providing assistance in training, planning, operations, organization and member involvement. **Services:** Provides referral and technical information. Offers annual reports, brochures/pamphlets, informational newsletters, library facilities (limited) and photos (limited). **How to Contact:** Write or call. Responds to most inquiries within a month. "We have very limited resources and very limited time." **Tips:** "We answer questions about our projects and help with any inquiry to our best ability."

496• AGRICULTURAL MARKETING SERVICE
Department of Agriculture, Washington DC 20250. Contact Person: Director, Information Division. **Description:** AMS is responsible for standardization and grading for various farm

commodities, marketing agreements and orders, market news services, promoting fair trade practices, food purchasing for distribution through programs of the Food and Nutrition Service, research and promotion programs, enhancing food safety, and market research and development. It provides various marketing services for nearly all agricultural commodities. **Services:** Provides advisory, analytical, interpretative, referral, technical and trade information on its programs. Offers publications, photos, a catalog of available publications and other assistance. **How to Contact:** Write. Responds to most inquiries immediately. Varying fees are charged for some marketing services and for some reports and publications. "Reports and publications are not copyrighted and may be used by the public without restriction—credit is appreciated." **Tips:** "Questions should be specific and well defined." Recent information request: "What are marketing orders and how do they work?"

497• AGRICULTURAL STABILIZATION AND CONSERVATION SERVICE
Department of Agriculture, Box 2415, Information Division, Washington DC 20013. (202)447-5237. Contact Person: Director. **Description:** "A service agency dedicated to providing the best possible administration of farm programs." **Services:** Provides advisory, historical and referral information covering (Commodity Credit Corporation) government loans and payments to farmers; conservation assistance for farmers; farm programs and federal farm acts. Offers statistics and brochures/pamphlets. Publications include material on many agricultural topics, particularly those related to farm programs. **How to Contact:** Write or call. Responds to most inquiries immediately. Charges for photocopying. **Tips:** "Because of the decreasing availability of funds, we need your help. Try us; we may not have the information, but we are willing to help you find it." Recent information requests: Background material on the US dairy surplus; related questions on the distribution of government-owned stocks.

498• AMERICAN ANGUS ASSOCIATION
3201 Frederick Blvd., St. Joseph MO 64501 (816)233-3101. Contact Person: Director of Communications and Public Relations. **Description:** Organization keeping ancestral and production records on purebred Angus cattle. "We have a complete advertising and promotion program; a junior activities program involving some 11,000 young cattle breeders; and 30,000 active life members who produce registered beef cattle as seedstock for the commercial cattle industry. We are the largest beef cattle registry association in the world, as determined by annual registrations." **Services:** Provides information covering agriculture, food, history, self-help and technical data. Offers aid in arranging interviews, annual reports, biographies, statistics, brochures/pamphlets, placement on mailing lists and photos. Publications include *How to be Successful with Your Small Angus Herd*; *History of the Angus Breed*; *Crossbreeding, Tool for Profit or Financial Disaster*; *Angus Sire Evaluation and Production Records* and *Star of Your Future*, a booklet for youngsters who want to get into the cattle business. **How to Contact:** Write or call. "There is no fee for services except for special requests that would involve a great deal of time or research."

499• AMERICAN BAKERS ASSOCIATION
2020 K St. NW, Suite 850, Washington DC 20006. (202)296-5800. Contact Person: President. **Description:** The chief emphasis of the association is on legislative and regulatory issues affecting wholesale bakers, their suppliers and customers. **Services:** Offers aid in arranging interviews, statistics, brochures/pamphlets, placement on mailing list, newsletter and speakers. **How to Contact:** "Telephone contact is preferred, unless a great deal of information is needed." **Tips:** "Make sure you've got your questions well thought out in advance."

500• AMERICAN DIETETIC ASSOCIATION
430 N. Michigan Ave., Chicago IL 60611. (312)280-5000. Contact: Public Affairs. **Description:** Association of 47,000 dietitians "dedicated to improving the nutrition of human beings and advancement of the science of dietetics and nutrition and the promotion of education in these and allied fields." **Services:** Provides bibliographical, technical, professional and consumer information. Publications include *Food Facts Talk Back*; *Allergy Recipes*; *Handbook of Clinical Dietetics*; *Nutrition: What's It All About?*; *Food 2* and *Food 3*; *National Nutrition Time Materials*; *Sodium, Think About It*; *Nutrition Services for Older Americans: Food-service Systems and Technologies*. Publications catalog available. **How to Contact:** Write or call. Charges for publications.

501• AMERICAN FARM BUREAU FEDERATION
225 Touhy Ave., Park Ridge IL 60068. (312)399-5700. Contact Person: Senior Economist.
Description: "The American Farm Bureau Federation (AFBF) is local, statewide, national and international in scope and influence and is nonpartisan, nonsectarian, nonsecret in character. AFBF is a free, independent nongovernmental and voluntary organization of farm and ranch families united for the purpose of analyzing problems and formulating action programs to achieve educational improvement, economic opportunity and social advancement, thereby promoting the national well-being." **Services:** Provides analytical, referral, technical and trade information covering farm economics and general economics. Offers brochures/pamphlets, statistics and commentary on farm and general economic policies. **How to Contact:** Write or call. Responds to most inquiries within a month; "depends on the inquiry." **Tips:** "Think through your questions; make them specific; quote us accurately." Recent information request: "What are the economic implications of this year's federal wheat program?"

502• AMERICAN HOMEBREWERS ASSOCIATION
Box 287, Boulder CO 80306. (303)447-0816. Contact Person: Editor. **Description:** "Our purpose is educational and literary, to benefit homebrewers of beer, 'microbrewing' on a small commercial scale; also to provide network of information for all those interested in beer and brewing." **Services:** Provides advisory, bibliographical, historical, how-to, technical and trade information. Offers informational newsletters, photos, press kits, research assistance and statistics. Publications include *Zymurgy* magazine. **How to Contact:** Write. Responds to most inquiries within a week. Give credit to association. **Tips:** Recent information requests: How-to information; photos and illustrations; questions about homebrewing and small-scale commercial brewing in a specific area.

503• AMERICAN MUSHROOM INSTITUTE
Box 373, Kennett Square PA 19348. (215)388-7806. Contact Person: Director of Communications. **Description:** "The AMI is an organization that acts on legislative and marketing problems faced by US mushroom growers." **Services:** Provides advisory, analytical, how-to, interpretative, referral, technical and trade information including how to grow mushrooms; statistics on fresh and processed mushrooms; consumer consumption; recipes and nutritional information. Offers aid in arranging interviews, brochures/pamphlets, informational newsletters, library facilities, placement on mailing lists and statistics. Publications include *Mushroom News*, a trade magazine for the mushroom industry; *The Great American Mushroom*; *Six Steps to Composting*; *Crop Report for Mushrooms*. **How to Contact:** Write or call. Responds to most inquiries within a week. Charges nominal fee for some publications. **Tips:** "Ask specific questions." Recent information requests: "How many mushroom growers are there in the US?"; "How have imports from the People's Republic of China hurt the American mushroom industry?"

504• AMERICAN SHEEP PRODUCERS COUNCIL
200 Clayton St., Denver CO 80206. (303)399-8130. Contact: Communications Services Department. **Description:** Organization promoting and marketing the American sheep industry, including lamb and wool products. **Services:** Provides educational information on lamb and wool products and the American sheep industry. Offers brochures/pamphlets and press kits. Publications include *Lamb Cookery Basics*; *Lamb Around the World*; *The History of Sheep*; *Story of Wool*. Complete list of publications available. **How to Contact:** Write. Responds to most inquiries within a month. Charges for some publications.

505• AMERICAN SPICE TRADE ASSOCIATION (ASTA)
Box 1267, Englewood Cliffs NJ 07632. (201)568-2163. Contact Person: Secretary. **Description:** Organization for firms producing, trading or processing spices; using spices in industrial quantities; or selling products or services to the spice industry. "American Spice Trade Association's (ASTA) purpose is that of an aggressive trade association designed to protect the interests and promote the welfare of its industry and to assume as a group those functions which the individual member firm cannot perform as effectively itself." **Services:** Provides advisory, analytical, how-to, interpretative, referral, technical and trade information covering agriculture, business, food and history of the industry. Offers aid in arranging interviews, bibliographies, statistics and brochures/pamphlets. Publications include several booklets, brochures and article reprints. Publications guide available. **How to Contact:** Write Mr. M. Neale, Lewis and Neale, Inc., 928 Broadway, New York NY 10010. "This firm has handled our PR and has operated our test kitch-

ens for over 30 years." Responds to most inquiries within a week. **Tips:** "Know what you want. Don't ask to 'send me all your information about spices.' "

506• ASSOCIATED MILK PRODUCERS, INC.
Box 32287, San Antonio TX 78284. Contact Person: Communications Coordinator. **Description:** Dairy marketing cooperative organized into three regions. **Services:** Provides trade information. Offers placement on mailing list. Publications include *Dairymen's Digest*, monthly. **How to Contact:** "Contact region in which information is needed." For mid-states region, write 8550 Bryn Mawr, Chicago IL 60631. For Southern region, write Box 5040, Arlington TX 76010. For North Central region, write Box 455, New Ulm MN 56073. Responds to most inquiries within a month. "We're limited in personnel to handle extensive research. Try USDA first—they specialize in many dairy research items." **Tips:** "Use information provided accurately and properly."

507• C. BREWER—KILAUEA AGRONOMICS
Box 1826, Honolulu HI 96805. (808)536-4461. Contact Person: Public Relations Manager. **Description:** "Producers, processors and marketers of tropical products, including guava fruit. The parent company produces sugar and macadamia nuts." **Services:** Provides advisory, historical and referral information covering the growing, processing, and marketing of guava products. Offers aid in arranging interviews, annual reports and brochures/pamphlets. **How to Contact:** Write. Responds to most inquiries within a week.

508• CALORIE CONTROL COUNCIL
5775 Peach St., Dunwoody Rd. NE, Suite 500-D, Atlanta GA 30342. (404)252-3663. Contact Person: Director of Communications. **Description:** "The Calorie Control Council is an association of manufacturers and suppliers of dietary foods and beverages." **Services:** Offers a quarterly newsletter, *Commentary*; and *Saccharin* (data on history, safety and benefits of this sweetener). **How to Contact:** Write or call. Responds to most inquiries within a week. Charges for brochure: $9/hundred (0-499); $8.25/hundred (500-999); and $7/hundred (1000-Over). **Tips:** "We answer many requests for updated information on the regulatory status of sweeteners and for reports on upcoming and new sweeteners."

509• CAMPBELL SOUP COMPANY
Campbell Place, Camden NJ 08101. (609)964-4000. Contact Person: Manager, Public Relations. **Description:** Campbell Soup Co. manufactures "prepared convenience foods." **Services:** Provides bibliographical and historical information on corporate operations. Offers aid in arranging interviews, annual reports, biographies, photos and press kits. Publications include *The Eleventh Decade*, and material covering company history and chronology. **How to Contact:** Write. Responds to most inquiries immediately.

510• CANADA GRAINS COUNCIL
760-360 Main St., Winnipeg, Manitoba, Canada R3C 3Z3. (204)942-2254. Contact Person: Communications Officer. **Description:** "We provide a forum for discussion for the grains industry in Canada, as well as a liaison with government. We work toward increasing markets for Canadian grains overseas and at home. We seek general improvements for the grains industry, coordinate research and disseminate information." **Services:** Provides advisory, analytical, historical, interpretative, referral and technical information covering all facets of the Canadian grains industry. Offers statistics, brochures/pamphlets and placement on mailing list. Publications include *Statistical Handbook* ($7.50); *Open Door* (6 copies of a marketing newsletter for $3); and reports on many specific subjects (free). **How to Contact:** Write or call. Responds to most inquiries within a week.

511• CASTLE AND COOKE FOODS
50 California St., San Francisco CA 94111. (415)986-3000. Contact Person: Publicity Manager. **Description:** "Castle and Cooke markets food under the Dole and Bumble Bee brands, including bananas, pineapple, coconut, mushrooms, tuna, salmon, crab, lobster and shrimp at retail and food service markets." **Services:** Provides in-depth information about the nutrition and home usage products, recipes and photos for publication and free cookbooklets. Offers brochures/pamphlets, placement on mailing list and newsletter. Publications include a 4-page fact sheet for each product and many recipe booklets. **How to Contact:** Write. Responds to most inquiries within a

week. **Tips:** Recent information requests: Recipes; information about specific foods; help arrange a tour of the Dole pineapple plant in Hawaii.

512• CENTER FOR RURAL STUDIES

Box 8445, Minneapolis MN 55408. (612)825-0138. Contact Person: Executive Director. **Description:** "Our activities include research on food, agriculture, environment and rural affairs." **Services:** Provides analytical, historical, interpretative, referral and trade information on food, nutrition, farming, agribusiness, ecology, environment. Offers aid in arranging interviews, biographies, clipping services, computerized information searches, informational newsletters, library facilities, placement on mailing lists, press kits, research assistance and statistics. Publications include *Monthly Intelligence Service*. **How to Contact:** Write. Responds to most inquiries within a week. Services by contract.

513• CHAMPAGNE NEWS AND INFORMATION BUREAU

220 E. 42nd St., New York NY 10017. (212)907-9382. Contact Person: Director. **Description:** "We are the educational arm in the US for the champagne industry of France. We serve as a resource for press, writers, commentators and the public. We maintain a library, photo file and staff to answer specific requests for information concerning champagne (both the wine and the region where it is produced). We will also assist writers in developing angles for articles." **Services:** Provides information on champagne wine and champagne region: agriculture, business, celebrities, economics, entertainment, food, health/medicine, history, how-to, industry, law, new products, technical data and travel. Offers aid in arranging interviews, statistics, brochures/pamphlets, information searches, photos and press kits. Publications include *Entertaining with Champagne*; *There it is . . . but . . . Wait . . .*; *Champagne-Wine of France*; a brand sheet; and schedule of visiting hours in the cellars. **How to Contact:** Write or call. Responds to most inquiries immediately. **Tips:** "Our cooperation is limited to authentic champagne, i.e., the wine made only in the limited area in northern France. We have no information on other sparkling wines. Be specific when making inquiries." Recent information requests: questions on pink champagne resulting from current interest by consumers in Rosé champagnes; inquiry on champagne for ship launchings.

514• COGNAC INFORMATION BUREAU

c/oCarl Byoir & Associates, 380 Madison Ave., New York NY 10017. (212)986-6100. Contact Person: Account Executive. **Description:** The bureau provides information on the history, production, uses and enjoyment of French cognac. **Services:** Provides historical, referral and trade information covering history, production, culinary uses, enjoyment of cognac—plus market information, photos and recipes. Offers aid in arranging interviews, brochures/pamphlets, library facilities, photos, press kits, research assistance and statistics. **How to Contact:** Write or call. Responds to most inquiries within a week. **Tips:** "We don't provide information for specific brands of cognac, but we will refer you to appropriate people." Recent information requests: "What do the labels on a cognac bottle mean?"; "Why is cognac different from other brandies?"

515• CORN REFINERS ASSOCIATION, INC.

1001 Connecticut Ave. NW, Washington DC 20036. (202)331-1634. Contact Person: Director, Public Affairs. **Description:** "Our organization represents the corn refining (wet milling) industry of the US, producers of starches, syrups, feeds and oil from corn. Primary areas of activity are research on corn products and processing, government relations and public relations." **Services:** Offers annual reports, brochures/pamphlets, placement on mailing list and press kits. Publications include *Corn Annual*; *Tapping the Treasure of Corn*; booklets on corn sweeteners and corn products. **How to Contact:** Write. Responds to most inquiries within a week. Small charge for some printed material. **Tips:** "Usually, a writer calls or writes for one of our publications; then, calls back with specific questions."

516• COUNCIL FOR AGRICULTURAL SCIENCE AND TECHNOLOGY

250 Memorial Union, Ames IA 50011 (515)294-2036. Contact Person: Executive Vice President. **Description:** "The Council for Agricultural Science and Technology (CAST) advances the understanding and use of food and agricultural science and technology in the public interest. It serves as a resource group to which the public and government may turn for information on food and agricultural issues; organizes task forces of agricultural scientists and technologists to assemble and interpret factual information on these issues; and disseminates this information in a usable form to the public, news media and the government." **Services:** Provides referral information covering food

and agriculture. Offers aid in arranging interviews, brochures/pamphlets, reports on scientific facts of current issues and newsletters. Publications include *News from CAST* (bimontly newsletter) and *Directory of Environmental Scientists in Agriculture*. **How to Contact:** Write or call. Responds to most inquiries immediately. **Tips:** "CAST services are available to assist writers in making contact with responsible scientists, thus providing them with accurate information in developing stories." Recent information request: "What is the validity of the National Academy of Science's report on *Diet, Nutrition and Cancer?*"

517• COUNCIL FOR RESPONSIBLE NUTRITION
1735 Eye St. NW, Suite 805, Washington DC 20006. (202)872-1488. Contact Person: Executive Director. **Description:** "Trade association of nutrient supplement manufacturers, dedicated to enhancing the health of the US population through responsible nutrition, including the appropriate use of nutrient supplementation." **Services:** Provides technical and trade information on vitamin/mineral supplements: sales and marketing information, scientific/technical, and government relations oriented. Offers aid in arranging interviews, brochures/pamphlets, press kits and statistics. **How to Contact:** Write. Responds to most inquiries within a week.

518• DEPARTMENT OF AGRICULTURE
Office of Governmental and Public Affairs, 12th and 14th Sts. SW, Washington DC 20250. (202)447-8005. Contact Person: Deputy Director, Public Affairs. **Description:** "The Department of Agriculture is directed by law to acquire and diffuse useful information on agricultural subjects in the most general and comprehensive sense. The Office of Governmental and Public Affairs provides direction, leadership and balance in the development and delivery of this information to the public on the USDA's research, educational and regulatory activities. Public Affairs also provides centralized services to USDA in the areas of photography, motion picture and design exhibits." **Services:** Various agencies of the USDA provide information on research, education, conservation, marketing, regulation, nutrition, food programs and rural development. **How to Contact:** Write or call. Responds to most inquiries as soon as possible. **Tips:** "Requests for information of a specific nature should be sent directly to the appropriate agency in the USDA. For example, requests for information on insects would go to the Agricultural Research Services; requests related to forest and forest products would go to Forest Services. If you're not sure which agency within the USDA to contact, call this office which will refer you to the appropriate agency."

519• DEPARTMENT OF AGRICULTURE, NATIONAL AGRICULTURAL LIBRARY
10301 Baltimore Blvd., Room 1402, Beltsville MD 20705. (301)344-3755. Contact: Educational Resources Staff. **Description:** "The National Agricultural Library (NAL), with a collection of 1.7 million volumes, is the largest agriculture collection in the world. Collected from all over the world, it is made available to farmers, scientists and educators. NAL is tied to a worldwide network of agriculture data collections. Agricultural OnLine Access (Agricola) is the library's data base." **Services:** Provides information on biology and chemistry and related fields as applied to agriculture. Offers brochures/pamphlets, computerized information searches, informational newsletters, library facilities, placement on mailing lists, kits, research assistance, statistics and telephone reference services. Publications include *Agriculture and Hydroponics, 1968-1978*; *Structure of US Agriculture* (bibliography); *Guide to Services*. **How to Contact:** Write or visit. Responds to most inquiries within a week, bibliographic searches, 2 weeks. Charges 20¢/page for photocopying; $1/microfilm. **Tips:** The National Agricultural Library operates the Food and Nutrition Information Center (FNIC) which offers customized service and educational materials in the area of food and nutrition. *Editor's Note:* See entry 525.

520• PETER ECKRICH AND SONS, INC.
Box 388, Fort Wayne IN 46801. (219)481-2448. Contact Person: Director, Public Affairs and Communications. **Description:** "Meat processing company with a line of sausage, frankfurters and luncheon meats that are distributed mainly in the Midwest, but also market by market, coast to coast." **Services:** Provides bibliographical, historical, interpretative, referral and trade information on processed meats. Offers aid in arranging interviews, brochures/pamphlets, information searches, photos and press kits. "We can provide information on meat processing, meat research and consumer issues." **How to Contact:** "We prefer an initial written contact and promise a quick follow-up for urgent matters; phone calls are welcome." **Tips:** "Suggest as other sources for meat information: American Meat Institute (Arlington, VA) and National Livestock

and Meat Board (Chicago).'' Recent information requests: ''Does recent USDA rule on mechanically deboned meat affect Eckrich?''; ''Can you supply information on the history of sausage?''

521• ECONOMIC RESEARCH SERVICE REFERENCE CENTER
500 12th St. SW, Room 147, Washington DC 20250. (202)447-4382. Contact Person: Director. **Description:** ''Government agency library serving the research needs of agricultural economists.'' **Services:** Provides advisory, bibliographical, historical, how-to and referral information on agricultural economics and related topics, e.g., marketing, transportation, cooperatives, foreign trade, agricultural policy, farm management, food economics, world hunger, agriculture in developing countries, land economics, and the like. Offers aid in arranging interviews, brochures/pamphlets, computerized information searches, library facilities and telephone reference services. **How to Contact:** Call or visit. Responds to most inquiries within a week. ''Agency researchers and the general public may use reference center materials on-site. Agency personnel may borrow materials for photocopying only. Online search services and in-depth reference services are available to agency personnel only.'' **Tips:** Recent information requests: ''What has been published recently on livestock futures?''; ''How many cooperatives are in Indiana, Kentucky, Tennessee and Ohio? What is their total business volume and membership?''; ''What legislation has been passed recently that affects small farms?''

522• FARM CREDIT ADMINISTRATION
490 L'Enfant Plaza SW, Washington DC 20578. (202)755-2170. Contact Person: Division Director, Public Affairs Division. **Description:** ''The Farm Credit Administration is responsible for the supervision and coordination of activities of the farm credit system, which consists of federal land banks and federal land bank associations, federal intermediate credit banks and production credit associations, and banks for cooperatives.'' **Services:** Provides information on agricultural credit and finance. Offers annual reports, brochures/pamphlets and placement on mailing list. Publications include *Farm Credit Facts* (a summary of operations of Farm Credit Banks and Associations); *Investor's Guide to Farm Credit Securities* (answers to frequently asked questions about Farm Credit Bonds); *Banks for Cooperatives: How They Operate* (an explanation of lending operations); *The Cooperative Farm Credit System* (an explanation of the functions and organization of the system); *Federal Land Banks: How They Operate* (a description of lending operations of the banks); *Production Credit Associations: How They Operate.* **How to Contact:** Write or call. Responds to most inquiries within a week. **Tips:** Recent information request: How to obtain a farm credit loan.

523• FATS AND PROTEINS RESEARCH FOUNDATION, INC.
2250 E. Devon Ave., Des Plaines IL 60018. (312)827-0139. Contact Person: Technical Director. **Description:** ''We provide technical support for the rendering industry (recyclers of animal byproducts) to expand existing markets and open new markets through research results.'' **Services:** Provides how-to, interpretative, referral, technical and trade information on animal production, industrial uses and other applications for products. Offers aid in arranging interviews and brochures/pamphlets. **How to Contact:** Write. Responds to most inquiries within a month.

524• FOOD AND DRUG ADMINISTRATION
5600 Fishers Lane, Rockville MD 20857. Contact: Press Relations Staff. **Description:** The FDA is concerned with the ''protection of consumers in the areas of food (except meat and poultry); medicines, cosmetics, medical devices, biologicals and electronic equipment emitting radiation.'' **Services:** Provides interpretative, referral and technical information on regulation and safety of medical products—drugs, vaccines, devices—veterinary feeds and drugs, cosmetics and food. Offers press releases, placement on mailing list and brochures on many subjects. Publications include *FDA Consumer* magazine, available by subscription through the Government Printing Office. **How to Contact:** Write for addition to mailing list, brochures. Telephone with press inquiries to (301)443-4177, or 443-3285. Responds to most inquiries immediately. **Tips:** ''We are too busy to do 'general' background research writer could do in library.''

525• FOOD AND NUTRITION INFORMATION CENTER, USDA
National Agricultural Library Bldg., Room 304, Beltsville MD 20705. (301)344-3719. Contact Person: Acting Deputy Administrator. **Description:** ''Specialized information center on food and human nutrition—primarily serves food and nutrition professionals and nutrition

educators." **Services:** Provides bibliographical, referral and technical information on human nutrtion, nutrition education, food service management and management (general). Offers library facilities and telephone reference services. **How to Contact:** Write, call or visit. Responds to most inquiries within a week. **Tips:** Recent information request: Fad diets.

526• FOOD RESEARCH AND ACTION CENTER, INC. (FRAC)
1319 F St. NW, Washington DC 20004. Contact Person: Director of Public Information. **Description:** "Food Research and Action Center (FRAC) operates as a law firm and advocacy center representing the interests of poor people who participate and who are entitled to participate in the federal food programs (food stamps, school lunch and breakfast, elderly nutrition, and other child nutrition programs.) The staff is composed of lawyers, nutritionists, researchers, lobbyists and community organizers. They work with local and state antihunger groups to expand and improve the federal food programs and to encourage the development of poor people's organizations. FRAC also works on welfare reform issues." **Services:** Provides analytical, historical, how-to, interpretative and referral information on Social Welfare—federal food programs, nutrition issues and low-income persons, budget issues affecting low-inome persons. Offers aid in arranging interviews, bibliographies, statistics, brochures/pamphlets and placement on mailing list. Has "information on the governmental and private-sector efforts to end hunger in this country and reform the welfare system. There is also material on legislative matters affecting poverty issues." **How to Contact:** Write or call. Responds to most inquiries within a week. Cost of mailing lists, $20/year; various charges for publications. "The only stipulation for writers/researchers using our services is that FRAC is given credit for the information and that if any reproduction is involved, the material be distributed free of charge." **Tips:** When writing for information, request the *Profile of Federal Food Programs* which describes FRAC, its publications, and the type of work we are involved in. It is free. Recent information requests: Inquiries on statistical information on the participation data for the food stamp program; characteristics of persons participating in the food stamp program; the purchase requirement for the food stamp program (historical background); and request for assistance in improving meal quality in school meals program.

527• FROZEN FOOD ACTION COMMUNICATION TEAM (FACT)
Box 10163. Grand Central Station, New York NY 10163. (212)887-8063. Contact: Public Relations—FACT. **Description:** Promotional and communications program of the frozen food industry working to educate consumers in understanding the frozen food industry. **Services:** Provides analytical, historical, referral and trade information. Offers brochures/pamphlets, press releases, some statistics and telephone reference services. Publications include *Frozen Foods Value and You*; *Frozen Foods—Microwave Cooking*. **How to Contact:** Write (preferred) or call. Responds to most inquiries "before deadline" or within a month. **Tips:** Recent information requests: Trends and costs involved in the frozen food industry.

528• GENERAL FOODS CORPORATION
250 North St., White Plains NY 10625. (914)683-2415. Contact Person: Communications Associate. **Description:** "We are a foods manufacturer and manufacture dry goods and pet foods." **Services:** Offers aid in arranging interviews, annual reports, biographies, statistics, brochures/pamphlets, information searches, placement on mailing list, photos and press kits. Publications include an annual report. **How to Contact:** Write or call. Responds to most inquiries within a week. "Freelancers must be writing for a bona fide publication."

529• GENERAL MILLS, INC.
9200 Wayzata Blvd., Box 1113, Minneapolis MN 55440. (612)540-2460. Contact Person: Director of Communications. **Description:** Manufacturer of consumer goods. Products include Gold Medal Flour, Wheaties, Cheerios, and Betty Crocker mixes. Affiliates include Red Lobster Inns, David Crystal Fashions, Ship 'n Shore, Kenner and Parker Brothers, Eddie Bauer and The Talbots. **Services:** Provides advisory, analytical, historical, interpretative, referral, technical and trade information covering all subjects relating to General Mills and its subsidiary companies. Offers aid in arranging interviews, annual reports, bibliographies, biographies, statistics, brochures/pamphlets, information searches, placement on mailing list, photos, press kits and news releases. **How to Contact:** Write. Responds to most inquiries within a week. "Sometimes, a writer will be referred to an industry trade organization." **Tips:** Recent information request: Describe General Mills's origins as a milling company and its subsequent diversification.

530• HIGGINS LIBRARY OF AGRICULTURAL TECHNOLOGY
Department of Special Collections, University of California Library, Davis CA 95616.
(916)752-1621. Contact Person: Curator. **Description:** "We support teaching and research on the
university campus and research of scholars in the field of agricultural technology." **Services:**
Provides bibliographical, historical and technical information on agricultural technology, agricultural history. Offers brochures/pamphlets, library facilities, photos, research assistance and telephone reference services. **How to Contact:** Write, call or visit. Responds to most inquiries within
a month. Charges for photocopying and photographic reproduction of materials in the collection.
"Credit lines must accompany all reproductions of items from the collection."

531• INSTITUTE OF FOOD TECHNOLOGISTS
221 N. LaSalle St., Chicago IL 60601. (312)782-8424. Contact Person: Director of Public
Information. **Description:** The IFT is a professional scientific society whose members are active
in academic, industrial and governmental institutions and are concerned with food science and
food technology. **Services:** Provides referral and technical information on nutrition and food
safety, also processed foods and food additives. "To help provide editors of trade and popular
publications with factual information, IFT produces both background material and up-to-date
status summaries on current scientific topics of food-related concern. It also maintains a group of
trained volunteers who meet regularly with the press. These 'Regional Communicators' also
appear as guests on radio and TV, and help local media people find additional expert sources."
Offers aid in arranging interviews and brochures/pamphlets. Publications include *Food
Technology* (monthly, official journal of the IFT, free to members); *Journal of Food Science* (bimonthly); *IFT World Directory and Guide* (annual, free to members); and career guidance booklets and materials. **How to Contact:** Write or call. Responds to most inquiries within a week. **Tips:**
Recent information requests: Safety of irradiated food; nutritional value of apples; reasons for including fats in the diet.

532• INTERNATIONAL FOOD INFORMATION SERVICE
Lane End House, Shinfield, Reading RG2 9BB, England 0734-883895. Contact Person:
Managing Director. **Description:** "We provide a world information service in food science and
technology. We have a data base of 18,000 items (abstracts) from world literature. Data base
information is available as a monthly journal (*Food Science and Technology Abstracts*) and on
magnetic tape." **Services:** Provides advisory, bibliographical and technical information on food
science and technology. Offers bibliographies, information searches and newsletter. Publications
include information kit describing service. **How to Contact:** Write. Responds to most inquiries
within a week. Charges for online searches and photocopying.

533• KAHN'S AND COMPANY
3241 Spring Grove Ave., Cincinnati OH 45225. (513)541-4000. Contact Person: Director of
Public/Consumer Relations. **Description:** "We are a processed meats manufacturer owned by
Consolidated Foods Corp. in Chicago." **Services:** "We can provide or put a writer in contact with
someone who can provide information on Rudy's Farm and Hillshire Farm (brand names)."
Provides information on food, health/medicine (related to meat). "We also have information on
Hillshire Farm, Rudy's Farm, the food service trade (restaurants, schools, etc.), and government
regulation in regard to meat." Offers annual reports, biographies, statistics and
brochures/pamphlets. **How to Contact:** Write. Responds to most inquiries within a week. "We
will help in any way we can, but we like to know what kind of article is being written, what type of
tone/theme/angle will be used, and where it will be placed."

534• KITCHENS OF SARA LEE
500 Waukegan Rd., Deerfield IL 60015. (312)945-2525. Contact Person: Manager of Public
Affairs. **Description:** Manufacturer of frozen bakery products for retail and food service
outlets. **Services:** Provides advisory, analytical, bibliographical, historical, how-to,
interpretative, referral, technical and trade information on the baking industry. Offers aid in
arranging interviews, biographies, brochures/pamphlets, photos, press kits, research assistance
and statistics. **How to Contact:** Write or call. Responds to most inquiries immediately. "No
comments on financial details (referred to parent company, Consolidated Foods Corp., Chicago)
or on new product or advertising plans."

535• KRAFT, INC.
Kraft Court, Glenview IL 60025. (312)998-2000. Contact Person: Public Relations Manager.
Description: Manufacturer of prepared foods. **Services:** Offers annual reports and brochures/
pamphlets. **How to Contact:** Write. Responds to most inquiries within a week.

536• THE KROGER COMPANY
1014 Vine St., Cincinnati OH 45201. (513)762-4440. Contact Person: Manager, Public
Information. **Description:** Activities include food processing and operation of supermarkets and
drug stores. **Services:** Offers aid in arranging interviews, annual reports, biographies, statistics,
brochures/pamphlets, and "general information about the food and supermarket industry." **How
to Contact:** Write. Responds to most inquiries within a week.

537• LIVESTOCK CONSERVATION INSTITUTE
239 Livestock Exchange Bldg., South St. Paul MN 55075. (612)457-0132. Contact Person:
Director of Information. **Description:** "The LCI serves as a clearinghouse for all sectors of the
livestock and meat industry in sponsoring research and educational programs designed to control
and eradicate livestock diseases and reduce the losses that result from parasites, bruises, injuries
and deaths incurred in handling." **Services:** Provides advisory, interpretative, referral and trade
information on LCI committees: brucellosis, pseudorabies, parasites, trichinosis, emergency
diseases, livestock handling, swine abscess, swine dysentery, chemicals/additives/residues,
feeder cattle health, identification and swine mycobacteriosis and TB. Offers annual reports,
brochures/pamphlets, informational newsletters, research assistance and statistics. Publications
include: Official Proceedings of annual meeting (covering all committee areas); pamphlets on
handling livestock, disease control, and background papers on subjects of interest to the various
committees listed. **How to Contact:** Write or call. Responds to most inquiries within a week.
Charges for some services; nominal cost for pamphlets and livestock handling slide sets, quantity
prices available. LCI members receive discount. For single copies of pamphlets, send SASE. *No
charge for information-type questions.* **Tips:** Recent information requests: Handling of veal calves
and feeder calves from farm to market; new brucellosis interstate movement regulations;
eradication of pseudorabies.

538• MAPLE RESEARCH LABORATORY
University of Vermont, Life-Sciences Bldg., Burlington VT 05405. (802)656-2930, 656-2931.
Contact Person: Research Associate Professor. **Description:** "We are involved in basic and
applied research about the sugar maple tree and its products; teaching undergraduate and graduate
students sugar maple science; and consulting to the sugar maple industry in the US and Canada."
Services: Provides advisory, bibliographical, historical, referral, technical and trade information
related to the sugar maple (physiology, anatomy, ecology, etc.; biochemistry and microbiology of
sap; chemistry of syrup, etc.; technology of sap and syrup production, etc.); historical and modern
perspective. Offers annual reports, brochures/pamphlets, technical papers, informational newsletters, library facilities, photos, placement on mailing lists, press kits, research assistance, statistics
and telephone reference services. Publications include: list of publications, sugar maple research
newsletter (annual), reprints and photocopies. **How to Contact:** Write, call or visit. Responds to
most inquiries within a week. Charges for photocopies and cost of handling the request (if
lengthy). "We require accuracy in reporting research information and citing sources." **Tips:**
"Write us or phone first in order to set up a personal contact visit to our facilities: laboratories,
sugarbush and sugarhouses. We have completed successfully a collaborative study with 6 other
research laboratories to test a new method of detecting adulteration of maple syrup with cane sugar
and corn syrup."

539• MIGRANT LEGAL ACTION PROGRAM
806 15th St. NW, Suite 600, Washington DC 20006. (202)347-5100. Contact Person:
Librarian. **Description:** "Our legal services support center provides legal services to migrant and
seasonal farm workers." **Services:** Provides advisory, analytical, historical, interpretative and
referral information on migrant and seasonal farm workers, working conditions, state and federal
labor legislation, pesticides, housing, migrant education and temporary foreign workers. Offers
aid in arranging interviews, library facilities, research assistance, statistics and telephone
reference services. **How to Contact:** Write or call. Responds to most inquiries within a
week. **Tips:** Recent information request: "How many states have eliminated the 'fellow worker'
exception to negligence liability of an employer of farm labor?"

540• NATIONAL ASSOCIATION OF ANIMAL BREEDERS
Box 1033, Columbia MO 65205. (314)445-4406. Contact Person: Director of Communications. **Description:** ''The National Association of Animal Breeders (NAAB) is the trade association for the artificial insemination (IA) industry.'' **Services:** Provides advisory, analytical, bibliographical, historical, how-to, interpretative, referral, technical and trade information covering artificial insemination and the reproductive physiology of beef and dairy cattle. Offers statistics about semen sales, brochures/pamphlets and magazine. Publications include *The Advanced Animal Breeder*, magazine published 9 times/year (subscription $4); *Beef Proceedings*, covering the annual Beef Artificial Insemination convention ($2); *Annual Convention Proceedings*; (covering the annual NAAB convention ($1); *Technical Proceedings*, covering the biennial Artificial Insemination Technical Conference ($6); *Better Beef with AI* (50¢); *AI Industry of the U.S.A.* (15¢); *Dairy Sire Evaluation in the U.S.A.* (9¢); *Career Opportunities in Artificial Insemination* (free); *Recommended Standards for Health of Bulls Producing Semen for Artificial Insemination* (free); *Recommended Minimum Standards for Training Artificial Insemination Technicians and Herdsman Inseminators* (8¢ and postage); *Beef Artificial Insemination Regulations* (20¢ each; minimum order—$1); *Artificial Insemination Requirements of Members of PDCA* (4¢ and postage); and *CSS Serving the Livestock Industry* (free). **How to Contact:** ''Write and ask. Prices are subject to change. Most of our material is copyrighted. Written permission must be obtained to use it.'' Responds to most inquiries within a week.

541• NATIONAL BOARD OF FUR FARM ORGANIZATIONS, INC.
3055 N. Brookfield Rd., Brookfield WI 53005. (414)786-4242. Contact Person: Administrative Officer. **Description:** Organization designed to educate and inform people about US farm-raised mink and foxes, excluding the promotion and marketing of mink and fox furs. **Services:** Provides analytical, historical, how-to, referral and technical information covering the raising of mink and foxes on farms. Offers aid in arranging interviews, bibliographies, statistics and brochures/pamphlets. Charges for publications including *Mink Farming in the United States*; *Research References on Mink and Foxes* and *Nature's Jewels, a History of Mink Farming in the United States*. **How to Contact:** Write. Responds to most inquiries within a week. '''We do not do literature searches or other work which writers themselves can do. Tell us exactly why you want the information and how you propose to utilize it and in what media. We do not provide information which can be obtained in libraries of major cities and universities.'' **Tips:** ''Gather all possible factual data before contacting us.'' Recent information request: ''What is the economic future for mink farming in the US?''

542• NATIONAL BUFFALO ASSOCIATION
Box 706, Custer SD 57720. (605)683-2073. Contact Person: Executive Director/Editor. **Description:** Organization that ''promotes buffalo and buffalo products; encourages the raising of buffalo; distributes information on buffalo breeding, health, etc., monitors legislation that affects buffalo and promotes research on buffalo nutrition and immunity to cancer.'' **Services:** Provides advisory, analytical, historical, how-to and trade information covering live animal breeding and buffalo management. Resources include collections of buffalo-related items. Offers brochures/pamphlets and newsletter. Publications include *Buffalo: America's Original Inhabitants* (SASE); a buffalo cookbook ($1.75); *Buffalo!* (bimonthly magazine $10/year); and information on the association. **How to Contact:** Write. Responds to most inquiries immediately. Charges for services to nonmembers; free information to members (SASE). Associate membership ($20) includes magazine, newsletter and all NBA mailings. Active membership ($30) for the person training buffalo includes all the above services and marketing assistance. **Tips:** ''We are the only information source on the subject of buffalo.'' Recent information requests: Statistics, telephone interviews and general background on the industry.

543• NATIONAL COLONIAL FARM
3400 Bryan Point Rd., Accokeek MD 20607. (301)283-2113. Contact Person: Director. **Description:** ''The National Colonial Farm is a living historical farm museum. Its purposes are to educate the public through a re-creation of an 18th century, middle-class tobacco plantation. It also conducts research into historical agriculture. The farm is involved in genetic research into crops and is attempting to develop a blight-free American chestnut.'' **Services:** Provides advisory, historical, how-to and interpretative information covering historic agriculture and living historical farm operations. Offers annual reports, brochures/pamphlets and newsletter.

Publications include *A Companion Planting Dictionary; Herbs; Tobacco: The Cash Crop Along the Colonial Potomac; Corn: The Production of a Subsistence Crop Along the Colonial Potomac; An Update on Maize; English Grains Along the Colonial Potomac; The American Chestnut; Of Fast Horses, Black Cattle, Woods Hogs and Rat-Tailed Sheep: Animal Husbandry Along the Colonial Potomac; Investigations into the Origins and Evolution of Zea Mays (Corn); History and Experience of the Accokeek Foundation—A Case Study in Open Space Conservation; A History of the Legislation for the Creation and Development of Piscataway Park; Living Historical Farms: The Working Museums; A Conflict of Values: Agricultural Land in the United States; Farmers and the Future: Opinions and Views of Maryland Farmers; The Development of Wheat Growing in America; Investigations into the Origins and Evolution of the Genus Nicotiana (Tobacco); Root Crops in Colonial America; Colonial American Legume Crops.* **How to Contact:** Write, requesting specific title or information. Responds to most inquiries within a month. "Some materials are restricted to use on the site of the National Colonial Farm." Charges 50¢-$12/publication, including postage and handling. Requires acknowledgment of source. **Tips:** "Organize research data; take complete notes; check quotes whenever possible." Recent information request: "What were the nutrient requirements that made a crop of small grains possible after growing crops of tobacco and corn?"

544• NATIONAL COTTON COUNCIL
Box 12285, Memphis TN 38112. (901)274-9030. Contact Person: Public Relations Director. **Description:** "The council's purpose is to increase use of cotton, cottonseed and their products." **Services:** Provides information on agriculture, economics, history and technical data. Offers aid in arranging interviews, statistics, brochures/pamphlets, photos and press kits. Publications include *Cotton, the First Fiber . . . Yesterday, Today, and Tomorrow*; *Cotton From Field to Fabric*; *The Story of Cotton*; and *Cotton: The Perennial Patriot.* **How to Contact:** Write or call. Responds to most inquiries immediatey. Most literature is available free for single copies; charges for quantity orders. **Tips:** "Be specific in requesting information."

545• NATIONAL DAIRY COUNCIL
6300 N. River Rd., Rosemont IL 60018. (312)696-1020. Contact Person: Manager, Nutrition Information. **Description:** "The National Dairy Council provides nutrition research, nutrition information dissemination and nutrition education materials and program. Our mission is to contribute to optimal health through leadership in nutrition research and education by encouraging food selection patterns that include dairy foods and other major food categories in accordance with scientific recommendations." **Services:** Provides advisory, analytical, how-to, referral, technical, technical and trade information covering dairy foods as they relate to human nutrition; education and nutrition; and limited information or referrals on the marketing of dairy foods. Offers aid in arranging interviews, statistics, brochures/pamphlets, information searches, and photos. "We provide specific information on the nutritional value of dairy foods as part of a balanced diet." Publications include consumer information sheets and *Nutrition Source Book.* **How to Contact:** Write or call. Responds to most inquiries immediately, "depending on the nature of inquiry. We charge only for certain materials, such as brochures, that are normally sold to the public. Background information, searches in our own library and other information are normally provided without cost to media. Specific permission must be granted to quote from copyrighted materials. National Dairy Council requires that all uses be enumerated as to context and application." **Tips:** "Be specific. Fishing expeditions are difficult to handle and frequently are unproductive. National Dairy Council's library is one of the most specialized libraries available on dairy foods and nutrition. It includes data search capabilities, original manuscripts, etc. The nutrition research program supports more than 30 grant-in-aid projects annually which are often the source of news stories." Recent information requests: A statement responding to a recent report from the National Academy of Science on the relationship between diet and cancer; the role of National Dairy Council in nutrition education in the schools.

546• NATIONAL FOOD PROCESSORS ASSOCIATION
1133 20th St. NW, Washington DC 20036. (202)331-5900. Contact Person: Vice President, Public Communications. **Description:** The National Food Processors Association "provides laboratory services to member companies and represents the interests of the food processing industry in Congress and before various regulatory agencies." **Services:** Provides advisory, historical and technical information. Offers brochures/pamphlets. Publications include pamphlets on the food processing industry. **How to Contact:** Write or call. Responds to most inquiries within

a week. "We will generally try to assist in a variey of ways anyone seeking information on the food processing industry."

547• NATIONAL GRANGE
1616 H St. NW, Washington DC 20006. (202)628-3507. Contact Person: Director of Information/Public Relations. **Description:** "We are the oldest and second largest farm organization. There are 500,000 members in this fraternal organization." **Services:** Provides information on agriculture and history of the Grange. Offers aid in arranging interviews and brochures/pamphlets. Publications include *Blue Book*, a summary of Grange history and structure, and legislative policies and programs. **How to Contact:** Write or call. Responds to most inquiries within a week. "We do not provide information on how to become a farmer or on methods of farming, etc."

548• NATIONAL HOT DOG & SAUSAGE COUNCIL
400 W. Madison, Chicago IL 60606. (312)454-1242. Contact Person: Executive Secretary. **Description:** "We are a service to the meat industry. Our objective is encouraging the increased consumption of sausage products and furthering the consumer's knowledge of processed meats (sausage)." **Services:** Offers aid in arranging interviews, brochures/pamphlets, information searches, newsletters and photos. Publications include a hot dog fact sheet. **How to Contact:** Write or call. Responds to most inquiries immediately. **Tips:** Recent information request: "How many hot dogs are consumed in a year?"

549• NATIONAL PEACH COUNCIL
Box 1085, Martinsburg WV 25401. (304)267-6024. Contact Person: Executive Director. **Description:** "The only national organization devoted solely to the interests of the peach industry." **Services:** Provides referral and trade information covering the fresh market peach industry. Offers aid in arranging interviews and information searches. **How to Contact:** Write or call. Responds to most inquiries within a week.

550• NATIONAL RESTAURANT ASSOCIATION
311 First St., NW, Washington DC 20001. (202)638-6100. Contact Person: Director of Research and Information Services. **Description:** "The association represents more than 125,000 food service units nationally, promoting and protecting their interests as business people." **Services:** Provides analytical, historical, how-to, interpretative, referral, technical and trade information covering food service industry, consumer behavior and attitudes, market and economic research and broad areas of legislation. "We are the leading information source for information pertaining to food service." **How to Contact:** Write or call. Responds to most inquiries within a week. Charges for photocopying and special consumer surveys. **Tips:** "Contact us for an Information Service brochure; visit our library in person." Recent information request: "What is the size of the food service industry?   What are the trends in new menu items?   How do you conduct a feasibility study?"

551• NATURAL ORGANIC FARMERS ASSOCIATION
Box 335, Antrim NH 03440. (603)588-2760. Contact Person: Membersip Coordinator. **Description:** "We promote biological farming practices and support small-scale diversified farming in the Northeast only." **Services:** Provides advisory, historical, how-to and referral information on crops, soil amendments, biological pesticides, herbicides, marketing, tillage, cover cropping, etc. Offers aid through conferences, workshops, brochures/pamphlets, informational newsletters and research assistance. Publications include *The Natural Farmer* (quarterly) and *Organizing Farmers Markets* (pamphlet). **How to Contact:** Write, call or visit. Responds to most inquiries within a month. Charges for some services. Give credit to Natural Organic Farmers Association. **Tips:** "Make questions specific." Recent information requests: "Is biological/organic farming economically feasible?"; inputs vs. outputs by crop.

552• PEPSI-COLA COMPANY
c/o Robert Marston & Associates, 485 Madison Ave., New York NY 10022. (212)371-2200. Contact Person: Vice President. **Description:** "Pepsi-Cola Company is a major US soft drink manufacturer engaged in a wide variety of marketing activities, including an extensive promotional effort that includes sports promotions, (bicycling, road running, drag racing, stock car racing, triathlons, skiing) and many special events." **Services:** Provides analytical, historical, how-to,

interpretative, referral and trade information on the size, growth and trends in the soft drink industry; new product launches; sports promotions and the soft drink industry; changing American beverage trends and tastes. Offers aid in arranging interviews, biographies, brochures/pamphlets, photos, placement on mailing lists, press kits and statistics. **How to Contact:** Write or call. Responds to most inquiries within a week. Give credit to Pepsi; give reason for inquiry. **Tips:** Recent information request: Predictions on what's ahead for the soft drink industry and why.

553• THE POTATO BOARD
1385 S. Colorado Blvd., Suite 512, Denver CO 80222. (303)758-7783. Contact Person: Public Relations Manager. **Description:** "The Potato Board is a nonprofit organization supported by the nation's 17,000 potato growers. Its purposes are to educate consumers about the nutritional and low calorie benefits of potatoes; increase potato consumption; and develop new markets for potatoes." **Services:** Provides analytical, referral and trade information on the nutrition of potatoes; marketing and promotion of potatoes; consumer attitudes towards potatoes; purchase incidence of potatoes; potato recipes. Offers aid in arranging interviews, annual reports, brochures/pamphlets, informational newsletters, library facilities, photos, placement on mailing lists, press kits and statistics. Publications include *Spotlight* (bimonthly newsletter); *The Whole Potato Catalog*; *Consumer Usage and Attitude Study*; *Nutrition* leaflet; *The Potato Lover's Diet Cookbook*; and *Potato Bar Kit* (information for foodservice operators). **How to Contact:** Write or call. Responds to most inquiries within a month. **Tips:** "We do not have the staff to do any extensive research for writers." Recent information requests: "What nutrients do potatoes provide based on the US RDA's?"; "How many potatoes does the average American eat and how does he like to fix them?"; "How are potatoes marketed, promoted on a nationwide basis?"

554• SALT INSTITUTE
206 N. Washington St., Alexandria VA 22314. (703)549-4648. Contact Person: Director of Public Relations. **Description:** "We provide research, information services and government relations to member companies; also information and educational materials to consumers and field services to users of salt." **Services:** Provides advisory, historical, referral and technical information on salt (general), agricultural salt, food grade salt, water conditioning salt, highway salt and sodium and health. Offers aid in arranging interviews, brochures/pamphlets, informational newsletters, photos (limited), placement on mailing list and statistics. Publications include *Highway Digest*; *Agricultural Digest*; *Straight Talk about Salt* (diet); *Salt, the Necessary Nutrient*; *Salt for Livestock, Poultry and Other Animals*; *Salt Tidbits* (general); *Salt Secrets* (tips on various salt uses around the home); *Salt and the Environment*; and four brochures on salt use advantages in water conditioning. **How to Contact:** Write or call. Responds to most inquiries within a week. **Tips:** "When requesting information, give us plenty of lead time."

555• SHERRY INSTITUTE OF SPAIN
220 E. 42nd St., New York NY 10017. (212)907-9381. Contact Person: Director. **Description:** "We are the educational/promotional arm of the Sherries of Spain which we represent as a generic product. **Services:** Provides historical, technical and trade information on all matters pertaining to the Sherries of Spain and the sherry-producing region. Offers aid in arranging interviews, brochures/pamphlets, photos, research assistance and statistics. Publications include *Gracious Hospitality with Sherry from Spain* and *Sherry, Noble Wine of Spain*. **How to Contact:** Write or call. Responds to most inquiries immediately. "Information and materials are strictly generic and deal only with the Sherries of Spain." **Tips:** "Be specific regarding your needs and interests." Recent information requests: Type of foods which should accompany various styles of sherry; production methods, growing conditions, styles.

556• SOCIETY FOR RANGE MANAGEMENT
2760 W. 5th Ave., Denver CO 80204. (303)571-0174. Contact Person: Executive Secretary. **Description:** A nonprofit organization with the following objectives: "to develop an understanding of range ecosystems and of the principles applicable to the management of range resources; to assist all who use range resources to keep abreast of new findings and techniques in the science and art of range management; to improve the effectiveness of range management to obtain from range resources the products and values necessary for man's welfare; to create a public appreciation of the economic and social benefits to be obtained from the range environment; to promote the professional development of its members." **Services:** Provides bibliographical and

referral information on various aspects of range (grazing, grassland) management, including: soils, animal nourishment, insects, watershed management, the physiology and morphology of range plants, reclamation and the economics of the management of range lands. Offers brochures/pamphlets and informational newsletters. Publications include bimonthly *Rangelands* and *Journal of Range Management* for members and subscribers. **How to Contact:** Write. Responds to most inquiries within a month. Charges for photocopying. "We don't have a librarian or staff to answer questions, but we can refer you to a journal or other publication which may offer you the information you need."

557• THE SUGAR ASSOCIATION, INC.
1511 K St. NW, Washington DC 20005. (202)628-0189. Contact Person: Director, Public Relations. **Description:** "Our purpose is to communicate the scientific facts about sugar's role in nutrition and health to the consuming public." **Services:** Provides bibliographical, historical, interpretative and referral information on sugar, nutrition, food technology and statistics. Offers brochures/pamphlets, informational newsletters, library facilities, press kits, research assistance, statistics and telephone reference services. **How to Contact:** Write or call. Responds to most inquiries within a month.

558• TEA COUNCIL OF THE USA, INC.
230 Park Ave., New York NY 10017. (212)986-6998. Contact Person: Executive Director. **Description:** "The Tea Council of the USA is a nonprofit organization established in 1953 for the purpose of increasing US sales and consumption of tea. It is supported by the major firms of the US tea industry and the major tea producing countries. Its aim is to extend and increase the consumer's knowledge and awareness of the benefits of tea drinking. It uses all media in its educational, promotional, public relations and publicity programs. It prepares and sends material to a wide variety of individuals including food and women's page editors, radio and television commentators, program directors, news and business editors, sports editors and teachers." **Services:** Offers brochures/pamphlets and photos. "We also offer food releases and background information on tea (its history, legends, growing, processing, etc.). Publications include *The Story of Tea* (16 pages; the romance, history, growing and processing of tea shown in captioned drawings; preparation methods); *Two Leaves and a Bud* (16 pages; the legends and history connected with tea; how and where it is grown and processed; types of tea; preparation methods); and *What You Should Know About Tea* (16 pages; how to prepare hot tea; using loose tea; teabags; instant and iced tea mixes; and tea party serving suggestions and recipes. Illustrated). **How to Contact:** Write or call. Responds to most inquiries immediately.

559• TOBACCO GROWERS INFORMATION COMMITTEE
Box 12046, Raleigh NC 27605. (919)832-3766. Contact Person: Managing Director. **Description:** "Tobacco information and public relations/promotion." **Services:** Provides analytical, historical, interpretative, referral and trade information covering the economic contribution of tobacco to the US; tobacco price support and production control program; the smoking and health controversy; punitive legislation regarding tobacco (public smoking restrictions and discriminatory taxation). Offers aid in arranging interviews, clipping services, information searches, placement on mailing list, statistics and newsletter. **How to Contact:** Write or call. Responds to most inquiries within a week. **Tips:** "Writers need objectivity to approach this subject which is often the victim of misinformation. Recent information requests: Explanation of price support program for tobacco; arranging interviews with farmers; description of the impact of doubling federal excise tax on cigarettes.

560• TWININGS TEA
c/o Ruth Morrison Associates, 509 Madison Ave., New York NY 10022. (212)838-9221. Contact Person: President or Assistant Account Executive. **Description:** Blenders and sellers of quality teas. **Services:** Provides bibliographical, historical and how-to information on tea history and lore; Twinings history; tea blending, growing, brewing, serving, varieties. Offers photos, press kits, and research library. **How to Contact:** Write or call. Responds to most inquiries within a month. **Tips:** "Allow enough lead time (particularly important when dealing with an overseas company) to gather information from all sources." Recent information requests: History of Earl Grey tea; "Where is afternoon tea served around the world?"

561• UNITED FRESH FRUIT AND VEGETABLE ASSOCIATION
727 N. Washington St., Alexandria VA 22314. (703)836-3410. Contact: Library. **Description:** Trade association promoting all facets of the fresh fruit and vegetable industry. **Services:** Provides historical, referral, technical and trade information on nutrition and consumer-related topics pertaining to fruits and vegetables. Offers brochures/pamphlets and library facilities. Publications include bimonthly magazine and weekly newsletter. **How to Contact:** Write or call. Responds to most inquiries within a week. Charges for photocopying. Research services for members only.

562• UNITED STATES TOBACCO MUSEUM
100 W. Putnam Ave., Greenwich CT 06830. (203)661-1100. Contact Person: Curator. **Description:** Museum and research library. Collects antiques related to tobacco. **Services:** Provides advisory, bibliographical, historical, referral and trade information covering art, business, economics, history and new products of the tobacco industry. Offers annual reports, bibliographies, biographies, statistics, brochures/pamphlets, information searches, placement on mailing lists, photos and press kits. Has 2,000 b&w and "several thousand" color photos: "prints, paintings, old advertising art, slides of our collection, transparencies and glossy prints of a variety of objects. Photographs can be taken with permission of the museum curator." **How to Contact:** Write or call (203)869-5531 and a private tour or conference with the curator can be arranged. Responds to most inquiries within a week. "In most cases, we do not lend research material; work must be done here." **Tips:** "Call or write ahead for appointment to use the library. U.S. Tobacco has recently opened a new museum, The Museum of Tobacco Art and History, 800 Harrison St., Nashville TN 37202. The museum has no library or research material available, but houses displays of tobacco-related antiques, lithography, and collectibles." Recent information request: Specific advice on collectibles.

563• THE WINE MUSEUM OF SAN FRANCISCO
633 Beach St., San Francisco CA 94109. (415)673-6990. Contact Person: Director. **Description:** "Funded by Fromm & Sichel, Inc. of San Francisco, distributors of Christian Brothers wine and brandy, this is a free museum presenting the Christian Brothers collection of wine in the arts, consisting of original prints, drawings and watercolors, sculpture, silver and rare drinking vessels. There is also a 1,000 volume library of rare wine books (1550 to present), and a 150-volume library on glass drinking vessels." **Services:** Provides bibliographical, historical, interpretative and referral information. Offers brochures and photo reproductions of all artworks in the collection. Publications include: books, *In Celebration of Wine and Life* ($19.95), *Wine and the Artist* (Dover, $5.95); a 16-page illustrated brochure describing the museum ($1.50 plus postage); and a free fact sheet on the museum and its collections. Also offered are two traveling exhibitions: 1) "500 Years of Wine in the Arts," consisting of 120 original prints, drawings and watercolors; and 2) "Nineteenth Century American Pressed Wine Glasses," 116 early pressed glasses dating from 1840-1900. **How to Contact:** Write or call for appointment; visit. Responds to most inquiries within a week. Charges $5-10/photo. Credit must be given to the collection and the museum when quoting materials or reproducing the photographs.

SECTION·TEN

FASHION

The truly fashionable are beyond fashion.
—Cecil Beaton

This section identifies resources in the apparel and textile industries; fashion design and modeling; cosmetics, jewelry and accessories; skin and hair care.

Bibliography

American Fabrics Magazine, eds. *Encyclopedia of Textiles*. 2d ed. New York: Doric Publishing, 1973.

Boughton, Patricia and Martha Ellen Hughes. *The Buyer's Guide to Cosmetics*. New York: Random House, 1981.

Calasibetta, Charlotte. *Dictionary of Fashion*. New York: Fairchild Publications, 1975.

Gioello, Debbie Ann. *Profiling Fabrics: Properties, Performance & Construction Techniques*. New York: Fairchild Publications, 1981.

Lambert, Eleanor. *World of Fashion: People, Places, Resources*. New York: Bowker, 1976.

Lenz, Bernie, ed. *New Complete Book of Fashion Modeling*. rev. ed. New York: Crown Publishers, 1982.

Rubin, Leonard G. *World of Fashion: An Index*. New York: Harper & Row Publishers, 1976.

Zizmore, Jonathan and Sharon Sabin. *Complete Guide to Grooming Products for Men: A Vital Handbook for Every Man Who Wants to Look His Best*. New York: Playboy Press, 1982.

564• AESTHETICIANS INTERNATIONAL ASSOCIATION, INC.
4818 Cole Ave., Suite 101, Dallas TX 75205. (800)527-5448. In Texas (214)526-0752. Contact Person: Founder/Chairman of the Board. **Description:** "Our purpose is to promote education in skin care (aesthetics) and public awareness." **Services:** Provides advisory, how-to, referral, technical and trade information on skin care, make-up and body therapy. Offers brochures/pamphlets, informational newsletters, library facilities, photos, placement on mailing lists, press kits and research assistance. Conducts educational seminars. Publications include *Dermascope*, AIA newsletter. **How to Contact:** Write or call. Responds to most inquiries within a week. Charges for some services depending upon the amount of work involved. "Credit must be given to the Aestheticians International Association, Inc." **Tips:** "Be direct and specific in your request; don't ask for 'all information!' " Recent information request: "How do I go about getting into the profession of aesthetics?"

565• AMERICAN APPAREL MANUFACTURERS ASSOCIATION
1611 N. Kent St., Suite 800, Arlington VA 22209. (703)524-1864. Contact Person: Director of Communications. **Description:** "We provide service to the US apparel industry—research, government relations, other educational services." **Services:** Provides advisory, historical, how-to, interpretative, referral, technical and trade information on manufacturing aspects of apparel manufacturing and legislative and trade concerns. Offers aid in arranging interviews, biographies, brochures/pamphlets, informational newsletters, photos, press kits, position papers and special reprints. **How to Contact:** Write or call. Responds to most inquiries within a week.

566• AMERICAN GEM SOCIETY
2960 Wilshire Blvd., Los Angeles CA 90010. (213)387-7375. Contact Person: Public Relations Administrator. **Description:** "The American Gem Society, founded in 1934, is a nonprofit organization of jewelers and gemologists in the US and Canada. AGS is dedicated to consumer protection and gemological proficiency in the industry itself." **Services:** Provides advisory, analytical, bibliographical, historical, how-to, interpretative, referral, technical and trade information on jewelry, gems, gold and precious metals. Offers aid in arranging interviews, biographies, brochures/pamphlets (including consumer tips), informational newsletters, photos, placement on mailing lists, press kits, research assistance, statistics and telephone reference

services. Publications include newsletter. "AGS offers a free consumer kit with membership roster and brochures on a variety of topics. An active speaker's bureau and spokesperson program are administered by the public relations department." **How to Contact:** Write. Responds to most inquiries within a month. Use of material should be for publication or broadcast. **Tips:** "We have access to the world's experts and a spokesperson list of over 3,000."

567• ASSOCIATION OF BRIDAL CONSULTANTS, INC.
29 Ferriss Estate, New Milford CT 06776. (203)355-0464. Contact Person: President. **Description:** "Our purpose is to promote the professional bridal/wedding consultant and improve the consultant's professionalism." **Services:** Provides advisory, analytical, bibliographical, how-to, interpretative, referral and trade information on all aspects of the wedding industry. Offers aid in arranging interviews, brochures/pamphlets, informational newsletters, research assistance, statistics and telephone reference services. **How to Contact:** Write or call. Responds to most inquiries within a week. Charges for reproduction and postage. "Specific questions are preferred. Please identify intended market; attribution is a must. We prefer to deal with written inquiries, but phone calls are acceptable." **Tips:** "There are few hard statistics available nationally on the wedding market. Specific questions allow reasonable search and interpretation of data." Recent information requests: Wedding market statistics, trends; interviews; local/regional data.

568• BEAUTY WITHOUT CRUELTY INTERNATIONAL
175 W. 12th St., New York NY 10011. Contact Person: USA Chairperson. **Description:** "A humane society that provides information on cruelties imposed on animals by the fashion and cosmetic industries, and how to obtain cruelty-free garments and personal care products including cosmetics. This is the only animal welfare society of its kind. It has a field director who travels worldwide to investigate cruelties in the production of garments and toiletries. This include the production of civet musk used in perfumes, methods of capture and slaughter of snakes and crocodiles for leather and the poaching of elephants and other animals on the endangered species list. This information is passed onto members in 25 countries throughout the world. **Services:** Provides bibliographical, how-to and referral information on fashions and personal care products including cosmetics, toiletries and perfumes; maintains an up-to-date list of companies producing cruelty-free cosmetics. Offers tri-annual reports, brochures/pamphlets, placement on mailing list, newsletter and press kits. **How to Contact:** Write. Responds to most inquiries within a week. **Tips:** "If wanting to find out whether or not a product is cruelty free, ask factual questions of the scientist in charge of safety evaluation and of the chemist (if it is a cosmetic)." Recent information request: A list of the manufacturers of cosmetics which do not involve slaughterhouse products and which are not tested on animals.

569• CLAIROL, INC.
345 Park Ave., New York NY 10154. (212)546-3509. Contact Person: Publicity Director. **Description:** "Leading manufacturer of hair coloring and hair care products." **Services:** Provides advisory, how-to, referral, technical and trade information on hair coloring, hair styling and care, product use, industry trends and image enhancement. Offers aid in arranging interviews, brochures/pamphlets, photos and press kits. **How to Contact:** Write or call. Responds to most inquiries within a week. "No charge to the press. Give credits for photos; confirm quotes."

570• COSMETIC, TOILETRY AND FRAGRANCE ASSOCIATION, INC.
110 Vermont Ave. NW, Washington DC 20005. (202)331-1770. Contact Person: Director of Public Information. **Description:** "We are a leading US trade association for the cosmetic industry, representing manufacturers of roughly 90% of US sales in cosmetics, toiletries and fragrances. We are the industry voice on industry issues. We will handle inquiries on cosmetics in general, but not specific brands. We encourage consumers and press to contact the Cosmetic, Toiletry and Fragrance Association (CTFA) for information about cosmetics." **Services:** Offers aid in arranging interviews, annual reports, bibliographies, biographies, statistics, brochures/pamphlets, placement on mailing list, photos, press kits, and in-depth background information on product categories or specific issues relating to the cosmetic industry. Publications include *Who's Who in the Cosmetic Industry* ($40 charge); *CFTA Annual Report* and *CFTA Cosmetic Journal* ($16/year). "Individual issues might be sent free if they contained material valuable to the writer's purpose." **How to Contact:** Write or call. Responds to most inquiries

immediately, if phone call; within a week, if letter. "We would be glad to talk to or correspond with any serious writer." **Tips:** "Statistics on cosmetic industry sales are difficult to come by and are frequently out-of-date. When attempting to write an article about a cosmetic product or an issue affecting the cosmetic industry, the writer should be prepared to understand a wide variety of scientific information. Disciplines related to this industry include microbiology, chemistry and toxicology. Recent information request: A novelist who wanted to include a small cosmetic company in his book was referred to a small company.

571• EMBROIDERY COUNCIL OF AMERICA
500 5th Ave., 58th Floor, New York NY 10110. (212)730-0685. Contact Person: Director. **Description:** "We maintain a library of samples from different embroidery manufacturers which is open to designers and the press." **Services:** Provides trade information on Schiffli machine-made embroidery. Offers aid in arranging interviews, statistics, brochures/pamphlets, photos and fashion and trend information about present and future uses of embroidery, lace and eyelet in apparel and home furnishings. Publications include *This Is Embroidery* ($1) and *Sewing with Lace and Embroidery* (35¢). **How to Contact:** Write or call. Responds to most inquiries immediately. Publications are available from the Embroidery Manufacturers Promotion Board, 513 23rd St., Union City NJ 07087. **Tips:** Recent information request: "What is Schiffli embroidery?"

572• FAN CIRCLE INTERNATIONAL
24 Asmuns Hill, London, England NW11 6ET. (01)458-1033. Contact Person: Honorary Secretary. **Description:** "Fan Circle International is a fine arts society which promotes the interest and knowledge of the fan in all aspects, its place in all parts of the world in fashion and social history." **Services:** Provides advisory, analytical, bibliographical, historical, how-to, interpretative, referral and technical information on all aspects of fans, related to textiles, fashion, advertising and art. Offers aid in arranging interviews, biographies, informational newsletters, placement on mailing lists and research assistance to members. Publications include *Bulletin* (to members); book list for research. **How to Contact:** Write, call or visit. Responds to most inquiries within a week. "Return postage costs are a courtesy we appreciate." **Tips:** Recent information request: "How can we restore/conserve a worn/torn/broken lace/ivory 18th century fan?"

573• FASHION INSTITUTE OF DESIGN AND MERCHANDISING
Resource and Research Center, 818 W. 7th St., Los Angeles CA 90017. (213)624-1200. Contact Person: Director. **Description:** Resource center for a 2-year college of fashion and design. **Services:** Provides advisory, analytical, bibliographical, historical, how-to, interpretative, referral, technical and trade information on fashion design, fashion merchandising, interior design, etc. Maintains 10,000-volume reference library; periodicals division (foreign, domestic, consumer and trade); media lounge; textiles division; rare books and periodicals; interior design workroom; costume library (covering women's, men's and children's fashions and accessories from 1855-present). Offers biographies, brochures/pamphlets, clipping services (designer file and newspaper clipping file), informational newsletters (quarterly), library facilities, placement on mailing lists, research assistance, statistics and telephone reference services. Publications include bibliographies by discipline/major (apparel manufacturing, textiles, etc.). List of publications available. **How to Contact:** Write or call. Responds to most inquiries immediately. **Tips:** Recent information requests: "Where can I buy candy pants (edible underwear)?"; "What's the formula for red dye that most stimulates the palate?"; "Name the 10 most famous women in history with the smallest waists?"

574• FASHION INSTITUTE OF TECHNOLOGY
Shirley Goodman Resource Center, 227 W. 27th St., New York NY 10001. (212)760-7695. Contact Person: Library Director. **Description:** The FIT is a specialized college offering programs of study in fashion, jewelry, interior design, cosmetics, fragrance and toiletries, merchandising and technology. The Resource Center houses both the library and the design laboratory for FIT students. **Services:** Provides historical, referral, technical and trade information on the fashion industry. "An assortment of sketch books, periodicals and business records donated by designers, manufacturers and merchants is available in the library as are slides, tapes, films and clipping files." **How to Contact:** Write or visit. Responds to most inquiries within a month.

575• FEDERATION OF APPAREL MANUFACTURERS
450 7th Ave., New York NY 10123. (212)594-0810. Contact Person: Executive
Director. **Description:** FAM is a national organization (headquartered in New York City) which
"represents women's and children's apparel manufacturers in all government and industry-related
matters." **Services:** Provides information on the apparel industry and related concerns. **How to
Contact:** Write or call.

576• THE FOOTWEAR COUNCIL
51 E. 42nd St., New York NY 10017. (212)697-0663. Contact Person: Fashion Director or
Executive Director. **Description:** "Our purpose is to promote the shoe industry; we serve as a
clearinghouse for all inquiries concerning the industry." **Services:** Provides historical,
interpretative and trade information on footwear and shoes. Offers aid in arranging interviews,
brochures/pamphlets, library facilities, photos, press kits, statistics and telephone reference
services. **How to Contact:** Write or call. Responds to most inquiries immediately **Tips:**
"Footwear is a very fragmented industry." Recent information request: "What are the trends in
the sales, production (domestic and imported) of shoes by classification?"

577• FRAGRANCE FOUNDATION
116 E. 19th St., New York NY 10003. (212)673-5580. Contact Person: Executive Director.
Description: Manufacturers and other members of the perfume industry seeking to educate the
public on the use and care of perfume and related products. "The nonprofit, educational organization encourages increased use and enjoyment of fragrance products; disseminates information on
the manufacture, care and application of such products; and inspires keener interest in the role of
the sense of smell and fragrance in people's lives." **Services:** Provides historical, cultural and referral information on perfumes. Offers aid in arranging interviews and research assistance. Publications available. **How to Contact:** Write (preferred) or call. Responds to most inquiries within a
week. Charges only if any costs are incurred.

578• GUILD OF PROFESSIONAL DRYCLEANERS
c/o Sommers/Rosen Public Relations, 1405 Locust St., Philadelphia PA 19102. (215)735-8943.
Contact Person: Vice President. **Description:** "Professional trade association dedicated to
upholding the highest standards of quality in the industry." **Services:** Provides advisory, how-to,
referral, technical and trade information on fabrics and fabric care including wardrobe and
household items. Offers aid in arranging interviews, brochures/pamphlets, placement on mailing
lists and telephone reference services. **How to Contact:** Write or call. Responds to most inquiries
within a month. Charges for laboratory testing through the International Fabric Care
Institute. **Tips:** Recent information request: "What is the best way to store winter attire?"

579• HAIR SCIENCE INSTITUTE
39 Milltown Rd., East Brunswick NJ 08816. (201)257-1990. Contact Person:
Consultant. **Description:** The institute reverses the balding pattern with a unique system of
treatment, based on natural therapies. **Services:** Provides advisory and how-to information on hair
growth, nutrition, herbs, diet. Offers informational newsletters. **How to Contact:** Write or call.
Responds to most inquiries immediately. **Tips:** Recent information request: "What does growing
hair involve?'

580• HEADWEAR INSTITUTE OF AMERICA
1 W. 64th St., New York NY 10023. (212)724-0888. Contact Person: Executive
Director. **Description:** "Our association represents the activities and promotes the sales of men's
headwear nationwide. Our members include retailers, wholesalers and manufacturers." **Services:**
Provides referral and trade information including sales forecasts; latest stylings and fashion trends;
headwear facts and issues including names of firms and products they offer; and history of headwear. Offers aid in arranging interviews, clipping services, informational newsletters, photos,
placement on mailing lists, press kits, research assistance and statistics. Publications include HIA
newsletter. "We also refer writers to the *Hat Life Yearbook and Directory*." **How to Contact:**
Write or call. Responds to most inquiries immediately. **Tips:** "It is important to go to the right
source for accurate, reliable information—deal with the experts in a given field. Know exactly
what it is you're looking for; have a clear-cut purpose." Recent information request: Trend in
men's headwear—types of fabrics and predominant colors.

581• INSTITUTE OF TEXTILE TECHNOLOGY
Box 391, Charlottesville VA 22902. (804)296-5511. Contact: Library. **Description:** Educational and research organization of the textile industry. The institute's library is an information center providing current textile information to members and non-members. **Services:** Provides bibliographical, historical and referral information. Offers computerized information searches, library facilities, interlibrary loans and research assistance. Publications include *Textile Technology Index*, "an abstract coverage of current periodicals, books and patents in the field of textile technology." **How to Contact:** Write. Responds to most inquiries immediately. Charges 60¢/page and 50¢ handling charges for photocopies. **Tips:** Recent information request: Latest weaving techniques and machinery.

582• INTERNATIONAL ASSOCIATION OF CLOTHING DESIGNERS
7 E. Lancaster Ave., Ardmore PA 19003. (215)896-7010. Contact Person: Executive Director. **Description:** Professional organization of men's designers; in-house designers for major apparel manufacturers throughout the world. **Services:** Provides advisory, analytical, historical, interpretative, referral, technical and trade information on fabrics, machinery, style, designs. Offers aid in arranging interviews, annual reports, biographies, brochures/pamphlets, informational newsletters, library facilities, photos, placement on mailing lists, press kits and telephone reference services. **How to Contact:** Write. Responds to most inquiries within a month. "No confidential information on members." **Tips:** Recent information request: "What are the latest trends in men's apparel?"

583• INTERNATIONAL FABRICARE INSTITUTE
12251 Tech Rd., Silver Spring MD 20904. (301)622-1900. Contact Person: Director of Communications. **Description:** Trade association of dry cleaners and launderers. **Services:** Provides advisory, analytical, technical and trade information on garment cleaning care procedures to members. Offers brochures/pamphlets, library facilities and press kits. Publications include newsletter (members only). **How to Contact:** Write. Responds to most inquiries within a week.

584• JEWELRY INDUSTRY COUNCIL
608 5th Ave., New York NY 10020. (212)757-3075. Contact Person: President. **Description:** "We are the nationwide nonprofit public information organization of this entire industry which supplies generic facts about gems and jewelry of all kinds." **Services:** Provides advisory, historical, how-to, referral and trade information covering gems and jewelry of all kinds; as well as fashions and trends, precious metals, fashion jewelry, watches and consumer tips and guidelines. Offers aid in arranging interviews, brochures/pamphlets, photos, generic facts, and related information about gems and jewelry products of all kinds, including history and lore. Publications include leaflets and booklets on diamonds, pearls, watches, silver, gold, fashion tips for teenagers, jewelry for the woman of today, men's jewelry, birthstones, china, crystal, stainless, planning the wedding, gifts for the wedding party, the modern wedding anniversary list, fashion jewelry, the romance of rings and birthstones. **How to Contact:** Write or call. Responds to most inquiries immediately. "The Jewelry Industry Council does not publicize or promote individual companies or brand names." Writers must give credit to Jewelry Industry Council. **Tips:** "Pinpoint your specific area of editorial interest. Contact us as industry experts to insure accuracy and authority." Recent information request: Background on colored gems.

585• MEN'S FASHION ASSOCIATION OF AMERICA
1290 Avenue of the Americas, New York NY 10104. (212)581-8210. Contact Person: Executive Director. **Description:** The Men's Fashion Association supplies information to the media in an effort to help inform the public about new trends in men's fashion; provides information on how to build a wardrobe for career purposes. **Services:** Provides advisory, analytical, historical, how-to, interpretative, referral and trade information on fashion materials, construction, design, fabrics and quality control. Offers aid in arranging interviews, annual reports, biographies, brochures/pamphlets, clipping services, informational newsletters, library facilities, photos, placement on mailing lists, press kits and telephone reference services. **How to Contact:** Write. Responds to most inquiries within a week. Charges for extensive photocopying. Some material may be restricted. **Tips:** Recent information request: "What is the origin of the blue blazer?"

586• NATIONAL ASSOCIATION OF BARBER SCHOOLS, INC.
304 S. 11th St., Lincoln NE 68508. Contact Person: Secretary/Treasurer. **Description:**
Organization existing "to promote and advance barber education and to promote and advance the
barber industry." **Services:** Provides advisory, historical, interpretative, technical and trade information covering the barber-stylist industry. Offers brochures/pamphlets. Publications include a
description of the barber industry—history, educational requirements, opportunities, training and
future. **How to Contact:** Write. Responds to most inquiries immediately. **Tips:** Recent information request: Career information on the barbering profession.

587• NATIONAL ASSOCIATION OF JEWELRY APPRAISERS
7414 E. Camelback Rd., Scottsdale AZ 85251. (602)941-8088. Contact Person: Executive
Director. **Description:** "Our purpose is to promote professionalism and ethics in the jewelry
appraisal field and advance education in jewelry appraising. Our membership consists of experts in
all fields relating to jewelry and gem appraising." **Services:** Provides advisory, analytical,
historical, how-to, referral, technical and trade information on gemological news, methods of
establishing value, certification news, new products, legal aspects, gem prices, new equipment,
new forms, association news, etc. Offers aid in arranging interviews, annual reports, biographies,
brochures/pamphlets, informational newsletters, photos, placement on mailing lists, press kits,
research assistance, statistics, telephone reference services, guest editorials, surveys and book
reviews. Publications include *The Jewelry Appraiser*. **How to Contact:** Write. Responds to most
inquiries within a week. Indicate how information will be used. **Tips:** "Please be specific. If we
are unable to provide data requested we can usually refer you to a source." Recent information
request: "How does one determine if a diamond is real?"

588• NATIONAL BEAUTY CAREER CENTER
3839 White Plains Rd., Bronx NY 10467. (212)881-3000. Contact Person:
Director. **Description:** "Our purpose is to disseminate career information relative to cosmetology
(hairdressing and barber styling) careers." **Services:** Provides advisory and trade information on
cosmetology and barber styling. Offers brochures/pamphlets. Publications include *Picture
Yourself as a Professional Hairstylist*; and *A Profitable Professional Career Awaits You in Barber
Styling*. **How to Contact:** Write. Responds to most inquiries within a week. "Name and address
must be identified as source of the materials." **Tips:** Recent information request: "What is the
average earnings of a hairdresser after five years in the field?"

589• NATIONAL HAIRDRESSERS AND COSMETOLOGISTS ASSOCIATION
3510 Olive St., St. Louis MO 63103. (314)534-7980. Contact: Public Relations
Department. **Description:** "We represent and support cosmetologists and hairdressers in the
US." **Services:** Provides advisory, analytical, historical, how-to, interpretative, referral,
technical and trade information on hairdressing, cosmetology, men's hair styling, hair fashion, old
and new. Offers aid in arranging interviews, brochures/pamphlets, clipping services,
informational newsletters, photos, press kits and telephone reference services. Publications
include *Beautiful Hair Magazine*. **How to Contact:** Write. Responds to most inquiries within 10
days. **Tips:** Recent information request: Annual sales in salons in the US.

590• NATIONAL HANDBAG ASSOCIATION
350 Fifth Ave., New York NY 10118. (212)947-3424. Contact Person: Executive
Director. **Description:** "We are a full-service association of domestic/import manufacturers
(public relations, collections, seminars and marketing segmentation)." **Services:** Provides how-to
and trade information on handbags, personal leathergoods, belts (sales training), buyer directory
resource listings and fashion forecasting information. Offers brochures/pamphlets, informational
newsletter, placement on mailing lists, press kits and research assistance. Publications include
How to Sell Handbags; and *Fashion Forecast*. **How to Contact:** Write. Responds to most
inquiries within a week. Charges for services "depending upon the request—anywhere from 50¢
to $50." Give credit to the National Handbag Association. **Tips:** Recent information request: "I
am writing a book, article, story on effective dressing and need information on accessories. Can
you help me?"

591• SAGA FURS OF SCANDINAVIA
509 Madison Ave., New York NY 10022. (212)888-1888. Contact Person: Public Relations
Manager. **Description:** "We promote mink and fox by making consumers more fur-conscious,

and we support the fur trade in all its efforts. Publicity efforts include news releases, photographs, public speaking." **Services:** Provides analytical (limited), historical (limited), how-to, interpretative, referral, technical (limited) and trade information on mink; fox; fur fashion trends; how to buy and care for fur; Scandinavian fur farming; fur auctions; grading system; international market outlook; limited market analysis; referral to designers and manufacturers. Offers aid in arranging interviews, brochures/pamphlets, photos, placement on mailing lists, press kits, research assistance and statistics. Publications include *Saga Mink* brochure and color chart; and *Saga Fox* brochure. **How to Contact:** Write or call. Responds to most inquiries immediately. "A Saga Furs credit/mention is requested." **Tips:** "Saga represents Scandinavia's finest mink and fox pelts, the raw materials used by fur manufacturers all over the world. We do not manufacture any garments, but we do have extensive contacts in the trade, and we do provide photographs of international fur fashions." Recent information requests: "How do you judge the quality of a fur garment?"; "What are the trends in fur fashion?" ˙

592• IRMA SHORELL, INC.
c/o Barnes Associates, Inc. 1 Astor Plaza, 4th Floor, New York NY 10036. (212)719-5420. Contact Person: President. **Description:** "We manufacture and distribute 20 basic skin care products to 600 specialty and department stores across the nation." **Services:** Provides advisory, how-to and interpretative information on skin care for women, men and teenagers. Offers "interview and consultation on skin care in connection with books and articles being written on the subject." Publications include descriptive brochures and flyers; sample ads on the development of the company and its products. **How to Contact:** Write or call. Responds to most inquiries immediately. "Only those writers with specific assignments should request consultation meetings. Establish writing credentials; assignment verification and outline of information requested." **Tips:** "General knowledge of cosmetic industry is essential." Recent information requests: Aspects of skin care such as what type of cleansers/moisturizers to use; plastic surgery pros and cons; skin care for men.

593• WORLD MODELING ASSOCIATION
Box 100, Croton-on-Hudson NY 10520. (914)737-8512. Contact Person: President. **Description:** The association's purpose is "to promote the career of fashion modeling through educational programs and materials, modeling competitions and promotions; to upgrade the field through information; and to protect the young people who wish to enter the field by giving direction and accurate information." **Services:** Provides advisory, analytical, historical, how-to, referral and trade information, including statistical information about job opportunities, how much is paid, how many are employed; trends in the field; resources; history of modeling; who's who in modeling; preparation for career; how to get started; courses of instruction; tools of the trade; state of the art; and fashion for men and women. Offers aid in arranging interviews, brochures/pamphlets, informational newsletters, photos, placement on mailing lists, press kits, research assistance, statistics, telephone reference services, and advice on avoiding unscrupulous operators. Publications include textbooks on personal development and fashion for men and women; newsletters; model head sheets; photographs; and courses on specific areas of modeling, including: photography, fashion shows, and TV commercials. **How to Contact:** Write. Responds to most inquiries immediately. "Usually there is no charge for questions that do not require research on our part. If research is necessary, fee depends upon amount of time required. Fee is $200/day. Writers/researchers should identify themselves as being involved in a project that requires accurate information and knowledge about the fashion modeling field." **Tips:** "Write rather than call and give complete information about the type or types of information required. Writers should search out facts and not use hearsay or generalities; get the facts from those in a position to know what they are; use libraries, especially the Library of Congress for information; research the history as well as the current trends on the subject; double check any information that is subjective rather than objective." Recent information request: Case study involving the head of a modeling agency handling questions from a prospective model.

SECTION · ELEVEN

GOVERNMENT AND MILITARY

Any system of government will work when everything is going well. It's the system that functions in the pinches that survives.
—John F. Kennedy

This section includes resources on the various general operations and activities of American government, as well as information sources for military history and the armed forces. For additional government information sources consult Leila Kight's and Matthew Lesko's article, page 14.

Specialized government agencies/departments are listed throughout the book in the subject category appropriate to their concerns (e.g., Department of Energy is found in the Environment/The Earth category; Department of Agriculture, in Farming and Food; Supreme Court, in Law/Law Enforcement). Additional military history resources (Civil War listings, for example) may be found in the History section along with government-related historical information (such as presidential libraries). Political parties are covered in the Public Affairs category. Information on foreign governments is found in the World Scope section.

Bibliography

Andriot, John, ed. *Guide to US Government Publications.* 2 vols. McLean, VA: Documents Index, 1982.

Holler, Fredrick L., ed. *Information Sources of Political Science.* 3d ed. American Bibliographical Center. Santa Barbara, CA: Clio Press, 1981.

Kane, Joseph Nathan, ed. *Facts About the Presidents.* 4th ed. New York: H.W. Wilson Co., 1981.

Lesko, Matthew. *Information USA.* Washington Researchers. New York: Viking Penguin, 1983. (Guide to government information sources)

Quick, John. *Dictionary of Weapons and Military Terms.* New York: McGraw-Hill, 1973.

Safire, William. *Safire's Political Dictionary: The New Language of Politics.* New York: Random House, 1978.

Sullivan, Linda E., ed. *Encyclopedia of Governmental Advisory Organizations.* 3d ed. Detroit: Gale Research Co., 1980.

US Congress Joint Committee on Printing. *Congressional Directory.* Annual. 1809-date. Washington DC: Government Printing Office. (Biographical sketches of members of Congress; the committees on which they serve; maps of Congressional districts)

US Government Manual. Annual. Washington DC: Government Printing Office. (Detailed information on the organizations, activities and chief officers of all government agencies)

Webster's American Military Biographies. Springfield, MA: G&C Merriam, 1978.

Who's Who in American Politics. Edited by Jaques Cattell Press. 8th ed. New York: Bowker, 1981-2.

Young, Peter, ed. *The World Almanac Book of World War II.* New York: World Almanac Publications, 1981.

594· ADMINISTRATIVE CONFERENCE OF THE UNITED STATES
2120 L St. NW, Suite 500, Washington DC 20037. Contact Person: Information Officer. **Description:** An independent federal agency organized to identify the causes of inefficiency, delay and unfairness in administrative proceedings affecting private rights and to recommend improvements to the president, the agencies, the Congress and courts. **Services:** Provides advisory, bibliographical and historical information covering administrative law, administrative procedure and regulatory reform. Publishes multivolume *Recommendations and Reports of the Administrative Conference of the U.S.* which contain the official texts of recommendations adopted by the assembly and *Annual Report* describing ongoing projects. **How to Contact:** Write. Responds to most inquiries within a week. "Our library is for reference use only on the premises." **Tips:** Call ahead to make an appointment. Recent information request: "Has ACUS done any research on some particular area of administrative law?"

595• AIR FORCE HISTORICAL FOUNDATION
Eisenhower Hall, Manhattan KS 66506. (913)532-6733. Contact Person: Editor. **Description:** Individuals interested in the history of aviation with emphasis on that of the USAF and its predecessors. **Services:** Provides advisory, bibliographical, historical and referral information on worldwide aviation history. Publications include *Aerospace Historian* (quarterly). Publications list available. **How to Contact:** Write. Responds to most inquiries within a week "except in the summer when responses may take a few months due to limited staff." Give credit to foundation.

596• AIR FORCE OFFICE OF PUBLIC AFFAIRS
Magazines and Books Division, AFOPA-MB, 1221 S. Fern St., Rm. D-159, Arlington VA 22202. (202)695-5331. Contact Person: Chief. **Services:** Provides advisory, historical, interpretative, referral and technical information on all facets of the United States Air Force. "Established writers and publishers seeking information, assistance or photographic support for use in articles or books, concerning any aspect of the United States Air Force, should work through the Magazines and Books Division. This division also provides a referral service for those authors and researchers engaged in historical research on the Air Force." **How to Contact:** Write or call. Responds to most inquiries within a month. Possible photo or document reproduction fee if request is unusually large. "Current information must be unclassified. The Air Force will not provide comment about completed manuscripts other than to review on a limited basis those portions taken from material given for technical accuracy." **Tips:** "It's best to approach the research process with an open mind or explain main idea—often suggestions can be made for additional or alternate information which would better suit writer's purpose. Writers should be prepared to travel to do their own research. They should not send duplicate requests to other levels of organization unless instructed by this office."

597• AMERICAN BATTLE MONUMENTS COMMISSION
5127 Pulaski Bldg., 20 Massachusetts Ave. NW, Washington DC 20314. Contact Person: Director of Operations. **Description:** "Our principal functions are to commemorate the services of the American forces where they have served since April 6, 1917; to design, construct, operate and maintain permanent American military burial grounds." **Services:** Offers "reference information concerning the cemeteries, photographs, individual cemetery booklets, and a general information pamphlet which briefly lists and describes the cemeteries under our care. The commission publishes an information newsletter and periodically updates it as required. A copy of the newsletter may be obtained by writing to the commission." **How to Contact:** Write. Responds to most inquiries within a week.

598• AMERICAN LEGION
700 N. Pennsylvania St., Indianapolis IN 46206. (317)635-8411. Contact Person: Public Relations Director. **Description:** Organization designed "to uphold and defend the constitution of the US; to maintain law and order; to foster and perpetuate 100% Americanism; to preserve memories and incidents of our associations in the great wars; and to promote peace and goodwill on earth." **Services:** Provides advisory, bibliographical, how-to and interpretative information covering the entire scope of the American Legion organization. Offers aid in arranging interviews, annual reports, bibliographies, biographies, brochures/pamphlets, information searches, placement on mailing list, news releases, statistics and video tape programs. Publications available. **How to Contact:** Write. Responds to most inquiries immediately. "Writers should use our information for the benefit and interest of veterans."

599• AMERICAN LOGISTICS ASSOCIATION
5205 Leesburg Pike, Suite 1213, Falls Church VA 22041. (703)998-5400. Contact Person: Assistant Editor. **Description:** "The association's purpose is to educate and promote the interests of members in industry forums and in liaison with the federal government and Congress. We represent businesses who do business with the armed forces." **Services:** Provides analytical, how-to, referral, technical and trade information on the supply of products and services to the government, for resale in military commissaries, exchanges, clubs and for troop subsistence. Offers annual reports, brochures/pamphlets, informational newsletters, placement on mailing lists, press kits and statistics. Publications include *Executive Briefing Newsletter*; *Annual Directory*; and *Interservice* (quarterly journal). **How to Contact:** Write or call. Responds to most inquiries within a week. Charges for subscriptions to publications for nonmembers. "Obtain appropriate clearances prior to publication." **Tips:** "Send an informal letter explaining interests.

ALA itself has only limited staff resources. The watchword is 'patience.' '' Recent information request: Total military exchange sales for previous fiscal year.

600• CENTER FOR DEFENSE INFORMATION
600 Maryland Ave. SW, # 303W, Washington DC 20024. Contact Person: Research Director. **Description:** ''We conduct research and analyses of military issues.'' **Services:** Provides advisory, analytical, bibliographical, historical, interpretative, referral and technical information on arms trade and exports, defense budget, weapons systems, nuclear war issues/US policy, arms control, US-Soviet military comparisons. Offers aid in arranging interviews, brochures/pamphlets, informational newsletters, library facilities, photos, placement on mailing lists, press kits, research assistance and statistics. Publications include *The Defense Monitor* (monthly); *The Nuclear War Prevention Kit.* **How to Contact:** Write, call or visit. Responds to most inquiries within a week.

601• COMMANDANT OF MARINE CORPS
Washington DC 20380. (202)694-4309. Contact Person: Director of Public Affairs. **Description:** ''Our purpose is to inform the Marine Corps family of important matters and to inform public of Marine Corps matters.'' **Services:** Offers aid in arranging interviews, annual reports, bibliographies, biographies, statistics, brochures/pamphlets, clipping services, and photos. **How to Contact:** Write or call. Responds to most inquiries within a week. **Tips:** Recent information requests: Permission to observe recruit training; appointment to interview the commandant on current Marine Corps policies.

602• CONGRESSIONAL INFORMATION SERVICE, INC. (CIS)
4520 East-West Highway, Suite 800, Bethesda MD 20814. (800)638-8380. In Maryland (301)654-1550. Contact Person: Customer Services Representative. **Description:** ''The CIS is the leading commercial indexer, abstracter and micropublisher of government publications.'' It provides access to government and statistical publications through a wide variety of print, microform and computer-readable products. It publishes 3 major monthly indexes and microfiche collections: *CIS/Index*, covering the working papers of the US Congress; *American Statistics Index* (ASI), a guide to statistical publications of the US government; *Statistical Reference Index* (SRI), which covers statistical publications from American sources other than the federal government; and *Index to International Statistics* (IIS), which provides access to statistical publications issued by major international, inter-governmental organizations. **Services:** Provides bibliographical and historical information on law and ''virtually any topic investigated by Congress or on which the federal government publishes statistics; also, foreign statistics.'' The CIS/Index and ASI databases are searchable online on DIALOG and ORBIT. CIS also publishes the *CIS Legislative History Service*, which provides comprehensive citations and documentation for all significant public laws enacted by the 97th and succeeding Congresses. Major retrospective indexes and microfiche collections include: *CIS US Congressional Committee Prints Index*, mid-1800s-1969; *CIS US Congressional Committee Hearings Index*, 1833-1969; *CIS US Serial Set Index*, 1789-1969; and *State Constitutional Conventions, Commissions and Amendments*, 1776-1978. Other microfiche collections include *Current National Statistical Compendiums on Microfiche*; *CIS/Congressional Bills, Resolutions and Laws on Microfiche*; and *CIS Periodicals on Microfiche.* **How to Contact:** Visit a major academic or public library that subscribes. To order individual goverment documents or legislative histories from CIS, call the CIS Documents on Demand Service at the numbers listed above. Responds to most inquiries immediately.

603• CONGRESSIONAL RECORD CLIPPINGS
Suite 402, 1868 Columbia Rd. NW, Washington DC 20009. (202)332-2000. Contact Person: General Manager. **Description:** ''We monitor the Senate and House of Representatives and the daily *Congressional Record* appendix.'' **How to Contact:** Write or call. Responds to most inquiries immediately.

604• CONGRESSIONAL RECORD INDEX
Room B104, US Government Printing Office, North Capitol and H Sts. NW, Washington DC 20402. (202)275-9009. Office hours 7:30 a.m. to 5:00 p.m. **Description:** ''*Congressional Record Index* is a biweekly and annual index of the proceedings, debates, additional statements and history of legislation as reported in the *Congressional Record*.'' **Services:** Provides analytical, interpretative, legislative, procedural and historical information on material contained in the

Congressional Record. "We supply needed references or offer expertise in locating them." Biweekly and annual *Indexes to the Congressional Record* are sent to all subscribers of the *Record* on request, and all depository libraries. Issues may be purchased from the Superintendent of Documents, Government Printing Office, Washington DC 20402 at $1/biweekly issue and $43 for latest printed annual. **How to Contact:** Write or call. **Tips:** "*Index* is referenced by member, subject, bill (by subject and legislative number), year, month, date and page. The History of Legislation reflects all action taken on proposed bills and all new bills introduced during an issue period. Anyone using the *Index* and having a problem should write us and we will be happy to help them. We cannot, however, provide copies of pages or entire issues of the *Congressional Record.*"

605• COUNCIL OF STATE GOVERNMENTS
States Information Center, Box 11910, Iron Works Pike, Lexington KY 40578. (606)252-2291. Contact Person: Coordinator of Public Affairs. **Description:** The council is a national organization of the 50 states and supported by them to promote exchange of information, provide assistance in state-federal relations and promote cooperation at all levels of government. The States Information Center is the council's collection of resources. It provides a loan service and a variety of resource publications to state officials, and serves as a reference source for state officials and others. **Services:** Provides analytical, bibliographical and referral information on state government and related topics, such as human services, taxation, intergovernmental relations, etc. Offers computerized information searches, informational newsletters, library facilities, research assistance and telephone reference services. Offers *State Government Research Checklist* (bimonthly). **How to Contact:** Write or call. Responds to most inquiries within a week. Charges for newsletter. "Our first priority is to state officials; requests by others are handled as time and staff permit." **Tips:** Recent information request: "What tax practices are used in Iowa and surrounding states to give money back to the local government?"

606• COUNCIL ON AMERICA'S MILITARY PAST
Box 1151, Ft. Myer VA 22211. (202)479-2258. Contact Person: National Secretary. **Description:** "A national, nonprofit, educational organization dedicated to the identification, location, restoration, preservation, and memorialization of old military installations and their history and traditions. We emphasize military history and historic preservation." **Services:** Provides advisory, bibliographical, historical, referral and technical information on military history and historic preservation with emphasis on sites. Offers aid in arranging interviews, brochures/pamphlets, informational newsletters, press kits, research assistance and telephone reference services. Publications include *Headquarters Heliogram* (monthly newspaper) and *Periodical* (quarterly journal), both by membership/subscription only. Back copies of publications and a list of books and pamphlets are available. **How to Contact:** Write. Responds to most inquiries within a month. "We do not charge for the publication of a research query in our newspaper. Other research priority goes to members as this is a member-supported nonprofit organization." Charges for back issues of publications, books and pamphlets.

607• DEFENSE LOGISTICS AGENCY
Cameron Station, Alexandria VA 22314. Contact: Public Affairs Office (DLA-BP). **Description:** "The agency is responsible for supply support to the military services, administration of defense contracts and various other logistics services." **Services:** Offers information on Defense Logistics Agency areas of activity. Publications include *Introduction to the Defense Logistics Agency.* **How to Contact:** Write. Responds to most inquiries immediately. **Tips:** Recent information request: How to do business with the DLA; general inquiries about the DLA and its areas of activity.

608• DEPARTMENT OF DEFENSE, OFFICE OF ASSISTANT SECRETARY
Room 2E-772, The Pentagon, Washington DC 20301. **Description:** The Defense Department is responsible for providing the military forces to deter war and protect the country's security. The office of Assistant Secretary "provides the national news media with coverage (press releases, speech texts, film, photos) on the activities of the Defense Department." **Services:** Offers aid in arranging interviews, annual reports, bibliographies, biographies, statistics, brochures/pamphlets, photos and press kits. **How to Contact:** Write. "Be as specific as possible. Due to limited staff, priorities must be made and requests will be answered as time permits." Responds to most inquiries within a month.

609• DEPARTMENT OF DEFENSE, AUDIO-VISUAL DIVISION
Room 2E-773, The Pentagon, Washington DC 20301. **Services:** Offers assistance in gathering information about the Department of Defense and its components; motion pictures and stills. **How to Contact:** Write. Responds to most inquiries within a month.

610• DEPARTMENT OF STATE
2201 C St. NW, Washington DC 20520. Press Office/(202)632-2492, Contact Person: Director. Freedom of Information Office/Room 1239, (202)632-0425, Contact Person: Coordinator, Information and Privacy Staff. Office of Historian/(202)632-8888. Contact Person: General Editor. **Description:** "Our purpose is to inform the press on daily activities of the Department of State. The Freedom of Information Office can provide access to classified documents under the Freedom of Information Act. The Office of Historian declassifies and publishes documents of United States foreign policy of the past 20 years." **Services:** Offers aid in arranging interviews, annual reports, bibliographies, biographies, statistics, brochures/pamphlets, information searches, placement on mailing list, photos (of department heads), daily press briefings and document searches under Freedom of Information Act. Publications available. **How to Contact:** Write or call. Responds to most inquiries immediately. Charges for some documents; $12/hour for information searches and 10¢/page copied material from Freedom of Information Office. **Tips:** "Journalists must apply for press status and press pass. Response from the Freedom of Information Office usually averages 6 weeks. The Office of Historian arranges occasional briefs on research procedures which would benefit in-depth scholarly research."

611• DEPARTMENT OF THE ARMY
Office Chief of Public Affairs, The Pentagon, Washington DC 20310. (202)695-5135. Contact: Chief of Public Affairs. **Description:** The Office Chief of Public Affairs "is directly responsible to the Secretary of the Army and Chief of Staff and is charged with formulating army public affairs to include public information, command information and community relations policies and programs." **Services:** Provides information on army activities and referrals to appropriate offices within the department. **How to Contact:** Write or call. Response time depends on scope of research required. **Tips:** "The more specific you can be, the faster we can respond." Recent information requests: "How many people are in the army?"; "What's the ratio of men to women?"

612• DEPARTMENT OF THE NAVY, OFFICE OF INFORMATION
Attention: Media Services Branch, The Pentagon, Washington DC 20350. (202)695-0911. Contact Person: Head, Media Services Branch. **Description:** The Office exists "to keep the public informed about historical, current and future activitites pertaining to the Department of the Navy, within security requirements, and not classified." **Services:** Provides bibliographical, historical, referral, technical and trade (book, magazine) information covering unclassified material related to the Department of the Navy. Offers "aid in arranging interviews with cognizant officials on naval subjects; arranges, insofar as possible, media requests for orientation flights, ship embarkations; provides unclassified fact sheets, materials and information, or appropriate sources for same. Photographs are available for a fee from Still Photography Branch, Office of Information, Department of the Navy, Washington DC 20350. Thousands of unclassified government documents are for sale by the Government Printing Office and the National Techncial Information Service, 5285 Port Royal Road, Springfield VA 22161 at nominal costs." **How to Contact:** Write. Responds to most inquiries within a month; "it depends on the scope of the questions and the availability of information." **Tips:** "Materials provided by the Navy, a component of the federal government, may not be copyrighted. In requesting Navy information, be as specific as possible regarding subject, whether a publisher's contract exists, and deadline." Recent information requests: "What is the status of the Battleship Reactivation program?"; background on ships, aircraft and weapons of the US Navy.

613• DEPARTMENT OF THE NAVY, OFFICE OF NAVAL RESEARCH
800 N. Quincy St., Arlington VA 22217. (202)696-5031. Contact Person: Public Affairs Officer. **Description:** Agency for support of basic research and technology. **Services:** Provides analytical, historical, referral, technical and trade information on mathematical and physical, environmental, engineering, and life sciences; aviation and aerospace, undersea, communications and computer, electronic and electro magnetic, and materials technology; manpower, personnel, and training technology; and advanced conformal submarine acoustic sensor. Offers aid in arranging inter-

views, biographies, brochures/pamphlets, photos, press kits, research assistance and statistics. Publications include *Contract Research & Technology Program; Naval Research Reviews*; *Naval Research Logistics Quarterly*; *U.S. Navy Journal of Underwater Acoustics* (ONR-1 NAVSO P-3589 April 1982); and *Shock and Vibration Digest*. **How to Contact:** Write, call or visit. Responds to most inquiries within a week. **Tips:** ''Be precise and avoid generalizations when asking your questions. For detailed information of a technical nature, submit questions in writing and allow 1-2 weeks for a response.'' Recent information request: ''What is the recent development in the robustness theory of multivariable systems?''

614• FEDERAL ELECTION COMMISSION
1325 K St. NW, Washington DC 20463. (800)424-9530. In District of Columbia (202)523-4068. Contact Person: Information Specialist. **Description:** ''Government agency providing public disclosure of campaign finance reports filed by candidates for federal office and political committees that support them; and administration of the Federal Election Campaign Act and the public financing of presidential elections.'' **Services:** Provides advisory, analytical, bibliographical, historical, how-to, interpretative, referral, technical and trade information on campaign financing of federal elections. Arranges interviews. Provides computerized information searches, library facilities, placement on mailing lists, press kits, research assistance, statistics, campaign finance reports of all federal candidates and political committees and telephone reference services. Publications include brochures and Campaign Guide series explaining the election law; monthly newsletter; copies of election laws and regulations; and annual reports. **How to Contact:** Call (on toll-free line). Responds to most inquiries immediately. ''Generally, telephone inquiries are answered immediately; publications and reports ordered take 1 to 2 weeks for delivery; and letters take approximately 1 month to be answered.'' Charges for photocopying of documents and campaign finance reports. ''The election law provides that any information copied from FEC reports not be used or sold by any person for the purpose of soliciting contributions or for commercial purposes.'' **Tips:** ''When identifying the documents or information you want, please try to include as many details as possible, such as names of candidates or committees, dates of the activity and your name, address and telephone number.'' Recent information request: ''What individuals and political groups have contributed to candidate X running from my state or district?''

615• FEDERAL EMERGENCY MANAGEMENT AGENCY
500 C St. SW, Washington DC 20472. (202)287-0300. Contact Person: Director, Office of Public Affairs. **Description:** A government agency whose activities involve ''preparedness for natural and man-made disasters, including war.'' **Services:** Provides advisory, historical, how-to, referral and technical information on nuclear war (civilian aspects); earthquakes, hurricanes, tornadoes, floods, etc.; fire prevention; and strategic materials stockpile. Offers aid in arranging interviews, annual reports, brochures/pamphlets, photos and statistics. **How to Contact:** Write or call. Responds to most inquiries within a month. In some cases material and subject matter may be classified.

616• FEDERAL INFORMATION CENTERS (FIC)
Description: Government agency ''providing a single point for the public to address questions about federal agencies and programs. Callers receive the desired information or are told how to contact the office that can assist them.'' **Services:** Provides advisory, how-to, referral and technical information on the federal government and its activities. Offers aid in arranging interviews, research assistance and telephone reference services. ''We do not have publications of our own but can help callers find sources of documents of other government agencies.'' **How to Contact:** Call. Responds to most inquiries immediately. **Tips:** ''Try to be as specific as possible with your question. The most difficult part of researching any question or starting any research is making sure that you know your real question. Sometimes, identifying all the factors behind the question is an enormous help in answering it.'' Recent information request: ''A writer asked one FIC for assistance with a novel he was working on. His story called for a man to be stranded on a beach just before the onset of winter. The writer wanted government survival guides that would allow him to portray the character's actions realistically.'' FICs and their phone numbers and tielines are arranged geographically on the following pages.

Federal Information Centers

ALABAMA
Birmingham (205)322-8591
Mobile (205)438-1421

ALASKA
Anchorage (907)271-3650

ARIZONA
Phoenix (602)261-3313
Tucson (602)622-1511

ARKANSAS
Little Rock (501)378-6177

CALIFORNIA
Los Angeles (213)688-3800
Sacramento (916)440-3344
San Diego (619)293-6030
San Francisco (415)556-6600
San Jose (408)275-7422
Santa Ana (714)836-2386

COLORADO
Colorado Springs (303)471-9491
Denver (303)234-7181
Pueblo (303)544-9523

CONNECTICUT
Hartford (203)527-2617
New Haven (203)624-4720

FLORIDA
St. Petersburg (813)893-3495
Tampa (813)229-7911

From elsewhere in Florida-
(800)282-8556

GEORGIA
Atlanta (404)221-6891

HAWAII
Honolulu (808)546-8620

ILLINOIS
Chicago (312)353-4242

INDIANA
Gary/Hammond (219)883-4110
Indianapolis (317)269-7373

IOWA
Des Moines (515)284-4448

From elsewhere in Iowa-
(800)532-1556

KANSAS
Topeka (913)295-2866

From elsewhere in Kansas-
(800)432-2934

KENTUCKY
Louisville (502)582-6261

LOUISIANA
New Orleans (504)589-6696

MARYLAND
Baltimore (301)962-4980

MASSACHUSETTS
Boston (617)223-7121

MICHIGAN
Detroit (313)226-7016
Grand Rapids (616)451-2628

MINNESOTA
Minneapolis (612)349-5333

MISSOURI
Kansas City (816)374-2466
St. Louis (314)425-4106

From other Missouri locations in
Area Code 314-(800)392-7711

From other Missouri locations in
Area Codes 816 & 417-(800)892-5808

NEBRASKA
Omaha (402)221-3353

From elsewhere in Nebraska-
(800)642-8383

NEW JERSEY
Newark (201)645-3600
Paterson/Passaic (201)523-0717
Trenton (609)396-4400

NEW MEXICO
Albuquerque (505)766-3091
Santa Fe (505)983-7743

NEW YORK
Albany (518)463-4421
Buffalo (716)846-4010
New York (212)264-4464
Rochester (716)546-5075
Syracuse (315)476-8545

NORTH CAROLINA
Charlotte (704)376-3600

OHIO
Akron (216)375-5638
Cincinnati (513)684-2801
Cleveland (216)522-4040
Columbus (614)221-1014
Dayton (513)223-7377
Toledo (419)241-3223

OKLAHOMA
Oklahoma City (405)231-4868
Tulsa (918)584-4193

OREGON
Portland (503)221-2222

PENNSYLVANIA
Allentown/Bethlehem (215)821-7785
Philadelphia (215)597-7042
Pittsburgh (412)644-3456
Scranton (717)346-7081

RHODE ISLAND
Providence (401)331-5565

TENNESSEE
Chattanooga (615)265-8231
Memphis (901)521-3285
Nashville (615)242-5056

TEXAS
Austin (512)472-5494
Dallas (214)767-8585
Fort Worth (817)334-3624
Houston (713)229-2552
San Antonio (512)224-4471

UTAH
Odgen (801)399-1347
Salt Lake City (801)524-5353

VIRGINIA
Newport News (804)244-0480
Norfolk (804)441-3101
Richmond (804)643-4928
Roanoke (703)982-8591

WASHINGTON
Seattle (206)442-0570
Tacoma (206)383-5230

WISCONSIN
Milwaukee (414)271-2273

617• GENERAL SERVICES ADMINISTRATION
18th and F Sts. NW, Washington DC 20405. (202)566-1231. Contact Person: Director of Information. **Description:** The General Services Administration (GSA) establishes policy and provides for a system for the management of federal property and records, including construction and operation of buildings, procurement and distribution of supplies, utilization and disposal of property, transportation, traffic and communications management, stockpiling of strategic materials and management of government-wide Automated Data Processing resources program. **Services:** Provides advisory, interpretative, referral and technical information covering the scope of GSA's operations. **How to Contact:** Write or call. Responds to most inquiries immediately. "No restrictions exist except for classified information and that not releasable under the Freedom of Information Act."

618• GOVERNMENT PRINTING OFFICE
N. Capitol and H Sts. NW, Washington DC 20402. Contact Person: Legislative Liaison/Public Affairs Officer. **Description:** Printing and binding services for the Congress, judicial and executive branches of the federal government; distribution of 18,000 titles of federal documents to the public. Programs include printing production and innovations and a mail order sales program. **Services:** Provides advisory, bibliographical, historical, how-to, technical and trade information. "There are 300 subject bibliographies covering the topics dealt with by government publications available through the sales program." Offers "reference materials or information on an individual request basis. Writers may obtain federal reference publications on a broad range of subjects— available through mail order or in bookstores throughout the country." **How to Contact:** Write. Responds to most inquiries within a month. "All government publications made available through the sales program are priced so as to allow GPO to recover costs; prices for specific documents are obtainable upon request." **Tips:** Two free catalogs of GPO sales publications are available. The quarterly *US Government Books* lists about 1,000 bestselling publications; *New Books*, issued on a bimonthly basis, lists all government publications placed on sale in the preceding 2-month period. To receive copies of these catalogs, write to: Superintendent of Documents, Washington, D.C. 20402.

619• MARINE CORPS
Historical and Museums Division, Headquarters, United States Marine Corps, Washington DC
20380. (202)433-3840. Contact Person; Chief Historian. **Description:** "The Division oversees
the Marine Corps Historical Program which includes Marine Corps museums. Its offices are
located in the Marine Corps Historical Center in the Washington Navy Yard (9th & M St. SE). The
Historical Center is a comprehensive archival and museum facility which houses artifact
collections of personal papers, oral history interviews, military music, art, reference files, writing
and publications offices, and administrative offices. All collections and activities are oriented
toward Marine Corps history and amphibious operations." **Services:** Provides advisory,
bibliographical, historical, interpretative, referral and technical information on art, history, music
and technical data. Offers bibliographies, brochures/pamphlets, information searches, statistics,
newsletter, personal papers and oral history interviews of United States Marines. Publications
available. **How to Contact:** Write. Responds to most inquiries within a month (non-priority
requests). Currently charges 7¢/page for copying of lengthy documents and $14/hour for
professional/clerical time. "Basically, there are few restrictions except those on access to
classified documents (the majority of holdings are not classified) and those placed on personal
papers and oral history holdings by donors (which are not extensive)." **Tips:** "We will not do
involved research or extensive copying as it detracts from our primary mission." Recent
information request: Material on the alleged Marine involvement in the search for Amelia Earhart.

620• MARINE CORPS AVIATION MUSEUM
Marine Corps Museums Branch Activities, Bldg. 2014, Quantico VA 22134. (703)640-2606.
Contact Person: Officer in Charge. **Description:** "We preserve, document and dramatize Marine
Corps aviation history." **Services:** Provides advisory, historical and technical information on
U.S. Marine Corps aviation history and historical materials and equipments. Offers
brochures/pamphlets, photos (limited), research assistance and reference material. **How to
Contact:** Write or call; visit by appointment only. Responds to most inquiries within a month.
Research must be conducted on site.

621• NATIONAL ARCHIVES AND RECORDS SERVICE
Pennsylvania Ave. at 8th St. NW, Washington DC 20408. (202)523-3054. Contact Person:
Archivist. **Description:** The National Archives is the repository for valuable, official records of
the US government. All treaties, laws, proclamations, executive orders and bills are retained. It is
also authorized to accept some private papers which deal with government transactions.
Administering all presidential libraries and 15 federal records centers across the nation, the
National Archives was created to serve the government, scholars, writers, students. Offers
pictorial records (primarily b&w) from some 140 federal agencies illustrating all aspects of
American history from the colonial period to the recent past, and many aspects of life in other parts
of the world. Included are several large collections such as the Mathew Brady Civil War
photographs, the picture file of the Paris branch of the *New York Times* (1923-1950), and the
Heinrich Hoffmann files illustrating activities of the Nazi party in Germany (1923-45). **Services:**
Offers sound recordings, films, some artifacts, and five million photos (available for purchase).
"Most are in the public domain and may be freely reproduced." **How to Contact:** Write. Re-
sponds to most inquiries within six weeks. **Tips:** *Editor's Note:* In addition to the Presidential li-
braries listed in the History section are these: Gerald R. Ford Library, 1000 Beal Ave., Ann Arbor
MI 48109. (313)668-2218. Contact Person: Director. John F. Kennedy Library, Columbia Point,
Dorchester MA 02125. (617)929-4500. Contact Person: Director. Franklin D. Roosevelt Library,
259 Albany Post Rd., Hyde Park NY 12538. (914)229-8114. Contact Person: Director. Harry S.
Truman Library, US Highway 24 and Delaware St., Independence MO 64050. (816)833-1400.
Contact Person: Director. Richard M. Nixon's papers are currently in Washington DC and not
available to the public. Jimmy Carter's library is currently under development in Atlanta.

622• NATIONAL ASSOCIATION OF TOWNS AND TOWNSHIPS
1522 K St. NW, # 730, Washington DC 20005. (202)737-5200. Contact Person:
Communications Coordinator. **Description:** "We provide technical assistance, educational
services and public policy support to local government officials in 13,000 small communities
across the country." **Services:** Provides trade information on small town officials' duties and
responsibilities; impact of federal programs/legislation on small towns. Offers annual reports,
brochures/pamphlets, informational newsletters and photos. Publications include *National*

Community Reporter; seminar reports; testimony. **How to Contact:** Write or call. Responds to most inquiries within a month. Charges for some reports and subscriptions.

623• OFFICE OF AIR FORCE HISTORY
HQ USAF/CHO, Bldg. 5681, Bolling Air Force Base, Washington DC 20332. (202)767-5088. Contact: Office of Air Force History. **Description:** "The Office of Air Force History formulates policy for, directs and administers the Air Force historical program. Our historians prepare objective, comprehensive and accurate historical accounts of USAF activities in peace and war. Provides historical reference services to the Air staff, other public and private agencies, and individuals. Our historical records cover military aeronautics from its early beginnings to the early 1980s. Unclassified records are available to any individual or organization. Records are not loaned; must be used here." **Services:** Offers bibliographies, biographies, brochures/pamphlets, information searches and statistics. "We will make available all unclassified materials, including microfilm, to any researcher who wishes to utilize our facilities. Our microfilm holdings include most Air Force unit histories for World War II, pre-World War II and post-World War II. A brochure describing the Albert F. Simpson Historical Research Center of the United States Air Force is available. The center maintains the offical Air Force historical document collection. A few pamphlets pertaining to Air Force history and aircraft and answering pertinent questions are available. Although these are published by the Office of the Secretary of the Air Force, Office of Information, we have a small quantity available for distribution." **How to Contact:** "Because of a very limited staff, only minor research requests can be taken care of by mail. Researchers and writers should make arrangements to perform their research in our facilities. Our office hours are Monday through Friday, 7:45 a.m. to 4:15 p.m. Responds to most inquiries within a month. "Public queries for information do not get priority; Air Force requests come first. Researchers and writers can also make arrangements with Albert F. Simpson Historical Research Center, Maxwell Air Force Base, AF SHRC/RI, Maxwell AL 36112. (205)293-5963."

624• OFFICE OF MANAGEMENT AND BUDGET
Old Executive Office Bldg., Washington DC 20503. (202)395-3080. Contact: Public Affairs Office. **Description:** The Office of Management and Budget advises the President on fiscal and economic policies, prepares the budget and formulates the government's fiscal program among other responsibilities outlined in the publication *The Work of the Office of Management and Budget*. The Office of Public Affairs handles inquiries from the press, other government agencies and the public regarding OMB activities. **Services:** Prepares speeches, organizes briefings for press officials and visitors, coordinates outside speaking activities of the OMB staff, issues general descriptive materials about OMB activities. Publications include *The Budget of the United States Government*; *The United States Budget in Brief* and *The Catalogue of Federal Domestic Assistance*. **How to Contact:** Write or call. "Response time varies according to nature of inquiry." Those interested in obtaining publications should contact the publications office, (202)395-7332. **Tips:** "Know exactly what you're asking." Recent information requests: Statistical information from the budget books.

625• P.T. BOATS, INC.
Box 109, Memphis TN 38101. (901)272-9980. Contact Person: Director. **Description:** "P.T. Boats, Inc. is a nonprofit, historical corporation compiling the operational histories of the 43 operating squadrons, 25 bases and 20 tenders (mother ships); maintaining museum and library; publishing newspaper and roster for over 7,500 on list." **Services:** Provides information on history. Offers aid in arranging interviews, information searches, newsletter and photos. Publications include squadron histories. "We have published 2 books on P.T boats and are in the process now of publishing a 40-year book of P.T. boaters." **How to Contact:** Write, call or visit. Responds to most inquiries immediately. "Any research or service is $10/hour or part of an hour; photos vary in price."

626• PACIFIC SUBMARINE MUSEUM
Naval Submarine Base, Pearl Harbor HI 96860. (808)471-0632. Contact Person: Curator. **Description:** "Our purpose is to preserve submarine historical artifacts and memorabilia; depict history of the American submarine from Revolutionary War through the current Trident submarine; maintain a research library with war patrol reports from WWII and film library; and arrange special group tours." **Services:** Provides advisory, historical, interpretative and referral information on submarine warfare World War I, World War II; every US Navy submarine ever con-

structed; Japanese midget submarines, Japanese Army submarines (limited data); and disposition of various Fleet submarines. Offers research library facilities (by reservation), research assistance, statistics and photographic analysis/interpretation of submarine materials. **How to Contact:** Write. Responds to most inquiries within a week. **Tips:** "Since the museum staff is very small, our capability to do major research is limited. It may be advisable to submit a letter outlining your needs and the museum will follow-up with what we do or do not have . . . and, a suggestion where the remaining data may be procured. The Naval Historical Center, Washington, D.C., provides microfilm copies of all war patrol reports for Navy submarines during WWII. Photographs of warships may be procured from Photo Services, Naval Institute, Annapolis, MD 21402. We do not provide photo service or extensive copy work on war patrol reports. Obtain these from the above." Recent information requests: "Was the Submarine Base attacked on 7 December 1941? If so, could you detail the damage inflicted?"; "What ships were present at the Submarine Base on 7 December 1941?"

627• POSTAL RATE COMMISSION
2000 L St. NW, Washington DC 20268. (202)254-5614. Contact Person: Public Information Officer. **Description:** "The Postal Rate Commission is a public forum for consideration of domestic postal rate fee, service and classification changes proposed by the Postal Service." **Services:** Provides historical, referral, technical and trade information on postal rates and mail classifications. Offers aid in arranging interviews, biographies, statistics and placement on mailing list. **How to Contact:** Write or call. Responds to most inquiries immediately. "Writers must pay duplicating costs when supplies of copies of original documents have been exhausted." **Tips:** "Be aware that the Postal Rate Commission is NOT the US Postal Service. The Postal Rate Commission (PRC) is the Federal agency which serves as the legal forum for proposed changes in postal rates, fees, mail classifications (which are official definitions of the different services available from the Postal Service); or changes in the nature of available postal service; or appeals from Postal Service decisions to close or consolidate small post offices. The commission also investigates complaints concerning postal rates, fees, mail classifications, or services. Be prepared to read through testimony and/or hearing transcripts if researching past or present postal proceedings."

628• RESEARCH PUBLICATIONS, INC.
12 Lunar Dr., Drawer AB, Woodbridge CT 06525. (203)397-2600. Contact Person: Managing Editor, Declassified Documents. **Description:** "Research Publications, a microform publisher, is the principal compiler of material declassified as a result of Freedom of Information Act requests and by mandatory review." **Services:** Provides historical information on US foreign relations since 1945, including involvement in Korea and Vietnam; international events and crises; defense and national security policy; domestic intelligence. Publications include *The Declassified Documents Reference System*, consisting of Annual Collections and the Retrospective Collection, which provides access to over 20,000 formerly classified CIA, Defense Department, State Department, National Security Council, and White House documents. "Researchers can examine the full texts of the documents on microfiche; abstracts and subject indexes keyed to the documents can be used as separate research tools. Annual Collections are published in quarterly installments." **How to Contact:** Write or call. Responds to most inquiries within a week. While there is a subscription fee ($725 for the current year's collection of abstracts, indexes, and microfiche; $375 for abstracts and indexes only), writers and researchers can contact RPI's Washington office (Suite 905, 1911 N. Ft. Myer Drive, Arlington VA 22209, (703)525-5940) for information on the locations of subscribing university and public libraries and on the specific subject areas covered in the collections.

629• RESERVE OFFICERS ASSOCIATION OF THE UNITED STATES
1 Constitution Ave. NE, Washington DC 20002. (202)479-2258. Contact Person: Director of Public Affairs. **Description:** "We are chartered by Congress to support policies which will ensure adequate national security for the United States. There are 125,000 members representing officers of all branches of military service, reserve and regular." **Services:** Provides bibliographical, historical, interpretative and referral information on national security, national defense policies of the U.S. and current programs of all the Armed Forces with emphasis on Reserve Components. Offers aid in arranging interviews, brochures/pamphlets, informational newsletters, library facilities, press kits and research assistance. The William J. Reilly Memorial Library contains 5,000 volumes on military subjects. Books may be used on site only. Publications include *The

ROA Story (a history of ROA and the Reserve Components from 1922-1982); and *The Officer* (monthly magazine). Projected publication *Defense Education Report* (monthly newsletter). **How to Contact:** Write. Responds to most inquiries within a week. **Tips:** "We have limited staff time." Recent information request: General Hershey's relationship with the ROA.

630• UNITED STATES AIR FORCE MUSEUM
Wright-Patterson Air Force Base, Dayton OH 45433. (513)255-3284. Contact Person: Public Affairs Officer. **Description:** Museum portraying the history of the United States Air Force and its predecessor organizations. **Services:** Provides advisory information covering the United States Air Force and the history of military aviation. Offers aid in arranging interviews, brochures/pamphlets and press kits. **How to Contact:** "Call to discuss requirements, or preferably, write to the museum explaining what is desired." Responds to most inquiries within a week. Charges for extensive photocopying; "10¢/copy for documents from the research files. Credit the US Air Force Museum for assistance or photos." **Tips:** "Avoid short fuse requests. Plan on personal visits if possible. We prefer writers to visit and do their own research/photography because of our limited staff, but we do provide minimum service where possible to qualified writers with credentials. We do not provide complete research services for writers. We can generally provide a picture or stock news release, but writers cannot expect the museum to provide them a complete package of stories, pictures, etc. Our volume of requests does not permit this service. Our research department is open Mon.-Fri. 9 a.m.-4 p.m."

631• UNITED STATES ARMY AIR DEFENSE ARTILLERY MUSEUM
Attn: ATZC-DPT—PA, Ft. Bliss TX 79916. (915)568-5412, 568-6848. Contact Person: Director. **Description:** "Our Museum contains anti-aircraft artillery from World War I to the present." **Services:** Provides information on the history of the Air Defense. Offers brochures/pamphlets, library facilities, photos and research assistance. Publications include *The Reasons Why*. **How to Contact:** Write, call or visit. Responds to most inquiries immediately.

632• UNITED STATES ARMY MILITARY HISTORY INSTITUTE
Carlisle Barracks PA 17013. (717)245-3152. Contact Person: Director. **Description:** The library and museum collects, preserves and provides for public use materials relating to the history and traditions of the United States Army, 1775-present and military history in general. **Services:** Provides advisory, bibliographical, historical and referral information on United States Army military history and military history in general. Offers bibliographies and special studies, brochures/pamphlets, informational newsletters, library facilities, photos, placement on mailing lists, research assistance and telephone reference services. Publications include bibliographies and semi-annual newsletter. **How to Contact:** Write, call or visit. Responds to most inquiries within a month.

633• UNITED STATES COMMISSION ON CIVIL RIGHTS
1121 Vermont Ave. NW, Room 500, Washington DC 20425. (202)254-6345. Contact Person: Director, Community Relations Division. **Description:** "The U.S. Commission on Civil Rights is an independent government agency established by Congress in 1957 to collect and study information on discrimination and denial of equal protection of the laws, to appraise the laws and policies of the Federal Government, to serve as a national clearinghouse for information on civil rights, and to report to the President and the Congress. The commission's jurisdiction covers race, color, religion, national origin, sex, age, handicap and the administration of justice." **Services:** Provides advisory, analytical, bibliographical (limited basis), interpretative and referral information on denial of equal protection of the laws in education, employment, housing, the administration of justice, and voting rights based upon race, color, religion, national origin (ethnicity), sex, age and/or handicap. Offers aid in arranging interviews, brochures/pamphlets, informational newsletters, library facilities, placement on mailing lists and statistics (in USCCR Reports). Publications include commission reports, without charge, on studies; proceedings of conferences and consultations; quarterly magazine *Prespectives*; newsletter *Update*; a *Directory of Civil Rights Organizations*; a catalog of commission publications; and the commission brochure. **How to Contact:** Write, call or visit. Responds to most inquiries within a week. "Write or call in advance for personal interviews or use of commission library." Give credit to commission. **Tips:** Recent information requests: Programs related to battered women and domestic violence; income differentials among blacks and whites and men and women; "What evidence is there that denial of voting rights is still a problem in the U.S.?"

BEHIND THE BYLINE

Matthew Lesko
Writer and researcher

"I hated doing research in school; to me, it meant sitting in some stuffy library. It seemed like the most boring thing in the world. But now I approach research differently."

So differently, in fact, that Matthew Lesko finds himself doing research for the business community. He's a partner in a research firm called Washington Researchers. Lesko's "library" is Washington, DC but his approach to research goes far beyond the printed word.

"If it's information you need for decision making or writing a book, looking for sources in other books is very limited. By the time an idea actually comes out in print, it's an idea the author had three or four years ago. But if you find that person who specializes in some kind of information, then you get from that person's head what will be published a few years from now."

Information is a people business, Lesko says. "There's an information explosion going on right now. You can get eighty-five thousand citations on anything; but you don't have the time to get it all, read it all and find out what's worthwhile. But with a half-dozen phone calls (Lesko's average is seven), you can find an expert who's read it all. He'll probably be glad to share it with you and he'll be able to tell you what's been published and what's unpublished."

Lesko believes some of the best information is found in "unpublished documents"—one-of-a-kind studies; testimonies on Capitol Hill; a report on some bureaucrat's shelf. "An expert in the field will know about it."

Doing research with people instead of card catalogs and computer terminals presents unique challenges for writers. "The key to getting information is treating people right. It's a series of one-night stands, and first impressions (especially on the phone) really count. Be open about what you are doing because you want another person to be open with you. And don't ask a battery of questions. Get people to talk; you'd be surprised what comes out."

Lesko puts the fruits of his research labor to

use by writing for consumers. His monthly inflation-fighting column in *Good Housekeeping* offers money-saving insights; his book, *Getting Yours: A Complete Guide to Government Money* and his other consumer-oriented publications offer information about what's available in the marketplace.

What does he decide to pass along to consumers? "Projects germinate. I try to force myself to think about the things people need. Sometimes the ideas I come out with sound terrible, but I just run with what I've got. That's important for building up to a better idea. You can't just sit back and wait for a rocket to come out of the sky. Follow through with an idea as far as you can." (Lesko sold his book, *Getting Yours*, on just the *idea* of identifying the funding and programs available to consumers through the government. Following discussions with his editors and others, the actual book turned out to be not only a list of programs, but also real-life accounts of people who tapped into those programs.) "Talk to other people. What will happen is they're going to change the idea for you."

It's that stick-to-it-iveness that Lesko credits for much of his research/writing success. It's a long-term philosophy, a strategy of sorts. "The trick is to keep getting leads; once you're out of leads, you're out of the game."

634• UNITED STATES MILITARY ACADEMY
West Point NY 10996. (914)938-4011. Contact: Public Affairs Office. **Description:** "Military academy with 4,200 students." **Services:** Offers biographies, brochures/pamphlets and informational papers. **How to Contact:** Write. Responds to most inquiries immediately. **Tips:** "Specify exactly what type of information or brochure you're looking for."

635• UNITED STATES NAVAL ACADEMY MUSEUM
Annapolis MD 21402. (301)267-2108. Contact Person: Director. **Description:** "Our purpose is to collect, preserve and utilize historic objects germane to the history and traditions of the US Navy with particular emphasis on the officer corps and graduates of the US Naval Academy." **Services:** Provides advisory, bibliographical, historical, interpretative and referral information on US naval history, ship models, paintings, prints, medals, uniforms, weapons, flags, etc. Special collections include The Rogers Ship Models Collection, The Beverley R. Robinson Collection of Naval Battle Prints, Malcolm Storer Naval Medal Collection, The US Navy Trophy Flag Collection; significant groups of objects and documentary material; and over 750 oil paintings and pieces of sculpture. Offers biographies, brchures/pamphlets, library facilities, photos and research assistance. Publications include small catalogs of ship models, medals, manuscripts, prints, etc. **How to Contact:** Write, call or visit. Responds to most inquiries within a week. **Tips:** Recent information requests: "Did John Paul Jones command *Providence* and when?"; "Please provide a ship's history of *USS Providence*"; "Could you provide a picture of the battle between *USS Constitution* and *HMS Guerriere*, War of 1812?"; "I think my uncle graduated from the Naval Academy—what class was he in?"

636• VETERANS ADMINISTRATION
Office of Public and Consumer Affairs (063), 810 Vermont Ave. NW, Washington DC 20420. Contact Person: Director, News and Media Liaison Division. **Description:** The VA administers laws authorizing benefits principally for former members and certain dependents of former members of the armed forces. Major Veterans Admistration (VA) programs include medical care and research, education and training, compensation, pension, loan guaranty, death benefits, rehabilitation and insurance. **Services:** Offers specialized pamphlets describing individual VA benefits. **How to Contact;** Write. Information is available at 58 VA regional offices and 172 hospitals. Phone any VA office or (202)389-2741 in Washington DC.

637• VETERANS OF FOREIGN WARS OF THE UNITED STATES
34th and Broadway, Kansas City MO 64111. (816)756-3390. Contact Person: Publisher. **Description:** "The purpose of this organization shall be fraternal, patriotic, historical and educational; to preserve and strengthen comradeship among its members; to assist worthy comrades; to perpetuate the memory of our dead and to assist widows and orphans; to maintain true allegiance to the government of the United States of America, and fidelity to its Constitution and laws; to foster true patriotism; to maintain and extend the institution of American freedom; and to preserve and defend the United States from all her enemies whomsoever." **Services:** Offers brochures/pamphlets and newsletters. Publications include *V.F.W. Magazine* (10 times/year); *Washington Action Reporter* (monthly); *Speak Up for Democracy* (monthly radio/TV script); *The Communicator* (bimonthly newsletter). **How to Contact:** Write or call. Responds to most inquiries within a week.

638• WAR MEMORIAL MUSEUM OF VIRGINIA
9285 Warwick Blvd., Huntington Park, Newport News VA 23607. (804)247-8523. Contact Person: Curator. **Description:** "The War Memorial Museum of Virginia exists to reveal the military history of the United States from the Revolutionary War to the present. Exhibits include World War I and II posters, weapons, uniforms and insignia from all over the world. The library (which includes books, periodicals, historical files, tapes, photos and films) contains information covering the US and world military history, especially concerning World War I and II." **Services:** Provides advisory, historical, referral and technical information covering US military history— 1775 to the present; European military history—WWI & II. Offers brochures/pamphlets and information searches. "We are presently preparing pamphlets about our collection of posters, weapons and local military history. We will assist a qualified researcher, as best as possible, in using our library, historical films and tapes when he is researching at the museum or through written correspondence." Publications include *Excavated Artifacts from Battlefields and Campsites of the Civil War*; *Bullets Used in the Civil War*; *German Medals and Decorations of World War II*; *Officers and*

Men at the Battle of Manila Bay; *Shoulder Patch Insignia of the United States Armed Forces*; *Aviation Badges and Insignia of the United States Army, 1913-1946*; and *British Cut and Thrust Weapons*. **How to Contact:** Write or call. Responds to most inquiries within a month. Charges 50¢ entrance fee to the museum and copying fees. "No materials of any form can leave the museum. Films, historical files, tapes, books and name books are cataloged and located in a central position to ease research at the museum. No artifacts can be loaned to private individuals; films are available on a limited basis." **Tips:** "We can offer techniques in identification of military history artifacts. We can also advise researchers of additional materials and information from governmental sources." Recent information requests: Identification of US and foreign military equipment; local and state military events and personages; background on military artwork—posters, especially.

639• WEST POINT MUSEUM
US Military Academy, West Point NY 10996. (914)938-2203. Contact Person: Director of the Museum. **Description:** "This military museum has been open to the public since 1854." Information covers "exhibits from the American Revolution until now, including uniforms, flags, arms, art, history and technical information." **Services:** Offers aid in arranging interviews, biographies, brochures/pamphlets, placement on mailing lists, photos and press kits. Publications include a portrait catalog. **How to Contact:** Write. Responds to most inquiries within a month. **Tips:** "We answer questions on all phases of American military history."

640• WRITERS FOR THE 80'S
Box 3797, Washington DC 20007. Contact Person: Vice President. **Description:** "We are a political writer's resource service. We provide computer back-up on data for all political candidates, publish a monthly newsletter and our staff writers prepare documents as requested by clients." **Services:** Provides advisory, analytical and interpretative information on all forms of public information from Congress, Administration, public sector sources including state and local governments, agencies, commissions, etc. Offers annual reports, brochures/pamphlets, computerized information searches, informational newsletters, research assistance and statistics. Publications include a monthly newsletter on services available and recent developments in the field. **How to Contact:** Write. Responds to most inquiries within a week. Charges for services on an individual basis with qualified clients. **Tips:** "We can provide either the raw data, or work it up in a narrative format. With our substantial computer records, we can obtain accurate information quickly, and for an extra fee can provide 24-hour turn-around time on emergency request for specific information and/or data. Be sure you know specifically what it is you are interested in . . . this saves you both time and money." Recent information request: "What is the status of state laws dealing with sales taxes on food stuffs, and what are the general taxing trends for states and local governmental subdivisions on sales taxes?"

SECTION · TWELVE

HEALTH AND MEDICINE

All interest in disease and death is only another expression of interest in life.

—Thomas Mann

Information resources in the fields of health and medicine cover physical and mental health care and alternatives, as well as health professionals, disease and prevention, drugs and pharmaceuticals, abuse and wellness.

Other health-related contacts are found in the Human Services section. Fitness and sports medicine are covered in the Sports category; nutrition, in the Farming and Food section. Occupational health sources are listed in the Workplace section. For contact information on the government's Department of Health and Human Services, consult page 19 of the government information article.

Bibliography

American Hospital Association Guide to the Health Care Field. Chicago: American Hospital Association, 1980. (Directory of hospitals)

Berkow, Robert, ed. *Merck Manual of Diagnosis & Therapy*. 13th ed. Rahway, NJ: Merck Sharp & Dohme Research Laboratories, 1977.

Bricklin, Mark. *Rodale's Encyclopedia of Natural Home Remedies*. Emmaus, PA: Rodale Press, Inc., 1982.

Brody, Jane. *New York Times Guide to Personal Health*. New York: Times Books, 1982.

Hulke, Malcolm, ed. *Encyclopedia of Alternative Medicine and Self-Help*. New York: Schocken Books, 1979.

Kruzas, Anthony T., ed. *Health Services Directory*. Detroit: Gale Research Co., 1981. (Clinics, centers, programs, services treating health and social problems)

Kruzas, Anthony T., ed. *Medical and Health Information Dictionary*. Detroit: Gale Research Co., 1982. (Agencies, companies, associations concerned with health care)

National Directory of Mental Health. New York: Neil-Schuman Publishers, Inc., John Wiley & Sons, 1980.

Physician's Desk Reference. Annual. Oradell, NJ: Medical Economics Co., Litton Industries. (Pharmacology reference with objective information on thousands of drugs)

Taber's Cyclopedia Medical Dictionary. Philadelphia: F.A. Davis Co., 1981.

Weise, Freida, ed. *Health Statistics: A Guide to Information Sources*. Detroit: Gale Research Co., 1980.

641• ACUPUNCTURE RESEARCH INSTITUTE
313 W. Andrix St., Monterey Park CA 91754. (213)722-7353. Contact Person: Secretary. **Description:** Persons in the medical professions interested in investigating the application of acupuncture in America. **Services:** Provides how-to, interpretative and referral information on medicine, homeopathy, acupuncture, dentistry, nutrition, etc. Offers informational newsletters, placement on mailing lists and telephone reference services. Publications include journal (semiannual). **How to Contact:** Write. Responds to most inquiries immediately.

642• ALCOHOL, DRUG ABUSE AND MENTAL HEALTH ADMINISTRATION
National Clearinghouse for Alcohol, National Clearinghouse for Drug Abuse, National Clearinghouse for Mental Health, 5600 Fishers Lane, Rockville MD 20857. (301)443-3783. Contact Person: Director of the Office of Communications and Public Affairs. **Description:** "The administration provides research, service and training in the areas of alcohol, drugs and mental health." **Services:** Provides support for research on alcohol, drug abuse and mental health problems and technical assistance for communication and prevention activity relating to these problem areas. Offers brochures/pamphlets, newsletter, placement on mailing list, press kits and photos. Three publication lists available—one each on alcohol, drug abuse and mental

health. **How to Contact:** Write or call the National Clearinghouse for Alcohol (301)468-2600, the National Clearinghouse for Drug Abuse (301)443-6500 or the National Clearinghouse for Mental health (301)443-4513. Charges only for Freedom of Information request or for some publications that are available only from the Superintendent of Documents. **Tips:** ''Be very clear about what information you want.''

643• AMERICAN ACADEMY OF ALLERGY AND IMMUNOLOGY
611 E. Wells St., Milwaukee WI 53202. Contact Person: Public Relations Agent, Ted Klein & Co., 118 E. 61st St., New York NY 10021. (212)935-1290 or academy executive office. **Description:** The object of the academy is ''the advancement of the knowledge and practice of allergy and immunology, by discussion at meetings, by fostering the education of students and the public, by encouraging union and cooperation among those engaged in this field, and by promoting and stimulating research and study in allergy and immunology.'' **Services:** Provides advisory, referral, technical and trade information on asthma, allergy and immunology. ''We have an extensive list of referrals. The writer should call our office or our PR agent to obtain this list. We also have a 'hot line' which provides a 5-minute crash course on a variety of allergic diseases.'' Offers statistics, brochures/pamphlets, placement on mailing list and press kits. Publications include an abstract book (papers presented at annual meeting), position statements and material on hymenoptera (insect) stings. **How to Contact:** Write or call. Responds to most inquiries immediately. **Tips:** Recent information request: ''A writer called because a local resident had been stung by a fire ant and had a severe reaction. She wanted to know who she could talk to about fire ants, and if the sting should be reported and to whom.''

644• AMERICAN ACADEMY OF FAMILY PHYSICIANS
1740 W. 92nd St., Kansas City MO 64114. (800)821-2512. Contact Person: Manager, Public Relations Services. **Description:** ''The AAFP is a nonprofit national medical organization representing 54,000 family physicians. It was founded in 1947 to promote and maintain high standards for family doctors providing continuing, comprehensive health care to the public.'' **Services:** Provides advisory, historical, how-to, interpretative and referral information on health care delivery. Offers aid in arranging interviews, annual reports, biographies, brochures/pamphlets, informational newsletters, photos, placement on mailing lists, press kits and statistics. Publications include *AAFP Reporter* and *American Family Physician*. **How to Contact:** Write or call. Responds to most inquiries within a week.

645• AMERICAN ACADEMY OF PERIODONTOLOGY
c/o The Siesel Co., 845 3rd Ave., New York NY 10022. (212)759-6500. Contact Person: Senior Vice President. **Description:** ''An association of dentists who have completed two years of graduate study in periodontics; examines applicants for Board Certification and sponsors National Foundation for the Prevention of Oral Disease.'' **Services:** Provides advisory, analytical, bibliographical, historical and referral information on all aspects of gum (periodontal) disease. Offers aid in arranging interviews, brochures/pamphlets, research assistance and telephone reference services. Publications include *Journal of Periodontology*, scientific journal reporting on research and clinical advances in treating gum disease; background information on gum disease. **How to Contact:** Write or call. Responds to most inquiries immediately.

646• AMERICAN ACADEMY OF PHYSICIAN ASSISTANTS
2341 Jefferson Davis Hwy., Suite 700, Arlington VA 22202. (703)920-5730. Contact Person: Director of Public Education and Publications. **Description:** ''The American Academy of Physician Assistants (AAPA) is a nonprofit organization representing physician assistants. Its range of activities includes many specific membership services, meetings and conferences, research on the profession, public relations, publications and legislative activity. The AAPA has the most complete demographic information on the PA profession and is dedicated to providing the public with a greater understanding of the role of PAs in the health care delivery system. We serve as the only national information resource center on the PA profession.'' **Services:** Offers aid in arranging interviews, annual reports, bibliographies, statistics, brochures/pamphlets, placement on mailing list, newsletter and press kits. Publications include *The P.A. Profession . . . What You Should Know* and *AAPA National Health Practitioner Program Profile* (catalog of physician assistant programs). **How to Contact:** Write. Responds to most inquiries within a week. Charges $7/copy for programs catalog, 10¢/copy for pamphlets/brochures in quantities greater than 10. ''Give credit to the AAPA.'' **Tips:** Recent information request: ''What is a physician assistant?''

647• AMERICAN ASSEMBLY FOR MEN IN NURSING
600 S. Paulina, Room 474H, Chicago IL 60612. Contact Person: Chairman of the Board. **Description:** Men and women in the assembly work to meet the following goals: "to encourage men to become nurses and join together with all nurses in strengthening and humanizing health care for Americans; to encourage men who are now nurses to grow professionally and demonstrate to each other and to society the increasing contributions being made by men within the nursing profession; to have all members be full participants in the nursing profession and organizations and to use the assembly to meet these goals." **Services:** Offers brochure explaining membership in the organization and statistics on the assembly. **How to Contact:** Write or call. Responds to most inquiries within a week. **Tips:** Recent information request: "What percentage of nurses in America are males?"

648• AMERICAN ASSOCIATION OF BLOOD BANKS
1117 N. 19th St., Suite 600, Arlington VA 22207. Contact Person: Director of Communication. **Description:** "We are the largest association of blood banking professionals in the world. The membership is made up of hospitals and transfusion services and individual scientists, administrators, technicians and donor recruiters. Our areas of research include blood composition, diseases, transfusions and the need for blood." **Services:** Provides advisory, analytical, interpretative, referral and trade information on blood banking, blood diseases, and blood collection and distribution. Offers aid in arranging interviews, annual reports, brochures/pamphlets, statistics and newsletter. Publications available. **How to Contact:** Write or call. Responds to most inquiries immediately. **Tips:** "Call and give us time to refer you to an expert in the field, or check with our sources for accurate information." Recent information requests: "How much blood is collected, donated in the US?"; questions regarding blood shortage, diseases.

649• AMERICAN ASSOCIATION OF POISON CONTROL CENTERS
San Diego Regional Poison Center, 225 Dickenson St., San Diego CA 92103. Contact Person: Secretary/Treasurer. **Description:** "Our purpose is to set up standards of operation for poison control centers; to encourage poison prevention programs at public and professional levels; to provide information to the public and develop information services concerning toxicology; to stimulate educational programs and scientific research on toxic substances; and to assist federal, state and local officials and voluntary agencies in the field of poison control." **Services:** Offers annual reports, brochures/pamphlets and newsletter. Publications include *What If a Poisoning Occurs?*; *What about Plants?*; *Emergency Action for Poisoning* (chart); *Do You Know about Ipecac Syrup?*; *Animal and Human Toxicology* (journal). **How to Contact:** Write. Responds to most inquiries within a month.

650• AMERICAN CANCER SOCIETY, INC.
4 W. 35th St., New York NY 10001. (212)736-3030. Contact Person: Assistant Director, Magazine and Book Relations. **Description:** A voluntary health organization composed of 58 divisions and about 3,000 local units around the country with a threefold program: research, education and service to the cancer patient. **Services:** Provides advisory and referral information on cancer and the American Cancer Society programs in research, education and service to the cancer patient. **How to Contact:** Write or call. Responds to most inquiries within a week. **Tips:** "Freelancers must have a firm assignment. Give adequate time for handling of requests."

651• AMERICAN COLLEGE OF EMERGENCY PHYSICIANS (ACEP)
Box 61911, Dallas TX 75261. (214)659-0911. Contact Person: Public Relations Director. **Description:** ACEP's purpose is "to improve the quality of emergency medical care through the educational association of practitioners of emergency medicine." Information covers health/medicine and emergency health care. **Services:** Provides historical and referral information on ACEP, history of emergency medicine, policies and position statements on various areas, Emergency Care Guidelines, freestanding emergency facilities, trauma centers, prehospital care, facts and figures on emergency medicine. Offers aid in arranging interviews, bibliographies, statistics, brochures/pamphlets, placement on mailing list, photos and press kits. Publications include a brochure on services to members; CME requirements; *1968-1978: ACEP's First Decade of Achievement*; a fact sheet; a monthly newsletter (*ACEP News*); a clinical journal (*Annals of Emergency Medicine*); and general information about emergency medicine. **How to Contact:** Write or call. Responds to most inquiries immediately. **Tips:** "Formulate your question clearly.

The more specific the question, the easier it will be for us to search the appropriate file. Call early enough before deadlines to allow written materials to be mailed." Recent information requests: "How many freestanding emergency facilities are there?"; "What is the best method of removing fish hooks?"

652• AMERICAN DENTAL ASSOCIATION
211 E. Chicago Ave., Chicago IL 60611. (312)440-2806. Contact Person: Manager of Media Services. **Description:** A voluntary national health organization with 140,000 members. **Services:** Provides historical, referral, technical and trade information on all dental topics. **How to Contact:** Write or call. Responds to most inquiries immediately. **Tips:** Recent information request: The amount of money spent annually on dental care, the type of care most frequently received and by whom.

653• AMERICAN DENTAL HYGIENISTS' ASSOCIATION
211 E. Chicago Ave., Chicago IL 60611. (312)440-8923. Contact Person: Director, Communications Division. **Description:** "American Dental Hygienists' Association (ADHA) is an organization of dental hygiene professionals dedicated to promoting the oral health of the public." **Services:** Provides bibliographical, historical, referral and technical information on dental hygiene and other related subjects. Offers aid in arranging interviews and brochures/pamphlets. Publications include two journals, *Dental Hygiene* and *Educational Directions.* **How to Contact:** Write or call. Responds to most inquiries immediately. **Tips:** Recent information request: Career opportunities for dental hygienists.

654• AMERICAN DIABETES ASSOCIATION, INC.
2 Park Ave., New York NY 10016. (212)683-7444. Contact Person: Director of Public Relations. **Description:** "We are a national voluntary nonprofit health organization serving 11 million diabetics through programs of research, patient and public education and community services. The national headquarters in New York works in conjunction with 600 affiliates in all 50 states and locations in the US. The association has a dual mission: to promote the search for a cure or prevention of diabetes; and to improve the health and well being of people with diabetes and their families." **Services:** Offers aid in arranging interviews, annual reports, brochures/pamphlets, placement on mailing list, statistics, newsletter and press kits. **How to Contact:** Write or call. Responds to most inquiries within a week. "We really stress use of local offices and prefer written information requests if questions are involved." **Tips:** "One of our major program objectives is to provide an increased understanding of the life-shortening complications of the disease—blindness, heart disease, kidney failure and amputation from gangrene." Recent information requests: Background on new treatments, insulin pumps, blood-glucose monitoring devices and research in the field.

655• AMERICAN HEALTH CARE ASSOCIATION
1200 15th St. NW, Washington DC 20005. (202)833-2050. Contact Person: Director of Communications. **Description:** "The American Health Care Association is the nation's largest federation of nursing homes and long-term health care facilities for the aged and the convalescent. It is composed of 48 state associations with more than 8,000 facility members providing over 750,000 long-term care beds, half of all such beds in America. AHCA was founded in 1949 to provide leadership in promoting high standards of professional operation and administration of long term and related convalescent health care facilities and to ensure quality care for patients and residents in safe surroundings, on a basis of fair payment for services." **Services:** Offers aid in arranging interviews, statistics, brochures/pamphlets, placement on mailing list, newsletter and press kits for members only. Publications include *Weekly Note* and *Journal of the American Health Care Association,* (bimonthly). No cost for single copies of *Facts in Brief on Long-Term Care* and *Thinking About a Nursing Home.* **How to Contact:** Write or call. Responds to most inquiries within a week. "Obtain permission to use copyrighted material; give credit to American Health Care Association." **Tips:** Recent information request: How to choose a nursing home; the number of nursing homes in the country.

656• AMERICAN HEARING RESEARCH FOUNDATION
55 E. Washington St., Suite 2105, Chicago IL 60602. (312)726-9670. Contact Person: Executive Director. **Description:** "The American Hearing Research Foundation is a nonprofit organization that has three fundamental purposes: to provide financial assistance for medical research into the

causes, prevention and cure of deafness, impaired hearing and balance disorders; to encourage the collaboration of clinical laboratory research; and to broaden teaching of the medical aspects in hearing problems and disseminate the latest and most reliable scientific knowledge to physicians and the public." **Services:** Provides bibliographical and historical information on hearing research and education. Offers aid in arranging interviews, annual reports, biographies, brochures/pamphlets, informational newsletters, placement on mailing lists, research assistance, statistics and telephone reference services. Publications include newsletter, annual report and research papers. **How to Contact:** Write. Responds to most inquiries within a month. **Tips:** Recent information request: "I have nerve deafness. Can I be helped by an ear operation?"

657• AMERICAN HEART ASSOCIATION
7320 Greenville Ave., Dallas TX 75231. (214)750-5397. Contact Person: Director of Science and Public Information. **Description:** The Heart Association works "to reduce death and disability from cardiovascular diseases through research, education and community service projects." **Services:** Offers aid in arranging interviews, annual reports, biographies, statistics, brochures/pamphlets and press kits. **How to Contact:** Write or call. Responds to most inquiries within a week. "Obtain permission to use copyrighted material." **Tips:** Recent information request: Statistical data on the number of deaths in the US which are the result of heart disease.

658• AMERICAN HOLISTIC HEALTH SCIENCES ASSOCIATION
1766 Cumberland, Suite 208, St. Charles IL 60174. (312)377-1929. Contact Person: Secretary. **Description:** "We provide a forum for exchanges between the various health philosophies. We promote preventative health care, natural non-toxic therapies, and the dissemination of self-care and holistic health education." **Services:** Provides advisory, bibliographical and referral information on self-responsibility for health, nutrition information, natural health methods and unconventional medicine. Offers informational newsletters. Publications include over 100 books and tapes on alternative/holistic health subjects; and *Alternative Health-Subjects Schools* (annual directory). **How to Contact:** Write. Responds to most inquiries within a week. Charges for newsletters or specific books. **Tips:** Recent information requests: "Where would one get information that is anti-immunization for children?"; "What are the alternatives to drugs, surgery, and radiation for cancer therapy?"

659• AMERICAN HOLISTIC MEDICAL ASSOCIATION
6932 Little River Turnpike, Annandale VA 22003. (703)642-5880. Contact Person: Executive Director. **Description:** "Our purpose is to provide education and member services to physicians, to educate the public and health professionals, to promote research in holistic medicine." **Services:** Provides bibliographical, historical, referral and trade information on holistic medicine and holistic health. Offers aid in arranging interviews (referrals), brochures/pamphlets, informational newsletters and placement on mailing lists. Publications include membership directory, monthly newsletter, semi-annual *Journal*. **How to Contact:** Write. Responds to most inquiries within a week. Charges for publications, but newsletter sample is free. "We expect writers to present material objectively, and to provide us with a copy of the article beforehand if at all possible. We request a clipping after publication." **Tips:** "We answer most questions concerning the Association itself, e.g., its history, demographics, purposes, etc. Many writers contact us with specific medical questions, and we refer them to appropriate physicians."

660• AMERICAN HOSPITAL ASSOCIATION
840 N. Lake Shore Dr., Chicago IL 60611. (312)280-6000. Contact: Department of Media Relations or Library. **Description:** "The American Hospital Association is a membership organization for hospitals and hospital workers. The AHA's purpose is education, research and the offering of statistical data. Current membership of 6,300 works to provide the best possible health care. The AHA also represents hospitals and hospital workers in issues of legislation and regulations." **Services:** Offers aid in arranging interviews, bibliographies, statistics, brochures/pamphlets, placement on mailing list, newsletter, press kits and press releases. Publications include *AHA Guide to Health Care*; *AHA Hospital Books*; and *Hospital Week*. **How to Contact:** Write. Responds to most inquiries immediately. "Media calls are handled by the Department of Media Relations; public information is handled by the library." **Tips:** Recent information requests: Statistical data on occupancy rates for community hospitals; expenses per patient per day.

661• AMERICAN LUNG ASSOCIATION
1740 Broadway, New York NY 10019. (212)245-8000. Contact Person: Director of Communications. **Description:** "The association is concerned with the control and prevention of all lung disease including asthma, emphysema, tuberculosis—as well as some of their associate causes such as smoking, air pollution and occupational living hazards." **Services:** Offers aid in arranging interviews and brochures/pamphlets. A publication list is available. **How to Contact:** Write. Responds to most inquiries within a week. "You may wish to contact your local lung association; give credit to the association and obtain copyright permission where necessary." Recent information requests: Statistics on lung disease; history of tuberculosis.

662• AMERICAN MEDICAL ASSOCIATION
535 N. Dearborn St., Chicago IL 60610. Contact Person: Director of Media Relations. **Description:** The AMA "informs physicians on progress in clinical medicine, pertinent research and landmark evolutions." **Services:** Provides advisory, interpretative and referral information on medicine, health care and science. Offers statistics, brochures/pamphlets, clipping services, library searches, placement on mailing list and newsletter. Publications include a publications list. **How to Contact:** Write or call. Responds to most inquiries immediately. "Contact Media Relations Department first rather than calling others in the AMA." **Tips:** "Allow enough time for research. Be specific in asking a few questions. We respond to more than 500 calls per month on everything imaginable."

663• AMERICAN MEDICAL TECHNOLOGISTS
710 Higgins Rd., Park Ridge IL 60068. (312)823-5169. Contact Person: Public Relations Director. **Description:** "American Medical Technologists (AMT) is a registry for medical laboratory personnel. It provides continuing education programs for these professionals." **Services:** Offers aid in arranging interviews and brochures/pamphlets. Publications include *Information on a Career in Medical Technology*. **How to Contact:** Write or call. Responds to most inquiries within a week. **Tips:** "We can provide interviews with working laboratorians on such topics as: Why the high cost of laboratory services in the hospital? What does modern technology offer the patient? What are career opportunities? Consult US Department of Labor's *Occupational Outlook Handbook* for background information on the medical lab occupation."

664• AMERICAN OPTOMETRIC ASSOCIATION
Communications Division, 243 N. Lindbergh Blvd., St. Louis MO 63141. (314)991-4100. Contact Person: Associate Director, News. **Description:** "The American Optometric Association represents 22,900 doctors and students of optometry. Its objectives are to improve the vision care and health of the public and to promote the art and science of the profession of optometry. Optometric care encompasses children's vision, vision care of children with learning problems, vision care of the aging, rehabilitation of the partially sighted, contact lenses, environmental vision in industry and agriculture, vision in sports and recreation and vision in driving." **Services:** Provides advisory, bibliographical, historical, how-to and referral information on vision problems; information on eye care for infants, children, teens, the middle-aged and older adults; advice about vision in school, on the job, on the farm, in the home, when driving, when participating in sports, when pursuing hobbies; care for the visually handicapped; eye safety; contact lenses; eyeglasses; sunglasses; and consumer advice about vision care. Offers aid in arranging interviews, bibliographies, statistics, brochures/pamphlets, information searches, placement on mailing list and photos. Publications include "specially prepared news backgrounders and news features on various vision care topics available exclusively to the media. These cover a subject in more depth than brochures and pamphlets. For example, *Contact Lens News Backgrounder* and *Consumer Advice on Vision Care: A News Backgrounder*." **How to Contact:** Write. Responds to most inquiries within a week. "Specify the vision care subject area in which you are interested, your audience, and, if known, the name of the publication for which you are writing. This helps us to pinpoint the exact background material you will find most useful and the exact interview subjects who will be most helpful to you. Writers should not abuse the privilege of receiving in-depth backgrounders from us by requesting them for their own personal use with no intention of passing the information in them along to others through their writing. We ask that, if our material is used either verbatim or paraphrased in the article, the American Optometric Association be given proper attribution. Also, we would appreciate receiving tear sheets of published articles and reports of broadcasts." **Tips:** "Be specific in your requests. The vision care field is so broad that it is impossible for us to answer

a request for 'information on vision care.' But it is easy for us to respond with information on specific topics such as contact lenses, children's vision, older adults' vision, etc. Also, don't wait until you are up against a deadline to contact us.'' Recent information request: "I'm looking for material and individuals in the areas of behavioral optometry, vision therapy, myopia prevention and control, and the effects of stress on eyesight.''

665• AMERICAN OSTEOPATHIC HOSPITAL ASSOCIATION
55 W. Seegers Rd., Arlington Heights IL 60005 (312)398-7700. Contact Person: Editorial Assistant. **Description:** "The purpose of this organization is to promote the public health and welfare through effective hospital leadership; provide member hospitals a channel through which to act collectively in areas of common interest; collect and analyze appropriate data; and provide management services and programs that improve the ability of member hospitals to deliver quality osteopathic health care.'' **Services:** Provides advisory, referral and trade information covering hospital management. Offers aid in arranging interviews, annual reports, statistics, brochures/pamphlets, placement on mailing lists and newsletter. Publications include *OH* magazine ($12/year) and *Focus: PR Innovations* newsletter. **How to Contact:** Write or call. Responds to most inquiries within a week. "We represent hospitals and have only general information on physicians.''

666• AMERICAN PSYCHIATRIC ASSOCIATION
1400 K St., NW, Washington DC 20005. Contact Person: Public Affairs Director. (202)682-6000. **Description:** "The American Psychiatric Association is a professional medical society representing 27,000 US and Canadian psychiatrists. Our goals are to improve treatment, rehabilitation and care of the mentally ill; to promote research; to advance standards of all psychiatric services and facilities; and to educate other medical professionals, scientists and the general public.'' **Services:** Provides advisory, analytical, bibliographical, historical, how-to, interpretative, referral and technical information on psychiatric care, psychiatric insurance and mental illnesses. Offers aid in arranging interviews, bibliographies, biographies, statistics, brochures/pamphlets and placement on mailing list. Publications include "advance and post-convention articles and news releases each May concerning annual meetings and scientific proceedings; more than 400 individual papers on a wide range of topics are typically available each year; intermittent news releases throughout the year regarding new studies published in the APA journals. A wide range of publications on many aspects of human life are available, depending on the writer's specific interests.'' **How to Contact:** Write or call. Responds to most inquiries immediately; within a week if research is required. Fee for computer literature search; $2/copy for annual meeting papers over 50. Give credit to APA. **Tips:** "Always check credibility of sources with others in the field.'' Recent information requests: "I'd like to interview an expert on manic-depressive illness.''; "What research has been done on mental illness and lunar cycles?''

667• AMERICAN REYE'S SYNDROME ASSOCIATION
701 S. Logan, Suite 203, Denver CO 80209. (303)777-2592. Contact Person: Executive Director. **Description:** "The American Reye's Syndrome Association is a nonprofit organization dedicated to the treatment, cure and prevention of Reye's Syndrome through education, research, and family services.'' **Services:** Provides advisory, bibliographical, interpretative, referral and technical information relating to Reye's Syndrome. Offers aid in arranging interviews, biographies, brochures/pamphlets, informational newsletters, research assistance, statistics and conference and workshop reprints. **How to Contact:** Write, call or visit. Responds to most inquiries within a week. "We prefer to review final copy prior to publication, since one of our objectives is to correct misinformation about Reye's Syndrome which has appeared in the past.'' **Tips:** "We have copies of many articles relating to Reye's Syndrome and many potential human interest leads. Our files are open to writers at any time, but keep in mind that our staff time is limited.''

668• AMERICAN SOCIAL HEALTH ASSOCIATION
260 Sheridan Ave., Palo Alto CA 94306. (415)321-5134. Contact Person: Program Director. **Description:** "A nonprofit research and development corporation spearheading new strategies and techniques for solving the venereal disease problem through programs of research, public awareness, information dissemination, professional education and public advocacy.'' **Services:** Offers annual reports, statistics, brochures/pamphlets and newsletter. Publications include *The Sexually Active and VD*, *Some Questions and Answers About Penicillin Resistant Gonorrhea*,

Women and VD, *Body Pollution* and other materials related to VD. **How to Contact:** Write or call. Responds to most inquiries immediately. "Single copies of pamphlets are given free with SASE. All materials are copyrighted. Permission must be requested before any items can be duplicated."

669• AMERICAN SOCIETY FOR LASER MEDICINE AND SURGERY
425 Pine Ridge Blvd., Suite 203, Wausau WI 54401. (715)845-9282. Contact Person: Secretary. **Description:** "The society's purpose is to offer a forum for exchange of information on laser applications in medicine and surgery for all physicians and scientists interested in this subject." **Services:** Long-range goals are to provide advisory and technical information on any subject dealing with the applications of lasers in the field of medicine and surgery. Offers informational newsletters and placement on mailing lists. Publications include *Lasers in Surgery and Medicine* (journal); and *Laser Medicine and Surgery News*. **How to Contact:** Write. Responds to most inquiries within a week. "We request advance viewing of copy to be published if we are quoted directly."

670• AMERICAN SOCIETY OF CLINICAL PATHOLOGISTS
2100 W. Harrison St., Chicago IL 60612. (312)738-1336. Contact Person: Executive Vice President. **Description:** "The American Society of Clinical Pathologists (ASCP) is a professional society of clinical pathologists that conducts a year-round program of continuing medical education that is the largest of any medical organization in the world. The program is designed to enable pathologists and other medical laboratory personnel (medical technologists, technicians, microbiologists, etc.) to augment their professional knowledge with the latest advances in research and techniques of laboratory medicine." **Services:** Offers aid in arranging interviews, biographies, statistics, placement on mailing list, photos and press kits. Publications include "a basic information kit on the field of pathology and laboratory medicine." **How to Contact:** Write or call. Responds to most inquiries immediately. "Obtain permission to use copyrighted material. We are in the field of pathology and laboratory medicine and will be glad to assist in any research in that field. We will not comment on subjects outside our field. Please be definite in your questions."

671• THE ARTHRITIS SOCIETY
920 Yonge St., Suite 420, Toronto, Ontario, CN M4W 3J7. (416)967-1414. Contact Person: Director, National Communications. **Description:** "The society aims to help in the acquisition and dissemination of knowledge about the cause, cure and prevention of arthritis. Also, it aims to assist the health professions, hospitals, medical schools and governments to bring about a rapid and continuous improvement in the quality of care for arthritis. Its principal mechanism for the attainment of these purposes is the provision of grants in aid of research, associateships and fellowships." **Services:** Provides advisory, historical, how-to and referral information on technical and medical areas, coping and education. Offers brochures/pamphlets. Publications include *You, Your Child and Arthritis*, *Facts About Adult Arthritis*, *The Road to Discovery* and *About the Arthritis Society*. **How to Contact:** Write or call. Responds to most inquiries immediately. **Tips:** "Be specific in queries. Contact first to verify research sources." Recent information requests: "Is there a cure for arthritis?"; "Is this a valid medication?"

672• ASSOCIATION FOR ADVANCEMENT OF BEHAVIOR THERAPY
420 Lexington Ave., New York NY 10170. (212)682-0065. Contact Person: Executive Director. **Description:** Professional organization. "While primarily an interest group, AABT is also active in encouraging the development of the conceptual and scientific basis of behavior therapy as an empirical approach to applied problems; facilitating the appropriate utilization and growth of behavior therapy as a professional activity; serving as a resource and information center for matters related to behavior therapy." **Services:** Provides referral information on populations, settings, techniques, treatments and special areas of interest in behavior therapy. Offers aid in arranging interviews, brochures/pamphlets and telephone reference services. Publications list available. **How to Contact:** Write or call. Responds to most inquiries within a week. "We reserve right to see copy and make appropriate changes prior to publication." **Tips:** "Contact us with sufficient time to allow for mailing of articles and referrals." Recent information requests; Stress management in the workplace; child/spouse abuse.

673• ASTHMA AND ALLERGY FOUNDATION OF AMERICA
9604 Wisconsin Ave., Bethesda MD 20814. (301)493-6552. Contact Person: Director of Communications. **Description:** "The foundation promotes health/disease control and prevention

on behalf of over 35 million Americans who suffer from asthma/allergies. We provide research support, training fellowships, professional/public education." **Services:** Provides advisory, bibliographical, how-to, interpretative, and referral information on asthma and allergic diseases (including hayfever/rhinitis, food, insects, drug, occupational, mold, dust, skin). Offers aid in arranging interviews, brochures/pamphlets, informational newsletters, placement on mailing lists, press kits and statistics. Publications include *Advance* (bi-monthly national newspaper), subject brochures and reports. **How to Contact:** Write or call. Responds to most inquiries within a week. Single copies of most brochures at no cost; price list for printed publications available. Reprint permission required on copyrighted materials. **Tips:** Recent information requests: "What is the prevalence of hayfever in a certain region of the US?"; "What are generally accepted, standard diagnostic and treatment techniques for specific types of allergies?"

674• BAKKEN MUSEUM OF ELECTRICITY IN LIFE
3537 Zenith Ave. S., Minneapolis MN 55416. Contact Person: Director. **Description:** "Museum/library devoted to the history of electricity, particularly in its relation to medicine and biology." **Services:** Provides bibliographical, historical and referral information on the history of electricity in the life sciences. The collection is strong in 18th century electrotherapy and 19th century electrophysiology. Offers bibliographies, brochures/pamphlets, information searches and photos. Publications available. **How to Contact:** Write or call. Responds to most inquiries within a week. Charges for photocopies/photographs and slides. **Tips:** "When researching take the time to be careful and don't jump to quick conclusions. Be fair. We don't undertake major, i.e., several weeks or more research projects. When contacting the museum, try to be *specific*: dates, types of equipment, types of therapy, diseases that were treated." Recent information request: "How was a Wimshurst machine used for medical therapy?"

675• THE BETTER SLEEP COUNCIL
Box 275, Burtonsville MD 20866. (703)979-3962. Contact Person: Public Relations Director. **Description:** "The Better Sleep Council seeks to help the consumer become better informed about sleep—overcoming problems and learning how to get more out of sleep. We offer the latest information from the sleep research community: information on getting children to bed painlessly, whether rocking helps a baby sleep, 'beauty sleep' and what your dreams tell you." **Services:** Provides advisory, historical, how-to, referral, technical and trade information on sleep and bedding. Offers aid in arranging interviews and brochures/pamphlets. Publications include *The Guide to Better Sleep*. **How to Contact:** Write or call. Responds to most inquiries within a week. "Information must be credited to BSC if used for publication." **Tips:** "Be as specific as possible on the subject matter. We have a wide range of sleep information."

676• BETTER VISION INSTITUTE
230 Park Ave., New York NY 10017. (212)682-1731. Contact Person: Executive Secretary. **Description:** "The Better Vision Institute is a nonprofit public relations association which uses all the media to urge Americans to have regular eye examinations and to tell the public the importance of vision care. BVI is supported by the optical companies, optometrists, opthalmologists, opticians, and educational institutions. In our 50 years, we have gathered a lot of data on general vision subjects, eye care, eyeglasses, contact lenses, sunglasses, etc." **Services:** Provides advisory, bibliographical, historical, interpretative, referral and trade information. Offers aid in arranging interviews, statistics, brochures/pamphlets and photos. Publications include *Facts You Should Know About Your Vision* and *A Home Guide to Better Vision*, plus 12 other vision pamphlets on general subjects. **How to Contact:** Write or call. Responds to most inquiries immediately. **Tips:** "Our files, books, magazines, etc. are all open to writers at any time. Many writers/researchers like to come to our office and look through our files which go back 53 years. As we have copies of many articles written on the vision field, we can save a writer or researcher a lot of time. We also know who the experts are in each vision field. Recent information requests: "How many people wear eyeglases in the US?; Contact lenses?"; "What can happen to your eyes?"; "How often should you have your eyes examined?"

677• BRISTOL-MYERS COMPANY
345 Park Ave., New York NY 10154. (212)546-4000. Contact Person: Media Relations Director. **Description:** Pharmaceutical company. **Services:** Offers annual reports and publications. **How to Contact:** Write. Responds to most inquiries within a week.

678• CANADIAN SCHIZOPHRENIA FOUNDATION
2229 Broad St., Regina, Saskatchewan, Canada S4P 1Y7. (306)527-7969. Contact Person:
General Director. **Description:** "To improve diagnosis, treatment and prevention of children's
and adult's disorders. Many brochures, books and two periodicals are distributed." **Services:**
Provides advisory, bibliographical, how-to, referral and technical information on health, mainly in
the psychiatric field. Offers brochures/pamphlets, and newsletter. Publications include *The Journal of Orthomolecular Psychiatry* plus several books and brochures. List of publications available.
How to Contact: Write or call. Responds to most inquiries within a week. "We will not be able to
do investigative or research work for authors but will direct them to sources or supply literature and
references." **Tips:** "Try to assess and judge relevant research material and not take papers by
'experts' at face value." Recent information requests: Use of "pink" color in psychiatry and
correction; use of zinc in treating disorders; questions about allergies.

679• CENTERS FOR DISEASE CONTROL
1600 Clifton Rd. NE, Atlanta GA 30333. Contact Person: Director, Office of Public Affairs.
Description: "The Centers for Disease Control (CDC), a major agency of the US Public Health
Service, was established in 1946 as the Communicable Disease Center. While maintaining its expertise in infectious disease control, CDC now has the broader mission of preventing all unnecessary morbidity and mortality. Newer programs at CDC include environmental health, prevention
of occupational diseases and accidents, and promotion of health through education and information. It supports local, state, national and international prevention efforts in epidemiology, surveillance, laboratory science, and training." **Services:** Provides advisory and technical information
on the prevention of disease and injury. Offers reference and background materials and photographs on communicable diseases and other subjects. Publications include the *Morbidity and Mortality Weekly Report* and *Surveillance Reports.* "Mailing lists are maintained and anyone may
request these publications." **How to Contact:** Write. Responds to most inquiries within a week.

680• CONTACT LENS MANUFACTURERS ASSOCIATION
15 S. 9th St., Newark NJ 07107. (201)268-8053. Contact Person: Executive Director.
Description: The association works "to collect and disseminate information regarding contact
lenses and accessories to the public (for the betterment of public health); to recommend standards
for the improvement of the industry; to sponsor and promulgate research related to contact lenses
and accessories; to provide information to the eye care field regarding contact lenses and accessories; to provide information to the contact lens industry." **Services:** Offers brochures/pamphlets
and newsletter. Publications include *Living with Contact Lenses . . . And Enjoying Them*, *News
and Views* and membership directory. **How to Contact:** Write or call. Responds to most inquiries
within a week. **Tips:** Recent information request: New types of lenses; permalens lens for extended
wear.

681• CYSTIC FIBROSIS FOUNDATION
6000 Executive Bldg., Rockville MD 30326. Contact Person: Public Relations Communications
Director. **Description:** "Our main goal is to come up with a cure and control for cystic fibrosis."
Services: Provides advisory, how-to and interpretative information on research, publications,
public education and professional education. Offers aid in arranging interviews, annual reports,
bibliographies, biographies, brochures/pamphlets, information searches, placement on mailing
list, newsletter, press kits and films. **How to Contact:** "Write or visit." Responds to most inquiries within a week. **Tips:** "Gives writing awards for the best story written by or about a cystic fibrosis patient. The winners are published and cash awards are offered."

682• DENTAL LIBRARY
University of Southern California, Norris Dental Science Center, Los Angeles CA 90007. Contact
Person: Librarian. **Description:** Houses one of the major collections in dentistry on the West
Coast. The library has a book and journal collection of more than 32,000 volumes, and subscribes
to more than 450 current periodicals. **Services:** Provides advisory, bibliographical, historical,
how-to and referral information primarily on dental medicine. Offers bibliographies and
information searches. "Access to MEDLINE and other computer-generated bibliographies
prepared by a librarian is available through the dental library at a minimal fee." **How to Contact:**
Hours vary; call to arrange an appointment. "The library is mainly for the use of students and professionals in the field of dentistry. Use is restricted." Responds to most inquiries within a week.

Charges for computer-generated bibliographies—costs dependent on file accessed. "Writer/researchers will have to use journal/reference and reserve material in library."

683• DOCTORS OUGHT TO CARE (DOC)
c/o Dept. of Family Medicine, 456 Clinic Dr., Columbus OH 43210. (614)421-8007. Contact Person: Coordinator. **Description:** "We deal in health awareness and work with medical problems having to do with lifestyle-related and preventable diseases." **Services:** Provides advisory and how-to information on smoking; physicians and the media; counter-advertising techniques. Offers photos and health promotion/counter-advertising material. Publications include reprints of articles. **How to Contact:** Write or call. Responds to most inquiries within 2 weeks. Charges for publications and speakers bureau. **Tips:** Recent information request: Materials on smoking to be used for high school-age audience.

684• E.C.R.I.
5200 Butler Pike, Plymouth Meeting PA 19462. (215)825-6000. Contact Person: Editor. **Description:** "We conduct comparative evaluations of medical devices used by hospitals and publish a monthly journal, *Health Devices*. We investigate medical device hazards on behalf of hospitals and include many of our reports in our journal. We are involved in all medical devices, equipment and disposables. We are nonprofit, the hospitals' analog to Consumers Union, and accept no funds from medical device manufacturers for our evaluations. We also provide consultation services to hospitals under contract. We publish a weekly newsletter, *Health Devices Alerts*, that abstracts reported problems and hazards with medical devices, and other directories and publications on health care technology." **Services:** Provides advisory and technical information on health care technology. **How to Contact:** Write or call. Charges for copies of publications. **Tips:** "By 'services' we mean information to writers, not our technical services. While we do not charge for providing this information, understand that we are not offering any more than verbal statements on medical equipment, hospital regulation, device recalls, etc. We have no expertise in drugs or in personal health care; our interaction is primarily with hospitals." Recent information requests: "What does ECRI do?"; "How does ECRI help hospitals select the most appropriate technology?"

685• EASTER SEAL RESEARCH FOUNDATION
2023 W. Ogden Ave., Chicago IL 60612. (312)243-8400. Contact Person: Director. **Description:** "The purpose of the Easter Seal Research Foundation is to support, stimulate and advance research." **Services:** Provides information on the rehabilitation of physically disabled persons. Offers brochures/pamphlets and information on applying for grants. **How to Contact:** Write or call. Responds to most inquiries within a week.

686• EPILEPSY FOUNDATION OF AMERICA (EFA)
4351 Garden City Dr., Suite 406, Landover MD 20785. (301)459-3700. Contact Person: Director, Public Information Department. **Description:** "EFA provides parent/patient information; counseling and referrals, employment assistance; medical services, advocacy; special programs such as parent education; training grants and publication for physicians and other professionals; EEG training grants and programs; sponsorship of national conferences to train volunteer and staff members; education programs for teachers (School Alert); support of medical research; and public health education." **Services:** Provides advisory, bibliographical, historical, how-to, referral and technical information on epilepsy and all that relates to it. Offers aid in arranging interviews, annual reports, bibliographies, statistics, brochures/pamphlets, newsletter, photos and press kits. Publications include publications list. "Specialized information is also available from the EFA National Library and Resource Center on Epilepsy. **How to Contact:** Write or call. Responds to most inquiries within a week. Some restrictions on reprint permission. **Tips:** "Much of the most current information is not widely disseminated. However, EFA is able to direct writers to most current and authoritative sources and has established a new National Library and Resource Center on Epilepsy with on-line computer access to existing medical collections."

687• INSTITUTE FOR BURN MEDICINE
3737 Fifth Ave., #206, San Diego CA 92103. (714)291-4764. Contact Person: Executive Director. **Description:** "Our purpose is to educate the public about various aspects of burn prevention and fire safety; and to do epidemiological research into burn injuries." **Services:** Provides analytical, historical, how-to, referral and trade information on all aspects of burn pre-

vention and fire safety. Offers brochures/pamphlets, informational newsletters, research assistance and statistics. Publications include *How to Make Your Home and Family Safe from Fire* (consumer guide). **How to Contact:** Write or call. Responds to most inquiries within a week. "Our materials are provided free of charge to people in San Diego and Imperial Counties; otherwise, there are nominal fees." Give credit to institute. **Tips:** Recent information requests: "What information do you have on self-extinguishing cigarettes?"; "How many deaths are caused by burns from fires started by cigarettes?"

688• INSTITUTE FOR CHILD BEHAVIOR RESEARCH
4157 Adams Ave., San Diego CA 92116. Contact Person: Director. **Description:** "ICBR is a nonprofit corporation founded for the express purpose of performing and assisting research leading to the prevention and treatment of severe learning and behavior disorders of childhood, e.g., autism, retardation and learning disabilities. The institute carries out its own research projects as well as serving as an international clearinghouse for researchers from throughout the US and many foreign countries." **Services:** Provides advisory and technical information on autistic children; and nutritional approaches to the treatment of learning and behavior disorders. Offers brochures/pamphlets/reprints, computerized information searches and library facilities. Publication list available. **How to Contact:** Write. Responds to most inquiries within a week. Reprints available at nominal cost.

689• INSTITUTE FOR RESEARCH IN HYPNOSIS & PSYCHOTHERAPY
10 W. 66th St., New York NY 10023. (212)874-5290. Contact Person: Director. **Description:** The Institute sponsors research, education and treatment in hypnosis and psychotherapy, medicine/psychology, and dentistry. **Services:** Provides advisory, analytical, bibliographical, historical, how-to, interpretative, referral and technical information on mental health, hypnotherapy, hypnoanalysis, hypnosis research and hypnosis-psychosomatics. Offers aid in arranging interviews, annual reports, biographies, brochures/pamphlets, informational newsletters, library facilities, placement on mailing lists, research assistance and statistics. The B.B. Reginsky Research Library contains numerous reprints, books, tape recordings and biographical archives. **How to Contact:** Write or call. Responds to most inquiries immediately. **Tips:** "Define area of interest." Recent information request: "How is hypnosis used in treating psychotropic drug addiction?"

690• INTERNATIONAL CHIROPRACTORS ASSOCIATION
1901 L St. NW, Washington DC 20036. (202)659-6476. Contact Person: Director: Special Projects. **Description:** "International Chiropractors Association (ICA) is dedicated to the objective of preserving chiropractic as a separate philosophy, science and art in the health care field. Its membership is composed of chiropractors and students of chiropractic. ICA works to promote chiropractic research and to ensure the passage of legislation that is in the best interests of chiropractic. It provides malpractice insurance for its members." **Services:** Provides advisory, referral and trade information about the history and philosophy of chiropractic, chiropractic colleges, current developments and practice in the field and current legislation affecting it. Offers brochures/pamphlets and placement on mailing list. Publications include *International Review of Chiropractic* (magazine), *ICA Today Newsletter* and *Washington Legislation Today* (newsletter). "Researchers may request individual issues or copies of articles in issues." **How to Contact:** Write. Responds to most inquiries within a month. Charges 10¢/page for photocopying. "We help as time and resources permit. Small staff limits our abilities to assist." **Tips:** "Be as specific as possible about what is needed; don't ask for 'everything about chiropractic.' "

691• INTERNATIONAL PHOTOTHERAPY ASSOCIATION, INC.
3260 Euclid Hts. Blvd., Cleveland Heights OH 44118. (216)929-8301, ext. 381. Contact Person: Chairman. **Description:** "We are an international, multidisciplinary association of mental health professionals who use still photos, motion pictures, videotape recordings and/or holography in practice and/or research." **Services:** Provides advisory, analytical, bibliographical, historical, how-to, interpretative, referral, technical and professional related information on both the diagnostic and therapeutic uses of all the various photographic media, in any and/or all mental health settings; using the state of the science in the mental health field. Offers aid in arranging interviews, annual reports, clipping services, informational newsletters, photos, placement on mailing lists, research assistance, statistics, telephone reference services and practice and research consultation referrals. Publications include *Phototherapy* (professional magazine format). **How to Contact:** Write or call. Responds to most inquiries within a month. Charges for

publications. **Tips:** Recent information request: "Please refer us to contemporary literature in the practice and research of still photography in mental health treatment with chronic depressives."

692• LEUKEMIA SOCIETY OF AMERICA, INC.
800 Second Ave., New York NY 10017. (212)573-8484. Contact Person: Assistant to Director: Public Education and Information Department. **Description:** "The Leukemia Society of America raises funds for support of research aimed at finding a cure or control for leukemia and allied diseases, and provides patient aid and professional/public information." **Services:** Provides bibliographical, interpretative, referral and technical information on the leukemias and related diseases. Offers aid in arranging interviews, annual reports, biographies, statistics, brochures/pamphlets and placement on mailing list. Publications include *What Is Leukemia?*, *Nature of Leukemia* (with slides), *Hodgkin's Disease*, *Management of a Child with Leukemia*, *Fact Sheet*, *Multiple Myelomas*, *Lymphomas* and *Annual Report*. **How to Contact:** Write or call. Responds to most inquiries immediately. **Tips:** "We ask that writers clearly define their needs." Recent information request: "Please tell me what leukemia is and how it progresses?"

693• MANDALA HOLISTIC HEALTH
Box 1233, Del Mar CA 92014. (714)481-7751. Contact: Publicity Department. **Description:** "Our purpose is to present holistic health to the conventional medical community in a professional responsible manner via a conference format and a yearly journal." **Services:** Provides advisory, historical and referral information on "new/old healing methods that have been used successfully and are not part of the general conventional medical knowledge/usage." Offers aid in arranging interviews, brochures/pamphlets, press kits, research assistance and contact with the people who are practicing the new/old methods. Publications include *Journal of Holistic Health* (annual-March). **How to Contact:** Write. Responds to most inquiries within a week. **Tips:** Recent information request: Use of herbs for disease prevention and healing.

694• MARCH OF DIMES BIRTH DEFECT FOUNDATION
1275 Mamaroneck Ave., White Plains NY 10605. (914)428-7100. Contact Person: Director of Public Relations. **Description:** The foundation works for the prevention of birth defects through support of basic and clinical research, medical services, public and professional education in genetics, perinatology, human biology and environmental factors affecting prenatal health. **Services:** Provides information on prenatal nutrition and related subjects. Offers aid in arranging interviews, annual reports, bibliographies, biographies, statistics, brochures/pamphlets, information searches, placement on mailing list, photos and press kits. Publications include *Maternal/Newborn Advocate* (quarterly newsletter reporting on government activity in prenatal health care at federal, state and local levels). Catalog available on books, films, publications and exhibits. **How to Contact:** Write or call. Responds to most inquiries as soon as possible. Give March of Dimes credit for information. **Tips:** Information on anticipated publication or type of audience for articles in preparation is helpful to us in selecting appropriate background material. Recent information request: Background on any of the 2,000 different birth defects.

695• MEDLINE DATA BASE
National Library of Medicine, 8600 Rockville Pike, Bethesda MD 20209. (301)496-6308. Contact Person: Chief, Office of Inquiries and Publications Management. **Description:** Data base containing 500,000 references to recently-published articles in health science. MEDLINE is accessible at about 2,000 medical schools, hospitals and government agencies. **Services:** Provides bibliographical information on health sciences. Offers information searches. Publications include an informational brochure. **How to Contact:** "Write or call for exact MEDLINE locations. Data base is online. The cost of a search varies from center to center." Various policies on restrictions/stipulations at MEDLINE user institutions.

696• MUSCULAR DYSTROPHY ASSOCIATION
810 7th Ave., New York NY 10019. Contact Person: Director, Public Health Education. **Description:** "Our purpose is to find the cause of and cure for muscular dystrophy and related neuromuscular diseases, while providing the best available daily care to patients and their families free of charge." **Services:** Provides referral and general and scientific information about activities and functions of the Muscular Dystrophy Association. Offers annual reports, brochures/pamphlets and newsletters on 40 neuromuscular diseases and patient information

brochures. **How to Contact:** Write. Responds to most inquiries within a week. **Tips:** Recent information request: "What type of research is going on in the area of Muscular Dystrophy?"

697• NATIONAL ASSOCIATION OF HEALTH UNDERWRITERS
145 North Ave., Hartland WI 53029. (414)367-3248. Contact Person: Executive Vice President. **Description:** "An association of disability and health insurance persons and companies who sell and service these products." **Services:** Provides trade information. Offers aid in arranging interviews. Publications include *Health Insurance Underwriter* (magazine). **How to Contact:** Write or call. Responds to most inquiries immediately.

698• NATIONAL CENTER FOR HEALTH SERVICES RESEARCH
OASH, PHS, Department of Health and Human Services, 3700 East-West Hwy., Hyattsville MD 20782. (301)436-8970. Contact Person: Chief, Publications and Information Branch. **Description:** "The National Center for Health Services Research (NCHSR) is the primary federal agency responsible for research to improve the delivery and quality of health services in the United States. Through grants and contracts, it supports research in the accessibility, acceptability, planning, organization, distribution, utilization, and quality of systems for the delivery of health care." **Services:** Offers brochures/pamphlets and placement on mailing list. **How to Contact:** Write or call. Responds to most inquiries within a week. List of publications available on request. **Tips:** "There is so much information available in the health care field; be as specific as possible."

699• NATIONAL CLEARINGHOUSE FOR ALCOHOL INFORMATION (NIAAA)
Box 2345, Rockville MD 20852. (301)468-2600. Contact: Reference Services. **Description:** "The National Clearinghouse for Alcohol Information has been established as a service of the National Institute on Alcohol Abuse and Alcoholism (NIAAA) to make available current knowledge on alcohol-related subjects. From worldwide sources, the clearinghouse collects information on studies and programs pertaining to prevention, training, treatment, and research aspects of alcohol abuse and alcoholism, and shares this knowledge with interested professional audiences as well as with the general public." **Services:** Provides bibliographical and referral information on alcohol abuse and alcoholism. Offers brochures/pamphlets, computerized information searches, library facilities, placement on mailing lists, research assistance, statistics and telephone reference services. Publications include *NIAAA Information and Feature Service* (published approximately monthly); *Alcohol Awareness Service* (bimonthly). **How to Contact:** Write, call or visit. Responds to most inquiries within a week. **Tips:** "Specify the area you are interested in and let us know the scope/target group of the article. A day-time telephone number is helpful when clarification is needed." Recent information request: "How many alcoholics are there in the U.S.?"

700• NATIONAL CLEARINGHOUSE FOR DRUG ABUSE INFORMATION (NCDAI)
Box 416, Kensington MD 20795. Contact Person: Chief. **Description:** "Our purpose is to provide information, usually in the form of publications, on the health consequences of drug abuse. Activities include maintaining mailing lists and operating a Resource Center (library) which is open to the public." **Services:** Provides bibliographical and technical information on physiological and psychological effects of drugs that are abused; incidence and prevalence of drug abuse; and treatment of drug abusers. (*No* information on drug traffic.) Offers annual reports, biographies, brochures/pamphlets, library facilities, placement on mailing lists and statistics (survey publications). "We maintain an inventory of over 200 publications that cover the following subjects as they relate to drug abuse: prevention, treatment, training, epidemiology and research." **How to Contact:** Write. Responds to most inquiries within 2 weeks. **Tips:** "Make your inquiries as specific as possible." Recent information requests: "What types of programs are available for treating adolescent drug abusers?"; "How do I start a drug abuse prevention program and evaluate its effectiveness?"

701• NATIONAL GENETICS FOUNDATION, INC.
555 W. 57th St., New York NY 10019. (212)586-5800. Contact Person: Genetic Counselor. **Description:** "We make clinical services and advances in medical genetics available to physicians and the lay public by responding to mail or telephone requests and providing information, family health history, review, and referrals to a network of Genetic Centers." **Services:** Provides advisory, analytical, referral and technical information on medical genetics/genetic disease; availability of prenatal diagnosis; genetic counseling; testing, screening

and evaluation. Offers reviews of genetic family health histories; provides access to genetic services by referral to medical genetics centers directly or through physician; conducts research projects on methods for the introduction of genetic services into primary medicine. Publications include *How Genetic Disease Can Affect Your Family*; *Can Genetic Counseling Help You?*; *For the Concerned Couple Planning a Family*; *Family Health History Scan*; *Should You Consider Amniocentesis?*. **How to Contact:** Write or call. Responds to most inquiries within a week. Requests review of articles in which the foundation is mentioned, quoted, or used for information. **Tips:** "Give us ample time prior to publicaton deadline for reviewing article. Literature searches are very useful. We answer specific questions on genetic dieseases and can give advice on conducting a literature search."

702• NATIONAL HEARING AID SOCIETY
20361 Middlebelt Rd., Livonia MI 48152. (313)478-2610. Contact Person: Executive Vice President. **Description:** "The National Hearing Aid Society's purpose is to promote welfare of hearing impaired; coordinate programs of society; provide communications among members in industry; improve methods of selling, fitting and using hearing aids; establish standards; examine qualifications of hearing aid specialists; create public education; and cooperate with medical professionals." The society also certifies qualified hearing aid specialists, approves and coordinates educational programs, enforces code of ethics, publishes information on hearing health care, cooperates with professional groups and government officials, and sponsors consumer protection programs. Publishes *Audecibel* and provides information packets. **Services:** Provides advisory, analytical, referral and trade information on hearing impairment and hearing aids. Offers statistics, brochures/pamphlets, information searches. Publications available. **How to Contact:** Write. Responds to most inquiries immediately. **Tips:** "Do some research first so questions will be specific." Recent information requests: "How many hearing impaired in US? How many wear hearing aids?"; "What are percentages of male/female hearing impaired in the US, incidence of hearing impairment by age group?"; "Volume sales by type of aid, what regulation is there?"

703• NATIONAL INSTITUTE OF NEUROLOGICAL AND COMMUNICATIVE DISORDERS AND STROKE (NINCDS)
National Institutes of Health, Bethesda MD 20014. (301)496-5751. Contact Person: Deputy Chief, Office of Scientific and Health Reports. **Description:** "We conduct and support research in neurological and communicative disorders and stroke. Information covers all areas within these general categories: research progress, current research activity, and health information literature for laymen." **Services:** Provides referral and technical information on health/medicine, science and technical data. Offers aid in arranging interviews, annual reports, bibliographies, statistics and brochures/pamphlets. Publications include material for physicians, scientists and other professional health workers, and for the general public. **How to Contact:** For publications, write to Publications Department, Room 8A-06, NINCDS, National Institutes of Health, Bethesda MD 20014. For work on specific features for magazines, contact Deputy Chief for discussion of what help can be offered. **Tips:** Recent information request: Background and statistics on epilepsy.

704• NATIONAL INSTITUTES OF HEALTH
Division of Research Resources, Bethesda MD 20014. (301)496-5545. Contact Person: Assistant Information Officer. **Description:** "The Division of Research Resources identifies and strives to meet the research resource needs and opportunities of the National Institutes of Health. The division conceives, develops and assures the availability of resources that are essential to the conduct of human health research. The division administers and manages six major programs that serve as the backbone for important health research at universities, hospitals and research institutes throughout the US. These programs are primate research centers (apes and monkeys), general clinical research centers (human patients), biotechnology resource centers (biomedical research computers, mass spectrometry, million-volt electron microscopes, nuclear magnetic resonance spectrometry, etc.), animal resources (laboratory animals other than apes and monkeys), and minority biomedical support (biomedical research activities at predominantly black, Indian, and Spanish-speaking colleges)." **Services:** Provides advisory, analytical, bibliographical, historical, interpretative, referral and technical information. Offers aid in arranging interviews, statistics, brochures/pamphlets and photos. Publications include *Division of Research Resources: Meeting the Research Resource Needs of the Biomedical Sciences*. **How to Contact:** Write or call. Responds to most inquiries immediately.

705• NATIONAL KIDNEY FOUNDATION
2 Park Ave., New York NY 10016. (212)889-2210. Contact Person: Director of Communications. **Description:** "Major voluntary organization seeking total answer to diseases of the kidney—prevention, treatment and cure. Each affiliate in the country conducts various programs of patient and community services, including patient visiting programs, early warning signs and detection, drug banks, summer camps, patient housing and transportation services." **Services:** Offers aid in arranging interviews, annual reports, bibliographies, brochures/pamphlets, placement on mailing list, statistics and quarterly newsletter. **How to Contact:** Write or call. Responds to most inquiries immediately. "Written requests will get prompt attention." **Tips:** "The foundation presents an annual public service award to the individual who highlights public awareness on problems of kidney disease." Recent information request: Questions on organ donation.

706• NATIONAL LEAGUE FOR NURSING
10 Columbus Circle, New York NY 10019. (212)582-1022. Contact Person: Media Relations Manager. **Description:** The National League for Nursing is "dedicated to improving the standards for nursing education and nursing service. Areas include education of nurses; nursing service in hospitals, long-term care institutions and community health agencies; public affairs; research; testing; and any other subject related to education or service." **Services:** Provides advisory, analytical, interpretative and referral information on nursing education, nursing practice, nursing manpower and nursing related health care issues. Offers aid in arranging interviews, annual reports, statistics, brochures/pamphlets and placement on mailing list. "We have hundreds of publications dealing with a variety of subjects." Publications catalog available. **How to Contact:** Write or call. Responds to most inquiries within a week. No charge for answering inquiry; may be nominal charge for some printed reference materials. **Tips:** "Use NLN as an initial resource. We can provide story suggestions, data, interpretation, commentary and referrals. Our statistical manpower data focuses on the supply side (i.e., nursing school admissions, enrollments, graduations); we can suggest possible sources for demand side data." Recent information request: Varied information on recent/ongoing changes in the nursing profession and its role in the health care delivery system; data on the current national nursing shortage.

707• NATIONAL LIBRARY OF MEDICINE
8600 Rockville Pike, Bethesda MD 20209. Contact Person: Chief, History of Medicine Division. **Description:** Medical library. **Services:** Offers b&w and color photos on the history of medicine (portraits, scenes and pictures of institutions); photos are not related to current personalities, events or medical science. **How to Contact:** Write. Responds to most inquiries within a month. Charges according to service provided; prices are subject to change without notice. Charges $6 minimum/copy print. No pictures sent on approval. Credit line required.

708• NATIONAL MIGRAINE FOUNDATION
c/o Norma A. Lee Co., 777 7th Ave., New York NY 10019. (212)247-4000, ext. M-62. Contact Person: Account Executive. **Description:** Clearinghouse for information on latest techniques and medication for prevention and care of severe headaches; serves both physicians and headache sufferers. **Services:** Provides advisory, referral and technical information on migraine headaches and other forms of severe headache. Offers aid in arranging interviews, brochures/pamphlets, informational newsletters, press kits, research assistance and statistics; conducts public awareness campaigns through free seminars in major cities and doctors' city media tours. **How to Contact:** Write or call. Responds to most inquiries immediately.

709• NATIONAL SOCIETY FOR AUTISTIC CHILDREN, INC.
1234 Massachusetts Ave. NW, # 1017, Washington DC 20005. (202)783-0125. Contact Person: Executive Director. **Description:** "NSAC is a national advocacy center serving people with autism and their families." **Services:** Provides bibliographical and referral information on bringing up a child with autism in the family, public education, individualized education program (IEP), evaluation and diagnosis, community services, education and treatment facilities, federal programs, etc. Offers research assistance and statistics. Updated booklist available from NSAC Bookstore. **How to Contact:** Write or call.

710• NATIONAL SOCIETY FOR MEDICAL RESEARCH
1029 Vermont Ave. NW, Suite 700, Washington DC 20005. (202)347-9565. Contact Person: Director of Scientific Affairs. **Description:** "The purpose of National Society for Medical Research (NSMR) is to generate public understanding of the benefits derived through responsible animal experimentation in biomedical research and teaching and to protect the rights of scientific investigators to use laboratory animals when appropriate for the betterment of mankind. Staff monitors state and federal legislation and regulations which might hinder animal research." **Services:** Provides advisory, bibliographical, historical, how-to, interpretative, referral and technical information on animals used in biomedical and behavioral research. Offers annual reports, monthly bulletin, news service, journalism award, special publications, data bank, exhibits, brochures/pamphlets, placement on mailing list, newsletter and press kits. Also operates a "news service for the media describing the benefits of animal experimentation." Publications include several booklets and brochures; write for publications list. **How to Contact:** Write or call. Responds to most inquiries within a week.

711• NATIONAL SOCIETY TO PREVENT BLINDNESS
79 Madison Ave., New York NY 10016. (212)684-3505. Contact Person: Director of Public Relations. **Description:** "The National Society to Prevent Blindness, founded in 1908, is the oldest voluntary health agency nationally engaged in the prevention of blindess through comprehensive programs of community services, public and professional education and research. Materials are available on eye health and eye safety." **Services:** Provides information on eye health and safety. Offers aid in arranging interviews, referrals, annual reports, bibliographies, statistics, films, teaching materials, posters, and brochures/pamphlets. *Catalog of Publications and Films* available. SASE. **How to Contact:** Write or call. Responds to most inquiries within a week. Charges handling fee for film loan.

712• NATIONAL STUTTERING PROJECT
1269 7th Ave., San Francisco CA 94122. (415)647-4700. Contact Person: Executive Director (letter) or Associate Director (phone). **Description:** "Our purpose is to educate the public on the nature of stuttering and to provide self-help for people who stutter." **Services:** Provides advisory, historical and referral information on stuttering. Offers brochures/pamphlets and informational newsletters. **How to Contact:** Write or call. Responds to most inquiries within a week. **Tips:** Recent information request: "How does a teenage girl who stutters behave?"

713• NATIONAL SUDDEN INFANT DEATH SYNDROME FOUNDATION, INC.
2 Metro Plaza, Suite 205, 8240 Professional Place, Landover MD 20785. (301)459-3388. Contact Person: Executive Director. **Description:** "The foundation attempts to ease the burdens on families who lose a child to SIDS or any other unexpected cause through educational and research programs; volunteer programs; public awareness campaigns; resource and referral mechanisms; and the ultimate elimination of Sudden Infant Death Syndrome." **Services:** Provides advisory and referral information on counseling for SIDS parents and families and information on Apnea Monitoring. Offers annual reports, bibliographies, statistics, brochures/pamphlets and newsletter. **How to Contact:** Write or call. Responds to most inquiries within a week. Publication price list available; publication charge for non-SIDS families. "We suggest that writers have their work checked by a person knowledgeable about SIDS. Staff at the national office can assist directly or refer requests for such services. There is no charge for such consultation. Because of the sensitive nature of all issues relating to SIDS, it is imperative that a writer have a broad perspective and be willing to research the interdisciplinary aspects."

714• OFFICE ON SMOKING AND HEALTH
Technical Information Center, Park Bldg., Room 1-16, 5600 Fishers Lane, Rockville MD 20857. (301)443-1690. Contact: Public Inquiries Office. **Description:** "The Office on Smoking and Health was established as part of the U.S. Public Health Service in March 1978 to provide leadership in education and research, and to serve as a clearinghouse for public and technical information on smoking and health." **Services:** Provides advisory, bibliographical, referral and technical information on all aspects of smoking and health. Offers annual reports, computerized information searches and placement on mailing lists. Publications include *Smoking and Health Bulletin* (abstracts of current technical literature on tobacco use, periodically); *Bibliography on Smoking and Health* (annual); *Health Consequences of Smoking* (annual); *Directory of On-Going Research in Smoking and Health* (biennial); and *State Legislation on Smoking and Health*

(annual). **How to Contact:** Write or call. Advance arrangements for visits to use reference collection are suggested. Requests for computer searches should be submitted on the Search Request Form printed in each issue of *Smoking and Health Bulletin* or available from TIC. **Tips:** For nontechnical information and publications contact Public Inquiries, Office on Smoking and Health, Park Bldg., Room 1-58, 5600 Fishers Lane, Rockville MD 20857. (301)443-1575.

715• THE PEOPLE-TO-PEOPLE HEALTH FOUNDATION, INC./PROJECT HOPE
2233 Wisconsin Ave. NW, Washington DC 20007. Contact Person: Director, Department of Information Services or Learning Resources Center, The HOPE Center, Millwood VA 22646. **Description:** The foundation conducts the medical education programs throughout the developing world, health sciences education and research projects centered at HOPE center, international symposia on health-related topics, and coordinates national committee investigating health and public policy. "We have a growing collection of literature on the various countries with whom we work—state of health care delivery, cultural aspects, political climate, level of technological development, etc. Our large collection of medical education program reports, written by staff, could be a valuable resource in various fields of inquiry." **Services:** Provides analytical, bibliographical and technical information on health education, policy. Offers annual reports, bibliographies, biographies, brochures/pamphlets, information searches, placement on mailing list, newsletters, photos and press kits. "We also have an educational monograph series, commissioned scholars' papers on the US health care system and a printed program summary series." **How to Contact:** Write. Responds to most inquiries within a week. "We request a credit line where applicable. We have limited staff and can offer little individual research assistance."

716• THE PSYCHOLOGY SOCIETY
100 Beekman St., New York NY 10038. (212)285-1872. Contact Person: Director. **Description:** "The society is an association of nearly 2,000 practicing psychologists (people who treat people) interested in the application of psychology to the solution of contemporary problems." **Services:** Provides information on social and marital relationships, prison reform, etc. Offers aid in arranging interviews and aid in securing specific data. **How to Contact:** Write or call. Responds to most inquiries within 48 hours. "We are interested in disseminating our findings in psychology and interested in dealing with writers. If writing for information, enclose SASE; if telephoning, call in the morning." **Tips:** Recent information requests: Background on the accident prone; the psychology of prisons and prisoners; ESP.

717• SHRINERS BURNS INSTITUTE
202 Goodman St., Cincinnati OH 45219. (513)751-3900. Contact Person: Director of Public Relations. **Description:** "We are a burn hospital (one of three in the US) supported by Shriners of North America, specializing in pediatrics (burns only—limit age up to 18). We provide treatment, research and teaching. Our staff currently is conducting research in skin grafting, skin banking, nutrition, skin substitutes and new burn dressings. We stress total patient treatment—rehabilitation emotionally as well as physically. The institute does have an out-patient clinic and follow-up care." **Services:** Provides advisory, analytical, how-to, interpretative and technical information on anything connected with pediatric burn treatment. Offers aid in arranging interviews, bibliographies, biographies, information searches and access to reprint file (most material is highly technical). "If writing on burns, we could assist in checking for medical accuracy." **How to Contact:** Write or call. Response time on inquiries depends on complexity of request and staff time/availability. "Case studies by request only. No access to patient records for any purpose." Give credit to Shriners Burns Institute. **Tips:** "Allow 3-4 weeks lead time. We are more likely to arrange interviews and/or spend time researching questions if given ample lead time." Recent information request: Check for medical accuracy for major magazine staff writer.

718• SICKLE CELL DISEASE FOUNDATION OF GREATER NEW YORK
209 W. 125th St., Suite 108, New York NY 10027. (212)865-1201. Contact Person: Executive Director. **Description:** "We are a nonprofit, charitable, informational and educational organization." **Services:** Offers aid in arranging interviews, statistics and brochures/pamphlets. Provides both professional and lay seminars and information on genetic counseling and screening for the SC trait. **How to Contact:** Write or call. Responds to most inquiries immediately. **Tips:** Recent information request: "What's currently happening in the area of SC research?"

719• THE TOBACCO INSTITUTE
1875 I St. NW, Suite 800, Washington DC 20006. Contact Person: Information Specialist. **Description:** "The Tobacco Institute is a nonprofit, noncommercial organization that fosters public understanding of the smoking and health controversy, and public knowledge of the historic role of tobacco and its place in the national economy. It is a communicator of information and viewpoints on such matters to the public, news media and government bodies at local, state and federal levels." **Services:** Offers brochures/pamphlets. **How to Contact:** Write. Responds to most inquiries within a week. "The library is not open to the general public and publications are limited to no more than 10 copies." Recent information request: "How many smokers are there in the US?"

720• VASCULAR DIAGNOSTIC SERVICES, INC. (VDS)
111 W. Monroe, Suite 1212, Phoenix AZ 85003. (602)254-6552. Contact Person: Public Relations Consultant at (213)417-3038. **Description:** Health management company and public education resource "encouraging early detection of blood vessel disease in susceptible individuals." **Services:** Provides advisory, bibliographical, how-to, referral, technical and trade information on all aspects of noninvasive diagnostic vascular testing and current trends in vascular disease detection. Offers aid in arranging interviews, brochures/pamphlets, informational newsletters, photos, press kits, research assistance and statistics. **How to Contact:** Write, call or visit. Responds to most inquiries immediately. **Tips:** Recent information requests: "How does vascular diagnostic testing fit into the realm of the annual physical?"; "What kinds of physicians do vascular testing?"; "What type of equipment is needed?"; "Does noninvasive testing carry any risks?"

721• WARNER-LAMBERT
201 Tarbor Rd., Morris Plains NJ 07950. (201)540-2000. Contact Person: Director, Public Communications. **Description:** "We do research, development, manufacturing and marketing of pharmaceuticals, scientific instruments and consumer items." **Services:** Provides advisory, historical, referral and technical information on pharmaceuticals, scientific instruments, diagnostics and consumer products. Offers aid in arranging interviews, annual reports and placement on mailing list. **How to Contact:** Write or call. Responds to most inquiries immediately.

HISTORY

History repeats itself in the large because human nature changes with geological leisureliness.

—*Will and Ariel Durant*

Historical information sources included here cover American, ancient and world history, archaeology and historical preservation.

Specific entries dealing with "the history of . . . dolls, the Marine Corps, etc.," are listed in the appropriate subject category (Hobby and Leisure, Government and Military, respectively). Anthropology and additional humanities resources are found in the Society and Culture section.

Bibliography

Adams, James T., ed. *Dictionary of American History*. 8 vols. New York: Charles Scribner's Sons, 1976.

American Council of Learned Societies. *Dictionary of American Biography*. 17 vols. + supplement (1981). New York: Charles Scribner's Sons.

Champion, Sara. *Dictionary of Terms & Techniques in Archeology*. New York: Everest House, 1982.

Collings, Rex. *Chronology of World History: A Calendar of Principal Events from 3000 BC to AD 1976*. 2d ed. London. Totowa, NJ: Dist. by Rowman & Littlefield, 1978.

DeFord, Miriam Allen & Joan S. Jackson, eds. *Who Was When? A Dictionary of Contemporaries*. 3d ed. New York: H.W. Wilson Co., 1976.

Finley, M.I., ed. *Atlas of Classical Archaeology*. New York: McGraw-Hill, 1977.

Great Historic Places: An American Heritage Guide. New York: Fireside Book, Simon & Schuster, 1980.

Jackson, Kenneth T., ed. *Atlas of American History*. rev. ed. New York: Charles Scribner's Sons, 1978.

Kane, Joseph Nathan, ed. *Famous First Facts: A Record of First Happenings, Discoveries and Inventions in American History*. 4th ed. New York: H.W. Wilson Co., 1981.

Platt, Colin. *The Atlas of Medieval Man*. New York: St. Martin's Press, 1980.

Poulton, Helen J. and Marguerite S. Howland. *The Historian's Handbook: A Descriptive Guide to Reference Works*. Norman, OK: University of Oklahoma Press, 1977.

722• AMERICAN ANTIQUARIAN SOCIETY

185 Salisbury St., Worcester MA 01602. (617)755-5221. Contact Person: Head of Readers' Services. **Description:** The Society "collects, preserves and makes available for study and research materials relating to American history and culture through 1876." **Services:** Provides bibliographical information on American history and culture through 1876. Offers brochures/pamphlets, library facilities (of nearly 5 million books, pamphlets, prints, manuscripts, maps, newspapers, etc.) and photos. Publications include *Proceedings* and books on related subjects. **How to Contact:** Write or visit. Responds to most inquiries within a week. Charges for photocopying; write for fee schedule. Curatorial fees vary.

723• AMERICAN ASSOCIATION FOR STATE AND LOCAL HISTORY

708 Berry Rd., Nashville TN 37204. (615)383-5991. Contact Persons: Publications Director or History News Managing Editor. **Description:** "Our organization has a membership of 7,700 professional historians, librarians, and museologists. We have an active publishing program of books, technical leaflets and a monthly magazine. Our *Directory of Historical Societies and Agencies in the United States and Canada* lists 5,865 state and local history agencies which are an excellent source of local history records. Information covers art, history and how-to for history professionals, museologists and historians. The magazine, *History News*, reports current events and activities and covers topics of immediate concern in the history field through full-length feature articles, while offering practical help to those at work in historical organizations through its

regular columns and technical leaflets." **Services:** Provides advisory, analytical, bibliographical, historical, how-to, interpretative, referral, technical and trade information covering historical societies and programs; historical preservation, restoration and interpretation; genealogy; archives; oral history; conservation; museum management; historic sites; museum exhibits; educational opportunities; historical collections and professional activities. Offers bibliographies, brochures/pamphlets, magazine and books. Publications include *Researching, Writing, Publishing Local History; Using Local History in the Classroom; Transcribing and Editing Oral History; Bibliography on Historical Organization Practices* (4 vols.) **How to Contact:** Write or call. Responds to most inquiries immediately. Charges for publications. Individual association membership is $25. **Tips:** "Become a member of AASLH to receive *History News*, information on seminars and workshops and technical leaflets which offer practical and theoretical knowledge." Recent information request: "How can we improve our interviewing skills to write a history of medicine for our area?"

724• THE AMERICAN COMMITTEE TO ADVANCE THE STUDY OF PETROGLYPHS AND PICTOGRAPHS (ACASPP)
Box 260, 1100 Washington St., Harpers Ferry WV 25425. (304)535-6977. Contact Person: Executive Secretary. **Description:** "Our purpose is the study and documentation of prehistoric and historic rock art as part of the overall study of human cultures (petroglyph—signs pecked into surface of rock; pictograph—signs/markings painted onto surface of rock)." **Services:** Provides advisory, analytical, bibliographical, historical, interpretative, referral and technical information covering archaeological materials of primarily North America but also Middle and South America and some Old World. "Millions of rock paintings/carvings are known from virtually everywhere in the world." Offers brochures/pamphlets, informational newsletters, photos, placement on mailing lists, research assistance and statistics. Publications include newsletter ($5/year) and occasional papers. **How to Contact:** Write. Responds to most inquiries within a week. Charges "depend entirely on services requested and time/labor involved. We negotiate this with person requesting the service; call to discuss. We would prefer to see a copy of the intended submission using our material before it is published." **Tips:** "Send us a detailed letter outlining your project and particular needs, so we can see what you are driving at and help accordingly. Prehistoric rock art is an area often ignored by the academic world and by the public. Vandalism is widespread, especially so in California. This is an area that desperately needs more public attention. We can supply bibliographic and expert-referral assistance and sometimes do limited research. We compile state-by-state statistics, too."

725• AMERICAN HISTORICAL ASSOCIATION
400 A St. SE, Washington DC 20003. (202)544-2422. Contact Person: Executive Director. **Description:** "We promote historical studies; the collection and preservation of historical manuscripts and dissemination of historical research." **Services;** Provides advisory, bibliographical, historical and referral information on aspects of American history. Offers annual reports, brochures/pamphlets, statistics, newsletter and employment information. **How to Contact:** Write. Responds to most inquiries within a week. **Tips:** Recent information request: Careers in the history field.

726• AMERICAN INDIAN ARCHAEOLOGICAL INSTITUTE
Box 260, Rte. 199, Washington CT 06793. (203)868-0518. Contact Person: Executive Vice President. **Description:** "AIAI is a research and education museum dedicated to the discovery, preservation and interpretation of the past—the study of prehistoric and historic man in New England." **Services:** Provides historical and interpretative information on prehistoric and historic archaeology in New England and American Indians. Offers brochures/pamphlets, informational newsletters, library facilities, exhibits, lectures, press kits and research assistance. Publications available. **How to Contact:** Write or call. Responds to most inquiries within a month. Charges $15 for membership.

727• ANCIENT STUDIES/RELIGIOUS STUDIES CENTER
153 JSB , Brigham Young University, Provo UT 84602. (801)378-3498. Contact Person: Director, Ancient Studies. **Description:** "We research and publish in Ancient Studies with emphasis on art; archaeology; Greek, Latin, and Coptic manuscripts; history; and ancient religions (especially Judaism and Christianity)." **Services:** Provides analytical, bibliographical, historical, interpretative, referral and technical information in the field of ancient studies. Offers library

facilities and research assistance. Publications include monographs of symposium proceedings, journal articles, etc. **How to Contact:** Write, call or visit. Responds to most inquiries within a week. **Tips:** "As expected in a university setting, we offer seminars and classes in our ancient studies program." Recent information requests: "What is the significance of the Dead Sea Scrolls and the Nag Hammadi texts?"

728• ANTIETAM NATIONAL BATTLEFIELD
Box 158, Sharpsburg MD 21782. (301)432-5125. Contact Person: Librarian or Curator. **Description:** "We provide a museum and interpretation of the Battle of Antietam, one of the bloodiest battles of the Civil War, September 17, 1862; we work to preserve and conserve cultural and natural resources of the park." **Services:** Provides advisory, historical, interpretative and referral information on the Civil War (battles of South Mountain, Antietam and Monocacy) and certain local history of Washington County and Sharpsburg, Maryland. Offers annual reports, biographies, brochures/pamphlets, library facilities, photos, placement on mailing lists, press kits and research assistance. "We provide visitor reference services." **How to Contact:** "Call for appointment to use our library on the premises; our collection includes Civil War histories, copies of letters and diaries and regimentals." Responds to most inquiries "within 2 weeks or 1 month, or as time permits." Charges 25¢/page for photocopying. **Tips:** "Be prepared with specific information requests and to spend time to perform the major portion of research with the references provided by our staff." Recent information requests: Background on Civil War personalities; regimental involvement in the Battle of Antietam.

729• THE ASSOCIATION FOR PRESERVATION TECHNOLOGY
Box 2487, Station D, Ottawa, Ontario, Canada K1P 5W6. (613)238-1972. Contact Person: Executive Secretary. **Description:** The APT works to improve the quality of practices in the field of historical preservation and rehabilitation; promotes research. **Services:** Provides advisory, bibliographical, historical, referral and technical information covering historical preservation, restoration and building technology. Offers brochures/pamphlets, computerized information searches, informational newsletters and research assistance. Publications include a quarterly bulletin, bimonthly newsletter and supplements devoted to specific topics in the historic preservation field. **How to Contact:** Write, call or visit. Responds to most inquiries within a week. Charges for publications. Research fees are handled on an individual basis.

730• BERLIN HISTORY PROJECT, INC.
Box 164, Berlin Heights OH 44814. Contact Person: Director. **Description:** "Primarily, we are a group of professionals dedicated to the historic preservation of Victorian communitarian sites (e.g., utopian experiments) and to allied research efforts. Our network of historians can provide information relative to Victorian perfectionism, socialism, free love, spiritualism, and a plethora of other reform doctrinal experiments. We are especially interested in the literary contributions of Victorian female writers and editors." **Services:** Provides advisory, bibliographical, historical and referral information on midwestern perfectionism, genealogy (limited to study of members of the 19th century "Berlin Movement"), free thought, free love and spiritualism. Offers aid in arranging interviews (with appropriate scholars) and information searches. **How to Contact:** Write. Responds to most inquiries within a month. "While we do not charge any fees for services, we do expect reimbursement for the cost of photocopied materials, and we do require acknowledgment in published works as well as a copy of the published article/book." **Tips:** "Writer/researchers should provide a brief *vita* describing their qualifications and interests, as well as a brief statement indicating how the materials will be used and in what context. It is always helpful if we know precisely what the researcher needs in terms of sources or expert aid in order to match the writer with the appropriate professional." Recent information request: Inquiry concerning the career of editor-reformer Cordelia Barry.

731• THE BETTMANN ARCHIVE, INC.
136 E. 57th St., New York NY 10022. (212)758-0362. Contact: Research Department. **Description:** Collection of historical and editorial photos and fine art. **Services:** Provides analytical, bibliographical, historical, interpretative and technical information on agriculture, art, business, celebrities, economics, entertainment, food, health/medicine, history, how-to, industry, law, music, nature, new products, politics, recreation, science, self-help, sports, technical data and travel. Offers 5 million black and white photos, engravings, etc. and 150,000 color photos. Offers one-time rights, editorial rights, advertising rights, reproduction rights or all

rights. **How to Contact:** Write or call. Responds to most inquiries immediately. Research fee (minimum $35) required on most orders. Rental fees vary with exact use. Holding period: 90 days for book publication, 30 days for other uses. Credit line "The Bettmann Archive" obligatory. Will send free brochure or the *Bettmann Portable Archive* for $35. **Tips:** "Be specific with respect to subject matter and technique. If you want a bespectacled country doctor in a horse-and-buggy, don't merely say 'doctors' or 'medicine.' Also specify color or black-and-white photos or line cuts, horizontal or vertical, etc."

732• AMON CARTER MUSEUM
3501 Camp Bowie, Fort Worth TX 76107. (817)738-1933. Contact Person: Public Relations Coordinator. **Description:** "The Amon Carter Museum is devoted to the westering of North America. The program consists of special exhibitions, collections of American paintings, sculpture and photography, and special programs such as film series and seminars. Represented in the collection are such artists as Winslow Homer, Frederic Remington, Thomas Moran, Martin Johnson Heade, Georgia O'Keeffe, Charlie Russell, Albert Bierstadt and Ben Shahn. The photographic collection includes works by W.H. Jackson, Edward Weston and Laura Gilpin." **Services:** Provides bibliographical and historical information. Offers bibliographies, biographies, statistics and photos. "We have an extensive library devoted chiefly to Western history, plus nearly 6,000 microfilm rolls of 19th century newspapers." **How to Contact:** "Call or write for an appointment. Responds to most inquiries within a week. The reseach library is open by appointment only. Interested writers who wish to do research in the photographic collections should contact the Curator of the photographic collection. We have frequently been used as a research source by writers throughout the country and are happy to cooperate. We only ask that interested parties make appointments in advance and have specific requests. We require a credit line for any published reproduction of any item in the permanent collection." Charges for reproduction of art in the permanent collection. "Fees vary according to subject."

733• CIVIL WAR PRESS CORPS
3d Finance Co., APO NY 09036. Contact Person: Editor. **Description:** "We provide information on current activities and publications that relate to the American Civil War and the period of Southern history from 1812-1890." **Services:** Provides advisory, historical, interpretative, referral and technical information covering the American Civil War and Southern history 1812-1890 including slavery, battles, leaders and politics. Offers brochures/pamphlets, informational newsletters, library facilities, placement on mailing lists and research assistance. Publications include monthly newsletter. **How to Contact:** Write. Responds to most inquiries immediately. "Membership in the Civil War Press Corps ($10) entitles member to monthly newsletter, free advertising." **Tips:** "We believe that the CWPC has a very good idea what the public would like to see researched and what needs additional research." Recent information requests: "Where could I go to see a genuine re-enactment unit in action?"; "Is there a Civil War-related history organization that meets regularly in my area?"; "What are the top ten books on the Civil War?"

734• CIVIL WAR ROUND TABLE ASSOCIATES
Box 7388, Little Rock AR 72217. (501)225-3996. Contact Person: National Chairman. **Description:** "We are dedicated to a continuing interest in the history of the American Civil War and to the protection and preservation of Civil War historic sites." **Services:** Provides advisory and historical information on preservation problems at Civil War sites, Civil War history and study of contemporary activities based on interest in Civil War history. Offers newsletter and reports on developmental pressures facing Civil War historic sites; also offers names and addresses of other information sources. **How to Contact:** Write or call. Responds to most inquiries within a week. Charges $10/year for newsletter.

735• COLLIER STATE PARK LOGGING MUSEUM
Box 428, Klamath Falls OR 97601. Contact Person: Curator. **Description:** "The museum's theme is the evolution of logging equipment from the days of brute strength to the present day of modern equipment. We have 600 + exhibits and 600 + acres of pine forest. We like to tape history of loggers; that way we get back to the source and don't have to rely on memory. Pictures also preserve accuracy." **Services:** Provides historical information. "We have about 105 collections of pictures which can be copied." **How to Contact:** Write or "come and see us." Responds to most

inquiries within a month. Give credit for pictures and quotations. **Tips:** Recent information request: Background on operations of Segoma Lumber Company and details of their incline.

736• CONNER PRAIRIE PIONEER SETTLEMENT
30 Conner Lane, Noblesville IN 46060. (317)773-3633. Contact: Public Relations. **Description:** "Conner Prairie is a living museum of some 25 buildings located on 55 acres. Since 1975, lives of ordinary people of central Indiana in the 1830s have been portrayed through historical buildings, artifacts of the period and craft demonstrations, and through first-person historic role interpretation. This role-playing allows the visitor to participate in the site interpretation on more than one level. By being involved in the recreated environment and treated as a drop-in visitor in the lives of the 1836 villagers, the visitor can hopefully gain insight into the past. The activities in the recreated village are dictated by the seasons, and special events are planned accordingly." **Services:** Provides information on Central Indiana 1836 (religion, education, agriculture, medicine, etc.); first-person interpretation. Offers aid in arranging interviews, placement on mailing list, newsletter, photos and press kits. Publications include *Conner Prairie Peddler, Conner Prairie Pioneer Settlement* and other material. **How to Contact:** Write. "Response time depends on the inquiry and number of departments involved to acquire answer. Simple requests answered immediately. Our season runs from April 1 through December 19, closed on Mondays. Information we have in file is readily shared; however, if we must spend time preparing any information, we must charge. Prices include personnel hourly time and, if slides, cost of materials. Quotes must be accurate." **Tips:** "Simplify requests. Don't ask for a thesis when a prepared questionnaire would serve both the writer's and the museum's needs. Concentrate on central Indiana history of the 1830s and specifically of 1836." Recent information request: "Background on development of our first-person interpretation program; when did it begin, what training is involved, where do you select your interpreters, the cost of the program and any other pertinent details."

737• DWIGHT D. EISENHOWER LIBRARY
Abilene KS 67410. (913)263-4751. Contact Person: Director. **Description:** "We provide research and education on the life and times of Dwight D. Eisenhower, 34th President. We have 18.5 million pages of manuscripts, 24,000 books, 300,000 still photographs and 300 oral history interviews." **Services:** Provides historical information. Offers brochures/pamphlets and information searches. **How to Contact:** Write. Responds to most inquiries immediately. Charges for photos, photocopies and audiovisual reproduction; write for current rates. **Tips:** "Be as specific as possible in requests. Searches are limited to manuscript resources. Please check out printed sources first."

738• THE EPIGRAPHIC SOCIETY
6625 Bamburgh Dr., San Diego CA 92117. Contact Person: President. **Description:** Society interested in the deciphering of ancient inscriptions. "We serve as a publishing center for papers contributed by members engaged in the discovery or decipherment of ancient inscriptions." **Services:** Provides advisory, analytical, bibliographical, historical, how-to, interpretative, referral and technical information covering ancient inscriptions. Offers aid in arranging interviews, annual reports, library facilities and annual volume of reports. Publications include *Occasional Publications* which "reports the discovery and decipherment of ancient inscriptions, especially those of the Americas." **How to Contact:** Write, call or visit. Responds to most inquiries immediately. **Tips:** Recent information request: "What ancient inscriptions are recorded from the Ohio area?"

739• ESSEX INSTITUTE
132 Essex St., Salem MA 01970. (617)744-3390. Contact Person: Community Relations Coordinator. **Description:** "Essex Institute is one of the oldest and largest privately endowed regional historical societies in the US. The collections include material associated with the civil history of Essex County, Massachusetts, and adjacent areas since the early 17th century. The institute owns 13 buildings, all of which are listed in the National Register of Historic Places. It maintains a research library of extensive printed and manuscript materials, a museum collection of approximately 39,000 objects, and a publications department. The institute offers special exhibits, public lectures, guided period house tours, publications and library facilities." **Services:** Provides historical and interpretative information on genealogy, history, art and educational programs. Offers annual reports, brochures/pamphlets, placement on mailing list, newsletter, photos and press kits. Publications include descriptive brochures, booklets on historic houses and collections,

a quarterly newsletter and other materials. **How to Contact:** "Write or call for an appointment. Responds to most inquiries within a week. "Freelance writers may use our materials for publicity purposes without a fee. We charge a fee for photo reprint service unless the writer is doing a publicity piece." **Tips:** "Travel writers, including foreign writers, doing travel books are encouraged."

740• FLAG RESEARCH CENTER
3 Edgehill Rd., Winchester MA 01890. (617)729-9410. Contact Person: Director. **Description:** "The oldest and largest resource center for matters relating to flags." **Services:** Provides advisory, analytical, bibliographical, historical and referral information on flags and state heraldry. Offers clipping services, informational newsletters, library facilities, photos and original artwork, research assistance and telephone reference services. Publications include *Flag Bulletin* (bimonthly). **How to Contact:** Call. Responds to most inquiries immediately. Charges for research, artwork, photocopying, etc. Library and files are not open to the public. **Tips:** "We are a consulting business interested in expanding both interest in and knowledge of flags." Recent information requests: "Where can data be found on the Tennessee Civil War flags?"; "What personal banner did Pope Pius IX use?"

741• HENRY FORD MUSEUM/GREENFIELD VILLAGE
Box 1970, Dearborn MI 48121. (313)271-1620, ext. 350. Contact Person: Head of Press Relations. **Description:** The museum and village—under the corporate title The Edison Institute—comprise the world's largest indoor-outdoor museum of Americana. The collection areas cover all aspects of day-to-day life from the Colonial period through the Second World War, with the concentration being in the period from 1840 to 1920. The village has more than 85 historic structures and the 12 acres of indoor museum include collections ranging from a 600-ton steam locomotive to miniature portraits. The archives and research library contain more than 8,000 cubic feet of records and more than 40,000 negatives. There are operating steam-powered industries including a circular sawmill and gristmill in the village. **Services:** Provides advisory, historical, some how-to and interpretative information on agriculture, art, business, celebrities, entertainment, food, industry, music, politics, recreation, science, travel and all areas relating to collection items. Offers aid in arranging interviews with the museum staff of experts, annual reports, brochures/pamphlets, information searches, placement on mailing list, photos and press kits. **How to Contact:** Write or call. Responds to most inquiries within a week. Photographs and slides promoting the village, museum or its collections and activities are available without charge. Historical photos are available at set rates from the archives and library. Advertising and commercial use of materials not available.

742• FORT GEORGE NATIONAL HISTORIC PARK
Box 787, Niagara-on-the-Lake, Ontario, Canada L0S 1J0. (416)468-2741. Contact Person: Superintendent. **Description:** "We are a historic park emphasizing the War of 1812." **Services:** Provides historical information on the War of 1812. Offers brochures/pamphlets. Publications include *Fort George*; *British Soldiery in Canada*; and *Battle of Queenston Heights Battlefield Walking Tour.* **How to Contact:** Write or call. Responds to most inquiries within a month. **Tips:** "We appreciate receiving requests for information but have only limited personnel to answer inquiries. We are not professional researchers, and have limited source material. Be specific and precise in your requests. If this is not done, all we can do is send brochures." Recent information requests: Question about the Parks Canada System; role of the Militia or Indians in a particular battle of the War of 1812.

743• FREEDOM CENTER COLLECTION
Library-Freedom Center, California State University, Box 4150, Fullerton CA 92634. (714)773-2633. Contact Person: Freedom Center Librarian. **Description:** "Our purpose is to collect controversial political literature—mostly ephemeral. We have more than 10,000 pamphlets, 4,000 newspaper and periodical titles, 100 linear feet of folders. Material covers the extreme right to the extreme left." **Services:** Provides bibliographical and referral information on 20th century American political ephemera, extreme right to extreme left; British socialism; much information on almost any subject with political overtones. **How to Contact:** Visit. "Material can be used in library only; because of its value and ephemeral nature, the material does not circulate. Some materials will be sent out through interlibrary loan." Responds to most inquiries within a week. Charges 5¢/page for photocopies. **Tips:** "Be specific about what you want so that we may

let you know quickly if we have the material." Recent information requests: Names of extreme labor groups in Southern California and the West Coast; information on the local Ku Klux Klan; history of tax rebellion in the US.

744• THE HAKLUYT SOCIETY
The Map Library, The British Library, Reference Division, Great Russell St., London, England WC1B 3DG. (025)125-4207. Contact Person: Administrative Assistant. **Description:** "Established in 1846, we are dedicated to the advancement of education by the publication of scholarly editions of records of voyages, travels and other geographical material of the past." **Services:** Provides information on "the literature of travel and the history of geographical science and discovery." Offers publications list. **How to Contact:** Write. Charges for publications.

745• RUTHERFORD B. HAYES PRESIDENTIAL CENTER
Spiegel Grove, Fremont OH 43420. (419)332-2081. Contact Person: Director. **Description:** The Hayes Center Research Library contains books, pamphlets, newspapers, manuscripts and photographs covering the last half of the nineteenth century and the early twentieth century, with emphasis on President Hayes' life and major interests. The Hayes Center Museum contains articles used by President and Mrs. Hayes, including clothing, the Presidential carriage, two large doll houses, as well as furniture and china from the White House. The museum also houses interesting collections of American Indian artifacts, old weapons from three continents and children's toys. The Hayes Residence, a lovely Victorian mansion, is on the grounds and open to the public. **Services:** Provides advisory, bibliographical, historical, interpretative and referral information on American history, mid-nineteenth century to early twentieth century, with emphasis on politics, race relations, prison reform, Indian affairs and veterans affairs. Publications include *The Statesman* (quarterly newsletter); and *Hayes Historical Journal* (semiannual). **How to Contact:** Write, call or visit. Responds to most inquiries within a week. Museum and residence hours: Tuesday-Saturday, 9 a.m.-5 p.m.; Sunday, Monday, and Holidays, 1:30-5 p.m. Admission fee. Library hours: the same except closed on Sundays and holidays. Open to the public without charge. Research assistance $10/hour after the first 15 minutes. Copyright restrictions must be observed; credit the Hayes Center where practical **Tips:** Recent information request: Genealogical question; "Do you have any paintings by the American portraitist John Antrobus?"

746• HERSHEY MUSEUM OF AMERICAN LIFE
Box 170, Hershey PA 17033. (717)534-3439. Contact Person: Director. **Description:** "The Museum of American Life has extensive collections of artifacts illustrating the life of German settlers in Pennsylvania in the 18th and 19th centuries. Also, it has fine collections of American Indian and Eskimo objects; military objects, especially Pennsylvania rifles; china; etc." **Services:** Provides advisory, historical and how-to information. Offers aid in arranging interviews, brochures/pamphlets and photos. "We try to aid in all requests for information about our collections, individual objects, pictures, loans, etc." **How to Contact:** Write or call. Responds to most inquiries within a week. Charges for photos; "rates vary according to what is required. Credit must be given. Permission is generally given for one-time use." **Tips:** "Do not expect museum staff to do free research. We can suggest and advise only. Recent information requests: Early Pennsylvania German measuring tools; a particular artist; Pennsylvania rifles; etc.

747• HOLT-ATHERTON PACIFIC CENTER FOR WESTERN STUDIES
University of the Pacific, Stockton CA 95211. (209)946-2404. Contact Person: Director. **Description:** "The center collects and organizes material on western history." **Services:** Provides advisory and historical information on California and Pacific Slope of North America. Offers bibliographies, biographies, brochures/pamphlets, information searches, newsletters and photos. Publications include quarterly journal and monograph series. **How to Contact:** Write. Responds to most inquiries within a week. Charges for publications, research and photos. "Writers must come here to do research, but first apply to the center for research use of the archives and the Stuart Library. Hours: 9 a.m.-5 p.m., Mon.-Fri. only." **Tips:** "Do not expect the staff to do your research." Recent information requests: Do you have a certain book (name of author and title given in full)?"; "Do any of your collections have information on Mr. ABC (name in full and some identification)?"

748• HERBERT HOOVER PRESIDENTIAL LIBRARY
West Branch IA 52358. (319)643-5301. Contact Person: Director. **Description:** "The Hoover

Presidential Library is a museum and reseach center focusing on the public service of Herbert Hoover, the times in which he lived, and the changing character of American society and the institutions by which it is governed.'' **Services:** Provides advisory and historical information on the Hoover presidency and related American history. Offers library facilities, photos, research assistance and telephone reference services. Publications include historical materials in the Hoover Library. **How to Contact:** Write or visit. Responds to most inquiries immediately. Charges for photocopying. ''A few collections contain very small quantities of donor-restricted materials. Over 95% of our holdings are open for research.'' **Tips:** ''Inquiries should be reasonably specific and indicate whether information desired will be used in a biographical article or in a discussion of a specific topic or issue. Requests that others *not* be advised of an ongoing research project will be honored.''

749• INDIAN AND COLONIAL RESEARCH CENTER
Main St., Old Mystic CT 06372. Contact Person: Librarian. **Description:** ''We are a research library housing the collection of Eva L. Butler—2,000 notebooks containing her vast research in colonial and Indian history, from old town records, deeds, diaries and letters. We also have over 3,000 books on colonial history and life and Indian history and customs, plus many rare photos from our glass plate negatives of this area for 1895-1920. We have one department for genealogy containing hundreds of names of families of this area, also old maps and manuscripts.'' **Services:** Provides historical information on colonial history, Indian life and lore and genealogy. Offers brochures/pamphlets and information searches. Publications available. **How to Contact:** Write or call. Responds to most inquiries within a week.. ''We are only open on Tuesday, Thursday and Saturday.'' Charges 25¢ for photocopies; $5 minimum fee for genealogy research. ''All material must be used at the center, none can be taken out.'' **Tips:** ''Call before coming as we are all volunteers who run the center.''

750• LYNDON B. JOHNSON LIBRARY
2313 Red River, Austin TX 78705. (512)482-5137. Contact Person: Supervisory Archivist. **Description:** This presidential library makes available for research the papers of Lyndon B. Johnson and his associates. **Services:** Provides bibliographical, historical and referral information covering the career of Lyndon B. Johnson, the American Presidency, Congress and American history (1908-present). Offers brochures/pamphlets, informational newsletters, library facilities, photos, placement on mailing lists, research assistance, telephone reference services, oral history interviews, xerographic reproduction of documents, microfilm copies of some holdings, museum sales desk and interlibrary loan of oral history transcripts and finding aids. Publications include draft list of holdings (interlibrary loan); searches of materials in the LBJ Library of various topics (such as the Congress); LBJ Library brochure. **How to Contact:** Write, call or visit. Contact by mail or phone is preferred. Responds to most inquiries within a week. Charges for xerographic reproduction, 20¢/page if ordered at the library; 25¢/page if ordered by mail. ''Please write to the library for appropriate fee schedules, for museum sales desk items and reproduction of audiovisual materials. Researchers under 16 years of age must be accompanied by an adult.'' **Tips:** ''Write or call in advance of a personal visit.'' Recent information request: List of materials on Medicare and the Detroit riots.

751• LIBRARY COMPANY OF PHILADELPHIA
1314 Locust St., Philadelphia PA 19107. (215)546-3181. Contact Person: Reference Librarian. **Description:** ''The Library Company is a rare book and research library founded by Benjamin Franklin in 1731. It is open to the public without charge.'' **Services:** Provides bibliographical and historical information on American books in its collection printed before 1880, including education, agriculture, and Afro-Americana. ''The print and photograph collection is strong in 18th and 19th century Philadelphia.'' Offers library facilities. Publications include exhibition catalogs; *Nineteenth-Century Photography in Philadelphia*; *Negro History 1553-1903*; *Quarter of a Millennium: The Library Company of Philadelphia, 1731-1981*. **How to Contact:** Write or visit. Mon.-Fri. 9 a.m. to 4:45 p.m. Responds to most inquiries within a week. Charges for photocopying, microfilming and photographing items in the collection, and for publications. **Tips:** ''All items from the collection must be used at the Library Company. The staff cannot provide research services over the phone or through the mail; we can only answer whether a particular item is in our collection. Writers are encouraged to do their own research in the library. Because the card catalog is arranged by author, a writer should know specifically what he or she needs.''

752• LIBRARY OF CONGRESS, MANUSCRIPT DIVISION
Washington DC 20540. (202)287-5383. Contact Person: Chief. **Description:** The Manuscript
Division is a collection of 40 million pieces—consisting of the personal papers and drafts of the
writings of presidents, members of their Cabinet, officers of the armed services, authors, poets and
scientists. Users of the collection are mainly engaged in scholarly research. **Services:** Provides
information on American history. Offers annual reports, computerized information searches,
library facilities and photos. **How to Contact:** Write. Responds to most inquiries within a week.
Some materials in the collection are restricted. "Contact us in advance."

753• MUSEUM OF THE CONFEDERACY
1201 E. Clay St., Richmond VA 23219. (804)649-1861. Contact Person: Curator of
Manuscripts. **Description:** "The Museum of the Confederacy was founded in 1896 for the
purpose of collecting, preserving, exhibiting, and interpreting artifact and manuscript materials
relating to the Civil War. The Eleanor S. Brockenbrough Library serves as a research facility and
repository for the manuscripts and photo collection." **Services:** Provides advisory,
bibliographical, historical, how-to, interpretative and referral information covering the Civil War
and southern history 1850-1890 with special emphasis on Confederate history. Offers biographies,
library facilities, photos, research assistance and limited telephone reference services.
Publications include brief biographies and bibliographies of major southern leaders; museum
newsletter focuses on various aspects of Confederate history (available with museum
membership). **How to Contact:** Write, call or visit. Responds to most inquiries within 2 weeks.
Charges for photographs, photocopying and postage. Include SASE. Allow several weeks for
photograph and copying orders. "Appointments are required so the curator has time to assemble
items which would allow researchers to utilize collection to the ultimate. Researchers are required
to seek written permission from museum for use of manuscripts and photographs in publications,
audio/visual presentations, etc." **Tips:** "Be prepared to narrow your topic. Be open to possible
changes in topic, especially if primary source material proves sparse." Recent information
request: Verification that crew of *CSS Shenandoah* left cannon on Australian island, 1865.

754• MUSEUM OF THE FUR TRADE
Rt. 2, Box 18, Chadron NE 69337. (308)432-3843. Contact Person: Director. **Description:**
"Museum is devoted to the materials and methods of the North American fur trade." **Services:**
Provides advisory, analytical, bibliographical, historical, referral and technical information on
materials and methods of the North American fur trade 1600-1900. Offers brochures/pamphlets,
information searches and professional services in reviewing manuscripts and artists' sketches for
historical accuracy (fur trade period only, 1600-1900). **How to Contact:** "Write or call, outlining
in specific detail what help is needed. Responds to most inquiries within a month. There is a standard professional consulting fee of $150/day plus any travel or reproduction expenses. Normal
searches for data are $10/hour for an assistant with supervision. Photos and copies at regular com-
mercial rates." Credit for illustrations must be given. **Tips:** "Be specific—general questions are
expensive to answer." Recent information requests: Questions about costumes or equipment of a
specific time and place or defining terms encountered in perusal of old records.

755• NATIONAL COUNCIL FOR THE ENCOURAGEMENT OF PATRIOTISM, INC.
Box 3271, Munster IN 46321. (219)838-1796. Contact Person: Executive Director. **Description:**
The council encourages love of country through education. **Services:** Provides advisory and historical information on the council's history. "We maintain the Highway of Flags Servicemen's
Memorial at US 41 and Rodge Road in Highland, Indiana. We offer information on the memorial's
history and on flags." Offers brochures/pamphlets and tours of the memorial all summer. Provides
speakers for a fee. Publications include citizenship responsibility booklet (for donation) and *You
Bet I'm a Flag Waver* 45 rpm record ($1). **How to Contact:** Write or call. Responds to most in-
quiries within a week. Charges $50-100 plus expenses for lectures. **Tips:** "Arrange a personal in-
terview with the council director." Recent information request: The council's reaction to MIA
Day.

756• NATIONAL COWBOY HALL OF FAME
1700 NE 63rd St., Oklahoma City OK 73111. (405)478-2250. Contact Person: Director of Public
Relations. **Description:** "The National Cowboy Hall of Fame is dedicated to the preservation of
the history and heritage of the American West, and honors the men and women living and deceased
who pioneered there." Includes a $40 million western art collection. **Services:** Provides historical

information on agriculture (ranching), celebrities (great western performers), art, history and sports (rodeo). Offers brochures/pamphlets, photos and press kits. "Literature and a general information sheet on the museum library are available for in-person research." **How to Contact:** Write, stating needs and intended use of material. Responds to most inquiries within a week. "Charges will be made individually on the basis of use. Restrictions are placed on all photography of the museum." **Tips:** "Make appointment if interested in using research services." Recent information request: General press kits on the Cowboy Hall of Fame.

757• NATIONAL MUSEUM OF AMERICAN HISTORY
Smithsonian Institution, 14th St. and Constitution Ave., Washington DC 20560. (202)357-3129. Contact Person: Public Affairs Officer. **Description:** "The National Museum of American History is a bureau of the Smithsonian which conducts scholarly research and administers the national collections of American history, including science and technology, and the national philatelic and numismatic collections. In addition to installation of objects from the collections, it offers major special exhibitions devoted to topics within its purview." **Services:** Provides historical and referral information on US social, cultural, scientific and technological history from the colonial period to the present; also philatelics and numismatics. Offers brochures/pamphlets, photos and press kits, placement on mailing list, aid in arranging interviews. **How to Contact:** Write or call. Responds to most inquiries within a week. "There is often a charge for brochures and exhibition catalogs. Photos are available to publicize installations and exhibitions while they are on view." **Tips:** "Questions should be within the purview of the museum's collections and preferably related to installations and special exhibitions on view. Please allow as much lead time as possible for a response." Recent information request: "When did the Star-Spangled Banner enter the collections? Please describe its significance and provenance."

758• NATIONAL SOCIETY, DAUGHTERS OF THE AMERICAN REVOLUTION
1776 D St. NW, Washington DC 20006. (202)628-1776. Contact Person: President General. **Description:** National society of more than 208,000 members—descendants of soldiers and patriots of the Revolutionary War. "We are dedicated to promoting historical, educational and patriotic activities." **Services:** Provides historical, how-to, and referral information on Revolutionary War history, genealogy, citizenship and how to use and display the flag. Offers aid in arranging interviews, annual reports, biographies, brochures/pamphlets, library facilities, photos, placement on mailing lists and research assistance. Publications include *Know the D.A.R.* **How to Contact:** Write or call. Responds to most inquiries within a week.

759• NATIONAL SOCIETY, SONS OF THE AMERICAN REVOLUTION
1000 S. 4th St., Louisville KY 40203. (502)589-1776. Contact Person: Executive Secretary. **Description:** National society of 22,500 members who provide educational, historical and genealogy information of the Revolutionary War. **Services:** Provides historical, how-to, and referral information on Revolutionary War, history and genealogy. Offers brochures/pamphlets, library facilities and telephone reference services. Publications include *S.A.R.* magazine. $4 (non-members). **How to Contact:** Write. Responds to most inquiries within a week. Charges for extensive materials. **Tips:** Recent information request: "How can I join the S.A.R.?"

760• NATIONAL TRUST FOR HISTORIC PRESERVATION IN THE UNITED STATES
1485 Massachusetts Ave. NW, Washington DC 20036. (202)673-4000. Contact Person: Media Information Assistant. **Description:** "The National Trust is a private, nonprofit organization chartered by Congress in 1949 with the responsibility to encourage public participation in the preservation of sites, buildings and objects significant in American history and culture. Support for the National Trust is provided by membership dues, endowment funds and contributions and by federal grants, including matching grants from the Department of the Interior. The Trust owns 8 historic properties; publishes a monthly newsletter, bimonthly color magazine, books and newsletters; provides advisory services; awards matching grants; conducts conferences and workshops; and administers 6 regional offices in the areas of history, architecture, conservation, archaeology, planning, and preservation law. The National Trust serves as a clearinghouse for preservation groups and programs, financing, ordinances, aesthetic guidelines and restoration techniques." **Services:** Provides advisory, how-to, referral and technical information on preservation; rehabilitation; tax and law; historic museum properties; financial aid programs; conferences; regional, state and local programs; and tours. Offers aid in arranging interviews, annual reports, bibliographies, statistics, brochures/pamphlets, information searches, placement

on mailing list, newsletter and press kits. "Preservation Press provides advisory services for publications. Public Affairs provides assistance to press and other media. Library provides research assistance to members." Publications include *Preservation News*; *Historic Preservation*; *Conserve Neighborhoods*; *Annual Report*; *Preservation Law Reporter*; various press releases and brochures describing publications; and the *Information* series of technical advice. "The library is a major depository of preservation research materials in the US. A list of preservation periodicals and newsletters, both national and state, is also available from the library." **How to Contact:** "Writers may contact the Public Affairs staff and request information—the more specific, the more appropriate the response." Responds to most inquiries within 10 days. "The 6 regional offices will provide information on preservation groups and activities and issues in their areas. Library services must be by appointment. Send letter of inquiry for manuscript review and advice to the Magazine Editor. Membership in the trust is encouraged, magazine and newspaper are available as benefits of membership." Charges $15/year for membership. **Tips:** "Another source is the state historic preservation office of each state, as well as city historic district or landmark commissions in most US cities. Check with local historical societies. *National Register of Historic Places* has documentation of historic buildings, sites or objects of national, state and local significance. *Historic American Buildings Survey* has an excellent collection of architectural drawings and photographs (available through the Library of Congress)." Recent information request: "Provide a list of reused/rehabilitated railroad depots."

761• ORIGINAL PONY EXPRESS HOME STATION, INC.
106 S. 8th St., Marysville KS 66508. (913)562-3726. Contact Person: Curator. **Description:** History museum. The Pony Express Barn, built in 1859 and subsequently restored, is the only original station on the old horse mail route. **Services:** Provides historical information on Pony Express and related memorabilia. Offers aid in arranging interviews, brochures/pamphlets, photos, research assistance and tours. **How to Contact:** Write. Responds to most inquiries immediately.

762• PILGRIM SOCIETY
Pilgrim Hall, 75 Court St., Plymouth MA 02360. (617)746-1620. Contact Person: Curator of Manuscripts and Books. **Description:** "The Pilgrim Society was founded in 1820 to study and interpret Pilgrim history, to preserve Pilgrim artifacts and to promote a continuing awareness of the Pilgrims' contributions to the founding of our nation. We maintain a museum, library and manuscript collection relating to the Pilgrim experience and to the founding and continuing development of Plymouth town and colony." **Services:** Provides bibliographical and historical information on Pilgrims and Plymouth history. Offers brochures/pamphlets, information searches and "assistance with historical research within the Pilgrim experience—scholarly and, to a lesser extent, genealogical." Publications include *The Pilgrim Society (1820-1970)*; *A Guide to Manuscripts of the Pilgrim Society*; *The Pilgrim Story* and *Sparrow Hawk*. **How to Contact:** Write. Responds to most inquiries within a week. "If coming in person, arrange beforehand with curator, as office is open only on part-time basis." Minimal charge $1; 25¢ per photocopy (10¢ to members) plus postage; varying rates for published material. **Tips:** "Most requests for genealogical information would have greater success with other organizations, such as the New England Historic Genealogical Society in Boston." Recent information requests: Photocopies of specified newspaper articles, 1838; early maps showing historical development of given coastal area.

763• SANTA FE TRAIL CENTER MUSEUM/LIBRARY
Route 3, Larned KS 67550. (316)285-2054. Contact Person: Archivist. **Description:** The archives provide researchers with information concerning the history of the Santa Fe Trail. Also functions as the Pawnee County (Kansas) archives. **Services:** Provides historical information. Offers annual reports, brochures/pamphlets, library facilities and photos. **How to Contact:** Write, call or visit. Responds to most inquiries within a week. Charges 25¢/page for photocopying. "The collection may be used only under the supervision of a staff member. The materials may not be taken from the archives. Since we are normally not open on weekends, contact the archivist in advance if you plan to use the archives on Saturday or Sunday so that arrangements can be made." **Tips:** Recent information requests: The history of caravans, routes, distances and traders on the Santa Fe Trail.

764• SHAKERTOWN AT PLEASANT HILL, KENTUCKY, INC.
Rt. 4, Harrodsburg KY 40330. (606)734-5411. Contact Person: Director of Public Relations. **Description:** "Shakertown at Pleasant Hill was incorporated as a living outdoor history

museum to preserve 27 original Shaker buildings and to interpret the way of life of this unusual 19th century religious sect. We provide visitors with an exhibition tour, dining, lodging, craft shops, rides on a paddlewheel riverboat up the Kentucky River and a conference facility. All touring, dining, lodging and shopping services are housed in original buildings on 2,200 acres.'' **Services:** Provides advisory, analytical, bibliographical, historical, interpretative and referral information covering history, preservation, antiques, crafts, arts, country inns, agriculture, historic pharmacy, and folk music. ''We would be happy to supply writers with historical information about our Shaker heritage—architecture, furniture, music and advanced ecological and social concepts, or information on the restoration and adaptive uses of our buildings, or information on our year-round visitor services.'' Offers annual reports, brochures/pamphlets, placement on mailing list, photos and press kits. Publications include color brochure, calendar of events, hours and rates sheet, and *Writer's Fact Packet*, which covers the history of the Shakers and the restoration. ''We cannot make available our original source documents. They are not kept at Pleasant Hill, but are in a university library under climate control.'' **How to Contact:** Write or call. Responds to most inquiries within a week. ''Photos can be used for educational and/or promotional uses only with our approval—not for commercial advertising. We request tearsheets.'' **Tips:** ''Indicate the main thrust of your story; specify black and white or color transparencies; include deadline. If story is specialized rather than a general travel piece, give us time to put information together. Explore secondary sources first; source documents require a lot of time, so plan for it.'' Recent information request: Background on the uses of herbs by Shakers.

765• THE SOCIETY FOR CREATIVE ANACHRONISM, INC.
Box 743, Milpitas CA 95035. (408)262-5250. Contact Person: Corporate Secretary. **Description:** Persons interested in researching and re-creating the Middle Ages. Events are held and members attend as persons from the medieval period. Events include tourneys, revels, sword combat, dancing, needlework, armoring, feasts, equestrian, archery, etc. **Services:** Provides ''information relating to many medieval topics as they are practiced in the world today. We know about calligraphers, dance instructors, early music ensembles, armorers, illuminators, etc.'' Publications include *Tournaments Illuminated* (quarterly journal on medieval and current topics); *Fighters Handboke* (the art of armed combat in the SCA); *Known World Handboke* (the Current Middle Ages). **How to Contact:** Write. Responds to most inquiries within a month. Charges for publications. **Tips:** ''Volunteers have lots of enthusiasm and knowledge about subjects of much interest but they rarely answer letters within a week. Don't overwork us.'' Recent information requests: ''Where can I find a professional calligrapher?''; ''Who can design a coat of arms for our church's bishop?''; ''Where can I find a full-sized poster of a knight in armor?''; ''Please supply knights and ladies on horseback for photo session.''

766• THE SOCIETY FOR THE PRESERVATION OF OLD MILLS
Box 435, Wiscasset ME 04578. Contact Person: Secretary. **Description:** ''The purpose of the society is to preserve the history of old mills.'' **Services:** Provides advisory, how-to, referral, technical and trade information on little old mills of all kinds. Offers newsletters and cross index (1972 thru 1981). ''We are not a writer's service bureau; our newsletters are for our members. Dues are $8/year. We do have many mill-oriented books but these are in private houses at two locations and visits must be arranged first.'' **How to Contact:** Write. ''We prefer letters; do not phone.'' Responds to most inquiries within a week. Photocopied letters of inquiry not answered.'' Charges the regular published price for back issues of *Old Mill News* and for cross index. **Tips:** Recent information requests: Inquiries on milling processes, particular mills, equipment, etc.

767• STONEHENGE STUDY GROUP
2821 De La Vina St., Santa Barbara CA 93105. (805)687-9350. Contact Person: Editor. **Description:** Individuals interested in astronomy, archaeology, geology and related arts and sciences; conducts field trips to megalithic sites in England, Scotland, Wales, Ireland, France, Sweden, Malta. **Services:** Provides interpretative and referral information on prehistory, archaeoastronomy, archaeometeorology, megalithic site analysis, ley line and canopy research, halo patterns, symbol analysis, dragon lore and Druids, Merlin/King Arthur and ancient myths/legends, ancient religions and ''hidden halo'' research. Offers aid in arranging interviews, computerized information searches, informational newsletters, library facilities, photos, research assistance and statistics. Publications include *Stonehenge Viewpoint* (6 issues/year); books on related subjects; list of organizations with comparable interests. **How to Contact:** Write, call or vis-

BEHIND THE BYLINE

Stephen Birmingham
Writer

Stephen Birmingham writes about rich and famous people. He writes about groups of people with identities linked to race, religion, state in life or address. His books command national attention, and his numerous articles appear in top magazines. But the former New York advertising copywriter didn't begin writing as a full-time endeavor.

"I didn't think I'd be writing about rich people either. It happened almost by chance. Cleveland Amory was the resident writer of high society at *Holiday*, but he had become uninterested in covering such topics. Since I had been to many society affairs, I volunteered to do a piece. I was able to gradually cut back my advertising work, until I quit it altogether in 1973-74 and started writing full time. That was a scary thing: no regular paycheck, no free insurance, no Blue Cross."

The risk paid off. His interest in the rich has been translated into a successful career. "Though I didn't come from a rich family, I went to school with a lot of Mellons, Pillsburys, Vanderbilts and Rockefellers. I knew a little about their world. I've always been interested in the craziness of the rich—the funny things they do, the silly things, the good things they do. I really write for myself, I guess."

He enjoys doing the research for his books, especially when that involves talking to people. Birmingham reaches into his own past to seek out potential contacts. "I use my Williams College address book and my Hotchkiss school directory. The Williams alumni are listed by city. If I'm going to a certain place, I'll look up a couple of classmates. It's safe to assume the kids who went to Williams and Hotchkiss are reasonably prosperous." He looks for connections. "Sometimes you have to do some detective work on the phone. But I'm a great believer in it; it saves time and gives people less of a chance to say 'no.' I generally find that people are anxious to help.

"If I don't have any acquaintances in a city, I still use the phone. I contact children or friends of the people I want to write about. If you find two or three contacts in a city, each of those will suggest two or three more. I talk to people until I begin hearing the same stories. That's when I know I've done enough."

Birmingham has learned many things in his research. "You find out people lie a lot. There's plenty of exaggeration in what they tell you—even your most unimpeachable sources. I have to do a lot of checking of facts when I'm dealing with word-of-mouth memories. And still people are always coming back with 'I was misquoted' which generally means 'I shouldn't have said that.' "

In addition to people research, Birmingham does his own library research. "I tried using other researchers a few times, but they didn't give me what I wanted. I look for amusing things." Birmingham says he reads between the lines of history; he questions, interprets, analyzes and then makes conclusions about what he reads.

"And I try to entertain. The things I write are not Barbara Tuchman, great sweeping histories of the fourteenth century. I like to look at the little footnotes to history that perhaps wouldn't make it into the *Encyclopaedia Britannica*."

Birmingham is currently working on a novel and recognizes the value in checking on details. "You can't have someone humming a tune before it was written. In one of my books, I had tulips and irises blooming at the same time. I got a lot of letters from readers telling me that irises bloom much later than tulips. You can get tripped up on the details if you don't do the research."

it. Responds to most inquiries immediately. Charges for books; *Stonehenge Viewpoint* ($10/15 issues)—one issue sent free. **Tips:** "Be familiar with our topics of interest. Our material would be 'a natural' for borderline science writers." Recent information requests: "Are there any Druid organizations in existence?"; "How can one get permission to visit Stonehenge after hours?"

768• TITANIC HISTORICAL SOCIETY, INC.
Box 53, Indian Orchard (Springfield) MA 01151. Contact Person: Secretary. **Description:** "The society was founded to perpetuate the history of the *Titanic* and her sister ships by the establishment of an archives and a quarterly newsletter for distribution to members." **Services:** Provides bibliographical, historical, referral and technical information on steamship history of the North Atlantic, Cunard, White Star, etc. Offers newsletter. **How to Contact:** Write and include # 10 SASE. Responds to most inquiries within a week. **Tips:** "Be specific, giving us as much information as possible . . . check libraries and local museums first." Recent information requests: "Were my cousins on the *Titanic*?"; "I have a *Titanic* life-ring, what is it worth?"; "Whatever happened to the *Titanic's* lifeboats?"

769• UNITED STATES CAPITOL HISTORICAL SOCIETY
200 Maryland Ave. NE, Washington DC 20002. (202)543-8919. Contact Person: Chief Historian. **Description:** The society promotes the history of the Capitol building and Congress. **Services:** Provides bibliographical and historical information covering Congressional history. Offers aid in arranging interviews, bibliographies and newsletter. Publications include a calendar and journal; also has informational recording. **How to Contact:** Write or call. Responds to most inquiries within a week. Charges for photocopying. **Tips:** "Call us. Every inquiry is different; our staff is limited, and research requests are best handled on an individual basis."

770• WESTERN HISTORICAL RESEARCH ASSOCIATES
1052 Meridian Rd., Victor MT 59875. (406)961-3612. Contact Person: Secretary-Treasurer. **Description:** "We promote the factual history of the western expansion of the US. The WHRA is composed of people from all walks of life who have a true love for the factual history of our western expansion." **Services:** Provides historical information on all phases of the western expansion of the United States. Offers library facilities, photos and research assistance. Publications include *The Pony Express*. **How to Contact:** Write. Responds to most inquiries immediately. Charges for postage. **Tips:** Recent information request: Background on the Chisholm Trail by section, township and range in immediate vicinity of Fort Worth, Texas.

771• WOMEN'S HISTORY ARCHIVE
Sophia Smith Collection, Smith College, Northampton MA 01063. Contact Person: Director. **Description:** The archive contains thousands of manuscripts and about 5,000 photos emphasizing women's history and general subjects: abolition and slavery, American Indians, outstanding men and women, countries (culture, scenes), US military history, social reform, suffrage and women's rights. Mainly b&w or sepia. **Services:** Provides historical information on women's history. Publications include *Picture Catalog*, which includes a fee schedule, and a *Manuscript Catalog*. **How to Contact:** Write. Responds to most inquiries within a week. Offers US rights, one-time use only. "We charge for reproduction of photographs plus a permission fee." Charges $6 for *Picture Catalog*, $3 for *Manuscript Catalog*. All material is non-circulating.

772• WORLD ARCHAEOLOGICAL SOCIETY
Star Rte. 445, Hollister MO 65672. Contact Person: Director. **Description:** "We publish, promote, and protect the antiquities and provide information and services to the related fields of archaeology, anthropology and art history (globally). Our motto is 'Ut Prosit'—to be of service." **Services:** Provides advisory, analytical, bibliographical, how-to, interpretative, referral and technical information covering archaeology, anthropology and art history. ("The antiquity studies have become a multi-field endeavor borrowing from such fields as zoology, botany, also geology, astronomy, agriculture, etc.") Offers clipping services, informational newsletters, library facilities, photos and research assistance. Publications include *W.A.S. Newsletter* and other special publications. **How to Contact:** Write. Enclose SASE. Responds to most inquiries within a week, "sometimes within a month." Charges for clippings and lengthy projects; "we will quote a fee." Library materials cannot be borrowed. **Tips:** "We are happy to work with writers." Recent information requests: Name and address of prominent woman archaeologist; title of book on Inca agriculture.

SECTION · FOURTEEN

HOBBY AND LEISURE

It is a happy talent to know how to play.
—Ralph Waldo Emerson

This category includes resources related to spare time activities—hobbies of making and/ or collecting; games and toys; amusement parks and circuses; recreation and pastimes.

Additional information sources related to leisure may be found in both the Tourism and Travel and Sports sections; those pertaining to radio, television and motion pictures are listed in the Communications/Entertainment section.

Bibliography

Gale, Janice & Stephen, eds. *Guide to Fairs, Festivals & Fun Events*. Miami, FL: Sightseer Publications, 1981.

Jensen, Dean. *The Biggest, The Smallest, The Longest, The Shortest: A Chronicle of the American Circus from Its Heartland*. Madison, WI: Stanton & Lee Publications, Inc., 1975.

Kovel, Ralph and Terry, eds. *Kovel's Antique Collectibles and Price List*. 15th ed. New York: Crown, 1982.

Liman, Ellen and Lewis Liman. *The Collecting Book*. New York: Penguin Books, 1980.

Morehead, Albert H. and Geoffrey Mott-Smith, eds. *Hoyle Up-to-Date: Official Rules for All Important Games*. New York: Grosset & Dunlap, 1959.

Savage, George. *Dictionary of Antiques*. 2d ed. New York: Mayflower Books, Smith Publications, 1978.

Wilmeth, Don B., ed. *American and English Popular Entertainment: A Guide to Information Sources*. Detroit: Gale Research Co., 1980.

773• AMERICAN BACKGAMMON PLAYERS ASSOCIATION
12333 W. Washington Blvd., Los Angeles CA 90066. Contact Person: National Director. **Description:** An organization of backgammon enthusiasts at all levels of playing skill. The association is an information center for local and national tournaments. **Services:** Provides analytical, how-to, technical and trade information on backgammon, its rules and related topics. Offers brochures/pamphlets, informational newsletters, placement on mailing lists, statistics and backgammon clinics. Publications include *Backgammon Is Everywhere* (quarterly); and papers on backgammon-related topics. **How to Contact:** Write. Responds to most inquiries within a week. "Occasionally, writers expect more than source information. We'll conduct surveys, studies, etc.—and bill them." **Tips:** "We're delighted to help, especially when the inquirer already has a direction and not just a curiosity." Recent information request: "Where can we find a history of the game?"

774• AMERICAN CAMPING ASSOCIATION
Bradford Woods, Martinsville IN 46151. (317)342-8456. Contact Person: Editor. **Description:** "American Camping Association (ACA) is an accrediting agency of organized children's camps, both private and agency, in the US." **Services:** Provides information on training, direction, legislative lobbying, workshops, publications and conventions aimed at continuous updating and improvement of organized camping and camp management. Offers statistics, brochures/pamphlets and media kits. Publications include *Camping Magazine*; *Author's Guide* and general informational brochures on the subject of organized camping and ACA. "Our services are generally restricted to the rather narrow field of organized children's camps. We can't help with Winnebagos and KOAs, etc., but if you're patient, we'll help all we can in our discipline." **How to Contact:** Write or call. Responds to most inquiries within a month.

775• AMERICAN KITEFLIERS ASSOCIATION
1104 Fidelity Bldg., Baltimore MD 21201. (301)752-3320. Contact Person: Business Manager. **Description:** Nonprofit hobby organization of persons interested in kiteflying. **Services:** Provides

advisory, historical, how-to, interpretative, referral, technical and trade information on how to build and fly kites, conduct kite contests, etc. Offers aid in arranging interviews, annual reports, biographies, informational newsletters, research assistance, statistics and telephone reference services. Publications include *American Kitefliers Association News*. **How to Contact:** Write. Responds to most inquiries within a week.

776• AMERICAN NUMISMATIC ASSOCIATION
Box 951, Colorado Springs CO 80901. (303)632-2646. Contact Person: Editor. **Description:** "Nonprofit, educational body chartered by Congress as such to aid the enjoyment and research of and for collectors of coins, tokens, medals and paper money." **Services:** Provides advisory, bibliographical, historical, how-to, referral and technical information. Offers biographies, library facilities, photos, research assistance and statistics. "We have the world's largest circulating library relating to numismatics and the collecting trends and activities in the field." Publications include *The Numismatist* (monthly journal) and assortment of brochures and pamphlets explaining our services. **How to Contact:** Write. Responds to most inquiries within a week. Charges for photos. **Tips:** "Numismatics is a very large area of study and can usually be related to just about any other subject." Recent information requests: "When was the US half dollar first struck?"; "How many designs have existed throughout our history?"

777• AMERICAN PHILATELIC SOCIETY
Box 8000, State College PA 16801. (814)237-3803. Contact Person: Director of Administration. **Description:** "We are the largest organization of stamp collectors (50,000) in this country." **Services:** Provides how-to, bibliographical and referral information on philately, stamp collecting and postal history. Services include research library. **How to Contact:** Write or call. Responds to most inquiries within a week. "Information is free, but we do charge for photocopies of articles or book loans." **Tips:** Recent information request: "Please send listings from your library about the squared circle postal markings of Canada."

778• AMERICAN RECREATION COALITION
1901 L St. NW, Suite 700, Washington DC 20036. (202)466-6870. Contact Person: President. **Description:** "ARC is a nonprofit association of national and regional organizations and corporations dedicated to the protection and enhancement of every citizen's right to pursue health and happiness through leisure-time activities. ARC members range from the United States Ski Association to the Experimental Aircraft Association, from the Recreation Vehicle Industry Association to Kampgrounds of America, Inc. ARC was created to help ensure that the benefits of recreation are recognized by the general public and government at all levels. It provides communication, coordination and cohesion to the American recreation community and provides a unified approach to the major national issues that affect recreationists throughout the country." **Services:** Provides advisory, analytical, interpretative, referral and trade information. Offers aid in arranging interviews, brochures/pamphlets, photos, research assistance and statistics. Publications include *Energy and Recreation* (1980); *Recreation Industry Forum Proceedings* (annual); *Recreation Roundtable Series* (annual); and a bimonthly advisory to its members. **How to Contact:** Write or call. Responds to most inquiries within a week. **Tips:** "Be candid about your focus and target; this allows us to be more helpful. Send a copy of your work when completed." Recent information request: Trends in recreation participation, equipment sales.

779• AMERICAN SHORTWAVE LISTENER'S CLUB (ASWLC)
16182 Ballad Lane, Huntington Beach CA 92649. (714)846-1685. Contact Person: General Manager, ASWLC. **Description:** "We are dedicated to the principle of 'World Friendship Through Shortwave', which means our activities are directed toward advancement of the SWL hobby and development of the individual's interest in listening to shortwave radio broadcasts." **Services:** Provides advisory, analytical, historical, how-to, referral and technical information covering international broadcast bands, utility broadcast frequencies, international shortwave schedules, frequency monitoring, hour by hour frequency monitoring, feature articles and general news on international broadcasting. Offers biographies, brochures/pamphlets, computerized information searches, informational newsletters, library facilities, photos, placement on mailing lists, research assistance and statistics. Publications include *SWL* monthly publication and *Proper Reporting Guide*. **How to Contact:** Write, call or visit. Responds to most inquiries immediately. When our services are used, we simply request that credit be given to the ASWLC and/or our publi-

cation, *SWL*. **Tips:** "Our files, books, magazines, etc., are open to interested parties at anytime." Recent information requests: "How many SWLs in the USA/world?"; "How many receivers are in the USA?"; "What is the range of age and occupation of the hobbyists?"

780• THE AMERICAN SOCIETY OF DOWSERS, INC.
Danville VT 05828. (802)684-3417. Contact Person: Director of Operations. **Description:** "Nonprofit, educational and scientific society with 50 chapters dedicated to preserving an open forum of ideas. Dowsing is the name given to a quest for information, with or without the assistance of a device such as a forked stick or pendulum. The society exists to give dowsing a stature of authority; to help members with their dowsing problems; to give guidance to beginners; and to disseminate knowledge and information on dowsing." **Services:** Provides how-to information on dowsing. Offers brochures/pamphlets, informational newsletters and library facilities. Publications include *The American Dowser*, quarterly publication sent to membership. **How to Contact:** Write or call. Responds to most inquiries immediately.

781• AMERICAN SPOON COLLECTORS
Box 260, Warrensburg MO 64093. (816)429-2630. Contact Person: Club Sponsor. **Description:** "Nonprofit hobby club that promotes interest in the hobby of souvenir spoon collection—antique and modern, American and foreign." **Services:** Provides advisory, bibliographical, historical and how-to information covering the history of souvenir spoons; varieties of souvenir spoons; specific persons, places, events commemorated on souvenir spoons; and current news on the hobby. Offers aid in arranging interviews, informational newsletters, library facilities (private) and research assistance. Publications include *Spooners Forum* (monthly membership newsletter). **How to Contact:** Write. Responds to most inquiries within a week. Charges for secretarial time. Approval of material to be used prior to publication is required.

782• AMERICAN VECTURIST ASSOCIATION
Box 1204, Boston MA 02104. (617)277-8111. Contact Person: Editor. **Description:** Individuals interested in "the study of transportation fare tokens and the transportation systems (past or present) that have issued them." **Services:** Provides bibliographical, historical, referral and trade information covering metal and plastic fare tokens, urban transit fare structures and urban transportation history. Offers informational newsletters, research assistance and statistics. Publications include *The Fare Box*, monthly publication about transportation tokens; *The Atwood-Coffee Catalogue of U.S. & Canadian Transportation Tokens* (2 Vols.). **How to Contact:** Write or call. Responds to most inquiries within a week. Charges for books and periodicals. Give credit to American Vecturist Association. **Tips:** Recent information requests: "What is the most valuable transportation token ever issued, and what is it worth?"; "When were transportation tokens first used, and where?"; "What other cities use tokens the same size as we use on our system?"

783• AMERICANA COLLECTOR'S SHOP
1120 N. Westwood, Santa Ana CA 92703. (714)547-1355. Contact Person: Owner. **Description:** A collection of country store collectibles, paper Americana, etc. **Services:** Provides advisory, historical, how-to and referral information on tin containers and other collectibles. Offers appraisals and display work, brochures/pamphlets, photos, research assistance and statistics. **How to Contact:** Write, call or visit. Responds to most inquiries within a week. Enclose SASE with written inquiries. Charges for services "depending on the time involved"; $25/hour for appraisals. Give credit for any information furnished. **Tips:** Recent information request: How to care for tins; questions on their value and age.

784• AMUSEMENT AND MUSIC OPERATORS ASSOCIATION
2000 Spring Rd., Suite 220, Oak Brook IL 60521. Contact Person: Director of Communications and Research. **Description:** An association of music and amusement operators; clearinghouse for industry information. **Services:** Provides advisory, analytical, historical, how-to, interpretative, referral, technical and trade information on pinball machines, jukeboxes; coin-operated video games; cost-of-doing-business surveys; national lobbying and legislation affecting the industry; and research being done in the field of video games. Offers aid in arranging interviews, annual reports, brochures/pamphlets, photos, press kits, research assistance, statistics (some), telephone reference services, technical schools (on repair of equipment), educational cassettes on the industry. Sponsors yearly exhibition, The International Exposition of Games and Music.

Publications include *The Location* (monthly newsletter); *The Quarternote* (quarterly newsletter to state associations). **How to Contact:** Write. Responds to most inquiries within a week. Charges for publications and cassettes. **Tips:** Recent information requests: "I'd like to start an arcade; what's involved?"; questions on the state of the video game industry.

785• AUTOMOBILE LICENSE PLATE COLLECTORS ASSOCIATION, INC. (ALPCA)
Box 712, Weston WV 26452. (304)842-3773. Contact Person: Secretary-Treasurer. **Description:** "A nonprofit organization promoting interest in the collecting of motor vehicle license plates, fraternizing with fellow hobbyists and exchanging information about the hobby with other members of the organization." **Services:** Provides historical information on license plates. Offers informational newsletters. **How to Contact:** Write, call or visit. Responds to most inquiries within a week. Charges membership dues; newsletter available only to members. **Tips:** "There is very little information on license plates and old registration systems." Recent information request: "I found a 1948 New York license plate in our garage. What is it worth?"

786• BOYS TOWN PHILAMATIC CENTER
Box 1, Boys Town NE 68010. (402)498-1360. Contact Person: Curator. **Description:** "We are a stamp, coin and currency museum exhibiting the collections donated to Boys Town over the years. The main thrust of the subject matter is philatelic and numismatic; however, we show artwork, artifacts, old newspapers (related to historic figures and events), documents, memorabilia and miscellaneous flat 'collectibles.' We also have a supportive library, which has been built through donations rather than on a constructive basis. We are reputed to exhibit more bank notes than anyone else in the world. Our purpose is to support the boys of Boys Town in their numismatic and philatelic hobbies, as well as to offer for exhibit the collections of Boys Town to philatelists, numismatists and general tourists." **Services:** Provides historical and technical information covering numismatics and philatelics. Offers "background material along historical and documentary lines about the exhibits here, research material for books authored on subject matter relating to our exhibits, and documentation of authentic bank notes for the purposes of prospective numismatic authors." Publications include a brochure on the Philamatic Center. **How to Contact:** Write. Responds to most inquiries within a week. "We suggest that requests be tentative and explicit. There is no charge provided request does not involve considerable time—more than an hour of research." **Tips:** "Try us. We may have something you will find nowhere else. A personal visit would be more beneficial than correspondence. Tell us all the information you already have so that we might add to it." Recent information request: Identification of foreign coins.

787• THE BUCKEYE STATE SOCIETY CIRCUS WORLD WIDE ATTRACTIONS, INC.
Box 74, Barnesville PA 18214. (717)467-2316; toll-free (800)824-7888, ext. A263. Contact Person: Manager/Owner. **Description:** "A circus playing schools and colleges as a fundraiser, supported by circus stars as well as trained animals; also a program lecturing on chimps and having them perform. It's the only educational show of its kind in America." **Services:** Provides how-to information on chimpanzees; a lecture series plus act. Offers brochures/pamphlets, photos and press kits. **How to Contact:** Write or call. Responds to most inquiries immediately. Give credit to the circus. **Tips:** "I have owned and trained chimps for over 34 years; I've owned 24 in my life and am considered an authority." Recent information request: "How do you train chimps?"

788• CIRCUS WORLD MUSEUM LIBRARY AND RESEARCH CENTER
415 Lynn St., Baraboo WI 53913. (608)356-8341. Contact Person: Chief Librarian and Historian. **Description:** "The center preserves the records, materials, history and nostalgia of the circus and makes some materials available to researchers and inquirers under the protected facilities of our library, which includes circus lithographs, photographs, negatives, programs, route books, personnel records, heralds and couriers." **Services:** Provides advisory, bibliographical, historical, some how-to, referral, technical and trade information on the circus. Offers aid in arranging interviews, annual reports, bibliographies, biographies, statistics, brochures/pamphlets, limited information searches, photos, photo services, book lending service and reproduction service (of collection pieces). Publications include booklets on holdings and services. **How to Contact:** Write or call. Responds to most inquiries within a month; "sometimes longer if extensive research is involved. We will do research on an inquiry for up to one hour as a public service. Research time beyond one hour is done for a fee. Persons calling at our premises and doing their own research may do so without charge. There is a charge for having photo prints or reproductions made, and a service charge for book and movie rentals. A publication fee is charged for images published. The inquirer should

not, however, expect replies by return mail. Inquiries requiring research are handled by a limited staff." **Tips:** "Do not ask general questions that defy answering in the confines of one letter. We will not write your epistle for you, but will answer precise and direct questions which have answers. We are an open, free public library and research center to which researchers are invited to come, utilize our resources and do their own in-depth research."

789•   CLASSIC AUTOMOTIVE APPRAISALS
2220 21st St., Boulder CO 80302. (303)449-1128, days. (303)447-2786, evenings. Contact Person: President. **Description:** Commercial appraisal of classic or collectible automobiles for historical, legal, insurance or personal purposes. Development of community information services to dispense accurate information on the automobile. **Services:** Provides advisory, bibliographical, historical, how-to, referral and technical information on the historical development and social impact of the automobile; the fair and realistic market value of interesting automobiles; technical (how-to) information for consumers (not engineers). Offers biographies, brochures/pamphlets, clipping services, computerized information searches and computer-assisted appraisals, library facilities and research assistance. **How to Contact:** Write. Responds to most inquiries within a week. Charges for research services, but not routine inquiries. **Tips:** "Focus your needs in this field. Make sure that local sources have first been explored. We are interested in filling the gap between your library and the Smithsonian." Recent information requests: Name of the car driven by Geronimo; first one-way street; first car in a movie; background information on Ralph Nader and the Corvair story.

790•   DELTIOLOGISTS OF AMERICA
10 Felton Ave., Ridley Park PA 19078. (215)521-1092. Contact Person: Director. **Description:** "To supply collectors with information about pre-1915 picture postcards, their artists and publishers." **Services:** Provides historical and referral information. Offers bibliographies, brochures/pamphlets and placement on mailing list. Publications include *Deltiology*. **How to Contact:** Write with SASE. Responds to most inquiries immediately. Call only in emergency. There is a fee for publications and services.

791•   WALT DISNEY WORLD
Box 40, Lake Buena Vista FL 32830. (305)824-2222, 824-4531. Contact Person: Manager of Publicity. **Description:** "Most popular vacation destination in America." **Services:** Offers aid in arranging interviews, annual reports, bibliographies, biographies, statistics, brochures/pamphlets, information searches and press kits. "Press kits are made to suit the writer's needs." Publications include *The Story of Steam Locomotives in the Magic Kingdom; Biography of Walt Disney*; and special press kits for special events. **How to Contact:** Write or call. Responds to most inquiries immediately. No charge to "the author or working pressperson." Requires an editor's OK on a story to give help to a writer. Written requests preferred. "We like to work with people, especially if they are writing from a new angle on our large and many-faceted operation. We must have control of Disney material."

792•   DISNEYLAND
1313 Harbor Blvd., Anaheim CA 92801. (714)533-4456. Contact Person: Manager, Publicity/Public Relations. **Description:** Amusement park. **Services:** Offers press kits. Publications include a guide book. **How to Contact:** Write or call. "We deal only with working journalists with credentials. A freelancer needs a letter from editor or managing editor."

793•   DOLL COLLECTORS OF AMERICA, INC.
14 Chestnut Rd., Westford MA 01886. Contact Person: Treasurer. **Description:** Doll collectors who encourage the doll collecting hobby and preservation of early dolls. **Services:** Provides historical and how-to information on the origin and history of dolls; including doll making, doll repair and doll collecting in general. Offers research assistance. Publications include manuals on doll collecting. **How to Contact:** Write. Responds to most inquiries within a month. Charges for publications. "We do not provide a doll evaluation service." **Tips:** "We can help writers by giving them information on where to find answers about doll collecting in their own area." Recent information request: Questions about china dolls, Barbie dolls.

794• THE EPHEMERA SOCIETY OF AMERICA, INC.
124 Elm St., Bennington UT 05201. Contact Person: North American Director. **Description:** Persons interested in collecting "the minor documents of everyday life"—tickets and letterheads, labels, timetables, magazines and newspapers, greeting cards, catalogs, etc. The organization is concerned with the preservation, study and educational uses of printed and handwritten ephemera. **Services:** Provides advisory, historical and referral information on all topics related to ephemera. Offers aid in arranging interviews and informational newsletters. Publications include *Ephemera News.* **How to Contact:** Write. Responds to most inquiries within a week. **Tips:** "Ephemera in general is now an accepted social history tool. We will put individuals in touch with experts. Be specific in your area of interest." Recent information request: "Do you have any ephemera on the history of the Brooklyn Bridge or know where I can locate some?"

795• FEDERATION OF HISTORICAL BOTTLE CLUBS
Star Route 1, Box 3A, Sparrow Bush NY 12780. (914)856-1766. Contact Person: Director, Public Relations. **Description:** Organization designed "to promote the collection and preservation of historical containers (bottles, jars and insulators); to foster research of these containers and related items; and to encourage the display of historical containers." **Services:** Provides historical, how-to and referral information covering bottles, jars, insulators and related items of glass and stoneware. Offers aid in arranging interviews, brochures/pamphlets, research assistance and aid to clubs specializing in antique bottles. Publications include *The Federation Letter* (monthly); brochure with information on dating bottles; list of clubs. **How to Contact:** Write or call. Responds to most inquiries within a week. Enclose legal-size SASE for publications and inquiries. Charges $17.50 for use of FOHBC logo; 2 courtesy copies of material published. Give credit to the Federation of Historical Bottle Clubs. **Tips:** "An exploratory letter indicating possible areas of interest would be the best first approach; intended audience is also important." Recent information request: Comment on the popularity of bottle collecting.

796• FLORIDA CYPRESS GARDENS
Box 1, Cypress Gardens FL 33880. (813)324-2111. Contact Person: Public Relations-Publicity Manager. **Description:** "This is a family tourism total destination attraction." **Services:** Provides advisory, how-to, referral and technical information covering entertainment and recreation. Offers aid in arranging interviews, annual reports, brochures/pamphlets, information searches, placement on mailing list, photos and press kits. Publications include *Ski Like a Pro.* Photos include pictures of flowers, plants, scenics, boating, water skiing, fishing, camping and animals. **How to Contact:** Write or visit. Responds to most inquiries within a week. "All Cypress Garden photos must carry a credit line." Charges if photo used without credit line: "Photo courtesy of Florida Cypress Gardens." Return of pictures required. **Tips:** "Plan to spend the whole day. Have questions to cover a specific area." Recent information request: "What has been the key to the success of Cypress Gardens, and what did Mr. Pope start with?"

797• FREE BEACHES DOCUMENTATION CENTER
Box 132, Oshkosh WI 54902. (414)231-9977. Contact Person: Information Coordinator. **Description:** "We exist to coordinate the efforts of persons and groups working to gain full recognition for clothing-optional sunbathing, swimming and other modes of recreation." **Services:** Provides information on nude resorts and recreation areas. Offers aid in arranging interviews, bibliographies, brochures/pamphlets, placement on mailing list, photos and press kits. Publications include pertinent legal documents and *Guide to Nude Beaches of the World* (annual). **How to Contact:** Write. Responds to most inquiries within a week. "We provide an overview of the current acceptance, the problems and historical origins of nude beaches and related activities. Writers are encouraged to contact local advocates and sources as well; we may or may not be able to facilitate such contacts." **Tips:** " 'Participatory' practices by reporters and photographers going to skinny-dipping sites in their area will result in greater cooperation by sources."

798• GOLDFISH SOCIETY OF AMERICA
Box 1367, South Gate CA 90280. Contact Person: Editor. **Description:** Individuals interested in promoting interest in the goldfish-keeping hobby. **Services:** Provides advisory, how-to and technical information on goldfish caring, breeding, showing, doctoring, buying and related aspects of the goldfish hobby. Offers brochures/pamphlets, informational newsletters, library facilities and photos. Publications include *The Goldfish Report* (periodical) and *Goldfish*

Beginner's Guide. **How to Contact:** Write or call. Responds to most inquiries within a month. Charges for publications; 12 monthly issues of the *Goldfish Report* and free consulting service are included with the annual membership fee of $10 in the US. **Tips:** "Goldfish are the most highly developed of all *domesticated* creatures. The Chinese and Japanese people are responsible for nearly all of the more than 200 varieties that have been developed in the past 1,000 years. The most authentic books on the subject were published in the US prior to 1930. There have been a lot of new developments since then." Recent information requests: "What is a detailed description of a particular variety of goldfish?"; "What is wrong with a goldfish showing the following symptoms and what course of treatment is recommended?"

799• HOLLYWOOD STUDIO COLLECTOR'S CLUB
Box 1566, Apple Valley CA 92307. Contact Person: Executive Officer. **Description:** Collectors and other interested individuals who encourage the trading and selling of information and ideas concerning movie memorabilia and motion picture history. **Services:** Provides historical, how-to and motion picture industry-related information. Offers biographics, brochures/pamphlets, clipping services, photos and research assistance. Publications include *Hollywood Studio Magazine*. **How to Contact:** Write. Responds to most inquiries within a week. **Tips:** "Subscribe to the magazine for information on prices of movie memorabilia." Recent information request: "What is the value of a robot from a 1960 movie?"; "What is an 8x10 photo (June, 1938) of Rosalind Russell worth?"

800• INTERNATIONAL DOLL MAKERS ASSOCIATION
420 N. Broad St., Suffolk VA 23434. Contact Person: President. **Description:** The organization "furthers the interest in doll making and the study of doll making either in the original or reproduction areas." **Services:** Provides advisory, historical, how-to, referral and technical information on doll making. Offers informational newsletters and photos. Publications include *The Broadcaster* (quarterly magazine). **How to Contact:** Write. Responds to most inquiries within a week. "A self-addressed, stamped envelope would be appreciated. We will not provide marketing listings." **Tips:** "Be thorough in requests and define the exact area of interest." Recent information request: The steps in producing an original doll through sculpting to finished product.

801• INTERNATIONAL FESTIVALS ASSOCIATION
702 Wayzata Blvd., Minneapolis MN 55403. (612)377-4621. Contact Person: Managing Director. **Description:** "We serve as a clearinghouse for nonprofit civic celebrations." **Services:** Provides travel-oriented information and "how-to's" of organization and execution of civic festivals. Offers brochures/pamphlets, informational newsletters and photos. Publications include bi-monthly newsletter. **How to Contact:** Write. Responds to most inquiries immediately. **Tips:** Recent information requests: Typical organization, audience sizes, trends in the industry.

802• INTERNATIONAL GAMERS ASSOCIATION
5465 Atlantic Ave., N. Long Beach CA 90805. (213)422-2369. Contact Person: President/ **Description:** Individuals interested in strategy simulation games. "We design strategy simulations and provide a bank of information regarding such activities. We give information and design assistance for simulations using the theory of education and marketing through the osmosis of entertainment." **Services:** Provides advisory, historical, how-to (on occasion), referral and trade information on design techniques and concepts, industrial history, practical application, historical military research, distribution techniques. Offers direct assistance in design, distribution, and manufacturing of products in the field and research assistance. **How to Contact:** Call. Responds to most inquiries immediately. Charges "depend on the service requested and the man hours to be expended. Each job is bid separately. We do some work free of charge depending on the circumstances. Membership lists strictly confidential. We must be credited with the part of the project we performed." **Tips:** "Call for an interview to ascertain viability of using our services. Many of the things writers need are available at no charge if transmitted verbally and due credit is given." Recent information request: Extrapolation on the outcome of the Falkland Islands confrontation. "This was asked in the 2nd week of the situation. We provided what we felt would be the course of events and the eventual outcome of the crisis."

803• INTERNATIONAL SEAL, LABEL AND CIGAR BAND SOCIETY
8915 E. Bellevue St., Tucson AZ 85715. (602)296-1048. Contact Person: Executive Secretary. **Description:** Individuals interested in "collecting cigar bands, cigar box labels and all

other poster stamps and labels.'' **Services:** Provides advisory, bibliographical, historical, how-to, interpretative and referral information covering the history and location of manufacturers and lithographers; values of cigar bands, cigar box labels and all other label types. Offers informational newsletters, research assistance and sales and trade exchange for above items/collectibles. Publications include quarterly newsletter. **How to Contact:** Write. Responds to most inquiries within a month. ''Specify exact needs and time restraints.'' Charges postage and research costs; $6.50/yr. membership; $25 and up for appraisal services. Recent information requests: ''What is the history of the cigar band?''; ''What year were they instituted, where and why?''

804•   KEY COLLECTORS INTERNATIONAL
Box 9397, Phoenix AZ 85068. Contact Person: Executive Director. **Description:** The organization works to promote and educate key and lock collectors. **Services:** Provides advisory, historical, referral and technical information on all types of locks and keys. Offers research assistance. **How to Contact:** Write. Responds to most inquiries within a week. Charges for photocopying and postage. **Tips:** ''Almost all our questions are to identify locks and keys, who manufactured them and when.''

805•   KINGS ISLAND
Kings Island OH 45034. (513)241-5600, ext. 461. Contact Person: Manager of Public Relations. **Description:** Family entertainment center. Special features are the College Football Hall of Fame, 18-hole Jack Nicklaus Sports Center, Wild Animal Safari, and a major amusement park. **Services:** Provides bibliographical, historical and general information about the family entertainment center, and especially KI theme park. Offers aid in arranging interviews, annual reports, statistics, information searches, placement on mailing list, photos (color transparencies) and press kits. **How to Contact:** Write, call or visit. Responds to most inquiries within a week. **Tips:** ''Start with a press kit. Call a few days in advance for help.''

806•   KNOTT'S BERRY FARM
8039 Beach Blvd., Buena Park CA 92801. (714)533-4456. Contact Person: Public Relations Manager. **Description:** Amusement park. Features 150-year old operating stage coaches, an Old West ghost town, the largest miniature collection in the world, demonstrations of panning for gold, a narrow-gauge railroad manufactured in 1881, thrill rides, shows, and a 2,100-seat theatre. **Services:** Provides bibliographical, historical and trade information. Offers press kits. Publications include general farm brochures. **How to Contact:** Write or call. ''Start in the publicity department and state an area of specific interest.'' Responds as soon as possible. Material ''must be used for publicity on Knott's Berry Farm in the media.'' Must have credentials to use services.

807•   LEAGUE OF AMERICAN WHEELMEN
Box 988, Baltimore MD 21203. (301)727-2022. Contact Person: Administrative Director. **Description:** ''The purposes of the league are: to advance and defend the rights and interests of bicyclists; to disseminate information about bicycling to its members and other interested persons; to encourage the formation and development of local and regional bicycling organizations; and to organize and conduct bicycle rallies and other bicycling activities.'' **Services:** Provides historical, how-to, interpretative, referral and technical information on non-competitive bicycling—how, where, with whom, experts, political action, books, maps. Offers aid in arranging interviews, brochures/pamphlets, library facilities and telephone reference services. Publications include *American Wheelmen* (monthly magazine). **How to Contact:** Write, call or visit. Responds to most inquiries within a week. ''Not a lending library; need SASE if copies requested.'' **Tips:** ''It is very helpful to know who your intended audience is and what you are trying to convey. Our maps, books and files are open to all. We can refer writers both to national experts and to local contacts.'' Recent information requests: Names of older women cyclists to be interviewed; comment on new technology; advice on how to get started cycling; history of special shoes for cycling.

808•   LEISURE STUDIES DATA BANK
University of Waterloo, Waterloo, Ontario, Canada N2L 3G1. (519)885-1211, ext. 2204. Contact Person: Coordinator. **Description:** ''The Leisure Studies Data Bank is a nonprofit research facility that maintains machine-readable data on leisure and leisure-related topics. The bank provides all researchers with ready access to diverse data sources and provides assistance in their use and analysis. Services are available in both official languages of Canada (English and French).'' **Services:** Provides advisory information on leisure, tourism, sport, fitness, outdoor

recreation, time use and related topics. "Most files are national or provincial in scope but files related to local aspects of leisure as well as international studies are also maintained. Files dealing with recreation facilities and environments are maintained as well as studies of leisure behaviour, attitudes, expenditures, etc." Offers research assistance and statistics. Publications include descriptive brochure on LSDB and *LSDB: Catalogue of Holdings* (English/French) $8. **How to Contact:** Write. Responds to most inquiries within a week. Charges recovery cost. **Tips:** "Be as specific as possible about your information request."

809• MAGIC LANTERN SOCIETY OF THE US AND CANADA
819 14th St. NE, Auburn WA 98002. (206)833-7784. Contact Person: Chairman. **Description:** Nonprofit organization interested in the magic lantern and other kinetic "vintage" type optical devices, both professional and toy. "We encourage the exchange of knowledge and collect and tabulate information on magic lantern manufacturers, slide makers, and lantern slide artists." **Services:** Provides advisory, bibliographical, historical, how-to, interpretative, referral and technical information. Offers informational newsletters. Publications include *Magic Lantern Society* (quarterly bulletin). **How to Contact:** Write. Responds to most inquiries immediately. Charges for photocopying and postage. **Tips:** "We are nonprofit so would appreciate questions that can be answered in one paragraph. Queries from the public are answered to the best of our ability." Recent information request: Materials on Sy Lubin, film and slide maker, Philadelphia, 1890-1920.

810• MARBLE COLLECTORS SOCIETY OF AMERICA
Box 222, Trumbull CT 06611. Contact Person: Executive Director. **Description:** "Nonprofit organization dedicated to gathering and disseminating information relating to marbles." **Services:** Provides advisory and historical information on marbles. Offers brochures/pamphlets, informational newsletters, library facilities, photos, research assistance and statistics. **How to Contact:** Write. Responds to most inquiries within a week.

811• MARRIOTT'S GREAT AMERICA
Box 1776, Gurnee IL 60031. (312)249-1776. Contact Person: Public Affairs Manager. **Description:** "We are a theme park featuring over 130 rides, shows and attractions." **Services:** Provides advisory, bibliographical, historical, how-to, interpretative, referral and trade information covering celebrities, entertainment, history, music, recreation and travel. Offers aid in arranging interviews, statistics, brochures/pamphlets, placement on mailing list, newsletters, photos and press kits. **How to Contact:** Write and specify purpose for which information is needed. Responds to most inquiries within a week.

812• NATIONAL ASSOCIATION OF BREWERIANA ADVERTISING
2343 Met-To-Wee Lane, Wauwatosa WI 53226. (414)257-0158. Contact Person: Executive Secretary. **Description:** The organization encourages the collection, preservation and study of American breweriana advertising—trays, labels, mirrors, signs, etc. It conducts research on brewery histories. **Services:** Provides advisory and historical information on breweriana advertising. Offers informational newsletters to members only. Publications for members include *The Breweriana Collector* (quarterly) and annual membership directory. **How to Contact:** Write. Responds to most inquiries within a month.

813• NATIONAL ASSOCIATION OF MINIATURE ENTHUSIASTS
Box 2621, Anaheim CA 92804. (714)871-6263. Contact Person: Executive Secretary. **Description:** Nonprofit organization of over 12,000 members promoting the collecting and crafting of miniatures. **Services:** Provides advisory, historical, how-to, referral, technical, and trade information covering scale and types of miniatures, decorating tips, craft ideas and sources of miniatures. Offers annual reports, biographies, brochures/pamphlets, informational newsletters, research assistance and telephone reference services. Publications include *Miniature Gazette* (available to members). **How to Contact:** Write or call. Responds to most inquiries within two weeks. **Tips:** Recent information request: "What does scale mean?"

814• NATIONAL ASSOCIATION OF ROCKETRY
182 Madison Dr., Elizabeth PA 15037. (412)384-6490. Contact Person: President. **Description:** Nonprofit organization which sanctions model rocket competition for the United States; selects the US team to fly in the World Spacemodeling Championships; charters local sections; provides hob-

by insurance; publishes monthly magazine; safety certifies model rocket motors; offers education program for hobby advancement. **Services:** Provides historical, referral and technical information on the model rocket hobby, model rocket research and development, and model rocket rules and regulations. Offers brochures/pamphlets, informational newsletters and research assistance. Publications include *Model Rocketeer* (monthly membership magazine). **How to Contact:** Write. Responds to most inquiries within a week. Give credit to the National Association of Rocketry. **Tips:** Recent information requests: "Where can I find someone doing hobby research with R/C boost gliders?"; "Where can I find the nearest model rocket competition for this coming month?"

815• NATIONAL ASSOCIATION OF WATCH & CLOCK COLLECTORS MUSEUM, INC.
Box 33, Columbia PA 17512. Contact Person: Museum Director. **Description:** Organization of hobbyists, historians, collectors and others interested in time-keeping devices; seeks to preserve, display, and promote horology as a hobby. "The NAWCC Museum has the largest collection of printed material dealing with horology in the United States with the exception of the Library of Congress. Its Horological Data Bank is largely computerized." **Services:** Provides historical and referral information on horology (clocks, watches, and related materials). Offers aid in arranging interviews, computerized information searches, library facilities and photos. **How to Contact:** Write or visit. Responds to most inquiries within a week. Charges for photos, photocopies and other costs which depend on the research needed. Give credit to the NAWCC Museum Horological Data Bank. **Tips:** Recent information requests: History of advertising clocks; photos of advertising clocks and captions; sources for further information (major collectors), etc.

816• NATIONAL BALLROOM AND ENTERTAINMENT ASSOCIATION
Box 65338, West Des Moines IA 50265. (515)223-1341. Contact Person: Secretary. **Description:** The association's purpose is "to promote dancing to live music; to get dancers into the ballroom; to promote big band ballroom dancing." **Services:** Offers brochures/pamphlets, newsletter, annual yearbook and an annual convention. **How to Contact:** Write or call. Responds to most inquiries within a week.

817• NATIONAL BUTTON SOCIETY
2733 Juno Place, Akron OH 44313. Contact Person: Secretary. **Description:** "A nonprofit organization devoted to the promotion of the hobby of button collecting; members include collectors, libraries, museums, members of the button trade and others from all states and several foreign countries." **Services:** Provides historical and referral information on buttons. Offers brochures/pamphlets, library facilities and statistics. Publications include *State* and *National Button Bulletins*. **How to Contact:** Write. Responds to most inquiries immediately. "Credit must be given to the National Button Society." **Tips:** Recent information requests: Questions on military buttons.

818• NATIONAL CAVES ASSOCIATION
Box 106, Rt. 9, McMinnville TN 37110. (615)668-3925. Contact Person: Secretary/Treasurer. **Description:** "The National Caves Association (NCA) brings together show cave operators to share, discuss, and, if necessary, take action regarding various subjects of interest and concern. The organization strives to set high standards of cave operation throughout the country." **Services:** Provides referral and trade information on America's show caves. Offers aid in arranging interviews, brochures/pamphlets and press kits (from some members). "We can usually arrange to make suitable photos or slides available." Publications include *Caves and Caverns*, directory brochure; *Great Show Caves of America*, illustrated b&w booklet. **How to Contact:** Write. Responds to most inquiries within a week. "We do not supply business or confidential material."

819• NATIONAL EUCHRE PLAYERS ASSOCIATION
1775 Woodview Ct. W, #J, Columbus OH 43068. (614)868-8465. Contact Person: President. **Description:** "We hold euchre tournaments; provide rule and testing material concerning the game of euchre; compile statistics and draw inferences from them. We also promote the varied interests of the entire membership." **Services:** Provides analytical, historical, interpretative, referral and technical information on the game of euchre: variations of the rules relative to area in the United States; complete numerical analysis of the basic partnership game; where the game entered the United States scene; interpretative abilities of other numerical systems; statistical analysis; proof of the extinction of the 32- and 28-card packs. Offers aid in arranging

interviews, brochures/pamphlets, informational newsletters, placement on mailing lists, research assistance, statistics and telephone reference services. Publications include "mailings that we send to our entire membership"; Brandly theory publications concerning mathematical analysis. **How to Contact:** Write. Responds to most inquiries within a week. "Do not violate existing copyrights; give minimal footnote acknowledgement in any published works." **Tips:** "Feel free to contact us. We are eager to establish credibility and are very confident of our accuracy of information." Recent information requests: "How is the game of euchre played in the United States today?"; "What is known about probability of differing situations in euchre play?"; "What parts of published works are outdated?"

820• NATIONAL SPA AND POOL INSTITUTE
2000 K St. NW, Washington DC 20006. (202)331-8844. Contact Person: Publications Editor. **Description:** "The institute is a trade association representing 2,800 member firms in all segments of the swimming pool, spa and hot tub industry. It includes manufacturers, distributors, builders/installers, retail stores and service companies. NSPI monitors government activity affecting this industry and promotes the benefits of swimming, etc." **Services:** Provides how-to, referral, technical and trade information on various types of pools and spas; chemical maintenance; health and fitness; number of pools in USA, etc.; construction and design standards; safety; how to buy a good pool . . . ." Offers aid in arranging interviews, brochures/pamphlets, photos, press kits and statistics. **How to Contact:** Write or call. Responds to most inquiries immediately. Charges *only* for publications ordered. "Entire membership list is not available; sales information on individual firms is not available, nor are member only publications." **Tips:** "Be as specific as possible in your request. Freelancers should always identify themselves as such and identify their purpose— many who call don't or refuse to." Recent information requests: "How many pools are installed each year?"; "Where are they?"; "Average cost?"; "What is the difference between gunite, vinyl-lined, and fiberglass pools?"

821• NATIONAL VALENTINE COLLECTOR'S ASSOCIATION
Box 1404, Santa Ana CA 92702. (714)547-1355. Contact Person: Editor. **Description:** The organization promotes education and good fellowship among fellow collectors of antique valentines. **Services:** Provides advisory, historical, how-to and referral information covering the history of valentines, current price trends, care and preservation of collection, etc. Offers informational newsletters and photos. Publications include quarterly newsletter. **How to Contact:** Write, call or visit. Responds to most inquiries within a week. Enclose SASE. Charges $2/issue of newsletter; $25/hour on appraisals. "Give us credit for any material used from our files." **Tips:** "Many museums around the country have some good examples of early American and English lacy valentines; but most don't know too much about what they do have on hand, and much is poorly researched!" Recent information requests: Questions on the age and possible value of valentines.

822• OPRYLAND ENTERTAINMENT COMPLEX
2802 Opryland Dr., Nashville TN 37214. (615)889-6600. Contact Person: Public Relations Manager. **Description:** Entertainment complex whose major components are the Opryland USA theme park, the Grand Ole Opry, the Opryland Hotel and the Opryland Productions television production company. **Services:** Provides advisory, historical, referral and trade information covering theme park, lodging, convention, television, radio, tourism and music industries. Offers aid in arranging interviews, brochures/pamphlets, photos, press kits, site tours. **How to Contact:** Call or write. Responds to most inquiries immediately.

823• THE PHILATELIC FOUNDATION
270 Madison Ave., New York NY 10016. Contact Person: Director of Education. **Description:** The organizaton was "chartered by the state of New York for philatelic study and research in 1945. Some of our activities are expertizing (examination) of stamps and other philatelic items (for a fee). Each item receives a Certificate of Opinion which is universally recognized. We hold frequent seminars on philately and also publish books on philatelic subjects." **Services:** Provides analytical, historical and technical information covering technical problems and advanced techniques for examining stamps. Offers aid in arranging interviews, brochures/pamphlets, informational newsletters, library facilities, photos, placement on mailing lists, research assistance, statistics and analysis leaflets "which give historical background and list numbers of items examined along with findings." Publications include *The Foundation Bulletin; Color In Philately; The Foundations of*

Philately; *The Typographed Issues of the Confederate States*; *Philatelic Vocabulary in Five Languages*. **How to Contact:** Write. Responds to most inquiries immediately. "There is a fee for our expertizing service, depending on the catalogue or fair market value of the item. Some of our publications are free, some are not. A free listing is available. Advance appointments must be made for the use of our facilities or to speak to any of our curators or staff. Information gathered from us requires giving us a credit line." **Tips:** "We can (and do) refer people to what libraries or other sources are available for their specific request. Most important is to give us as much specific information as possible." Recent information request: "What were the mail routes from San Francisco to China in 1858?"; "When were the first airmail flights to Europe?"; "What is the value of a US stamp on an envelope dated 1847?"; "Where can I get current stamps from Ireland?"; "What types of scientific examination are used in examining stamps?"; "Where can I find records on the Pony Express?"

824• POSTCARD HISTORY SOCIETY
Box 3610, Baltimore MD 21214. Contact Person: Executive Secretary. **Description:** Society promoting the hobby of collecting old picture postcards. **Services:** Provides advisory, bibliographical, historical, how-to and referral information on old picture postcards. Offers annual reports, brochures/pamphlets, informational newsletters, placement on mailing lists and research assistance. Publications include quarterly newsletter. **How to Contact:** Write. Responds to most inquiries within a week. Include SASE. **Tips:** Recent information request: "Where can I obtain books or catalogs on old picture postcards?"

825• RAGGEDY ANN ANTIQUE DOLL AND TOY MUSEUM
171 Main St., Flemington NJ 08822. (201)782-1243. Contact Person: Owner. **Description:** "The museum provides guests with a look into the past—over 6,000 antique dolls and over 2,000 antique toys, all with cards telling what they are." **Services:** Provides historical and referral information on antique dolls, toys, games, music boxes, china, glass and furniture. Offers biographies, brochures/pamphlets and research assistance. Publications include *Encyclopedia of Dolls* and *Doll Castle News*. **How to Contact:** Visit. Contact owner for appointment. Responds to most inquiries immediately. Closed January; open weekends only in February and March; Wed.-Sun. 10 a.m.-5 p.m. from April 1-December 31. **Tips:** "Museum represents 50 years of research into antique dolls and their values."

826• RATHKAMP MATCHCOVER SOCIETY
1312 E. 215th Pl., Carson CA 90745. (213)834-9717. Contact Person: Secretary. **Description:** Collectors of matchbook covers. **Services:** Provides how-to information. Offers aid in arranging interviews and research assistance involving the collection of matchcovers. **How to Contact:** Write or call. Responds to most inquiries within a week.

827• REMINGTON GUN MUSEUM
Remington Arms Co., Inc., Ilion NY 13357. (315)894-9961. Contact Person: Curator. **Description:** "We are a firearms manufacturer with an in-plant gun museum." **Services:** Provides historical and technical data. Offers information searches. **How to Contact:** Write, call or visit. Responds to most inquiries within a month. **Tips:** "Writers are welcome to visit museum and talk about their area of research." If question is specific, phone call preferred. Recent information requests: "Many people call asking for the history of a particular firearm."

828• RINGLING BROS. AND BARNUM & BAILEY CIRCUS
3201 New Mexico Ave. NW, Washington DC 20016. (202)364-5000. Contact: Public Relations Department. **Description:** "World's largest and oldest (109 years old) circus. Popularly known as the Greatest Show on Earth." **Services:** Offers aid in arranging interviews, bibliograhies, biographies, statistics, clipping services, placement on mailing list, photos and press kits. **How to Contact:** Write or call. "Always better to write than call." Responds to most inquiries within a month. **Tips:** "We get a lot of requests for historical information."

829• JOHN AND MABLE RINGLING MUSEUM OF ART/RINGLING MUSEUM OF THE CIRCUS
Ringling Museums, Information Dept., Box 1838, 5401 Bayshore Rd., Sarasota FL 33578. (813)355-5101. Contact Person: Chief, Information Department. **Description:** "The

newly-renovated galleries of the Ringling Museum of Art house one of the largest collections of baroque art in the United States and a growing collection of contemporary art. The Museum of the Circus is one of two authentic circus museums in the country, and offers a brilliant collection of parade wagons, posters and circus memorabilia.'' **Services:** Offers aid in arranging interviews, annual reports, brochures/pamphlets, placement on mailing list, newsletter, photos and press kits. Publications include *Souvenir Book; Fifty Masterpieces in the Ringling Museum of Art;* and *Ringling Museum of the Circus.* **How to Contact:** Write, call or visit.

830• ROUGH AND TUMBLE ENGINEERS' HISTORICAL ASSOCIATION, INC.
Box 9, Kinzers PA 17535. (717)442-4249. Contact Person: Secretary. **Description:** Museum. "Our purpose is the restoration and preservation of antique equipment, primarily of the steam era." **Services:** Provides advisory, historical, how-to and referral information on antique equipment, primarily steam and farm related. Offers brochures/pamphlets, informational newsletters, placement on mailing lists and telephone reference services. **How to Contact:** Write, call or visit. Responds to most inquiries within a month. **Tips:** "Please allow enough time for an answer. Our association's work is all done by volunteers." Recent information request: "What's the value of a particular piece of equipment?"

831• SIX FLAGS, INC.
515 S. Figueroa St., Los Angeles CA 90071. (213)680-2375. Contact Person: Manager Of Corporate Communications. **Description:** "Six Flags owns/operates the following theme amusement parks: Six Flags Over Georgia (Atlanta), Six Flags Over Texas (Dallas/Fort Worth), Six Flags Over Mid-America (St. Louis), Astroworld (Houston), Magic Mountain (Los Angeles), and Six Flags Great Adventure (New Jersey). Six Flags also operates the Movieland Wax Museum (Southern California) and the Stars Hall of Fame (Orlando, Florida)." **Services:** Offers aid in arranging interviews, biographies, statistics, brochures/pamphlets, photos, press kits and historical information on theme parks, amusement park rides and attractions. **How to Contact:** Write or call. Responds to most inquiries within a week. "We have individual PR people at each of our parks. You may want to contact them if you want information on a specific park." **Tips:** Recent information request: "A children's magazine contacted us for information on our Southern California parks."

832• SOCIETY OF PHILATELIC AMERICANS, INC.
Box 30286, Cleveland OH 44130. (216)843-8607. Contact Person: Executive Secretary. **Description:** "As a hobby organization we disseminate knowledge about stamp collecting through a monthly magazine and provide other services related to the expertizing, selling and buying of stamps." **Services:** Provides advisory, historical and referral information on the "expertization of stamps." Offers annual reports, informational newsletters, research assistance, statistics and telephone reference services. Publications include monthly *SPA Journal.* **How to Contact:** Write. Responds to most inquiries immediately. **Tips:** Recent information requests: Cataloging of a specific stamp; identification as to whether a stamp is good or not (counterfeit); watermarks of printing paper.

833• STEIN COLLECTORS INTERNATIONAL
Box 463, Kingston NJ 08528. (201)329-2567. Contact Person: Executive Director. **Description:** Hobby group which collects beer steins and other antique drinking vessels; disseminates information about steins, etc., via publications, meetings and conventions. **Services:** Provides advisory, historical, how-to and technical information on antique beer steins and other drinking vessels. Offers aid in arranging interviews, informational newsletters, photos and research assistance. Publications include *Prosit*, quarterly magazine devoted entirely to beer steins, and related articles from other hobby magazines. **How to Contact:** Write. Responds to most inquiries within a week. **Tips:** "We cannot do extensive research; we offer background information, reprints, etc." Typical information request: "When were most beer steins manufactured; where, and who were the important manufacturers?"

834• SWIGART MUSEUM
Box 214, Museum Park, Huntington PA 16652. (814)643-0885 or 634-3000. Contact Person: Owner. **Description:** The purpose of the museum is "to preserve, renew and display the American antique automobile (classic and vintage) for the enjoyment of the private individual and groups. Research material is limited to the history and development of the American

car." **Services:** Offers statistics and photos. **How to Contact:** Write or call. Responds to most inquiries within a week. Charges for "the time spent in research and development of the topics." Charges up to $10/hour. "Topics must be researched by our staff. Materials are not open to the public." **Tips:** Recent information requests: Help in identifying old cars.

835• TOY MANUFACTURERS OF AMERICA
200 Fifth Ave., New York NY 10010. (212)675-1141. Contact Person: Public Information Manager. **Description:** "TMA is the trade association for domestic producers and importers of toys, games and holiday decorations. It is recognized as the authoritative voice of the US toy industry. TMA's membership includes approximately 245 toy makers which account for 90% of total sales. The association sponsors and manages the American Toy Fair, one of the world's largest toy trade shows and counsels members in such areas as marketing and sales, safety and quality control, credit and collection, distribution management, import/export trade, legal advice, public relations, statistics, consumer information, media relations and advertising guidelines." **Services:** Provides advisory, bibliographical, historical, referral, and trade information on various toy industry-related topics from advertising to video games. Offers brochures/pamphlets, photos, placement on Toy Fair invitational mailing lists (working press only), press kits, press releases, some research assistance and statistics. "We also provide a service for writers sent to our membership's public relations contacts called 'Publicity Opportunity Bulletins.' It is done about once a month. In it, we tell our members about a writer's plans for an upcoming feature and, to a great degree, our members do most of the work for the writer. The writer tells us the theme of the feature, information on particular items wanted, age groups, price ranges, etc., giving a deadline date for press materials to be sent and/or whether samples are needed for photography. Writers should have a lead time of 3-4 weeks (comfortably) in order to participate in this highly successful service." Publications include *Toy Industry Fact Book*; *The ABC's of Toys & Play*, consumer information pamphlet on safety and selection tips. **How to Contact:** Write or call. Responds to most inquiries within a week. **Tips:** "We maintain an article file from which we can cull much information for writers. Please try to be specific about information needed and do not contact us at the last minute, when our help would be restricted due to limited staff. Tell us where and when the article will be published."

836• UNICORNS UNANIMOUS
248 N. Larchmont Blvd., Los Angeles CA 90004. (213)464-5000. Contact Person: Executive Officer. **Description:** Organization serves members interested in unicorns, unicorn lore and collecting unicorns. "We are also a retail store with thousands of collectible fantasy items, mainly unicorns." **Services:** Provides advisory, bibliographical and historical information on unicorns, dragons, Pegasus and wizards. Offers brochures/pamphlets, informational newsletters, placement on mailing lists and research assistance. Publications include occasional newsletters. **How to Contact:** Write. Responds to most inquiries within a week. Charges $12.50/year membership.

837• UNITED STATES TRIVIA ASSOCIATION, LTD.
Box 5213, Lincoln NE 68505. (402)476-3586. Contact Person: Editor/Publisher, *Trivia Unlimited*. **Description:** "Our purpose is to promote trivia and trivia-related projects: National Trivia Hall of Fame, *Trivia Unlimited* magazine." **Services:** Provides information in the field of trivia: television, radio, movies, music, sports, comic books. Offers informational newsletters, research assistance and telephone reference services. Publications include *Trivia Unlimited* magazine (monthly). **How to Contact:** Write or call. Responds to most inquiries immediately. "Writers/researchers using our services must subscribe to the magazine ($12/year)." **Tips:** Recent information request: "Had anyone ever refused an Oscar prior to George C. Scott in 1971?"

838• WORLD AIRLINE HOBBY CLUB
3381 Apple Tree Lane, Erlanger KY 41018. (606)342-9039. Contact Person: President. **Description:** "Individuals interested in the collecting and study of airline memorabilia and history." **Services:** Provides historical, how-to and referral information on airline and airliner history and various types of airline memorabilia. Publications include *The Captain's Log*, quarterly magazine. **How to Contact:** Write. Responds to most inquiries within a week. Charges for any costs the club incurs in obtaining information requested. **Tips:** "We are not technically or politically involved with the airlines or government. We can help those researching airline/airliner history

through articles already published in our quarterly magazine, *The Captain's Log* and via other means.''

839• WORLD LEISURE AND RECREATION ASSOCIATION
345 E. 46th St., New York NY 10017. (212)697-8783. Contact Person: Executive Director. **Description:** ''Our purpose is to promote awareness of the importance leisure and recreation play in social and individual development.'' **Services:** Provides advisory, bibliographical, interpretative, referral and technical information on leisure, recreation, tourism, play, parks. Offers aid in arranging interviews, brochures/pamphlets, computerized information searches, informational newsletters and library facilities. **How to Contact:** Write. Responds to most inquiries immediately. ''Services for members only—membership is open.''

840• WORLD'S FAIR COLLECTORS SOCIETY, INC.
148 Poplar St., Garden City NY 11530. (516)741-4884. Contact Person: President. **Description:** Individuals interested in preserving the heritage of the various world expositions in America and abroad; collects literature, postcards, spoons, medals, souvenirs; concerned with historical, intellectual and administrative aspects of the expositions as well. **Services:** Provides information on all World's Fairs—past, present, and future. Offers brochures/pamphlets, informational newsletters, library facilities and telephone reference services. Publications include *Fair News*, bimonthly bulletin, $8/year; and several hundred publications on World's Fairs in the library. **How to Contact:** Write. Responds to most inquiries within a month. Enclose SASE for reply. Charges $15/hour for in-depth research. **Tips:** Recent information requests: Value of various collectible items; listing of new products introduced at World's Fairs.

SECTION · FIFTEEN

HOUSE AND HOME

There is much virtue in a window. It is to a human being as a frame is to a painting, as a proscenium to a play, as "form" to literature. It strongly defines its content.

—Max Beerbohm

House and Home resources reflect the areas of housing and shelter, construction, real estate, home products and furnishings and home improvement.

Cooking-related sources are listed in the Farming and Food category; architecture information is available in The Arts section. Consult the subject index under *design* for references to interior design.

Bibliography

Aronson, Joseph, ed. *The Encyclopedia of Furniture*. 3d ed. New York: Crown Publishers, 1965.

Back to Basics: How to Learn & Enjoy Traditional American Skills. Pleasantville, NY: Reader's Digest Association, 1981. (How-to activities for in and around the home)

Brooks, Hugh, ed. *Illustrated Encyclopedic Dictionary of Building and Construction Terms*. Englewood Cliffs, NJ: Prentice-Hall, 1975.

Brownstone, David M. and Irene M. Franck. *The VNR Real Estate Dictionary*. New York: Van Nostrand Reinhold, 1981.

Brushwell, William, ed. *Painting & Decorating Encyclopedia*. South Holland, IL: Goodheart Willcox Co., 1982.

Conran, Terence. *The Home Book*. New York: Crown Publishers, 1982. (Also see *The Bed & Bath Book*, *The Kitchen Book*, etc.) (Interior design)

Heyn, Ernest and Herbert Shuldiner. *Popular Science Book of Gadgets: Ingenious Devices for the Home*. New York: Crown, 1981.

Horbostel, Caleb, ed. *Construction Materials: Types, Uses and Applications*. New York: John Wiley & Sons, 1978.

The Household Handbook: Answers & Solutions You Need to Know. Deephaven, MN: Meadowbrook Press, 1981.

Popular Science Complete Manual of Home Repair. New York: Beekman House, 1981.

The Ultimate Householder's Book. Edited by Consumer Guide. New York: A&W Publications, Inc., 1982. (Thousands of time and money-saving tips for use around the house)

841• AMERICAN OLEAN TILE COMPANY
1000 Cannon Ave., Lansdale PA 19446. (215)855-1111. Contact Person: Director, Public Relations. **Description:** "American Olean Tile Company is the largest producer of ceramic tile in the US. We have eight manufacturing plants across the country and make a wide variety of ceramic tile. We work closely with a number of magazines and supply photographic material, resource information and articles." **Services:** Provides how-to, technical and trade information on ceramic tile. Offers brochures/pamphlets, photos and press kits. **How to Contact:** Write or call. Responds to most inquiries within a week. "We like to approve copy for accuracy. I would suggest that a telephone conversation would be more helpful than a letter, because we could have a better exchange of material needed and services available." **Tips:** Recent information requests: "What are the basic kinds of ceramic tile?"; "How can the beauty of ceramic tile be maintained?"

842• AMERICAN STANDARD HOMES CORPORATION
700 Commerce Ct., Box 4908, Martinsville VA 24112. (703)638-3991. Contact Person: Public Relations Director. **Description:** "We manufacture preassembled homes and spaces in six areas: small two-bedroom homes; econo-line two- and three-bedroom homes; two- three- and four-bedroom homes; vacation and second homes; commercial line-office, restaurants, motels, clinics, etc.; and multifamily housing, duplexes, condominiums, townhouses and apartments. A

seventh area of our production would be in our ease at working with 'specials'—in other words, our availability to work, design and manufacture some home outside of our standard line." **Services:** Offers brochures/pamphlets and newsletter. **How to Contact:** "Write, call or arrange for an office visit and tour of our manufacturing plant. We refer written inquiries to the appropriate sales representative; people who write us can expect a reply within 10 days." **Tips:** Recent information request: "What is panelized housing?"

843• AMERICAN WOOD COUNCIL
1619 Massachusetts Ave. NW, Suite 500, Washington DC 20036. (202)265-7766. Contact Person: Vice President of Marketing. **Description:** "The council promotes the use of wood products in new single-family houses built in metropolitan areas." **Services:** Offers photos. **How to Contact:** Write or call. Responds to most inquiries within a month. **Tips:** "Be specific and cite the source of your information." Recent information requests: Many questions on the All-Weather Wood Foundation and the Plen-Wood System.

844• APARTMENT OWNERS-MANAGERS ASSOCIATION OF AMERICA (AOMA)
65 Cherry Plaza, Box 238, Watertown CT 06795. (203)274-2589. Contact Person: President. **Description:** Organization for apartment construction and management. **Services:** Provides information on apartment management—everyday duties of a manager, pool maintenance, security, zoning problems, etc. Offers brochures/pamphlets. Publications include descriptions of association services. **How to Contact:** Prefers written inquiries. Responds to most inquiries within 2 weeks.

845• ASSOCIATION OF HOME APPLIANCE MANUFACTURERS
20 N. Wacker Dr., Chicago IL 60606. (312)984-5818. Contact Person: Director of Public and Consumer Relations. **Description:** The AHAM "promotes the general welfare of the appliance industry and the homemaking public. It represents the manufacturers of household appliances and is independent of fuel sources and other non-appliance interests." **Services:** Provides historical, referral and trade information (all generic) on appliance purchase, use, care and maintenance (both major and portable home appliances). Offers aid in arranging interviews, brochures/pamphlets, educational materials, informational newsletters, placement on mailing lists and statistics. Publications include certification directories, safety and appliance energy conservation brochures and other consumer information. **How to Contact:** Write. Responds to most inquiries within a month. Charges for most publications. **Tips:** "Give us enough time to send information rather than calling the day of your deadline." Recent information request: "Are today's appliances more energy efficient than those of ten years ago?"

846• CARDINAL INDUSTRIES
2040 S. Hamilton, Columbus OH 43227. (614)861-3211. Contact Person: Vice President of Communications. **Description:** "The nation's largest manufacturer of multifamily dwellings and motels in the United States; the firm also constructs and manages all aspects regarding the construction of apartment or motel projects." **Services:** Offers aid in arranging interviews, annual reports, brochures/pamphlets, placement on mailing list, statistics, newsletter, photos and press kits. **How to Contact:** Write or call. Responds to most inquiries within a week. **Tips:** "Be very precise. It's very expensive to send out all of our publications."

847• CARPET AND RUG INSTITUTE
Box 2048, Dalton GA 30720. (404)278-3176. Contact Person: Director of Consumer Affairs. **Description:** "Trade association of carpet and rug manufacturers and those allied industries supplying services and products to the industry." **Services:** Provides advisory, analytical, how-to, referral and trade information covering economics and history of the industry, as well as technical data. Offers annual reports, statistics, brochures/pamphlets and press kits. Publications include information to help consumers with carpet purchases and carpet care. **How to Contact:** Write or call. Responds to most inquiries within a week. "We like to read writers' rough copies and to have our association given credit." **Tips:** "We can answer any question related to carpets and rugs."

848• CENTURY 21
18872 MacArthur Blvd., Irvine CA 92715. (714)752-7521. Contact Person: Vice President/Marketing. **Description:** "We provide services to real estate brokers who are

independently owned and franchised to operate under the name 'Century 21.' Our system includes about 7,000 offices in the US and Canada.'' **Services:** Provides information covering business, economics, how-to, industry, law, new products, politics and technical data. Offers aid in arranging interviews, annual reports, bibliographies, biographies, statistics, brochures/pamphlets, information searches, placement on mailing list, photos and press kits. Publications include *Real Estate Investment Journal* (bimonthly). **How to Contact:** Write.

849• COATS AND CLARK, INC.
225 W. 34th St., New York NY 10122. (212)736-5353. Contact: Public Relations. **Description:** ''We are a privately-owned company that manufactures thread, yarn and zippers.'' **Services:** Provides information on the business and new products. Offers aid in arranging interviews, bibliographies, biographies, brochures/pamphlets, information searches, placement on mailing list, photos and press kits. Publications available. **How to Contact:** Write. Responds to most inquiries within a week.

850• ELECTRONIC REALTY ASSOCIATES (ERA)
Box 2974, Shawnee Mission KS 66201. (800)255-6623. In Kansas (913)341-8400. Contact Person: Public Affairs Director. **Description:** ''We are the second-largest real estate franchise and America's largest marketer of home warranty programs. We operate through 3,500 offices in 50 states and 5 foreign countries. We do not buy or sell properties. All offices are independently owned. We are also the exclusive sponsor of the Muscular Dystrophy Association for the entire real estate industry.'' **Services:** Provides information on business, economics, industry, law, nature, politics, self-help and travel. Offers aid in arranging interviews, bibliographies, biographies, statistics, brochures/pamphlets, information searches, placement on mailing list, newsletter, photos and audiovisual materials. Publications include *ERA News* (bimonthly). **How to Contact:** Write or call. Responds to most inquiries within a week. **Tips:** ''Our press kits contain some story ideas on moving, etc. They could be a great source of ideas on the industry.'' Researchers may also contact Fleishman-Hillard, Kansas City MO. (816)474-9407.

851• ESCAPEE CLUB FOR FULL-TIME ROVERS
Box 2870-MCCA, Estes Park CO 80517. Contact Person: Director. **Description:** ''We provide advice and help to those who want to learn about living and traveling full time in an RV (recreational vehicle) home on wheels.'' **Services:** Provides advisory, how-to, referral, technical and trade information on numerous subjects related to RV living. Offers brochures/pamphlets, informational newsletters and statistics (annual report). Publications include bimonthly 34-page newsletter; directory of RV sources and information; booklets and pamphlets on RV living and how-to books such as *Home Is Where You Park It* and *Survival of the Snowbirds*. **How to Contact:** Write. Responds to most inquiries within a week. ''Staff limitations require that responses will usually be with existing booklets and pamphlets. We are not set up to offer individual research or reference services. If writers are seriously interested in the full-time RV lifestyle, we will be happy to send our pamphlets, booklets and informational directory for postage charge only.'' Charges for books (10% discount) and bimonthly newsletter. **Tips:** ''We are a specialized field—FULL TIME RV Living—but in this specialized field we are the best source of material and have access to all of the top authorities in our field. Our greatest help to writers/researchers is our *Directory of RV Informational Sources* which we will send for $1 in cash or postage.'' Recent information requests: ''How does the RV traveler handle mail; cashing checks that are out of state; buy auto licenses; get a doctor; pay taxes; provide a way for family to reach him when an emergency arises?''

852• FEATHER AND DOWN ASSOCIATION
4441 Auburn Blvd., Suite O, Sacramento CA 95841. (916)481-3812. Contact Person: Executive Director. **Description:** The association's purpose is ''to publicize and promote feather and down products, such as pillows, comforters, sleeping bags, garments and furniture filled with feathers and down.'' **Services:** Provides advisory, analytical, how-to, referral, technical and trade information on feather and down. Offers statistics, photos and press kits. **How to Contact:** Write or call. Responds to most inquiries within a week. **Tips:** Recent information request: Production statistics.

853• FEDERATION OF MOBILE HOME OWNERS OF FLORIDA, INC.
4020 Portsmouth Rd., Largo FL 33541. Contact Person: Executive Director. **Description:** ''Our

organization enables mobile home owners to receive fair treatment through our legislative efforts, information service and volunteer officer network." **Services:** Provides advisory, referral and trade information on mobile home living in Florida. Offers informational newsletters. Publications include *FMO News*. **How to Contact:** Write. Responds to most inquiries immediately. Charges for information if significant time, effort is spent to get it. **Tips:** "Mobile homes account for over 10% of all housing in the state of Florida and the growth of the mobile home lifestyle is accelerating."

854• FOUNDATION OF THE WALL AND CEILING INDUSTRY
25 K St. NE, Washington DC 20002. (202)783-2924. Contact Person: Librarian. **Description:** "Our purpose is to support and expand the industry's educational and research activities; to provide industry specifications, technical publications and reports, manufacturers' catalogs, books, periodicals and government reports." **Services:** Provides advisory, analytical, bibliographical, historical, how-to, interpretative, referral, technical and trade information on building codes; asbestos abatement; lien and contract law; estimating; Portland cement; stucco; walls and ceilings; fire resistant/fire proof materials; ASTM and CSI Standards—all areas as they apply to the wall and ceiling industry. Offers brochures/pamphlets, informational newsletters, library facilities, photos, placement on mailing lists, research assistance and telephone reference services. Publications include *Construction Dimensions* (monthly); *Who's Who in the Wall & Ceiling Industry*; *Buyer's Guide*; and many technical bulletins as applied to the industry. **How to Contact:** Write or call. Responds to most inquiries immediately. Charges for some services. **Tips:** Recent information request: Plastering techniques in Old Town San Juan.

855• THE GALLERY OF HOMES, INC.
1001 International Blvd., Atlanta GA 30354. (404)768-2460. Contact Person: Advertising Manager. **Description:** "The Gallery of Homes is a real estate franchising organization." **Services:** Provides historical and trade information about the Gallery of Homes and real estate franchising as well as referrals to experts reporting on the trends of commercial and residential real estate sales, interest rates, laws, etc. Offers aid in arranging interviews, bibliographies, biographies, statistics, brochures/pamphlets, clipping services, information searches, placement on mailing list and newsletter. Publications include *Keynote* (monthly). **How to Contact:** Write or call. Responds to most inquiries within a week. "A written request must be submitted for approval by Gallery's Legal Department." **Tips:** "Follow a written request with a phone call. When calling or writing to any company for research information, leave behind an address or phone number which will verify the legitimacy of your request. Be patient, but persistent." Recent information request: Samples of Gallery's national and local advertising for a student author working on a book concerning real estate advertising.

856• GEORGIA-PACIFIC CORPORATION
c/o Gross & Associates, 592 Fifth Ave., New York NY 10036. Contact Person: Account Executive. **Description:** "Georgia-Pacific, headquartered in Atlanta, manufactures and distributes a wide variety of building products—lumber, plywood, sidings, gypsum products, prefinished panelings, hardboard, particleboard, metal products, insulation, roofing and doors." **Services:** Provides advisory and how-to information on building products, and technical data. Offers brochures/pamphlets, placement on mailing list, photos, annual reports, aid in arranging interviews, research assistance and statistics. **How to Contact:** Write. Responds to most inquiries immediately.

857• GLIDDEN COATINGS AND RESINS
Division of SCM Corp., 900 Union Commerce Bldg., Cleveland OH 44115. (216)344-8140. Contact Person: Manager, Public Relations. **Description:** "Glidden manufactures and markets a wide range of coatings which are used by do-it-yourselfers, painting contractors, plant maintenance engineers, and original equipment manufacturers. Coatings are applied on residential, commercial, industrial and institutional properties, as well as yachts and other boating vehicles. All types of coatings are sold: alkyds, epoxies, latex, oil, polyurethane, wood stains, etc. Our coatings technologies for original equipment manufacturers include: powder coatings, water-borne coatings, electrocoating, high solids, and conventional solvent-borne coatings. Literature and data sheets are available upon request for the majority of products." **Services:** Provides analytical, how-to and trade information on coatings for residential, commercial, institutional and industrial use. Offers SCM annual reports, brochures/pamphlets and placement on mail-

ing list. **How to Contact:** Write or call. Responds to most inquiries within a week. "Information used which is obtained from Glidden must be attributed to Glidden Coatings & Resins, Division of SCM Corporation, and in some cases the Glidden specialist must be identified." **Tips:** "Be prepared to be specific about what your needs are, what use you are planning for the information, and how you plan to give Glidden credit as a source of the material. Recent information request: What is Insul-Aid® and how does it help to protect the structure of a home?"

858• HOME ECONOMICS READING SERVICE, INC.
1341 G St. NW, Washington DC 20005. (202)347-4763. Contact Person: President. **Description:** "We can make available information from 1,350 daily metropolitan newspapers on homemaking interests and publicity." **Services:** Provides advisory and analytical information on food, household equipment, home furnishings and styles. **How to Contact:** Write or call. Responds to most inquiries immediately. Charges a monthly rate plus a per-clipping fee.

859• HOMEMAKERS' EQUAL RIGHTS ASSOCIATION (HERA)
48 Rollingwood Dr., Voorhees NJ 08043. (609)783-6102. Contact Person: Co-Director. **Description:** HERA works "to raise the legal and social status of homemakers and to change inequitable laws that govern the married woman." **Services:** Provides advisory, historical and interpretive information. Offers brochures/pamphlets, informational newsletters, press kits, research assistance and statistics. **How to Contact:** Write. Responds to most inquiries within a week.

860• HUD USER
Box 280, Germantown MD 20874. (301)251-5154. Contact Person: Project Manager. **Description:** Government contract providing information retrieval and access to Department of Housing and Urban Development-sponsored research results. **Services:** Provides bibliographical and referral information on housing and development. Offers computerized information searches, library facilities, placement on mailing lists and telephone reference services. **How to Contact:** Write or call. Responds to most inquiries within a week. Charges $50/custom data base searches; $5/standard searches; prices vary for documents. **Tips:** "Be specific." Recent information request: "What information is available on the construction of affordable housing?"

861• IMPERIAL KNIFE
c/o Ruth Morrison Associates, 509 Madison Ave., New York NY 10022. (212)838-9221. Contact Person: Account Executive. **Description:** Cutlery manufacturer (both kitchen and sports knives). **Services:** Provides how-to, technical and trade information on knife care; maintenance; kitchen cutting and outdoor/hunting chores; trade information for retailers. Offers brochures/pamphlets, photos and press kits. **How to Contact:** Write or call. Responds to most inquiries immediately. **Tips:** Recent information request: "If one were to set up 'housekeeping,' what are the best basic knives to purchase and why?"

862• INTERNATIONAL MASONRY INSTITUTE
Market Development Program, 823 15th St. NW, Suite 1001, Washington DC 20005. (202)783-3908. Contact Person: Publicist or Director of Engineering. **Description:** "We provide information about the use of masonry (brick, concrete masonry, tile, stone, marble, terrazzo) in both residential and non-residential building, and promote masonry construction by union craftsmen and contractors." **Services:** Provides advisory, historical, technical and trade information on loadbearing construction, passive solar, restoration of buildings, fireplaces, architecture, all-weather construction, craftsmanship in construction and masonry materials. Offers annual reports, brochures/pamphlets, photos, placement on mailing lists, press kits and statistics. Publications include brochures on energy efficiency with masonry; union craftsmen and contractors and all-weather construction; press releases on masonry fireplaces, passive solar, glass block, etc. **How to Contact:** Write. Responds to most inquiries within a week. **Tips:** Recent information requests: "What are the principles at work in a passive solar home built with masonry?"; "What types of masonry fireplaces are available today to achieve energy efficiency?"; "What are the advantages of construction by union craftsmen and contractors?"

863• ITALIAN TILE CENTER
c/o The Siesel Co., 845 Third Ave., New York NY 10022. (212)759-6500. Contact Person:

Account Executive. **Description:** "The Italian Tile Center is an information center providing material to broaden public understanding and awareness of Italian ceramic tile and to increase usage of tile in the US." **Services:** Provides how-to, referral, technical and trade information. Offers brochures/pamphlets, informational newsletters, photos, placement on mailing lists, press kits and films. Publications include booklets on tile installation, tile applications. **How to Contact:** Write or call. Responds to most inquiries immediately. **Tips:** Recent information requests: Types and manufacturers' products available in US; properties of Italian ceramic tile.

864• KNIFEMAKERS GUILD
401 W. 700 South, Richfield UT 84701. (801)896-5319. Contact Person: Director. **Description:** Organization whose objectives are to promote knives and knifemakers, assist those in the industry and encourage professional business practices. **Services:** Offers brochures/pamphlets, informational newsletters and video tape of the organization. **How to Contact:** Write, call or visit. Responds to most inquiries within a week. **Tips:** "Study as much material as possible about knives; not just contemporary pieces, but the works of the old masters. Attend as many knife shows as possible; ask questions and observe the knives being displayed." Recent information request: "What do you see as the future trend in knifemaking?"

865• LOAN-A-HOME
18 Darwood Place, Mt. Vernon NY 10553. Contact Person: Proprietor. **Description:** "We are a housing service for academic families going on sabbatical; also a business and retirement community for those looking for long-term (4 months minimum, excluding July and August) housing." **Services:** Provides information on housing available worldwide. Offers brochures/pamphlets and directories and supplements. **How to Contact:** Write. Responds to most inquiries within a week. Charges for directories and supplements. **Tips:** Recent information request: "I have a home available in Washington DC for a certain academic year, and I'm looking for housing in Paris. What's available?"

866• THE MAYTAG COMPANY
403 W. 4th St. N., Newton IA 50208. Contact Person: Public Information Specialist. **Description:** Manufacturer of laundry and kitchen appliances. **Services:** Offers b&w and color photos and color transparencies of home laundry settings; kitchens; anything in the area of laundry appliances, laundering, kitchen appliances, use of dishwashers, disposers, microwave ovens, gas and electric ranges; laundering procedures. Also available are industrial shots, in-factory assembly line photos. **How to Contact:** Write. Responds to most inquiries immediately. Credit line and return of color transparencies required.

867• NATIONAL ASSOCIATION OF HOUSING COOPERATIVES
2501 M St. NW, Washington DC 20037. (202)887-0706. Contact Person: Executive Director. **Description:** "We are a nonprofit, tax-exempt organization of more than 425 cooperatives and 9 regional associations representing more than 100,000 families living in cooperative housing communities across the United States. Our major goals are to educate people about the advantages of housing co-ops, and to improve and make more efficient the organization and operation of housing cooperatives, especially those whose members are primarily low-, moderate- and middle-income families. We publish the monthly *Cooperative Housing Bulletin*, books, pamphlets and educational materials. We also sponsor conferences, seminars, education programs, research services and government relations programs. Cooperatives are an excellent method of removing housing from the speculative market, of offering people control over where and how they live. Co-ops are not condominiums." **Services:** Offers bibliographies, brochures/pamphlets, statistics, newsletter and photos. Publications available. **How to Contact:** Write or call. Responds to most inquiries immediately. Charges for membership and publications. **Tips:** "We have a general information packet. We don't get into high level research." Recent information request: A list of cooperatives throughout the country.

868• NATIONAL ASSOCIATION OF SOLAR CONTRACTORS (NASC)
236 Massachusetts Ave. NE, # 610, Washington DC 20002. (202)543-8869. Contact Person: Media Specialist. **Description:** "Not-for-profit trade association for installers and manufacturers of solar equipment; involved in national contractor referral, lobbying, technical referral, and product education." **Services:** Provides advisory, how-to, referral, technical and trade information on passive/active solar (including design, installation and servicing of equipment) and

all types of renewable energy technology. Offers aid in arranging interviews and photos ("to some extent"). Publications include *Solar Energy: An Installer's Guide to Domestic Hot Water*; *NASC News* (newsletter). **How to Contact:** Call. Responds to most inquiries within a week. **Tips:** "Know the basics of solar before contacting NASC. Required reading: *Passive Solar Energy Book*, by Edward Mazria; get a subscription to *Solar Age* magazine." Recent information request: "What standards exist to insure a homeowner he has hired a reliable solar contractor?"

869• THE NATIONAL HOUSING PARTNERSHIP
1133 15th St. NW, Washington DC 20005. (202)857-5700. Contact Person: Director of Corporate Affairs. **Description:** "The largest private producer in the nation of housing for families of low and moderate income, The National Housing Partnership (NHP) enters into partnerships with builders, developers, and nonprofit and community groups at local levels for the construction of housing, either multifamily rental or single-family sales. Providing equal capital and joint venture funds, NHP supplies also guidance and assistance from its staff of professionals during the planning and building stages of a project, plus management responsibility upon completion. In its nationwide operations, NHP fulfills the objective of its Congressional charter by stimulating the production by private enterprise of low and moderate income housing and by assisting the building industry in general." **Services:** Provides referral and technical information on operations of The National Housing Partnership. Offers annual reports, brochures/pamphlets, placement on mailing list and photos. Publications available. **How to Contact:** Write. Responds to most inquiries within a month. **Tips:** "Our information pertains primarily to the operations of The National Housing Partnership, and we are not a source for government statistics." Recent information request: "What is The National Housing Partnership and how does it operate?"

870• THE NATIONAL PAINT AND COATINGS ASSOCIATION
1500 Rhode Island Ave. NW, Washington DC 20005. (202)462-6272. Contact Person: Associate Director, Product Promotion. **Description:** "We represent paint and coatings manufacturers." **Services:** Provides advisory, how-to, referral and technical information on interior and exterior decorating with paint (color trends and selection, special techniques); how-to directions; maintenance and problem solving advice. Offers brochures/pamphlets, information searches, placement on mailing list, photos, fact sheets on various products or techniques, and articles for use as background material. "All of our material deals with paint and coatings in generic terms; we never mention company names or product trade names in our material." Publications list is available. **How to Contact:** Write or call. Responds to most inquiries immediately. "Give credit lines for photos and for magazine articles we help with; also copies of published articles." **Tips:** Recent information request: "Suggest innovative uses of paints and stains and supply before and after photos."

871• NATIONAL RURAL HOUSING COALITION
1016 16th St. NW, # 8G, Washington DC 20036. (202)775-0046. Contact Persons: Legislative Director or Legislative Analyst. **Description:** "Nonprofit organization which provides legislative information and advocacy; coordinates a network of state rural housing coalitions; advocates at the national level for legislation supporting federal housing and community development." **Services:** Provides analytical, interpretive and referral information covering federal housing and community development programs which serve low income people in small towns and rural areas. Offers brochures/pamphlets, informational newsletters and telephone reference services. "For information on legislation as it develops, we can provide verbal explanations (on the phone or in person) and background materials on specific pieces of legislation." Publications include *Congressional Round-Up* (monthly when Congress is in session, $100/year for organizations; $25/year for individuals); *Legislative Updates* (weekly when Congress is in session, $250/year). **How To Contact:** Write or call. Charges for publications. **Tips:** Recent information request: Statistics and referrals on the role of women in tenant organizing.

872• NICHOLS-KUSAN, INC.
c/o Sumner Rider & Associates, Inc., 355 Lexington Ave., New York NY 10017. (212)661-5300. Contact Person: Account Supervisor. **Description:** Manufacturer of Old Jacksonville and American Pride ceiling fans. Conducts market and technical studies on ceiling fans and their energy-saving benefits. **Services:** Provides advisory, analytical, historical, how-to, interpretive, referral, technical and trade information on all aspects of ceiling fans. Offers aid in arranging interviews, brochures/pamphlets, photos, placement on mailing lists, press kits,

research assistance and statistics. **How to Contact:** Write or call. Responds to most inquiries immediately.

873• PRIVATE ISLANDS UNLIMITED
17538 Tulsa St., Granada Hills CA 91344. (213)360-8683. Contact Person: Owner. **Description:** "We offer a clearinghouse for information regarding islands and island properties for sale throughout the world for the purpose of bringing sellers and buyers together." **Services:** Provides advisory, interpretative and trade information on island properties. Offers brochures/pamphlets, informational newsletters and placement on mailing lists. **How to Contact:** Write or call. Responds to most inquiries within a week. "Island inventory and supplements are available at $15/year. Supplemental information available at low or no cost." **Tips:** "We are glad to offer advisory and other informational services to writers." Recent information requests: Questions regarding purchase or sale of an island property, typical purchasers and their end uses for such properties and range of prices and locations.

874• THE PROCTER AND GAMBLE COMPANY
301 E. 6th St., Box 599, Cincinnati OH 45201. (513)562-1100, 562-5311. Contact (for general information requests): Information Services Assistant. Contact (562-4185 for media queries): Manager of Corporate Media Relations. **Description:** "Procter and Gamble is primarily a manufacturer and distributor of household and industrial cleaning products sold throughout the US and abroad. P&G also markets a variety of products for business and industry, including cellulose pulp, industrial chemicals, industrial cleaning products and industrial food products." **Services:** Provides information on marketing, corporate responsibility, advertising and company history. Offers annual reports, brochures/pamphlets, photos and speeches. **How to Contact:** Write or call. "A written request is preferable." Responds to most inquiries within a month. Contact Consumer Services Department for bulletins on specific brands, pricing, how a brand is named, etc.

875• SHARED HOUSING RESOURCE CENTER, INC.
6344 Greene St., Philadelphia PA 19144. (215)848-1220. Contact Person: Director of Educational Projects. **Description:** "A national nonprofit organization that promotes shared housing options through education, research, networking, technical assistance and public policy analysis." **Services:** Provides advisory, analytical, bibliographical, historical, how-to, interpretative, referral and technical information. Offers informational newsletters, library facilities, placement on mailing lists, research assistance and statistics. Publications include *Shared Housing Quarterly; Pilot Study of 21 Shared Housing Residences; National Policy Workshop on Shared Housing Report.* **How to Contact:** Write or call. Responds to most inquiries within a month. Charges for services.

876• SHELTERFORCE/NATIONAL TENANTS UNION
380 Main St., East Orange NJ 07018. (201)678-6778. Contact Person: Information Officer. **Description:** SHELTERFORCE community legal education project runs training programs and produces video and other media presentations. NTU is the national network of tenant associations. **Services:** Provides advisory, analytical, how-to, referral and technical information on housing, landlord-tenant law, organizing, community activity, media, etc. Offers aid in arranging interviews, brochures/pamphlets, informational newsletters and statistics. Publications include *Shelterforce*, quarterly nationwide housing newspaper that focuses on tenants' rights and public policy. **How to Contact:** Write. Responds to most inquiries within a week. Charges $8/6 issues of *Shelterforce*; information and advice on tenants' rights given to subscribers. Press contacts available. **Tips:** "In the area of housing, too often the views of housing consumers—especially tenants—are neglected. We can help give a tenants' movement viewpoint on the facts and on policy options." Recent information requests: "What current laws directly affect rental housing?"; "What are the names of tenant and housing groups in other parts of the US?"

877• THE SINGER COMPANY
8 Stamford Forum, Box 10151, Stamford CT 06940. Contact Person: Manager, Corporate Communications. **Description:** "The Singer Company develops and produces aerospace and other high-technology systems for government and industry, and manufactures or markets sewing and consumer durable products in the United States and approximately 100 other nations." **Services:** Provides historical information and specific and current data on corporate

developments. Offers aid in arranging interviews, annual reports, brochures/pamphlets, statistics and press kits. **How to Contact:** Write. Responds to most inquiries within a week.

878• THE SOAP AND DETERGENT ASSOCIATION
475 Park Ave. S., New York NY 10016. (212)725-1262. Contact Person: Assistant Public Affairs Director. **Description:** "The Soap and Detergent Association (SDA) is a national trade group representing the manufacturers of well over 90% of the soap and detergents made in the US. Member companies include producers of consumer and industrial cleaning products, raw materials suppliers and producers of fatty acid and glycerine." **Services:** Provides historical, how-to, referral, technical and general trade information on the industry; as well as "generic consumer and industrial/institutional information relating to cleanliness and washing/cleaning products; and statistical data (mostly from government or other public sources)." Offers statistics and brochures/pamphlets. Publications list available. **How to Contact:** Write or call. Responds to most inquiries immediately. Charges for *some* brochures and informational materials. **Tips:** "The information we offer is generic. Information about trade name products and specific companies is not compiled."

879• UNITED FARM AGENCY, INC.
612 W. 47th St., Kansas City MO 64112. (816)753-4212. Contact Person: Director of Corporate Information. **Description:** "We market farms, ranches, town and country homes; recreational, business and commercial real estate in 46 states through 550 sales offices and customer service centers in several cities. Except for business and commercial properties, our activities are mainly in rural communities." **Services:** Provides advisory, analytical, bibliographical, historical, how-to, interpretative, referral, technical and trade information on real estate sales, primarily in rural areas. Offers aid in arranging interviews, biographies, statistics, brochures/pamphlets, placement on mailing list and press kits. Publications include "our seasonal catalog, published three times a year to provide an idea of what is selling and where." **How to Contact:** Write or call. Responds to most inquiries immediately. "We will assist in researching articles pertaining to our business and will provide other leads for related information. We'd appreciate receiving as much advance notice as possible. Not all information is readily available, and special computer programs may have to be written to obtain some data." **Tips:** "Be as specific as possible." Recent information requests: "What are current trends in rural real estate?"; "What's selling and what's most in demand?"

880• UPHOLSTERED FURNITURE ACTION COUNCIL (UFAC)
Box 2436, High Point NC 27261. (919)885-5065. Contact Person: Program Director. **Description:** The council's major task is "to research, conduct and publicize a program which will reduce the hazard of cigarette ignition of upholstered furniture." **Services:** Provides historical, technical and trade information including technical advice and instruction to furniture manufacturers and suppliers. Offers aid in arranging interviews, brochures/pamphlets, informational newsletters, press kits, research assistance and statistics. Publications include *Reducing the Hazard*; *Directory of Supply Resources*; *Honor Roll of Participating Companies*. **How to Contact:** Write or call. Responds to most inquiries within a week. **Tips:** Recent information request: "What chemical treatments are required for a furniture manufacturer to participate in your program?"

881• VINYL SIDING INSTITUTE
c/o Sumner Rider & Associates, Inc., 355 Lexington Ave., New York NY 10017. (212)661-5300. Contact Person: Account Supervisor. **Description:** "The Vinyl Siding Institute is a national trade association whose basic objective is to promote new technology and increase the vinyl siding market." **Services:** Provides advisory, analytical, bibliographical, historical, how-to, interpretative, referral, technical and trade information on "anything related to the vinyl siding industry." Offers aid in arranging interviews, brochures/pamphlets, photos, placement on mailing lists, press kits and research assistance. Publications include *What Homeowners Want to Know About Solid Vinyl Siding*; *Cleaning of Vinyl Siding*; *Rigid Vinyl Siding Application*. **How to Contact:** Write or call. Responds to most inquiries immediately. **Tips:** Recent information request: "How does the application of new siding enhance a home's aesthetics and value?"

882• WALLPAPERS TO GO
c/o Russom & Leeper, 350 Pacific Ave., San Francisco CA 94111. (415)397-7878. Contact

Person: Account Executive. **Description:** Retail merchandiser of wallcoverings, wallpapering supplies and decorating aids. **Services:** Provides how-to information on decorating with wallcoverings; do-it-yourself tips; wallcovering trends; unusual uses of wallcoverings. Offers brochures/pamphlets, photos and press kits. Publications include *10 Common Mistakes* (in decorating with wallcoverings); *How Many Rolls Do You Need?*; *Decorating Basics*; *Wallpapering Crafts*; *Wallpapering Techniques.* **How to Contact:** Write or call. Responds to most inquiries within a week. Give credit to Wallpapers to Go. **Tips:** "Ask lots of questions." Recent information requests: "How do you hang wallcovering?"; "How can I assure I'll like the wallcovering once I get it home?"

883• WHIRLPOOL CORPORATION
Public and Government Relations Administrative Center, Benton Harbor MI 49022. Contact Person: Public Information Manager. **Description:** Manufacturer of major home appliances. **Services:** Provides information on the manufacture of major home appliances, new products and technical data. Offers aid in arranging interviews, annual reports, biographies, statistics, brochures/pamphlets, information searches, placement on mailing lists, photos and press kits. **How to Contact:** Written requests preferred. Responds to most inquiries within a week. May charge for some publications.

SECTION · SIXTEEN

HUMAN SERVICES

Too many have dispensed with generosity to practice charity.

—Albert Camus

Information sources in the human services are those social welfare organizations (charities, volunteer groups, counseling centers, information centers, etc.) providing assistance to those in need.

Additional health-related organizations are listed in the Health and Medicine category; family-oriented services are found in the Family section.

Bibliography

Croner, Helga B., comp. *National Directory of Private Social Agencies* (with monthly supplements). Queen's Village, NY: Social Service Publications.
Handicapping Conditions & Services Directory. 2d ed. Detroit: Gale Research Co., 1981. (National level organizations offering information and services for the handicapped)
Kruzas, Anthony T., ed. *Social Service Organizations and Agencies Directory*. Detroit: Gale Research Co., 1982.
Schmidt, Alvin J., ed. *Fraternal Organizations*. Westport, CT: Greenwood Press, 1980.
Weinstein, Amy, ed. *Public Welfare Directory*. Annual. Washington DC: American Public Welfare Association.
Women's Action Alliance. *Women Helping Women: A State by State Directory of Services*. New York: Dist. by Neil-Schuman Publishers, 1981.

884• THE ABORTION FUND
1801 K St. NW, # 200, Washington DC 20006. (202)244-1510. Contact Person: Executive Director. **Description:** "The Abortion Fund provides direct assistance to women in need of an abortion in states with no governmental assistance. We work with participating clinics to defray the cost of first trimester abortions for women on Medicaid or women that are Medicaid-eligible." **Services:** Provides referral information. Offers statistics. **How to Contact:** Write or call. Responds to most inquiries within a week. **Tips:** "Call—any help we can give we will be happy to do so. Naturally, we would expect any information we provide to be used in a positive way; we do not lobby, but our aim is actively pro-choice." Recent information requests: "How many states have no funding for indigent abortions?"; "What are they?"; "What is the profile of a woman using the fund?"

885• ACCENT ON LIVING/ACCENT ON INFORMATION
Box 700, Bloomington IL 61701. Contact Person: Publisher and Editor. **Description:** "*Accent* is edited for people with physical disabilities, their families and rehabilitation professionals. AOI is a computerized information system with a data base consisting mostly of aids and assistive devices for disabled." **Services:** Provides advisory, bibliographical and technical information on products, aids, services and how-to information for persons with physical disabilities. Offers computerized information searches. Publications include *Accent* magazine and books which provide "detailed information whether you want to take a vacation, make your home accessible or manage with only one hand." **How to Contact:** Write. Responds to most inquiries within a week. Charges $12 "for a computer search for up to the latest 50 references." **Tips:** Recent information requests: Materials on housing and architectural barriers; mobility aids; furniture for the physically disabled.

886• AMERICAN EUTHANASIA FOUNDATION, INC.
95 N. Birch Rd., Fort Lauderdale FL 33304. Contact Person: Vice President. **Description:** Organization whose objective is to distribute the "Mercy Will," which expresses the wish that no remarkable means be used to maintain the existence of a terminally ill patient. **Services:** Provides advisory and how-to information. Offers *The Will to Die*. **How to Contact:** Write. Responds to

most inquiries within a week. Give credit to American Euthanasia Foundation. **Tips:** Recent information request: "Is the 'Mercy Will' a legal document?"

887• AMERICAN RED CROSS
17th and D Sts. NW, Washington DC 20006. (202)737-8300. Contact Person: Information Research Specialist. **Description:** "The aims of the American Red Cross are to improve the quality of human life and to enhance individual self-reliance and concern for others. It works toward these aims through national and chapter services governed and directed by volunteers. American Red Cross services help people avoid emergencies, prepare for emergencies and cope with them when they occur. To accomplish its aims, the Red Cross provides volunteer blood services to a large segment of the nation, conducts community services, and, as mandated by its congressional charter, serves as an independent medium of voluntary relief and communication between the American people and their armed forces; maintains a system of local, national and international disaster preparedness and relief; and assists the government of the United States to meet humanitarian treaty commitments." **Services:** Provides bibliographical and historical information covering ARC history, services and personnel as well as health/medicine, disasters and military welfare services. Offers annual reports, bibliographies, biographies, statistics, brochures/pamphlets, information searches and photos. Publications include *Publications of the American Red Cross*; a catalog of materials is available. Publications cover American Red Cross services, including safety services, (general information, first aid, small craft, water safety), nursing and health services, international services, youth services, volunteer services, disaster services, blood services, and general and historical information about the organization. Also publishes first aid and safety textbooks. Red Cross publications are available from local American Red Cross Chapters. **How to Contact:** "Writers may query by letter, asking for information as specifically as possible. Or, they may visit our library. For library visits, researchers must advise us in advance of their date of visit." Responds to most inquiries within a week. Charges $6/photo; 5¢/page for photocopying. **Tips:** Recent information requests: Questions on POWs in WWII; the ARC in the Vietnam conflict.

888• AMERICANS UNITED FOR LIFE
230 N. Michigan Ave., # 915, Chicago IL 60601. (312)263-5029. Contact Person: Director of Education. **Description:** Groups of individuals "providing legal and educational resources on the human life issues such as: abortion, infanticide, euthanasia, and *in vitro* fertilization procedures and other genetic issues." **Services:** Provides analytical, bibliographical, historical, interpretative and referral information on abortion, infanticide, genetic prenatal screening, euthanasia, *in vitro* fertilization and eugenics. Offers brochures/pamphlets, informational newsletters, photos, placement on mailing lists, press kits and statistics. **How to Contact:** Write or call. Responds to most inquiries within a week. Give credit to Americans United for Life. **Tips:** "Writers should try to carefully define their terms and questions before calling or writing." Recent information request: Legal background for Supreme Court's 1973 decision legalizing abortion.

889• AMERICA'S KIDS ON CAMPUS, INC.
155 W. Hospitality Lane, Suite 215, San Bernardino CA 92408. (714)824-0492. Contact Person: President. **Description:** "We are a nonprofit, community service-oriented national organization teaching kids positive ways to a drug abuse-free life. We use positive success motivation and present drug education programs for school age children and parent groups." **Services:** Provides advisory, how-to and interpretative information covering drug education, drug and alcohol abuse, success motivation, positive lifestyle. Offers annual reports, brochures/pamphlets, informational newsletters, photos, press kits and information on service clubs in junior and senior high schools. Publications include *The Winner* (for elementary age children); *America's Kids* (elementary and junior high); *Compass Magazine* (high school and adult). **How to Contact:** Write. Responds to most inquiries within a week. Charges for magazines. **Tips:** "We approach drug abuse from a positive 'prevention' point of view by putting kids to work on community service projects and recognizing their efforts." Recent information request: "How can we start an America's Kids On Campus Club in our local schools?"

890• ASSOCIATION FOR RETARDED CITIZENS OF THE UNITED STATES
2501 Avenue J, Box 6109, Arlington TX 76011. (817)640-0204. Contact Person: Public Information Specialist. **Description:** "The ARC is the largest national voluntary health organization and is devoted solely to improving the welfare of *all* mentally retarded people without

regard to race, creed, geographic location or degree of handicap. It provides help to parents and other individuals, organizations and communities in jointly solving the problems caused by retardation." **Services:** Provides advisory, bibliographical, historical, how-to, interpretative, referral and technical information on mental retardation. Offers aid in arranging interviews, biographies, brochures/pamphlets, informational newsletters, photos, placement on mailing lists, press kits, research assistance, statistics and telephone reference services. Publications include *The Arc.* **How to Contact:** Write or call. Responds to most inquiries within a week. **Tips:** "Before we provide names/contact information for families of retarded people or retarded people for interviews, we may interview 15-20 families to select an appropriate subject and then will clear with the family or person their desire to cooperate in an interview. Depending on the complexity of the request, it may take a month to find an appropriate interview subject." Recent information requests: "Can you help us locate a family who has been advised to withhold medical treatment from their retarded child; verify the following facts; locate a retarded adult in a work program; provide a list of laws affecting mentally retarded people?"

891• ASSOCIATION OF HALFWAY HOUSE ALCOHOLISM PROGRAMS OF NORTH AMERICA, INC.
786 E. 7th St., St. Paul MN 55106. (612)771-0933. Contact Person: Office Manager. **Description:** "The association is a voluntary vehicle by which halfway house alcoholism programs have bound themselves together to promote the role of supportive residential facilities in the continuum of care and rehabilitation in the recovery process of those with alcoholism." **Services:** Provides advisory, how-to, referral, technical and trade information covering alcoholism and recovery homes. Offers statistics, brochures/pamphlets and newsletter. **How to Contact:** Write or call. Responds to most inquiries within a week. Charges nonmembers for services. "Our materials are, for the most part, descriptive, firsthand reports and experiences."

892• BIG BROTHERS/BIG SISTERS OF AMERICA
117 S. 17th St., Suite 1200, Philadelphia PA 19123. (215)567-2748. Contact Person: Supervisor. **Description:** "Big Brothers/Big Sisters is the only national youth-serving organization based on the warmth of one-to-one friendship between an adult volunteer and a child from a one-parent home." **Services:** Provides historical, interpretative and referral information. Offers aid in arranging interviews, annual reports, biographies, brochures/pamphlets, informational newsletters, library facilities, photos, placement on mailing lists, press kits, research assistance and statistics. **How to Contact:** Write, call or visit. Responds to most inquiries within a week. **Tips:** "We always welcome inquiries from writers and researchers." Recent information requests: Statistics on the effectiveness of the program; referrals to experts in the social service field.

893• CHILD FIND, INC.
Box 277, New Paltz NY 12561. (914)255-1848. Contact Person: Executive Director or Information Director. **Description:** Nonprofit organization involved in the prevention and location of missing children. Serves as a national registry for locating missing children. **Services:** Provides advisory, bibliographical, how-to and referral information on missing children—location, prevention, referral and updates on current legislation. Offers aid in arranging interviews, annual reports, biographies, brochures/pamphlets, informational newsletters, photos, press kits, research assistance, statistics and telephone reference services. Publications include Directory of Missing Children. **How to Contact:** Write or call. Responds to most inquiries within a month. "Writers are encouraged to make modest contribution for information received." **Tips:** "Observation of confidentiality and exclusivity is required where appropriate." Recent information request: "What's being done to prevent child abduction?"

894• CLEARINGHOUSE ON THE HANDICAPPED
Department of Education, Switzer Bldg., Room 3119, Washington DC 20202. (202)245-0080. Contact Person: Chief, Clearinghouse. **Description:** "The Clearinghouse on the Handicapped was created by the Rehabilitation Act of 1973 to enhance the flow of disability-related information to handicapped individuals and service providers." **Services:** Provides analytical, bibliographical and referral information in all subject areas relevant to handicapping conditions; "especially strong in legislation, funding, federal programs and who has what information." Offers brochures/pamphlets, informational newsletters and library facilities. "The information contained

in the *Directory of National Information Sources on Handicapping Conditions and Related Services* has been put into a computerized data base which is available through Bibliographic Retrieval Services, 1200 Route 7, Latham NY 12110, (518)783-1161." Publications include *Programs for the Handicapped*, bimonthly newsletter focusing on federal activities affecting the handicapped. Publications list available. **How to Contact:** Write or call. Responds to most inquiries within a month. **Tips:** "Be specific; do not ask for everything in the field of handicaps or education of handicapped children."

895• COMMITTEES OF CORRESPONDENCE, INC.
Box 232, Topsfield MA 01983. (617)774-2641. Contact Person: Secretary. **Description:** Nonprofit, educational and philanthropic organization working to combat drug abuse, especially in youth. Encourages letter writing to effect change. **Services:** Provides how-to and referral information on drug use (cocaine, marijuana, alcohol) as health hazard to children. Offers brochures/pamphlets, informational newsletters and placement on mailing lists. Publications include educational pamphlets on health hazards of marijuana and alcohol use; newsletter on specific drug-abuse issues. **How to Contact:** Write. Responds to most inquiries within a week. Charges for newsletter subscription. "Material may be copied as long as credit is given Committees of Correspondence." **Tips:** Recent information request: "What are the health consequences to adolescents using marijuana?"

896• CONCERN FOR DYING, AN EDUCATIONAL COUNCIL
250 W. 57th St., New York NY 10107. (212)246-6962. Contact Person: Executive Director. **Description:** "CFD is a nonprofit, educational organization serving the general public, the medical, nursing and legal professions, hospital administration, the clergy, social workers, educators and the media, through the distribution of the Living Will and other literature on death and dying, the sponsorship of conferences and educational programs, a legal advisory service, consulting library and film rentals." **Services:** Provides advisory, analytical, bibliographical, historical, how-to, interpretative and referral information covering the areas of death and dying, ethics and philosophy thereof, terminal and critical illness, patient rights, current status of "Living Will" or "Right to Die" legislation in different states, professional education and death and dying. Offers aid in arranging interviews, annual reports, brochures/pamphlets, informational newsletters, library facilities, placement on mailing lists, press kits, research assistance, telephone reference services and legal referrals. Publications available. **How to Contact:** Write, call (preferred) or visit. Responds to most inquiries within a month. No charge, "but we request contributions to help us cover our costs."

897• FACE LEARNING CENTER
12945 Seminole Blvd., Largo FL 33706. (813)586-1110, 585-8155. Contact Person: Director, Career/Community Development. **Description:** "We are a nonprofit service through which women learn self-sufficiency, emotional stability and financial independence." **Services:** Provides advisory, bibliographical, how-to, referral and trade information covering career/job development, educational/grant opportunities, personal growth/support services, emotional/physical/legal/financial well-being and resumé preparation. "We specialize in data on displaced homemakers and single female heads of households, women's issues and divorce counseling." Offers aid in arranging interviews, bibliographies, brochures/pamphlets, placement on mailing list, community programs and classes. **How to Contact:** Write or call. Responds to most inquiries within a week. "There are no fees for information and referral; initial counseling visit, no charge; specific career/employment/resume preparation counseling, by appointment only, (on a sliding fee scale). Most services free to displaced homemakers. If coming in person, please call ahead for appointment. Center is open Monday-Friday, 9 a.m.-5 p.m." **Tips:** "We welcome and enjoy working with writers. We have a very comprehensive resource library on employment/careers/personal development topics/women's issues and more. Call/write for appointment. We also have an internship program." Recent information requests: How to adjust personally/professionally after divorce/separation/death of spouse; background on job market re-entry; how-to start a business, day care information; assertiveness training.

898• FAMILIES IN ACTION DRUG INFORMATION CENTER
3845 N. Druid Hills Rd., Suite 300, Decatur GA 30033. (404)325-5799. Contact Person: Executive Director or Assistant Director of Information. **Description:** A drug information center with 90,000 documents. "We collect all relevant information about drug and alcohol abuse

(particularly as it relates to children) and disseminate that information to prevent abuse." **Services:** Provides advisory, analytical, bibliographical, historical (limited), how-to, interpretative, referral, technical and trade information in 740 subject categories under broad divisions, including: athletics, bibliographies, conferences, crime, education, entertainment, health care, government, industry and business, media, organizations, parent groups, paraphernalia, people, publications, sexuality, surveys. Offers aid in arranging interviews, brochures/pamphlets, clipping services, library facilities, photos (few), placement on subscription lists, research assistance, statistics and telephone reference services. Publications include *Drug Abuse Update* (12-page quarterly); 162-page parent group organizational manual. **How to Contact:** Write, call or visit. Responds to most written inquiries within a week. Charges for publications, photocopying and postage. **Tips:** "It is best to visit our center to sample the vast collection and to take advantage of our holdings. Quick questions can be answered by phone." Recent information requests: Extent of drug abuse among children and adolescents; health effects of various drugs of abuse; "What is the parents' movement?"; "What are some drug lobbies working for legalization?"

899• FATHER FLANAGAN'S BOYS' HOME
Boys Town NE 68010. (402)498-1301. Contact Person: Director of Public Relations. **Description:** Nonprofit youth care home. "Boys Town provides several services to youth. Father Flanagan's Boys' Home provides residential care for more than 400 abused, neglected and needy youths. Communication-impaired children are diagnosed and treated at the Boys Town Institute for Communication Disorders in Children. In Omaha's inner city, the Boys Town Urban Program is an alternative educational program for at-risk youth. Boys Town USA is an effort to help needy youth right in their own community." **Services:** Provides advisory, historical, how-to, referral and technical information on Boys Town, communication disorders, inner-city youth, adolescent abuse, suicide, divorce, cults, runaways' school problems, learning disabilities, friendless children, television, parenting, status offenders. Offers aid in arranging interviews, brochures/pamphlets, informational newsletters, photos, placement on mailing lists and press kits. Publications include Boys Town history and program guides; booklets about specific problems of youth including *Adolescent Suicide*; *Divorce*; *Children and Television*; *America's Runaways*; *Helping Friendless Children*; *Cults and Kids*; *Active Parenting*; *Television and Youth*; *Juvenile Delinquency and Learning Disabilities*; *Tips on Discipline*; *Parent's Guide to the Periodic Progress Report*; and *What to Do if Your Child Is an Underachiever in School*. **How to Contact:** Write, call or visit. Responds to most inquiries within a week. Charges for some books. "We ask that writers check facts about Boys Town orally with the public relations staff." **Tips:** "Writers are more than welcome to visit Boys Town, America's leading provider of quality care to troubled youth. In addition to its role in the care of youth, Boys Town, founded in 1917, is a national historic travel site." Recent information requests: Historical materials; research-based information on helping troubled youth.

900• FORUM FOR DEATH EDUCATION AND COUNSELING
14-Z-3 Laurel Hill, Greenbelt MD 20770. Contact Person: Executive Director. **Description:** "An association of professional death educators and counselors interested in upgrading the quality of education and counseling in the areas of death, dying and bereavement." **Services:** Provides advisory, bibliographical and interpretative information. Offers brochures/pamphlets, informational newsletters, workshops, annual conference proceedings. Publications include *Forum Newsletter*; *New Directions in Death Education and Counseling* (enhancing the quality of life in the nuclear age). **How to Contact:** Write. Responds to most inquiries within a month. "Obtain permission to use items from Forum publications." **Tips:** "Use *Forum Newsletter* to seek others interested in a particular phase of the movement."

901• FOSTER GRANDPARENT PROGRAM
Action, 806 Connecticut Ave. NW, M1006, Washington DC 20525. (202)254-7605. Contact Person: Chief of Foster Grandparent Program. **Description:** Program of low-income volunteers aged 60 and over providing person-to-person services to children with special or exceptional needs. **Services:** Provides historical and referral information on the Foster Grandparent Program. Offers brochures/pamphlets and press kits. Publications include *Handbook for Sponsors*. **How to Contact:** Write. Responds to most inquiries within a month.

902• FOSTER PARENTS PLAN, INC.
155 Plan Way, Warwick RI 02887. (401)738-5600. Contact Person: Associate Director of Development. **Description:** "International child welfare agency providing services to poverty-stricken children and their families in overseas countries. Funds are provided through sponsorship of the children by caring Americans. Sponsorship funds are used to provide additional food and clothing, medical care, and an education. All services are extended to the immediate family." **Services:** Provides referral information on social service delivery in Third World countries. Offers annual reports, brochures/pamphlets and informational newsletters. **How to Contact:** Write or call. Responds to most inquiries immediately.

903• FOUR-ONE-ONE
7304 Beverly St., Annandale VA 22003. (703)354-6270. Contact Person: President. **Description:** Resource center for volunteerism; serves as national clearinghouse for community/volunteer programs, national organizations and agencies in the human service/community needs area. **Services:** Provides analytical, bibliographical, how-to, referral and technical information covering volunteerism in some 30 human services areas. Offers aid in arranging interviews, computerized information searches, informational newsletters, library facilities (3,000 volumes on volunteerism at the local level), press kits, research assistance and telephone reference services. Publications include *Green Sheets*, annotated listings of resource organizations and publications providing how-to advice for volunteers and program administrators. **How to Contact:** Write, call or visit. Responds to most inquiries as soon as possible "depending on the request." Charges for publications and 25¢/page for information after the first ten pages. **Tips:** Recent information request: "What are some current legislative incentives to encourage volunteers?"

904• GOODWILL INDUSTRIES OF AMERICA
9200 Wisconsin Ave., Bethesda MD 20814. Contact Person: Assistant Director of Communications. **Description:** "We provide leadership and assistance to organizational members in their efforts to help the handicapped, disabled and disadvantaged attain their fullest potential. The primary purpose of Goodwill is to provide rehabilitation services, training, employment and opportunities for personal growth for handicapped, disabled and disadvantaged persons who cannot fit into the competitive labor market or the usual facets of society." **Services:** Provides advisory, historical, how-to, referral, technical and trade information covering vocational rehabilitation and communication strategy. Offers aid in arranging communications, interviews, annual reports, placement on mailing list and newsletter. **How to Contact:** Write. Responds to most inquiries immediately. "Material is available on a limited basis. We do not charge our member Goodwill Industries. Additional consultation services to outside agencies would be negotiable. We reserve the right to review and approve all copy written about our organization." **Tips:** "Give reasonable time for your requests to be answered."

905• HAZELDEN FOUNDATION
Box 11, Center City MN 55012. Contact Person: Managing Editor. **Description:** The foundation works to aid in the prevention and recovery of drug and alcohol abuse. **Services:** Provides advisory, analytical, bibliographical, historical, how-to, interpretative, referral, technical and trade information on drug and alcohol addiction; other addictions and compulsive behavior; rehabilitation; values clarification; "wellness" items. Offers brochures/pamphlets, library facilities, placement on mailing lists and research assistance. **How to Contact:** Write. Responds to most inquiries within a month.

906• KIWANIS INTERNATIONAL
3636 Woodview Trace, Indianapolis IN 46268. (317)875-8755. Contact Person: Public Relations Director. **Description:** "International service organization, providing fellowship and helping youth, community and nation." **Services:** Offers aid in arranging interviews, biographies, statistics and brochures/pamphlets. "We also have service reports and a library." Publications available. **How to Contact:** Write or call. Responds to most inquiries "as soon as possible." **Tips:** Recent information requests: "How big is the Kiwanis organization?"; "Is the service club movement still viable today?"

907• LIONS CLUB INTERNATIONAL
300 22nd St., Oak Brook IL 60570. (312)986-1700. Contact Person: Manager of Public Relations

Division. **Description:** "We are a world organization in 155 countries with volunteers in humanitarian services in these areas or countries." **Services:** Offers brochures/pamphlets, placement on mailing list, statistics, photos and press kits. Publications available. **How to Contact:** Write or call. Responds to most inquiries within a week. **Tips:** "Be as specific as possible."

908• MAKE TODAY COUNT, INC.
Box 303, Tama Bldg., Suite 514, Burlington IA 52601. (319)754-7266 or 754-8977. Contact Person: Executive Director. **Description:** "An international organization with 211 chapters, bringing together terminally ill persons (especially cancer patients), family members, members of the health care professions and other interested persons to help patients and family members cope with the emotional problems of depression, rejection, etc., associated with an illness such as cancer. Make Today Count sponsors seminars on Death and Dying and Living with a Life-Threatening Illness. In addition, Make Today Count individual chapters are located in approximately 34 states. Most chapter members are willing to talk with writers and representatives of the news media." **Services:** Offers brochures/pamphlets, information searches, newsletter and photos. Publications available. **How to Contact:** Write or call. Responds to most inquiries immediately. **Tips:** "Please let us know when you're including us in a reference work." Recent information requests: Location of the nearest chapter; information on specific diseases.

909• METROPOLITAN ORGANIZATION TO COUNTER SEXUAL ASSAULT
2 W. 40th St., # 104, Kansas City MO 64111. (816)931-4527. Contact Person: Associate Director. **Description:** "We provide sexual assault counseling, mental health and public education and legal aid on sexual assault." **Services:** Offers aid in arranging interviews, bibliographies, brochures/pamphlets, placement on mailing list, statistics and newsletter. Publications available. **How to Contact:** Write or call. Responds to most inquiries immediately. "The staff does not have the manpower to aid in the actual research process."

910• NATIONAL ASSOCIATION OF RECOVERED ALCOHOLICS
Box 95, Staten Island NY 10305. (212)448-6094. Contact Person: Executive Director. **Description:** Organization which assists recovering alcoholics economically, legally and socially. **Services:** Provides advisory, historical, referral and trade information on current trends in alcoholism recovery and employment opportunities. Offers aid in arranging interviews, brochures/pamphlets, informational newsletters, placement on mailing lists and research assistance. **How to Contact:** Write or call. Responds to most inquiries within a week.

911• NATIONAL ASSOCIATION OF SOCIAL WORKERS (NASW)
7981 Eastern Ave., Silver Spring MD 20910. (301)565-0333. Contact Person: Public Affairs Director. **Description:** Membership association and lobbying organization. **Services:** Provides bibliographical, interpretative and referral information covering social work, social welfare and social services. Offers aid in arranging interviews, statistics, newsletter, photos and press kits. Publications include *NASW News* (monthly newspaper) and *The Advocate* (roundup of social service legislation); policy statements on such issues as immigration, racism, social services, housing, confidentiality; and standards booklets for social workers in schools, hospitals, personnel practices and social service manpower. **How to Contact:** Call or write the Public Affairs Director. Charges $6/year for *NASW News*, $20/year for *The Advocate.* "Cite NASW as source of information." **Tips:** "When possible, allow enough time to adequately research requests and/or arrange interview." Recent information request: NASW's comments on federal social services budgets.

912• NATIONAL COUNCIL ON ALCOHOLISM
733 Third Ave., New York NY 10017. (212)986-4433. Contact Person: Public Information Director. **Description:** The National Council on Alcoholism, Inc., "founded in 1944, is the only national voluntary health agency founded to combat the disease of alcoholism. There is no duplication between NCA and Alcoholics Anonymous; they cooperate fully and supplement each other's work." **Services:** Offers programs in labor-management, prevention and education, community services and public information. Offers statistics and speakers. Publications available. **How to Contact:** Write or call. Responds to most inquiries "as soon as possible."

913• THE NATIONAL COUNCIL ON COMPULSIVE GAMBLING, INC.
99 Park Ave., New York NY 10016. (212)686-6160. Contact Person: President/Executive Director. **Description:** "The National Council on Compulsive Gambling, Inc., was organized to disseminate information, education, training and research on compulsive gambling as a treatable illness." **Services:** Provides bibliographical and historical information on compulsive (pathological) gambling. Offers brochures/pamphlets, informational newsletters and statistics. Publications include quarterly newsletters and various pamphlets. **How to Contact:** Write. Responds to most inquiries within a week. Charges $25/membership which includes newsletter and publications. **Tips:** Recent information requests: "How many compulsive gamblers are there in the US?"; "What treatment is available?"

914• NATIONAL HOSPICE ORGANIZATION
1311A Dolly Madison Blvd., McLean VA 22101. (703)356-6770. Contact: Public Information or Research Department. **Description:** "Hospice is a specialized health care program emphasizing the management of pain and other symptoms associated with terminal illness while providing care for the family as well as the patient." **Services:** Provides bibliographical, historical and how-to information on the hospice movement. Offers brochures/pamphlets, informational newsletters, research assistance, statistics and telephone reference services. Publications include *Standards of Hospice Care; Frequently Asked Questions About Hospice; Directory of Hospices in the United States*; various bibliographies. **How to Contact:** Write. Responds to most inquiries within a month.

915• NATIONAL LIBRARY SERVICE FOR THE BLIND AND PHYSICALLY HANDICAPPED
Library of Congress, 1291 Taylor St. NW, Washington DC 20542. (202)882-5500. Contact Person: Head, Publications Service. **Description:** "We provide braille and talking books and magazines to blind and physically handicapped individuals. We also have the same range of books/magazines as in any public library." **Services:** Provides advisory, analytical, bibliographical, historical, interpretative, referral, technical and trade information on the library service. Offers bibliographies, brochures/pamphlets and newsletters. Publications include *Reading Is for Everyone; Books That Talk?; Volunteers in Library Services*; talking books for physically handicapped readers, and many others. **How to Contact:** Write. Responds to most inquiries within a week.

916• NURSING HOME INFORMATION SERVICES
925 15th St. NW, Washington DC 20005. (202)347-8800. Contact: National Council of Senior Citizens. **Description:** Organization furnishing information and referrals concerning long term care in nursing homes. **Services:** Provides advisory, analytical, bibliographical, how-to, interpretative, referral and technical information on regulations; social work agencies; analysis of inspections of nursing homes; finding long term nursing home care. Offers aid in arranging interviews, brochures/pamphlets, informational newsletters, library facilities, placement on mailing lists and telephone reference services. Publications include newsletter; *How to Choose a Nursing Home; Patient's Rights; Directory of Long Term Care Services.* **How to Contact:** Write, call or visit. Responds to most inquiries within a week. **Tips:** Recent information request: Suggested guidelines for deciding when someone needs nursing home care.

917• OPTIMIST INTERNATIONAL
4494 Lindell Blvd. St. Louis MO 63108. (314) 371-6000. Contact Person: Public Relations Director. **Description:** "We are active in youth activities, community service and aid to the deaf." **Services:** Provides advisory and historical information on the work of the Optimist Clubs. Offers aid in arranging interviews, brochures/pamphlets, statistics, newsletter, photos and press kits. **How to Contact:** Write. Responds to most inquiries within a week.

918• PEOPLE TO PEOPLE COMMITTEE FOR THE HANDICAPPED
1111 20th St., NW, Washington DC 20036. (202)653-5024. Contact Person: Chairman. **Description:** "We have long been the 'international arm' of the President's Committee on Employment of the Handicapped. We work with the public and private sectors to create a better climate of acceptance for handicapped persons in employment and all other forms of human endeavor." **Services:** Provides historical, how-to and referral information on

rehabilitation and employment of handicapped persons, including education, accessibility, housing and transportation. Offers aid in arranging interviews, brochures/pamphlets, informational newsletters and placement on mailing lists. Publications include *Directory of Organizations Interested in Handicapped* and quarterly newsletter. **How to Contact:** Write. Responds to most inquiries within a week. Charges $3 for *Directory*, but would be happy to send it free to anyone mentioning *Writer's Resource Guide*. Give credit to People to People Committee. **Tips:** "We are generalists, all volunteers, mostly senior retired federal executives or recognized private citizen volunteers. We know the federal byways and we know Washington. We are anxious to be helpful and have international, national, and state ties. Drop us a line indicating specific story leads of interest; ask us for leads to specialists in specific disabilities. If urgent, call (703)525-4047 and ask for Colonel McCahill, chair emeritus." Recent information requests: "What can you do to help a new network of publications on Spina Bifida?"; "Can you help us publicize an international seminar on public relations in rehabilitation?"

919• PROJECT SHARE
Box 2309, Rockville MD 20852. (301)251-5170. Contact Person: Reference Specialist. **Description:** Government contract providing information on how to improve the management and delivery of human services. **Services:** Provides bibliographical and referral information on planning, managing, and delivering all human services except health care and education ("limited resources in these areas as other clearinghouses deal exclusively with these subjects"). Offers computerized information searches, informational newsletters, library facilities, placement on mailing lists, research assistance and telephone reference services. Publications include *Journal of Human Services Abstracts*; *Sharing* (a newsletter); human service monographs and bibliographies. **How to Contact:** Write or call. Responds to most inquiries within a week. Charges for computer searches and documents. **Tips:** "Be specific." Recent information request: "Do you know of any program in New England where volunteer data banks have been established?"

920• REPRODUCTIVE RIGHTS NATIONAL NETWORK
17 Murray St., New York NY 10007. (212)267-8891. Contact Person: National Coordinator. **Description:** Reproductive rights (abortion rights) organization serving as an education and outreach group. **Services:** Provides advisory, analytical, bibliographical, how-to and referral information on abortion, sterilization abuse, population control in US and abroad, reproductive hazards in the workplace, child care, lesbian rights and infant mortality. Offers aid in arranging interviews, brochures/pamphlets, informational newsletters, research assistance, statistics, telephone reference services and information on reproductive rights issues. Publications include pamphlets on the human life amendment and sterilization abuse. **How to Contact:** Write or call. Responds to most inquiries within a month. Charges for publications, photocopying, extensive consultations and in-depth research. "We want to know how and where the information will be used." Give credit to Reproductive Rights National Network. **Tips:** "Be clear and concise about what you want. We cannot write your paper, book etc., for you." Recent information requests: "How many women have died from illegal abortions prior to 1973?"; "What's happening in Congress regarding abortion?"; "What's the difference between birth control and population control?"

921• ROTARY INTERNATIONAL
1600 Ridge Ave., Evanston IL 60201. (302)328-0100. Contact Person: Public Relations Manager. **Description:** "We are an organization of business and professional men, united worldwide who provide humanitarian service, encourage high ethical standards in all vocations and help to build goodwill for peace in the world. We operate in 157 countries and geographical regions." **Services:** Provides advisory, analytical, historical and how-to information on public relations guidance for volunteer groups and rotary programs and activities: aiding the disabled, elderly, youth, students and international organizations. Offers aid in arranging interviews, annual reports, statistics, brochures/pamphlets and press kits. Publications and audio-visual materials available. **How to Contact:** Write or call. Responds to most inquiries "as soon as feasible. Depends on nature of request." Charges for extended consultation on a selective and individual basis on public relations techniques for voluntary groups. Nominal costs for some publications and audio visual materials, depending on request.

922• RURITAN NATIONAL, INC.
Ruritan Rd., Dublin VA 24060. (703)674-5431. Contact Person: Executive Secretary. **Description:** Civic service organization "designed to meet the needs of rural people and rural communities and to foster greater understanding between rural and urban people on the problems of each, as well as on mutual problems." **Services:** Provides information on Ruritan's activities. Offers brochures/pamphlets. Publications include *The Ruritan* (for members) and various handbooks and brochures on community service. **How to Contact:** Write. Responds to most inquiries within a week. Charges for some publications. **Tips:** Recent information request: An example of public/private cooperation.

923• THE SALVATION ARMY ARCHIVES AND RESEARCH CENTER
145 W. 15th St., New York NY 10011. (212)620-4392. Contact Person: Assistant Archivist. **Description:** The archives collects, preserves and makes available records and historical data on the activities of The Salvation Army in the United States. **Services:** Provides bibliographical and historical information on The Salvation Army (both current and historical information). "Researchers with the following interests may find material: religion, women, adult rehabilitation, alcoholism, ethnicity." Offers biographies, brochures/pamphlets, informational newsletters, library facilities, photos, research assistance and telephone reference services. Publications include *Historical News/View* (newsletter). **How to Contact:** Write, call or visit. Responds to most inquiries immediately. Charges for photos and photocopying. **Tips:** "Researchers who wish to visit the archives for research are requested to telephone before their arrival. Material is available to the public. Unpublished records are available 25 years after their creation unless covered by a specific restriction." Recent information request: "Please send me some information on my father who served as an officer in The Salvation Army."

924• THE SEEING EYE
Box 375, Morristown NJ 07960. (201)539-4425. Contact Person: Assistant Director, Development and Public Information. **Description:** Nonprofit, philanthropic organization. "Breeds or obtains dogs by purchase or gift; places puppies with 4-H children who raise the puppies in a family setting; educates the dogs to serve as guides; matches the dogs with qualified blind people who are taught how to use them for greater freedom." **Services:** Provides advisory, analytical, bibliographical, historical and interpretative information covering qualifications of dog guide users, mobility, history of dog guides and seeing eye program, 4-H program, legal rights of blind people with dog guides and seeing eye dogs in various settings. Offers aid in arranging interviews, annual reports, biographies, brochures/pamphlets, informational newsletters, photos, press kits, research assistance and statistics. Publications include *Love in the Lead*, by Peter Putnam; *History of Dog Guides*; various pamphlets and brochures. **How to Contact:** Write or call. Responds to most inquiries within a week. "We like to review copy and photos for accuracy when possible. **Tips:** "Please have an open mind. Some journalistic ideas are not possible because of our need to protect the privacy of our students. Also, we only have 4 weeks to develop a good working relationship between student and dog; therefore, we must restrict visitors. We like to give writers and producers individualized attention and go to great lengths to answer questions thoroughly." Recent information request: "How does a seeing eye dog know when to cross the street?"

925• UNITED WAY OF AMERICA
United Way Plaza, Alexandria VA 22314-2088. (703)836-7100. Contact Person: Director, Media Relations. **Description:** "United Way of America is a nonprofit, voluntary membership association providing a variety of services to over 2,100 local independent United Way organizations in the United States and abroad. We maintain a Center for Charitable Statistics, Corporate Support Resource Center, Volunteer Leadership Development Program, National Information and Referral, Management Assistance Programs and training and development programs for agency volunteers and staff." **Services:** Provides advisory, analytical, bibliographical, historical, how-to, interpretative, referral, technical and trade information on philanthropy. "Our Information Center contains loan folders on voluntarism, national agencies, fund raising and marketing research; in addition, we have films and videotapes, national fact sheets, *Community* magazine, the *Executive Newsletter* and publications covering a range of topics relevant to the voluntary sector." **How to Contact:** Write. Responds to most inquiries within a week. **Tips:** "United Way of America is an important resource for writers interested in gaining a better understanding of the local operations of United Way organizations—how funds are collected

and disbursed in the community. Charitable groups funded by United Way contain the seeds of a multitude of human interest stories linked with the human care service agencies United Way supports.'' Recent information request: ''What effect would a flat tax rate have on charitable giving?''

926• VOCATIONAL REHABILITATION
Box 1118, Hato Rey PR 00919. (809)725-1792. Contact Person: Assistant Secretary. **Description:** ''Through counseling, physical and/or mental restoration services, evaluations, vocational training, economic assistance, job placement and other services on an individualized, as-needed basis, we help handicapped people become productive and independent.'' **Services:** Offers aid in arranging interviews and answers to requests for specific information, when available. Publications include *State Plan of Operations* (annual). **How to Contact:** Write or call. Responds to most inquiries within a month.

927• VOLUNTEER: THE NATIONAL CENTER FOR CITIZEN INVOLVEMENT
Box 4179, Boulder CO 80306. (303)447-0492. Contact Person: Manager of Information Services. **Description:** The organization ''promotes volunteerism, and acts as a technical assistance resource group for volunteer programs.'' **Services:** Provides bibliographical, historical, how-to, referral, technical and trade information on all facets of volunteering: establishing volunteer programs—planning, recruiting, funding, evaluating; expanding volunteer opportunities; grantsmanship. Offers brochures/pamphlets, computerized information, informational newsletters, library facilities, placement on mailing lists, research, assistance and telephone reference services. Publications include *Voluntary Action Leadership*; *Volunteering*; *Exchange Networks*; *Volunteer Readership* (annual catalog). **How to Contact:** Write, call or visit. Responds to most inquiries within a week. Charges $20/hour for detailed library searches. **Tips:** ''Be sure your inquiries pertain to the issues concerned with volunteers. This is our only area of expertise.'' Recent information requests: ''What is the national dollar value of volunteer time?''; ''What are the most recent national statistics on volunteers?''; ''How do you set up a volunteer program?''

928• VOLUNTEERS OF AMERICA
National Headquarters, Suite 202, 3939 N. Causeway, Metairie LA 7002. (504)837-2652. Contact Person: National Director. **Description:** ''As a national Christian human services organization, Volunteers of America gives spiritual and material aid to those in need regardless of race or creed. A variety of human service programs are provided by the organization to serve families, children and youth, the disabled, alcoholics and drug abusers, offenders, ex-offenders, and the elderly. Some of the services and facilities offered include: emergency shelters, adoption services, low and moderate income housing, day care centers, boys' ranches, summer camps, group homes for the emotionally disturbed, communication centers for the deaf, detox centers, pre-release centers for offenders, halfway homes and vocational training for ex-offenders, congregate and home-delivered meals, nursing homes, and foster grandparent and senior volunteer programs.'' **Services:** Provides referral information on various services and client populations. Offers brochures, *The Volunteer Gazette*; an internal newspaper and *VOAgape*, a human services magazine. **How to Contact:** Write. Responds to most inquiries immediately.

929• WOMEN FOR SOBRIETY, INC.
Box 618, Quakertown PA 18951. (215)536-8026. Contact Person: Executive Director. **Description:** Self-help program for women alcoholics. **Services:** Provides advisory and referral information on alcoholism and women. Offers annual reports, brochures/pamphlets and informational newsletters. **How to Contact:** Write. Responds to most inquiries immediately. Enclose SASE. **Tips:** Recent information requests: ''What is the difference between AA and WFS?''; ''Why isn't Alcoholics Anonymous adequate for women alcoholics?''

INFORMATION SERVICES

Somewhere, something incredible is waiting to be known.

—Carl Sagan

This section is divided into three categories—clipping services, information retrieval and libraries. Each section highlights general resources whose business is information (obtaining, storing and providing it).

Bibliography

American Library Association. *American Library Directory*. 35th ed. Annual. Edited by Jaques Cattell Press. New York: Bowker.

Bragonier Jr., Reginald and David Fisher, eds. *What's What: A Visual Glossary of the Physical World*. Maplewood, NJ: Hammond, Inc., 1981. (Names and illustrations for hundreds of whatchamacallits)

Ethridge, James M. *Directory of Directories: An Annotated Guide to Business and Industrial Directories, Professional and Scientific Rosters and Other Lists and Guides of All Kinds*. 2d ed. Detroit: Gale Research Co., 1982.

Facts on File Yearbook. Annual. New York: Facts on File, Inc. (Cumulation of the weekly service covering US and world affairs and general current events)

Fenner, Peter and Martha C. Armstrong. *Research: A Practical Guide to Finding Information*. Los Altos, CA: William Kaufmann, Inc., 1981.

Harris, William H. and Judith S. Levey, eds. *The New Columbia Encyclopedia*. 4th ed. 1 vol. New York: Columbia University Press, 1975.

Kruzas, Anthony and John Schmittroth. *Encyclopedia of Information Systems and Services*. 5th ed. Detroit: Gale Research Co., 1982.

Miller, Mara. *Where to Go for What*. Englewood Cliffs, NJ: Prentice-Hall, 1981. (Information-gathering sources and techniques)

National Directory of Addresses and Telephone Numbers. Annual. New York: W.C.C. Directories, Inc.

New York Times Index. 1851 to date, semi-monthly. Annual Cumulation. New York: The New York Times.

Newspaper Enterprise Association. *World Almanac and Book of Facts*. Annual. New York: World Almanac.

Polking, Kirk. *Writer's Encyclopedia*. Cincinnati: Writer's Digest Books, 1983. (One-volume reference of terms, facts and figures, organizations and illustrations of the writing life)

Reader's Guide to Periodical Literature. 1900 to date, semi-monthly. New York: H.W. Wilson Co.

Sheehey, Eugene P. *Guide to Reference Books*. 9th ed. and supplement. Chicago: American Library Association, 1980. (Lists and annotates thousands of reference books by subject and type)

Thomas, Robert C. and James A. Ruffner. *Research Centers Directory*. 7th ed. Detroit: Gale Research Co., 1982. (University-related and other nonprofit research operations)

Todd, Alden. *Finding Facts Fast*. Berkeley, CA: Ten Speed Press, 1979. (Approaches to the process of finding facts)

Wasserman, Paul and J. O'Brien, eds. *Statistics Sources*. Detroit: Gale Research Co., 1982. (Identifies primary sources of statistical data on over 12,000 subjects)

Williams, Martha E. *Computer Readable Databases: A Directory and Data Sourcebook*. White Plains, NY: Knowledge Industry Publications, 1982.

Young, Harold C. and Margaret L., eds. *Directory of Special Libraries and Information Centers*. 6th ed. Detroit: Gale Research Co., 1981.

Clipping Services

Clipping bureaus are in the business of collecting information produced by the media. Writers needing up-to-the-minute, extended coverage of a particular topic or trend may consider using the services of a clipping bureau. In addition to providing print information from newspapers and magazines, some bureaus also monitor radio and television.

The range of coverage may be regional, national or international. Some clipping bureaus provide coverage of specific subjects.

The list below represents a sample of general clipping bureaus. Other clipping services may be found in *Literary Market Place* (New York: Bowker) or in the business/commercial directory of the Yellow Pages of larger cities.

930• ALLEN'S PRESS CLIPPING BUREAU
657 Mission St., San Francisco CA 94105. (415)392-2353. Contact Person: Manager. **Description:** "We've been in business for 90 years. We supply information from local (California), national and international newspapers." **Services:** Provides clippings from over 9,000 newspapers and 4,000 trade and consumer magazines covering many subject areas. **How to Contact:** Write or call. Responds to most inquiries immediately. Charges vary.

931• BACON'S CLIPPING BUREAU
332 S. Michigan Ave., Chicago IL 60604. (312)922-8419. Contact Person: President. **Description:** "To keep pace with today's information explosion, more and more businesses are using Bacon's services both here and abroad. With over 50 years experience in reading, evaluating and analyzing magazines and newspapers, Bacon's provides you with a highly trained staff that gives you the specific information required." **Services:** "As a press clipping bureau, we cover 4,000 business magazines and 500 newspapers." **How to Contact:** Write or call. Responds to most inquiries immediately. Charges $90/month plus 55¢/clipping for clipping services (3 months minimum), and $120 plus $3 shipping for publicity checker.

932• BURELLE PRESS CLIPPING BUREAU
75 E. Northfield, Livingston NJ 07039. (800)631-1160. (201)992-6600. Contact Person: Sales Manager. **Description:** "Burelle covers all national newspapers and consumer trade magazines on any subject." **Services:** Offers clipping services covering agriculture, art, business, celebrities, economics, entertainment, food, health/medicine, history, how-to, industry, law, music, nature, new products, politics, recreation, science, self-help, sports, technical data and travel. **How to Contact:** Write or call. Responds to most inquiries within a week. Charges for services.

933• CANADIAN PRESS CLIPPING SERVICE
481 University Ave., Toronto, Ontario, Canada M5W 1A7. (416)596-5223. Contact Person: Customer Liaison Representative. **Description:** Clipping service searching all Canadian press and magazines (English and French). **Services:** Provides news reference, advertising, technical and trade information on all subjects. **How to Contact:** Write, call or visit. Responds to all inquiries immediately. Charges for services.

934• INTERNATIONAL PRESS CLIPPING BUREAU, INC.
1868 Columbia Rd. NW, Washington DC 20009. (202)332-2000. Contact Person: President. **Description:** Clipping service. **Services:** Provides coverage of domestic and foreign publications and information on a broad range of subjects. **How to Contact:** Write or call. Responds to most inquiries immediately. Charges for services.

935• LUCE PRESS CLIPPINGS, INC.
420 Lexington Ave., New York NY 10017. (800)528-8226. Contact: Publicity Department. **Description:** Clipping bureau offering national coverage. **Services:** Provides information covering "all subjects, specific companies, institutions, etc." **How to Contact:** Write or call; prefers written requests. Charges for reading plus a per-clipping fee.

936• NEW ENGLAND NEWSCLIP AGENCY, INC.
5 Auburn St., Framingham MA 01701. (617)879-4460. Contact Person: Vice President/General

Manager. **Description:** "New England Newsclip Agency reads newspapers and magazines which cover the New England area." **Services:** Provides clippings covering a broad spectrum of subject areas. Material is also available from television and radio. **How to Contact:** Write or call. Responds to most inquiries immediately. Charges for services based on coverage. Copyright based on media standards of re-usage. **Tips:** "We read on a specific order from the present into the future. We do not do back-reading. Users should be ready to define informational needs in fairly specific fashion." Recent information requests: Detective story writer requested clippings of true crimes; newsletter writer sought stories on people overcoming physical handicaps.

937• NEWSVERTISING
Suite 603, 1868 Columbia Rd. NW, Washington DC 20009. (202)332-2000. Contact Person: General Manager. **Description:** Clipping service. **Services:** Offers "all media monitoring, clipping and retrieval services—news, editorial, TV-radio commentary, legislative, diplomatic researching on any subject." **How to Contact:** Write or call. Responds to most inquiries immediately.

938• PRESS INTELLIGENCE, INC.
1341 G St. NW, Washington DC 20005. (202)783-5810. Contact Person: President. **Description:** "We provide information from most of the nation's newspapers, magazines, weeklies, etc." **Services:** "We can cover every subject from private corporations to rock stars," including agriculture, art, business, celebrities, economics, entertainment, food, health/medicine, history, how-to, industry, law, music, nature, new products, politics, recreation, science, self-help, sports, technical data and travel. **How to Contact:** Write or call; prefers calls followed up with a letter for the file. Responds to most inquiries within a week. Charges for services; write for information.

939• PRESSCLIPS, INC.
47 Lawrence St., New Hyde Park NY 11040. (516)437-1047. Contact Person: Vice President, Sales. **Description:** "We tailor our clipping service to the client's requirements. Our coverage is local, regional or national." **Services:** Provides clippings in any field, "specific or general." **How to Contact:** Write or call. Responds to most inquiries immediately. Charges monthly reading fee that varies with coverage required plus 40¢/clipping. Annual contract also available. **Tips:** "Contact us by phone for specific suggestions." Recent information request: Clippings on a recently-published book.

Information Retrieval

The information services listed below are a multidisciplinary sample of "what's out there." Writers today have options galore for finding information they need by using the technology available. Included here are data base publishers who produce machine-readable data bases and related print products; online vendors who offer computerized search services by providing user access to their own or someone else's data bases; information brokers who gather information and facts (either via computers or manual searching) on a fee or contractual basis. Any of these organizations may also offer one or more additional information-related services. An entry for the trade association of the information industry is also included.

References to some of the more specialized information retrieval centers (ERIC Clearinghouse on Rural Education and Small Schools, Engineering Information, Inc., for example) are listed in the appropriate subject section of the book.

For a comprehensive roster of organizations engaged in information production and/or retrieval, consult *Computer-Readable Databases: A Directory and Sourcebook* (White Plains, NY: Knowledge Industry Publications). For a quick reference to the tools and products of the information industry, consult *Information Industry Market Place* (New York: Bowker). In addition, the *Encyclopedia of Information Systems and Services* (Detroit: Gale Research Co.) and its periodic supplements identify national and international information sources.

940• ACCESS INNOVATIONS, INC.
Box 40130, Albuquerque NM 87196. (505)265-3591. Contact Person: President. **Description:** "Information storage and retrieval systems, literature searches and document delivery services." **Services:** Provides bibliographical, how-to and referral information. "We provide literature searches, document delivery, data base design, abstracting, indexing, and data entry/word processing services." Offers computerized information searches, library facilities and research assistance. **How to Contact:** Write, call or visit. Responds to most inquiries immediately. Charges for consultations $35/hour; literature searches $25 minimum.

941• ASLIB
3 Belgrave Square, London, SW1X 8PL England. (LON)235-5050. Contact Person: Director. **Description:** Center for promoting the effective use of all kinds of information. Conducts research in information handling. **Services:** Provides advisory, analytical, bibliographical, historical, how-to, interpretative, referral, technical and trade information in all subject areas. Offers computerized information searches, informational newsletters, library facilities, placement on mailing lists, research assistance, statistics and telephone reference services. Publications catalog available. **How to Contact:** Write. Responds to most inquiries within a week. Charges nonmembers for services rendered. **Tips:** "Contact us for more details."

942• BIBLIOGRAPHIC RETRIEVAL SERVICES
1200 Route 7, Latham NY 12110. (800)833-4707. In New York and Canada (518)783-7251 (call collect). Contact: Customer Service. **Description:** "BRS is a major online search service which provides its users with access to major data bases in all areas of the life, physical, social and engineering sciences as well as business, economics and news." **Services:** "Our data bases provide advisory, analytical, bibliographical, historical, how-to, interpretative, referral, technical and trade information covering science and medicine, business and finance, education, social science-humanities, energy and environment and reference data bases." Offers brochures/pamphlets, informational newsletters and research assistance. Publications include *BRS Bulletin* (monthly); *System Reference Manual*; various *Data Base Guides*; brief papers exploring in-depth topics related to online searching. **How to Contact:** Write or call. Responds to most inquiries within a week. Charges for online access and some publications.

943• CAPITAL SYSTEMS GROUP, INC.(CSG)
11301 Rockville Pike, Kensington MD 20895. (301)881-9400. Contact Person: President. **Description:** "A technically-oriented information services firm, CSG, through its Infoquest program, can serve writers in the following ways: information research; reference assistance; manual literature searching; automated data base searching with emphasis on science, technology, business, medicine, and aviation; library research; monitoring federal agency activities; locating hard-to-find resources and document delivery of journal articles, government reports, proceedings, research reports, patents, foreign materials, and other identifiable documents. Located in the Washington DC area, we have direct access to the information resources of the federal government, trade associations, professional societies, special libraries, and major universities in the area. InfoQuest's trained librarians and information specialists can also directly search over 225 of the world's major computerized data bases." **Services:** Offers bibliographies, statistics, information searches and document delivery. Publications include a description of CSG's information research services, and a fee schedule. **How to Contact:** "Call or write for a preliminary consultation, for which there is no charge."

944• COMPUSERVE, INC.
Information Services Division, 5000 Arlington Centre Blvd., Columbus OH 43220. (800)848-8990. In Ohio (614)457-8650. Contact: Customer Service. **Description:** Videotex service to people who own personal computers or computer terminals and have them in their homes or offices. **Services:** Provides advisory, analytical, bibliographical, historical, how-to, interpretative, technical and trade information covering news, finance, entertainment, electronic shopping and banking, electronic mail, professional services and personal computing. Offers biographies, brochures/pamphlets, clipping services, computerized information searches, informational newsletters, press kits, research assistance and statistics. Publications include *Update* (monthly newsletter); *Today* (monthly magazine). **How to Contact:** Visit a local computer store. Responds to most inquiries immediately. Charges for search service and

publications. "Material online is not reproducible in any form." **Tips:** "Go to a Radio Shack Computer Center for a live demonstration."

945• THE DATA CENTER
464 19th St., Oakland CA 94612. (415)835-4692. **Description:** "The Data Center is a unique library of books, periodicals and well-organized clipping files. It is an independent, nonprofit, user-supported public interest research library. We organize and retrieve information for clients on political, economic, and social events from a local, national and international perspective. Our files include clippings that span the decade from over 350 periodicals. Specific areas of focus include corporations, labor, environmental issues, industries, government organizations and countries." **Services:** Provides advisory, bibliographical, how-to, technical and trade information on over 5,000 corporations; major industries; trade union activities; international labor organizations; working conditions; affirmative action; plant closures; occupational safety and health issues; banking and finance; international aid and trade; military, police, and intelligence agencies, national governments and economies; Central America social and human rights conditions; new right and neo conservatives and people in the news. Offers annual reports, biographical articles, brochures/pamphlets, clipping services, information searches, library facilities, line graphics, research assistance, statistics, and telephone reference services. Publications include press profiles on timely subjects; research methodology guide. **How to Contact:** Write, call or visit. Responds to most inquiries within a week. Charges vary according to service.

946• DATA COURIER, INC.
620 S. 5th St., Louisville KY 40202. (502)582-4111. Contact: Customer Service. **Description:** Publisher of 2 data bases: ABI/INFORM, business and management information data base and a pharmaceutical news index. **Services:** Offers "information services by calendar-year subscription; magnetic tape leasing of data bases." Publications include catalog of services. **How to Contact:** Write or call and request catalog. Responds to most inquiries within a week, "depending on what is needed." **Tips:** Recent information requests: Custom searches in business and management, quality control, fringe benefits, women in management.

947• DIALOG INFORMATION SERVICES, INC.
3460 Hillview Ave., Palo Alto CA 94304. (800)227-1927. Contact: Marketing Department. **Description:** "DIALOG Information Services, Inc. offers an online information retrieval system with more than 170 data bases covering every topic from art to zoology. DIALOG is accessible with any standard computer terminal or personal computer and an ordinary phone line." **Services:** Provides bibliographical, historical, how-to, referral, technical and trade information in virtually all subject areas from agriculture and chemistry to business, humanities, law, medicine and current affairs. **How to Contact:** Write or call. Responds to most inquiries immediately. "DIALOG charges are based on the amount of time a client is connected to the system; each data base has an hourly rate. To use DIALOG, one must complete an order form to initiate service and get a password. Purchasing the system manual, *Guide to DIALOG Searching*, and attending the System Seminar are highly recommended." **Tips:** "Writers should search applicable DIALOG data bases before going to the library—thereby, saving hours of researching for information manually."

948• DOW JONES NEWS/RETRIEVAL SERVICE
Box 300, Princeton NJ 08540. (800)257-5114. Contact: Customer Service. **Description:** "Dow Jones News/Retrieval Service provides online information from the *Wall Street Journal*, *Barron's*, Dow Jones News Wire and other sources for corporations, financial institutions, small businesses and consumers. This information enables them to make informed decisions on business and financial matters." Also offers consumer data bases not related to business and finance. **Services:** Provides analytical, bibliographical, historical and trade information on companies, industries, economics and finance as well as data bases covering movie reviews, sports, weather and an entire encyclopedia (Academic American). Offers annual reports online (1OK) and free text search capabilities. **How to Contact:** Write or call. Responds to most inquiries within a week. Charges for online access of data bases; various pricing plans. "Users must have a personal computer, terminal or word processor on which to access Dow Jones News/Retrieval."

949• FIND/SVP
500 5th Ave., New York NY 10110. Contact Person: Business Development

Manager. **Description:** "FIND/SVP is a total information resource offering a wide variety of research services. Small and large projects are undertaken. Searching of computer bibliographic data bases is a specialty." **Services:** Provides analytical, bibliographical and trade information covering health care, advertising, food and beverages, company information, energy, finance, foreign trade and demographics. Offers bibliographies, biographies, statistics, brochures/pamphlets and information searches. Publications include *How to Win with Information or Lose Without It*; *The Information Catalog*; *Findex: The Directory of Market Research Reports, Studies and Surveys*; and a brochure describing the services of FIND/SVP. **How to Contact:** Call. Responds to most inquiries (for retainer clients) immediately. Charges monthly fee, based on usage. "Information searches generally cost between $25-50/hour. Computer data base searches start at $50, plus computer online costs."

950• GATHERFACTS
255 Kennedy Ct., Louisville KY 40206. (502)896-0943. Contact Person: Owner. **Description:** "We do library research, computer searches, compile bibliographies, organize files, compile indexes." **Services:** Provides bibliographical, historical and how-to information in subject areas including business, management, sociology, psychology, political science, religion, Kentucky history and mining. Offers aid in arranging interviews, computerized information searches, library facilities, photos (local to Louisville only), research assistance and telephone reference services. **How to Contact:** Write or call. Responds to most inquiries within a week. Charges $30/hour plus costs of photocopies, computer searches, long distance phone calls, mileage, (i.e., any expenses incurred in the search). **Tips:** "If some sources have already been consulted, list those to avoid duplication."

951• IN-FACT, RESEARCH AND INFORMATION SERVICES
Righter Rd., Rensselaerville NY 12147. (518)797-5154. Contact Person: President. **Description:** Library research and copy editing firm. **Services:** Provides bibliographical and historical information on any subject. Offers research assistance and copy editing. **How to Contact:** Write, call or visit. Responds to most inquiries within a week. Charges are determined on an individual basis. **Tips:** "Be specific." Recent information requests: "Locate a photo of a local brewery's beer wagon"; "Summarize a series of legislative hearings."

952• INFO-MART
Box 2400, Santa Barbara CA 93120. (805)965-5555, 965-0265. Contact Person: Owner. **Description:** Computerized library research service. **Services:** Provides bibliographical, historical, referral and technical information in all subject areas. Offers computerized information searches at $50/hour, manual searches and research assistance at $30/hour. **How to Contact:** Call. Responds to most inquiries within a month. Basic computerized search/$175; comprehensive search/$450. **Tips:** "Call us early in the project."

953• INFORMATION ACCESS COMPANY
404 Sixth Ave., Menlo Park CA 94025. (800)227-8431. In California (415)367-7171. Contact: Customer Services or Marketing Department. **Description:** "We are a data base publisher, publishing indexes and bibliographic information in microfilm, computer-readable and print formats. Indexes/data bases are available on a subscription basis as well as online through DIALOG Information Services. We publish indexes to meet the needs of librarians, library users, writers, students, professionals, information specialists and other researchers." **Services:** Provides bibliographical information from general, widely-read periodical literature (multidisciplinary); national newspapers—business and news; legal periodical literature; trade and industry-related periodical literature. Publications include *The Magazine Index*™; *The National Newspaper Index*™; *The Legal Resource Index*™; *The Business Index*™; *Trade and Industry Index*™; *Newsearch*™; *Current Law Index*™. **How to Contact:** Write or call. Responds to inquiries within a week. Charges for services. Microfilm products available on a subscription basis; online data bases available on a per use basis through DIALOG. **Tips:** "Use your local library (be it public, academic, corporate). Libraries usually have microfilm indexes or access to online data bases."

954• INFORMATION/DOCUMENTATION
Box 17109, Dulles International Airport, Washington DC 20041. (703)979-5363. Contact Person: Research Specialist. **Description:** "INFO/DOC primarily furnishes US government publications, documents, reports, freedom of information items, domestic and foreign patents and literature. We

retrieve articles from the vast holdings of Washington area libraries, including the Library of Congress, the National Library of Medicine and many others." **Services:** Provides government publications, document delivery, library research; advisory, analytical, bibliographical, historical, how-to, interpretative, referral, technical and trade information in all subject areas. Offers annual reports, biographies, brochures/pamphlets, computerized information searches, informational newsletters, library facilities, photos, placement on mailing lists, research assistance and statistics. **How to Contact:** Write or call. Responds to most inquiries within a week. Charges for documents, research time and handling fees. "Ask for our information packet."

955• INFORMATION FUTURES
2217 College Station, Pullman WA 99163. (509)332-5726. Contact Person: Director. **Description:** "We provide research and reports in areas of futuristics, educational technology, and applications of information or telecommunications technology. We currently specialize in micro-computers." **Services:** Provides advisory, how-to, interpretative, referral and trade information on educational technology, micro-computers (specializing in utilization), futuristics. Owns and operates Community Computer Center providing full service in rural cities of the Northwest. Offers aid in arranging interviews, computerized information searches, research assistance, telephone reference services and access to micro-computer product listings. Publications catalog available. **How to Contact:** Write, call or visit (by appointment). Responds to most inquiries within a week. Fees charged according to specific task. "If professional time is assigned, fees are assessed. Estimates for all fee-based services available in advance. Professional reference or contacts to colleagues generally at no cost." **Tips:** "Our interest is high in areas exploring utilization of 'new' technologies supportive of human communication resulting in learning. Writers should be aware (need not be specialists) in the field."

956• INFORMATION INDUSTRY ASSOCIATION
316 Pennsylvania Ave. SE, Washington DC 20003. (202)544-1969. Contact Person: Communications Director. **Description:** Trade association of companies involved in products and services related to information transfer and the information industry in general. **Services:** Provides trade information; offers aid in arranging interviews with member firms. Publications include *Information Sources*, annual directory of information providers "that package and deliver data bases via the new technologies." **How to Contact:** Write or call. Responds to most inquiries within a week.

957• INFORMATION ON DEMAND
Box 9550, Berkeley CA 94709. (800)227-0750. In California (415)841-1145. Contact Person: President. **Description:** "We do all types of information gathering including literature searching, market research and document delivery." Sources include over 150 computer data bases, trade associations, government agencies and experts. **Services:** Provides bibliographical, historical and referral information in all subject areas. Offers computerized information searches, research assistance and telephone reference services. "We provide copies of any published document." **How to Contact:** Write, call or visit. Responds to most inquiries immediately. Charges $45/hour plus costs (2 hour minimum) for literature searches. "Call us to discuss your needs and our capabilities. We always give you a quote before we start."

958• NATIONAL REFERRAL CENTER
Library of Congress, Washington DC 20540. (202)287-5670. Contact: Head, Referral Services Section. **Description:** "The NRC refers people who have a question, on any subject, to organizations that can provide the answer. To serve this purpose effectively, the center maintains and keeps up-to-date a data base in which more than 13,000 'information resources' are described in detail. The data base may be searched online at the Library of Congress, and also through the DOE/RECON network maintained by the Department of Energy; it is also used by the center for publishing listings and directories." **Services:** Provides referral information in all subject areas. "We refer the inquirer free of charge to organizations that have the competence to provide answers and have indicated a willingness to do so. All subject areas are covered, from science and engineering to the humanities and the performing arts. Responses may be in the form of computer print-outs describing the information capabilities and services of one or more organizations. Some responses—on topics of apparent current interest—are 'canned' in advance and issued free on request in the informal *Who Knows?* series. More formal volumes are published in the series

Directory of Information Resources in the United States, available for purchase from the US Government Printing Office." **How to Contact:** Write, call or visit. "Calls are welcome, since they afford an opportunity to discuss and 'fine-tune' the request." Responds to most inquiries within a week. **Tips:** "The center's referral specialists have numerous personal contacts that they will use if the data base doesn't seem to cover a given topic. Our services are based on the premise that it is often quicker and more efficient to discuss a topic directly with someone who knows than to search the literature." Recent information request: The average per-acre yield of sugar beets in the US. ("We referred caller to American Society of Sugar Beet Technologists!")

959• NATIONAL TECHNICAL INFORMATION SERVICE
5285 Port Royal Rd., Springfield VA 22161. (703)487-4737. Contact Person: Chief Officer of Market Development in Charge of Promotion. **Description:** "The National Technical Information Service (NTIS) is a self-supporting, nonprofit, information service organization. It promotes the general welfare by channeling information about technological innovations and other specialized information to business, industry, government and the public. Its products and services are intended to increase the efficiency and effectiveness of the US research and development enterprise; to support US foreign policy goals by assisting the social and economic development of other nations; and to increase the availability of foreign technical information in the US. NTIS undertakes and develops products and programs having the potential for self-support and which are appropriate for government, instead of private enterprise." **Services:** "Offers help in location of useful reports through published searches and online computer search service; lease of the NTIS bibliographic data file (on magnetic tape); and current summaries of new research reports in 26 abstract newsletters—each devoted to a different subject (usually published weekly); Selected Research in Microfiche (SRIM) automatically sends subscribers full texts of new research reports in their selected field of interest." **How to Contact:** Write or call.

960• THE NEW YORK TIMES INFORMATION SERVICE (NYTIS)
Mt. Pleasant Office Park, 1719A Route 10, Parsippany NJ 07054. (201)539-5850. Contact Person: Marketing Services Manager. **Description:** Computerized information retrieval system containing a number of different news and business information data bases. NYTIS is accessible with standard computer terminals, or personal computer, modem and phone line. **Services:** Offers the following data bases: The Information Bank (current affairs); *The New York Times* Online; Disclosure II (business and finance); Deadline Data on World Affairs; Advertising and Marketing Intelligence; SUMM (news summaries). **How to Contact:** Write or call. Responds to inquiries as soon as possible. Subscription to NYTIS data bases is by contract only. Contact Marketing Services Manager for more information.

961• PACKAGED FACTS
274 Madison Ave, New York NY 10016. (212)532-5533. Contact Person: President. **Description:** "Packaged Facts is a research company with files of clippings on literally thousands of topics. We will research historical background; we have access to any material desired." **Services:** "Our files cover all areas of library research including agriculture, art, business, celebrities, economics, entertainment, food, health/medicine, history, how-to, industry, law, music, nature, new products, politics, recreation, science, self-help, sports, technical data and travel. **How to Contact:** Write or call. Responds to most inquiries immediately. Charges for services; write for free estimate.

962• RESEARCH VENTURES
3050 College Ave., Berkeley CA 94705. (415)654-4810. Contact Person: Coordinator. **Description:** Research and information organization. "We'll do your research for you or teach you how to do it, as well as how to organize it and/or how to present it. We will supervise or train researchers; advise on formats or annotations; do light editing and offer advice on structure." **Services:** Provides advisory, analytical, bibliographical, how-to, interpretative and referral information in "just about every field. Specialties are social sciences, children, education, environment and ecology, peace, and the arms race." Offers computerized information searches and research assistance. "Annotated bibliographies or bibliographic guides are a specialty." **How to Contact:** Write, call or visit. Responds to most inquiries within a week. Charges $10-20/hour. **Tips:** "Try to think through questions before calling. Know what you want to know and know what your biases and areas of ignorance are in these areas."

963• SOURCE TELECOMPUTING CORPORATION (THE SOURCE)
1616 Anderson Rd., McLean VA 22102. (703)734-7500. Contact Person: Manager, Corporate Communications. **Description:** The Source is a large news and information data base subscribed to by over 25,000 users. "We provide electronic information and communication services to professionals and business decision makers." **Services:** Provides advisory, analytical, how-to, interpretative, referral, technical and trade information on the teletext and videotex fields; electronic shopping and transactions; electronic opinion research; use of The Source to meet others, get advice, solve problems, obtain needed information; electronic publishing; new professions; future use of electronics in home and business; electronic communication (i.e., electronic mail computer conferencing); how subscribers in a wide variety of businesses and professions use videotex. Offers aid in arranging interviews, biographies, brochures/pamphlets, clipping services, computerized information searches, informational newsletters, photos, placement on mailing lists, press kits, research assistance, statistics, telephone reference services and "online research among subscribers in specific professions, locales; information on uses of our system." Special new service "Scribs" facilitates freelance assignments on computer telecommunications. Publications include *Information Kit*; *Computer Center Kit*; monthly newsletter; news releases. **How to Contact:** Write or call. Responds to most inquiries immediately. Charges for subscription to use The Source. **Tips:** "Those who subscribe to our service are in the forefront of the personal computing field. We are a 'one stop' reference for anyone writing about uses, applications for personal computing and videotex services." Recent information request: "Is anyone using The Source who is a student, business entrepreneur, or physician from Minneapolis?"

Libraries

People have long recognized the value in and the need for collecting, organizing and preserving information—be it in books, on microform or clay tablets. Today, according to the 35th edition of the *American Library Directory*, there are nearly thirty thousand libraries in the United States alone: public, academic, corporate, private and other special libraries with services as diverse as the patrons they serve. Unless writers know of a particular library with a specialized collection which can provide needed information, they should probably begin their library research with their own public library. (See page 10.) Even if the information is not available there, it is likely that the librarians on staff will have communications with a network of other libraries (see American Library Association entry below) and their state library. Local libraries can often provide referrals—places to look next.

Some special libraries (e.g., National Agricultural Library, National Library of Medicine, etc.) are listed in the appropriate subject sections of this book. A complete list of special libraries may be found in the *Directory of Special Libraries and Information Centers* (Detroit: Gale Research Co.). Another valuable reference for locating university-related and nonprofit organizations and their libraries is the *Research Centers Directory* (Detroit: Gale Research Co.).

The libraries listed below are recognized for the size of their collections and/or the depth of the resources they have in certain fields. They have supplied information about their unique services and programs of interest to writers and the general public. These largest of libraries are bustling places. As such, they do not always have the time or staff to handle questions from around the country that could easily be tackled on a local level. But after writers have "looked everywhere else," it may be one of these information giants that can ultimately provide an answer—or yet another lead.

964• AMERICAN LIBRARY ASSOCIATION
50 E. Huron St., Chicago IL 60611. (312)944-6780. Contact Person: Public Information Director. **Description:** "Founded in 1876, the American Library Association has 38,000 members, 200 staff and 56 local groups. Members include libraries, librarians, publishers, educators, trustees, friends of libraries and others interested in the responsibilities of libraries in the educational, social and cultural needs of society. Our objective is to promote and improve library

service and librarianship. We establish standards of services; promote access to information and intellectual freedom; conduct liaison with federal agencies; promote popular understanding and public acceptance of the value of library services; maintain a special library and publish monographs, pamphlets, books and journals.'' **Services:** Offers bibliographies, brochures/pamphlets, placement on mailing list, newsletter and press information on libraries and library issues. Publications available. **How to Contact:** Write or call. Responds to most inquiries within a week. "Communication by mail is preferred."

965• CHICAGO PUBLIC LIBRARY

425 N. Michigan Ave., Chicago IL 60611. (312)269-2900. **Description:** "Our collection totals more than 8 million resources, over 4 million of which are books. We maintain 90 facilities including the central library, branches, and regional libraries, a library for the blind and physically handicapped, a library in the Cook County Jail and a cultural center.'' **Services:** Provides bibliographical, historical, referral and technical information in all subject areas. Offers aid in arranging interviews (Contact Department of Public Information 269-2986), annual reports, biographies, brochures/pamphlets, computerized information searches, library facilities, research assistance and telephone reference services. **How to Contact:** Write, call or visit. Charges for some computer information searches. "Special collections and rare books do not circulate.'' **Tips:** "Of special interest for writers is Chicago Public Library's Literature and Language Division which has materials on creative writing, language and communication skills improvement, journalism, publishing and how to get published, as well as all types of literary periodicals. The library's specialized services include the Computer-Assisted Reference Center, which is part of the Business/Science/Technology Division (269-2915); the Government Publications Department's computer search services on state and federal legislation; the Information Center (269-2800) for answering quick reference questions; Dial-Law (644-0800), which offers information on laws and the legal system; and Dial-Pet (342-5738), which provides pet care information. Library collections have materials for research on a wide variety of subjects, and all departments answer reference questions in person and by telephone. Materials on careers in writing can be found in the Business Information Center's special section on Careers.''

966• LIBRARY OF CONGRESS

1st and Independence Aves. SE, Washington DC 20540. (202)287-5108. Contact: Information Office. **Description:** "The Library of Congress, the research arm of the US Congress, also serves as the national library of the United States. It acquires resources in all forms—books, periodicals, maps, music, manuscripts, prints and photographs, motion picture and television film, records and discs, and microform—and makes them available for research. Collections number over 78 million items (more than 19 millions books) available on the premises. The Library of Congress is not a circulating library, but does make material available to serious investigators in their own libraries available on interlibrary loan.'' **Services:** Provides information in "every subject but agriculture and clinical medicine which are covered by two other national libraries.'' Offers aid in arranging interviews, annual reports, bibliographies, biographies, statistics, brochures/pamphlets, placement on mailing list, newsletter, photos and press kits. "The Information Office can provide brochures about various activities and holdings of the library. A *List of Library of Congress Publications in Print*, revised annually, includes both free and priced publications. Review copies of library publications may be requested by book reviewers and review journals.'' **How to Contact:** "Writers interested in covering the Library of Congress, its services, activities and events may write, call or visit the Information Office, Room LM-103, James Madison Memorial Building. The office will provide information, arrange interviews and facilitate photographing or filming on library premises. Writers may also contact this office for guidance in using the collections of the library. The library cannot undertake research on behalf of any of its patrons. Reference questions that can be answered in 15 minutes are accepted; inquirers with more difficult problems are invited to do their own research.'' Charges for photocopying services and duplication of sound recordings. **Tips:** *Editor's Note*: Consult the title index under "Library of Congress" for listing locations of the various divisions of the national library.

967• LOS ANGELES PUBLIC LIBRARY

630 W. 5th St., Los Angeles CA 90071. (213)626-7461. **Description:** "Collection of resources numbers in excess of 2 million volumes covering a broad range of subject areas.'' **Services:** Provides advisory, analytical, bibliographical, historical, how-to, interpretative, referral, technical and trade information in all subject areas with emphasis on material from and about the West

and southern California in general. ''In addition, we have a strong genealogy collection; a complete US patent collection; much material on the Pacific Basin; a collection of orchestral scores; a children's literature historical collection; in excess of 200,000 volumes in the fiction collection; resources in 28 different languages; and a collection of US federal and military standards and specifications. We also maintain the Security Pacific National Bank collection of more than 225,000 historical photos.'' Offers annual reports, biographies, brochures/pamphlets, clipping services, computerized information searches, library facilities, photos, research assistance, statistics and telephone reference services. **How to Contact:** Write, call or visit. Charges for computer searches and photocopying. **Tips:** ''Be specific in your inquiry. Many times a telephone call will help identify the materials we have available for writers. Anyone in the country can get a free library card at the LAPL; show us something with your name and address on it. The best time to get telephone reference assistance is Saturday.''

968• NATIONAL LIBRARY OF CANADA/BIBLIOTHEQUE NATIONALE DU CANADA
395 Wellington St., Ottawa, Ontario, Canada K1A 0N4. (613)995-9481. Contact: Reference and Bibliographies Services Division. **Description:** National Library of Canada provides ''interlibrary loan, location, reference, referral, advisory and consulting services; compiles and publishes a national bibliography (entitled *Canadiana*) in which books produced in Canada, written or prepared by Canadians or of special interest or significance to Canada may be noted and described; compiles and/or publishes other bibliographies, checklists, indexes and union lists, coordinating the library services of government departments, branches, and agencies; collects, by purchase or other means, books for the library; compiles and maintains a Canadian Union Catalogue in which the contents of the principal library collections throughout Canada may be listed; ensures the availability of Canadian materials in the context of universal availability of publications.'' **Services:** Provides advice, instruction and referrals, as well as factual and bibliographic reference services in social sciences and humanities; Canadiana; music; Canadian children's literature; library science. Offers computerized literature searches and current awareness services, research assistance, telephone reference services; provides Canadian Theses on Microfiche. Publications catalog available. **How to Contact:** Write, call, visit or use electronic mail. Responds to most inquiries within a week. Charges for online retrospective searches and photocopying. *Guide for Researchers* (free on request) explains services and facilities available. **Tips:** ''Study rooms exist for long term (3 months) researchers; lockers for short term use. Building pass and registration required for after-hours library use. Regular hours 8:30-5:00 Mon.-Thurs.; extended to 6:00 on Fridays in certain public service areas. For general questions about the library itself, contact Public Relations Office (613)995-7969.''

969• NEW YORK PUBLIC LIBRARY
5th Ave. and 42nd St., New York NY 10018. (212)661-7220. **Description:** ''We are a research library, museum and archive. We provide resources in various subjects; our collection numbers 6 million volumes and about 12 million non-book resources, such as manuscripts, maps, prints, etc.'' **Services:** Provides bibliographical, historical, referral and technical information in all subject areas except medicine and law. Offers annual reports, biographies, clipping services, computerized information searches, informational newsletters, library facilities, photos, research assistance and telephone reference services (212)340-0849. ''We also have special study rooms available to writers and researchers.'' **How to Contact:** Write, call or visit. Responds to most inquiries within a month. Charges for photocopying. ''All materials must be used on the premises.'' **Tips:** The NYPL has special collections in the performing and visual arts, ethnic subjects, humanities and social sciences, science and technology, as well as a patents collection, rare book and manuscript collection and a newspaper annex. ''The best place to start is in the public catalog of the general research division.''

LANGUAGE AND LITERATURE

Literature is language charged with meaning.
—Ezra Pound

These resources cover the areas of English and foreign languages, linguistics and usage, literature and translation.

Additional writing-related resources are available in both The Arts and Communications/Entertainment categories.

Bibliography

Benét, William Rose. *Reader's Encyclopedia*. 2d ed. New York: Thomas Y. Crowell, 1965. (Classic one-volume reference to the authors, characters, works, intellectual forces, terminology of world literature)

Brewer, E. Cobham, ed. *Brewer's Dictionary of Phrase and Fable*. Centenary Edition. rev. ed. New York: Harper and Row Publishers, 1981.

Carroll, David, ed. *Dictionary of Foreign Terms in the English Language*. New York: Hawthorn Books, 1979.

Cassell's Encyclopedia of World Literature. 3 vols. New York: Morrow and Co., 1973.

Chicago Manual of Style. 13th ed. rev. and enl. Chicago: University of Chicago Press, 1982. (or other manuals: *The Elements of Style*; *Words into Type*, etc.)

Clarke, Jack A., ed. *The Reader's Adviser*. 12th ed. New York: Bowker, 1977. (Especially useful for booksellers and librarians—3 volumes cover American and British book industry, literature and reference works; includes bibliography and annotations)

Copperud, Roy H. *American Usage & Style: A Consensus*. New York: Van Nostrand Reinhold, 1979. (or other usage books: *Shaw's Dictionary of Problem Words and Expressions*; *Harper Dictionary of Contemporary Usage*, etc.)

DeSola, R., ed. *Abbreviations Dictionary*. 6th ed. New York: Elsevier, 1981.

A Dictionary of Literary Terms. Garden City, NY: Doubleday, 1977.

Granger's Index to Poetry. New York: Columbia University Press, 1982.

Koster, Donald N. *American Literature and Language: A Guide to Information Sources*. Detroit: Gale Research Co., 1982.

March's Thesaurus & Dictionary of the English Language. New York: Abbeville Press, 1980. (or other thesauri: *Roget's Thesaurus*; *Webster's New World Thesaurus*, etc.)

Miller, Don Ethan, ed. *The Book of Jargon: An Essential Guide to the Inside Language of Today*. New York: Macmillan, 1981.

Oxford Dictionary of Quotations. 3d ed. New York: Oxford University Press, 1979. (or other quotation books: *Bartlett's Familiar Quotations*; *Know or Listen to Those Who Know*, etc.)

Pearl, Anita. *Dictionary of Popular Slang*. Middle Village, NY: Jonathan David Publishers, Inc., 1980.

Urdang, Laurence and Nancy La Roche, eds. *Picturesque Expressions: A Thematic Dictionary*. Detroit: Gale Research Co., 1980.

Webster's Third New International Dictionary Unabridged: The Great Library of the English Language. Springfield, MA: G&C Merriam, 1981.

970• HORATIO ALGER SOCIETY
4907 Allison Dr., Lansing MI 48910. Contact Person: Secretary. **Description:** "The society was founded to further the philosophy of Horatio Alger Jr., and to publicize through its bimonthly publication information on the life and writings of this famous 19th century American author." **Services:** Provides advisory, bibliographical, historical, referral information on the life and works of Alger. Offers biographies and informational publication. Publications include *Newsboy*, (bimonthly). **How to Contact:** Write. Responds to most inquiries within a week.

Enclose SASE with all inquiries. Give credit to the Horatio Alger Society. **Tips:** "Virtually all of the information on Alger in libraries is fictitious, based on a 1928 hoax biography. Don't be surprised if the books we steer you to or information we provide contradicts that which you have already found." Recent information requests: "I have an old Alger book. What is it worth?"; "Horatio Alger knew Edward Statemeyer, who started the Hardy Boys and Nancy Drew series. Do you have any material on him?"

971• AMERICAN DIALECT SOCIETY
English Dept., MacMurray College, Jacksonville IL 62650. (217)245-6151, ext. 284. Contact Person: Executive Secretary. **Description:** "ADS is a national association of scholars concerned with studying the English language in North America—especially variations in vocabulary, pronunciation, grammar." **Services:** Provides analytical, bibliographical, historical, interpretative, referral and technical information "in our publications." Information covers contemporary American English (vocabulary, pronunciation, grammar, points of usage); regional and social variation in American English; dialects of other languages in North America. Offers aid in arranging interviews and research. Publications include newsletter of the ADS (3 times a year; gives meetings, notices of current activities) and 2 journals: *American Speech* (quarterly) and *PADS* (occasional monographs). **How to Contact:** Write. Responds to most inquiries within a week. Charges subscription fee for journals and newsletter. "Be patient and understanding; we're all part-time volunteers and have no paid staff." **Tips:** "Write for a free sample newsletter, which gives a good idea of the range of our activities and interests and lists coming meetings. Talks given at our meetings and papers in our journals are often non-technical and readily lend themselves to feature articles of general interest. Our *Dictionary of American Regional English* (DARE), edited by Frederic Cassidy (University of Wisconsin), will be an especially rich and fascinating source of information." Recent information requests: "Where can I find information about Brooklynese, Southern accents and Utahn?"; "What experts could I interview?"

972• AMERICAN LITERARY TRANSLATORS ASSOCIATION
University of Texas at Dallas, Box 688, Mail Section 1102, Richardson TX 75080. (214)690-2093. Contact Person: Executive Secretary. **Description:** ALTA "provides essential services to literary translators of all languages and a professional forum for the exchange of ideas on the translator's art." The association works to enhance the art of literary translation. **Services:** Provides advisory, bibliographical and referral information on the translation of literary material into the English language. Offers brochures/pamphlets, computerized information searches, informational newsletters, library facilities (on matters of translation) and statistics. Publications include *Translation Review*; newsletter. **How to Contact:** Write. Responds to most inquiries within a week. Charges membership fee. Inquiries must come from individuals involved in literary translation.

973• AMERICAN SCIENCE FICTION ASSOCIATION
Box 10, Port Neches TX 77651. Contact Person: Executive Vice President. **Description:** Individuals interested in all science fiction and fantasy arts and promoting all aspects of writing and publishing of science fiction and fantasy items. **Services:** Provides advisory, analytical, how-to, referral information on science fiction and fantasy writings of all nature. Offers aid in arranging interviews, annual reports, informational newsletters, library facilities and statistics. Publications include *Journal of the ASFA* (monthly) and newsletter (monthly)—both to members only. "We also publish books of members and non-members." **How to Contact:** Write. Responds to most inquiries within a week. Offers service to members only.

974• AMERICAN TRANSLATORS ASSOCIATION (ATA)
109 Croton Ave., Ossining NY 10562. (914)941-1500. Contact Person: Staff Administrator. **Description:** ATA works "to advance the standards of translation and promote the intellectual and material interests of translators and interpreters in the United States." **Services:** Provides advisory information and referrals to translators as well as general information on the profession of the translator, "ranging from what training is needed to various types of translating jobs." Offers brochures/pamphlets. Publications include *ATA Chronicle* (monthly newsletter); *Translator Training Guidelines* (includes a model curriculum for training translators at university level, bibliography of source material, list of institutions offering translation courses). **How to Contact:** Write or call. Responds to most inquiries within a week. Charges for newsletter and some publications.

975•   JANE AUSTEN SOCIETY OF NORTH AMERICA
Box 621, Nanuet NY 10954. (914)425-9548. Contact Person: President. **Description:** "Literary society which provides a meeting place for members to discuss the life, works, critical essays and biographical studies of Jane Austen and encourages interest in the field of Jane Austen studies." **Services:** Provides bibliographical and referral information related to Jane Austen studies. Offers bibliographies and library facilities. "We maintain a library of 1,000 volumes including recordings, tapes, slides and memorabilia." Publications include newsletter. **How to Contact:** Write. Responds to most inquiries within a month. **Tips:** Recent information request: Background on Jane Austen and her music.

976•   BERLITZ TRANSLATION SERVICE
Research Park, Bldg. 0, 1101 State Rd., Princeton NJ 08540. (609)924-8500. Contact Person: Director. **Description:** "We provide language services—specifically translation, interpretation, language consultation services." **Services:** Provides advisory and translation services in any subject area. **How to Contact:** Write, call or visit. "Each project is evaluated individually; translation rates are based on language combination requested, nature of the material, volume, deadline, final format required, etc. National network of sales offices and production facilities; worldwide resources; communications by word processor, computer, telecopier and telex."

977•   THE BIBLIOGRAPHICAL SOCIETY OF AMERICA
Box 397, Grand Central Station, New York NY 10163. Contact Person: Executive Secretary. **Description:** An organization of collectors, librarians and others interested in books; encourages bibliographical scholarship. **Services:** Provides bibliographical information on rare books. Publications include scholarly journal. **How to Contact:** Write.

978•   PEARL S. BUCK BIRTHPLACE FOUNDATION, INC.
Box 126, Hillsboro WV 24946. (304)653-4430. Contact Person: Executive Director. **Description:** The foundation exists to "operate the Historic House Museum of 1892 (Pearl S. Buck birthplace); to establish a national and international center for arts and humanities; and to contribute to educational and cultural development of the region, state and nation. We conduct tours of the museum and restored barn seven days a week, all year long. Also, we have an annual Pearl S. Buck birthday celebration (June 26th); an author's day in August; and St. Nicholas Day (a Dutch celebration of Pearl S. Buck's ancestors) in December." **Services:** Provides bibliographical, historical and referral information. Offers aid in arranging interviews, bibliographies, brochures/pamphlets, information searches and newsletters (to members). Publications include *The Works of Pearl S. Buck* (a bibliography); manuscripts of Pearl S. Buck available to researchers on a limited basis. **How to Contact:** Write or call. Responds to most inquiries within a week.

979•   LEWIS CARROLL SOCIETY OF NORTH AMERICA
617 Rockford Rd., Silver Spring MD 20902. Contact Person: President. **Description:** Individuals interested in the life and works of Lewis Carroll "and his continuing effect on our culture." **Services:** Provides information on the life and writing of Lewis Carroll. Offers informational newsletters. Publications include *Knight Letter* and various chapbooks. **How to Contact:** Write. Responds to most inquiries within a week. Charges for membership and publications.

980•   JOSEPH CONRAD SOCIETY OF AMERICA
Dept. of English, SUNY, New Paltz NY 12561. Contact Person: President and Editor. **Description:** Professors, students and others interested in promoting the study of Joseph Conrad's work and life. **Services:** Provides bibliographical, interpretative, referral information. Offers annual reports, biographies and informational newsletters. Publications include *Joseph Conrad Today* (newsletter). **How to Contact:** Write. Responds to most inquiries within a month. Charges for newsletter subscriptions.

981•   THE DICKENS HOUSE MUSEUM
48 Doughty St., London, WC1N 2LF, UK. Tel. (01)405-2127. Contact Person: Curator. **Description:** "The museum spreads knowledge and appreciation of Charles Dickens and his works. **Service:** Provides advisory, analytical, bibliographical, historical and interpretative information on Dickens's life, works, times and circle. Offers library facilities, photos, research assist-

ance and telephone reference services. Publications include *The Dickensian*, journal of the Dickens Fellowship (3 times/year) and *Mr. Dick's Kite*, news sheet of the Dickens Fellowship (occasional). **How to Contact:** Write, call or visit. Responds to most inquiries immediately. Charges research fee for any services requiring more than routine checking of information. Give credit to the Dickens House Museum. **Tips:** Recent information request: "Do you have any information about Dickens's relationship to Thomas Cooper, the poet?"

982• THE EIGHTEEN NINETIES SOCIETY (INCORPORATING THE FRANCIS THOMPSON SOCIETY)
28 Carlingford Rd., Hampstead, London, NW3 1RX, UK. Contact Person: Honorable Secretary. **Description:** Individuals interested in promoting interest in the literary, artistic and theatrical areas of the last decade of 19th century England. **Services:** Provides advisory information. Offers biographies and informational newsletters. "The society publishes critical biographies of neglected and forgotten authors and artists of the Nineties, as well as reprints of the extremely rare and important publications of the period; and also uncollected or unpublished works of the authors and artists of the Nineties. These are published under the general title of *Makers of the Nineties*." **How to Contact:** Write. Responds to most inquiries within a month. "Please include SASE for reply." **Tips:** "Use your local libraries extensively. Get in touch with us only when the information you are looking for is not available elsewhere nearer to your place of work."

983• ERIC CLEARINGHOUSE ON LANGUAGES AND LINGUISTICS (FL)
Center for Applied Linguistics, 3520 Prospect St. NW, Washington DC 20007. (202)298-9292. Contact Person: User Services Coordinator. **Description:** "ERIC (Educational Resources Information Center) is a national information system which obtains and makes available hard-to-find, often unpublished information in all areas of education." Conducts computer searches on languages and language sciences. **Services:** Provides bibliographical information covering languages and language sciences; theoretical and applied linguistics; all areas of foreign language and linguistics instruction; pedagogy and methodology, psycholinguistics and the psychology of language learning; cultural and intercultural context of languages; application of linguistics in language teaching, bilingualism and bilingual education; sociolinguistics, study abroad and international exchanges; teacher training and qualifications specific to the teaching of foreign languages; commonly and uncommonly taught languages including English as a second language; related curriculum developments and problems. Will refer researchers to other ERIC clearinghouse agencies if needed. Publications include information packets. **How to Contact:** Write, call or visit. Responds to most inquiries within a week. Charges for information searches. Computer searches (of the ERIC database) cost $30 and cover search, postage and up to 100 citations—10¢ each for citations over 100. "Writers may use materials on premises free of charge." **Tips:** "Narrow your research question."

984• ESPERANTIC STUDIES FOUNDATION
6451 Barnaby St. NW, Washington DC 20015. (202)362-3963. Contact Person: President. **Description:** Research and educational foundation working on international language problems and solutions. **Services:** Provides advisory, bibliographical, historical, interpretative and referral information on language problems in international communications; Esperanto—history, status, trends in use; literature. Offers aid in arranging interviews, brochures/pamphlets, library facilities and research assistance. Publications include *Esperanto and International Language Problems: A Research Bibliography*. **How to Contact:** Write or call. Responds to most inquiries immediately. Charges $2 for bibliography; pamphlets and reprints free for SASE and 40¢ postage. **Tips:** Recent information request: "What is the current status of Esperanto?"

985• FOLGER SHAKESPEARE LIBRARY
201 E. Capitol St. SE, Washington DC 20003. (202)544-7077. Contact Person: Director of Public Relations. **Description:** "The Folger Library houses the largest collection of Shakespeare materials in the world and one of the most complete bodies of Renaissance materials in North America. It is also the home of a professional, classical theatre company, and the Folger Consort, ensemble for early music. The library's educational and museum programs are extensive." **Services:** Provides bibliographical and historical information on performing arts, arts in education, research libraries. Offers aid in arranging interviews, annual reports, brochures/pamphlets, informational newsletters, library facilities (restricted to those engaged in doctoral or post-doctoral study), photos, placement on mailing lists and press kits. **How to**

Contact: Write or call. Responds to most inquiries immediately. "Because the Folger is an advanced research library, use of the collection is limited to those pursuing doctoral or post-doctoral study. Services of the Folger Theatre Group and Public Programs Department are open to all." **Tips:** Recent information requests: "How does the Folger work with DC public schools in sharing its resources with teachers and students?"; "How do you make Shakespeare appeal to young students?"

986• INSTITUTE OF GENERAL SEMANTICS
RR 1, Box 215, Lakeville CT 06039. (203)435-9174. Contact Person: Director. **Description:** The institute is dedicated to improving communication. It "functions as a center for training and research in general semantics and as a clearinghouse for workers in the discipline." **Services:** Provides information on the institute's programs, which include seminars and workshops. Publications include *General Semantics Bulletin* (members only). **How to Contact:** Write. Responds to routine inquiries immediately; response time for others depends on the nature of the request.

987• INTERLINGUA INSTITUTE
Box 126, Canal Street Station, New York NY 10013. (212)929-0264. Contact Person: Executive Director. **Description:** The institute promotes interlinguistics and international communications. **Services:** Provides analytical and technical information on interlinguistics, linguistics and foreign languages. Offers brochures/pamphlets, informational newsletters, placement on mailing lists and press kits. Publications include *Currero International de Interlingua.* **How to Contact:** Write. Responds to most inquiries within a week.

988• THE INTERNATIONAL SAVE THE PUN FOUNDATION
Box 5040, Station A, Toronto, Ontario, Canada M5W 1N4. Contact Person: "Chairman of the Bored." **Description:** "The world's largest apocryphal society, committed to building a greater appreciation of the English language by having fun with words." **Services:** Foundation members receive the monthly newsletter, *The Pundit,* and an annual report on the Ten Best-Stressed Puns of the Year. **How to Contact:** Write. Responds to most inquiries immediately. Charges for membership. "*The Pundit* supplies a monthly source of new and unpublished humor from members around the world. Useful for scripts, articles, etc. The foundation's motto is: 'A day without puns is like a day without sunshine; there is gloom for improvement!' "

989• KIPLING SOCIETY, UNITED STATES BRANCH
420 Riverside Dr., 12G, New York NY 10025. (212)222-3375. Contact Person: US Secretary. **Description:** The society promotes the study and appreciation of the life and works of Rudyard Kipling (1865-1936), writer of English prose and verse. Headquarters are in London, England. **Services:** Provides bibliographical, historical, interpretative and referral information on the life, works and opinions of Rudyard Kipling. Offers research assistance. Publications (In London) include *Kipling Journal* (quarterly). **How to Contact:** Write or call. Responds to most inquiries within a month. **Tips:** "Routine questions can be answered by the US Branch, but more specialized ones may be referred to our headquarters in London." Recent information requests: "How tall was Kipling?"; "Where is Furdurstrandi mentioned in Kipling's *Finest Story in the World?*"

990• VACHEL LINDSAY ASSOCIATION
603 S. 5th St., Springfield IL 62703. (217)528-9254. Contact Person: President. **Description:** "We provide information on the heritage of poet/artist Vachel Lindsay." (The home includes manuscripts and artwork.) **Services:** Offers brochures/pamphlets. "Home is being renovated and tours are by appointment only." **How to Contact:** Write or call. Responds to most inquiries within a week. "Large groups are requested to donate $1/person. All revenue will go directly to the renovation of the home and to building program in the community that will highlight the Lindsay contribution. A single individual or family desiring an extended tour should contact the President."

991• JACK LONDON RESEARCH CENTER
Box 337, Glen Ellen CA 95442. (707)996-2888. Contact Person: Owner. **Description:** Private center providing access to authentic information on Jack London. **Services:** Provides advisory, bibliographical and historical information covering all secondary research material on Jack London. Offers biographies, brochures/pamphlets, clipping services, library facilities, photos,

BEHIND THE BYLINE

Edwin Newman
Writer and news commentator

Edwin Newman's journalistic roots go back to the days when "it was mostly newspaper and wire service work." Over the last forty years, he has anchored documentaries, covered political conventions, hosted numerous radio and TV news broadcasts, written for top magazines and authored three books.

He reflects on the news business then and now. "In those days people in news were expected to have a varied and considerable range of knowledge and a certain curiosity about things. You were lucky there was a newspaper morgue. You got what you could there and relied on your memory a lot.

"This isn't the case any longer," he continues. "The range of knowledge and allusion—which is important to a writer—is not present to the same degree because the news business has changed. It's a lot easier to find information today. And to the extent that the same information is available to everybody, there may be a greater uniformity in news coverage."

Newman isn't sold on technology for its own sake. "There are vast amounts of pointless information being accumulated, pumped out without point. Whether it's for better or worse or if it will contribute to more or less originality, I don't know. I do know that all this information makes the job less personal. I think if you are sitting at the typewriter, there's nothing more valuable as having ideas of your own ignited by something that's happened. That's what makes writing personal. It's not going to be the same information everybody else has; it's having your own information or your own attitude toward that information—and knowing what to do with it."

Being able to call on your own resources is a kind of research. Newman recalls the day President Reagan was shot. "I was sitting in front of a camera. I knew the Twenty-fifth Amendment to the Constitution governed the matter of succession to the presidency." During a break in the coverage, he asked his secretary for a copy of the amendment and told her she'd find it in the *World Almanac*. "That's research, I suppose. It's knowing where to look. And especially in the broadcast end of the business, it's being able to get it fast.

"You can always get a computer print-out, but there are times when you have to connect what is before you right now with something else. To do that, there has to be something in your head."

It was that kind of awareness that brought Newman to write two books on language. "I found there were so many examples of the language I was writing about that the research wasn't difficult. It was a matter of listening, keeping my eyes open, clipping the papers and magazines."

Newman takes a reverent attitude toward language and its use by journalists. "There's a tendency to substitute slogans for thoughts; that's something a writer ought to resist. We talk about 'The Great Society,' 'The Grand Design' and 'The Ford Doctrine.' These things ought to be looked at with a fishy eye. When it becomes difficult to see through the language which foists ideas upon us, or to see the language which conceals the fact that there *are* no ideas, then maybe we don't have the skeptical attitude we need. Language is the chief asset, the principal instrument we have; we ought to be particularly devoted to preserving and defending it. As a writer, you either take a critical attitude to what you read and hear, or you contribute to the spread of misinformation."

research assistance and telephone reference services. **How to Contact:** Write, call or visit. Responds to most inquiries immediately. **Tips:** "Research enough to write factual material." Recent information request: "Exactly how did Jack London die?"

992• THE WILLIAM MORRIS SOCIETY, UNITED STATES BRANCH
420 Riverside Dr., 12 G, New York NY 10025. (212)222-3375. Contact Person: US Secretary. **Description:** Persons interested in encouraging the spread of information about, and the study of, the life, works, circle, times and opinions of William Morris (1834-1896) English author, artist, designer, reformer, socialist and printer. Headquarters of the society are in London, England. **Services:** Provides bibliographical, historical, interpretative and referral information on Morris's literary works (poetry, fiction, lectures, essays, editorial work); his designs for wallpaper, fabrics, stained glass; his book design, printing, calligraphic manuscripts, wood cuts; illuminations; his social views, socialism, preservation of significant buildings and the environment; additional information on Morris's life and activities and of the persons associated with him. Offers annual reports, informational newsletters and research assistance. Publications include quarterly newsletter and journal. **How to Contact:** Write or call. Responds to most inquiries within a month. **Tips:** "The US Branch's secretary has a reasonably good reference library on Morris and Sir Edward Burne-Jones and their works from which most questions may be answered or leads given. For literary criticism Morris's influence on American book arts and specialized details, the inquirer can be referred to experts." Recent information requests: "Where can I find a photo of the east front of the Kelmscott Manor?"; "What book(s) would give me illustrations of Morris's designs for wallpaper and fabrics?"

993• THE MYTHOPOEIC SOCIETY
Box 4671, Whittier CA 90605. Contact Person: Correspondence Secretary. **Description:** "We're an educational organization devoted to the study, discussion, and enjoyment of the works of J.R.R. Tolkein, C.S. Lewis and Charles Williams. We believe these writers can be better understood by studying the realm of myth; the genre of fantasy; and the literary, philosophical and spiritual traditions which underlie their work." **Services:** Provides analytical, bibliographical, historical and interpretative information on Tolkein, Lewis and Williams as well as other fantasy literature, film and myth. Offers annual reports and informational newsletters. **How to Contact:** Write. Responds to most inquiries within a month. "You must become a member of the society to receive the journal and other publications."

994• NATIONAL CENTER FOR BILINGUAL RESEARCH
4665 Lampson Ave., Los Alamitos CA 90720. (213)598-0481. Contact Person: Director. **Description:** "The center conducts research on language learning, bilingualism, bilingual education, and language minorities in the US. We conduct research in these areas and disseminate information to researchers, practitioners, and policymakers." **Services:** Provides analytical, bibliographical and interpretative information on language learning, bilingualism and bilingual education, language assessment and instruction and language minority issues. Offers brochures/pamphlets, computerized information searches, informational newsletters, placement on mailing lists and research assistance. Publications include research reports, professional papers, research bulletins. **How to Contact:** Write. Responds to most inquiries within a week. Charges for publications. **Tips:** "Have a well-thought-out question in mind before contacting us—not a vague, general one, such as, 'I'm doing a paper on bilingual education and need to know everything there is on the subject.' " Recent information request: "What are some reasons why language minority youths drop out of high school before graduation?"

995• NATIONAL POETRY DAY COMMITTEE, INC./WORLD POETRY DAY COMMITTEE, INC.
1110 N. Venetian Dr., Miami Beach FL 33139. (305)373-9790. Contact Person: National Director. **Description:** "We keep interested writers informed as to what the market offers; where to obtain information; how to search for material of all kinds, including pictures and artwork relating to writing of poetry and prose; how to design/edit/publish your own books, etc. We keep members informed as to what is going on in the literary field, and provide information about contests and other pertinent subjects." **Services:** Provides advisory, analytical, bibliographical, historical, how-to, interpretative, referral and technical information covering prose, poetry, all arts and crafts. Offers aid in arranging interviews, annual reports, biographies, brochures/pamphlets, clipping services, information searches, statistics, newsletter and photos.

"We also have information about courses for members and about special meetings to attend other than our own. We have information about other places that offer services (with or without fees) to writers." **How to Contact:** Write or call. Responds to most inquiries within a week. "All receivers of information from us must be members. It would not be fair to spend our members' money to send out free information to nonmembers. We assist our members in any way we can, but we are a nonprofit organization. We supply anything that a writer wants in the way of information." **Tips:** Recent information request: "When/where is the next World Congress?"

996• ORCHARD HOUSE HISTORICAL MUSEUM
Louisa May Alcott Memorial Association, Box 343, Concord MA 01742. (617)369-4118. Contact Person: Director. **Description:** "This is the home of the Alcott family where *Little Women* was written in 1868 by Louisa May. The family lived here from 1858 to 1877 and Louisa May's father, Amos Bronson Alcott, prominent transcendentalist, founded the Concord School of Philosophy here." **Services:** Offers brochures/pamphlets and "help in finding documents for historical research. Most of the manuscripts have been deposited by the Louisa May Alcott Memorial Association at the Houghton Library, Harvard University." Publications include *Story of the Alcotts.* **How to Contact:** "Write well in advance to arrange to do research in the house. The house is often crowded with tourists in summer and fall, so writers need to make an appointment with the director so that we can be of assistance. The museum is closed from mid-November to mid-April. Plan any on-site visits for seasons when we are open and let us know you are coming." **Tips:** "We go out of way to be of help. Recently, many writers have been interested in Amos Bronson Alcott's transcendentalist studies."

997• PROUST RESEARCH ASSOCIATION
Department of French and Italian, University of Kansas, Lawrence KS 66045. (913)864-3388. Contact Person: Editor. **Description:** "The *Proust Research Association Newsletter* aims to provide a forum for the discussion of problems relating to current research on Marcel Proust. We are a very small and very loose organization of Proust scholars primarily in the United States, England, Canada, France and about a dozen countries." **Services:** Provides analytical, bibliographical, interpretative and referral information "dealing with Proust manuscripts and current scholarship and research dealing with Marcel Proust's life and works, with some attention to his relations to the society of the Belle Epoque." Offers informational newsletters. Publications include *Proust Research Association Newsletter.* **How to Contact:** Write or call. Responds to most inquiries within a month. **Tips:** "Have a thorough grounding in the basic critical materials surrounding the life and work of Marcel Proust, as well as good knowledge of the principal texts of Marcel Proust. Generally, the nature of our journal is such that it is of interest only to serious scholars either as doctoral candidates preparing a dissertation on Proust or as publishing professionals." Recent information requests: Identification of the source of a quotation from Proust; bibliographical information about Proust's articles on Chardin; advice on dealing with the Proust manuscripts.

998• REVIEW ON FILE
Box 215, Walton NY 13856. Contact Person: Owner. **Description:** Book review clippings from newspapers and magazines 1929-1970. **Services:** "Our service covers fiction, nonfiction and technical works; only back clips from the years listed above." **How to Contact:** Write or call. Responds to most inquiries immediately. Clippings indexed according to author. Charges a per-clipping fee.

999• THE SOCIETY FOR NEW LANGUAGE STUDY
Box 10596, Denver CO 80210. Contact Person: Treasurer. **Description:** "The society studies ancient and modern languages and literatures from a perennial perspective." **Services:** Provides analytical, historical, interpretative and technical information on ancient/modern languages and literatures. Offers brochures/pamphlets. Publications include *In Geardagum: Essays on Old and Middle English Language and Literature* (series). **How to Contact:** Write. Responds to most inquiries within a month. Charges for publications.

1000• SOCIETY FOR THE STUDY OF SOUTHERN LITERATURE
Box 2625, Mississippi State MS 39762. (601)325-3644. Contact Person: Secretary/Treasurer. **Description:** Scholars and persons interested in encouraging the study of

Southern literature. **Services:** Provides bibliographical and referral information on Southern literature. Offers informational newsletters. Publications include *Newsletter of the Society for the Study of Southern Literature* (semiannual). **How to Contact:** Write. Responds to most inquiries within a week. Charges for membership $2 in US; $4.50 outside US (includes *Newsletter*).

1001•   STEINBECK SOCIETY
English Department, Ball State University, Muncie IN 47306. (317)285-4044. Contact Person: President. **Description:** "International learned society of scholars, critics, biographers, teachers, collectors and students promoting Steinbeck studies and teaching." **Services:** Provides bibliographical and biographical studies and biographical and literary criticism of Steinbeck's major works. Offers *Steinbeck Quarterly*, 2 combined issues published twice/year. **How to Contact:** Write. Responds to most inquiries within a week. Services to members only; $15/year.

1002•   THE THOREAU FOUNDATION, INC.
Thoreau Lyceum, 156 Belknap St., Concord MA 01742. (617)369-5912. Contact Person: Curator. **Description:** "Thoreau Learning Center for schools, colleges and people who are teaching, writing or reading." **Services:** Provides bibliographical and historical information covering Henry David Thoreau and other 19th century transcendentalists and writers. Offers brochures/pamphlets, informational newsletters, library facilities, photos, research assistance and telephone reference services. Publications include *The Concord Saunterer* and booklets. Bookshop has rare out-of-print books on Thoreau and his contemporaries, as well as in-print hardcovers and paperbacks. **How to Contact:** Visit, write or call. Responds to most inquiries within a month. Charges for books and photos. Give credit to the Thoreau Foundation. **Tips:** "Come to the Lyceum, if possible."

1003•   THE MARK TWAIN MEMORIAL
351 Farmington Ave., Hartford CT 06105. (203)247-0998. Contact Person: Director. **Description:** "The MTM owns and operates the house Mark Twain and his family lived in from 1874 to 1891, his most productive literary period. In 1881 the High Victorian Gothic structure's interior was decorated in part by Louis Comfort Tiffany and associates. The house is open to visitors and we also maintain a research library and photo collection." **Services:** Provides bibliographical, historical and interpretative information on Mark Twain and literary and decorative arts of the late 19th century. Offers biographies, brochures/pamphlets, library facilities, photos, research assistance and telephone reference services. **How to Contact:** Write or call. Responds to most inquiries immediately "depending on their complexity". Usual credits are required. A copy of the publication is requested in lieu of reference fee (or use fee for photographs). "Contact us in advance." **Tips:** Recent information requests: Verification of a Twain quotation; Signet information on whether "The" appears in title of *Adventures of Huckleberry Finn.*

1004•   WALT WHITMAN BIRTHPLACE ASSOCIATION
246 Old Walt Whitman Rd., Huntington Station NY 11746. (516)427-5240. Contact Person: Curator. **Description:** "The association maintains Walt Whitman's birthplace and sponsors poets in residence, concerts and other cultural events." **Services:** Provides biographical, historical and interpretative information on the local history of the Whitman family and their relation to Long Island. Offers brochures/pamphlets, library of 200 volumes, research assistance and musical settings of Whitman's poetry. Publications include *West Hills Review*, a journal of poetry and scholarship. **How to Contact:** Write. Responds to most inquiries within a month. "Arrange in advance to use the facilities. Books do not circulate." **Tips:** Recent information requests: "How tall was Walt Whitman?"; "What interested him in the natural history of Long Island?"

1005•   WRITER'S HOTLINE
Emporia State University, Emporia KS 66801. (316)343-1200, ext. 380. **Description:** "We provide assistance in the solution of specific writing questions." **Services:** Provides advisory, analytical, bibliographical, how-to, interpretative and technical information on writing. Offers library facilities and research assistance. **How to Contact:** Write, call or visit. Responds to most inquiries immediately. "Be sure the questions you ask over the phone are answerable over the phone." **Tips:** Recent information requests: Placement of a hyphen; suggestions on how to make a sentence less confusing; sources of information for writing clearly and concisely.

LAW/LAW ENFORCEMENT

Unless we have a safe society, we are not going to have a free society.

—Robert C. Byrd

This category includes resources in the areas of crime, punishment, legal services and investigation, laws and regulations and the judicial system.

Bibliography

Black, Henry Campbell, ed. *Black's Law Dictionary*. 5th ed. St. Paul, MN: West Publishing Co., 1979.

Cohen, Morris L., ed. *How to Find the Law (Methods & Materials of Doing Legal Research)*. St. Paul, MN: West Publishing Co., 1976.

Cushman, Robert F., ed. *Leading Constitutional Decisions*. 16th ed. Englewood Cliffs, NJ: Prentice-Hall, 1982.

Dobelis, Inge N., ed. *Family Legal Guide: An Encyclopedia of Law for the Layman*. Pleasantville, NY: Reader's Digest Association, 1981.

Index to Legal Periodical Literature. 1908 to date, monthly. New York: H.W. Wilson Co.

Johnstone, Donald F. *Copyright Handbook*. New York: Bowker, 1982.

Nash, Jay R., ed. *Almanac of World Crime*. New York: Doubleday, 1981.

Rothenberg, Robert E. *The Plain Language Law Dictionary*. New York: Penguin Books, 1981.

Scanlon, Robert A., ed. *Law Enforcement Bible*, No. 2. South Hackensack, NJ: Stoeger Publishing Co., 1982. (Police techniques, equipment, resources, etc.)

Smith, Gregory White and Steven Naifeh. *What Every Client Needs to Know About Using a Lawyer*. New York: Putnam, 1982.

Wasserman, Paul, ed. *Law and Legal Information Directory*. Detroit: Gale Research Co., 1980.

1006• AMERICAN ACADEMY FOR PROFESSIONAL LAW ENFORCEMENT
444 W. 56th St., Brooklyn NY 11220. (212)489-3982. Contact Person: Administrative Assistant. **Description:** Organization "dedicated to further professionalization of law enforcement and to achieving the highest levels of standards and ethical practices in the field." **Services:** Provides advisory, how-to, referral and trade information on police services. Offers annual reports, brochures/pamphlets and books (text), informational newsletters, placement on mailing lists, research assistance and telephone reference services. Publications list available. **How to Contact:** Write. Responds to most inquiries within a week. Charges for membership and publications. **Tips:** Recent information request: "Are there any computer crime courses being given in the US at this time?"

1007• AMERICAN BAR ASSOCIATION
1155 E. 60th St., Chicago IL 60637. (312)947-4000. Contact Person: Director, ABA Press. **Description:** The ABA works "to improve the justice system and the practice of law." **Services:** Provides information on law. Catalog ($2) lists available audio-visual materials, books, periodicals, and pamphlets produced by the ABA. *ABA Catalogue* includes consumer guides, professional responsibilities, legal history and education. Computer system, AMBAR, allows research on all activities and publications of the ABA; contact Information Services. **How to Contact:** Write or call. Contact Communications Division for press releases; Director, for *ABA Journal*. Contact Circulation Department for information on publication. Charges for some publications. "If a writer wishes to use copyrighted material, he should contact us first."

1008• AMERICAN POLYGRAPH ASSOCIATES
Box 74, Linthicum Heights MD 21090. Contact Person: Editor-in-Chief. **Description:** "Formed

in 1966, the APA has been the national representative of the polygraph field in its effort to establish standards of ethical practices, instrumentation, training and techniques.'' **Services:** Provides advisory, bibliographical, historical, referral, technical and trade information on polygraph techniques, operations, applications, training, history, activities, etc. Offers aid in arranging interviews, biographies, brochures/pamphlets, informational newsletters, placement on mailing lists, research assistance and statistics. Publications include *The Polygraph Profession*, an APA pamphlet; specific materials on request. **How to Contact:** Write. Responds to most inquiries within a week. Charges for some publications and for photocopying in excess of 10 pages. **Tips:** ''Provide us with an outline or information on what aspect of polygraph technique you plan to write about.''

1009• CITIZENS' LEGAL PROTECTIVE LEAGUE
Box 2115, Sanford FL 32771-0026. (305)322-7011. Contact Person: National Chairman. **Description:** Persons interested in representing themselves in court. The organization educates people in the areas of court procedure and preparation for ''being your own lawyer.'' **Services:** Provides advisory and how-to information on filing lawsuits, answering lawsuits, defending against criminal charges, preparing motions, affidavits, appeals and all essential legal papers involved in any kind of court action. Offers brochures/pamphlets, informational newsletters, placement on mailing lists, cassette tapes, speakers (as available) and course entitled ''Be Your Own Lawyer.'' Publications include brochures on the right to use the courts without hiring a lawyer, citing Faretta vs. California, 1975 (US Supreme Court). **How to Contact:** Write. Responds to most inquiries within a week. Charges for basic course; accepts donations for publications. ''All material is covered by US Copyright. Excerpts, with proper credit are permissible. Lengthy reprints are not. Request free brochures; specify source of information, *Writer's Resource Guide* and include SASE (business size) for reply.'' **Tips:** ''If access to a law library is denied, check to see if books are in any way 'public property' to the extent that public funds are used to purchase them. (If Bar members only pay the costs, then refusal may be legitimate; but if housed in a public building, access can be compelled by mandamus action.) Take copious notes and file by subject for future reference. Attend trials in local courts to gain on-the-spot guidance on trial procedures. Listen, take lots of notes!'' Recent information request: ''Does your course cover how to defend oneself in a traffic case?''

1010• COPYRIGHT CLEARANCE CENTER, INC.
21 Congress St., Salem MA 01970. (617)744-3350. Contact Person: Marketing Manager. **Description:** Established in compliance with 1978 copyright law requiring that permission of copyright holder be obtained by persons doing systematic photocopying or other photocopying not permitted by the law. ''CCC provides authorizations to photocopy to 1,400 corporations, academic and research libraries, information brokers, government agencies and other users of copyrighted information. Royalties for photocopying beyond exemptions contained in US Copyright Law are collected on behalf of 600 member publishers and 5,000 participating titles.'' **Services:** Provides bibliographical, how-to and referral information on photocopying from: journals, books, proceedings, newspapers and newsletters, consumer and trade magazines. Offers brochures/pamphlets and placement on mailing lists. ''Authorization to photocopy copyrighted material provided by CCC is limited to personal or internal use or personal or internal use of specific clients. Authorizations do not extend to secondary publishing or use of copyrighted material in one's written work.'' Publications include *Publishers' Photocopy Fee Catalog (PPC)*; *Directory of Users; Directory of Publishers; Guide to CCC—Participating Document Delivery Services; Handbook for Libraries and Users*; instruction booklets for publishers. **How to Contact:** Write or call. Responds to most inquiries within a week. ''There is no charge to open an account; photocopy royalty fees are set by publishers and are billed to users when photocopying is reported.'' **Tips:** ''CCC is the only centralized service for photocopying authorization in the United States, and exists to facilitate the flow of information from creator to user.''

1011• COPYRIGHT OFFICE
Office of Information and Publications, Library of Congress, Washington DC 20559. Contact Person: Public Information Specialist. **Description:** The Copyright Office registers claims to copyright. **Services:** Provides advisory and how-to information on copyright and how to register claims to copyright. Offers copyright searches, free circulars on copyright subjects, and other related services. **How to Contact:** Write or call (202)287-8700 to speak to a Public Information Specialist; or call (202)287-9100 to leave a recorded message requesting specific copyright

application forms. Responds to most inquiries within a week. "No charge for most information services; a $10 fee must accompany each application for copyright registration; please write for charges for other fee services. Contact the Information and Reference Division, LM-453, Copyright Office, Library of Congress, Washington DC 20559, for special information on services such as research into the status of copyrights and copies of certificates and documents." **Tips:** "Write to the Copyright Office for Circular R1, 'Copyright Basics,' and Circular R22, 'How to Investigate the Copyright Status of a Work.' " Recent information request: "How should I register my novel/song/poster for copyright?"

1012• CRIMINAL JUSTICE STATISTICS ASSOCIATION
444 N. Capitol St. NW, Suite 305, Washington DC 20001. (202)347-4608. Contact Person: Director. **Description:** Clearinghouse for state criminal justice statistical information. "We also provide state statistical analysis centers (SACS) with workshops and technical support." **Services:** Provides analytical, how-to, interpretative, referral and technical information. Offers informational newsletters, research assistance and statistics. **How to Contact:** Write or call. Responds to most inquiries immediately. **Tips:** "Have very specific questions in mind." Recent information request: "Which states use computerized prison population forecasting methods?"

1013• CUSTOMS SERVICE
1301 Constitution Ave. NW, Room 6313, Washington DC 20229. (202)566-5288. Contact Person: Chief, Media & Public Services Group, Public Affairs Office. **Description:** "The US Customs Service is the principal border enforcement agency of the US. It enforces the Tariff Act of 1930 as well as some 400 other provisions of law for 40 other federal agencies concerned with international trade. The service collects duties and other revenues; regulates the movement of commerce and people between the US and other nations; and detects and investigates contraband smuggling and other activities, including arms trafficking, unreported movement and other law violations." **Services:** Provides bibliographical, historical, referral and technical information. Offers aid in arranging interviews, annual reports, bibliographies, biographies, statistics, brochures/pamphlets, clipping services, placement on mailing list, photos and press kits. Publications include publications list. **How to Contact:** Write or call. "We have a limited staff, but will do our best to answer requests; give us as much lead time as possible. We've worked successfully in the past with a number of article and book authors." **Tips:** Recent information requests: Customs law enforcement or trade programs or interviews on these topics.

1014• DEPARTMENT OF JUSTICE
Office of Public Information, 10th St. and Constitution Ave. NW, Room 5114, Washington DC 20530. (202)633-2007. Contact Person: Public Information Officer for specific area. **Description:** "As the largest law firm in the nation, the Department of Justice serves as counsel for its citizens. It represents them in enforcing the law in the public interest. Through its thousands of lawyers, investigators and agents, the department plays the key role in protection against criminals and subversion; in ensuring healthy competition of business in our free enterprise system; in safeguarding the consumer; and in enforcing drug, immigration and naturalization laws. The department also plays a significant role in protecting citizens through its efforts for effective law enforcement, crime prevention, crime detention, and prosecution and rehabilitation of offenders." **Services:** Provides information on anti-trust laws, civil rights, criminal justice, drug law enforcement, federal prisons, activities of US marshals, law suits against the government, enforcement of federal statutes. **How to Contact:** Write or call. Responds to most inquiries within a week. **Tips:** Recent information request: Caseload comparisons between this year and last.

1015• ENVIRONMENTAL LAW INSTITUTE
1346 Connecticut Ave. NW, Suite 620, Washington DC 20036. (202)452-9600. Contact Person: Librarian. **Description:** The institute gathers information in the area of environmental law. **Services:** Provides bibliographical, historical and referral information covering environmental law, toxic substances, air and water pollution and environmental economics. Offers bibliographies and information searches. Publications include several books and periodicals. **How to Contact:** Write or call. Responds to most inquiries within a week. Charges 10¢/page for photocopying. **Tips:** "Call first to make an appointment." Recent information requests: Interlibrary loans; computer search for question on environmentalists and poverty.

1016• EQUAL JUSTICE FOUNDATION
1346 Connecticut Ave. NW, # 525, Washington DC 20036. (202)452-1267. Contact Person: Executive Director. **Description:** The foundation works to "increase access to decision making forums for underrepresented persons by removing procedural and financial barriers. Issues include continuation of Legal Services Corporation, preserving Freedom of Information Act, defeating court-stripping legislation." **Services:** Provides advisory, analytical, interpretative, referral and technical information on attorneys' fees, the federal regulatory process, various pending legislation. Offers brochures/pamphlets, informational newsletters and press kits. Publications include *The Tither* (quarterly newsletter). **How to Contact:** Write. Responds to most inquiries within a week. Charges for newsletter; "other fees vary according to information request." **Tips:** "Be as specific as possible in your written request." Inform the requestee at the outset how the information will be used. Recent information request: "What information do you have on the conservative organization called the Pacific Legal Foundation?"

1017• FEDERAL BUREAU OF INVESTIGATION
9th St. and Pennsylvania Ave. NW, Washington DC 20535. (202)324-3000. Contact Person: Assistant Director, Office of Congressional and Public Affairs. **Description:** "The Federal Bureau of Investigation (FBI) investigates violation of certain federal statutes, collects evidence in cases in which the United States is or may be an interested party and performs other duties specified by law or presidential directive." **Services:** Provides advisory, bibliographical, historical and referral information on current and historical FBI operations such as fingerprinting, training, laboratory procedures and famous cases in general. Offers aid in arranging interviews. Will furnish annual reports, brochures/pamphlets, statistics and some news clippings. Publications available. **How to Contact:** Write. Responds to most inquiries within a month. "We assist authors and members of the media. We can provide information regarding cases which have been fully adjudicated. Freedom of Information document requests are processed through separate channels." **Tips:** "Be as specific as possible." Recent information request: Questions on the gangsters of the 1930s.

1018• FEDERAL JUDICIAL CENTER
1520 H St. NW, Washington DC 20005. (202)633-6011. Contact: Information Service Office. **Description:** "To further the development and adoption of improved judicial administration in the courts of the US. Information service collection consists of books, articles, and periodicals in the field, especially court management and the federal judicial system." **Services:** Offers annual reports, bibliographies and brochures/pamphlets. **How to Contact:** Write or call. Make appointment in advance of visit. Responds to most inquiries within a week. Judicial personnel are given priority on requests. However, the information service is open to the public for viewing files. **Tips:** Recent information requests: "How many judges are in the federal system?"; addresses of particular courts.

1019• FEDERAL LAW ENFORCEMENT TRAINING CENTER
Public Affairs Office, Building 94, Glynco GA 31524. (912)267-2447. Contact Person: Public Affairs Specialist. **Description:** "The Federal Law Enforcement Training Center is a bureau of the Department of the Treasury, which serves as an interagency training center for federal police officers and investigators. The center provides basic training for new officers and investigators from more than 48 federal law enforcement organizations. In addition, the center provides administrative and logistical support for the organizations to conduct advanced and specialized training required to meet their individual needs." **Services:** Provides technical information on FLETC programs and activities. Offers annual reports, brochures/pamphlets and photos. **How to Contact:** Write. Responds to most inquiries within a month.

1020• HALT—AN ORGANIZATION OF AMERICANS FOR LEGAL REFORM
201 Massachusetts Ave. NE, Suite 319, Washington DC 20002. (202)546-4258. Contact Person: Public Relations Director. **Description:** Citizens united "to educate the public about the US legal system and to make civil legal services less costly and more responsive to the needs of average Americans." **Services:** Provides advisory, how-to, interpretative and referral information covering reform of various aspects of the US civil justice system, e.g., simplified probate, plain language, no-fault auto insurance, no-fault divorce, etc. Offers informational newsletters, research assistance (some) and telephone reference services. Publications include *Citizens Legal Manuals* on topics such as shopping for a lawyer, probate, real estate, small claims court and using

a law library. **How to Contact:** Write or call. "We may request postage charge if we mail a great deal of material." **Tips:** "We have an excellent manual on legal research, written specifically for the layman." Recent information requests: "In what areas of the law can people reduce legal fees by doing some of the work themselves?"; "What is Plain Language and where have Plain Language laws been passed?"

1021• INSTITUTE OF CRIMINAL LAW AND PROCEDURE
Georgetown University Law Center, 600 New Jersey Ave. NW, Washington DC 20001. (202)624-8220 or 625-4205. Contact Person: Deputy Director. **Description:** The institute conducts research on the administration of criminal justice. **Services:** Provides advisory, analytical, interpretative and referral information on plea bargaining, sentencing, the police, prosecutors, the criminal courts (felony and misdemeanor), preventive detention, public defender and other systems of defense for indigents. Offers research assistance and telephone reference services. Publishes reports of research studies as they are completed. **How to Contact:** Call or visit. Responds to most inquiries within a week. **Tips:** "Call and explain your interest, we will provide what information and leads we have." Recent information requests: Plea bargaining—what is it?; whether it can be eliminated; whether it is unethical to accept a plea while the jury is out deciding a case.

1022• INTERNAL REVENUE SERVICE (IRS)
1111 Constitution Ave. NW, Washington DC 20224. (202)566-4024. Contact Person: Public Information Specialist. **Description:** The IRS "administers federal tax laws of the United States." **Services:** Provides how-to, interpretative and technical information covering federal taxes and related information bearing on income received and deductions claimed. Offers aid in arranging interviews, annual reports, brochures/pamphlets, statistics, placement on mailing list and press kits. Publications available. **How to Contact:** Write or call. Responds to most inquiries within a week. "We do not divulge individual tax information and no research is performed here. We will read the final draft of freelance articles for technical accuracy of tax information." **Tips:** "Read free IRS publications first. Become familiar with the various commercial tax services and their indexing procedures." Recent information request: "Under the law what are the restrictions that apply to an Individual Retirement Account?"

1023• LIBEL DEFENSE RESOURCE CENTER
708 Third Ave., 32nd Floor, New York NY 10017. (212)687-4745. Contact Person: General Counsel. **Description:** "We provide libel defendants and their counsel with information on current libel cases and on nationwide trends in libel law." **Services:** Provides advisory, analytical, bibliographical, interpretative, referral and technical information on defamation/libel/invasion of privacy. "Our information focuses primarily on media libel law but also covers developments in non-media libel law. We maintain state-by-state files on current libel cases and provide legal assistance of an informational and advisory capacity through telephone and correspondence." Offers annual reports, brochures/pamphlets, informational newsletters, library facilities, placement on mailing lists, press kits, research assistance, statistics and telephone reference services. Publications include *LDRC Bulletin* (quarterly); *LDRC 50-State Survey—Current Developments in Media Libel* and *Invasion of Privacy Law* (annual). **How to Contact:** Write or call. Responds to most inquiries immediately. Charges for photocopying, postage and specific publications. **Tips:** Recent information requests: Comments on libel cases, trends, developments.

1024• LIBRARY OF CONGRESS, LAW LIBRARY
James Madison Memorial Bldg., Room 40, 1st St. and Independence Ave. SE, Washington DC 20540. (202)287-5079. Contact Person: Head, Law Library Reading Room. **Description:** "Although the Law Library serves primarily as the foreign law research arm of Congress, its reference and legal specialists also provide American law reference and foreign law research and reference to the other branches of government and to the public." **Services:** Provides bibliographical, how-to and referral information covering all known legal systems, present and past. Offers library facilities, research assistance and telephone reference services. **How to Contact:** Write, call or visit. Responds to most inquiries within a month. **Tips:** "Assistance to the public is limited by Congressional priorities."

1025• LONDON CLUB
Box 4527, Topeka KS 66604. Contact Person: Chairman. **Description:** "An organization serving

as a clearinghouse for criminal research. Specializing in researching unsolved crimes both past and present: Jack the Ripper; Whitechappel Murders; and Lincoln and Kennedy assassinations, as well as current unsolved crimes in the US and abroad. Seeks to become a mass private sector for researching unsolved crime on a local level by bringing together experts from various fields.'' **Services:** Provides analytical information covering criminology, especially unsolved crimes. Offers aid in arranging interviews, brochures/pamphlets and press kits. **How to Contact:** Membership in the organization is a prerequisite. Write. Responds to most inquiries within a week. Apply for membership ($20/year) by writing the chairman. ''Services are available only to members in good standing. We expect members to contribute articles, essays and research to *The London Club Journal* for consideration by the editors. If the article is sold to another publication as a reprint, the author will be paid a royalty on the sale. The London Club employs the same standard of accuracy as does any major news reporting service in the US. The London Club is seeking professionals in all fields who feel that they have something to contribute to the fields of criminology as researchers and investigative reporters. The organization is also open to individuals who feel they have an interest in criminology and something worthwhile to contribute.''

1026• NATIONAL ASSOCIATION FOR CRIME VICTIMS RIGHTS, INC.
Box 16161, Portland OR 97216. (503)252-9012. Contact Person: Executive Director.
Description: The association works ''to raise the level of awareness of America's 220 + million potential victims of criminal violence; to inspire their active support in programs designed to aid victims of crime; to increase the rights of all victims within the justice systems.'' **Services:** Provides advisory, historical, how-to and referral information on all categories of crime and human suffering and additional information on controversies related to gun control and parole boards. Offers aid in arranging interviews, brochures/pamphlets, clipping services, informational newsletters, library facilities, placement on mailing lists and research assistance. **How to Contact:** Write. Responds to most inquiries within a week. Charges for services ''in order to defray our operating costs.'' Requests tax deductible donations in proportion to size of project. **Tips:** ''We are a volunteer group. Be specific, don't ask us to review the entire criminal justice system; don't ask our views relating to criminal benefits.'' Recent information request: ''What rights do today's crime victims have?''

1027• NATIONAL ASSOCIATION OF LEGAL INVESTIGATORS
303 N. Shamrock, Box 210, East Alton IL 62024. (618)259-4405. Contact Person: Secretary-Treasurer. **Description:** Association which promotes professionalism among legal investigators. **Services:** Provides referral information in all areas of investigation regarding personal injury or criminal defense. Offers aid in arranging interviews and informational newsletters. Publications include *The Legal Investigator* (quarterly by subscription). **How to Contact:** Write or call. Responds to most inquiries within a week.

1028• NATIONAL AUTOMOBILE THEFT BUREAU
Public Relations Department, 10330 S. Roberts Rd., Palos Hills IL 60465. (312)430-2430. Contact Person: Director of Public Relations. **Description:** ''The National Automobile Theft Bureau formulates and implements policies for the prevention of vehicle theft, vehicle arson and vehicle fraud. NATB cooperates with duly constituted public authorities in the prosecution of individuals engaged in vehicle crime and fraud. The bureau is an agency for the location and identification of stolen vehicles and for the promotion of anti-vehicle theft activities. NATB is a crime prevention organization supported by more than 550 property-casualty insurance companies providing assistance to law enforcement, insurance and the public.'' **Services:** Provides historical and referral information on vehicle theft, including background on overall problem, summary of actions to control the problem and tips for consumers. Offers aid in arranging interviews, annual reports, statistics, brochures/pamphlets, placement on mailing list, newsletter and press kits. Publications include annual report and *Your Car Could Be Stolen This Year.* **How to Contact:** Write or call. Responds to most inquiries immediately.

1029• NATIONAL CENTER FOR COMPUTER CRIME DATA
2700 N. Cahuenga Blvd., Suite 2113, Los Angeles CA 90068. Contact Person: Director. **Description:** The library collects and disseminates information about computer crime. **Services:** Provides information on computer crimes and experts in computer crimes. Offers informational newsletters, placement on mailing lists and telephone reference services. Publications include *Computer Crime Digest* (monthly); *Computers and Security*

(quarterly). **How to Contact:** Write. Responds to most inquiries within a week. "Quick questions we handle for free. Ones involving lengthy research we handle through contract. If you're local, visit us."

1030• NATIONAL CLEARINGHOUSE FOR LEGAL SERVICES, INC.
500 N. Michigan Ave., Suite 1940, Chicago IL 60611. (312)670-3656. Contact Person: Librarian.
Description: Nonprofit organization funded by the Legal Services Corp. to provide support services both to attorneys representing the poor and to the general public. **Services:** Provides bibliographical and referral information. Distributes material on over 20 areas of law including poverty law, consumer, family, employment, housing, immigration, juvenile, landlord-tenant, public utilities, civil rights laws and attorneys' fees. Offers brochures/pamphlets, library facilities, placement on mailing lists, press kits, research assistance and telephone reference services; distributes "pleadings, opinions and legislation to attorneys." Publications include *The Clearinghouse Review* (monthly journal). **How to Contact:** Write or call. Responds to most inquiries within a week-10 days. Charges for publications. **Tips:** Recent information requests: Publications dealing with compulsory education/home education programs; material and debt collection practices related to harassment.

1031• NATIONAL CLEARINGHOUSE ON MARITAL RAPE
2325 Oak St., Berkeley CA 94708. (415)548-1770. **Description:** "Our purposes are to make marital rape recognized as another crime against women and to help outlaw it legally; to provide data for researchers, legislators, and others studying the subject of marital rape; to provide a network to connect victims with each other; and to coordinate contact between those involved in cases or in changing the laws." **Services:** Provides advisory, analytical, bibliographical, historical, how-to, interpretative, referral and technical information on marital rape, cohabitation rape and date rape specifically, as well as current studies, research and articles on the above subjects; legislative information including bills passed, proposed, and defeated on marital rape, and rape/assault laws; information on marital rape cases in California, and in other states where marital rape is illegal, including a pamphlet on the Rideout case in Oregon; case histories, especially on marital rape victims charged with manslaughter for killing their husbands in self-defense. Offers biographies, brochures/pamphlets, clipping services, library facilities (members only), research assistance and statistics. "Our services include acting as a clearinghouse for all information pertaining to marital, cohabitation, and date rape. We also serve as a networking agency that connects victims, legislators, district attorneys, etc., with those interested in working with others in their situation—especially to end the feeling of isolation among victims; to aid district attorneys in their prosecution of marital rape cases; and to facilitate the passage of legislation." Publications include *Guide to the Clearinghouse Library* $3 (lists the over 700 files, including a bibliography of major articles, subject heading list, and a contact list); summary of Greta Rideout's rape and subsequent trial against her husband $2; socio-legal chart of California marital rape cases $4; socio-legal chart of cases in states other than California where marital rape is a crime $4; pamphlet on marital rape victims who have killed their husbands in self-defense $2. **How to Contact:** Write. Responds to most inquiries within a week. Charges for membership. "Ours is not an open library: all material/information searches are performed by staff. (Research for members only.) Membership is not required for purchase of publications." Include SASE for further information requests. **Tips:** "Perform general background reading to clarify goals before commencing in-depth research. Be specific and thorough versus broad and superficial in the examination of a subject." Recent information requests: "Which states have abolished the marital rape exemption?"; "How many cases have there been in (state)?"; "Who are the experts in the field?"

1032• NATIONAL COALITION TO PREVENT SHOPLIFTING
100 Edgewood Ave., NE, Suite 1804, Atlanta GA 30303. (404)577-3437. Contact Person: Director. **Description:** The coalition works "to educate the public particularly the young, as to the consequences of shoplifting; to increase public awareness of the fact that merchants' shoplifting losses are passed on to the consumer; to build a national volunteer coalition to organize and coordinate anti-shoplifting activities; to develop and implement a model system of treatment for juveniles." **Services:** Provides analytical, how-to, interpretative, referral, technical, trade and statistical information on cost of shoplifting; educational materials; shoplifting prevention materials; juvenile shoplifting court diversion program; upper elementary school curriculum; model code and overview of 50 state laws. Offers aid in arranging interviews,

brochures/pamphlets, informational newsletters, placement on mailing lists, research assistance and statistics. Publications include *Shoplifting and the Law* (a model code); *1981-82 National Research Report on Shoplifting*; *Project First Stop Manual* (how to implement juvenile diversion program); *The Golden Touch* (shoplifting prevention play). **How to Contact:** Write, call or visit. Responds to most inquiries immediately. Charges for material. **Tips:** Recent information requests: "What are the current losses to retailers from shoplifting?"; "Is shoplifting increasing because of the depressed economy?"

1033• NATIONAL CRIME PREVENTION INSTITUTE
University of Louisville, Shelby Campus, Louisville KY 40292. (502)588-6987. Contact Person: Manager, Information Services. **Description:** The institute is a "training agency for crime prevention/security topics. NCPI also provides technical assistance to industry, government and communities; maintains a crime prevention resource center." **Services:** Provides advisory, bibliographical, how-to, referral and technical informaton on crime prevention and security for private industry. Offers brochures/pamphlets, library facilities, placement on mailing lists, statistics and telephone reference services. Publications include *Understanding Crime Prevention*. **How to Contact:** Write or call. Responds to most inquiries within a month. No charges "unless substantial materials are involved." **Tips:** Recent information request: Statistics on the effect of "Neighborhood Watch" on residential burglaries.

1034• NATIONAL INSTITUTE OF JUSTICE/NCJRS
Box 6000, Rockville MD 20850. (301)251-5500. **Description:** Information clearinghouse; "provides information about the causes of crime and its prevention, the functioning of criminal justice/juvenile justice systems in US and other countries, research and operations in law enforcement, private security, courts and corrections." **Services:** Provides bibliographical and referral information covering police and law enforcement, courts (adult and juvenile), corrections (adult and juvenile) all aspects of criminal justice and criminology, private security, crime prevention. Offers brochures/pamphlets, computerized information searches, library facilities, research assistance and telephone reference services. Publications include *Selective Notification of Information* (bimonthly abstracts of recent additions to document data base); topical bibliographies. The National Juvenile Justice Clearinghouse operates within the NCJRS, (800)638-8736, and provides information on everything from delinquency prevention to treatment of juvenile offenders. **How to Contact:** Write or call. Responds to most inquiries within a week. Charges for most products and services. Price list available. **Tips:** "Call a reference specialist and describe your specific research needs. The National Criminal Justice Reference Service document data base has descriptions of more than 65,000 books, journal articles, government documents and audio-visual items, growing at a rate of approximately 500/month."

1035• NATIONAL LEGAL AID AND DEFENDER ASSOCIATION
1625 K St. NW, Washington DC 20006. (202)452-0620. Contact Person: Director of Communications. **Description:** Legal offices and organizations working "to ensure that poor persons in America receive high quality legal help in both civil and criminal matters, when they need it." **Services:** Provides advisory, bibliographical, historical, referral, technical and trade infomation. Offers aid in arranging interviews, annual reports, brochures/pamphlets, "access to our clips," informational newsletters, statistics and telephone reference services. Publications include *Cornerstone*, a monthly newspaper covering legal services news; *Briefcase*, a magazine discussing issues related to legal services for the poor. **How to Contact:** Write or call. Responds to most inquiries within a week. Charges for photocopying; other fees "depend on the nature of the service." **Tips:** Recent information requests: Questions about the current crisis in funding for attorneys and programs that defend poor people accused of crime.

1036• NATIONAL NOTARY ASSOCIATION
23012 Ventura Blvd., Woodland Hills CA 91364. (213)347-2035 or (800)423-5752. Contact Person: Public Relations Manager. **Description:** "We serve and educate the nation's notaries public and keep the general public and legislators informed and aware of the purpose and needs of notaries. We cover every area that affects or could affect the notary, usually changes in law or in business and economic conditions." **Services:** Offers aid in arranging interviews, annual reports, bibliographies, statistics, brochures/pamphlets, newsletter and press kits. Publications include *What Is a Notary Public?*; *11 Questions about the NNA*; *The National Notary Magazine*; *Viewpoint*

newsletter; notary primers for the states of California, Texas, Missouri and Florida; and *Notary Public Practices & Glossary*. **How to Contact:** Write or call. Responds to most inquiries within a week.

1037• NATIONAL RESOURCE CENTER FOR CONSUMERS OF LEGAL SERVICES
3254 Jones Ct. NW, Washington DC 20007. (202)338-0714. Contact Person: Director. **Description:** Legal service program. Clearinghouse conducts research and advises groups and individuals on legal services delivery issues; special focus is on legal service plans. **Services:** Provides information on the delivery of legal services, "especially for individuals of moderate means." Offers aid in arranging interviews, annual reports, brochures/pamphlets, informational newsletters, library facilities, placement on mailing lists, research assistance and statistics. Publications list and bibliography available. **How to Contact:** Write, call or visit. Responds to most inquiries immediately.

1038• ORGANIZATION OF WOMEN FOR LEGAL AWARENESS
17 N. Clinton St., East Orange NJ 07019. (201)762-5208. Contact Person: President. **Description:** "OWLA was founded to help make women aware of their legal rights, primarily in divorce, and the implementation of these rights. OWLA seeks to eliminate the mystique from the law and is dedicated to helping women to help themselves; to become assertive in dealing with their legal and financial problems, their lawyers and in public issues that can foster changes whenever and wherever necessary." **Services:** Provides advisory and referral information on the legal rights of women, divorce and marriage laws, credit laws. Offers library facilities, 24-hour hotline for emergencies, workshops. Publications include OWLA's *Guide to Marriage and Divorce Laws*. **How to Contact:** Write, call or visit. Responds to most inquiries immediately. Donations suggested for publications; sliding scale fees for membership and counseling. "Board approval" needed to use OWLA's services. **Tips:** Recent information request: The differences between community property and equitable distribution laws.

1039• PATENT AND TRADEMARK OFFICE
Department of Commerce, Washington DC 20231. (703)557-3158. Contact: Public Information Officer. **Description:** The office administers the patent and trademark laws, examines applications, and grants patents when applicants are entitled to them under the law. **Services:** Offers patent information, maintains search files of US and foreign patents and a patent search room for public use, and supplies copies of patents and official records to the public. Performs similar functions relating to trademarks. **How to Contact:** Write or visit. Responds to inquiries as soon as possible.

1040• SECRET SERVICE
1800 G St. NW, Washington DC 20223. (202)535-5708. Contact Person: Assistant to the Director, Office of Public Affairs. **Description:** "Responsibilities and jurisdiction of the Secret Service as prescribed by law include detection and arrest of persons committing any offense against US laws relating to coins, currency, and other obligations, and securities of US and foreign governments; protection of the US President and other government officials and their immediate families, and visiting heads of foreign states and governments." **Services:** Provides advisory and historical information. "Our various brochures discuss the historical development and current responsibilities of the US Secret Service. In additon, our recruitment brochures outline the qualifications and requirements for employment with our agency." **How to Contact:** Write or call. Responds to most inquiries within a week. "The information we provide is a matter of public record; therefore, no restrictions exist." **Tips:** Recent information request: "I am writing an article in which I want to reflect a bit of history about your organization. Can you provide me with background material?"

1041• SUPREME COURT
1 1st St. NE, Washington DC 20543. (202)252-3211. Contact Person: Public Information Officer. **Description:** It is the power of the Supreme Court to examine national and state laws and executive acts and determine whether they are in accord with the provisions of the Constitution. **Services:** Offers annual reports, biographies, statistics and brochures/pamphlets. **How to Contact:** Write or call. Responds to most inquiries within a month.

1042• UNITED STATES MARSHALS SERVICE
One Tysons Corner Center, McLean VA 22102. (703)285-1131. Contact Person: Public Affairs Office. **Description:** The US Marshals Service is a government agency which "provides support and protection to the Federal Judiciary and carries out law enforcement functions for the Attorney General." **Services:** Provides advisory and historical information on the functions of US Marshals including fugitive investigations and arrests; witness protection; court security; prisoner custody and transport; special operations group; and enforcement of court orders. Offers aid in arranging interviews and brochures/pamphlets. Publications include *Then . . . and Now*, a descriptive brochure on past and present operations of US Marshals Service. **How to Contact:** Write or call. Responds to most inquiries within a week. Prefers to review copy for accuracy.

1043• VOLUNTEER LAWYERS FOR THE ARTS
1560 Broadway, Suite 711, New York NY 10036. (212)575-1150. Contact Person: Administrator. **Description:** Not-for-profit corporation. "VLA was founded in 1969 to provide the artistic community with free legal assistance; nearly 800 attorneys in the New York City area now donate time to artists through VLA. Publications, conferences and workshops are designed to give artists the information they need in order to avoid legal problems." **Services:** Provides advisory information on copyright, publishing contracts, tax issues, immigration problems, loft problems, and other legal issues affecting the practice of one's art (music, dance, print, film, theatre, multi-media). Offers brochures/pamphlets and books. Publications list available. "Some publications e.g., *The Tax Guide: Fear of Filing*, apply to any artist; others e.g., *The Writer's Legal Guide*, are targeted to specific groups." **How to Contact:** Write or call. Responds to most inquiries within a month. "VLA charges an administrative fee for referrals to volunteers: $20 for an individual, $30 for a nonprofit organization. Many workshops are free. There is no charge for legal services for eligible artists apart from this fee. In order to qualify for free legal services, writers must demonstrate a gross income from all sources of under $7,500 per year, or up to $15,000 with Schedule C tax deductions of $7,500 or more. All other programs are available to anyone regardless of income." **Tips:** "It's a good idea to come to VLA with a specific legal problem, rather than a hypothetical one." Recent information requests: Questions on publisher's contracts; copyright issues.

1044• WORLD ASSOCIATION OF DETECTIVES
Box 5068, San Mateo CA 94402. (415)341-0060. Contact Person: President. **Description:** "Association for the professional upgrading and training of private investigators." **Services:** Provides advisory, bibliographical, historical and how-to information covering law and all facets of private investigation. Offers aid in arranging interviews and information searches. **How to Contact:** Write or call. Responds to most inquiries immediately. Give credit to association.

1045• WORLD ASSOCIATION OF DOCUMENT EXAMINERS
111 N. Canal, Chicago IL 60606. (312)930-9446. Contact Person: Executive Secretary. **Description:** Professional document examiners interested in advancing training and recognition of document examiners by the public, bar, and judiciary. Conducts research and keeps members informed of new techniques and discoveries in document work. **Services:** Provides historical and referral information on the work of document examiners e.g., disputed check signatures, wills, deeds, petitions, letters, etc. Offers aid in arranging interviews and informational newsletters. **How to Contact:** Write. Responds to most inquiries within a week. **Tips:** "Be sure your inquiries fall into association activities."

SECTION·TWENTY

PHILOSOPHY AND RELIGION

Philosophy is the microscope of thought.
                           —*Victor Hugo*

Religion is behavior and not mere belief.
                       —*S. Radhakrishnan*

Philosophy and Religion resources include various denominations and church groups; or-ganizations concerned with church business, history and service; and groups interested in ethics, metaphysics, the future and such philosophies as humanism and atheism.

Psychic and paranormal references are available in the Science, Engineering, Technology category; information on vegetarian, homosexual and feminist philosophies is included in the Special Interest Groups category.

Bibliography

Coggins, Richard. *Who's Who in the Bible*. Totowa, NJ: Barnes & Noble Books, 1981.
Edwards, Paul, ed. *Encyclopedia of Philosophy*. 4th ed. New York: Macmillan, 1973.
Jacquet Jr., Constant H., ed. *Yearbook of American and Canadian Churches*. Annual. New York: National Council of Churches of Christ in the USA.
Mead, Frank S., ed. *The Handbook of Denominations in the US*. 7th ed. Nashville, TN: Abingdon Press, 1980.
Neil, William, ed. *Concise Dictionary of Religious Quotations*. Grand Rapids, MI: William B. Eerdman's Publishing Co., 1974.
Reese, William L. *Dictionary of Philosophy and Religion: Eastern and Western Thought*. Atlantic Highlands, NJ: Humanities Press, 1980.
Strong, James. *The Exhaustive Concordance of the Bible*. Nashville, TN: Abingdon Press, 1980. (Comprehensive alphabetical index and analysis of the principal words, passages, persons in the Bible)
Wiener, Philip P., ed. *Dictionary of the History of Ideas*. 5 vols. New York: Charles Scribner's Sons, 1973-74.

1046• THE ACADEMY OF RELIGION AND PSYCHICAL RESEARCH
326 Tunxis Ave., Bloomfield CT 06002. (203)242-4593. Contact Person: Executive Secretary. **Description:** "Our purpose is to encourage dialogue, exchange of ideas and cooperation between clergy and academics of religion and philosophy and scientists, researchers and academics of all scientific and humanistic disciplines in the fields of psychical research and new disciplines, as well as the historic sciences; and to conduct an education program for these scholars in the area where religion and psychical research interface." **Services:** Provides advisory and referral information in the areas in which religion and psychical research interface. Offers brochures/pamphlets (of annual conferences), library facilities (for members only), tapes, and abstracts of conference presentations. Publications include *The Journal of Religion and Psychical Research* ($2/issue). List of cassette tapes available. **How to Contact:** Write or call. Responds to most inquiries immediately. Include SASE with information request. **Tips:** "We can provide the names/addresses of experts in the field and other sources for research data in the field of parapsychology, psychical research and their interface with religion, especially Christianity." Recent information request: "I'm doing research on spiritual healing for my dissertation. Do you have any bibliographical material on this subject?"

1047• AMERICAN ATHEISTS
Box 2117, Austin TX 78768. (512)458-1244. Contact Person: Editor, *American Atheist* magazine. **Description:** "We labor for complete separation of church and state." Purposes of the organization include education about atheism. **Services:** Provides analytical and historical information on atheism, history of religion, and legal aspects of separation of church and state.

Offers brochures/pamphlets, informational newsletters, information packet, placement on mailing lists, research assistance and telephone reference services. Publications include *American Atheist* magazine; books (our catalog lists over 100 titles). **How to Contact:** Write. Responds to most inquiries within a week. Charges for magazine ($25/year); average $3 for paperback books. **Tips:** Ask for an information packet.

1048•   AMERICAN BAPTIST CHURCHES IN THE UNITED STATES
Valley Forge PA 19481. (215)768-2000. Contact: Division of Communication. **Description:** "We are a national church body (6,000 congregations) located in 49 of the 50 states. We have 3 boards and 37 regional divisions and are also involved in foreign mission programs." **Services:** Offers aid in arranging interviews, brochures/pamphlets and statistics. Publications available. **How to Contact:** Write or call. Responds to most inquiries within a week. **Tips:** "A lot of people call for articles that have appeared in our magazine, *The American Baptist.*"

1049•   AMERICAN BAPTIST HISTORICAL SOCIETY
1106 S. Goodman St., Rochester NY 14620. (716)473-1740. Contact Person: Executive Director. **Description:** Historical research. **Services:** Provides advisory, analytical, bibliographical, historical, how-to and interpretative information on American Baptist life and thought and American religious history. Offers biographies, library facilities, photos, research assistance and telephone reference services. Publications include *A Baptist Bibliography*, 26 vols.; *The Primary Source*; and *American Baptist Quarterly.* **How to Contact:** Write or visit. Responds to most inquiries within a month. "Normal 'fair use' photocopy restriction on most material; some restrictions on use of confidential items in archives." **Tips:** "We have a wide range of published and unpublished materials—books, periodicals, archives, and personal papers. The researcher with a reasonable background in his topic will find a great deal of information on almost anything related to American Baptists. The staff assists in every way possible." Recent information request: "Can you supply information on the founding of First Baptist Church in (a particular city)?"

1050•   AMERICAN HUMANIST ASSOCIATION
7 Harwood Dr., Amherst NY 14226. (716)839-5080. Contact Person: Administrator. **Description:** "The purpose of the association is to promote the philosophy of humanism through publications, conferences, local chapter organizations, the United Nations, and through our own speakers bureau." **Services:** Provides bibliographical, historical, interpretative and referral information on "humanism as a philosophy, our association, church/state separation issues, the creation-evolution controversy, and the major social issues of our time which we have treated in our publication *The Humanist.*" Offers brochures/pamphlets, library facilities, press releases and access to copies of our publications. Publications include *The Humanist; Free Mind* (membership publication); and *Creation/Evolution* (specialized journal on this controversy). **How to Contact:** Write. Responds to most inquiries within a week. Charges $3 for back issues of publications, $2.50 each in quantity. "Quotations from our materials beyond 'fair use' require permission and often a fee. Use of our library is by appointment only, preferably a month in advance." **Tips:** Recent information request: Background information on the attacks against humanism by the Moral Majority.

1051•   AMERICAN JEWISH COMMITTEE
165 E. 56th St., New York NY 10022. (212)751-4000. Contact Person: Director of Public Relations. **Description:** "This is a human relations agency, founded in 1906, mandated to protect the civil and religious rights of Jews in the US and abroad, and to advance the cause of improved human relations for all people. Our information covers issues of Jewish concern, human rights, intergroup activities generally." **Services:** Provides information covering the following as they apply to the Jewish community: agriculture, art, business, celebrities, economics, entertainment, food, health/medicine, history, how-to, industry, law, music, nature, politics, recreation, science, self-help, sports, technical data and travel. Offers aid in arranging interviews, annual reports, bibliographies, statistics, brochures/pamphlets, information searches, placement on press mailing list, newsletters and press kits. "We have an excellent library given over to subject matter of our concern and acknowledged experts who can offer authoritative comment on such subject matter." **How to Contact:** *Publications of the American Jewish Committee Institute of Human Relations* is a catalog of materials available. "These materials are available free to writers, and we will send the catalog in response to serious inquiries from writers."

1052• THE AMERICAN MUSLIM MISSION
7351 S. Stony Island Ave., Chicago IL 60649. (312)667-7200. Contact Person: Resident Imam.
Description: "AMM is concerned with Islam in the United States. The objectives of the AMM are
education, jobs primarily for husbands and fathers who accept family responsibility, and moral
excellence. The AMM is engaged in a number of projects and programs which demonstrate its
commitment to improve every aspect of the human life, including communications,
health/medicine, and economic development." **Services:** Offers annual reports,
brochures/pamphlets (historical) and statistics. Publications include *World Muslim News* (weekly
newspaper). **How to Contact:** Write or call. "Write for specific information, call if there is a
simple question that can be answered on the phone."

1053• AMERICANS UNITED FOR SEPARATION OF CHURCH AND STATE
8120 Fenton St., Silver Spring MD 20910. (301)589-3707. Contact Person: Director of
Research. **Description:** "Our purpose is to defend and preserve the First Amendment's religious
liberty provisions." **Services:** Provides advisory, analytical, bibliographical, historical,
interpretative and referral information on church-state relations. Offers aid in arranging
interviews, brochures/pamphlets, library facilities, research assistance and statistics. Publications
include *Church and State*, a monthly magazine. **How to Contact:** Write or call. Responds to most
inquiries within a week. **Tips:** Recent information requests: "How do the states aid parochial
schools?"; "What constitutional provisions in the states exist to aid religious liberty?"

1054• ASSOCIATION FOR RESEARCH AND ENLIGHTENMENT, INC.
Box 595, 67th and Atlantic, Virginia Beach VA 23451. (804)428-3588. Contact Person:
Communications Department Manager. **Description:** "Our purpose is to make available the
Edgar Cayce psychic legacy through research, publications, seminars, individual and group study
aids." **Services:** Provides advisory, bibliographical, how-to, interpretative and referral
information on parapsychology; psychology; self-help; dreams; comparative religions; health,
nutrition, prevention of disease; meditation; parent/child/family relationships; prophecy;
reincarnation and Karma; and ancient civilizations (Egypt and Atlantis). Offers aid in arranging
interviews, brochures/pamphlets, informational newsletters, library facilities, photos, press kits
and telephone reference services. Publications include *A.R.E. Journal*; and *Perspective on
Consciousness and Psi Research*. **How to Contact:** Write, call or visit. "In-person research is
preferable to research through the mail."Responds to most inquiries within a week. "When using
copyrighted Cayce readings for publication, permission must be obtained in writing." **Tips:**
Recent information requests: "What is the purpose of existence?"; "What do the Edgar Cayce
readings say about Jesus and Christianity?"; "Do you have materials on Kerlian photography?"

1055• BAHA'I FAITH
Baha'i Office of Public Affairs, 112 Linden Ave., Wilmette IL 60091. (312)869-9039. Contact
Person: Public Affairs Officer. **Description:** "An independent, worldwide religion based on the
teachings of Baha'u'llah. Some of the principles of the faith are the oneness of mankind, the
independent investigation of truth, equality of men and women, the elimination of all forms of
prejudice (racial, social, religious, class, etc), the essential harmony of science and religion, a
spiritual solution to the economic problem, universal education, a universal auxiliary language,
and the need for a world government to maintain world peace." **Services:** Provides advisory,
analytical, bibliographical, historical, how-to, interpretative and referral information on world
peace, disarmament, elimination of racial prejudice, human rights, education and child
development, family issues, equality of men and women, international development, individual
spiritual growth. Offers brochures/pamphlets "pertaining to the history and teachings of the faith.
A number of topics are covered, from death to racial unity." **How to Contact:** "Write or phone
and specify the type of information desired. A phone call is usually the most efficient and
effective." Responds to most inquiries within a week. Observe copyright restrictions. **Tips:** "The
Baha'i international community at the United Nations is a valuable source of information relating
to international affairs. Most libraries, especially university libraries, carry thorough collections of
Baha'i materials. The best starting point is the office of public affairs, though." Recent
information requests: "What is the Baha'i faith?"; "Who are the Baha'is?"

1056• B'NAI B'RITH INTERNATIONAL
1640 Rhode Island Ave. NW, Washington DC 20036. (202)857-6536. Contact Person: Press
Officer. **Description:** "We are designed to foster Jewish unity and the future of Judaism in the

world. Programs generally aimed at young people—education, cultural, religious orientation—nonsectarian programs are also offered the elderly." **Services:** Offers aid in arranging interviews, brochures/pamphlets, placement on mailing list and photos. **How to Contact:** Write or call. Responds to most inquiries immediately.

1057• BOARD OF CHURCH AND SOCIETY OF THE UNITED METHODIST CHURCH
100 Maryland Ave. NE, Washington DC 20002. (202)488-5600. Contact Person· Director of Communications. **Description:** "We are a religious organization." Information covers social issues from a Christian viewpoint. **Services:** Offers annual reports, brochures/pamphlets, information searches, statistics and monthly publication. **How to Contact:** Write or call. Responds to most inquiries in 2 weeks. **Tips:** Recent information request: "What is the United Methodist Church's stand on abortion?"

1058• BUDDHIST VIHARA SOCIETY
5017 16th St. NW, Washington DC 20011. (202)723-0773. Contact Person: President. **Description:** The society is a religious and educational center; its purpose is to spread Buddhism. **Services:** Provides advisory, bibliographical and technical information related to Theravada Buddhism. Offers brochures/pamphlets, informational newsletters and placement on mailing lists. Publications include *Washington Buddhist* (newsletter). **How to Contact:** Visit. Responds to most inquiries within a month.

1059• CATHOLIC INFORMATION CENTER
741 15th St. NW, Washington DC 20005. (202)783-2062. Contact Person: Receptionist. **Description:** The center provides information, counseling and teaching services. **Services:** Offers information leads, statistics, a lending library of some 4,000 titles on theology, church history, philosophy, social science, etc. and a reference library for in-depth information. Publications available. **How to Contact:** Write or call. Responds to most inquiries immediately, "unless some research is involved." Charges for paperbacks and magazines. **Tips:** Recent information request: "Where is Archbishop LeFevbre headquartered?"

1060• THE CATHOLIC UNIVERSITY OF AMERICA
620 Michigan Ave., Washington DC 20064. (202)635-5000. Contact Person: Director of Public Relations. **Description:** "Catholic University continues to fulfill the mission for which it was conceived by the American bishops and for which it received a papal charter. The document designated the institution as a graduate and research center for the study of 'all branches of literature and science, both sacred and profane.' But today undergraduates also participate in the benefits of Catholic University's unique tradition. The university's location in the nation's capital, its easy access to the cultural, scientific, governmental, clinical and research sources have enhanced the fulfillment of its original mission, as have the following research centers located on the campus: the centers for Advanced Training in Cell and Molecular Biology, Congressional and Governmental Affairs, National Policy Review, Pastoral, Pastoral Studies, Study for Pre-retirement and Aging, Study of Youth Development, Ward Method Studies, Curriculum Development, National Rehabilitation Information, and Family Studies; the Institutes for Christian Oriental Research, Communications Law Studies, and The Leonine Commission, as well as the distinguished Vitreous State Laboratory. Other programs which are noted for excellence include the School of Music and the Drama Department." **Services:** Provides advisory and analytical information. Offers biographies and brochures/pamphlets, referral to experts on the faculty. **How to Contact:** Call. Responds to most inquiries immediately. Give credit to Catholic University of America.

1061• CEDAR SPRINGS LIBRARY
42421 Auberry Rd., Auberry CA 93602. Contact Person: Librarian. **Description:** The library provides information in special fields such as humanism, free thought, euthanasia, creation/evolution controversy, social concerns, peace. "This is a 'hobby' library with a growing collection of over 250 periodicals and several thousand monographs." **Services:** Provides advisory, bibliographical and referral information on humanism, free thought and agnosticism. Offers biographies, brochures/pamphlets, informational newsletters and library facilities. Publications include selected list of humanist groups and publications; bibliographies of selected collections in the library. **How to Contact:** Write. Responds to most inquiries within a month. "No fees are charged; but contributions are expected to cover the cost of reprints, copies, and

postage. Library is usually open only on weekends and holidays (we have no full-time staff), but extended use can sometimes be arranged for after visiting the library." **Tips:** Recent information requests: "Can you provide the address of the Atheist Connection?"; "I understand you have an outline in parallel columns of the two stories of creation in Genesis?"; "Can you provide a copy of an article on Hume and Boswell in *Free Inquiry*?"; "Are there books on contradictions in the Bible?"

1062• CENTER FOR BIOETHICS LIBRARY
Kennedy Institute, Georgetown University, Washington DC 20057. (202)625-2383. Contact Person: Librarian. **Description:** "We collect and disseminate all literature related to moral, ethical, value issues in biomedicine and medical research." **Services:** Provides advisory, analytical, bibliographical, historical and referral information on applied ethics, bioethics, philosophy of medicine, science/technology and society, sociology of medicine, professional-patient relationship, informed consent, confidentiality, right to health care, allocation of health resources, sexuality, contraception, abortion, population, reproductive technologies (including in vitro fertilization, cloning, sperm banking), genetic counseling and screening, genetic engineering, mental health therapies (including psychopharmacology, psychosurgery, involuntary commitment), human experimentation, transplantation, death and dying (including euthanasia, allowing infants to die, living wills), physician's attitudes to nuclear war. Offers clipping services, computerized information searches, informational newsletters, library facilities, research assistance and telephone reference services. Publications include *New Titles in Bioethics*; and subject bibliographies. **How to Contact:** Write, call or visit. Responds to most inquiries within a week. "Materials may not be removed from the library—photocopying facilities available." **Tips:** "We can provide bibliographies of the literature (comprehensive) on all biomedical issues, can isolate major statements by important spokesmen, provide legal cases related to specific issues." Recent information requests: "How many test-tube babies are there to date?"; "How do I prepare a living will?"; information on research on prisoners; material on reproductive technologies; legal cases dealing with allowing infants to die.

1063• CENTER FOR RELIGION, ETHICS AND SOCIAL POLICY (CRESP)
Anabel Taylor Hall, Cornell University, Ithaca NY 14853. (607)256-6486. Contact Person: Coordinator. **Description:** "Through programs, workshops, journals and ongoing projects CRESP, a nonprofit educational organization, explores the relationships between values, ethics and social life. We recognize the present as a turning point in human history, and our work promotes the transition to a more sustainable, equitable and joyful pattern of living." **Services:** Provides advisory, analytical, bibliographical, how-to, interpretative and referral information on the eco-justice crisis; changing world-views; appropriate technologies; mentor-apprentice learning; international relations (especially Latin-America); peace; holistic health; self-sufficiency; draft counseling, etc." Offers aid in arranging interviews, annual reports, brochures/pamphlets, informational newsletters, library facilities and placement on mailing lists. "We have a unique and very complete 'Alternatives Library' with books, periodicals, tapes, slide shows and films, all for lending." Publications include *The Egg*, quarterly journal of the Eco-Justice Project; the *CUSLAR Newsletter* (Committee on US-Latin American Relations). **How to Contact:** Write, call or visit. Responds to most inquiries within a week. Availability of staff time to assist writers/researchers is limited. **Tips:** Recent information request: "What is 'superinsulation'?"

1064• CENTER FOR THE STUDY OF ETHICS IN THE PROFESSIONS
Illinois Institute of Techonolgy, Chicago IL 60616. (312)567-3017. Contact Person: Director. **Description:** "We develop and promote research and education programs relating to professional responsibility and ethics." **Services:** Provides advisory, analytical, bibliographical, interpretative and referral information on professional and business ethics, professional self-regulation and licensing, professional continuing education, ethics education, and professions and public policy. Offers informational newsletters, library facilities and research assistance. More than 500 codes of ethics of various types of organizations are on file at CSEP. Publications include *Perspectives on the Professions* (quarterly); Occasional Paper Series; and specialized bibliographies and reports relating to professional ethics. Publications list available. **How to Contact:** Write or call. Responds to most inquiries within a month. "CSEP publications are free, but processing fee applied. Bibliographic items available for costs of photocopying. Visitors are welcome, but contact center in advance by phone or mail." **Tips:** Recent information request: Copies of codes of ethics of pro-

fessional associations which include provisions regarding professional disability (e.g., drug abuse, alcoholism, mental impairment).

1065• CHURCH AND SYNAGOGUE LIBRARY ASSOCIATION
Box 1130, Bryn Mawr PA 19010. (215)853-2870. Contact Person: Executive Secretary. **Description:** "The purpose of the Church and Synagogue Library Association is to provide educational guidance in the establishment and maintenance of library service in churches and synagogues. We hold an annual national conference and workshop and have 17 chapters throughout the country that hold regional meetings." **Services:** Provides advisory, bibliographical, historical, how-to, interpretative, referral and technical information on church and synagogue librarianship. Offers aid in arranging interviews, annual reports, bibliographies, statistics, brochures/pamphlets, information searches and newsletter. "Our publications include *Church and Synagogue Libraries* (bimonthly), eight guides for congregational libraries, two tracts and two bibliographies. Our library services also distribute small publications designed to be of help to librarians. A number of graduate students have done research papers for their degrees on the subject of congregational libraries. We have a list of these, plus other publications by denominations, etc., which are available." **How to Contact:** Write. Responds to most inquiries within a week. Charges for some publications. Give credit to Church and Synagogue Library Association.

1066• CHURCH OF THE NAZARENE
6401 The Paseo, Kansas City MO 64131. Contact Person: Division Director, Christian Life and Sunday School. **Description:** "Kansas City is the location of the International Headquarters for the Church of the Nazarene and also Nazarene Publishing House. The Paseo location houses the offices of five divisions: Finance, Church Growth, World Missions, Communications, and Christian Life and Sunday School. The publishing house is located at 29th & Troost, Kansas City, Missouri 64141." **Services:** Offers aid in arranging interviews, bibliographies, statistics and brochures/pamphlets. Publications include *Herald of Holiness, World Mission, Preacher's Magazine* and *Resource*. **How to Contact:** "We prefer a written request so letters can be forwarded to the proper office." Responds to most inquiries within a week.

1067• CONCORDIA HISTORICAL INSTITUTE
801 DeMun Ave., St. Louis MO 63105. (314)721-5934, ext. 320. Contact Person: Director. **Description:** The institute's purpose is "to promote interest in Lutheran history; to collect and preserve historical articles; to stimulate and publish history and research; to serve as an official depository for the Lutheran church and other agencies; and especially to encourage students from all over the world in historical research." **Services:** Provides advisory, analytical, bibliographical, historical, how-to, interpretative and referral information covering Lutheran history and theology in America; immigration, history and pre-immigration history (esp. German-American); archives, theory and practice. Offers bibliographies, biographies, brochures/pamphlets and information searches. Publications include series of bulletins on such topics as developing an archive, writing congregational histories, restoring historic sites. **How to Contact:** Write, requesting specific information. Responds to most inquiries within a month. Charges for some services; write for summary of costs. Stipulations for use of material "vary with specific resources used. Generally, acknowledge use of our resources and provide us two copies of finished product." **Tips:** "Write before coming; have specific questions or areas you wish addressed. Plan your research; don't expect or ask archivist and librarians to do your footwork; take careful notes; check your resources." Recent information requests: "What were Lutheran reactions in America to World War I?"; "Can I have biographical information on a specific pastor or teacher?"; "What Lutheran church was pastored by a Rev. Schmidt in Milwaukee during this particular year?"

1068• CREATION RESEARCH SOCIETY
2717 Cranbrook Rd., Ann Arbor MI 48104. (313)971-5915. Contact Person: Membership Secretary. **Description:** The society conducts research and disseminates information on science and creation. **Services:** Provides bibliographical, historical and interpretative information on science, apologetics, creation and evolution. Offers research assistance. Publications include *Creation Research Society Quarterly*. **How to Contact:** Write. Responds to most inquiries within a month. Charges for photocopies. Give credit to society.

1069• EPISCOPAL CHURCH CENTER
Office of Communication, 815 2nd Ave., New York NY 10017. Contact Person: Editorial

Coordinator. **Description:** National headquarters. **How to Contact:** "We prefer requests in writing so the office can evaluate the merit of the piece. State the specific information you wish to have." Responds to most inquiries within a month. **Tips:** Recent information requests: Many questions about Episcopal Church's stand on the ordination of women, ecumenical dialogues with Catholics, and the Episcopal Church's history.

1070• ETHICS RESOURCE CENTER, INC.
1730 Rhode Island Ave. NW, Washington DC 20036. (202)223-3411. Contact Person: Executive Director. **Description:** "The purpose of our organization is to restore public trust in government, business, education and the other institutions of our society by strengthening their ethical values and practices." **Services:** Provides advisory, analytical and bibliographical information on ethics oriented issues, including code of ethics/standards of conduct collection. Offers aid in arranging interviews, library facilities and research assistance. Publications include *Common Sense and Everyday Ethics.* **How to Contact:** Write. Responds to most inquiries within a week. Give credit to Ethics Resource Center.

1071• THE FIRST CHURCH OF CHRIST, SCIENTIST
Christian Science Center, Boston MA 02115. (617)262-2300. Contact Person: Manager of the Committees on Publication. **Description:** "Christianity in a scientific age; restoration of Christian healing." Information includes history of Christian Science Church, its theology and organization. Also biographical information on its founder, Mary Baker Eddy. **Services:** Furnishes scholarly material as well as more general facts. Publications available. **How to Contact:** Write or call. "The time necessary to respond to an individual depends largely on the nature of the information requested. We do all we can to accommodate those with academic or publishers' deadlines."

1072• FREEDOM FROM RELIGION FOUNDATION, INC.
Box 750, Madison WI 53701. (608)256-8900. Contact Person: President. **Description:** "Our purpose is to promote the constitutional principle of state-church separation and to educate the public about nontheistic beliefs." **Services:** Provides advisory and referral information on nontheism and bible-debunking. Publications include a monthly newsletter. **How to Contact:** Write or call. Responds to most inquiries within a week.

1073• GENERAL CONFERENCE OF SEVENTH-DAY ADVENTISTS
6840 Eastern Ave. NW, Washington DC 20012. (202)723-0800. Contact Person: Director of Communication. **Description:** "We are the highest administrative body of the Seventh-Day Adventist Church, with 550,000 members in North America, three million worldwide. We are especially active in health education, cancer research and operation of hospitals (over 200). We are involved with a large educational system (400,000 students in kindergarten through Ph.D. programs worldwide). Our popular Five-Day Plan to Stop Smoking is conducted in cooperation with American Cancer Society. A heavy disaster relief program SAWS (Seventh-Day Adventist World Service), is also headquartered here." **Services:** Offers aid in arranging interviews, biographies, statistics, brochures/pamphlets, clipping services, information searches, placement on mailing list, photos and press kits. Publication available. **How to Contact:** Write or call. Responds to most inquiries immediately. Adventist headquarters are located in each state and province of the US and Canada (local conferences). These can provide localized information. Contact the communication director in each case; conference names are available in the *SDA Fact Book* available from General Conference. **Tips:** Recent information request: "I'd like to know more about your church, its doctrines and history."

1074• GOSPEL MUSIC ASSOCIATION
Box 23201, Nashville TN 37202. (615)242-0303. Contact Person: Executive Director. **Description:** "Our purpose is to promote and perpetuate the use and heritage of gospel music." **Services:** Provides advisory, historical, how-to, referral and trade information on gospel music and related areas. Offers aid in arranging interviews, biographies, brochures/pamphlets, informational newsletters, research assistance and statistics. **How to Contact:** Write. Responds to most inquiries within a week.

1075• BILLY GRAHAM CENTER LIBRARY
Wheaton College, Wheaton IL 60187. (312)260-2525. Contact Person: Director. **Description:**

The library "assembles and makes available to the public for research, collections on evangelism, revivalism and missions." **Services:** Provides information on evangelism, revivalism, and missions. Offers bibliographies, biographies and information searches. **How to Contact:** Write. Responds to most inquiries within a week. Charges 10¢/page for photocopying services.

1076• GREEK ORTHODOX CHURCH IN THE AMERICAS/GREEK ORTHODOX ARCHDIOCESE OF NORTH AND SOUTH AMERICA
8-10 E. 79th St., New York NY 10021 (212)570-3529. Contact Person: Director, News and Information. **Description:** "We are a Greek Orthodox church with over two million members." **Services:** Provides advisory, analytical, bibliographical, historical, how-to, interpretative, referral and technical information on Greek Orthodox Christianity. Offers aid in arranging interviews, annual reports, bibliographies, biographies, brochures/pamphlets, information searches, placement on mailing list and press kits. **How to Contact:** Write or call. Responds to most inquiries within a week. "We prefer written requests but will answer urgent questions by phone. Give proper attribution and quote accurately." **Tips:** "Contact us first; we can refer you to local contacts. Locating information, particularly historical documents, requires time. Allow the maximum amount of time by contacting us early." Recent information request: "National magazine asked for the proper name, title, and jurisdiction of a Greek Orthodox bishop its writer had interviewed."

1077• HOOSE PHILOSOPHY LIBRARY
University of Southern California, Mudd Memorial Hall, Los Angeles CA 90089-0451. (213)743-2634. Contact Person: Librarian. **Description:** Broadly-based research library serving the academic community in philosophy, relating to its history, current problems, etc. **Services:** Offers 51,000 volumes ranging from medieval manuscripts and incunabula to the latest works of today's philosophers and scholars. "Its general strength is in metaphysics; epistemology; logic; ethics; and the philosophy of religion in various languages. Its holdings distinctively reflect the contributions of German philosophy. The *Gomperz Collection*, 3,500 volumes, concerns the Enlightenment and Romanticism periods. It's especially useful for the study of European philosophy from about 1700-1850. Complete, or nearly complete, runs of first editions of Kant; Schelling; Hegel; Schopenhauer; Wolff; Fichte; La Mettrie; and John Stuart Mill." **How to Contact:** Write or call for appointment. Nonstudents may not take material from facility. Student demand comes first. Rare books do not circulate.

1078• THE HYMN SOCIETY OF AMERICA, INC.
Wittenberg University, Springfield OH 45501. (513)327-6308. Contact Person: Executive Director. **Description:** "The society's purpose is to promote new hymns and tunes; to increase interest in writing texts and tunes; and to encourage the use of hymns by congregations of all faiths." **Services:** Provides bibliographical, historical, referral and technical information on hymnology—scholarly and practical. Offers biographies, brochures/pamphlets and research assistance. Publications include *The Stanza*, a semiannual newsletter containing practical suggestions for use of hymns in worship, reviews of materials, announcements of hymnic events, record and book reviews, and news about Hymn Society members; and *The Hymn*, a quarterly publication containing scholarly articles on hymnological topics plus book and hymnal reviews. **How to Contact:** Write. Responds to most inquiries immediately. **Tips:** Recent information request: Question on women hymn writers.

1079• INTERNATIONAL ASSOCIATION FOR RELIGION AND PARAPSYCHOLOGY
4-11-7 Inokashira, Mitaka-Shi, Tokyo, Japan 181. Tel. (0422)48-3535. Contact Person: Dr. Hiroshi Motoyama. **Description:** "We conduct research into 'paranormal' and religious phenomena. The association aims to unify science and religion and find a common basis for the various world religions. It aids and supports personal religious practice regardless of creed, and conducts lectures, workshops and study retreats on acupuncture and yoga." **Services:** Provides how-to, referral and technical information on "paranormal" phenomena (e.g., ESP, psychokinesis, psychic healing); religious experience and spiritual development; acupuncture; yoga; karma and reincarnation; and holistic health. Offers brochures/pamphlets. Publications include *Research for Religion and Parapsychology*, IRP Journal (3/year); *International Newsletter of the IARP* (bimonthly); plus periodic books and monographs. **How to Contact:** Write. Responds to most inquiries within a month. Charges for some services. "We would normally require a fee to cover expenses incurred. We are a non-profit-making organization. We prefer to provide services

for IARP members.'' Give credit to IARP and send copies of all resulting articles. **Tips:** "We are not really a 'service organization.' We are more a research institute and international association which conducts scientific research, publishes articles, etc. and deals with inquiries from others working in similar fields rather than aiming to provide specific services.'' Recent information requests: Questions relating to yogic practice, psychic experience, and scientific research in these areas.

1080• INTERNATIONAL ORDER OF KABBALISTS
25 Circle Gardens, Merton Park, London SW19 3JX England. (01)542-3611. Contact Person: Principal. **Description:** "An occult spiritual organization that teaches ancient wisdom in the interest of developing man's hidden potential.'' **Services:** Provides information to members only on meditation and related occult subjects including astrology, Egyptian and Greek mythology, Buddhism, etc. Publications include a quarterly magazine and other publications, also available to non-members. **How to Contact:** Write enclosing International Reply Coupons. Responds to most inquiries within a week. Membership: Lodge members $20; corresponding members $40.

1081• JEHOVAH'S WITNESSES
25 Columbia Heights, Brooklyn NY 11201. **Description:** Nonfundamentalist religious organization. **Services:** Provides analytical, historical and interpretative information. Offers explanatory publications on the Bible, on creation vs. evolution, on Bible authenticity, etc., including journals *The Watchtower* and *Awake!* published semimonthly. Brochure provided (free) on beliefs and missionary activities throughout the world. **How to Contact:** Write. Responds to most inquiries within a month. List of publications and prices available. *Yearbook* ($1) available from December through March. Order in advance. **Tips:** "Questions should be restricted to those pertaining to Bible or Jehovah's Witnesses.''

1082• LUTHERAN CHURCH—MISSOURI SYNOD
Department of Communications, 1333 S. Kirkwood Rd., St. Louis MO 63122. (314)231-6969. Contact: Department of Communications. **Description:** "We offer services, liaison and national organization membership to 6,100 congregations (with approximately 2.7 million members) who affiliate with the Lutheran Church—Missouri Synod (LCMS). We are the 6th largest Protestant church body. Our national body operates 13 colleges and three seminaries and has a partnership relation to mission outreaches in over 20 foreign lands. LCMS congregations operate the largest system of Protestant schools in the nation.'' **Services:** Offers bibliographies, statistics, brochures/pamphlets, placement on mailing list and photos. Publications include *Lift High the Cross* (history, beliefs and services of the LCMS); *A Brief Historical Sketch of the LCMS; Blessed To Serve* (description of LCMS programs); *That We May Grow* (descriptive brochure); *The Lutheran Witness* (monthly magazine); and *The Reporter* (weekly newspaper). "A number of other regular publications are offered.'' **How to Contact:** For brochures, write Department of Public Relations. For *Lutheran Witness* or *The Reporter*, write Concordia Publishing House, 3558 S. Jefferson Ave., St. Louis MO 63118. Charges $5.50/year subscription for *Witness*, $9/year for *Reporter*. **Tips:** Recent information requests: "What do Lutherans believe?''; "What are the differences between the three largest Lutheran bodies?''

1083• MENNONITE LIBRARY AND ARCHIVES
Bethel College, North Newton KS 67117. (316)283-2500. Contact Person: Director. **Description:** "Our purpose is the collecting and preserving of historical materials for research.'' **Services:** Provides historical information on Mennonite history and culture; and peace studies. Offers library facilities, photos, research assistance and telephone reference services. "We have about 300 Mennonite periodicals available.'' Publications include *Mennonite Life*. **How to Contact:** Write, call or visit. Responds to most inquiries within a week. **Tips:** Recent information requests: Primarily genealogical requests from Mennonites.

1084• MORMON HISTORY ASSOCIATION
Box 7010, University Station, Provo UT 84602. (801)378-2705. Contact Person: Secretary-Treasurer. **Description:** The Mormon History Association brings together historians united by interest in the Mormon experience. **Services:** Provides historical and referral information on Mormon history from its inception with the birth of Joseph Smith to the present. Offers informational newsletters and placement on mailing lists. Publications include quarterly newsletter and annual journal. **How to Contact:** Write or call. Responds to most inquiries within a

week. Charges for membership. **Tips:** Recent information request: Background on the participation of Joseph F. Smith in Senator Reed Smoot case in 1904.

1085• NATIONAL ASSOCIATION OF CHURCH BUSINESS ADMINISTRATORS
Suite 324, Northeast National Bank Tower, 7001 Grapevine Hwy., Fort Worth TX 76118. (817)284-1732. Contact Person: Executive Director. **Description:** The purpose of the association is "to extend the kingdom of God through a program of study, service, fellowship, exchange of information and problem discussion." **Services:** Provides advisory, bibliographical, how-to and referral information on matters pertaining to the management of the business of the church or religious institution—church budgeting, personnel, office, etc. Offers brochures/pamphlets and newsletter to members. "We provide a detailed salary survey of the church staff every 3 years." **How to Contact:** Write or call. Responds to most inquiries within a week. Charges for postage and printing. **Tips:** "Adequate lead time is a must!" Recent information request: "What is the average salary of pastors in the Southwest?"

1086• NATIONAL CONFERENCE OF CHRISTIANS AND JEWS
1425 H St. NW, Suite 735, Washington DC 20005. (212)678-9400. Contact Person: Director. **Description:** The conference is a nonprofit organization "concerned with human relations problems in metropolitan areas." **Services:** Offers aid in arranging interviews, brochures/pamphlets, clipping services, information searches and newsletter. **How to Contact:** Write. Responds to most inquiries immediately.

1087• NATIONAL COUNCIL OF CHURCHES OF CHRIST
News and Information Services, 475 Riverside Dr., Room 805, New York NY 10027. (212)870-2227. Contact Person: Assistant Director for Interpretation. **Description:** "We are composed of 32 member denominations; we are an ecumenical organization seeking to unify activities of members of the church. The NCCC is the largest ecumenical body in the US. It is a community of churches seeking to make a common Christian witness on a wide range of issues of concern to Christians." **Services:** Provides interpretative and referral information on the ecumenical efforts of US churches in the areas of overseas missions, domestic programs, Christian education and leadership, stewardship, communications, research and theological dialogue. Offers quarterly newsletter ($1/year) and guest placements on television and radio. List of publications available. **How to Contact:** Call. Responds to most inquiries within a week. **Tips:** Recent information request: Statistics on church membership, giving, etc.

1088• THE RELIGIOUS ARTS GUILD
25 Beacon St., Boston MA 02108. (617)742-2100. Contact Person: Executive Secretary. **Description:** "Our purpose is to create and foster interest in the fine arts within the life of churches; to increase appreciation of beauty in the lives of religious people and to provide materials and resource contacts in all the arts for liberal churches. We are an affiliate of the Unitarian Universalist Association." **Services:** Provides bibliographical, historical, how-to and referral information on promoting the use of the arts in church services and programming. Offers brochures/pamphlets. Publications include an awards folder describing annual competition in poetry, anthem and worship service; a catalog listing loan anthems; resources listing of worship services; and a listing of Unitarian Universalist performing artists. **How to Contact:** Write. Responds to most inquiries immediately "except during the summer (June—September 15) when the office is closed." Individual membership $10; church or fellowship $20. "Be explicit on Awards and Scholarship detail flyers. SASE (business size) for reply." **Tips:** "We no longer sponsor a drama competition. We have changed the focus of that award to anthems suitable for UU church/fellowship."

1089• RICHARD OWEN ROBERTS, BOOKSELLERS
205 E. Kehoe Blvd., Wheaton IL 60187. (312)668-1025. Contact: Sales Department. **Description:** "We stock and make available to the public approximately 150,000 volumes of rare and out-of-print religious and theological books in all the theological disciplines." **Services:** Provides bibliographical and historical information. Offers "catalogs of out-of-print religious and theological material." **How to Contact:** Write or call. Responds to most inquiries within a month. **Tips:** Request catalogs or specific information on authors and titles. Recent information request: "Is there any complete copy available in English of Justyn the Martyr's dialogue with Trypho?"

1090• THE BERTRAND RUSSELL SOCIETY
RD 1, Coopersburg PA 18036. (215)346-7687. Contact Person: Director of Public Information. **Description:** "The society's purpose is to encourage the study and teaching of Bertrand Russell's life, thoughts, and philosophy, and to promote the spirit of rational inquiry as applied to mankind's problems." **Services:** Provides bibliographical, historical and referral information on subjects covered in Russell's writings: logic, philosophy, happiness, education, peace, religion, marriage, science, etc. Offers informational newsletters and library facilities. Publications include Russell's books; films about him. **How to Contact:** Write or call. Responds to most inquiries within a week. Charges for books and rental of films. Give credit to society. **Tips:** "Visit the Bertrand Russell Archives at McMaster University, Hamilton, Ontario."

1091• THE SOCIETY OF EVANGELICAL AGNOSTICS
Box 515, Auberry CA 93602. Contact Person: Administrator. **Description:** SEA promotes the principles of agnosticism and disseminates information about agnosticism. **Services:** Provides advisory, bibliographical and historical information on agnosticism. Offers brochures/pamphlets and informational newsletters. Publications include *SEA Journal.* **How to Contact:** Write. Responds to most inquiries within a week. **Tips:** Recent information requests: "What is the relationship of agnosticism to atheism and theism?"; "How should agnostics celebrate such holidays as Christmas?"; "What techniques of child rearing do agnostics use?"

1092• SOCIETY OF METAPHYSICIANS, LTD.
Archers' Court, Stonestile Lane, The Ridge, Hastings, TN35 4PG, Sussex England. Tel. (0424)751577. Contact Person: Founder-President. **Description:** "The purpose of the society is to promote neometaphysics in high priority human affairs: (Neometaphysics: infinitely based general system)." **Services:** Provides advisory, analytical, bibliographical, historical, how-to, interpretative, referral, technical and trade information on parapsychology; paraphysics; esoterics; mysticism; religious codes; functional studies (fundamental laws and principles); psychics; social, economic and political reforms. Offers annual reports; biographies, brochures/pamphlets, computerized information searches, informational newsletters, library facilities, placement on mailing lists, press kits, research assistance, statistics and telephone reference services. **How to Contact:** Write. Responds to most inquiries immediately. Charges for services to non-members. Membership $54/annum. **Tips:** Recent information request: "Is there a fundamental structure which provides 'best for all' conditions in business?"

1093• SPIRITUAL COUNTERFEITS PROJECT, INC.
Box 2418, Berkeley CA 94702. (415)524-9534. **Description:** "The SCP examines the culture's shift from its Judeo-Christian heritage to a society of conflicting world views; it biblically critiques today's spiritual trends and movements that are based on Eastern philosophies and publishes its research." **Services:** Provides analytical, bibliographical, interpretative and referral information on broad cultural trends in philosophy, theology, education, art; information and analysis of specific new religious groups; referrals to counselors and other information sources. Offers brochures/pamphlets, informational newsletters, library facilities, placement on mailing lists and telephone reference services. Publications include bimonthly newsletter and annual journal; various pamphlets. **How to Contact:** Write. Responds to most inquiries within a month. Charges catalog prices for literature; cover charges for journal; free newsletter. There is an individual screening process for in-house use of services. **Tips:** "Contact us for information we have available on a specific religious group." Recent information request: "Do you have any information on The Unification Church?"

1094• UNITED CHURCH OF CHRIST
105 Madison Ave., New York NY 10016. Contact Person: Secretary. **Description:** "Founded in 1957, this is the congregational evangelical church of the Protestant denomination." **Services:** Provides interpretative and referral information on United Church of Christ program and organization. Offers brochures/pamphlets and statistics. Publications include *Minutes of General Synod* ($5); Yearbook ($10). **How to Contact:** Write. Responds to most inquiries within a week.

1095• UNITED PRESBYTERIAN CHURCH, UNITED STATES OF AMERICA
475 Riverside Dr. Room 1948, New York NY 10027. (212)870-2548. Contact Person: Director of Communications. **Description:** "We are a religious organization." **Services:** Provides

information on the beliefs, work and organization of the denomination. Offers information searches, placement on mailing list and press kits. **How to Contact:** Write or call. Responds to most inquiries immediately. "A written request for information is preferred, but we will answer simple questions on the phone." **Tips:** Recent information requests: The church's position on abortion and other social issues.

1096• WORLD FUTURE SOCIETY
4916 St. Elmo Ave., Bethesda MD 20814. (301)656-8274. Contact Person: Assistant Editor, *The Futurist.* **Description:** Association of persons interested in studying the future, i.e., forecasts, ideas, predictions about the future; and communicating the importance of conducting serious investigations into the future. **Services:** Offers library facilities, press kits and research assistance. Publications include: *Future Survey* (monthly); *Education Tomorrow*; *The Futurist* (bimonthly); *World Future Society Bulletin* (bimonthly); *Resource Guide* (directory of organizations, books dealing with the future). **How to Contact:** Write. Responds to most inquiries within 2 weeks.

1097• WORLD WIDE PICTURES
2520 W. Olive, Burbank CA 91505. (213)843-1300. Contact Person: Public Relations Secretary. **Description:** "We produce religious films for theatres, television and churches." **Services:** Offers aid in arranging interviews, biographies, photos and press kits. **How to Contact:** Write or call. Responds to most inquiries within a month.

PRODUCTS AND SERVICES

Honest transactions in a free market between buyers and sellers are at the core of individual, community and national economic growth.
—Ronald Reagan

This section is a selected marketplace potpourri—a brief sample of goods and services information provided by large, diversified companies, service-oriented businesses and professional organizations. Represented here are government agencies, trade associations and companies engaged in manufacturing, distribution, consultation and sales.

Additional product and service resources are listed in those categories reflecting their main interests: Clairol, in the Fashion section; Gallery of Homes, in the House and Home section, etc. *The Thomas Register of American Manufacturers* (see bibliography below) and the *Standard and Poor's Corporations* directories (see Business section bibliography) provide data on thousands of companies in today's marketplace.

Bibliography

Brand, Stewart, ed. *The Next Whole Earth Catalog—Access to Tools.* 2d ed. New York: Random House, 1981. (How and where to get useful, little-known, and/or unique tools/information for living)

Ellis, Iris, ed. *Save on Shopping.* 9th ed. New York: Grosset & Dunlap, 1982.

Thomas Register of American Manufacturers. Annual. New York: Thomas Publishing Co.

Trade and Professional Exhibits Directory. Detroit: Gale Research Co., 1982. (Lists conferences, conventions, trade shows, expositions and other events that use exhibits)

Wood, Donna, ed. *Trade Names Dictionary.* 2 vols. Detroit: Gale Research Co., 1982. (Directory of brands, product, model and trade names)

1098• AFFILIATED WAREHOUSE COMPANIES, INC.
Box 295, Hazlet NJ 07730. (201)739-2323. Contact Person: President. **Description:** "We do the national sales work and advertising for the 75 public merchandise warehouses that employ our services on a retainer basis." **Services:** Provides trade information. Offers brochures/pamphlets. Publications include an annual directory and direct mail advertising pieces. **How to Contact:** Write or call. Responds to most inquiries within a week.

1099• ALLRIGHT AUTO PARKS, INC.
1625 Esperson Bldg., Houston TX 77002. (713)222-2505. Contact Person: National Director, Public Relations. **Description:** "We are the world's largest auto parking company (United States and Canada). We offer all types of services, including consulting services, garages, open lots, etc. As the leader in the parking industry, we cover national information on parking and the history of parking. Our company occupies more downtown property than any other company and owns over 120 properties." **Services:** Provides advisory, bibliographical, historical and trade information. Offers aid in arranging interviews, annual reports, biographies, statistical information, brochures/pamphlets, placement on mailing list, newsletter and photos. Publications include *Parking News Quarterly* and individual sheets on specific areas of parking. **How to Contact:** Write or call. Responds to most inquiries within a week.

1100• ALUMINUM COMPANY OF AMERICA (ALCOA)
Alcoa Bldg., Pittsburgh PA 15219. Contact Person: Editor-Corporate Information. **Description:** Alcoa is a manufacturer of primary and fabricated aluminum and alumina chemicals. **Services:** Provides advisory, analytical, bibliographical, historical, interpretative, referral, technical and trade information—whatever is not restricted by patent or legal restraints. Offers descriptive literature, reference material, photos in color and b&w on aluminum and aluminum industry—mining,

refining, smelting, fabricating, products, uses, etc. **How to Contact:** Write. Responds to most inquiries within a week. Offers world rights. **Tips:** "Don't expect research and writing by Alcoa personnel on answers to lengthy questions. Be specific about information or material wanted. We will be helpful with meaningful research to knowledgeable researchers."

1101• AMERICAN BOARD OF FUNERAL SERVICE EDUCATION
Box 2098, Fairmont WV 26554. Contact Person: Administrator. **Description:** "We are an accrediting agency for funeral service programs. Our purpose is to further education in the field of funeral service and in fields necessary thereto or allied therewith, and to formulate standards of funeral service education and to give accreditation to proper colleges." **Services:** Provides advisory information on colleges of funeral service education accredited by the American Board, state board rosters, licensing rules and regulations, education requirements and scholarship information. Offers brochures/pamphlets. Publications include *Funeral Service State Examining Boards*; and *National Scholarships for Funeral Service*. **How to Contact:** Write, call or visit. Responds to most inquiries within a week.

1102• AMERICAN CAN COMPANY
American Lane, Greenwich CT 06830. (203)552-2000. Contact: Public Relations Department. **Description:** "We are a diversified corporation engaged in worldwide packaging, financial services, distribution and specialty retailing, and resource recovery and chemicals." **Services:** Offers aid to media in arranging interviews and distributing corporate literature. **How to Contact:** Write. **Tips:** "We're not available as a service for researchers writing papers or articles on involved subjects."

1103• AMERICAN COMMERCIAL COLLECTORS ASSOCIATION, INC.
4040 W. 70th St., Minneapolis MN 55435. (612)929-9669. Contact Person: General Manager. **Description:** "Our purpose is to further and promote the general welfare of the commercial collection profession in the US and elsewhere; to regulate practices, prescribe ethics, and enforce proper conduct among its members; to encourage and promote the adoption of legislation in the various states and in the US favorable to the rights of commercial collectors and the credit-granting public, and to gather and disseminate material relative to the commercial collection profession which may be valuable to members of the association." **Services:** Provides referral and trade information on commercial collections on accounts receivable for businesses from other businesses. Offers brochures/pamphlets, newsletter and press kits. Publications include *What ACCA Is*; *Collection Guidelines for Commercial Credit Grantors*; *Introducing the American Commercial Collectors Association, Inc.*; *Scope* (newsletter); and *Blue Book* (membership directory). **How to Contact:** Write. Responds to most inquiries within a week. Service fees vary. Charges for exceptional or out of the ordinary services. Advise how information will be used. **Tips:** "Prefer written requests on writer's stationery. Clearance must be obtained on some purchases. If we cannot help you, we will try to refer you to someone who may be able to assist."

1104• AMERICAN IRON AND STEEL INSTITUTE
1000 16th St. NW, Washington DC 20036. (202)452-7115. Contact Person: Director, Press Relations. **Description:** "We promote the interests of the iron and steel industry." **Services:** Provides advisory, analytical, historical, interpretative, referral, technical and trade information on steel manufacturing, distribution and uses. Offers aid in arranging interviews, annual reports, biographies (officers only), brochures/pamphlets, computerized information searches (limited), informational newsletters, library facilities (limited), photos, placement on mailing lists, press kits, research assistance, statistics and telephone reference services. Publications include routine monthly press releases and special bulletins on current issues. **How to Contact:** Write, call or visit. Responds to most inquiries immediately. "Attribution to source is welcome for factual material provided; analyses or interpretations are for guidance only and are provided on 'background' basis only." **Tips:** "Beware of assumption that there is a single monolithic entity called 'steel industry.' Analyses by types of producing companies, markets for individual product groups, or by geographical areas or types of consuming industries are much more realistic and useful. Avoid dependence on old morgue material; conditions have changed significantly in recent years." Recent information requests: Description of current production, employment, distribution conditions in steel industry; background data on imports relating to industry's complaints to government.

1105• AMERICAN MOVERS CONFERENCE
Box 2303, Arlington VA 22202. (703)521-1111. Contact Person: Director of Public Relations. **Description:** "National representative trade association of the interstate household goods moving industry, representing 1,000 moving companies and an underlying membership of over 8,000 movers worldwide. Each year, its member firms move interstate almost 1.5 million household goods shipments, 50% of which occur during June, July, August and September." **Services:** Offers aid in arranging interviews, biographies, statistics, brochures/pamphlets, placement on press mailing list and photos. Publications include *Guide to a Satisfying Move*, "a how-to booklet on the intricacies of moving," and *Moving and Children*, "a companion piece to the above with emphasis on including children in plans for moving, psychological impact, etc." **How to Contact:** Write or call.

1106• AMERICAN RECOVERY ASSOCIATION, INC.
Box 52076, New Orleans LA 70152. (504)367-0711. Contact Person: Executive Director. **Description:** "ARA is the world's largest organization of professional finance adjusters and repossession specialists. We serve lending institutions—including banks, credit unions, finance companies and leasing companies—in the recovery of collateral on defaulted time payment contracts." **Services:** Provides information on repossession of collateral on defaulted contracts. The association publishes 40,000 free membership directories (600 pages) to credit grantors; offers educational seminars (to help credit grantors handle collection and repossession problems) and monthly newsletters *News & Views*. **How to Contact:** Write. Responds to most inquiries immediately.

1107• ARMCO, INC.
General Offices, Middletown OH 45043. (513)425-5643. Contact Person: Supervisor, Public Information. **Description:** Armco is a multibusiness, multinational company. It is a major steelmaker, supplier of oilfield equipment, aerospace and strategic materials, metal buildings, architectural/engineering services and financial services. **Services:** Provides advisory, analytical, historical, interpretative, referral, technical and trade information. Offers annual and quarterly reports, biographies, pamphlets, speeches, photos, press kits and background on the businesses in which Armco is involved. **How to Contact:** Write or call. Responds to most inquiries within a week. "Please give as much lead time as possible."

1108• AUTO BABY SITTERS/AUTO DEAD STORAGE SYSTEMS, INC.
827 Sterling Place, Brooklyn NY 11216. (212)493-9800. Contact Person: Manager. **Description:** "We provide storage of vehicles for travelers/persons who wish vehicle storage for various reasons." **Services:** Provides advisory and how-to information. Offers brochures/pamphlets. "Our brochures contain information regarding airport and pier pick-up and delivery service and vehicle storage." **How to Contact:** Write or call. Responds to most inquiries immediately.

1109• BETHLEHEM STEEL CORPORATION
8th and Eaton Aves., Martin Tower, Bethlehem PA 18016. Contact Person: Manager, News Media Division. **Description:** "We are the nation's second largest steel producer." **Services:** Offers aid in arranging interviews, annual reports, biographies, brochures/pamphlets, information searches, placement on mailing list and photos. "We have a library at our headquarters for serious researchers." Publications available. **How to Contact:** Write. Responds to most inquiries immediately. Charges for color photos. "Credit Bethlehem Steel for any of our photos or data used in a book or article." **Tips:** Recent information request: Information on computers and data information services used here at Bethlehem.

1110• THE BILTRITE CORPORATION
22 Willow St., Chelsea MA 02150. (617)884-1700. Contact Person: General Manager, Shoe Repair Products. **Description:** Leading manufacturer of heels and soles for shoes. Rubber products are marketed as Cat's Paw/Biltrite. **Services:** Provides analytical, historical, how-to, interpretative, referral, technical and trade information on shoe manufacturing and shoe repair. Offers aid in arranging interviews, brochures/pamphlets, informational newsletters, photos, press kits and statistics. Publications include *How Your Gifted Hands Can Put You On Your Own Two Feet.* **How to Contact:** Write or call. Responds to most inquiries within a week. **Tips:** "The shoe repair industry is a good barometer of the economy and the growing consumerism. Recent

information requests: "What kinds of people enter shoe repair?"; "Why are more consumers having their shoes repaired?"

1111• BUILDING OWNERS AND MANAGERS ASSOCIATION INTERNATIONAL
1221 Massachusetts Ave. NW, Washington DC 20005. (202)638-2929. Contact Person: Editor. **Description:** "Building Owners and Managers Association (BOMA) International represents the commercial office building industry, downtown and suburban. BOMA members own and/or manage over 2 billion square feet of class 'A' office space, the equivalent of 8,000 office buildings, or one-third of the office space in North America." **Services:** Provides analytical, bibliographical, how-to, interpretative and trade information on the management of commercial office space. Offers bibliographies, statistics, brochures/pamphlets, information searches, placement on mailing list and newsletter. "Through the association's monthly newsletter, *Skylines*, and semi-annual *Occupancy Survey* and annual *Experience Exchange Report*, the association provides information to members on legislative and regulatory topics, economic information and data on building, leasing and operations, including maintenance, energy conservation and joint venture projects and market conditions." **How to Contact:** Write or call. Responds to most inquiries within a week. Charges $25/year for newsletter subscription; $125 for *Experience Exchange Report*, "which compares expenses and income data from BOMA members. The report is designed to be a primary tool for ownership, management, mortgage, appraisal and investment." **Tips:** "Allow enough time for us to process your request."

1112• BUREAU OF ENGRAVING AND PRINTING
14th and C Sts. SW, Washington DC 20228. Contact Person: Information Specialist. **Description:** "The Bureau of Engraving and Printing manufactures US paper currency, postage stamps and approximately 800 miscellaneous security products." **Services:** Provides historical, technical and trade information on production of currency and postage stamps. Offers statistics, brochures/pamphlets and information searches. Publications include *Production of Government Securities*. **How to Contact:** Write. Responds to most inquiries within a month. Charges $5/hour if research exceeds one hour, and 10¢/photocopy.

1113• BY HAND & FOOT, LTD.: TOOLS DEPENDENT ON HUMAN ENERGY
Box 611, Brattleboro VT 05301. (802)254-2101. Contact Person: Publications Director. **Description:** A research and development network for integrated tool systems. **Services:** Provides advisory, analytical, bibliographical, historical, how-to, interpretative, referral, technical and trade information on tools in use in agriculture, and gardening, silviculture and transportation. Offers aid in arranging interviews, brochures/pamphlets, informational newsletters, photos, placement on mailing lists, research assistance and statistics. Publications include *The Scythe Book: Mowing Hay, Harvesting Small Grains* ($6.95); *Handcart Handbook* ($5.95); *Splitting Firewood* ($6.95); and *Guide to Grasses, Clovers and Weeds*. **How to Contact:** Write. Charges for publications. **Tips:** "When contacting us, write clearly, specifically, referring to sources already used." Recent information request: History and use of the peavey and cant hook.

1114• THE CHLORINE INSTITUTE, INC.
342 Madison Ave., New York NY 10173. (212)682-4324. Contact Person: Public Relations Manager. **Description:** "Our purpose is to ensure safe production, handling and use of chlorine; and to serve as the technical information center of the industry." **Services:** Provides advisory, analytical, bibliographical, how-to, technical and trade information. Offers biographies, brochures/pamphlets, informational newsletters, scientific specifications, research assistance, statistics, telephone reference services, audiovisual material and drawings. Publications include *Chlorine Manual*; *Thermodynamic Properties of Chlorine*; and *Chlorine: A Guide for Journalists*. **How to Contact:** Write or call. Responds to most inquiries within a week. Charges for pamphlets; service charges are imposed for certain services. "We ask that writers clear use of technical information through us." **Tips:** "We can offer a wealth of factual scientific background information." Recent information request: "What safety training programs are available through the institute and how can we have one conducted in our area?"

1115• CONTINENTAL ASSOCIATION OF FUNERAL & MEMORIAL SOCIETIES, INC.
1828 L St. NW, Suite 1100, Washington DC 20036. (202)293-4821. Contact Person: Executive Director. **Description:** "Continental Association of Funeral and Memorial Societies (CAFMS) aims to aid consumers by providing information about funerals; by encouraging pre-planning of

funerals; and by helping people to join memorial societies which provide their members with assistance in obtaining less expensive, simple and dignified funerals.'' **Services:** Provides advisory, analytical, bibliographical, historical, how-to and trade information on funerals, pre-planning, memorial societies, cremation and organ donation. Offers bibliographies, statistics, brochures/pamphlets and newsletter. ''We also frequently review TV and radio scripts and magazine articles on funerals. We check for accuracy and give leads in turning up stories, etc.'' **How to Contact:** Write or call. Responds to most inquiries within a week. ''A publication list gives prices if writer wishes to order books. We may charge an hourly fee ($25/hour) for review of scripts, etc. if the time spent is substantial. It is frequently difficult to obtain information on funeral laws in a particular state or get funeral directors to give their costs and explain them. This may be changing as the consumer movement grows. CAFMS regularly assists writers and is glad to do so.'' **Tips:** ''Accompany someone to a funeral home when they make arrangements; read some of the industry literature; read some of the testimony from Federal Trade Commission hearings.'' Recent information request: ''Are there changes in the funeral industry as a result of pressures from memorial societies and consumers?''

1116• FEDERAL EXPRESS CORPORATION

Box 727, Memphis TN 38914. (901)369-3613. Contact Person: Manager, Media Relations. **Description:** ''Federal Express provides highly-integrated, broad-based networks for reliable movement and transmission of high-priority business goods, documents and messages. Federal Express serves 250 major markets and more than 15,000 communities with 60 aircraft and more than 3,500 radio-equipped vans. The company handles more than 145,000 shipments nightly through its system.'' **Services:** Offers aid in arranging interviews, annual reports, biographies, placement on mailing list, photos and press kits. **How to Contact:** Write or call. Responds to most inquiries within a week. ''We deal only with writers that have assignments. Prearrange through PR department for interviews of top-level management.''

1117• FEDERATED DEPARTMENT STORES

7 W. 7th St., Cincinnati OH 45202. (513)579-7700. Contact Person: Media Relations Manager. **Description:** ''Corporate headquarters for Federated Department Stores. Our business consists of operating 19 department store divisions across the US, two mass merchandising divisions and a chain of grocery supermarkets in California.'' **Services:** Offers aid in arranging interviews, annual reports, brochures/pamphlets, placement on mailing list, statistics, press kits and corporate background materials. **How to Contact:** Write. Responds to most inquiries immediately. **Tips:** ''Have a clear outline of area or question. Give a clear understanding of what you need the material for, and what you intend to use it for. Please state if you intend to quote any material.''

1118• FIRESTONE TIRE AND RUBBER COMPANY

1200 Firestone Pkwy., Akron OH 44317. (216)379-6000. Contact Person: Director of Public Relations. **Description:** ''We are an industrial firm specializing in tire, rubber and diversified products.'' **Services:** Provides information related to the rubber industry. Offers aid in arranging interviews, annual reports, biographies, statistics, brochures/pamphlets, information searches, placement on mailing list, photos and press kits. **How to Contact:** Write or call. Responds to most inquiries within a week.

1119• FORD MOTOR COMPANY, DIVERSIFIED PRODUCTS OPERATION

Public Affairs Office, World Headquarters Bldg., Dearborn MI 48121. (313)323-4308. Contact Person: Diversified Products Public Affairs Manager. **Description:** ''Diversified Products Operation is the nonautomotive part of the Ford Motor Company. Its world-wide operations include steel; castings; plastics; paint; vinyl; automotive, architectural and mirror glass; automotive radiators and air conditioning components; electrical and electronic components; farm and industrial tractors and equipment; and aerospace and communications equipment (weather and communications satellites, command and control systems, and missile defense systems).'' **Services:** Provides technical and trade information. Offers aid in arranging interviews, annual reports, brochures/pamphlets, photos and press kits. Publications include a general descriptive brochure and brochures on glass, steel, casting, plastics and automotive electronics. ''Photos are limited generally to what we have in our files, but we are willing to shoot if the opportunity warrants. We welcome inquiries and the opportunity to explain our business.'' **How to Contact:** Write or call. Responds to most inquiries immediately. ''It would be helpful if writers provided their telephone numbers, the use for which the information is being sought (i.e., article in such-and-such publication), and a reasonable time to respond. We do not have time or staff to write term papers!'' Any restrictions/stipulations ''to be arranged at time of inquiry—release dates, review of copy, etc.'' **Tips:** ''Be specific in request; letter inquiry preferred to phone inquiry.'' Recent information request: Ford Glass Division growth; recent architectural glass sale (specific buildings); new electronic products and forward-year developments.

1120• HARDWOOD PLYWOOD MANUFACTURERS ASSOCIATION
Box 2789, Reston VA 22090. (703)435-2900. Contact Person: President. **Description:** ''We concentrate in six major areas of member services: information clearinghouse through publications; public relations/promotion in the form of news releases to the press; brochures and color slide presentations on the manufacture and uses of hardwood plywood to specifiers, purchasers and users of hardwood plywood; industry representation in various legislative issues affecting the hardwood plywood and veneer industry; semi-annual conventions as well as regional meetings providing a common forum for the industry to work toward solving common problems, exchanging information, and becoming better acquainted with other hardwood plywood manufacturers, prefinishers and suppliers to the industry; active committees on building codes, conventions, environment improvement, legislation, safety, technical, trade promotion and public relations; and technical activities featuring the most complete testing laboratory for hardwood plywood in the US.'' **Services:** Provides advisory, historical, how-to, referral, technical and trade information covering the hardwood plywood and veneer industry. Offers statistics, brochures/pamphlets, placement on mailing list and photos. Publication and price list available. **How to Contact:** Write or call. Responds to most inquiries within a month. Give credit to Hardwood Plywood Manufacturers Association.

1121• INDUSTRIAL FABRICS ASSOCIATION INTERNATIONAL
350 Endicott Bldg., St. Paul MN 55101. (612)222-2508. Contact Person: Director of Public Relations. **Description:** ''We are a vertical trade association for the industrial textile industry. Membership includes mills, fabric coaters, distributors and product fabricators involved with industrial textiles. Our textiles are found in almost every existing industry, including the design and architectural markets. Our membership includes members in 13 European countries, Canada and the US (1,400 members).'' **Services:** Provides advisory, how-to, referral, technical and trade information. Offers aid in arranging interviews, statistics, brochures/pamphlets, placement on mailing list, photos and press kits.Publications include various background information-type articles on the products of this industry (awnings, air structures, camping products, marine fabric products, sail making, industrial plant uses of fabric, etc.). ''We publish several magazines including the Industrial Fabric Products *Review*.'' **How to Contact:** Write or call. Responds to most inquiries within a week. **Tips:** ''We can help define questions and ideas on related topics as well as distribute or provide specific information.''

1122• INTERNATIONAL ASSOCIATION OF CONVENTION AND VISITOR BUREAUS
702 Bloomington Rd., Champaign IL 61820. (217)359-8881. Contact Person: Managing Director or Director of Information. **Description:** ''We promote sound professional practices in the solicitation and servicing of meetings and conventions and for the exchange of industry data on convention-holding organizations.'' **Services:** Provides referral and trade information including ''national statistics related to the convention/visitor industry; referral to convention and visitor bureau executives who can comment on trends, provide information related to their individual bureaus, cities.'' Offers aid in arranging interviews, biographies, brochures/pamphlets, placement on mailing lists, press kits and statistics. Publications include *General Information and Membership Directory*. **How to Contact:** Write or call. Responds to most inquiries immediately. Give credit to IACVB. **Tips:** ''Please do not call and ask for a list of the top convention cities. We do not rank cities; our information is provided in the aggregate only. We have a wealth of statistical information, much of which is available to writers in printed form. If you give us a call well in advance of your deadline, we can send it off to you rather than try to explain a lot of numbers over the phone.'' Recent information requests: ''What is the economic impact of a convention on the host city?''; ''What kinds of dollars do conventioneers bring into a city?''; ''How many meetings were there in the US last year?''; ''Is that up or down?''

1123• INTERNATIONAL COUNCIL OF SHOPPING CENTERS
665 Fifth Ave., New York NY 10022. (212)421-8181. Contact: Library or Information Services

Department. **Description:** "The International Council of Shopping Centers strives to promote professional standards of performance in the development, construction, financing, leasing, management and operation of shopping centers throughout the world." **Services:** Provides trade information on construction, consumer markets, design, energy, environment and land use, financing, furnishings and fixtures, geographical information, government regulations, leasing, legal considerations, operations and management, parking, planning, real estate industry, retailing, shopping center industry, tenant, urban planning and more. Offers annual reports, brochures/pamphlets, informational newsletters, library facilities, research assistance, statistics and telephone reference services. ICSC sponsors the annual University of Shopping Centers, offering courses which cover up-to-date information on shopping center development, retailing, leasing, financing and operations. Publications include an annual list of over fifty ICSC publications, some of which are available to members only. **How to Contact:** Write. Responds to most inquiries within 2 weeks. "Writers/researchers wanting to use our library facilities must make appointments with our librarian." **Tips:** Recent information request: "Is there a list of companies which provide software computers for shopping center management?"

1124• INTERNATIONAL HARVESTER COMPANY
401 N. Michigan Ave., Chicago IL 60611. Contact Person: Vice President/Corporate Communications. **Description:** "International Harvester is one of the world's largest producers of farm equipment, commercial trucks and construction equipment. We have been overseas since 1861 and currently do business in 168 countries." **Services:** Provides historical and current information. Offers aid in arranging interviews, annual reports, brochures/pamphlets, product lists, placement on mailing list, statistics, photos and press kits. **How to Contact:** Write or call. Responds to most inquiries within a month. "We prefer written requests. Writers who contact us should be accredited." **Tips:** Recent information request: "What products do you currently make?"

1125• INVENTORS WORKSHOP INTERNATIONAL
Box 251, Tarzana CA 91356. (213)344-3375. Contact Person: Vice President. **Description:** Invention organization helping inventors through the stages of bringing their idea to market-ready stage and then helping them to market their idea (invention). **Services:** Provides advisory and inventions information covering high technology, energy-related inventions and simple consumer products in all categories of inventive art. Offers computerized information searches and information on all stages of inventing. Publications include *Lightbulb*, a 48-page magazine dealing with subjects of interest to inventors. **How to Contact:** Write or call. Responds to most inquiries immediately. **Tips:** "Prepare concise questions." Recent information request: "How do inventors protect themselves from infringement of their ideas?"

1126• LIGHTNING PROTECTION INSTITUTE, INC.
48 N. Ayer St., Harvard IL 60033. (815)943-7211. Contact Person: Managing Director. **Description:** Manufacturers and installers of lightning protection equipment. **Services:** Provides advisory, analytical, historical, how-to, interpretative, referral, technical and trade information on lightning protection equipment. Offers aid in arranging interviews, brochures/pamphlets, informational newsletters, library facilities, photos, placement on mailing lists, press kits, research assistance, statistics and telephone reference services. Publications include *Lightning Protection for Home, Farm & Family*; and *Lightning Protection Installation & Inspection Standard (LPI-175)*. **How to Contact:** Write or call. Responds to most inquiries immediately. **Tips:** Recent information requests: How to protect a home or farm; how lightning losses occur.

1127• ELI LILLY AND COMPANY
307 E. McCarty St., Indianapolis IN 46285. (317)261-3570. Contact Person: Media Relations Director. **Description:** "Eli Lilly & Company is a manufacturer of pharmaceutical products, agricultural products and cosmetics." **Services:** Offers aid in arranging interviews, annual reports, bibliographies, statistics, brochures/pamphlets, placement on mailing list, photos and press kits. **How to Contact:** Write or call. Reponds to most inquiries within a week. **Tips:** "Contact us in plenty of time before your deadline."

1128• NATIONAL ASSOCIATION OF GREETING CARD PUBLISHERS
600 Pennsylvania Ave. SE, Suite 300, Washington DC 20003. Contact Person: Manager, Communications. **Description:** "NAGCP was established in 1941 to provide an information and

problem-solving network for greeting card publishers and their suppliers. Today, the association's major endeavors are centered in the areas of postal policymaking and industry-wide public relations.'' **Services:** Provides bibliographical, historical, referral and trade information. Offers aid in arranging interviews, statistics, and industry background. **How to Contact:** Write. Responds to most inquiries within a week. Include a business size SASE with information request. **Tips:** ''Contact us with general questions on the industry. We refer the more specific questions to our member companies.'' Recent information request: ''How many greeting cards are sold annually in the US?''

1129• NATIONAL ASSOCIATION OF LETTER CARRIERS
100 Indiana Ave. NW, Washington DC 20001. Contact Person: Director of Research and Education. **Description:** ''The association is a postal union for letter carriers.'' **Services:** Offers bibliographies, brochures/pamphlets, placement on mailing list and press kits. Publications available for members. **How to Contact:** Write. Responds to most inquiries within a week.

1130• NATIONAL ASSOCIATION OF MANUFACTURERS
1776 F St. NW, Washington DC 20006. (202)331-3700. Contact Person: Manager of Media Relations. **Description:** ''Trade association representing 80% of the nation's manufacturers. We represent members before Congress and regulatory agencies on national economics and business issues. We are nonprofit.'' **Services:** Offers aid in arranging interviews, brochures/pamphlets, placement on mailing list, statistics, newsletter and press kits. Publications available. **How to Contact:** Write or call. Responds to most inquiries immediately.

1131• NATIONAL ASSOCIATION OF RECYCLING INDUSTRIES
330 Madison Ave., New York NY 10017. (212)867-7330. Contact Person: Vice President of Communications. **Description:** ''We represent the processors and industrial consumers of recycled materials in the US, Canada and many countries overseas.'' **Services:** Provides information on the recycling of metals, paper, textiles and rubber. Offers aid in arranging interviews, statistics and brochures/pamphlets. A publications and price list is available. **How to Contact:** Write or call. Responds to most inquiries immediately. **Tips:** Recent information request: Statistical data on the recycling industry.

1132• NATIONAL ASSOCIATION OF UNIFORM MANUFACTURERS AND DISTRIBUTORS
1156 Avenue of the Americas, New York NY 10036. (212)869-0670. Contact Person: Director of Public Relations. **Description:** Trade association representing uniform manufacturers, distributors and suppliers to the industry. **Services:** Provides advisory, historical and how-to information on all tailored uniforms such as police, fire, postal, military, band, industrial and career apparel. Offers aid in arranging interviews, brochures/pamphlets and photos. **How to Contact:** Write. Responds to most inquiries within a week. **Tips:** Recent information request: Question on the increased influx of women into the uniformed work force.

1133• NATIONAL ELECTRIC SIGN ASSOCIATION
700 Princess St., Alexandria VA 22314. (703)836-4012. Contact Person: Vice President, Member Services. **Description:** Trade association representing the on-premise sign industry. **Services:** Provides advisory, analytical, historical, how-to, referral, technical and trade information. Offers aid in arranging interviews, brochures/pamphlets, informational newsletters, research assistance and statistics. Publications include *Sign Users Guide*; *Glossary* (of sign industry terminology); *Energy Report*; and other signage studies and reports. **How to Contact:** Write. Responds to most inquiries within a week. Charges for publications, and for some services depending on request. **Tips:** Recent information request: Importance of signage to resort hotel/motel industry.

1134• NCR CORPORATION
Main and K Sts., Dayton OH 45409. (513)445-2150. Contact: Press Relations. **Description:** ''NCR is a multi-national manufacturer and marketer of business information processing systems. Our primary markets are retail, financial, commercial, industrial, medical, educational and government sectors.'' **Services:** Provides historical, technical and trade information on the company and its products, including computers, terminals, communications systems and other areas such as electronic funds transfer. Offers annual reports, brochures/pamphlets, placement on mailing list, photos and press kits. **How to Contact:** Write or call. Responds to most inquiries within a

week. **Tips:** Recent information requests: Photos of equipment for illustrations; company history; publicly available financial and product information.

1135• PAPER BOX CORPORATION OF AMERICA
13 Lexington Ave., Brooklyn NY 11238. (212)857-3090. Contact Person: President. **Description:** "We are manufacturers of all styles of containers, including complete package coordination; design and production of all types of paperboard, cardboard, packaging containers." **Services:** Provides how-to and trade information. Offers research assistance. Product brochure available. **How to Contact:** Write. Responds to most inquiries within a week. Charges for services according to amount of time involved. Give credit to corporation.

1136• PRINCETON ANTIQUES BOOKSERVICE
2915-17-31 Atlantic Ave., Atlantic City NJ 08401. (609)344-1943. Contact Person: President. **Description:** "We are a library of architectural and historical photos on post cards dating from 1900-1940. Our reference library is a comprehensive historical collection covering the US marketplace of books and art of the last hundred years. One of the largest and finest private libraries of its kind, concentrating on prices, pricing and identification of books, art, antiques and collectibles, it totals over 12,500 volumes and we add 500 to 1,500 volumes annually. In addition, we have over 150,000 titles in stock, consisting primarily of hard-back books published in the 19th and 20th centuries in the US, and we are growing by 10,000-25,000 volumes each year to increase the probabilities of having the book you want." **Services:** Offers brochures/pamphlets and information searches. "If a book is available on the marketplace, we have a 75% chance of finding it in 45 days; 60 days if notification of price is necessary before purchase." **How to Contact:** Make an appointment or write, requesting author, title or subject area. Responds to most inquiries within a week. Charges for services. "We can obtain available material on any subject or by any author from the out-of-print book market. We are the leaders in the field."

1137• PYROTECHNICS GUILD INTERNATIONAL, INC.
5415 Bangert St., White Marsh MD 21162. (301)256-5144. Contact Person: Past President. **Description:** "We promote the safe and skillful display of fireworks; encourage public and private fireworks displays in conjunction with local and national holidays and celebrations; and promote the manufacture and sale of safe, high quality fireworks." **Services:** Provides advisory, historical, how-to, referral and technical information on all aspects of the fireworks market worldwide. Offers aid in arranging interviews, informational newsletters and statistics. Publications include *American Fireworks News* (11 issues/year); and tri-monthly bulletin. **How to Contact:** Write or call. Responds to most inquiries within a week. **Tips:** "Contact us prior to June 30." Recent information requests: "How are fireworks made?"; "What training is needed to shoot professional fireworks displays?"; "List the 36 states where fireworks are legal."

1138• R.J. REYNOLDS INDUSTRIES, INC.
World Headquarters Bldg., Winston-Salem NC 27102. (919)773-2732. Contact Person: Assistant Public Relations Representative. **Description:** R.J. Reynolds Industries is a diversified, multinational firm involved in the manufacture, distribution and sales of consumer packaged goods (foods, beverages, spirits, tobacco products) with strategic investments in the energy, transportation, restaurant and packaging industries. With about 100,000 full-time employees worldwide, R.J. Reynolds Industries is engaged in commerce in virtually every country and territory in the world. Corporate public relations provides information on the corporation, its subsidiaries and company-sponsored programs and organizations. **Services:** Provides analytical, bibliographical, historical, interpretative, referral, technical and trade information in areas relating to the corporation's lines of business: foods, beverages, tobacco, energy, transportation, packaging. Offers aid in arranging interviews; provides annual reports, brochures, biographies, photos, press kits, publications. Publications include a quarterly magazine for employees, retirees and stockholders; line of business books on subsidiaries; the "Commitment" book on programs supported by the corporation; employee information publications and recipe booklets. **How to Contact:** Write or call. Responds to most inquiries within a week. "Due to the sometimes technical subject matter involved, the corporation prefers to review articles in which its information has been used." **Tips:** "Please make requests for information as specific as possible." Recent information requests: Annual reports; historical data on product introduction and packaging; biographical information on executives.

1139• RSR CORPORATION
1111 W. Mockingbird Lane, Dallas TX 75247. (214)631-6070. Contact Person: Corporate Communications Coordinator. **Description:** "We recycle lead by purchasing lead-bearing scrap and smelting and refining it to very stringent specifications. The primary market is battery manufacturers and primary competition is lead miners/refiners." **Services:** Provides historical, technical, new product, financial and trade information. Offers aid in arranging interviews and annual reports. Publications include a technical industrial catalog of bulk lead alloys, and financial reports (annuals and quarterlies). **How to Contact:** Write or call. Responds to most inquiries within a week.

1140• RUNZHEIMER AND COMPANY, INC.
Rochester WI 53167. (414)534-3121. Contact Person: Vice President, Communications. **Description:** "Runzheimer and Company provides prime source, valid information to organizations in the areas of living costs (housing, transportation, taxes and goods and services) and travel costs (meals, lodging and transportation) for use with relocation and wage/salary policies, automobile reimbursement programs and monitoring of travel expenses." **Services:** Provides advisory, analytical, historical, how-to, interpretative and referral information on comparative international travel costs; comparative living costs throughout the world; management of transportation and travel budgets; site selection and relocation counseling; preretirement counseling. Offers aid in arranging interviews, brochures/pamphlets, computerized information searches, informational newsletters, placement on mailing lists, research assistance and statistics. Publications include *Runzheimer Reports on Transportation*; *Runzheimer Reports on Relocation*; *Runzheimer Reports on Travel Management*; *Runzheimer on Cars and Living Costs*; *Runzheimer Reports on Preretirement Counseling* and *Runzheimer Reports on Automotive Alternatives*. **How to Contact:** Write or call. Responds to most inquiries immediately. "Our firm must be properly credited and our information must be used accurately." **Tips:** "Call and discuss needs first." Recent information requests: "Cost of living comparisons among 10 US and foreign locations; cost of owning and operating an automobile."

1141• SANFORD CORPORATION
c/o Philip Lesly Co., 130 E. Randolph St., Chicago IL 60601. (312)565-1900. Contact Person: President. **Description:** Manufacturer of pens, markers, stationery supplies. **Services:** Provides how-to, technical and trade information on the uses of writing instruments and markers; lefthandedness; "how-to" involving writing, marking, decorating with markers, etc. Offers aid in arranging interviews, photos, placement on mailing lists and press kits. **How to Contact:** Write or call. Responds to most inquiries within a week. **Tips:** Recent information requests: "What are the latest facts about differences between lefthanders and righthanders?"; "How can you learn to do calligraphy easily?"; "How can you decorate with gold or silver ink?"

1142• SELF-SERVICE STORAGE ASSOCIATION
Box 110, Eureka Springs AR 72632-0110. (501)253-7701. Contact Person: Executive Director. **Description:** "We represent the self-service storage industry." **Services:** Provides referral and trade information on the self-service storage industry in general. Offers aid in arranging interviews. **How to Contact:** Write or call. Responds to most inquiries within a week.

1143• UNITED STATES POSTAL SERVICE
475 L'Enfant Plaza, Room 10912, Washington DC 20260. (202)245-4168. Contact Person: General Manager, Public Affairs. **Description:** "The US Postal Service (USPS) throughout the country (encompassing some 40,000 post offices) is charged with delivering the mail to its customers at a reasonable rate. The public and employee communications department is charged with providing information about all facets of the Postal Service to all external media and internal offices and departments through agency publications." **Services:** Provides information on "how USPS functions, and current and new ways to deliver messages, both printed and electronic." Offers aid in arranging interviews, annual reports, biographies, statistics, brochures/pamphlets, information searches, placement on mailing list, photos and press kits. Publications include *Annual Report of the Postmaster General* and "miscellaneous brochures/pamphlets on various services of USPS, e.g., *Presort*; *Express Mail*; *Parcel Post*; *Consumer's Guide to Postal Services & Products*; *Mailers Guide*; *Philately, Mail Fraud Laws* and *Memo to Mailers*, a free monthly publication for business mailers." **How to Contact:** Write or call. Responds to most inquiries

within a week. "Placement on press release lists is limited to accredited members of the press only."

1144• WHITTAKER CORPORATION
10880 Wilshire Blvd., Los Angeles Ca 90024. Contact Person: Corporate Communications Director. **Description:** "Whittaker is a publicly-held corporation with business activities in the metals, technology, marine, life sciences and chemical fields. The company is listed on the New York Stock Exchange." **Services:** Provides referral and trade information on healthcare supplies and services. Offers annual reports and placement on mailing list. Publications include annual and interim reports. **How to Contact:** Write. Responds to most inquiries within a month.

1145• WRITING INSTRUMENT MANUFACTURERS ASSOCIATION
c/o Liss Public Relations, 250 E. Hartsdale Ave., Hartsdale NY 10530. (914)472-5900. Contact: Public Relations Agency. **Description:** "An organization of manufacturers and industry suppliers of mechanical pencils, pens, marking instruments and parts disseminating information in an effort to stamp out illegible handwriting in the US." **Services:** Provides, advisory, analytical, bibliographical, historical, how-to, interpretative, referral, technical and trade information covering the history of the business, new products, technical data and sales. Offers aid in arranging interviews, biographies, statistics, brochures/pamphlets, placement on mailing list, photos and press kits. **How to Contact:** Write or call. Responds to most inquiries immediately.

SECTION·TWENTY-TWO

PUBLIC AFFAIRS

. . . public opinion is a giant which has frightened stouter-hearted Jacks on bigger beanstalks than hers.

—Louisa May Alcott

Information sources identified here represent those concerned with citizen, consumer and community affairs. Included are organizations concerned with public safety, arms control, nuclear power, citizen action, government re-form, politics, constitutional rights and responsibilities, fund raising, consumer protection and trade and community development.

Conservation groups are listed in both the Environment/The Earth and Animals and Plants sections. Human rights are covered in the Society and Culture section. Additional resources in the social welfare field are found in the Human Services section.

Bibliography

Consumer Information Catalog. Quarterly. Government Printing Office. Pueblo, CO: Documents Distribution Center. (Lists consumer-oriented government publications)

Consumer's Resource Handbook. US Office for Consumer Affairs. Pueblo, CO: Consumer Information Center. (Consumer guide to making effective complaints on unacceptable products/services)

Day, Alan J. and Henry W. Degenhardt. *Political Parties of the World*. Detroit: Gale Research Co.; 1980.

Murin, William J., Gerald M. Greenfield and John D. Buenker. *Public Policy: A Guide to Information Sources*. Detroit: Gale Research Co., 1981.

Public Affairs Information Service Bulletin. Weekly. New York: Public Affairs Information Service.

Rosenbloom, Joseph, ed. *Consumer Complaint Guide*. 8th ed. New York: Macmillan, 1981.

Schapsmeier, Edward L. and Frederick H. *Political Parties and Civic Action Groups*. Westport, CT: Greenwood Press, 1981.

Wasserman, Paul and Jean Morgan, eds. *Consumer Sourcebook: A Directory and Guide*. 2 vols. 3d ed. Detroit: Gale Research Co., 1981.

1146• AMERICAN ARBITRATION ASSOCIATION
140 W. 51st St., New York NY 10020. (212)484-4100. Contact Person: President. **Description:** Organization encouraging arbitration and mediation in the resolution of disputes. **Services:** Provides advisory, analytical, bibliographical, how-to, referral, technical and trade information on arbitration, mediation, private elections, negotiating, conciliation, etc. Offers aid in arranging interviews, annual reports, biographies, brochures/pamphlets, informational newsletters, library facilities (over 16,000 volumes in all areas of dispute resolution), placement on mailing lists, press kits, research assistance and telephone reference services. Publications include *Arb Journal*; *Arb News*; and case summaries. **How to Contact:** Write, call or visit. Responds to most inquiries immediately. Charges for some services.

1147• AMERICAN CIVIL LIBERTIES UNION
132 W. 43rd St., New York NY 10036. (212)944-9800. Contact Person: Public Relations Director. **Description:** "The American Civil Liberties Union exists to make sure people get their rights as stated in the Bill of Rights. We strive to achieve our goal through litigation, legislation and public education." **Services:** Provides advisory, analytical, historical, interpretative and referral information covering civil liberties, the Bill of Rights, Constitution, legislation, litigation and education. Offers aid in arranging interviews, annual reports, bibliographies, statistics, brochures/pamphlets, placement on mailing list, newsletter, photos and press releases. "We can arrange for people to go through our files." Publications include *Civil Liberties*. **How to Contact:** Write or call. Responds to most inquiries within a week.

1148• AMERICAN CONSERVATIVE UNION
38 Ivy St. SE, Washington DC 20003. (202)546-6555. Contact Person: Communications Director. **Description:** "The American Conservative Union is the nation's largest and oldest conservative lobbying group. Founded in 1964, ACU now has more than 350,000 members. We are active in lobbying and education on topics such as defense, foreign affairs, social issues, budget and taxes through special forums, seminars, research, publications and television documentaries. In late winter each year, ACU hosts the Conservative Political Action Conference which draws hundreds of people from across the country to hear the biggest names in the conservative movement." **Services:** Provides advisory, analytical, bibliographical, historical, how-to, interpretative, referral, technical and trade information on "most any issue that has a conservative side." Offers services to the media and to individual print and broadcast outlets, including special weekly columns, radio and video actualities on various topics, regular mailings to ACU's media list and briefings on special subjects. "We will help arrange interviews with members of Congress and the Administration, provide photos and press kits." Publications include *Battleline*, a monthly magazine, various special reports and annual ratings for all members of Congress. **How to Contact:** Write or call. Responds to most inquiries immediately, "depending on the scope of the inquiry." No charge "unless the service requested is extremely costly." Give credit to ACU where appropriate. **Tips:** "Give us as much notice as you can. We'll always do our best to accommodate writers' needs." Recent information requests: "What are the Congressional ratings for the Congressional delegation from Utah?"; "What amount of conservative change has occurred in Congress and why?"

1149• AMERICAN LIFE LOBBY
Box 490, Stafford VA 22554. (703)659-4171. Contact Person: President. **Description:** Pro-life individuals whose "primary goal is the passage of the Paramount Human Life Amendment to restore the legal protection of life for all human beings. Secondary goals include elimination of value-free sex education from schools; restoration of 'traditional' family values." **Service:** Provides advisory, analytical, bibliographical, historical, how-to and referral information on abortion, infanticide, sex education, pornography, secular humanism and school curricula. Offers aid in arranging interviews, brochures/pamphlets, informational newsletters, library facilities, placement on mailing lists, press kits, research assistance (limited) and statistics. Publications include *All About Issues* (monthly newsmagazine); over 100 different titles "stocked in our Resource Bank"; thousands of file references. **How to Contact:** Write or call. Responds to most inquiries within a week. Charges for photocopying and booklets when appropriate. Give credit to American Life Lobby. **Tips:** "Understanding the current position of the pro-life movement, legislation, etc. requires a reasonable medical and/or historical background. Our staff is happy to provide this." Recent information requests: statistics on abortion; historical background on the development of the pro-life movement; current status of pro-life legislation; medical information on the dangers of abortion.

1150• AMERICAN SEAT BELT COUNCIL
1730 Pennsylvania Ave. NW, Suite 460, Washington DC 20006. (202)393-1300. Contact Person: President. **Description:** "We are composed of manufacturers of active and automatic seat belts and webbing. The council was formed in 1961 to assist in the establishment of uniform production standards for seat belts. Since launching its first major nationwide buckle-up campaign in 1967, the American Seat Belt Council (ASBC) has worked with news media and other safety organizations to encourage greater use of seat belts. In addition to its public education campaigns, the council has cooperated with state legislatures to develop seat belt use laws. ASBC has information on both active and automatic seat belts, including pamphlets, films and studies." **Services:** Offers aid in arranging interviews, bibliographies, biographies, statistics, brochures/pamphlets, photos and press kits. Publications available. **How to Contact:** Write or call. Responds to most inquiries immediately. "We will put writers in contact with ASBC members."

1151• AMERICANS FOR DEMOCRATIC ACTION (ADA)
1411 K St. NW, Suite 850, Washington DC 20005. (202)638-6447. Contact Person: Press Secretary. **Description:** "ADA is actively engaged in political issues and political campaigns throughout the country." **Services:** Provides advisory, analytical and interpretative information on the economy, civil rights, peace, energy and the environment, and quality of life (education, housing, food and health care). Offers aid in arranging interviews, biographies, brochures/pamphlets, informational newsletters, photos, placement on mailing lists, press kits and

research assistance. Publications include *ADA World*; *For Your Information (FYI)*; *Courier* (foreign policy); and voting records. **How to Contact:** Write or call. Responds to most inquiries immediately. Charges for some publications. Give credit to ADA. **Tips:** Recent information requests: Voting record for a particular representative or senator.

1152• JOHN BIRCH SOCIETY
395 Concord Ave., Belmont MA 02178. (617)489-0600. Contact Person: Public Relations Director. **Description:** "We are a non-partisan group that stands for less government, more responsibility and, with God's help, a better world." **Services:** Provides political education on history and current events; specializing in traditional Americanism, anti-Communism, conservative economics, political interpretation. Fields covered include foreign affairs, government and politics. Offers bibliographies, books, pamphlets, research and information searches. Publications include *The Bulletin of the John Birch Society* (monthly); *The Birch Log* (weekly newspaper column); and *The Alan Stang Report* (daily radio commentary). "We also promote *American Opinion* (monthly journal of political thought) and *The Review of the News* (weekly newsmagazine)." **How to Contact:** Write or call. Responds to most inquiries immediately. Telephone interviews arranged; charges for extensive research. No periodic press mailings. "No obvious enemies will be cooperated with." **Tips:** "Go to the source, not to a third party." Recent information request: "What is the John Birch Society doing today?"

1153• CAMPAIGN FOR POLITICAL RIGHTS
201 Massachusetts Ave. NE, Washington DC 20002. (202)547-4705. Contact Person: Public Information Director. **Description:** "The campaign works to end US intelligence agency abuse, to defend the right to dissent and to promote government accountability. The campaign office provides public education materials and assists in organizing local and national campaigns on these issues." **Services:** Provides advisory, bibliographical, historical, how-to, and referral information on how to use the Freedom of Information Act; media and organizing; and all aspects of government policy, legislation, court decisions related to the US intelligence agencies and First Amendment rights. Offers aid in arranging interviews, annual reports, brochures/pamphlets, informational newsletters, press kits, research assistance and telephone reference services. Publications include *Organizing Notes*, newsletter published 8 times/year; *The Freedom of Information Act: Why It's Important and How to Use It* (single copies free); *Viewpoints: A Directory of Major Newspapers and Their Op-Ed Policies* ($2); and *Former Secrets: Government Records Made Public Through the FOIA* ($15); *US Covert Operations Against Nicaragua* (transcript of public forum $5); *Political Surveillance and the Law*. **How to Contact:** Write or call. Responds to most inquiries within a week. **Tips:** "We are primarily a networking/public education group in the field, so writers would probably want to call us in the beginning stages of research since we refer to experts." Recent information requests: "How do I file a Freedom of Information Act/Privacy Act request with the government?"; "What is the law regarding the government's ability to withhold certain information on national security grounds?"; "What laws govern the FBI? the CIA?"

1154• CENTER FOR A WOMAN'S OWN NAME
261 Kimberly, Barrington IL 60010. (312)381-2113. Contact Person: Assistant Director. **Descripion:** The center is an educational, not-for-profit organization whose purpose is "to help end discrimination against women in the choosing of names and the granting of credit." **Services:** Provides advisory and how-to information on name choices and consumer protection acts. Offers biographies, brochures/pamphlets and telephone reference services. **How to Contact:** Write or call. Responds to most inquiries within a week. Observe copyright restrictions. **Tips:** Recent information requests: "Do I have to change my name upon marriage?"; "How do I find out about my credit history?"

1155• CENTER FOR THE AMERICAN WOMAN AND POLITICS
Eagleton Institute, Rutgers University, New Brunswick NJ 08901. (201)828-2210. Contact Person: Secretary. **Description:** "We are a university-based research center active in research, service and education programs related to women in politics, government, and public leadership." **Services:** Provides analytical, bibliographical, historical, interpretative and referral information on women in politics and government, including statistics, background information, research data, information about organizations of women in government, etc. Offers computerized information searches, library facilities, fact sheets and statistical reports, mailing lists or labels for elected women, and assorted other data on women in politics. Publications include a publications list.

How to Contact: Write, call or visit. Responds to most inquiries within a week. Charges for lists or labels, for fact sheets in bulk, and for certain publications. "People who want to use our library must visit us during normal business hours (9-4:30 weekdays). Some inquiries that involve detailed historical information or listings cannot be answered completely due to limited staff and resources." **Tips:** "Call or write first to see if we have what you need; often we can make referrals to other appropriate resources. We are often aware of women's/feminist groups beyond our own sphere of interest." Recent information requests: "How many women are there in local/county/state/federal elective office?"; "Discuss advantages/disadvantages for women seeking public office."

1156• CENTRAL COMMITTEE FOR CONSCIENTIOUS OBJECTORS
2208 South St., Philadelphia PA 19146. (215)545-4626. Contact Person: Literature Coordinator. **Description:** "We provide counseling services and information to people with questions and problems concerning the registration and the draft, and give aid to members of the military who wish to obtain discharges." **Services:** Provides analytical, historical, referral and technical information on all registration, draft, and military questions with an emphasis on the conscientious objector status. Offers annual reports, brochures/pamphlets, informational newsletters, research assistance and statistics. Publications include *CCCO News Notes*; *The Objector*; and *Counter Pentagon*. **How to Contact:** Write or call. Responds to most inquiries within 2 weeks. Give credit to CCCO. **Tips:** "Keep questions as specific as possible, and please enclose SASE." Recent information request: "How many draft resisters were convicted during the Vietnam war?"

1157• CITIZENS COMMITTEE FOR THE RIGHT TO KEEP AND BEAR ARMS
Liberty Park, 12500 NE 10th Pl., Bellevue WA 98005. (206)454-4911. Contact Person: Project Director. **Description:** "We are a nonprofit organization defending the Second Amendment to the United States Constitution. We fight restrictive gun control legislation." **Services:** Provides information on the history, law and politics of guns. Offers aid in arranging interviews, annual reports, brochures/pamphlets, placement on mailing list, newsletter, filmstrips, speakers bureaus and attorney referral services. Publications available. **How to Contact:** Write or call. Responds to most inquiries immediately. **Tips:** Recent information request: "Are we going to lose the gun control battle nationally?"

1158• COMMITTEE FOR NUCLEAR RESPONSIBILITY
Box 11207, San Francisco CA 94101. Contact Person: Chairman. **Description:** "We serve as an independent source of solid information about low-level ionizing radiation; and as an environmental group which challenges the whole 'benefit-risk' justification of 'permissible' pollution—which is a violation of individual human rights and private property rights." **Services:** Provides interpretative and technical information on low-level ionizing radiation (medical, dental, environmental); public health principles applicable to both radioactive and chemical pollutants; and human rights. Offers brochures/pamphlets/books. Publications include *Radiation and Human Health* by John W. Gofman ($29.95 prepaid); *A No-Cost Way to Save a Million Lives* (25¢); and many others. **How to Contact:** Write. Responds to most inquiries within a week. **Tips:** "Keep an open mind, and always ask, 'Can this conclusion stand on its own merits thanks to evidence and logic, or is this conclusion interesting only because an expert or celebrity asserts it?' Read what we send and *then* ask questions; 99% of your questions will be answered more efficiently and better by print." Recent information request: "What's the *evidence* against there being a 'safe' dose of radiation?"

1159• COMMON CAUSE
2030 M St. NW, Washington DC 20036. (202)833-1200. Contact: Office of Media Communications. **Description:** "Common Cause is a citizens' lobby founded in 1970 by John Gardner to represent citizen interests in government decision making. Common Cause's agenda, voted on by members in an annual poll, includes reforms to make government more responsible to the people it is supposed to serve. Presently the organization is particularly concerned about the issues of campaign financing and nuclear arms control." **Services:** Offers brochures/pamphlets, information searches, placement on mailing list, statistics and *Common Cause* magazine (bimonthly). Charges for some publications. **How to Contact:** Write or call. Responds to most inquiries immediately. "There are limited quantities of material available. You may also contact the Common Cause office in each state, usually located in the state capital." **Tips:** "Be familiar with our areas of expertise." Recent information request: Material on political action committees.

1160• COMMUNIST PARTY, USA
235 W. 23rd St., 7th Floor, New York NY 10011. (212)989-4994. Contact: Media Department, Central Committee. **Description:** Political party. **Services:** Provides information on all aspects of economy, culture, ethnic groups (blacks, Latino-Americans, Mexican-Americans, native Indians, etc.). Offers aid in arranging interviews, bibliographies, brochures/pamphlets, placement on mailing list, press kits (irregularly) and books. Publications include *Daily World Newspaper*, listing all regional offices and progressive book stores. **How to Contact:** Write or call. Responds to most inquiries within a week.

1161• COMMUNITY SERVICE, INC.
Box 243, Yellow Springs OH 45387. (513)767-2161. Contact Person: Director. **Description:** "We are a national, nonprofit organization and a center where ideas and practices concerning community are appraised, developed and circulated." **Services:** Provides advisory, bibliographical and historical information on the small community, intentional community, community economics, education/schools, social change, simple living. Offers brochures/pamphlets, informational newsletters, library facilities, placement on mailing lists and research assistance. Publications include *Newsletter* (bimonthly, sample copy 50¢); community service and other publications; and current book list. **How to Contact:** Write, call or visit. Responds to most inquiries within a week. Charges for consultation. "We suggest a minimum contribution equal to that of the consulter's hourly wage for an hour of our time." Also sells reasonably priced books and pamphlets. "Visitors are welcome at the office from 9 a.m. to 3 p.m. where library resources and personal consultations are available." Library materials cannot be removed from the premises.

1162• CONSTITUTIONAL RIGHTS FOUNDATION
Box 2362, Texas City TX 77590. Contact Person: Executive Director. **Description:** "We give people information on how to use their constitutional rights to stop harassment from government agencies including the IRS, to repeal income tax, end deficit spending by a constitutional amendment, and return the United States to a free market economy. Our primary goal is to provide a society that respects the right of all Americans to life, liberty and property." **Services:** Provides advisory, bibliographical, historical and how-to information covering history, economics, income taxes and constitutional rights/civil liberties. Offers brochures/pamphlets, newsletter and lectures and speakers. Publications available. **How to Contact:** Write. Responds to most inquiries within a week. Membership fee $24/year; newsletter subscription $10/year, free sample copy; charges for publications. "Please describe your project and how you think we may be of assistance."

1163• CONSUMER FEDERATION OF AMERICA
1314 14th St. NW, 2nd Floor, Washington DC 20005. (202)387-6121. Contact Person: Executive Director. **Description:** Consumer advocacy organization lobbying on Capitol Hill and in regulatory agencies. **Services:** Provides information on legislative issues and voting records; how to organize a consumer group; product liability. Offers annual reports, biographies, brochures/pamphlets, placement on mailing list, newsletter (monthly) and photos. **How to Contact:** Write or call. Make appointment in advance of visit.

1164• CONSUMER PRODUCT SAFETY COMMISSION
Press Office, 1111 18th St. NW, Washington DC 20207. (202)634-7780. Contact Person (for media): Public Information Specialist. **Description:** An independent regulatory agency commissioned to protect consumer from unreasonable risks and injury associated with consumer products. Administers Consumer Product Safety Act, Federal Hazardous Substances Act, Flammable Fabrics Act, Poison Prevention Act and Refrigerator Safety Act. **Services:** Collects and provides data from a variety of sources and types of injuries associated with consumer products; identifies those on which it may take action; explores action requests to protect consumers. Offers aid in arranging interviews, annual reports, biographies, statistics, brochures/pamphlets (limited quantities), information searches, placement on mailing list. Publications include *CPSC Memo* (monthly newsletter). **How to Contact:** Write or call. Toll-free number for consumer complaints and product information (800)638-CPSC; Maryland (800)492-8363; Alaska, Hawaii, Puerto Rico, Virgin Islands (800)638-8333. "Give us time for extensive research." **Tips:** CPSC has 5 regional offices (Atlanta, Chicago, Dallas, New York City, San Francisco) that can serve reporters with answers to product safety questions. "We can't recommend one particular brand of product over other brands, or compare the quality of one particular brand with others."

BEHIND THE BYLINE

Norman Cousins
Writer and professor

"I think there are two ways to approach research: one is to have an idea or theory, think about it and then attempt to find the supporting data; the other way is to learn of research being done, be stimulated or inspired by it and then write about what you see."

Norman Cousins has served as editor, author, teacher, commentator, essayist and public servant. He piloted *Saturday Review* magazine for thirty-five years. He has written a book about his overcoming a debilitating illness and is currently an adjunct professor in the Department of Psychiatry and Biobehavioral Sciences at UCLA's School of Medicine.

Cousins has done a lot of thinking about the writing process. "Words on paper, it seems to me, come last. You've got to do an awful lot of noodling first. You let your subconscious fill up like a reservoir, and then you discover there's an almost automatic process of sorting and developing that goes on inside you. It gets to the point where it's like trying to hold back the tide."

Research is not always painless, and Cousins vividly recalls his toughest research assignment—the dropping of atomic bombs on Hiroshima and Nagasaki in 1945. "The most important research, it seems to me, is the process of solitary and organized thought where something seems true to you. It's a long process of persistent reflection that opens up the intellectual arteries; it gives you a sense of direction."

In that particular assignment, Cousins's direction was shaped by a logical deduction he made. He believed that President Truman's argument for why America dropped the bomb (i.e., "to save hundreds of thousands of lives that would have been lost in an invasion") was faulty. "If that had been the reason, why did we drop the second bomb?" he asks. "I started with that thought and dug into what was available. You'd be surprised at the amount of material that is not classified. Most people assume everything is buried in vaults."

Many research hours later, Cousins concluded that America had been working against a deadline toward unconditional Japanese surrender. "We let fly with everything we had to end the war ourselves, to prevent a Russian claim on the occupation." Cousins wrote essays reflecting his documented views.

But no two writers approach the process in exactly the same way, he says. "Writing is a personal process; inevitably, ideas have to be filtered through an individual's own experience, intelligence and taste. Then the real skill is putting those ideas into words in proper formation so as to have them say what you want them to say."

Cousins's writing success comes in part from his tendency to avoid writing strictly "out of the research. I try to write out of my own mind, using the reference materials as a backup resource and as documentation."

And, naturally, he surrounds himself with books—and other reference materials for use both in work and play. "I often consult my reference files and library out of fun and curiosity." Cousins says that much of research "ought to be like everything in life that's a joy." *March's Dictionary and Thesaurus* is his special word book. He names the Webster and Century dictionaries, the *Encyclopaedia Britannica*, *The Reader's Encyclopedia* and *Bulfinch's Mythology* as some "off-the-top-of-my-head" favorites.

1165• CONSUMERS FOR WORLD TRADE
1346 Connecticut Ave. NW, # 817, Washington DC 20008. Contact Person: President or Executive Director. **Description:** "CWT represents the consumer interest in the formulation of international trade policies—both imports and exports. We promote open trade policies and educate consumers on trade matters and their effects." **Services:** Provides trade information in all areas of international trade such as agriculture, services, manufactured goods, etc. Offers brochures/pamphlets and informational newsletters. Publications include *Consumers for World Trade Newsletter*; other pamphlets prepared by CWT or other groups. **How to Contact:** Write or call. Responds to most inquiries within a month. "Depending on size or amount of material, we occasionally charge postage or copying costs. Advise us how material will be used and where it will be published." **Tips:** "Due to staff limitation and heavy workload, we may not always be able to do independent research but can advise you where it might be found."

1166• CONSUMERS' RESEARCH, INC.
Box 168, Washington NJ 07882. (201)689-3300. **Description:** "A non-commercial (nonprofit) organization established to provide unbiased information and counsel on goods bought by consumers." **Services:** "We are not in a position to provide research services for writers, but on occasion we may be able to supply some limited services on a fee basis."

1167• CONSUMERS UNION
256 Washington St., Mt Vernon NY 10550. Contact Person: Public Information Officer. **Description:** "We provide consumers with information and counsel on consumer goods and services, give information on all matters relating to the expenditure of the family income, and initiate and cooperate with individuals and group efforts seeking to create and maintain decent living standards." **Services:** Provides advisory, analytical and interpretative information covering business, economics, entertainment, food, health/medicine, industry, law, new products, energy conservation and self-help. Offers publications. **How to Contact:** Write. Responds to most inquiries "according to nature of request and time available." Charges for publications, books, reprints, back issues, other CU publications and permission to excerpt or reprint CU material. "Because of the incredible number of unsolicited requests for information from all sectors of the domestic and international media, resources are severely strained. Therefore, we will do our best to try to help only writers who can verify that they are on a definite assignment. Please do your homework before you write us. Information may *not* be used for commercial gain, i.e., advertising, promotion, etc."

1168• THE COUNCIL FOR A LIVABLE WORLD
100 Maryland Ave. NE, Washington DC 20002. (202)543-4100. Contact Person: Administrative Assistant. **Description:** "Our purpose is to combat the menace of nuclear war. We do this through public education and lobbying." **Services:** Provides analytical, historical, interpretative and technical information on arms control issues. Offers brochures/pamphlets and informational newsletters. **How to Contact:** Write. Responds to most inquiries within a week. Charges for postage on orders of large quantity, such as 100 + brochures. **Tips:** Recent information request: "Do you have information on chemical weapons?"

1169• COUNCIL ON POSTAL SUPPRESSION (C.O.P.S.)
23088 L'Enfant Plaza, Washington DC 20024. Contact Person: Director. **Description:** "We publicize and oppose illegal and abusive activities by the US Postal Service and try to assure the USPS properly carries out its task of delivering mail." **Services:** Provides historical, how-to, interpretative, referral, technical and trade information on mail order laws, USPS activities. "We also keep an eye on USPS lobbying and political activities." Offers brochures/pamphlets, informational newsletters, photos and press kits. "We are developing booklets and background material on various aspects of USPS laws and activities, including explanations of mail fraud and false representation statutes, and analysis of USPS activities." **How to Contact:** Write. Responds to most inquiries within a week.

1170• DEMOCRATIC NATIONAL COMMITTEE
1625 Massachusetts Ave. NW, Washington DC 20036. (202)797-5900. Contact Person: Director. **Description:** Political party dedicated to promoting Democratic principles and interests. **Services:** Provides referral information covering elections and various political

activities. Offers party materials, charter bylaws. Publications include *Democrats Today* (newsletter). "Depending on the time of year, certain materials may not be available." **How to Contact:** Write. Responds to most inquiries within a week.

1171• DEMOCRATIC SOCIALISTS OF AMERICA
Suite 801, 853 Broadway, New York NY 10003. (212)260-3270. **Description:** "Our purpose is to build a humane social order based on popular control of resources and production, economic planning, equitable distribution, feminism, and racial equality. We are building a visible socialist presence within society." **Services:** Provides analytical, historical, interpretative information on politics, urban planning, economy, tax policy, feminism, racism, plant-shutdowns, sexism and socialism. Offers aid in arranging interviews, brochures/pamphlets, informational newsletters and placement on mailing lists. Publications include *Democratic Left* magazine; *Socialist Forum* (discussion bulletin); *Women Organizing* magazine; *Tax Policy and the Economy* pamphlet, etc. **How to Contact:** Write. Responds to most inquiries within a week. Charges for literature.

1172• EDGEWATER COMMUNITY COUNCIL
1112 W. Bryn Mawr Ave., Chicago IL 60660. (312)334-5609. Contact Person: Volunteer Coordinator. **Description:** This is a nonprofit community organization whose purpose is the "upgrading of neighborhoods—implementation of Operation WhistleSTOP/℠ program of the council. WhistleSTOP is a community safety program designed to fight crime on the streets, improve police-community relations, and foster a new sense of community spirit." **Services:** Provides information on how to implement Operation WhistleSTOP in neighborhoods. Offers brochures/pamphlets, informational newsletters, prospectus and organizers manual to aid sponsoring groups. Publications include brochure on WhistleSTOP; and crime prevention newsletters. **How to Contact:** Write. Responds to most inquiries within a week. Writers should emphasize that Operation WhistleSTOP is a trademarked program.

1173• FREE CONGRESS RESEARCH AND EDUCATION FOUNDATION
721 Second St., Washington DC 20002. (202)546-3004. Contact Person: Editor. **Description:** The organization conducts research, surveys, etc., in political and public policy issues as they affect the family. **Services:** Provides analytical information on political activities. Offers informational newsletters. "We publish four regular newsletters: *Political Report* (Congressional and Senate races); *Initiative and Referendum Report* (state ballot measures); *Family Protection Report* (social justice issues); and *Family Policy Insights* (special issues)." **How to Contact:** Write or call. Responds to most inquiries within a week. "We do not have a service charge for our newsletters. We provide the material free of charge to working journalists. For others the costs vary; *Political Report*, $100 a year, published weekly; *I&R Report*, $20 a year, monthly; *FPR*, $25 a year, monthly; *FPI*, periodic, varies."

1174• FREEDOM OF INFORMATION CLEARINGHOUSE
Box 19367, Washington DC 20036. (202)785-3704. Contact Person: Assistant Director. **Description:** Public interest organization providing information to writers, members of the press, and the general public on issues of access to government records. **Services:** Provides advisory and interpretative information on access to government records through such laws as the Freedom of Information Act (both state and federal), the Privacy Act, the government in the Sunshine Act and others. Offers brochures/pamphlets. Publications list available. **How to Contact:** Write or call. Responds to most inquiries immediately. **Tips:** "Often the legal process is not the fastest way to get information. Try to exhaust informal avenues of access first."

1175• IMPACT
100 Maryland Ave. NE, Washington DC 20002. (202)544-8636. Contact Person: Editor. **Description:** "Impact is an interfaith network which provides information on legislation and an opportunity for citizen action. We keep our membership informed about current legislative activities on a number of social issues, including human needs, civil rights, environment, arms control, etc." **Services:** Provides analytical, historical, how-to and referral information on the arms race, energy and environment, economic justice for women, immigration policy, economic security for the poor, global hunger and poverty, civil rights and liberties, human rights, and family farms and the food stamp program. Offers brochures/pamphlets, informational newsletters, placement on mailing lists and telephone reference services. Publications include *Update* (monthly

newsletter); *Action* (periodic alerts); periodic papers on Hunger; and *Prepare* (analytical papers on specific issues). **How to Contact:** Write, call or visit. Responds to most inquiries within a week. Membership receives monthly newsletter. Charges for *Action* alerts ($10.50); other publications cost from 3-25¢/copy. **Tips:** "Ask lots of questions. Even if you think someone may not know the answer, that person may be able to lead you to the right source. Keep digging! Feel free to call and ask questions, but we have limited staff and resources." Recent information requests: Current status of a specific piece of legislation; how to organize lobbying efforts.

1176• INTERNATIONAL ASSOCIATION OF FIRE FIGHTERS
1750 New York Ave., Washington DC 20006. (202)872-8484. Contact Person: Director of Research. **Description:** "International union concerned with providing its affiliates with the necessary tools to obtain better wages, benefits and working conditions for their members." **Services:** Provides historical, referral and trade information covering fire fighters and related subjects. Offers computerized statistical information relative to collective bargaining and fire fighters' safety and health and public relations assistance. Publications available. **How to Contact:** Write or call. Responds to most inquiries as soon as possible "depending on the request and current work load. Policy dictates that we can only answer questions about the international organization; for information about state or local affiliates, approval must first be secured from the principal officers of the affiliate(s)." Charges for publications.

1177• JOINT CENTER FOR POLITICAL STUDIES
1301 Pennsylvania Ave. NW, Washington DC 20004. (202)626-3500. Contact Person: Director of Information Resources. **Description:** "The Joint Center for Political Studies is a national nonprofit, nonpartisan institution that conducts research on public policy issues of special concern to black Americans and promotes informed and effective involvement in the governmental process." **Services:** Provides analytical, historical, interpretative and referral information. Offers aid in arranging interviews, annual reports, brochures/pamphlets, informational newsletters, library facilities, placement on mailing lists, press kits and press releases, research assistance, statistics and telephone reference services. Publications include *Focus* (monthly newsletter); *National Roster of Black Elected Officials* (annual). **How to Contact:** Write or call. Responds to most inquiries within a week. Charges for photocopying and some publications. Call for appointment to use library facilities. **Tips:** Recent information requests: "How many eligible black voters are there in the US?"; "What percentage of blacks voted in the last presidential election?"; "What is the total black population in the US?"

1178• LEAGUE OF WOMEN VOTERS OF THE UNITED STATES
1730 M St. NW, Washington DC 20036. Contact Person: Public Relations Director. **Description:** "We are a voluntary citizen education, public interest and lobbying organization whose aim is to involve people in the political process at all levels of government." **Services:** Offers bibliographies, statistics and newsletter. Publications catalog is available. Publications include *Tell It to Washington, Federal Environment Laws and You*, and newsletter and quarterly. **How to Contact:** Write. Responds to most inquiries within 10 days. Nominal fee for printed matter.

1179• LIBERAL PARTY
165 W. 46th St., Suite 615, New York NY 10036. (212)354-1100. Contact Person: Associate Executive Director. **Description:** "The Liberal party is the political vehicle for independent candidacy and corrective mechanism to the major parties. We advocate progressive liberalism and run candidates for office." **Services:** Provides advisory, analytical, historical, how-to, interpretative and technical information on the political process and the Liberal party. Offers biographies, statistics, brochures/pamphlets, placement on mailing list and press kits. Publications include *The Liberal Manifesto* and *History of the Liberal Party*. **How to Contact:** Write or call. Responds to most inquiries within a week. "A written request is preferred, and SASE is appreciated."

1180• LIBERTARIAN PARTY
1516 P St. NW, Washington DC 20005. (202)232-2003. Contact Person: Publications Director. **Description:** "The Libertarian Party exists to elect libertarians to office, effect the existing political structure, and educate the public about our philosophy and programs." **Services:** Provides referral and general information on current issues and campaign information pertaining to the Libertarian Party, foreign policy, politics and civil liberties. Offers aid in arranging interviews,

brochures/pamphlets, placement on mailing list, newsletter and press kits. **How to Contact:** Write or call. Responds to most inquiries within a week.

1181• NATIONAL ABORTION RIGHTS ACTION LEAGUE
1424 K St. NW, Washington DC 20005. (202)347-7774. Contact Person: Coordinator of News and Information. **Description:** "The National Abortion Rights Action League (NARAL) is the largest national membership and lobby organization dedicated to helping the pro-choice majority use the electoral process to keep abortion legal." **Services:** Provides advisory, analytical, historical, interpretative and referral information covering the politics of abortion. **How to Contact:** Write or call. Responds to most inquiries within a month.

1182• NATIONAL ACTION/RESEARCH ON THE MILITARY INDUSTRIAL COMPLEX
1501 Cherry St., Philadelphia PA 19102. (215)241-7175. Contact Person: Secretarial Assistant. **Description:** "NARMIC, a project of American Friends Service Committee, is active in research and production of printed and audio-visual resources on issues related to disarmament and human rights, with attention to corporations with military contracts." **Services:** Provides analytical, how-to, interpretative and trade information on military contractors; human rights in South Africa and Central America; nuclear weapons systems and their producers. Offers brochures/pamphlets, factsheets, map series, library facilities, photos, films, slide films and filmstrips, research assistance, and quarterly listings of military contracts by county or company. Publications include *How to Research Your Local War Industry: How to Read Defense Contract Listings.* **How to Contact:** Write. Responds to most inquiries within a week. Charges for publications and film slides/filmstrips; $2/quarter for military contract listings for each county or company; $3 for each state. No charge to people using materials at our office. Give credit to NARMIC. "Please make arrangements in advance to use library or military contract listings to be sure a staff member is on hand." **Tips:** Recent information requests: "Please send military contract listings for last 4 quarters available for Los Angeles County, California."; "What corporations make nuclear weapons?"

1183• NATIONAL COALITION TO BAN HANDGUNS
100 Maryland Ave. NE, Washington DC 20024. (202)544-7190. Contact Person. Executive Director. **Description:** The coalition is a public interest group engaged in educational and legislative programs to ban handguns from manufacture, sale, ownership and use by the public. The group conducts research on the effect of handgun control laws. **Services:** Provides advisory and referral information on the movement to ban handguns. Offers brochures/pamphlets and educational materials to increase awareness of the handgun situation. Publications include *Handgun Control News.* **How to Contact:** Call. Responds to most inquiries within a week.

1184• NATIONAL CONSUMER COOPERATIVE BANK
1630 Connecticut Ave. NW, Washington DC 20009. (202)745-4600. Contact Person: Information Officer. **Description:** "The Co-op Bank makes loans and provides technical assistance to consumer cooperatives." **Services:** Provides information on the bank's services. Offers annual reports, brochures/pamphlets and placement on mailing lists. **How to Contact:** Write. Responds to most inquiries within a week.

1185• NATIONAL PEOPLE'S ACTION
1123 W. Washington Blvd., Chicago IL 60607. (312)243-3038. Contact Person: Editor. **Description:** "A coalition of neighborhood groups, churches, unions, public interest groups organizing on issues such as unemployment, energy costs, housing, etc." **Services:** Provides advisory information on unemployment, health care, housing, energy costs, interest rates and insurance. Offers brochures/pamphlets, informational newsletters, placement on mailing lists, press kits, research assistance and referral to local organizing groups. (See listing for National Training and Information Center.) **How to Contact:** Write or call. Responds to most inquiries within 2 weeks. "We appreciate being given credit for research and seeing a copy of the writers'/researchers' works which use information about or from NPA."

1186• NATIONAL RIGHT TO LIFE COMMITTEE, INC.
419 7th St. NW, Suite 402, Washington DC 20004. (202)638-4396. Contact Person: Public Relations Director. **Description:** NRLC provides national leadership in the right-to-life movement and seeks passage of pro-life legislation. The NRLC Board of Directors is made up of

representatives from all 50 states; the organization has over 2,000 local right-to-life groups nationwide. NRLC maintains a lobbying staff on Capitol Hill and has regular communications with all the states through "Legislative Alerts" as well as educational publications from its NRL Educational Trust Fund. **Services:** Offers aid in arranging interviews, bibliographies, biographies, statistics, brochures/pamphlets, information searches, placement on mailing list, newsletter and press kits. Publications include *National Right to Life News* (biweekly); books dealing with abortion, infanticide, euthanasia, population, counseling, etc.; legislative updates and alerts; medical information; and reviews of literature available on subjects of interest to the pro-life movement. **How to Contact:** Write or call. Make appointment in advance of visit. "Specify exactly what your area of interest is and we will accommodate with any information we have—an up-to-the-minute accounting in most cases. If a writer has a specific area of interest which will require one-time use of our services, there is never a charge for this; we are more than happy to supply additional study material if needed." Charges for some publications. **Tips:** "Be prepared to search the libraries, especially the medical libraries, for statistics pertinent to the areas of medical concern with regard to abortion."

1187• NATIONAL SAFETY COUNCIL
444 N. Michigan Ave., Chicago IL 60611. (312)527-4800. Contact Person: Public Relations Director. **Description:** "We are a voluntary public-service organization of people and organizations acting to increase the safety and improve the occupational health of the American people." **Services:** Offers aid in arranging interviews, annual reports, bibliographies, biographies, statistics, brochures/pamphlets, information searches, placement on mailing list, photos and press kits. Publications include complete catalogs available in areas of farming, recreation, industry, school/college and miscellaneous related subjects. "The National Safety Council's *Accident Facts* magazine is available for quick reference with credit to the council where applicable. This service is a supplement to the council's research department which may be contacted for reference through the public relations department." **How to Contact:** Write or call. Responds to most inquiries immediately. "Information excerpted from National Safety Council materials must be credited to the council. All National Safety Council programs and/or products also must be attributed to the council." **Tips:** Recent information requests: "What can people do to help promote the 55 mph speed limit?"; "How can we solve the problem of drinking and driving?"

1188• NATIONAL SOCIETY OF FUND RAISING EXECUTIVES
1511 K St. NW, Washington DC 20005. (202)638-1393. Contact Person: Executive Vice President. **Description:** Individuals engaged in directing fund raising programs; the society holds workshops and seminars on all aspects of fund raising. **Services:** Provides advisory and referral information on philanthropy and fund raising. Offers placement on mailing lists, press kits and telephone reference services. **How to Contact:** Write. Responds to most inquiries within a week.

1189• NATIONAL TAXPAYERS UNION
325 Pennsylvania Ave. SE,, Washington DC 20003. (202)543-1300. Contact Person: Editor, *Dollars & Sense.* **Description:** "Our purpose is to organize a broad-based network of taxpayers in the country. We are nonpartisan, nonprofit representing 450,000 family members interested in reducing taxes, government waste, and spending." **Services:** Provides advisory, analytical, historical and referral information on balanced budget amendment, flat-rate tax, state and local taxes, and current legislation being considered on Capitol Hill affecting the US taxpayers. Offers brochures/pamphlets, informational newsletters and statistics. Publications include *Congressional Spending Study* (an annual analysis of congressional roll call votes which measures the performance of senators and representatives on spending issues); and *Dollars & Sense* (monthly newsletter). **How to Contact:** Write or call. Responds to most inquiries within a month. **Tips:** "Our ability to do extended research for others is limited, but we glady advise interested parties as to what sources, etc., to use." Recent information request: "How many states have passed a resolution calling for a Constitutional convention to add a balanced budget amendment to the Constitution?"

1190• NATIONAL TRAINING AND INFORMATION CENTER (NTIC)
1123 W. Washington Blvd., Chicago IL 60607. (312)243-3035. Contact Person: Training Director. **Description:** Resource center and clearinghouse for neighborhood organizations. **Services:** Provides research, training, technical assistance and on-site consultations with commu-

nity workers/leaders around the country. Offers how-to courses dealing with community organization, block clubs, housing concerns, etc. Publications include *NTIC Reports* and *Disclosure* (periodicals); also various booklets. **How to Contact:** Write or call. Responds to most inquiries within a week.

1191• NATIONAL URBAN LEAGUE
500 E. 62nd St., New York NY 10021. (212)644-6600, 644-6601. Contact Person: Director of Communications. **Description:** "An interracial, nonprofit community service organization that uses the tools and methods of social work, economics, law, business management and other disciplines to secure equal opportunites in all sectors of our society for black Americans and other minorities." **Services:** Provides analytical and interpretative information covering human and civil rights and data on black Americans. Offers aid in arranging interviews, annual reports, bibliographies, statistics, brochures/pamphlets, placement on mailing list and sometimes press kits. Publications include *Urban League Review.* **How to Contact:** Write or call. Responds to most inquiries immediately. "Request detailed information in writing. We will give interviews and place a writer on our mailing list only if we feel the project is worthwhile and the writer legitimate."

1192• NEGATIVE POPULATION GROWTH, INC.
16 E. 42nd St., New York NY 10017. (212)599-2020. Contact Person: President. **Description:** Nonprofit membership organization advocating reduction of size of US and world population. **Services:** Offers annual reports, brochures/pamphlets. Publications include position papers and newsletter, *Human Survival.* **How to Contact:** Write or call. **Tips:** Recent information requests: Effects of declining population on economic growth vs. GNP per capita income; age structure in declining population; ecological effects.

1193• NOT-SAFE (NATIONAL ORGANIZATION TAUNTING SAFETY AND FAIRNESS EVERYWHERE)
Box 5743W, Montecito CA 93108. (805)969-1185. Contact Person: Executive Director. **Description:** "Our purpose is to lampoon regulatory excess with 'satire' and overkill examples, and to promote libertarian ideas. We hope to use humor *first* to get peoples' attention . . . then to offer some *serious* solutions to paternalistic laws." **Services:** Provides advisory, analytical, historical, how-to and technical (statistical) information. "We use 'statistical' information to show how dumb laws can become the tools of 'extremist' or special interest groups. We try to show that 'good intentions' do not necessarily lead to good laws." Offers aid in arranging interviews, brochures/pamphlets, clipping services, press kits and statistics. Publications include "examples of 'letters-to-the-editors' (to show how to lampoon through the local media)." **How to Contact:** Write or call. Responds to most inquiries within a month. Give credit to organization. "We ask that each interview/article allow space for our mailing address."

1194• PEOPLE FOR THE AMERICAN WAY: A PROJECT OF CITIZENS FOR CONSTITUTIONAL CONCERNS, INC.
1015 18th St. NW, Suite 300, Washington DC 20009. (202)822-9450. **Description:** "We are a membership organization which promotes and defends citizens' constitutional freedoms and traditional American values through public education programs, citizen action, training, and the media." **Services:** Provides advisory, analytical, bibliographical and referral information on church/state separation, "electronic church," public education, the courts, school textbooks and curricula, family issues, school prayer, creationism, secular humanism, and radical right religious and/or political organizations. Offers brochures/pamphlets, clipping services, informational newsletters and library facilities. Publications include quarterly reports; monthly bulletins; issue papers; and *Liberty and Justice for Some* (primer on Constitutional concerns, $8.95 co-published with Frederick Ungar Publishing Co.). **How to Contact:** Write, call or visit. Responds to most inquiries within a week. **Tips:** "Please pose specific questions." Recent information request: "What are the activities of a certain Texas-based textbook censorship organization? How do they influence the textbook selection process nationwide?"

1195• PUBLIC CITIZEN, INC.
Box 19404, Washington DC 20036. (202)293-9142. Contact Person: Director. **Description:** "We provide support to the following groups: Congress Watch; Critical Mass Energy Project; Public Citizen Litigation Group; Freedom of Information Act Clearinghouse; Health Research Group;

Tax Reform Research Group; Center for Study of Responsive Law; Resident Utility Consumer Action Group.'' **Services:** Provides analytical and technical information on health, tax reform, safe energy, consumer protection, legislation, public interest litigation, corporate accountability research groups. Offers brochures/pamphlets and newsletter. Publications include *Public Citizen; People and Taxes; The Congress Watcher* and *Critical Mass Energy Journal*. **How to Contact:** Write, call or visit. Responds to most inquiries within a week. **Tips:** ''Call us. We have brochures, a list of publications that are free, and a staff of researchers glad to answer questions on specific topics.''

1196• PUBLIC CITIZEN'S CONGRESS WATCH
215 Pennsylvania Ave. SE, Washington DC 20003. (202)546-4996. Contact Person: Librarian. **Description:** ''We lobby for legislation in the public interest. We deal with issues in areas of consumer protection, energy, environment, government reform, waste/subsidy, tax reform.'' **Services:** Provides analytical and referral information. Offers informational newsletters, research assistance, statistics and telephone reference services. Publications include specific *PAC* studies; *Aid for Dependent Corporations*. **How to Contact:** Call. Responds to most inquiries within a week. Charges for extensive xeroxing of materials. **Tips:** Recent information requests: ''Journalists often ask for ratings from our annual Congressional Voting Index and information on specific legislation.''

1197• PUBLIC INTEREST ECONOMICS FOUNDATION
1525 New Hampshire Ave. NW, Washington DC 20036. (202)872-0313. Contact Person: Director of Education. **Description:** ''The Public Interest Economics Foundation was established for and remains committed to the development of innovative, equitable, and efficient economic policy. The foundation operates three broad programs: education, a clearinghouse and research.'' **Services:** Provides analytical, bibliographical, interpretative, referral and technical information on government policy in: environmental regulation, energy, maritime, social regulation, antitrust, employment, economics policy, and other areas on federal, state, and local level. ''We also deal with the general topic of economics.'' Offers aid in arranging interviews, placement on mailing lists and research assistance. Publications include a publications list. **How to Contact:** Write. Responds to most inquiries within a week. Charges for reproduction of material and for any significant amount of time required to respond to a request. Give credit to the foundation. **Tips:** ''Define your subject area carefully before contacting us.'' Recent information request: ''What has been the level of economic benefits derived from the Clean Air Act?''

1198• RENT-A-KVETCH, INC.
c/o B.L. Ochman Public Relations, 200 W. 57th St., New York NY 10019. (212)307-0585. Contact Person: President. **Description:** ''An organization dedicated to artful, legitimate complaining. We will handle any legitimate consumer complaint against any product, service, or person.'' **Services:** Provides advisory, how-to and interpretative information in all areas of consumerism. Offers aid in arranging interviews, brochures/pamphlets, case histories, press kits and ''philosophy of complaining for fun and profit.'' **How to Contact:** Write or call. Responds to most inquiries within a week. Charges $35 for each letter of complaint; $35 for gift certificates. **Tips:** ''Rent-A-Kvetch offers humorous, factual and useful information and believes that complaining about shoddy products and services is a healthy and economically viable activity.''

1199• REPUBLICAN NATIONAL COMMITTEE
310 1st St. SE, Washington DC 20003. (202)484-6500. Contact Person: Director of Communications. **Description:** ''The Republican National Committee is the national organization for the Republican party. The Chairman is spokesman for the party when there is no Republican president. The committee is made up of three represenatives from each state: the state chairman, a committee man and a committee woman. This is the headquarters of the national committee.'' **Services:** Provides advisory, analytical, bibliographical, historical, how-to and referral information on political issues, campaigning, fund raising and history of the Republican party. Offers aid in arranging interviews, statistics, brochures/pamphlets, placement on mailing list and press kits. Publications include *First Monday*, a monthly magazine to members; and a book about election results that is published after each election. **How to Contact:** Write or call. Responds to most inquiries within a week. ''Priority is given to members of the Republican National Committee and Republican party, although all inquiries are welcome.'' **Tips:** ''Write or call for information first.

We have limited facilities available for use by the public." Typical information request: Copy of the Republican platform for a specific year.

1200• RURAL AMERICA
1900 M St. NW, Washington DC 20036. (202)659-2800. Contact Person: Information Director. **Description:** "The purpose of our organization is to represent and empower low and moderate income rural and small town people." **Services:** Provides analytical, bibliographical, interpretative and referral information on a broad range of rural and social policy concerns. Offers brochures/pamphlets, informational newsletters and research assistance. Publications include *ruralamerica*, a bimonthly magazine, plus a complete selection of publications. **How to Contact:** Write or call. Responds to most inquiries within a month. Charges for publications. "Services are subject to availability of staff time and resources." **Tips:** "Be clear on exactly what you want. Talk to people actually involved in research/work in field." Recent information request: Contacts and information about structure of US agriculture.

1201• SANE, A CITIZENS' ORGANIZATION FOR A SANE WORLD
711 G St. SE, Washington DC 20003. (202)546-7100. Contact Person: Publications Director. **Description:** A nonprofit organization working to stop the arms race. "We have a membership of 40,000 and 28 chapters throughout the country. We do lobbying, research, and writing." **Services:** Provides advisory, analytical, historical and referral information on the arms race, the defense budget, military spending, and economic conversion. Offers brochures/pamphlets and informational newsletters. Publications include monthly newsletters, pamphlets and brochures, and complete resource lists. **How to Contact:** Write or call. Responds to most inquiries within a week. Charges for pamphlets and brochures in bulk.

1202• SMALL TOWNS INSTITUTE
Box 517, Ellensburg WA 98926. (509)925-1830. Contact Person: Director. **Description:** "Our purpose is to share new ideas and resources which will assist citizens and professionals to improve the quality of life in small communities." **Services:** Provides advisory, analytical, how-to, interpretative and referral information on "new or innovative ways of solving everyday problems in housing, land use planning, industrial development, community health, historic preservation, small business, solid waste and sanitation, local government finance, cultural development, and a wide range of other concerns." Offers informational newsletters and library facilities. Publications include *Small Town* (bimonthly, indexed). **How to Contact:** Write or call. Responds to most inquiries within a month. Charges for extensive time commitment. Give credit to institute. **Tips:** Recent information request: "What types of subsidized housing projects have been carried out in small towns recently?"

1203• SOCIAL SECURITY ADMINISTRATION
Office of Public Inquiries, 4100 Annex Building, 6401 Security Blvd., Baltimore MD 21235. (301)594-7700. **Description:** The SSA administers the federal retirement, survivors and disability insurance programs; health insurance for the aged and certain severely disabled people (Medicare); and a program of supplemental security income for the aged, blind and disabled. **Services:** Offers biographies, statistics, historical information, brochures/pamphlets, news releases, photos and "other information materials." **How to Contact:** Write or call. Responds to most inquiries within 3 weeks. "The Social Security Administration (SSA) can't provide information about any individual social security record or beneficiary. Under the law, all social security records are confidential." **Tips:** Recent information requests: "How will some particular legislation affect my social security benefits?"; "When was the SSA established and what were its original provisions?"; "What projections can you make about the SSA?"

1204• SOCIALIST LABOR PARTY
914 Industrial Ave., Box 50218, Palo Alto CA 94303. (415)494-1532. **Description:** "A political party formed 90 years ago to further the socialist view." **Services:** Provides information on the socialist view of the nuclear movement, the women's movement and the economy. Offers brochures/pamphlets and newspaper. Publications include *The People*, a biweekly newspaper. **How to Contact:** Write. Responds to most inquiries immediately. **Tips:** Recent information request: "What does the party represent?"

1205• SOCIALIST WORKERS PARTY
14 Charles Lane, New York NY 10014. (212)242-5530. **Description:** "The Socialist Workers party was started in 1938. Our view is a four-day work week with no cut in pay; the use of military budget for public works programs; an end to racism and oppression of women and gays; and an end to military and economic intervention abroad." **Services:** Provides information on politics. Offers bibliographies, biographies, brochures/pamphlets, newsletter and press releases for specific occasions. Publications include *The Militant*, a newspaper with socialist editorial policy. **How to Contact:** Write or call. "Written requests preferred. Responds to most inquiries within a week. Catalog may be ordered from Pathfinders Press, 410 West St., New York, New York."

1206• UNION FOR RADICAL POLITICAL ECONOMICS
41 Union Square, W., Room 901, New York NY 10025. (212)691-5722. Contact: National Office. **Description:** Professional economists and students interested in promoting the political-economic analysis of social problems. **Services:** Provides analytical, bibliographical, historical, interpretative, referral, technical and trade information on the political economy of women, racism, the state, taxation; analysis of social systems in the US, USSR, Third World, etc. Offers brochures/pamphlets, informational newsletters and statistics. Publications include *Review of Radical Political Economics*; *URPE Newsletter*. **How to Contact:** Write. Responds to most inquiries immediately. Charges for publications. **Tips:** "Please send your request for information in writing. We will refer you to one of our members or will send you copies of our articles at a low fee to cover photocopying." Recent information requests: "Is there a 'productivity decline' in the USA?"; "What is supply-side economics about?"; "How does discrimination based on sex and race affect labor?"

1207• UNITED STATES CIVIL DEFENSE COUNCIL
Box 6457, Great Falls MT 59406. (406)452-4221. Contact Person: Director Public Affairs. **Description:** "We inform our members (local Emergency Management Directors) of all activities in the field of E.M./Civil Defense; and inform and educate the public regarding individual responsibility to reduce death and injury due to disasters and emergencies." **Services:** Provides referral, technical and trade information on virtually every subject related to emergency preparedness (disaster preparedness by type—flood, earthquake, etc; fire safety; nuclear survival information). Offers aid in arranging interviews, brochures/pamphlets, placement on mailing lists and research assistance. Publications include *USCDC Bulletin* (monthly, 8-pages, to members); and *USCDC Impact* (quarterly magazine to members, Congress, governors). **How to Contact:** Write or call. Responds to most inquiries within a week. Give credit to council. **Tips:** "On topics of controversy, cross check your information and consider the source. We attempt to provide objective information, as the topics are normally life-threatening. We encourage writers to compare information from various sources and follow up on items that appear in conflict. Be as specific as possible in stating needs. We have limited time to devote to council activities and must know as clearly as possible what exactly is needed." Recent information requests: "What are the general qualifications for a local Emergency Manager (Civil Defense Director)?"; "What information do you have on sources of information on effects of nuclear weapons?"

1208• THE UNITED STATES JAYCEES
Box 7, Tulsa OK 74121. (918)584-2481. Contact Person: Director of Public Relations. **Description:** "We are an organization for 18- to 35-year-old men. The three areas of primary concentration are personal development, management training and community involvement. Through a balanced program including all three, the Jaycees help develop leaders for communities, states and the nation, while improving the quality of life in the communities served. Two programs worthy of special mention are the Outstanding Young Farmer recognition program and the Congress of America's Ten Outstanding Young Men. We have programs in youth activities, governmental involvement and family life, among others." **Services:** Provides historical and how-to information covering agriculture, self-help, individual, spiritual and community development. Offers annual reports, information searches and press kits. Publications available. **How to Contact:** Write. Responds to most inquiries within a week. "Our materials and publications may not be reproduced without written permission of the US Jaycees, and may not be used for profit under any circumstances. The Jaycees public relations department will cooperate in any way possible with writers who seek their assistance."

1209• WAR RESISTERS LEAGUE
339 Lafayette St., New York NY 10012. (212)228-0450. Contact: Staff. **Description:** "We resist all wars; seek to remove the causes of war; promote active nonviolent solutions to conflict." **Services:** Provides information on disarmament, draft and military recruitment, war tax resistance, nuclear weapons and power, foreign and military policy, local organizing. Offers aid in arranging interviews, biographies, brochures/pamphlets, informational newsletters and statistics. Publications include *WRL News*; literature list (over 200 titles). **How to Contact:** Write, call or visit. Responds to most inquiries within a week. Charges for postage. **Tips:** "We are an organization which does not exist to provide services for researchers; rather we seek to help those working to stop militarism, etc. If the information is buried in our files, you may have to come into our office to search." Recent information request: "How many war tax resisters are there in the US?"; "What happens if I don't register for the draft?"

1210• ZERO POPULATION GROWTH, INC.
1346 Connecticut Ave. NW, Washington DC 20036. (202)785-0100. Contact Person: Director of Communications. **Description:** "We promote public attitudes and policies favoring stabilization of US and world population size." **Services:** Provides advisory, interpretative and referral information on population, environment, resources, demographic trends, foreign aid (population related), immigration, local growth, fertility. Offers aid in arranging interviews, statistics, brochures/pamphlets, placement on mailing list and newsletter. Publications include leaflets on US population policy, statistics, school curricula, immigration, effects on economy and environment-related topics. **How to Contact:** Write or call. Responds to most inquiries immediately. Give credit to ZPG and send copies of articles or publications. **Tips:** "For a local angle, in many cities, we can give you the phone number for local ZPG activists or chapters. For specific population statistics and expert analysis, call the US Census Bureau, (301)763-5002. For perspective of a US group concerned about population growth, call ZPG. Be as specific as possible when requesting demographic information. Verify sources for consistency." Recent information requests: "How can the country still be growing when fertility is below 'replacement' level?"; "What are the benefits of population stabilization?"

SECTION·TWENTY-THREE

SCIENCE, ENGINEERING, TECHNOLOGY

The whole of science is nothing more than a refinement of everyday thinking.

—Albert Einstein

This category lists resources in science and mathematics; various engineering technologies; astronomy and space exploration; invention and discovery; parapsychology and research into the unexplained.

Specialized research and technological sources (in ocean science, health care or agriculture, for example) are found in the appropriate subject section of the book—in this case, Environment/The Earth; Health and Medicine; Farming and Food, respectively.

Bibliography

American Men and Women of Science. Edited by Jaques Cattell Press. New York: Bowker, 1979.

Applied Science and Technology Index. 1958 to date, monthly. New York: H.W. Wilson Co.

Asimov, Isaac, ed. *Asimov's Biographical Encyclopedia of Science and Technology.* 2d rev. ed. Garden City, NY: Doubleday, 1982.

Ballentyne, D.W.G. and D.R. Lovett, eds. *A Dictionary of Named Effects and Laws in Chemistry, Physics and Mathematics.* 4th ed. New York: Methuen, 1980.

Considine, Douglas M., ed. *Van Nostrand Scientific Encyclopedia.* 6th ed. 2 vols. New York: Van Nostrand Reinhold, 1982.

Davis, Henry B.O., ed. *Electrical & Electronic Technologies: A Chronology of Events and Inventors to 1900.* Metuchen, NJ: Scarecrow Press, 1981.

DeVore, Nicholas. *Encyclopedia of Astrology.* Totowa, NJ: Littlefield, 1977.

Engineering Index Annual. 5 vols. New York: Engineering Information, Inc.

General Science Index. 1978 to date, monthly. Annual Cumulation. New York: H.W. Wilson Co.

Hawley, Gessner G., ed. *The Condensed Chemical Dictionary.* 10th ed. New York: Van Nostrand Reinhold, 1981.

Industrial Research Laboratories in the US. Edited by Jaques Cattell Press. New York: Bowker, 1982.

James, Robert C., ed. *Mathematics Dictionary.* 4th ed. New York: Van Nostrand Reinhold, 1976.

Lapedes, Daniel N., ed. *Dictionary of Scientific and Technical Terms.* 2d ed. New York: McGraw-Hill Book Co., 1978.

McGraw-Hill Encyclopedia of Science and Technology. 5th ed. New York: McGraw-Hill Book Co., 1982.

McGraw-Hill Modern Scientists and Engineers. New York: McGraw-Hill Book Co., 1980.

McWilliams, Peter A. *The Personal Computer Book.* Los Angeles: Ingram Book Co., Prelude Press, 1982.

Riland, George, ed. *The New Steinerbooks Dictionary of the Paranormal.* New York: Steinerbooks, 1980.

Story, Ronald D., ed. *The Encyclopedia of UFOs.* New York: Dolphin Books, 1980.

Tver, David F. et al., eds. *Dictonary of Astronomy, Space and Atmospheric Phenomena.* New York: Van Nostrand Reinhold, 1982.

Walker, Benjamin. *Encyclopedia of the Occult, the Esoteric and the Unexplained.* New York: Stein & Day, 1980.

1211• ABRASIVE ENGINEERING SOCIETY
1700 Painters Run Rd., Pittsburgh PA 15243. (412)221-0909. Contact Person: Managing Editor. **Description:** "A technical society of manufacturers, users and others interested in abrasives such as abrasive wheels, coated abrasives, diamonds and their products, dressers and

dressing devices, abrasive grains and media used in blasting and tumbling." **Services:** Information covers business, industry, new product information and technical data. Offers aid in arranging interviews, statistics, information searches and photos. **How to Contact:** Write or call. Responds to most inquiries within a week.

1212• THE ADLER PLANETARIUM

1300 S. Lake Shore Dr., Chicago IL 60605. (312)322-0328. Contact Person: Supervisor of Development and Public Affairs. **Description:** The planetarium promotes astronomy to the general public through sky shows, exhibits and public events. **Services:** Provides information on the openings of each of the planetarium's five sky shows a year, and on celestial events of an astronomical nature. Offers aid in arranging interviews "with our staff of professional astronomers," library facilities, photos, placement on mailing lists, press kits and research assistance. Publications include press releases with diagrams of celestial events of an astronomical nature. **How to Contact:** Write. Responds to most inquiries immediately. "Use of our library is by appointment. Interviews with staff astronomers are usually conducted by phone, when an astronomer is available. Contact us by mail." **Tips:** "Most public libraries have basic astronomy books that will provide enough general knowledge of astronomy to a writer so that he/she will be prepared to ask intelligent questions (and understand the answers). In addition, The Adler Planetarium offers evening classes in astronomy and navigation ranging from beginners' level to advanced courses. A free brochure is available upon request." Recent information requests: Inquiries about the "Jupiter Effect;" causes of lunar and solar eclipses; the influence of the full moon on people; influence of the planets on people.

1213• AEROSPACE INDUSTRIES ASSOCIATION OF AMERICA

1725 De Sales St. NW, Washington DC 20036. (202)429-4600. Contact Person: Director of Publications. **Description:** "Aerospace Industry Association of America is a national trade association which represents major manufacturers of aerospace equipment. We deal with commercial, military, civil and private aviation and space activities as they relate to the design, development and manufacture of such equipment." **Services:** "We maintain statistical, historical and other information relative to the industry and speak on issues of industry wide significance." Offers aid in arranging interviews, statistics, brochures/pamphlets, placement on mailing list and newsletter. Publications include an annual report and *Aerospace*, quarterly magazine. **How to Contact:** Write or call; "we prefer written requests." Responds to most inquiries within a week. **Tips:** Recent information request: "Who makes the 747?"

1214• AMERICAN ASSOCIATION FOR THE ADVANCEMENT OF SCIENCE

1776 Massachusetts Ave. NW, Washington DC 20036. (202)467-4400. Contact Person: Head, Office of Communications. **Description:** The American Association for the Advancement of Science is a membership organization whose purpose is the advancement of science. **Services:** Provides advisory and referral information on all fields of science and science policy. Offers statistics, brochures/pamphlets, placement on mailing list and press releases. Publications include *Science*, a magazine free to members or available by subscription and *Science 83 (84, 85,* etc.), a general circulation magazine. **How to Contact:** Write or call. Written request preferable. Responds to most inquiries immediately. **Tips:** "Be as specific as possible. Ask researchers to suggest names of others doing work in your field of interest." Recent information request: Suggestions for researcher doing work on a specific area (left-handed sugars).

1215• AMERICAN ASSOCIATION OF META-SCIENCE

Box 1182, Huntsville AL 35807. Contact Person: President. **Description:** "A nonprofit organization devoted to exploring, understanding, utilizing and applying aspects of paranormal phenomena and spiritual energy to everyday life." **Services:** Provides analytical, interpretative, technical and trade information on paranormal phenomena, ESP, psychotronics, free energy, self-healing, dowsing, new science, UFOs, ELF energies, past lives, radionics, biofields, water monsters, Bigfoot. Offers brochures/pamphlets and informational newsletters. Publications include *Specula*, a journal published quarterly containing news, incidents, happenings, findings, detailed investigations and technical papers. **How to Contact:** Write. Responds to most inquiries within a month. Charges for "reproduction of a variety of materials."

1216• AMERICAN ASSOCIATION OF VARIABLE STAR OBSERVERS

187 Concord Ave., Cambridge MA 02138. Contact Person: Director. **Description:** Scientific

association which collects, analyzes and publishes observations from observers world-wide of stars that change in brightness (variable stars). **Services:** Provides technical information on astronomy—variable stars and sun. **How to Contact:** Write. Responds to most inquiries within a month. Charges for data on variable stars.

1217• AMERICAN ASTRONOMICAL SOCIETY
1816 Jefferson Place NW, Washington DC 20036. (202)659-0134 (executive office), (302)738-2986 (education office). Contact Person: Executive Officer or Education Officer. **Description:** Organization of professional astronomers in the US, Canada and Mexico whose objective is to promote the advancement of astronomy and closely related fields. **Services:** Provides interpretative, referral and technical information on astronomy, astrophysics and closely related fields. Offers aid in arranging interviews, brochures/pamphlets, informational newsletters, placement on mailing lists and press kits. Publications include *The Astrophysical Journal*; *The Astronomical Journal*; *The Bulletin of the American Astronomical Society*; *American Astronomical Society Photo-Bulletin*; *AAS Newsletter*. **How to Contact:** Write or call. Responds to most inquiries within a month. **Tips:** "We can probably direct you to a person who can answer just about any question on astronomy or a related field, ranging from questions regarding what's up in the sky right now to discussions of recent research developments. Sometimes we can answer questions directly. We mail out press releases on the most significant research developments reported at our meetings, held twice a year. Writers who wish to receive these releases should ask us to put them on our mailing list." Recent information requests: "Who can I talk to who will tell me more about black holes?"; "Tell me about the meteor shower coming in a couple of weeks."

1218• AMERICAN INSTITUTE OF CHEMICAL ENGINEERS (AIChE)
345 E. 47th St., New York NY 10017. (212)705-7660. Contact Person: Director of Public Relations. **Description:** Nonprofit technical society serving the profession of chemical engineering through publications, meetings and conferences for the exchange of technical information. **Services:** Provides advisory, analytical, bibliographical, historical, technical and trade information on energy (coal, oil, solar, nuclear, geothermal) and the environment (hazardous and toxic wastes, radioactive wastes, etc.) Offers aid in arranging interviews, biographies, brochures/pamphlets, informational newsletters, photos, placement on mailing lists, press kits, research assistance, statistics and telephone reference services. Publications include *Chemical Engineering Progress* (monthly); division and committee newsletters; *International Chemical Engineering Plant/Operations Progress*; *Energy Progress*; *Environmental Progress* (quarterlies) and *AICHE Journal* (bimonthly). **How to Contact:** Write or call. Responds to most inquiries within a week. **Tips:** "Try us for technical information on any chemical engineering subject as well as general information on the status and demand for chemical engineers." Recent information request: "Is it true that there's a process that eliminates pollutants (from coal's sulfur) and helps produce fertilizers at the same time?"

1219• AMERICAN INSTITUTE OF PHYSICS
335 E. 45th St., New York NY 10017. (212)661-9404. Contact Person: Manager, Public Information Division. **Description:** "AIP is a nonprofit scientific organization made up of nine member societies. Its purpose is to assist the member societies in their mission of promoting the advancement and diffusion of the knowledge of physics and its applications." **Services:** Provides advisory, analytical, bibliographical, historical, how-to, interpretative, referral, technical and trade information on physics, astronomy, solid state, optics, acoustics, rheology, vacuum, crystallography, physics in medicine, physics teaching, history of physics, manpower statistics, radio and TV services. Offers aid in arranging interviews, annual reports, brochures/pamphlets, computerized information searches, library facilities, photos, placement on mailing lists, press kits, research assistance and statistics. Runs news rooms and news conferences for scientific meetings; administers science writing awards. Publications include primary physics journals; press releases; radio and TV reports; annual booklet *Physics News in 19—*." **How to Contact:** Write, call or visit. Responds to most inquiries immediately. **Tips:** "We are in touch with most of the experts of physics. Give us a call." Recent information request: Clarification and further references regarding the discovery of Magnetic Monopole particle.

1220• AMERICAN MUSEUM—HAYDEN PLANETARIUM
Perkin Library, 81st St. and Central Parkway, New York NY 10024. (212)873-1300, ext. 478. Contact Person: Librarian. **Description:** "We are a department of astronomy, affiliated with a

natural history museum. We are a public department which offers a major planetarium, with topical sky shows, to the public. We have two floors of exhibits, two multimedia theatres, classrooms, a research library and a gift shop. Our library (and the department) specializes in astronomy, astrophysics, meteorology, navigation and space technology. Our research library is considered the best available to the general public in this field.'' **Services:** Provides advisory, bibliographical, historical, how-to and referral information on astronomy, astrophysics, space science, history, some math, physics, navigation, some meteorology. Offers bibliographies, information searches and photos for research only. Also offers NASA technical information and mission reports. **How to Contact:** ''The planetarium is open daily except Thanksgiving and Christmas. The library is open by appointment Monday through Friday, 1 p.m. to 5 p.m. We charge for photocopies and respond to most inquiries within a week.'' **Tips:** ''Come prepared with your own note-taking equipment; money for payment to use copier.'' Recent information request: ''Where can I find out about the next solar eclipse?''

1221• AMERICAN PRECISION MUSEUM ASSOCIATION, INC.
196 Main St., Windsor VT 05089. (802)674-5781. Contact Person: Director. **Description:** ''We have thousands of catalogs on pre-1930 mechanized industries, everything from stockyards to energy development. In addition, we have biographies, portraits, company histories and pictures of many industrial buildings and complexes.'' **Services:** Provides advisory, analytical, bibliographical, historical, interpretative, referral and technical information on hand and machine tools in a broad sense including the usual products of such equipment. ''We are not strong on hand tools of prehistoric times.'' Offers photos; ''10,000-12,000 photos are contained in our library.'' **How to Contact:** Write or call. Responds to inquiries within a week to six weeks, ''but we are able to do only minimum research, if at all, due to a small, busy staff.'' Charges according to work done. ''We do not lend material. Library stacks are not open, but any item in the catalog is readily available. Credit must be given on any material or assistance given when published.'' **Tips:** ''We find that many writers are not familiar with the subject they have elected to write on; they simply pick a salable topic and require more guidance than we could give on a regular basis. They should not expect museum staff to literally write or rewrite their work.''

1222• AMERICAN SOCIETY FOR CYBERNETICS
2131 G St. NW, Washington DC 20052. (202)676-7530. Contact Person: President. **Description:** Educational and scientific organization of individuals interested in theoretical, technical and applied cybernetics and in promoting education and research in cybernetics. **Services:** Provides advisory, historical and referral information on cybernetics, systems theory, artificial intelligence, robotics, experimental epistemology, managerial cybernetics. Offers aid in arranging interviews, brochures/pamphlets, informational newsletters, placement on mailing lists and telephone reference services. Publications include *Newsletter*; *Cybernetics*; annual conference proceedings. **How to Contact:** Call. Responds to most inquiries within a week. ''We charge for publications such as journals and conference proceedings but not for brochures and flyers.'' **Tips:** ''Contact us by phone first. We shall then refer you to the people who can be most helpful.'' Recent information request: ''What is cybernetics?''

1223• AMERICAN SOCIETY OF CIVIL ENGINEERS
345 E. 47th St., New York NY 10017. (212)705-7671. Contact Person: Manager, Public Information Services. **Description:** ''The society's goal is to advance the profession of engineering in its service to people.'' Membership of 80,000 individual civil engineers. **Services:** Provides historical and technical information on civil engineering. Offers aid in arranging interviews, bibliographies and a library. **How to Contact:** Write or call. Responds to most inquiries within a week. **Tips:** ''History of technology is virgin territory for research and writing.''

1224• AMERICAN SOCIETY OF MECHANICAL ENGINEERS
345 E. 47th St., New York NY 10017. (212)705-7740. Contact Person: Media Specialist. **Description:** Educational and technical society which seeks to aid members of the engineering profession in maintaining a high level of ethical conduct; to develop mechanical standards, codes, safety procedures, and operating principles for industry; to provide a forum for the development, exchange and dissemination of technical information, particularly on mechanical engineering; to encourage the personal and professional development of practicing and student engineers. **Services:** Provides advisory, analytical, bibliographical, historical, how-to, interpretative, referral, technical and trade information covering such areas as heat transfer,

lubrication, bioengineering, power, nuclear, fuels, gas turbines, ocean engineering, solar energy, advanced energy systems, petroleum, rail transportation, aerospace, air pollution control, solid waste, noise control, safety, textiles, materials, design, computers, high technology. Offers aid in arranging interviews, annual reports, biographies, brochures/pamphlets, informational newsletters, library facilities, photos, placement on mailing lists, press kits, research assistance, statistics and telephone reference services. Publications include *Mechanical Engineering* and *CIME* (Computers in Mechanical Engineering). ASME is the fourth largest technical publisher in the world. **How to Contact:** Write, call or visit. Responds to most inquiries immediately. "Some publications involve a nominal charge. Writers should indicate intended use of material and specific media."

1225• AMERICAN SOCIETY OF PHOTOGRAMMETRY
210 Little Falls St., Falls Church VA 22046. (703)534-6617. Contact Person: Program Assistant. **Description:** Individuals engaged in photogrammetry and photointerpretation as applied to various fields such as archaeology, geographic exploration, meteorological observation, etc. **Services:** Provides historical, referral, technical and trade information on photogrammetry, remote sensing, aerial mapping. Offers brochures/pamphlets, library facilities, press kits and telephone reference services. Publications list available. **How to Contact:** Write or call. Responds to most inquiries within a week. **Tips:** "We either refer people to where they can get the info they need or allow them to use our library independently."

1226• ASTRONOMICAL SOCIETY OF THE PACIFIC
1290 24th Ave., San Francisco CA 94122. (415)661-8660. Contact Person: Executive Officer. **Description:** "We are an international nonprofit scientific and educational organization, founded in 1889, whose main aim is to increase public understanding of astronomy. The society is unique in bringing together, in its membership and through its programs, professional astronomers, educators, amateur astronomers, and thousands of interested laypeople." **Services:** Provides advisory, bibliographical, referral and technical information on "astronomy, astrophysics, space, debunking pseudo-science, e.g., astrology, UFOs." Offers aid in arranging interviews, brochures/pamphlets, library facilities, placement on mailing lists, press kits, research assistance, and telephone reference services. "We make available many of the best photographs from the space program and large telescopes. There is a fee to cover costs." Publications include 2 journals and various bibliographical materials; information packets; and catalog of educational books, slides, prints, posters, tapes. **How to Contact:** Write or call. Responds to most inquiries as soon as possible. "If we can send a ready information packet, answer a quick question on the phone, or make a referral, there is no charge. For longer searches, and materials which cost us money, we must charge a fee. Try to be considerate of the fact that we are a nonprofit organization with a limited staff." **Tips:** "The Astronomical Society of the Pacific acts as a clearinghouse for reliable, up-to-date astronomy information for the media, providing news items on recent developments and the names of astronomers who can do longer interviews." Recent information requests: "Where can I get non-technical information on black holes and current research in this area?"; "I am doing a story on astrology. Can you give me the scientific perspective?"

1227• ATOMIC INDUSTRIAL FORUM
7101 Wisconsin Ave., Bethesda MD 20814. (301)654-9260. Contact Person: Media Relations Manager. **Description:** Organization promoting the peaceful uses of nuclear energy. **Services:** Provides advisory, analytical, bibliographical, historical, interpretative, referral, technical and trade information covering nuclear electricity generation, nuclear medicine, food irradiation, industrial uses of nuclear energy, science. Offers aid in arranging interviews, brochures/pamphlets, informational newsletters, library facilities, photos, placement on mailing lists, press kits and statistics. Publications include *Press Info* (monthly newsletter). **How to Contact:** Write or call. Responds to most inquiries immediately. Writers are expected to "honor any agreement as to attribution of information received." **Tips:** Recent information request: "How many nuclear power plants are there in Europe at present, and how many are under construction there?"

1228• GENE BARTCZAK ASSOCIATES, INC.
Box E, N. Bellmore NY 11710. (516)781-6230. Contact Person: President. **Description:** "Management consultants for high-technology industries, specializing in informational services." **Services:** Provides advisory, historical, referral and technical information on aviation, robotics, manufacturing. Offers aid in arranging interviews, brochures/pamphlets, informational

newsletters, photos, press kits, research assistance and statistics. **How to Contact:** Write. Responds to most inquiries immediately. Charges for information retrieval; "cost is by quotation, depending on requirements." **Tips:** "Write first, outlining scope of information sought, purposes, and references." Recent information requests: Status of R&D and industrial applications in the field of robotics internationally; forecast of markets by turn of century.

1229• BASIC FOUR CORPORATION
c/o Simon Public Relations, Inc., 11661 San Vicente Blvd., #903, Los Angeles CA 90049. (213)820-2606. Contact Person: Vice President. **Description:** "A Management Assistance, Inc. (MAI) company, Basic Four Corp. manufactures and sells small business computers and communications systems around the world." **Services:** Provides advisory, historical, interpretative, technical and trade information on business economics, new products and technical data. Offers aid in arranging interviews, brochures/pamphlets, information searches, placement on mailing list, photos, press kits and "case history articles on how the systems are used." **How to Contact:** Write or call. Responds to most inquiries within a week.

1230• BATTELLE MEMORIAL INSTITUTE
505 King Ave., Columbus OH 43201. (614)424-4160. Contact Person: Coordinator, Corporate Communications. **Description:** "Independent research institute whose purpose is to benefit mankind by the advancement and utilization of science through technological innovation and educational activities. A pioneer in contract research, the institute has major research centers in four locations." **Services:** Provides analytical, bibliographical, interpretative, referral, technical and trade information embracing the physical, engineering, life, and social/behavioral sciences. Scientific activities extend from fundamental studies for the sake of new knowledge to applied programs directed toward new products and processes. This work is supported largely by industry and government on a contract basis. Offers aid in arranging interviews, annual reports, biographies, brochures/pamphlets, informational newsletters, photos, placement on mailing lists and press kits. Publications include *Battelle Today* (newsletter). **How to Contact:** Write or call. Responds to most inquiries immediately. "Much of Battelle's research is of a proprietary nature and cannot be disclosed."

1231• THE BOEING COMPANY
Box 3707, Seattle WA 98124. (206)655-6123. Contact Person: Corporate Public Relations Director. **Description:** "The Boeing Co. is involved with commercial air transports, missiles and space programs." **Services:** Provides advisory, historical and trade information. Offers aid in arranging interviews, annual reports, bibliographies, biographies, statistics, brochures/pamphlets, information searches, placement on mailing list, photos and press kits. **How to Contact:** Write. Responds to most inquiries within a week. Charges for some photos. **Tips:** "Do your homework before approaching us."

1232• BUNKER RAMO INFORMATION SYSTEMS
An Allied Company, 35 Nutmeg Dr., Trumbull CT 06609. (203)377-4141. Contact Person: Director of Public Relations. **Description:** "Bunker Ramo Information Systems is the pioneer supplier of online data processing and communications systems. The division designs, builds, sells, and services online terminal systems to banks, insurance companies and other financially oriented users; operates a nationwide system to supply stock brokers with market quotations and other investment information; and specializes in terminals and communications control for online, real-time applications. It does not supply main-frame computers." **Services:** Provides advisory, historical, referral and technical information on branch office automation (banks, brokers, insurance, etc.). Offers aid in arranging interviews, annual reports, biographies, brochures/pamphlets, placement on mailing list, newsletters, photos and press kits. Publications include brochures/pamphlets for online systems for commercial banking, thrift banking, insurance operations and the financial community (stock, bond, and commodity exchanges; over-the-counter markets; options; order processing; instant news retrieval; ticker displays). **How to Contact:** Write or call. Responds to most inquiries within a week. Copy review if controversial. **Tips:** Recent information request: Photos and information on end user experiences.

1233• CENTER FOR SCIENCE IN THE PUBLIC INTEREST
1755 S St. NW, Washington DC 20009. (202)332-9110. Contact Person: Deputy to Director. **Description:** "The center provides information to consumers on nutrition and health and works for

progressive health policies by government and industry." **Services:** Provides analytical and interpretative information on nutrition, health and environmental toxins. Offers annual reports, brochures/pamphlets and informational newsletters. Publications include *Nutrition Action* magazines; books on cancer, diet and heart disease. **How to Contact:** Write. Responds to most inquiries within a month. Charges for publications. "All materials are copyrighted. Write for brochure."

1234• CONTROL DATA CORPORATION
Box O, HQNIIY, Minneapolis MN 55440. Contact: Public Relations Department. **Description:** Control Data Corp. is engaged in the sale and manufacture of computers, peripheral products information and financial services. **Services:** Provides trade information "only on the activities of Control Data Corp. and its products, including social commentary." Offers aid in arranging interviews, annual reports, biographies, brochures/pamphlets, photos, and press kits. **How to Contact:** Write. Responds to most inquiries within a week. "We prefer to work with writers who have assignments." **Tips:** "Please don't send surveys or expect our publicists to write stories for you. We do not have general information on 'the way a computer works' and receive too many requests of this kind." Recent information requests: "Send me information about your supercomputers."; "What is Control Data's business strategy?"

1235• DIVIDENDS FROM SPACE
1401 Mission Hts. Rd., De Pere WI 54115. (414)337-0847. Contact Person: Chairman. **Description:** "Our purpose is to illustrate the benefits that have come to mankind through space exploration, and to look at possibilities for the future. This is done through publications, a speakers bureau and by conferring honors upon those actively promoting space explorations." **Services:** Provides advisory and technical information on space exploration benefits. Offers brochures/pamphlets and newsletter. Publications available. **How to Contact:** Write or call. Responds to most inquiries within a month. Charges printing costs, plus postage (50¢-$1.50). **Tips:** "Written requests work better." Recent information request: Inquiry on past Mars explorations.

1236• THE DOW CHEMICAL COMPANY
2030 Dow Center, Midland MI 48640. (517)636-3912. Contact Person: Public Relations Director. **Description:** Manufacturer of chemicals, pharmaceuticals, plastics and agricultural products. **Services:** Offers aid in arranging interviews, annual reports, statistics, brochures/pamphlets, information searches, placement on mailing list, newsletter, photos and press kits. Publications include an extensive library of product literature. **How to Contact:** Write. Responds to most inquiries immediately. "When calling, dial the general information number above and explain your specific area of interest. Permission must be secured to release some materials to writers."

1237• E. I. DUPONT DE NEMOURS AND COMPANY
1007 Market St., Wilmington DE 19898. (302)774-2771. Contact Person: National and Financial Press Representative. **Description:** "We are a manufacturer of chemicals and allied products and an energy and natural resources company." **Services:** Offers aid in arranging interviews, annual reports, bibliographies, brochures/pamphlets, statistics, information searches, placement on mailing list and photos. Publications available. **How to Contact:** Write. Responds to most inquiries immediately. **Tips:** Recent information requests: "Typically, writers are looking for historical material about the company."

1238• EDISON ELECTRIC INSTITUTE
1111 19th St. NW, Washington DC 20036. (202)862-3837. Contact Person: Media Coordinator or Media Representative. **Description:** "Edison Electric Institute (EEI) is the association of America's investor-owned electric utility companies. Organized in 1933 and incorporated in 1970, EEI provides a principal forum where electric utility people exchange information on developments in their business, and maintains a liaison between the industry and the federal government. Its officers act as spokesmen for investor-owned electric utility companies on subjects of national interest. EEI ascertains factual information, data and statistics relating to the electric industry, and makes them available to member companies, the public and government representatives." **Services:** Provides referral, technical and trade information on energy and the electric utility industry. Offers aid in arranging interviews, statistics, brochures/pamphlets, information searches, placement on mailing list, photos, press kits, and access to the research

library. Publications include *Coal; Nuclear Power;* and *Emerging Energy Technologies.* **How to Contact:** Write, call or visit. Responds to most inquiries within a week. The library is accessible by appointment only. Charges for some publications. **Tips:** "Give us ample response time." Recent information requests: "How many nuclear plants are licensed?"; "What is the financial health of the utility industry?"

1239• EDUCATIONAL FOUNDATION FOR NUCLEAR SCIENCE
5801 S. Kenwood Ave., Chicago IL 60637. (312)363-5225. Contact Person: General Manager. **Description:** The foundation seeks "to develop informed opinion among scientists and to inform the general public on issues of science and public policy, in particular the implication of nuclear energy." **Services:** Provides analytical and historical information on science and public policy issues; nuclear weapons and war, arms control, disarmament, energy, food and resources, international relations, science and government secrecy, technology transfer, technology transfer to developing nations, human rights. Offers aid in arranging interviews and press kits. Publications include *The Bulletin of the Atomic Scientist.* **How to Contact:** Write or call. Responds to most inquiries within a week. Charges for *Bulletin.* **Tips:** Recent information request: History of the early scientists' movement for control of nuclear energy.

1240• ELECTRONIC INDUSTRIES ASSOCIATION
2001 Eye St. NW, Washington DC 20006. (202)457-4900. Contact Person: Vice President for Public Affairs. **Description:** The Electronic Industries Association is the full service national trade organization representing the entire spectrum of companies involved in the manufacture or distribution of electronic components, parts, systems and equipment for communications, industrial, government and consumer-end uses. **Services:** Provides advisory, analytical, bibliographical, historical, referral, technical and trade information on market growth and industry trends, government activities in terms of federal and state legislation and regulations, as well as consumer education and career guidance. Offers annual reports, biographies, brochures/pamphlets, photos, press kits and statistics. Publications index available free on request. Publications include *Trade Directory and Membership List; Audio Industry Consumer Study; DOD Electronics Market: Impact of the Administration; EIA Source Code and Date Code Book; Market Data Book;* various standards and regulations. **How to Contact:** Write or call. Responds to most inquiries within a week. Charges for some publications.

1241• ENGINEERING INFORMATION, INC.
345 E. 47th St., New York NY 10017. (212)705-7881. Contact Person: Communication Services Manager. **Description:** "Engineering Index, Inc. is a nonprofit organization recognized as the leading international publisher of engineering bibliographic information." **Services:** Provides information on civil, mechanical, electrical, petroleum and chemical engineering. Offers bibliographies, brochures/pamphlets and newsletter. **How to Contact:** Write or call. Responds to most inquiries within a week. "No information may be reproduced for resale." **Tips:** Recent information request: "What is the latest storage technology for nuclear waste?"

1242• ERIC CLEARINGHOUSE ON SCIENCE, MATHEMATICS AND ENVIRONMENTAL EDUCATION (SE)
1200 Chambers Rd., 3rd Floor, Columbus OH 43212. (614)422-6717. Contact Person: Professor, Science and Math Education. **Description:** "ERIC (Educational Resources Information Center) is a national information system which obtains and makes available hard-to-find, often unpublished information in all areas of education." Conducts searches on "all levels of science, mathematics and environmental education." **Services:** Provides advisory, analytical, bibliographical, historical, how-to, interpretative, referral, technical and trade information on science, mathematics and environmental education. Offers information searches, information packets, publications list, publications, consultant services, bulletins and newsletters. **How to Contact:** Write or call. "We will provide information of a general nature by phone, other services by written request." Responds to most inquiries within two weeks. Charges for searches, consulting vary, as do the charges for printed materials. **Tips:** "Our system provides access! We have both federal and local collections. Use our compilations. They are very cost effective compared to computers or other manual techniques." Recent information requests: Sources of information on the "crisis in science and math education," and "creationism vs. evolution."

1243• FUND FOR UFO RESEARCH, INC.
Box 277, Mt. Rainier MD 20712. (703)683-2786. Contact Person: Publicity
Director. **Description:** Nonprofit, scientific and educational organization which provides funds
for education and research into the phenomenon of unidentified flying objects (UFOs). "The
fund's basic goals are to seek public support and to channel money into worthwhile projects that
show promise of dispelling myths and/or acquiring reliable scientific information. No particular
theory is advocated; instead scientific data are sought that will help to evaluate current theories or
provide the basis for new ones." **Services:** Provides advisory, historical and referral information
on "all aspects of the UFO phenomenon—history, scientific research, and government secrecy."
Offers aid in arranging interviews, placement on mailing lists, press kits and research assistance.
Publications include a *Quarterly Report*; occasional news releases; interviews; and a compilation
of government documents recently released under the Freedom of Information Act regarding
UFOs. **How to Contact:** Write or call. Responds to most inquiries within a month. "We request
that our address be given so the public may contact us for more information." **Tips:** "Do a little
reading on the UFO subject before using our services." Recent information request: "What was
the latest sighting that is considered significant by your group?"

1244• HONEYWELL
200 Smith St., Waltham MA 02154. (617)895-6000, ext. 6529. Contact Person: Manager of
Public Relations. **Description:** "We manufacture and sell computers—minis, small, medium and
large, and office automation systems. The PR department disseminates information about these
activities." **Services:** Provides advisory, analytical, bibliographical, historical, referral,
technical and trade information on computers, office automation, company history, industry
trends and issues. Offers aid in arranging interviews, annual reports, biographies, statistics,
brochures/pamphlets, photos and press kits. "Dozens of brochures on Honeywell
products/services are available." **How to Contact:** "Send a formal request in writing. Be as clear
as possible when explaining why the information is needed and/or how it will be used." Responds
to most inquiries within a week. Stipulations for use of services: "Good taste and common
sense." **Tips:** "Don't ask 'shotgun' questions. Be specific enough to show the recipient of your
request that you know the territory." Recent information request: Purchase prices, lease prices and
maintenance prices for the typical Honeywell computer systems.

1245• INFORMATICS GENERAL CORPORATION
21031 Ventura Blvd., Woodland Hills CA 91364. (213)887-9040. Contact Person: Manager of
Marketing Communications. **Description:** Company providing software and computer services to
the information handling industry to help manage information overflow. **Services:** Provides
advisory, how-to, technical and trade information on computer software and services; applicability
to variety of vertical industries such as law, insurance or apparel. Offers aid in arranging interviews
or providing annual reports, biographies, brochures/pamphlets, informational newsletters, photos
and press kits. Publications include *Infostream*, newsletter on software and services field; speech
and article reprints. **How to Contact:** Write or call. Responds to most inquiries
immediately. **Tips:** "Call with a specific idea or a general thought. We'll send written material or
set up an interview with a company executive and help develop story line, if needed." Recent
information requests: "How is the recession affecting the computer industry?"; "Will software
ever reside on a silicon chip?"

1246• INTERNATIONAL BUSINESS MACHINES (IBM)
Old Orchard Rd., Armonk NY 10504. (914)765-1900. Contact: Information
Department. **Description:** "International Business Machine's (IBM) main activity is in the field
of information handling systems, equipment and services to help solve the increasingly complex
problems of business, government, science, space exploration, defense, education, medicine and
many other areas of human activity." **Services:** Offers such background materials as: annual
reports, biographies, brochures/pamphlets, photos and press kits. Publications include *IBM
Yesterday and Today*, a profile and history of the company. **How to Contact:** Write or call.

1247• INTERNATIONAL MICROWAVE POWER INSTITUTE (IMPI)
301 Maple Ave. W, Suite Tower 520, Vienna VA 22180. (703)281-1515. Contact Person:
Executive Vice President. **Description:** "International Microwave Power Institute (IMPI) is the
forum to foster the exchange of ideas in the science of microwave energy in the areas of domestic,
industrial, scientific and medical applications. Activities organized by IMPI are short courses,

workshops and annual symposium." **Services:** Provides bibliographical and referral information. Offers brochures/pamphlets and newsletter. Publications include *The Journal of Microwave Power*, (a quarterly, referred, scientific journal relating to microwave energy for noncommunication purposes) and *Microwave World* (bimonthly). **How to Contact:** Write. Responds to most inquiries within a month.

1248• INVENTORS CLUB OF AMERICA
121 Chestnut St., Box 3799, Springfield MA 01101. (413)737-0670. Contact Person: President-Chairman of the Board. **Description:** Individuals interested in problem solving and inventing; seeks to help the independent inventor in all phases of his work. **Services:** Provides advisory, analytical, how-to, referral, technical and trade information on all phases of inventing—patents, idea development, manufacturing, marketing, advertising, financial, business, invention sales exhibitions, lobbying, legal, evaluation, etc. Offers aid in arranging interviews, annual reports, brochures/pamphlets, computerized information searches, informational newsletters, library facilities, placement on mailing lists, press kits and research assistance. Publications include *Inventors News*. **How to Contact:** Write. Responds to most inquiries within a week. Charges "nominal fee for time and copies; minimum fee $10. We will not disclose any ideas that are not protected or give out membership information that is confidential." **Tips:** Recent information request: Background on our newest inventions and International Hall of Fame.

1249• LASER INSTITUTE OF AMERICA
5151 Monroe St., Toledo OH 43623. (419)882-8706. Contact Person: General Manager. **Description:** "The institute was organized to disseminate laser technology by local chapter activities, short courses, publications, conferences and support of student chapters at schools offering laser training." **Services:** Provides advisory, historical, interpretative, referral and technical information on laser technology. Offers aid in arranging interviews and brochures/pamphlets. Publications list available. **How to Contact:** Write or call. Responds to most inquiries within a week.

1250• LIBRARY OF CONGRESS, SCIENCE AND TECHNOLOGY DIVISION
10 First St. SE, Washington DC 20540. (202)287-5639. Contact Person: Chief. **Description:** "This division has primary responsibility for providing reference and bibliographic services and for recommending acquisitions in the broad areas of science and technology." **Services:** Provides bibliographical and referral information in all areas of science and technology, except for technical agriculture and clinical medicine. (The latter subjects are covered in the National Agricultural Library and the National Library of Medicine, respectively.) Offers brochures/pamphlets, computerized information searches, library facilities (3 million books, nearly 60,000 journals, 3 million technical reports) and telephone reference services. Publications include *LC Science Tracer Bullets*, "an informal series of literature guides designed to help a reader begin to locate published materials on a subject about which he or she has only a general knowledge. Included in the *Bullets* are subject headings for searching cards; books or computer catalogs; lists of basic texts, bibliographies, state-of-the-art reports, conference proceedings, government publications; a list of abstracting and indexing services; and names and addresses of organizations to contact for more information." **How to Contact:** Write, call or visit. Responds to most inquiries immediately. "Anyone may write to us. High school students must have a letter from their school principal to use the facilities of the library." **Tips:** "Submit inquiries in early stages of research to save time and to allow our staff to be as comprehensive as possible." Recent information request: "I plan to write a novel about a 'medicine man' living in Essex County, Massachusetts during the 18th century—a friend of Benjamin Franklin—where do I begin?"

1251• LICK OBSERVATORY
University of California, Santa Cruz CA 95064. (408)429-2513. Contact: Administrative Office. **Description:** Observatory. **Services:** Offers b&w $2^{1}/_{4}$x$2^{1}/_{4}$, 8x10 and 14x17 photos. Catalogs are 50¢ on written request. Information concerning color materials is contained in the catalog. **How to Contact:** Write. Responds to most inquiries within a week. "Users of astronomical photographs should make their selections from the standard list in the current catalog of astronomical photographs available as slides or prints from negatives obtained at Lick Observatory, since it is not possible to supply views of other objects or special sizes. Purchasers are

reminded that permission for use of Lick Observatory photographs for reproductions or commercial purposes must be obtained in writing from the director of the observatory."

1252• LOCKHEED MISSILES AND SPACE COMPANY
Box 504, Sunnyvale CA 94086. (408)742-5113. Contact Person: Public Relations Director. **Description:** "Lockheed is involved in aerospace development and manufacturing in the products, missiles, space and services division." **Services:** Offers aid in arranging interviews, annual reports, bibliographies, biographies, statistics, brochures/pamphlets, information searches, placement on mailing list, newsletter and press kits. **How to Contact:** Write or call. "Written requests are preferred—make an appointment to get into our plant." Responds to most inquiries within a week.

1253• METASCIENCE FOUNDATION
Box 32, Kingston RI 02881. Contact Person: Director. **Description:** Individuals interested in studying various subjects, such as consciousness, by use of scientific methods. **Services:** Provides analytical, bibliographical, historical, referral and technical information on consciousness, synchronicity, telepathy, precognition, psychokinesis, psychology, quantum physics of consciousness, graphology, UFOlogy and related topics. Offers biographies and library facilities. Publications include *Metascience Journal*. **How to Contact:** Write. Responds to most inquiries within a month. Charges for *Journal*. **Tips:** Recent information request: "Where is the Central Premonitions Registry?"

1254• MONSANTO COMPANY
1114 Avenue of the Americas, New York NY 10036. Contact Person: Eastern Public Relations Director. **Description:** "Monsanto is the 49th largest company in the US and the third largest chemical company." **Services:** Provides advisory, referral, technical and trade information on agriculture, business, economics, food, health/medicine, industry, new products, science and technical data. Offers aid in arranging interviews, annual reports, bibliographies, biographies, statistics, brochures/pamphlets, placement on mailing list, newsletter, photos and press kits. Publications include *Chemical Facts of Life*; *Chemical Facts of Life Bulletin*; and *Monsanto Public Affairs Bulletin*. **How to Contact:** Write or call. Responds to most inquiries immediately. **Tips:** Recent information request: "Is Monsanto engaged in DNA research in the agricultural area?"

1255• MORRISON PLANETARIUM
California Academy of Sciences, Golden Gate Park, San Francisco CA 94118. (415)221-5100, ext. 269. Contact Person: Director. **Description:** "Morrison Planetarium is part of the California Academy of Sciences, located in San Francisco's Golden Gate Park near the Japanese Tea Garden and the DeYoung Museum. Morrison Planetarium's unique Sky Theater consists of a 65-foot hemispherical dome which arcs above a comfortably appointed seating area. In the center stands the Academy Projector, designed and constructed at the California Academy of Sciences. This projector can depict the appearance of the sky as seen from the Earth, at any time—past, present or future. On the dome overhead can be seen the sun and moon, the five planets visible to the unaided eye, star clusters, nebulae and almost 4,000 stars. Special effects projectors and a new panorama system can take the viewer on a space voyage to Mars and Jupiter, enable one to land on the surface of an alien planet or vividly display such events as exploding stars, whirling galaxies and black holes." **Services:** Provides analytical, historical and interpretative information on astronomy and space sciences. Offers programs on astronomy. **How to Contact:** Write or call. Responds to most inquiries within a week. Admission charged for shows. **Tips:** "Give us plenty of notice; contact us during normal business hours. Don't plan to ask for specific information requiring more than 20 minutes to provide without arranging for us as independent consultants." Recent information request: "What time did the moon rise on December 8, 1982?"

1256• N.A.P. CONSUMER ELECTRONICS CORPORATION
Box 6950, Knoxville TN 37914. (615)521-4499. Contact Person: Public Affairs Director. **Description:** "We manufacture and market Magnavox, Odyssey, Philco and Sylvania brand consumer electronics products—color and b&w TVs, console and component stereo systems, video cassette recorders, videodisc players, video games, portable radios, and tape cassette players." **Services:** Provides advisory, historical, how-to, interpretative, referral, technical and trade information on consumer electronics. Offers aid in arranging interviews, brochures/pamphlets, and press kits. Publications include product brochures; product information

on technological advances; and information about the consumer electronics industry. **How to Contact:** Write. Responds to most inquiries within a week. **Tips:** Recent information request: "What was the first home video game system?"

1257• NATIONAL AERONAUTICS AND SPACE ADMINISTRATION
400 Maryland Ave. SW, Washington DC 20546. (202)755-8370. Contact: Public Information Branch. **Description:** Government agency responsible for civilian aerospace research and development. **Services:** Provides information on NASA programs and policies. Offers aid in arranging interviews, annual reports, biographies, statistics, brochures/pamphlets, placement on mailing list, photos and press kits with certain restrictions. Catalog of publications available. **How to Contact:** Write or call; response time varies according to the question asked. "Be specific in your request." **Tips:** Recent information request: "When is the next launch of the space shuttle?"

1258• NATIONAL AIR AND SPACE MUSEUM BRANCH LIBRARY
Washington DC 20560. (202)357-3133. Contact Person: Chief. **Description:** "The purpose of the library is to provide the research resources to support the programs and activities of the museum. These activities include collecting, restoring, documenting, and interpreting artifacts relating to aerospace through exhibition, publication and educational programs." **Services:** Provides advisory, bibliographical, historical and referral information covering the history of aviation; history of space sciences and exploration; flight technology; the aerospace industry; aerospace biography; rocketry; astronomy and earth and planetary science. Offers library facilities (and interlibrary loan), photos and research assistance. "Publications are available for use in the library." **How to Contact:** Write or visit. Responds to most inquiries within a month. Charges for photocopying. Give credit to the library for materials used. Some restrictions on use may have been established by donors. **Tips:** "Write to the library describing your research project. We will let you know the extent to which our collections will be useful and the amount of research assistance we can provide."

1259• NATIONAL BUREAU OF STANDARDS
Department of Commerce, Washington DC 20234. (301)921-3181. Contact Person: Chief, Media Liaison, Public Information Division. **Description:** "The National Bureau of Standards (NBS) is the nation's central laboratory for measurement and advanced physical science research. It develops and maintains the US system of physical, chemical and materials measurement, with the aid of centers devoted to absolute physical quantities, radiation research, chemical physics, analytical chemistry and materials science. The bureau provides services to industry and government, helps facilitate technological innovation, and operates centers dealing with applied mathematics, electronics and electrical engineering, chemical engineering, manufacturing engineering, building technology and fire research. NBS is organized into three major units: National Measurement Laboratory, National Engineering Laboratory and the Institute for Computer Sciences and Technology." **Services:** Provides analytical and technical information covering health/medicine (related to physical and measurement standards), industry, product information, science and technical data. Offers aid in arranging interviews, annual reports, bibliographies, biographies, brochures/pamphlets, information searches, placement on mailing list, photos and press kits. "Upon request, we will put writers on mailing list for news releases and *NBS Update*; writers should specify area of interest." Publications include general and technical press releases; special publications; technical notes; safety codes; handbooks; monographs and research reports. *NBS List of Publications* describes the bureau's publication program, including periodicals, nonperiodicals, NBS interagency reports, publications catalogs and many other items. **How to Contact:** Write. Responds to most inquiries immediately. "NBS scientists and engineers are happy to grant personal interviews. The courtesy of reviewing the writer's article for technical accuracy prior to publication is requested. NBS publications, reports and releases are in the public domain and may be used without restriction. We request credit to NBS when reprinting articles and similar items." **Tips:** Recent information requests: Questions on corrosion research; computer (federal information processing) standards; mechanical failure analysis; performance of building material.

1260• NATIONAL CENTER FOR STANDARDS AND CERTIFICATION INFORMATION
National Bureau of Standards, Washington DC 20234. (301)921-2587. Contact Person: Information Manager. **Description:** "NCSCI contributes to the NBS goal of strengthening and advancing the nation's science and technology by providing up-to-date information on standards

and certification programs. It works to meet the needs of government, industry, and the public for information on standards regulations, certification programs and related activities that affect trade and commerce." **Services:** Provides bibliographical, referral and trade information on standards, regulations, certification rules and programs, standards-related activities. Offers brochures/pamphlets, computerized information searches, library facilities and telephone reference services. **How to Contact:** Write or call. Responds to most inquiries within a week. **Tips:** Recent information requests: "What are the standards for electric toasters?"; "Have specifications for magnetic ink been established by a nationally recognized organization?"

1261• NATIONAL INVESTIGATIONS COMMITTEE ON UNIDENTIFIED FLYING OBJECTS
7970 Woodman Ave., # 103, Van Nuys CA 91402. (213)781-7704. Contact Person: President. **Description:** Individuals interested in UFO investigation. **Services:** Provides advisory, analytical, bibliographical, historical, interpretative and technical information on UFOs. Offers aid in arranging interviews, annual reports, brochures/pamphlets, informational newsletters, library facilities, photos and research assistance. Publications include *UFO Journal.* **How to Contact:** Write. Responds to most inquiries within a week. Charges for services. "Write for details."

1262• NATIONAL SCIENCE FOUNDATION
1800 G St. NW, Washington DC 20550. (202)632-5728. Contact Person: Public Information Officer. **Description:** "The foundation promotes the progress of science through the support of research and education in the sciences. Major emphasis is on basic research." **Services:** Provides referral and technical information on basic (and some applied) research in the sciences and engineering; research and development funding and participation in public and private sectors. Offers aid in arranging interviews, annual reports, bibliographies, statistics, brochures/pamphlets, placement on mailing list, newsletter and press kits. Publications available. **How to Contact:** Write or call. Responds to most inquiries within a week. **Tips:** "Be specific; the exact topic should be specified and the topic must be limited to the area of the National Science Foundation. Familiarity with science is helpful." Recent information requests: "Whom can I talk to about research in neuropeptides related to obesity?"; "How much R&D was done in the energy sciences between 1975-80?"; "Which universities get the most federal R&D money?"

1263• NATIONAL SOCIETY OF PROFESSIONAL ENGINEERS
2029 K St. NW, Washington DC 20006. (202)463-2300. Contact Person: Director of Public Relations. **Description:** Organization promoting the engineering profession and registration of engineers. **Services:** Provides referral and trade information covering subjects dealing with engineering science and technology. Offers aid in arranging interviews, annual reports, biographies, brochures/pamphlets, library facilities, placement on mailing lists, press kits and telephone reference services. Publications include *Professional Engineer Magazine*; *Engineering Times.* **How to Contact:** Call. Responds to most inquiries within a week. **Tips:** "Our membership is comprised of 80,000 licensed engineers in all technical branches of the engineering profession. A strong grassroots base provides information around the country."

1264• NATIONAL SPACE INSTITUTE
Suite 203W, 600 Maryland Ave. SW, Washington DC 20024. (202)484-1111. Contact Person: Executive Director. **Description:** The institute promotes all aspects of the space program—government, private, research, science, applications. **Services:** Provides advisory, analytical, bibliographical and referral information on space and astronomy. Offers aid in arranging interviews and telephone reference services. Publications include *Space World* magazine. **How to Contact:** Write or call. Responds to most inquiries within a week. Charges for publications. **Tips:** Recent information request: "What is the commercial sector doing in space?"

1265• NEW ALCHEMY INSTITUTE
237 Hatchville Rd., Hatchville MA 02536. (617)563-2265. Contact Person: Publications Coordinator. **Description:** Organization seeking "to research and demonstrate alternative strategies for energy design and organic food production in colder climates." **Services:** Provides how-to, interpretative, educational and technical information on agriculture, aquaculture, wind power design, solar design, horticulture, computer modeling, tree crops and science for application. Offers annual reports, brochures/pamphlets, informational newsletters, library

facilities, photos and placement on mailing lists. Publications include *New Alchemy Journal* (annual); *Village as a Solar Ecology*; *Water Pumping Windmill Book*; *Tomorrow is Our Permanent Address*; *The Book of the New Alchemists*; *The Back Yard Fish Farming Book*. **How to Contact:** Write. Responds to most inquiries within a month. **Tips:** "We welcome all researchers and writers who are interested in our work. Visit our demonstration site in person." Recent information request: "What makes your research different from any other organization in the country?"

1266• PARAPSYCHOLOGY FOUNDATION, INC.
228 E. 71st St., New York NY 10021. (212)628-1550. Contact Person: Associate Editor. **Description:** "The Parapsychology Foundation was established in 1951 to encourage and support impartial scientific inquiry into the psychical aspects of human behavior. The foundation observes objectively the many research and theoretical studies of parapsychology, and offers assistance to scientists and universities engaged in the interdisciplinary approach to a better understanding of telepathy, clairvoyance, precognition, psychokinesis and other psychic phenomena." **Services:** Provides information on parapsychology and various psychic concerns. Offers annual reports, brochures/pamphlets, informational newsletters, library facilities and research assistance. Publications include *Parapsychology Review*; *International Conference Proceedings*; *Monograph Series*. **How to Contact:** Write. Responds to most inquiries within a month. **Tips:** "The Eileen J. Garrett Library of the Parapsychology Foundation is open to all students and others pursuing studies in parapsychology. The library also serves as an information center for all who seek bibliographical data about publications in the field. No materials may be borrowed." Library is open Mon.-Fri. 9:30-4:30.

1267• QABEL FOUNDATION, INC.
Box 69, Santa Cruz CA 95063. Contact Person: President. **Description:** Nonprofit corporation which "conducts research and disseminates educational materials in the public interest concerning the optimization of resources. Research and educational activities are carried out through four study groups: Biological Resources, Energy Resources, Military Affairs, Economic Systems." **Services:** Provides advisory, analytical, bibliographical, historical, interpretative, referral, technical and trade information on weapon systems; public knowledge of military affairs; Freedom of Information Act use; energy information (including toll-free numbers); photovoltaic energy systems; arid lands plants (economic botany); male contraceptives; transnational corporations. Offers aid in arranging interviews, biographies, brochures/pamphlets, clipping services, informational newsletters, library facilities, photos, placement on mailing lists, press kits, research assistance and statistics. Publications include *Qabel Foundation Resources Letter* (semiannual); various bibliographies and information listings. **How to Contact:** Write. "We may arrange telephone or in-person appointments by mail." Responds to most inquiries within a week. Charges for publications. "Although the *Resources Letter* is copyrighted, we permit unlimited excerpting or reprinting without permission, provided the source and author (if bylined) is credited, and a copy of such use is provided to the foundation." **Tips:** Recent information requests: "What potential exists for commercialization of the buffalo gourd (Cucurbita foetidissima)?"; "What are the names (addresses, phone numbers) of manufacturers of photovoltaic cells?"

1268• ROCKWELL INTERNATIONAL CORPORATION
600 Grant St., Pittsburgh PA 15219. (412)565-7177. Contact Person: Manager, News Bureau. **Description:** "Rockwell International Corporation is a major international corporation applying advanced technology to a wide range of products." **Services:** Provides advisory, bibliographical, historical, interpretative, referral, technical and trade information on automotive, aerospace, electronics, general industries and energy. Offers aid in arranging interviews, annual reports, bibliographies, biographies, statistics, brochures/pamphlets, information searches, placement on mailing list, photos and press kits. **How to Contact:** Write or call. Responds to most inquiries immediately. **Tips:** "Be specific in your questions." Recent information request: Interview on space shuttle.

1269• SCIENTISTS' INSTITUTE FOR PUBLIC INFORMATION (SIPI)
Media Resource Service (MRS), 355 Lexington Ave., New York NY 10017. (212)661-9110. Contact Person: Associate Director, MRS. **Description:** Organization seeking to make information on science/technology and science policy both available and understandable to the public and various interest groups, particularly the media and government. **Services:** Provides

referral information on science, technology, science policy, medicine. Offers aid in arranging interviews, informational newsletters and placement on mailing lists. Publications include *SIPIscope* (bimonthly newsletter). **How to Contact:** Write or call (preferred). Responds to most inquiries within a week or "according to journalists' deadlines. Writers should have stories committed for publication when they call the Media Resource Service." **Tips:** "Our intent is to refer writers to experts in science and technology who faithfully represent various legitimate perspectives on the issues at hand." Recent information requests: "Who can comment on NAS study on cancer and diet, as well as on nutritional guidelines as a result of that study?"; "Who knows about ocean mineral exploration and development?"

1270• SOCIETY FOR COMPUTER APPLICATIONS IN ENGINEERING, PLANNING AND ARCHITECTURE, INC. (CEPA)
358 Hungerford Dr., Rockville MD 20850. (301)762-6070. Contact Person: Executive Director. **Description:** Organization working to further the effective application of computers in engineering, planning and architecture; to provide an exchange of information; and a means for exchange and cooperative development of computer programs and systems. **Services:** Provides technical information. Offers brochures/pamphlets and informational newsletters. Publications include quarterly newsletter; conference proceedings; special reports. Publications list available. **How to Contact:** Write. Responds to most inquiries within a week. The only restrictions that exist for nonmembers who contact us are the "limitations of office staff and time, etc." **Tips:** Recent information request: "I would like all the information you can give me on the use of microcomputers in engineering and architecture."

1271• SOCIETY FOR THE ENCOURAGEMENT OF RESEARCH AND INVENTION
100 Summit Ave., Box 412, Summit NJ 07901. (201)273-1088. Contact Person: Executive Director. **Description:** Independent organization devoted exclusively to the advancement of research and invention. "We recognize persons of diverse activities, of all ages, at different times in their lives, who have demonstrated significant achievements. We encourage researchers and scientists of all disciplines and in all fields and honor those who have particularly distinguished themselves by their activities and contributions furthering the evolution and growth of research, invention and innovation. We foster international understanding, relationships and the interchange of ideas." **Services:** Provides advisory, how-to, referral and technical information on any field of science and technology. Offers aid in arranging interviews, brochures/pamphlets, informational newsletters and library facilities. Publications include quarterly bulletin. **How to Contact:** Write or call. Responds to most inquiries within a week.

1272• SOCIETY FOR THE INVESTIGATION OF RECURRING EVENTS
157 Bellevue Ave., Summit NJ 07901. (201)277-4247. Contact Person: President. **Description:** A nonprofit, interdisciplinary, educational group "designed as a forum to promote the study and discussion, both pro and con, of recurring events, rhythms and cycles." S.I.R.E members are interested in the laws which account for patterns of recurrence—in economic, social, political and cultural arenas. **Services:** Offers informational newsletters. Publications include monthly letters to members. Cassette transcripts of meetings/speeches. Sample cassettes: *The Body Clock Diet and Other Personal Body Rhythms*; *The Geometry of Prediction*; *Public News as a Source for Investment Ideas*; *Forecasting History with Technical Analysis*. List of topics available. **How to Contact:** Write. Charges for membership and cassettes.

1273• SPERRY CORPORATION
1290 Avenue of the Americas, New York NY 10104. (212)484-4445. Contact Person: Director of Corporate Public Relations. **Description:** "Sperry is a worldwide enterprise, with almost $6 billion in revenues, and major interests in information processing systems and services, defense and aerospace systems, and machinery products, including farm equipment." **Services:** Provides historical (of company business), referral, technical and trade information. Offers aid in arranging interviews, annual reports, brochures/pamphlets, placement on mailing list, statistics, photos and press kits. **How to Contact:** Write or call. When time permits, written requests are preferred. Responds to most inquiries within a week. **Tips:** Recent information request: Application of a computer system to a particular industry segment.

1274• SPIRIT OF THE FUTURE CREATIVE INSTITUTE
Box 40296, 3027 22nd St., Suite 3B, San Francisco CA 94110. (415)821-7800. Contact Person:

Founder. **Description:** "We are in association with innovators, pioneers, inventors, futurist consultants, investigative researchers, research and development groups in private enterprise, educators, media persons, future consumers and creative, self-reliant applied thinkers engaging in a network of exchange of ideas and information." **Services:** Provides advisory forecasts, analytical, historical, how-to, referral, technical and trade information on future science/space technology and time travel; free enterprise; vital growth industries (renewable energy, transportation, housing, food); economics; conservation and recycling; survival and self-reliance planning; learning-improvement systems; natural health and therapy; historical re-discoveries; mysterious phenomena. Offers aid in arranging interviews, brochures/pamphlets, clipping services, computerized information searches, informational newsletters, placement on mailing lists, press kits, research assistance, statistics and telephone reference services. **How to Contact:** Write. Responds to most inquiries within a week. Charges for services. Enclose SASE and business card with information requests. **Tips:** "All requests should include a clear statement of purpose, objectives, subject areas and priorities; also, previously researched sources of information."

1275• 3M COMPANY
Public Relations Information Center, 3M Center, 225-5N, St. Paul MN 55144. Contact Person: Supervisor, Information Resources. **Description:** "We have information on some 50 major product lines in 17 basic technologies; also selected information on such 'social' issues as energy conservation, pollution control, the role of multinational corporations, etc." **Services:** Provides bibliographical, historical, referral and trade information on 3M history and products. Offers aid in arranging interviews, annual reports, biographies, brochures/pamphlets, placement on mailing list, newsletter, photos, press kits, speech reprints and position papers. Publications available. **How to Contact:** Write or call. Responds to most inquiries within a week. Charges for some publications, copying, etc. Might also bill for staff time on major searches. "Confidential or proprietary information will not be released but we may request 'copy check' on the use of some information." **Tips:** "Questions should be reasonably specific. Staff limitations require that initial response will usually be with existing 3M materials. The PR information center does not offer individual research or reference services. Indicate intended use of material and specific media, if possible." Recent information request: Detailed background on the history of "Scotch" brand tape.

1276• UNITED STATES METRIC ASSOCIATION
10245 Andasol Ave., Northridge CA 91325. (213)363-5606. Contact Person: President. **Description:** The association serves as a source for metric information and promotes both the *correct* usage of the metric system in the United States and the changeover to the metric system. **Services:** Provides historical, how-to, referral, technical and trade information on "the status of metric conversion in the US; correct metric units and symbols usage; where to find correct metric texts (as most off-the shelf texts contain glaring errors)." Offers aid in arranging interviews, brochures/pamphlets and informational newsletters. Publications include *USMA Newsletter*; and metric training aids; "we also have a few FREE handout sheets in return for requester's furnishing SASE." **How to Contact:** Write. Responds to most inquiries within a week. "USMA members ($10/yr.) get priority on answers. Nonmember queries are answered as time permits. All work is done by donated services and at times (where an answer has to be researched) there may be some delay in replying." **Tips:** "Too many books on the subject of the metric system contain inaccurate data or even give completely wrong rules for use of metric units and symbols (short forms). It is wise to ensure your data is correct and not based upon some author's imagination, or you will add to the nonfactual materials now rampant on the subject. USMA has what is probably the largest collection of metric system information in existence, and is willing to share it with anyone requiring the data. All that we ask is credit for our help in published materials where our help has been used." Recent information requests: "What is the metric unit that replaces the 'shot' in a shot-glass?''; "Is there a metric wrench that will handle a ¼-inch fastener?"

1277• UNITED STATES SPACE EDUCATION ASSOCIATION
746 Turnpike Rd., Elizabethtown PA 17022. (717)367-3265 after 12 p.m. (eastern time). Contact Person: International President. **Description:** "A worldwide organization dedicated to promoting the peaceful exploration of outer space. As a scientific, educational, and news-gathering organization, we seek to achieve goals through both professionals and non-professionals." **Services:** Provides advisory, analytical, bibliographical, historical, interpretative, referral, technical and trade information on space sciences, alternative energy

technologies, future studies and technologies and the historical aspects of space exploration. Offers aid in arranging interviews, brochures/pamphlets, informational newsletters, library and museum facilities, photos, press kits, research assistance and statistics. Publications include *Space Age Times* (bimonthly publication); *Update* (monthly publication). **How to Contact:** Write or call. Responds to most inquiries within a week. "Except for copying large documents, there are usually no charges for service of the USSEA Media Center. Appropriate credit must be given to the USSEA. A copy of any publication including information supplied by the USSEA is appreciated. Our mailing list is restricted and will not be made available. It will greatly assist us in processing your request for information if the question can be made as specific as possible. This will allow us to process your request more quickly by avoiding unnecessary research. We enjoy working with all media with space-related questions. Priority is given to USSEA members." **Tips:** "The USSEA is the only major space organization which maintains a Media Center and news bureau to serve the needs of the news media. We also have a full-time staff of reporters and photographers who are experienced in the space field and who can provide behind-the-scene insights unavailable through other space organizations. Explore the possibilities of using a local news angle in compiling your story. Are there local people or companies directly involved in the space field who can supply information or be the focus of a news story?" Recent information requests: "What sort of impact will result in the next decade as a direct result of the Space Shuttle?"; "What is a likely long-range scenario for space exploration?"

1278• UNIVERSITY OF TENNESSEE SPACE INSTITUTE (UTSI)
AEDC, Access Highway, Woods Reservoir, Tullahoma TN 37388. (615)455-0631. **Description:** "Graduate educational institution offering degrees in aerospace sciences, with heavy emphasis on research. The University of Tenneseee Space Institute (UTSI) is a leader in research activities, particularly the MHD process, the production of electricity directly from burning coal. MHD will lead to the production of about 50 percent of the possible energy in coal, versus the present 35 percent. Other research activities include high speed aerodynamics, low speed aerodynamics, modeling, remote sensing, weather phenomena, composite materials, jet propulsion, lasers, gas diagnostics, flight mechanics, aviation systems and mathematics computations. We would cooperate wtih writers in these fields." **Services:** Offers aid in arranging interviews and placement on mailing list. **How to Contact:** Write or call. Responds to most inquiries within a week. "Permission to release some information may be required."

SECTION·TWENTY-FOUR

SOCIETY AND CULTURE

Culture itself is neither education nor law-making: it is an atmosphere and a heritage.
—*H.L. Mencken*

The Society and Culture category identifies resources which reflect culture and provide information in the area of social science. Included are organizations dealing with demography, anthropology, sexuality, social process and behavior, philanthropy, the humanities, human rights and reflections of the times.

Information sources in the area of ethnic culture are listed in the Ethnic/Regional Heritage section. Additional references to long-ago societies and their respective cultures may be found in the History section.

Bibliography

The Annual Obituary. New York: St. Martin's Press. (Detailed information on individuals who have died in the past year)

Current Biography Yearbooks.1940 to date. New York: H.W. Wilson Co.

Gallup, George H., ed. *Gallup Poll: Public Opinion*. Annual. Wilmington, DE: Scholarly Resources, Inc.

Humanities Index, 1974 to date, quarterly. New York: H.W. Wilson Co.

Inge, M. Thomas, ed. *Handbook of American Popular Culture*. 3 vols. Westport, CT: Greenwood Press, 1978.

Marquis Who's Who Publications Index to All Books. Chicago: Marquis Publications, 1978.

Martin, Judith. *Miss Manner's Guide to Excruciatingly Correct Behavior*. New York: Atheneum, 1982.

Pick, Christopher, ed. *What's What in the 1980s*. Vol 1; others to follow. Europa Publications. Detroit: Dist. by Gale Research Co., 1982.

Post, Elizabeth. *The New Emily Post's Etiquette*. New York: Funk & Wagnall's Publishing Co., 1975.

Reading, Hugo F., ed. *A Dictionary of the Social Sciences*. Boston: Routledge & Kegan Paul, Ltd., 1977.

Robert, H.M., ed. *Robert's Rules of Order*. rev. ed. Old Tappan, NJ: Revell, 1980.

Saur, K.G., ed. *Museums of the World*. 3d ed. Detroit: Dist. by Gale Research Co., 1981.

Social Science Index. 1974 to date, quarterly. New York: H.W. Wilson Co.

US Bureau of the Census. *County and City Data Book*. Irregular. Washington DC: Government Printing Office, 1977. (A regional statistical abstract)

US Bureau of the Census. *Statistical Abstract of the United States*. Annual. Washington DC: Government Printing Office. (Current and comparative statistics on almost any aspect of American life)

White, Carl M. et. al., eds. *Sources of Information in the Social Sciences*. 2d ed. Chicago: American Library Association, 1973.

Winick, Charles. *Dictionary of Anthropology*. Totowa, NJ: Littlefield, 1977.

1279• AMERICAN ANTHROPOLOGICAL ASSOCIATION
1703 New Hampshire Ave. NW, Washington DC 20009. (202)232-8800. Contact Person: Director of Programs. **Description:** The association promotes anthropology and facilitates communication between anthropologists. **Services:** Provides information on the current status of the profession and referrals to anthropologists currently conducting research on any specified topics. Offers brochures/pamphlets and statistics. Publications include quarterly journal and monthly newsletter. **How to Contact:** Write or call. Make appointment in advance of visit. Responds to most inquiries within a week.

1280• AMERICAN ASSOCIATION OF MUSEUMS
1055 Thomas Jefferson St. NW, Washington DC 20007. (202)338-5300. Contact Person:

Program Assistant. **Description:** The association "promotes the welfare of museums and of museum professionals. Membership includes museums of all sizes and disciplines; zoos, botanical gardens, aquariums, planetariums. Activities include accreditation program, legislative program, publications, annual meeting." **Services:** Provides historical, interpretative, referral and technical information concerning the museum field, and related areas where available. Offers brochures/pamphlets and informational newsletters. Publications include *Official Museum Directory* (provides basic descriptive information on over 5,500 museums); *Museum News* (bimonthly magazine); *Aviso* (monthly newsletter); *AAM/ICOM Newsletter* (quarterly review of international programs); *Trustee Newsletter.* **How to Contact:** Write or call. Responds to most inquiries immediately. **Tips:** "We do not give out budget information about specific museums." Recent information request: "How have museums been affected by cuts in federal funding?"

1281• AMERICAN ENTERPRISE INSTITUTE FOR PUBLIC POLICY RESEARCH
1150 17th St. NW, Suite 1200, Washington DC 20036. (202)862-5800. Contact Person: Public Relations Officer. **Description:** Research organization dealing in public policy issues related to social and political processes, foreign policy, legal policy, economics, government regulations, etc. **Services:** Provides advisory, analytical, bibliographical, historical, how-to, interpretative, referral, technical and trade information on studies conducted. Offers aid in arranging interviews, annual reports, biographies, brochures/pamphlets, clipping services, computerized information searches, informational newsletters, library facilities, photos, placement on mailing lists, press kits, research assistance and statistics. Catalog of publications available. **How to Contact:** Write or call. Responds to most inquiries within a month.

1282• ANTHROPOLOGY FILM CENTER FOUNDATION
Box 493, Santa Fe NM 87501. (505)983-4127. Contact Person: Director. **Description:** Educational foundation furthering "scholarship, research and practice in the use of visual-aural media to record and communicate anthropological and ethnographic information and perform film production in anthropology and other related educational and scientific pursuits." **Services:** Provides bibliographical, historical, referral, technical and trade information on film, anthropology, and cultural communication. "Our library includes unpublished manuscript material, proceedings of the PIEF (Program in Ethnographic Film) and SAVICOM (Society for the Anthropology of Visual Communications) associations and history of the prominent individuals in native American filmmaking." Offers aid in arranging interviews, brochures/pamphlets, informational newsletters, library facilities and telephone reference services. Publications include *SAVICOM* newsletter; *Studies in Visual Communication*; *A Filmography for American Indian Education.* **How to Contact:** Call. Responds to most inquiries within a week. Charges for telephone reference ($35/hour with a 1 hour minimum); written reference material ($150 minimum); publications, mailing lists, copying costs and postage. "We prefer that freelance writers tell us where stories are going to be published. Our manuscript collection is restricted and requires AFCF approval for reporters or researchers to look at documents." **Tips:** "We appreciate specific questions after some groundwork has been done. Our staff has been involved in visual anthropology since the '50s and could offer leads and stories on both the historical and present situations." Recent information requests: "How can one enter ethnographic film work?"; "How can it be pursued as an avocational activity?"; "What are the important future directions of the field?"; "What is the relationship between filming and ethnographic fieldwork?"

1283• ANTHROPOLOGY RESOURCE CENTER
37 Temple Place, Room 521, Boston MA 02111. (617)426-9286. Contact Person: Director. **Description:** A public interest anthropology organization concerned with the rights of indigenous people in North and South America. **Services:** Provides analytical and interpretative information on anthropology and native North and South Americans. Offers brochures/pamphlets, clipping services, informational newsletters, library facilities, photos (some), placement on mailing lists, press kits (some) and research assistance (some). Publications include *ARC Newsletter* (quarterly); periodic special reports. **How to Contact:** Write. Responds to most inquiries within a week-10 days. Charges for publications and library search services. **Tips:** Recent information request: Material on the indigenous societies of Brazil.

1284• AQUARIAN RESEARCH FOUNDATION
5620 Morton St., Philadelphia PA 19144. (215)849-1259, 849-3237. Contact Person: Director. **Description:** The foundation conducts "research aimed at finding humanistic

alternatives to competitive society." **Services:** Provides information on natural birth control, new sciences, stopping the arms race, alternative lifestyles—especially alternative communities. Offers brochures/pamphlets and newsletters. Publications include *The Natural Birth Control Book*; *Unpopular Science*; and a newsletter published monthly in *Green Revolution Magazine*. **How to Contact:** Write or call; prefers calls or visits if a lot of information is needed. **Tips:** Recent information request: "What's the connection between the arms race and birth control?"

1285• ASSOCIATION FOR THE STUDY OF MAN-ENVIRONMENT RELATIONS, INC.
Box 57, Orangeburg NY 10692. (914)634-8221. Contact Person: President or Contributions Editor. **Description:** Nonprofit organization interested in man's interaction with his environment. Works to further the understanding of the role of the environment on human biological/sociological/psychological function, as well as the interface of individual/societal/institutional forces on the environment. **Services:** Provides advisory, historical, interpretive, and referral information. Publications include *Man-Environment Systems* (bimonthly journal); *International Directory of Behavior and Design Research*; various annotated bibliographies. Publications list available. **How to Contact:** Write or call.

1286• THE ASSOCIATION OF INTERPRETIVE NATURALISTS, INC.
6700 Needwood Rd., Derwood MD 20855. (301)948-8844. Contact Person: Executive Manager. **Description:** Nonprofit association fostering the advancement of education and development of skills in the art of interpreting the natural and cultural environment; supports the preservation of sites that have natural and historical value. Members maintain exhibits and programs at museums, zoos, schools, public and private institutions and other cultural environments. **Services:** Provides bibliographical, historical, how-to, interpretative, referral, technical and trade information on most aspects of natural and cultural resources. Offers biographies, brochures/pamphlets, computerized information searches, informational newsletters, placement on mailing lists and statistics. Publications include national newsletter (monthly); interpretive research bibliography; *Journal of Interpretation* (biannual). Publications list available. **How to Contact:** Write, call or visit. Responds to most inquiries immediately. Charges for membership and most publications.

1287• ATHENAEUM OF PHILADELPHIA
219 S. 6th St., Philadelphia PA 19106. (215)925-2688. Contact Person: Executive Director or Librarian. **Description:** "The Athenaeum is an independent research library founded in 1814 with a specialization in 19th century social and cultural history, especially architecture and decorative arts." **Services:** Offers bibliographies. Publications include books on Victorian culture. **How to Contact:** Write or visit. "Make an appointment by phone before coming in to do research." Responds to most inquiries immediately. Publications and price list available. "Ours is a rare book library with the usual restrictions. Researchers must complete reader application and have identification." **Tips:** Recent information request: "What colors for exterior decoration; what wallpaper and light fixtures are appropriate for a Victorian house?"

1288• BUREAU OF SOCIAL SCIENCE RESEARCH
1990 M St., Washington DC 20036. (202)223-4300. Contact Person: Research Associate. **Description:** Independent nonprofit organization engaged in research and analysis of social and public policy issues with particular emphasis on survey research; criminal justice; social science computing and computer networking; education; employment and training; aging, enhancing the capabilities of the disadvantaged; refugee adaptation; municipal governance and public opinion. **Services:** Conducts primary data collection through systematic sample surveys, secondary analyses of existing data, case studies, content analysis; provides analytical, biographical and technical information on crime statistics, victimization surveys and organizational studies of the police; survey methodology; conducts manpower and evaluation research; offers social science library with capability for online bibliographic searches; computing and data services which support statistical packages, online conferencing, computer graphics, data documentation and archiving. **How to Contact:** Write or call. **Tips:** "BSSR staff provide information and material as a courtesy to persons who share their research interests. They consider it a *professional* obligation to share freely information in their respective fields. Individual staff members are free to refuse information at their own discretion." Recent information request: "Why do the FBI's Uniform Crime Reports indicate

that crime is on the rise while the National Crime Survey indicates a stable crime rate over time? Is crime going up or down?''

1289• CENSUS BUREAU
Department of Commerce, Washington DC 20233. (301)763-4100. Contact Person: Chief, Customer Services Branch, Data User Services Division. **Description:** ''The Bureau of the Census is a general-purpose statistical agency whose primary function is to collect, process, compile and disseminate statistical data for the use of the general public and other government agencies. The Census Bureau occupies a unique place in the federal statistical system—it publishes more statistics than other federal statistical agencies do, covers a wider range of subjects, and serves a greater variety of needs. Through censuses and surveys, the Census Bureau collects data on population, housing, state and local governments, agriculture, construction, business, manufacturers, mineral industries, foreign trade, transportation and other subjects. Resulting statistics are available in printed reports, microform, and computer tape. Depending on the type of statistics, they are reported for city blocks, census tracts, ZIP code areas, cities, counties and various other geographic areas. The bureau also offers such related products and services as population estimates and projections, guides, maps, press releases, a monthly newsletter, statistical compendia, reports on survey methodology and training programs.'' **Services:** Provides analytical (statistical) information on a variety of areas relating to statistics for the United States and its constituent political areas. Statistics are included in population, housing, economics (retail trade, wholesale trade, manufacturing), agriculture and various current surveys such as on employment. Offers statistics, brochures/pamphlets and newsletter. ''A variety of pamphlets describing the statistical products and services of the Census Bureau are available.'' **How to Contact:** ''Write or call the Data User Services Division and indicate the types of statistical information needed. Relevant pamphlets and order forms will be sent. Responds to most inquiries within a week. We charge for statistical publications. We do not offer analytical services. For press releases and other news media services, write or call the public information office (301)763-4040. Statistical reports, reference publications, and statistical data on computer tape are sold by the Census Bureau or, in some cases, the Government Printing Office. Introductory materials, such as the pamphlets, and assistance in determining what relevant data are available are generally provided free of charge. The Census Bureau has user services specialists in its regional offices in the following cities: Atlanta, Boston, Charlotte, Chicago, Dallas, Denver, Detroit, Kansas City, Kansas, Los Angeles, New York, Philadelphia and Seattle. These specialists can assist users in locating data and obtaining publications. They also conduct training programs on census products and services.'' **Tips:** ''Contact libraries before calling us, to help determine which census resources are needed.'' Recent information request: ''What was the total population of the US in 1900 and how many people were aged 65 or older?''

1290• CENTER FOR RESPONSIVE PSYCHOLOGY
Brooklyn College, Brooklyn NY 11210. (212)780-5960. Contact Person: Manager. **Description:** ''We are an independent group of psychologists, students and legal professionals. We bring relevant social science information to the attention of the practitioner in the legal, judicial, academic and correctional fields. We endeavor to communicate recent research findings in clear, non-technical language in order to aid the practitioner in putting social science to work.'' **Services:** Provides advisory, analytical, bibliographical, historical, interpretative, referral, technical and trade information covering social psychology, law and related fields. Offers brochures/pamphlets, informational newsletters, placement on mailing lists, research assistance, statistics, telephone reference services, expert witnesses and other research-related services. Publications include *Social Action and the Law* (quarterly newsmagazine); relevant articles and reprints. **How to Contact:** Write, call or visit. Responds to most inquiries immediately. Charges for subscription and reprint services. **Tips:** ''Respect copyrights. Contact us; we will help in any way we can.''

1291• CENTER FOR THE STUDY OF HUMAN RIGHTS
Columbia University, 704 International Affairs Building, New York NY 10027. (212)280-2479. Contact Person: Administrative Assistant. **Description:** The center collects human rights research materials; develops human rights courses, seminars, conferences, publications. **Services:** Provides advisory, bibliographical and referral information on scholarly research; teaching and publications in human rights; information on human rights organizations. Sponsors residential fellowship program. Offers aid in arranging interviews, annual reports, brochures/pamphlets, informational newsletters, library facilities, placement on mailing lists, research assistance and

telephone reference services. Maintains "a library of human rights books, articles, magazines, and United Nations documents." Publications include classified human rights bibliography, newsletters, occasional papers and course curricula, conference proceedings. **How to Contact:** Write or call. Responds to most inquiries immediately. Charges for photocopying. "We are not a lending library."

1292• THE CIVIL SOCIETY
Box 6507, 2063 Pacheco St., Concord CA 94524. (415)682-4722. Contact Person: Chancellor (founding associate). **Description:** The society for advancing the art of civility and the art of cultural harmony. "This society is dedicated to helping create an atmosphere of cultural harmony by the practice of civility." **Services:** Provides advisory, analytical, bibliographical, historical, how-to and interpretative information on civility/manners/social customs in various societies. Offers commentaries. **How to Contact:** Write. Responds to most inquiries within a week. **Tips:** "Cross refer civility with morals (western and eastern); history and race relations (historical). We are in the process of building a bibliography. We will do anything in our power to help writers/researchers in our area of activity." Recent information request: "What causes incivility?"; "What can we do about it?"; "What are the benefits of civility?"

1293• ERIC CLEARINGHOUSE ON SOCIAL STUDIES/SOCIAL SCIENCE EDUCATION
Education and Demonstration Center, Social Science Education Consortium, 855 Broadway, Boulder CO 80302. (303)492-8434. Contact Person: Coordinator of User Services. **Description:** "ERIC (Educational Resources Information Center) is a national information system which obtains and makes available hard-to-find, often unpublished information in all areas of education." Conducts computer searches on "all levels of social studies and social science education." **Services:** Provides analytical, bibliographical, how-to, interpretative and referral information on social studies education. Offers bibliographies, information searches, placement on mailing list, newsletter and access to microfiche collection. Will refer researchers to other ERIC Clearinghouses or agencies if needed. Publications include publications list and information packets. **How to Contact:** Write, call or visit. Responds to most inquiries within a week. Charges $25 for computer search of up to 50 citations; each additional citation 10¢. "Writer may use materials on premises free of charge." **Tips:** "Be as specific as possible about the information you need." Recent information request: "What resources are available for teaching about global issues at the junior high school level?"

1294• THE FORD FOUNDATION
Office of Reports, 320 E. 43rd St., New York NY 10017. (212)573-5000. **Description:** "The Ford Foundation places a strong emphasis on the needs of people who suffer the brunt of economic, social, and cultural deprivation. It is equally concerned with the consequences of such deprivation for the larger society. In the United States, the foundation has a long-standing commitment to action on problems confronting blacks, Hispanics, native Americans, poor women, and other disadvantaged groups. Similarly, in the developing countries it focuses upon the most disadvantaged. Strategies to advance these commitments largely depend upon community self-help initiatives and link these local efforts to public and private resources in the greater society. The foundation's other interests span a range of domestic, international, and multinational issues, including the reduction of poverty and dependency, the quality of education, the vitality of cultural pursuits, world peace and interdependency, and the rights of individuals in free and closed societies." **Services:** Offers placement on mailing list and newsletter. Publications list available. **How to Contact:** Write.

1295• THE FOUNDATION CENTER
888 7th Ave., New York NY 10106. (212)975-1120. Contact Person: Director, Public Services. **Description:** "The Foundation Center is a national service organization which collects, analyzes and disseminates factual information about philanthropic foundations and their grants. It publishes a variety of reference publications which deal with foundations and their grants. It produces three computer data bases dealing with these topics. It also provides free library reference service to foundations, grant seekers and the general public in over 100 collections nationwide. It operates libraries in New York, Washington, Cleveland and San Francisco which offer special services to library users." **Services:** Provides private foundation information. Offers annual reports, bibliographies, biographies, statistics, brochures/pamphlets, information searches and placement on mailing list. Publications include *Foundation Directory*; *Grants Index*; *Directory of Grants to*

Individuals; *Foundation Center Source Book Profiles*; *National Data Book*; COMSEARCH printouts, *About Foundations*; *How to Find the Facts You Need to Get a Grant*; and several brochures on grant proposals. **How to Contact:** Write, call or visit. "Individuals must visit one of our collections. For information on the Foundation Center nearest you call (800)424-9836." Offers special service program for $250/year which includes telephone reference, copying and computer searches. **Tips:** Recent information request: "What organizations fund writers?"

1296• LOUIS HARRIS AND ASSOCIATES
630 Fifth Ave., New York NY 10111. (212)975-1600. Contact: Information Services. **Description:** Survey research firm conducting surveys in nearly every facet of society and culture. **Services:** Provides analytical and statistical information. Offers annual reports, informational newsletters, library facilities and statistics. Publications include various reports and surveys. **How to Contact:** "Facilities are not open to the public, but information requests may be submitted by mail or phone."

1297• THE HASTINGS CENTER
Institute of Society, Ethics and the Life Sciences, 360 Broadway, Hastings-on-Hudson NY 10706. (914)478-0500. Contact Person: Director, Public Relations. **Description:** The center conducts research and analysis on complex ethical issues in medicine and the life sciences, in the social and behavioral sciences, and in professional ethics. **Services:** Provides advisory, analytical, interpretative and referral information on ethical issues on death and dying; health policy; scarce medical resources; research on human subjects; behavioral studies; occupational health; the social sciences and public policy; legislative ethics; applied and professional ethics. Offers library facilities and research assistance. Publications include *The Hastings Center Report* (by subscription); *IRB: A Review of Human Subjects Research* (by subscription); various publications and readings. **How to Contact:** Write or call. Responds to most inquiries within a week. Charges for publications. "Library materials must be used on the premises." **Tips:** Recent information request: Questions on ethical decisions involved in medical care.

1298• HUMAN RIGHTS INTERNET
1502 Ogden St. NW, Washington DC 20010. (202)462-4320. Contact Person: Executive Director. **Description:** "We serve as a communications network and clearinghouse on international human rights information; our purposes are to stimulate communication and coordination among scholars, activists and policy-makers; to disseminate information about human rights through publications and to support teaching and research." **Services:** Provides advisory, bibliographical, interpretative and referral information on international human rights, minority rights, censorship, refugees, prisoners, children's rights, women's rights, development and self-determination, civil/political and economic rights. Primary focus is on all foreign countries, and migrants, native Americans and US immigration. Offers library facilities, research assistance and telephone reference services. Publications include *Human Rights Internet Reporter* (5 times/year); 3 directories of human rights organizations in use around the world; *Teaching Human Rights* (curricula and bibliographies). **How to Contact:** Write, call or visit. Responds to most inquiries within a week. Charges for publications and 10¢/page for photocopying on the premises. "Space and time in use of facilities and services may be restricted during certain periods when publications are being prepared. We request a call to make arrangements before visiting." **Tips:** Recent information requests: Bibliography on US human rights under President Carter; information on Soviet labor camps; number of assassinations during May 1982 in El Salvador.

1299• HUMANITIES RESEARCH CENTER (HRC)
The University of Texas at Austin, Box 7219, Austin TX 78712. (512)471-1833. Contact Person: Research Librarian. **Description:** "The HRC is a major research library housing numerous rare book, manuscript and other special collections. Special areas of interest include 19th- and 20th-century British, American and French literature and art, the history of science, photography, theater arts, and bibliography and book arts. The major units of the Humanities Research Center include the Reading Room, the Photography Collections, the Hoblitzelle Theatre Arts Library and the Iconography Collection and the academic center collections." **Services:** "We have something on almost every modern author. If you need information in this field, don't hesitate to call us." Offers brochures/pamphlets. **How to Contact:** Write or call. Responds to most inquiries within a month. Charges for photocopies. "We are very protective of copyrights. We do charge for the

commercial use of images from our art collection." **Tips:** "This is a research library. Unfortunately, we rarely have the staff or time to provide extensive searching and research services for commercial ventures. Each researcher should be aware of the size of the collection: 800,000 printed volumes, 9 million manuscripts, 4 million photographs, 60,000 art items, and several miles of clippings and ephemeral materials." Recent information requests: Information on the library of Leonard and Virginia Woolf; an unpublished manuscript by Salvador Dali; and biographical information on James Agee.

1300• INSTITUTE FOR SOCIAL RESEARCH
426 Thompson St., Ann Arbor MI 48104. (313)764-8363. Contact Person: Director. **Description:** Established at the University of Michigan in 1946, the Institute for Social Research conducts research in the social sciences. Its research goal is "to advance our understanding of society and behavior." It generates measurements of actual economic, sociological, psychological and political behavior through activities of its 4 basic research groups: The Survey Research Center, The Research Center for Group Dynamics, The Center for Research on Utilization of Scientific Knowledge and the Center for Political Studies. **Services:** Provides analytical, interpretative, referral and technical information on survey methodology, economics, journalism, politics, urban planning, education, psychology, sociology, organizational studies, use of time, etc. Offers aid in arranging interviews, informational newsletters, library facilities and archives, placement on mailing lists, research assistance and telephone reference services. Publications include newsletter (quarterly); *Economic Outlook USA* (quarterly); various other research reports and surveys. **How to Contact:** Write or call. Make appointment in advance of a visit. Responds to most inquiries within a week. **Tips:** Recent information requests: Economic surveys and consumer sentiment on various issues.

1301• INSTITUTE FOR THE STUDY OF CONSCIOUS EVOLUTION
2418 Clement St., San Francisco CA 94121. (415)221-9222. Contact Person: Executive Director. **Description:** The institute engages in research and education into the processes of conscious evolution, the act of intentional participation in human development. "We give seminars, conferences, courses; publish books and papers; have a number of projects." **Services:** Provides advisory, analytical, interpretative, referral, technical and trade information on ecology, interdisciplinary studies, governance, relationships, intuition, conscious evolution, intentional communities, planetary evolution, management consultation and organizational behavior, consensual decision-making, spiritual practices. Offers brochures/pamphlets, computerized information searches, informational newsletters, research assistance and "information on leading edge research in whole systems theory and societal evolution." Publications include *GAIA* (quarterly); *Conscious Evolution; Evolutionary Journey; The Applied Psi Newsletter;* various research papers. **How to Contact:** Write, call or visit. Response time varies "according to the request." Charges for printing and handling costs. **Tips:** "We operate on the assumption that there is a powerful interface between intellect and spirit, which can be accessed to open new avenues of perception. We have particular interest, research, expertise in the areas of futures research, in human consciousness, and human psychic potentials."

1302• THE KINSEY INSTITUTE FOR RESEARCH IN SEX, GENDER AND REPRODUCTION, INC.
Indiana University, Morrison Hall 416, Bloomington IN 47405. (812)335-7686. Contact Person: Information Service Officer. **Description:** "We are an independent, not-for-profit corporation located at Indiana University for research in human sexual development, attitudes and behavior and for dissemination of information. We have the world's largest library and art and photograph collections in this subject area." **Services:** Provides advisory, bibliographical, historical and referral information covering human sex behavior; erotic art, literature, photographs and films; sociological, psychological and historical aspects of human sexuality; gender identity. Offers aid in arranging interviews, brochures/pamphlets, computerized information searches, library facilities, photos, statistics and telephone reference services. Publications include *Sources of Information and Materials Related to Human Sexuality* (updated annually); approximately 200 subject bibliographies on specific sex-related topics. **How to Contact:** Write. Responds to most inquiries within a week. Charges for bibliographic searches; prepared bibliographies; films and photos for scholarly purposes only; "qualified individuals may do on-site research for a basic user fee; other costs on request. No restrictions for mail and telephone services related to bibliographic or statistical data. We have a strict policy of confidentiality in relation to information about

individuals. Access to erotica is limited to qualified scholars." **Tips:** "Avoid simplistic conclusions based on research conducted with small samples suggesting possible trends or indications. Avoid starting with a conclusion and simply selecting data to support it." Recent information request: "Is there a relationship between pornography and rape?"

1303• MARQUANDIA SOCIETY FOR STUDIES IN HISTORY AND LITERATURE
421 Scotland St., No. 6, Williamsburg VA 23185. (804)229-7049. Contact Persons: Curator and Co-Director. **Description:** "We encourage studies and discussion in the areas of regional history and use of fiction and unorthodox materials as sources of historical and cultural information. The society was founded in honor of the novelist, John P. Marquand." **Services:** Provides information on John P. Marquand and regional history (New England, Blue Grass, Tidewater, California). Offers biographies and research assistance. **How to Contact:** Write. Responds to most inquiries within a month. Charges for research advice and consultation on a per case basis. **Tips:** "Have realistic expectations and patience." Recent information request: "What are some good observations on life at Harvard in the 1920s?"

1304• NATIONAL INFORMATION BUREAU
419 Park Ave. S., New York NY 10016. (212)532-8595. Contact Person: Assistant Director. **Description:** Nonprofit organization working "to maintain sound standards in our field of philanthropy; to aid wise giving through advisory reports to contributors." **Services:** Provides advisory, analytical, referral, and technical information on "national, not-for-profit organizations which solicit the general public. NIB believes that agencies which solicit the public have a responsibility to make available information which will enable contributors to make informed decisions about giving. NIB does not generally undertake to report on religious, fraternal or political organizations and single or local institutions." Offers annual reports, brochures/pamphlets, placement on mailing lists and research assistance. Publications include monthly *Wise Giving Guide* giving NIB's ratings of several hundred national not-for-profit organizations based on NIB's standards; several hundred detailed reports about these organizations; booklet on NIB's interpretation of its standards. **How to Contact:** Write or call. Responds to most inquiries within a week. "Note dates of NIB ratings or reports; inform us of where articles are to be published; send us copy of article, if possible."

1305• POPULATION REFERENCE BUREAU
1337 Connecticut Ave. NW, Washington DC 20036. (202)785-4664. Contact Person: Technical Information Specialist. **Description:** "We are a nonprofit educational organization concerned with disseminating up-to-date and unbiased information on populations (and related topics) issues." **Services:** Provides analytical, interpretative and technical information on population, demography, environment, statistics. Offers computerized information searches, informational newsletters, library facilities, research assistance and statistics. Publications include *Population Bulletin* (quarterly); *Intercom* (bimonthly newsmagazine). **How to Contact:** Write, call or visit. Responds to most inquiries within a week. Charges for computerized information searches. Library hours Monday-Friday 8:30-4:30. **Tips:** Recent information request: "How many elderly people live in the US and what's the breakdown by certain states?"

1306• SMITHSONIAN INSTITUTION
1000 Jefferson Dr. SW, Washington DC 20560. (202)357-2627. Contact Person: Director, Office of Public Affairs. **Description:** "The Smithsonian, an independent trust establishment, conducts scientific and scholarly research; administers the national collections; and performs other educational public service functions, supported by its trust endowments, gifts, grants and contracts and funds appropriated to it by the Congress." **Services:** Provides historical and referral information on science, history and art. Offers aid in arranging interviews, annual reports and brochures/pamphlets. Publications include *Smithsonian Institution*, 20-page pamphlet with brief descriptions of 15 museums and 5 science centers; *Smithsonian Institution—Yesterday and Today*. **How to Contact:** Write. Responds to most inquiries within a month.

1307• YANKELOVICH, SKELLY AND WHITE
575 Madison Ave., New York NY 10022. (212)752-7500. Contact Person: Executive Vice President. **Description:** Public opinion and social research firm. **Services:** Provides statistical information. Offers reports (subject to availability) in the public domain on such topics as technological innovation, the Japanese economic challenge, etc. **How to Contact:** Write ("be specific"). Responds to most inquiries within a week.

BEHIND THE BYLINE

Nikki Giovanni
Poet

"Writing poetry is a profession of love. The rewards are predominantly personal as opposed to other writing fields. You write a poem and you may get twenty dollars. You won't see your poem mounted on a stage or done on TV. You write a poem and maybe half a dozen people will read it. You have to have a lot of inner strength and interest in the unique contribution you are making."

Nikki Giovanni has both. Her poems have been published and anthologized. She has earned honorary degrees and a bevy of awards for her writing. Her sixteenth and most recent book of verse is *Those Who Ride the Night Winds*. Giovanni works hard at her craft.

"Poetry is the most difficult of the writing arts. You have to know what you are saying and what you are not saying. You have a maximum of, say, two thousand words. You have to know everything in order to know what to eliminate. And to get to the point where you can do that, you have to think and grow. Writing is the art of maturation. It's like wine; you have to put in your time."

It's not just time that a poet needs, however. "You have to observe life and acquaint yourself with good writing and with history. Greeks, Egyptians, Chinese, Africans; you don't learn about them on TV. If you don't know what's gone before you, you'll come up with insights someone else had twelve thousand years ago."

Nikki's insights come from an awareness of her world. She was a part of the 60s movement; she thinks and feels strongly about her writing. "Poets go back a long way, to David and the harp really. And I think today we're back where we should be—to bringing the news and informing people and teaching them how to feel about their world. And the nice thing about being a poet is that we're not stuck with trying to make a statement via the form of a poem, but in fact, on the content. You can use anything—the new journalism or the classical, emotional poetry. You say what you have to say through the process of a poem. That process begins with an idea and it's a start-to-finish operation.

"The flow of a poem is important to me. It's like a painter and light. If a painter starts to paint with a northern light between 8:00 and 1:00, he can't pick up again at 4:00 because the light's changed. The flow of a poem is like that. I'm not locked into form; that's just not my personality. But the poem has to start and go—it has to be done in sequence. If I'm in the middle of a poem and have to stop for an interruption, it throws me off. I'm punching it out at the typewriter, and I need a block of time to do that.

"If I'm totally dissatisfied with a poem, I can throw it away or put it in the dead file, think about it and go back to it five or six years later. At some point, though, you've got to let it go and build another one. You are *not* going to write the perfect poem any more than you're going to live the perfect life, find the perfect love or make the perfect meat loaf. And some poems don't work. Sure you'd like to win a Pulitzer Prize and feel people like what you're doing. But you know what your best is and you know when what you have written is awfully good. If you know enough about the industry, you also know that it may be five years before anybody realizes what you have done."

SECTION · TWENTY-FIVE

SPECIAL INTEREST GROUPS

For is it not true that human progress is but a mighty growing pattern woven together by the tenuous single threads united in a common effort?

—Madame Chiang Kai-shek

This section speaks to the idea that human beings are a species of joiners. The information sources listed here are varied both in content and tone. Their common thread is dedication to a cause. Men, women, children and the elderly are special interest groups—as are homosexuals, lefthanders, little people and those interested in alternative lifestyles.

Bibliography

Akey, Denise, ed. *Encyclopedia of Associations*. Annual. Detroit: Gale Research Co. (The "bible" of institutional and professional associations)

Chase, William D. and Helen M., eds. *Chase's Calendar of Annual Events: Special Days, Weeks and Months In _____*. Annual. Flint, MI: Apple Tree Press.

McWhirter, Norris. *Guinness Book of World Records*. rev. ed. New York: Sterling Publishing Co., 1982.

Place, Linna Funk, Plinda Parker, and Forrest J. Berghorn, eds. *Aging and the Aged: An Annotated Bibliography and Library Research Guide*. Boulder, CO: Westview Press, 1981.

Wallace, Irving, et. al. *Book of Lists Two*. New York: Bantam, 1981.

Wasserman, Paul, ed. *Speakers and Lecturers: How to Find Them*. 2d ed. 2 vols. Detroit: Gale Research Co., 1981.

Weiser, Marjorie P. and Jean S. Arbeiter. *Womanlist: A Book of Lists to Celebrate Women*. New York: Atheneum, 1981.

Williamson, Jane et. al., eds. *Women's Action Almanac: A Complete Resource Guide*. Women's Action Alliance. New York: William Morrow & Co., 1979.

Wishard, Bill and Laurie. *Men's Rights: A Handbook for the 80s*. San Francisco: Cragmont Publications, 1980.

1308• ALL TOGETHER
3612-405 N. Wabash, Chicago IL 60611. (312)467-0465. Contact Person: President. **Description:** "We are a central resource on alternative lifestyles (homosexuals, swingers, bisexuals, etc.)." **Services:** Provides advisory and referral information. The organization works to eliminate economic descrimination against people with alternative lifestyles. "We provide marketing and consulting services to these groups." Offers aid in arranging interviews, informational newsletters, placement on mailing lists, research assistance, statistics, telephone reference services, specific project research, speakers and clipping file on alternative lifestyles. Publications include newsletter ($10/year, available to members). **How to Contact:** Write. Responds to most inquiries within a few weeks. Charges for some services. Include SASE with information request. **Tips:** Recent information request: Projections of future family.

1309• ALTERNATIVE PRESS CENTER
Box 7229, Baltimore MD 21218. (301)243-2471. Contact Person: Collective Member. **Description:** "We maintain a library of alternative and radical periodicals as well as publish the *Alternative Press Index*." **Services:** Provides bibliographical and historical information on anarchism, alternative energy, alternative culture, black movement, feminism, gay movement, liberation movements, labor movement, prisoners' rights, radical education, radical health, radical science, socialism, etc. Offers library facilities and research assistance. Publications include *Alternative Press Index*, published quarterly as a subject index to the Alternative Press. "It is a comprehensive guide to over 150 alternative and radical newspapers,

magazines, and journals. Format is similar to the *Readers Guide to Periodical Literature.*" **How to Contact:** Write, call or visit. Responds to most inquiries within a week. **Tips:** Recent information request: "Where do I find information on consumer co-ops?"

1310• AMERICAN ASSOCIATION OF RETIRED PERSONS (AARP)
1909 K St. NW, Washington DC 20049. (202)872-4700. Contact: Public Relations Department. **Description:** AARP is "the nation's largest organization of older Americans. It is legislation-oriented, nonprofit, nonpartisan. Activities include legislation, community service, education and information." **Services:** Offers aid in arranging interviews, bibliographies, statistics, brochures/pamphlets, information searches, placement on mailing list and newsletter. Publications include *Directory of Staff Specialists and Media Services* (general information on AARP policies, programs and services, including names and phone numbers of staff specialists, and media services available). **How to Contact:** Write or call. Responds to most inquiries within a week.

1311• AMERICAN ASSOCIATION OF UNIVERSITY WOMEN
2401 Virginia Ave. NW, Washington DC 20037. (800)424-9717. In Washington DC (202)785-7729. Contact Person: Public Relations/Media Coordinator. **Description:** "Our purpose is to lobby and educate on women's issues. Membership is 190,000 nationwide. We were the first organization involved in improving the position of women in society—founded in 1881. Large lobbying group also produces educational material on issues." **Services:** Provides advisory, analytical, bibliographical, historical and how-to information on women's issues: health/equity/women in government; and peace and national security issues. Offers aid in arranging interviews, annual reports, brochures/pamphlets, informational newsletters and press kits. Publications include *The Graduate Woman* (bimonthly); an in-depth look at issues important to women; and *Action Alert* (2 times a month). "When Congress is in session; *Action Alert* pushes and describes issues key to women." **How to Contact:** Call. Responds to most inquiries immediately. **Tips:** AAUW produces background information on all issues important to women.

1312• THE AMERICAN SUNBATHING ASSOCIATION, INC.
810 N. Mills Ave., Orlando FL 32803. (305)896-8141. Contact Person: Administrator. **Description:** "The association's purpose is to promote social family nudism." **Services:** Provides bibliographical and historical information on the history of nudism and source references. Offers brochures/pamphlets, informational newsletters, library facilities, press kits and research assistance. Publications include *The ASA Bulletin*; and *ASA Park Guide*. **How to Contact:** Write. Responds to most inquiries within a week. Member confidentiality must be maintained. **Tips:** "A visit to an affiliated club is encouraged."

1313• ANARCHIST ASSOCIATION OF THE AMERICAS (AAA)
Box 840, Benjamin Franklin St., Washington DC 20044. Contact Person: Corresponding Secretary. **Description:** "Our purpose is to build a mutual aid community between anarchist groups and individuals." Local groups have total autonomy and are organized regionally. **Services:** Provides interpretative information on current topics, Libertarian organization and anarchist alternatives. Offers brochures/pamphlets, library facilities, placement on mailing lists and press kits. Publications include *Emancipation* (Washington DC monthly); and *Social Anarchism* (Baltimore MD quarterly); Bayou La Rose (New Orleans LA quarterly). **How to Contact:** Write. Responds to most inquiries immediately.

1314• BALDHEADED MEN OF AMERICA
4006 Arendell St., Morehead City NC 28557. (919)726-1855. Contact Person: Executive Director. **Description:** "We attempt to eliminate the vanity that is associated with the loss of one's hair and to promote the fun of being baldheaded. If you don't have it, flaunt it or go topless." **Services:** Offers aid in arranging interviews, brochures/pamphlets, press kits and membership information. Publications available. **How to Contact:** Write or call. Responds to most inquiries within a month. **Tips:** Membership limited to those who are bald 6 inches from the forehead. Recent information requests: "How many members does the club have?"; "How did the club start?"; "What is the philosophy on being bald?"

1315• BOY SCOUTS OF AMERICA
1325 Walnut Hill Lane, Irving TX 75062. (214)659-2000. Contact: Communications Division.

Description: "Boy Scouts of America is a youth-serving organization stressing citizenship training, character building and physical fitness." **Services:** Provides bibliographical, historical and how-to information on activities by which youth meet the objectives of BSA; how churches, civic, and community groups use scouting in their outreach to youth in their community; how scouting serves as adjunct to schooling by bringing career information to young adults. Offers aid in arranging interviews, annual reports, brochures/pamphlets and photos. Offers numerous publications. **How to Contact:** Query the communications division of the national office or check the local Boy Scout or scouting supply outlet, where much of the information is available. "Use mail order forms for literature, available from the local scout office." Responds to most inquiries within a week. **Tips:** "Much help can be better provided by your local scout council rather than by the national office. Your needs should be specific." Recent information requests: "What is the membership of the BSA?"; "How many Eagle Scouts are there?"; "Name some famous people who were Scouts."

1316• THE BOYS' CLUBS OF AMERICA
771 1st Ave., New York NY 10017. (212)557-7755. Contact Person: Manager of Public Information. **Description:** Maintains clubs; "a place of their own for youth, 6-18 years of age, where a professional, guidance-oriented staff is available full time, offering diversified programs in social recreation, health, education and leadership development. There are currently 1,100 Boys' Clubs in all 50 states, Puerto Rico and the Virgin Islands. They are predominantly located in urban and inner city areas. Most Boys' Clubs professionals are experts in child care and development." **Services:** Provides information on juvenile justice, juvenile delinquency prevention and volunteerism. Offers aid in arranging interviews, annual reports, bibliographies, biographies, statistics, brochures/pamphlets, information searches, placement on mailing list, newsletter, photos and press kits. Publications include *The Bulletin* (quarterly). **How to Contact:** Write (preferred) or call for appointment. Responds to most inquiries within 2 weeks.

1317• CAMP FIRE, INC.
4601 Madison Ave., Kansas City MO 64112. (816)756-1950. Contact Person: Public Relations Executive. **Description:** "Camp Fire is a nationwide youth organization committed to providing a program of informal education and opportunities for youth to realize their potential in functioning effectively as caring, self-directed individuals responsible to themselves and to others. We seek to improve those conditions in society which affect youth." Members include girls and boys. **Services:** Provides historical, how-to and referral information on self-confidence and self-reliance for kids, socialization of kids, recreation, camping, cultural diversity. Offers aid in arranging interviews with experts in child development, education, recreation, camping, crafts, activities and games; photos on camping, recreation; annual 'Birthday Week' packet of activities in March; press kits; annual report; brochures; *Leadership* quarterly magazine for leaders; *Management* quarterly newsletter for staff and board members. **How to Contact:** Write. Responds to most inquiries within a week. **Tips:** Recent information requests: Self-reliance courses for kids and camping for senior citizens.

1318• CITIZEN'S FREEDOM FOUNDATION
Box 86, Hannacroix NY 12087. (518)756-8014. Contact Person: Acting Director. **Description:** "Our purpose is to create public awareness of the dangers of destructive cults." **Services:** Provides advisory, analytical and bibliographical information on activities, businesses and practices of destructive cults and information about their members. Offers aid in arranging interviews, biographies, brochures/pamphlets, informational newsletters, research assistance and telephone reference services. Publications include newsletter. **How to Contact:** Write or call. Responds to most inquiries within a month. "We accept donations to cover our costs." **Tips:** "We are the only nationwide organization that has in-depth information on most of the destructive cults."

1319• COMMITTEE TO HALT USELESS COLLEGE KILLINGS (C.H.U.C.K.)
Box 188, Sayville NY 11782. (516)567-1130. Contact Person: Founder. **Description:** Organization dedicated to preventing injuries, deaths, abuses (primarily fraternity-related) on college campuses; shares hazing data. **Services:** Provides statistics, legislative data (state laws, proposals), alternatives to hazing. Offers informational newsletters and statistics. **How to Contact:** Write or call. Responds to most inquiries within a month.

1320• DO-IT-YOURSELF RESEARCH INSTITUTE
770 North High School Rd., Indianapolis IN 46224. (317)241-1070. Contact Person: Executive Director. **Description:** "The institute's purpose is to build a data base of information on the do-it-yourself home, auto and lawn and garden consumer; and to act as a vehicle to communicate with the investment community." **Services:** Provides trade, industry-related information on size of DIY market, growth trends, activities undertaken, attitudes of DIYers and lifestyles of DIYers. Offers annual reports, informational newsletters, library facilities, research assistance, statistics and seminars. Publications include seminar materials. **How to Contact:** Write. Responds to most inquiries within a week. Some information available only to members.

1321• THE DULL MEN'S CLUB
2220 21st St., Boulder CO 80302. Answering Service: (303)449-1128. Contact Person: Founder. **Description:** "We provide support and refuge for dull men and women in an age of preposterous self-aggrandizement; we combat trendiness and slavish fads and fashions; we foster dull rights and dull pride." **Services:** Provides advisory, how-to and interpretative information on how to stay dull; rehabilitation of the interesting; the dull psyche; care of lawn tools; football, politics and quiz shows; and history of the fork. Offers aid in arranging interviews, brochures/pamphlets, informational newsletters, research assistance and speaker service. Publications include *Dull Men's Quarterly*; and texts of speeches. **How to Contact:** Write or call. Responds to most inquiries within a week. Charges for large printing or mailing. **Tips:** "Pursue tedious and painfully obscure subjects that no normal human being would be interested in. Not only will this virtually guarantee exclusivity in your research, but it will also make you a better person." Recent information requests: "What kind of men join the DMC?"; "What is the 'Museum of the Ordinary'?"; "Why was this club started?"; "How does one qualify for membership?"

1322• FEDERATION OF ORGANIZATIONS FOR PROFESSIONAL WOMEN
2000 P. St. NW, Suite 403, Washington DC 20036. (202)466-3544. Contact Person: Administrative Director. **Description:** "The Federation of Organizations for Professional Women is a national association of professional groups working together to enhance the status of women. Founded in 1972, the federation seeks to provide members with a mechanism to promote equality of opportunity in educational and all career fields." **Services:** Provides advisory, bibliographical, historical, how-to and referral information on women scholars, women's rights leaders, sexual harassment, women and psychotherapy, directory of women's organizations and public policy impact on professional women. Publications include *A Woman's Yellow Pages: 570 Organizations Concerned with Women's Issues*; *Women and Psychotherapy: Consumer Handbook*; Woman Scholar Poster Series (Leta Hollingworth and Jessie Bernard); Commemorative Seals of Women's Rights Leaders; and Sexual Harassment Kit. **How to Contact:** Write, call or visit. Responds to most inquiries within a week. Membership required to receive newsletter; individual members may join as "Friend" for $30/year. **Tips:** "Questions should be specific. Responses will be limited generally to existing FOPW materials. Staff will make referrals to individual and organizational members if appropriate. We recently arranged meeting of visiting foreign midwifery specialist with professional women doing research in this area."

1323• FEMINISTS FOR LIFE OF AMERICA, INC.
1918 Upton N., Minneapolis MN 55411. Contact Person: Secretary/Treasurer. **Description:** "Our purpose is to secure the right to life from conception to natural death of all human beings through passage of a Human Life Amendment, and to secure the legal and social equality of all persons regardless of sex through passage of an Equal Rights Amendment." **Services:** Provides advisory and interpretative information on pro-life feminism. Offers brochures/pamphlets and informational newsletters. Publications include *Pro-Life Feminism* (booklet); and *Sister Life* (journal/newsletter). **How to Contact:** Write. Responds to most inquiries within a month. Charges for publications: booklet $2; subscription to journal/newsletter $2.50/year. Give credit to organization. **Tips:** Recent information request: "Why should true feminists be pro life?"

1324• GIRL SCOUTS OF THE USA
830 3rd Ave., New York NY 10022. (212)940-7800. Contact Person: Corporate Relations Director. **Description:** "The Girl Scouts of the USA is the largest voluntary organization for girls in the world. We are dedicated to helping girls find their place in today's world and giving them the skills and confidence to do their share in making tomorrow's world a better one." **Services:**

Provides information on career exploration. Offers aid in arranging interviews, annual reports, biographies, statistics, brochures/pamphlets, information searches, placement on mailing list, newsletter and press kits. **How to Contact:** Write. Responds to most inquiries within a week. "Call to discuss ideas."

1325• GIRLS CLUBS OF AMERICA, INC.
205 Lexington Ave., New York NY 10016. (212)689-3700. Contact Person: Director of Public Relations. **Description:** "Girls Clubs of America is a national service and advocacy organization for girls age 6-18. More than 250 girls clubs serve nearly one-quarter of a million girls, regardless of race, creed or national origin. Clubs are located in urban areas and are open daily after school, weekends and during the summer. Programs in the arts, sports, education for sexuality, education/employment and juvenile delinquency prevention are featured." **Services:** Provides referral and technical information on a range of subjects on the special needs of girls. Offers aid in arranging interviews, annual reports, bibliographies, biographies, brochures/pamphlets, placement on mailing list, statistics, newsletter, photos and press kits. Publications available. **How to Contact:** Write or call. Responds to most inquiries within a week. **Tips:** "Writers may also call the GCA National Resource Center in Indianapolis, (317)634-7546, for information on girls." Recent information request: "Please put me in contact with runaway girls and those who work with them . . . etc."

1326• GOOD BEARS OF THE WORLD
Box 8236, Honolulu HI 96815. (808)946-2844. Contact Person: Founder. **Description:** "The Good Bears of the World is a nonprofit, tax exempt association believing in love and understanding for children. The primary goal of GBW is to provide teddy bears to comfort children of all ages in hospitals and institutions." **Services:** Provides general information and stories about teddy bears. Offers aid in arranging interviews, biographies, brochures/pamphlets, informational newsletters and photos. Publications include *Bear Tracks* (journal); news releases. **How to Contact:** Write. Responds to most inquiries within a week.

1327• GRAY PANTHERS
3635 Chestnut St., Philadelphia PA 19104. (215)382-3300. Contact Person: Executive Director. **Description:** Political advisory group for senior citizens. **Services:** Provides advisory, how-to and referral information on discrimination-related issues affecting senior citizens. Offers brochures/ pamphlets, informational newsletters, library facilities, photos, statistics and telephone reference services. Publications include *Network*. **How to Contact:** Write. Responds to most inquiries within a month. **Tips:** Recent information request: Senior citizens' rights on social security.

1328• RENE GUYON SOCIETY
256 S. Robertson Blvd., Beverly Hills CA 90211. Contact: Spokesperson. **Description:** "World's leading authority on child sexuality. We work for child sex law easement and cooperate with worldwide child sexual freedom movements." **Services:** Provides advisory, analytical, bibliographical, historical, interpretative and technical information on child sexuality in the very early years. Offers aid in arranging interviews, bibliographies and brochures/pamphlets. Publications available. **How to Contact:** Write or call. Responds to most inquiries within a month. "Please provide a # 10 SASE with 2 first class stamps. We provide free introductory data. For an extensive coverage of our field, we need co-author credit." **Tips:** Recent information request: Advice for writer for national TV series.

1329• THE HAUNT HUNTERS
c/o Goodwilling, 963 Clayton Rd., Ballwin MO 63011. (314)391-8256. Contact Person: Director or President. **Description:** "We investigate haunted houses and haunted people, and act as an international clearinghouse for tales of the uncanny and bizarre." **Services:** Provides advisory, how-to and referral information on ghosts and hauntings, ESP and PK, and demonology. Offers research assistance. Publications include *The Haunt Hunters Handbook for the Psychic Investigator*. **How to Contact:** Write. Responds to most inquiries within a week. Charges for handbook and membership (total $10). "In general, the people we investigate do not want notoriety attached to them." **Tips:** "Since our organization was founded, in 1965, we have investigated over 300 cases of ghosts and hauntings. The Haunt Hunters has over 350 members in every state and in 17 foreign countries."

1330• HEMLOCK SOCIETY
Box 66218, Los Angeles CA 90066. (213)391-1871. Contact Person: Executive Director. **Description:** The society's purposes are: "to raise consciousness about the option of active voluntary euthanasia for terminally ill people; and to change the law forbidding any assistance in suicide so that dying persons may ask a doctor or loved one to help them die." **Services:** Provides advisory, historical and interpretative information on euthanasia, also known as self-deliverance, sometimes called mercy killing. Offers brochures/pamphlets, informational newsletters, research assistance and statistics. Publications include *Hemlock Quarterly* (newsletter); *The Compassionate Crime* (booklet); *Jean's Way* (book); and *Let Me Die Before I Wake* (book). **How to Contact:** Write. Responds to most inquiries immediately. Charges for the more expensive books supplied. "Names of members of Hemlock never are revealed; no interviews with members are arranged by us. Make preliminary inquiries into subject of euthanasia before approaching us."

1331• HOMOSEXUAL INFORMATION CENTER, INC.
6758 Hollywood Blvd., #208, Los Angeles CA 90028. (213)464-8431. Contact Persons: Editors. **Description:** "We have the most complete file and library on issues and homosexuality in the world. Our library contains the archives of the homosexual movement. We have early newsletters, etc., which are unavailable anywhere else in the world. We as a staff have over 25 years experience dealing with homosexuality, having cooperated with such people as Evelyn Hooker and Kinsey. A co-founder, Don Slater, is the foremost thinker on the subject in the world. We present a balanced view." **Services:** Offers counseling/legal aid and referrals to qualified agencies; bibliographies, brochures/pamphlets and newsletter. Publications available. **How to Contact:** Write. Responds to most inquiries within a week. "Donations are tax-deductible." **Tips:** Recent information requests: Legal questions; changes in laws affecting homosexuals.

1332• INTERNATIONAL VEGETARIAN UNION
10, King's Drive, Marple, Stockport, SK6 6NQ England. (061)427-5850. Contact Person: Honorable General Secretary. **Description:** The International Vegetarian Union is dedicated to the furtherance of vegetarianism throughout the world; to keep world vegetarian organizations in touch; to answer queries about vegetarianism; to represent the vegetarian interest. **Services:** Provides advisory, bibliographical, historical, interpretative, referral and technical information on vegetarian health, diet and economics. Offers aid in arranging interviews, brochures/pamphlets, informational newsletters, library facilities (very limited), press kits, research assistance and statistics. **How to Contact:** Write. Responds to most inquiries within a week. "Depending on the services requested, some restrictions may exist. Write giving full details of requirements." **Tips:** Recent information requests: "How many vegetarians are there in the world, United States, U.K.?"

1333• INVISIBLE EMPIRE KNIGHTS OF THE KU KLUX KLAN
Box 700, Denham Springs LA 70726. (504)665-1018. Contact Person: Imperial Wizard. **Description:** "Our purpose is to represent the interests of white people and work politically to restore all people's right to practice their religious or personal preference to segregate." **Services:** Provides historical and interpretative information on Klan history, background, goals and present activity. Offers brochures/pamphlets, informational newsletters, placement on mailing lists and press kits. Publications include *The Klansman* (monthly newspaper); and *KYC Quarterly*. **How to Contact:** Write or call. Responds to most inquiries within a week.

1334• KNOW, INC.
Box 86031, Pittsburgh PA 15221. (412)241-4844. Contact Person: President. **Description:** "KNOW is dedicated to making known the needs brought about by the changing roles of women and men in our society. Specifically, we distribute information relevant to the concerns of persons interested in the Women's Liberation Movement." **Services:** Provides advisory, analytical, bibliographical, historical, how to, interpretative and referral information in all areas of women's rights: education, employment, the Equal Rights Amendment, psychology, religion, history, sports, language, rape, reproductive rights, sexuality, and other general topics. Offers biographies, brochures/pamphlets, informational newsletters, library facilities, placement on mailing lists, research assistance and telephone reference services. "We will provide a list of our over 300 publications free of charge upon request. Writers may also use our extensive files and library with

arrangements made in advance.'' **How to Contact:** Write or call. Responds to most inquiries within a week. Charges for publications. No material may be removed from library. **Tips:** "Write for a publication price list; two postage stamps would be helpful.''

1335• LEFTHANDERS INTERNATIONAL
3601 SW 29th, Topeka KS 66614. (913)273-0680. Contact Person: Vice President or Executive Director. **Description:** "We give recognition to outstanding lefthanded individuals; promote the good life of lefthandedness; work with manufacturers in order to get more lefthanded products made; and act as an information center for all things lefthanded.'' **Services:** Provides advisory, historical, how-to, interpretative, referral and technical information on anything pertaining to lefthandedness, including famous lefties in all walks of life (sports, entertainment, history, government, etc.); how-to information for lefties; stores that sell lefthanded equipment; how-to materials on lefthanders in the classroom for teachers and educators; a referral system for researchers in the field of brain research and handedness, etc. Offers aid in arranging interviews, brochures/pamphlets, informational newsletters, placement on mailing lists, press kits, research assistance and statistics. Publications include *Lefty Magazine* and Bill of Lefts. **How to Contact:** Write or call. Responds to most inquiries immediately. "No material may be reproduced without written permission of the publisher.''

1336• LITTLE PEOPLE OF AMERICA, INC. (L.P.A.)
Box 126, Owatonna MN 55060. (507)451-1320, 451-3842 (after 4:00 p.m. weekdays or weekends). Contact Person: Executive Officer. **Description:** "A nation-wide, voluntary organization, the Little People of America, Inc., is dedicated to helping people of short stature. LPA provides fellowship, moral support, and helpful information to those individuals accepting the unique challenges of being a little person.'' **Services:** Provides advisory information on vocational training and education, medical and scientific research, more convenient living for little people, difficulties of short statured persons, etc. Offers brochures/pamphlets and informational newsletters. Publications include *LPA Today* (newsletter); *My Child Is a Dwarf* (booklet); and *The Idea Machine* (manual). **How to Contact:** Write, call or visit. Responds to most inquiries within a month. **Tips:** Recent information request: "How does it feel to be short?''

1337• LIVE-FREE, INC.
Box 1743, Harvey IL 60426. (312)928-5830. Contact Person: President. **Description:** "We are a not-for-profit, tax deductible organization that provides organizing help to survivalists; conducts survival research and survival seminars; and supports and encourages all forms of self-sufficiency.'' **Services:** Provides advisory, analytical, historical, how-to, interpretative, referral and technical information on wilderness survival, survival foods, nuclear survival, the survivalist philosophy, survival first aid, survival organization, survival self defense, survival in the future, etc. Offers aid in arranging interviews, brochures/pamphlets, informational newsletters, photos, placement on mailing lists and press kits. Publications include *Directions* (monthly newsletter); *The Survivalist Papers* (list on request); *The Complete Guide to Freedom and Survival* ($14.95 per copy). **How to Contact:** Write. Responds to most inquiries within a month. Charges for books, newsletters and papers. Give credit to Live-Free. **Tips:** "Survivalists are all different and one or two interviews or a few newsletters from a few groups won't give a full and accurate concept.''

1338• LONERS ON WHEELS, INC.
2940 Lane Dr., Concord CA 94518. Contact Person: President. **Description:** "We provide information on activities for single people (primarily retired or soon to retire) who live or travel in recreational vehicles (trailers, campers, motor homes).'' **Services:** Provides information on trailer travel and vehicle maintenance. Offers informational newsletters and placement on mailing lists. Publications include monthly newsletter and membership directory. **How to Contact:** Write. Responds to most inquiries within a week. **Tips:** Recent information requests: data for several TV documentaries and books.

1339• MAN WATCHERS, INC.
8330 Sunset, # 363, Los Angeles CA 90046. Contact Person: President. **Description:** Man Watchers, Inc., is a worldwide women's organization whose purpose is the bettering of relationships between the sexes. Activities include presenting compliment cards to deserving men and doing woman/man opinion research. **Services:** "We release the results of our polls to our

members and to the press." Offers informational newsletters. Publications include *Man Watchers Official Newsletter*. Also markets a "Man Watcher's" Kit. **How to Contact:** Write. Responds to most inquiries within a month. **Tips:** "What men think women like, and what they really like is very different. We point that out through our pageants and research."

1340• MEN'S RIGHTS, INC. (MR, INC.)
Rindge Towers 402-8J, Cambridge MA 02140. (617)547-5054. Contact Person: Director. **Description:** "Our purpose is to raise public awareness about the range, depth, and seriousness of men's problems. We use legal action, legislative action, research, community programs, and publicity to further our goal of a non-sexist society." **Services:** Provides advisory, analytical, bibliographical, interpretative and referral information on fatherhood, military draft, divorce, life expectancy, violence, self-image, health, legal treatment, news media coverage, entertainment media portrayal, etc. Offers aid in arranging interviews, informational newsletters, library facilities, placement on mailing lists and press kits. Publications include news releases and newsletters. **How to Contact:** Write or call. Responds to most inquiries within a week. "Although we wish to exercise no control over editorial content, we expect to check articles for accuracy before publication." **Tips:** "Be prepared to find out that men's problems are far more serious than you assume." Recent information request: "What is men's liberation? Is it a backlash against women?"

1341• NATIONAL ACTION FORUM FOR MIDLIFE AND OLDER WOMEN
School of Allied Health Professionals, State University of New York, Stony Brook NY 11794. (516)246-2256. Contact Person: Director. **Description:** "The purpose of our organization is to increase public awareness, on a national and international basis, of the needs and potential of women over 40." **Services:** Provides information on health issues of women in midlife and late life—as well as transitional role concerns, economic and housing issues. Offers informational newsletters. Publications include *Hot Flash: A Newsletter for Midlife and Older Women*. **How to Contact:** Write. Responds to most inquiries within a week. Charges for subscription to newsletter: $10 annually.

1342• NATIONAL ANTI-KLAN NETWORK
Box 10500, Atlanta GA 30310. (404)221-0025. Contact Person: Coordinator. **Description:** "Our purpose is to counter the Ku Klux Klan and racist violence." **Services:** Provides advisory, analytical, historical, how-to, referral and technical information on the Klan, Nazis, history of racism, how to counter Klan hatred and violence and to help Klan victims. Offers aid in arranging interviews, brochures/pamphlets, informational newsletters, placement on mailing lists, press kits, research assistance, statistics and telephone reference services. **How to Contact:** Write. Responds to most inquiries within a week. Charges for mailing and literature costs. **Tips:** Recent information request: "How large is the Klan today? Is it really a threat? What can be done to counter it?"

1343• NATIONAL CONGRESS FOR MEN
10606 Wilkins Ave., Los Angeles CA 90024. (213)475-5352. Contact Person: President. **Description:** "A nationwide network of men's and father's groups dealing with societal goals and issues and with family law reforms." This is an organization of individual state and local organizations (with some individuals as associate members). **Services:** Provides advisory, analytical, bibliographical, historical, interpretative and referral information on child support, father deprivation, interstate jurisdiction, post-divorce family relations, rehabilitative allowances, stereotype and media portrayals, non-sexist draft, networking, support groups, legislative action and judicial monitoring. Offers aid in arranging interviews, biographies, brochures/pamphlets, informational newsletters, photos, placement on mailing lists, press kits, research assistance, statistics and telephone reference services. **How to Contact:** Write, call or visit. Responds to most inquiries within a week. **Tips:** Recent information request: "Are you in touch with a men's group in (a particular state)?"

1344• NATIONAL CONGRESS OF NEIGHBORHOOD WOMEN
249 Manhattan Ave., Brooklyn NY 11211. (212)388-6666. Contact Person: Educational Coordinator. **Description:** "We are a grassroots women's organization whose purpose is to help develop women's skills, leadership and role in community life through a variety of programs and networking." **Services:** Provides advisory, analytical, bibliographical, how-to and referral information on women's studies, scholarly writings and analysis of women's programs, status,

education; models of programs and trainings. Offers aid in arranging interviews, brochures/pamphlets, clipping services, informational newsletters, library facilities (research center), placement on mailing lists, statistics and telephone reference services. **How to Contact:** Write or call. Responds to most inquiries within a month. Resource guide/brochure carries prices for publications and mailing costs. Some materials are not to be taken out of the office. Charges for duplication. **Tips:** Recent information requests: "We have interviews with writers from different publications who wish to examine a facet of the organization (training, education programs, etc.)."

1345• NATIONAL COUNCIL ON THE AGING, INC.
600 Maryland Ave. SW, West Wing 100, Washington DC 20024. (202)479-1200. Contact Person: Media Director. **Desription:** "The National Council on the Aging (NCOA), founded in 1950, is a national, nonprofit, membership organization that seeks to improve the lives of older Americans through a variety of programs including technical assistance and training to corporations and other practitioners in the field of aging. Among other issues, NCOA is involved in employment, pre-retirement, senior centers, health care promotion and education, housing, the arts and humanities. We also confer with the producers and editors of prime time TV programming, provide information to other media outlets and testify before Congress." **Services:** Provides information on survey data, age discrimination, business, economics, the arts and entertainment and public policy affecting older Americans. Offers bibliographies, statistics, brochures/pamphlets and placement on mailing lists. Publications include *Aging in the 80s: America in Transition*, a major national survey conducted for NCOA by Louis Harris and Associates on trends in the aging experience and the public's attitude toward the status and problems of older Americans; *Perspective on Aging* (quarterly abstract); *Facts and Myths about Aging*; brochures on NCOA activities and programs. **How to Contact:** Write or call. Response time varies according to media and deadline.

1346• NATIONAL ORGANIZATION FOR WOMEN (NOW)
425 13th St. NW, Suite 1048, Washington DC 20004. (202)347-2279. Contact Person: Director of Communications. **Description:** NOW is concerned with federal and state legislation that affects the area of women's rights. Also provides educational services in women's rights, literature and annual conferences. **Services:** Offers aid in arranging interviews, statistics, brochures/pamphlets, placement on mailing list, newsletter, photos and press kits. Publications include *N.O.W. Times*. **How to Contact:** "We prefer phone requests." Responds to most inquiries immediately. Publications available by subscription or through membership. **Tips:** Recent information request: "What will NOW's focus be for the 80s?"

1347• NATIONAL YOUTH WORK ALLIANCE
1346 Connecticut Ave. NW, Washington DC 20036. (202)785-0764. Contact Person: Assistant Director. **Description:** "Our purpose is to increase the quality and quantity of service to youth. We focus on delinquency prevention, alcohol/drug abuse prevention, runaways and other youth problems." **Services:** Provides advisory, analytical, interpretative, referral and technical information. Offers aid in arranging interviews, brochures/pamphlets, informational newsletters, library facilities and research assistance. "We will put writers in contact with experts and programs in their city/state/region." Publications available. **How to Contact:** Write or visit. Responds to most inquiries within a week. Charges for publications, photocopies, and postage and handling. **Tips:** Recent information request: "Why do youths runaway? How many youths runaway? What happens to them? Names and addresses of local runaway centers."

1348• PHI KAPPA KAZE
717 Farragut Ave., Colorado Springs CO 80909. (303)632-9560. Contact Person: President. **Description:** "Our purpose is to unite men and women in one non-sexist fraternal organization across college campuses and to promote community activities. Our philosophy promotes positivism. We help others love life without spiritual guidance or religious specification." **Services:** Provides advisory and interpretative information on how to join and develop individual chapters as well as philosophies behind the frarority (fraternity and sorority). Offers "advice and support at this point of our development." **How to Contact:** Write. Responds to most inquiries within a week. **Tips:** Recent information requests: "What is the philosophy of Phi Kappa Kaze?"; "What are the advantages of being a member as well as advantages to the community?"

1349• PROCRASTINATORS' CLUB OF AMERICA
1111 Broad-Locust Bldg., Philadelphia PA 19102. (215)546-3861. Contact Person: President.
Description: "We promote the benefits of procrastination and bring together positive procrastinators. Activities, awards, celebrations (unusual), late parties, etc." **Services:** Offers aid in arranging interviews. **How to Contact:** Write. Responds to most inquiries within a month. Request by mail with SASE. **Tips:** Recent information request: Number of members, activities, age of organization, events celebrated, types of members, etc.

1350• SOCIETY FOR THE RIGHT TO DIE
250 W. 57th St., New York NY 10019. (212)246-6973. Contact Person: Executive Director. **Description:** "We work for the recognition of the individual's right to die with dignity through educational, legislative and judicial programs." **Services:** Provides advisory, analytical, bibliographical, historical, interpretative, referral and technical information on medical and legal developments relating to the right-to-die; advancement of patients' rights; and information on rights and options under enacted laws. Offers aid in arranging interviews, annual reports, bibliographies, brochures/pamphlets, placement on mailing list and newsletter. Publications available. **How to Contact:** Write or call. Responds to most inquiries immediately. "We provide information on the right-to-die movement including legal developments in legislatures and the courts." **Tips:** Recent information requests: "If my state has a 'natural death' law, how do I exercise my rights?"; "How can I exercise this right if I live in a state without such a law?"; "Why the need for legislation?"

1351• SOCIETY OF DIRTY OLD MEN
Box 18202, Indianapolis IN 46218. Contact Person: Vice President. **Description:** "We are dedicated to the principles of male supremacy." **Services:** Provides advisory, historical, how-to, interpretative and referral information on "the battle of the sexes"; man's place/women's place. Offers aid in arranging interviews, photos, some press kits, research assistance and statistics. **How to Contact:** Write. Responds to most inquiries within a week. Charges for services: $50/hour calculated to the $^1/_{10}$ of an hour. "We will respond to men only." **Tips:** Recent information request: "What do you feel are the respected roles of today's men and women?"

1352• SOCIETY TO CURTAIL RIDICULOUS, OUTRAGEOUS, AND OSTENTATIOUS GIFT EXCHANGES (SCROOGE)
1447 Westwood Rd., Charlottesville VA 22901. (804)977-4645. Contact Person: Executive Director. **Description:** "We advocate, in a low-key, good-humored fashion, the reduction of the more commercial aspects of the Christmas season." **Services:** Provides advisory and interpretative information: advice on how to reduce Christmas gift spending and *still* enjoy the holiday season; advice on inexpensive, thoughtful, and useful Christmas gifts; and moral support for those who want to avoid the "Christmas Shopping Frenzy Syndrome." Offers brochures/pamphlets, informational newsletters and research assistance. Publications include *The Annual Scrooge Newsletter*, published the week after Thanksgiving. **How to Contact:** Write or call. Responds to most inquiries within a week. Charges for postage for *overseas* mailings. Telephone inquiries preferred after 6:00 p.m. and on weekends. **Tips:** SCROOGE has over 600 members in the United States, Canada, and the United Kingdom. "A *main point* is that we are *not* anti-Christmas; we love Christmas but believe that some of the practices associated with it have gotten slightly out of hand." Recent information requests: "What advice would you offer to people who want to cut back on Christmas spending?"; "What general types of people join SCROOGE and what do they tell you about their reasons for joining?"

1353• TIPPERS INTERNATIONAL
Box 2351, Oshkosh WI 54903. (414)233-1588. Contact Person: President. **Description:** "We gather and compile information to establish tipping standards and foster understanding of tipping benefits for supporting members and the public." **Services:** Provides advisory, analytical, historical, how-to, interpretative and trade information on tipping in U.S.A. and 42 overseas nations for food service trade, hospitality and travel industries. Offers aid in arranging interviews, brochures/pamphlets, research assistance and statistics. Publications include *Guide for Tipping* (booklet); *Tipping Computer*; 3-way comment cards and referral envelope; and survey results. Materials description list available. **How to Contact:** Write or call. Responds to most inquiries within a week. Charges for materials plus postage. Give credit to Tippers International on all

copyrighted material; state where material can be purchased and the cost plus postage/handling. "We also request copies of articles for our files."

1354• TRANET (TRANSNATIONAL NETWORK)
Box 567, Rangeley ME 04970. (207)864-2252. **Description:** "We create links between individuals and groups concerned with alternatives and transformation." **Services:** Provides advisory, bibliographical, interpretative and referral information on alternative technology, world governance, Third World, alternative energy, organic gardening, communes and community, lifestyles and voluntary simplicity. Offers aid in arranging interviews, informational newsletters, library facilities and research assistance. "Much of TRANET's work is for U.N. agencies and in the Third World. Our files have 10,000 organizations active in appropriate technology and related activities. Our interest is in the changing paradigms globally." Publications include *TRANET*, quarterly newsletter. **How to Contact:** Write or call. Responds to most inquiries within a week. "For short projects up to ½ hour of research time, there is no cost; long-term consulting or studies $300/man day. Give details of your project and its expected social impact."

1355• VAMPIRE RESEARCH CENTER
Box 252, Elmhurst, New York NY 11373. Contact Person: Director. **Description:** "Research and study center in the field of vampirology (vampires); researches physical and psychological vampires, vampire-like people, S&M, blood cults, vampire tendencies." **Services:** Provides advisory, historical, how-to and interpretative information on parapsychology and vampirology. Offers aid in arranging interviews, biographies, brochures/pamphlets, placement on mailing lists and research assistance. Publications include *Vampires Are* (1983). **How to Contact:** Write. Responds to most inquiries within a month. Writers must submit biography and stated purpose of their request. Include SASE. **Tips:** Recent information requests: "Where are the vampires?"; "What proof do you have?"; history of vampirology.

1356• VEGETARIAN INFORMATION SERVICE, INC.
Box 5888, Bethesda MD 20814. **Description:** The Vegetarian Information Service, Inc. was founded in 1976 to enlighten the American public and government officials on the various merits of vegetarianism. Its specific objectives are: to collect and organize factual information on all aspects of vegetarianism; to produce and disseminate literature on vegetarianism; to disseminate information to the mass media and to government and commercial institutions; and to arrange conferences and symposia. **Services:** Provides advisory information on meatless diets, protection of farm animals and wildlife, humane education, speciesist language, etc. **How to Contact:** Write. **Tips:** "Action for Life was formed in 1980 to help unify and activate the vegetarian and animal rights movement. Its objectives are to train and mobilize concerned individuals for vegetarian and animal rights action through conferences and related task force activities."

1357• WOMEN USA
76 Beaver St., New York NY 10005. (212)422-1492. Contact Person: President. **Description:** "An action and information network for women who want to help win equality and justice for all women." **Services:** Provides advisory, how-to, interpretative, referral and technical information. Offers brochures/pamphlets, placement on mailing lists, statistics and telephone reference services. **How to Contact:** Write. Responds to most inquiries within a week. **Tips:** Call our hotline weekly (800) 221-4945. In New York (212)344-2531 and write us."

1358• WOMEN'S ACTION ALLIANCE, INC.
370 Lexington Ave., New York NY 10017. (212)532-8330. Contact: Information Services. **Description:** The Women's Action Alliance is a national center on women's issues and programs. Activities include a national information and referral service, the non-sexist child development project and the economic development project. **Services:** Collects analytical, bibliographical, historical, how-to, referral and trade information. Offers biographies, brochures/pamphlets, library facilities, photos, statistics and telephone reference services. Publications include *Women's Action Almanac*; *Non-Sexist Education for Young Children: A Practical Guide*; *How to Organize a Multi-Service Women's Center*; *Getting Your Share: An Introduction to Fundraising*; *Women Helping Women: A State-by-State Directory of Services* and mailing lists. **How to Contact:** Write, call or visit. Responds to most inquiries immediately. "If you wish to use library, call for an appointment; writers cannot take books out of library."

1359• YOUNG MEN'S CHRISTIAN ASSOCIATION OF THE USA (YMCA)
101 N. Wacker Dr., Chicago IL 60606. (312)977-0031. Contact Person: Public Relations Director. **Description:** The YMCA is a multiservice international organization promoting good health, fitness, and social service among young and old alike. **Services:** Provides advisory, analytical, bibliographical, historical, how-to, interpretative, referral and technical information on health and fitness, drug abuse, day care programs, family programming, social services and student activities. Offers aid in arranging interviews, annual reports, biographies, brochures/pamphlets, informational newsletters, library facilities, photos, placement on mailing lists, press kits, research assistance, statistics and telephone reference services. Publications include *Discovery YMCA*. **How to Contact:** Write or call. Responds to most inquiries within a week.

1360• YOUNG WOMEN'S CHRISTIAN ASSOCIATION OF THE USA (YWCA)
135 W. 50th St., New York NY 10020. (212)621-5115. Contact Person: Director of Communications. **Description:** "The YWCA is a multiservice, membership organization serving women and girls of all ages, ethnic and religious backgrounds, life-styles and socioeconomic levels. Women and girls 12 years and older are members. (Men and boys participate in YWCA as associates or registrants.) The YWCA concentrates on development of programs with the highest potential for serving women and girls and their families, and improving their lives. Key to this service program is a stress on the elimination of racism, implicit in all association work, as well as programs concerning racial justice, public policy, health, physical education and recreation. YWCAs are particularly concerned with education, self-improvement, growth, voluntarism, the individual's responsibility as a citizen within the community, emotional and physical health, employment. Nationally, the YWCA's public affairs program is working toward ratification and implementation of the Equal Rights Amendment and support of legislation ending sex-based discrimination against women; promotion of a national policy of full employment, mandating affirmative action and equal pay for work of comparable value; prevention of teenage pregnancy; protection against violence for every individual, particularly for those most vulnerable; and child care services." **Services:** Provides advisory, analytical, historical, interpretative and referral information. Offers aid in arranging interviews, annual reports, biographies, brochures/pamphlets, informational newsletters, library facilities, photos, placement on mailing lists, press kits (limited distribution), research assistance and statistics. Publications include *YWCA Interchange* (bimonthly national periodical for YWCA leaders); *Interact* (national student newsletter); *Public Policy Bulletin*; *National Board Annual Report*; *P.R. Update*; *Executive Bulletin*. **How to Contact:** Write or call. Responds to most inquiries within a week. Charges for historical photos. Give credit to YWCA of the USA in articles as appropriate. **Tips:** "Allow sufficient time for us to assemble information or do specific research." Recent information request: "How does the YWCA help women who are victims of domestic violence?"

1361• YOUTH POLICY INSTITUTE
917 G Place NW, Washington DC 20001. (202)347-3370. Contact Person: Co-Director. **Description:** "The institute monitors federal policies and programs for and affecting young people—done by keeping abreast of developments in Congress, executive agencies and significant non-governmental groups. We pay particular attention to money appropriated and spent." **Services:** Provides advisory, analytical, bibliographical, referral and technical information on budget, bilingual education, compensatory education, court cases, education, employment/vocational education, financial aid and testing, health, human services, juvenile justice, military and national service, nutrition, private sector funding and special education. Offers informational newsletters, research assistance and statistics. Publications include *Youth Policy* magazine; student press service *News Report*; *Profile of the Federal Effort in Juvenile Justice*; *Peace Corps: More Today Than 20 Years Ago*; *Youth Service & Conservation: Meeting National Needs in the 80s*; and *Stalking the Large Green Grant*. **How to Contact:** Write or call. Responds to most inquiries within a week. Charges for publications: *Youth Policy* $75/year; SPS *News Report* $36/year; other reports $5. Give credit to Youth Policy Institute.

SECTION · TWENTY-SIX

SPORTS

In America, it is sport that is the opiate of the masses.

—Russell Baker

Sports information sources cover professional and college sports; spectator sports; individual sports (running, walking, fitness); sports promotion and sports medicine.

Additional sports-related resources (bicycling, for example) may be found in the Hobby and Leisure section.

Bibliography

Arlott, John, ed. *The Oxford Companion to World Sports and Games*. New York: Oxford University Press, 1975.

Cuddon, J.A., ed. *The International Dictionary of Sports and Games*. New York: Schocken Books, 1980.

Koppett, Leonard. *New York Times Guide to Spectator Sports*. New York: Times Books, 1972.

McWhirter, Norris. *Guinness Book of Sports Records: Winners and Champions*. New York: Bantam, 1981.

Official World Encyclopedia of Sports and Games. New York: Paddington Press, Ltd., 1979.

Soderberg, Paul et. al., eds. *The Big Book of Halls of Fame in the US and Canada*. New York: Bowker, 1977.

Sparano, Vin T. *Outdoor Sportsman's Illustrated Dictionary*. New York: David McKay, 1980.

Various specialized directories—*The Baseball Encyclopedia*; *The Official NFL Encyclopedia of Pro Football*; *The Art of Freshwater Fishing*. (Consult the *Subject Guide to Books in Print* for individual titles.)

1362• ALL-AMERICAN SOAP BOX DERBY/INTERNATIONAL SOAP BOX DERBY
Box 7233, Derby Downs, Akron OH 44306. (216)733-8723. Contact Person: General Manager. **Description:** "We license Soap Box Derby programs worldwide; set rules and supervise programs; stage world championships with annual week long festival in Akron, Ohio." **Services:** Provides advisory, analytical, historical, how-to, interpretative, referral and technical information on all aspects of Soap Box Derby racing. Offers brochures/pamphlets, informational newsletters, photos, research assistance and statistics. **How to Contact:** Write, call or visit (by appointment). Responds to most inquiries within a week. Charges for services "only if requirement is so extensive it can't be completed on available staff time and requires overtime." **Tips:** "May-August is a bad time for extensive inquiries as that is the height of our annual program."

1363• AMATEUR ATHLETIC UNION OF THE UNITED STATES, INC.
3400 W. 86th St., Indianapolis IN 46268. (317)872-2900. Contact Person: Director of Public Relations. **Description:** "Our activities include local, regional and national competition in 20 Olympic sports in the AAU/USA Junior Olympics program at the AAU Physical Fitness Program offered in over 10,000 schools; also offer senior competition in 14 sports." **Services:** Provides historical, how-to and referral information on sports administration and youth sports. Offers aid in arranging interviews, brochures/pamphlets, informational newsletters, photos, press kits and statistics. Publications include *Media Guide*; *Code Book*; how-to brochures; and *Info AAU*. **How to Contact:** Write. Responds to most inquiries within a week. Give credit to AAU. **Tips:** Recent information requests: Results of national championships; outstanding young athletes; development programs for youth as part of Olympic development.

1364• AMERICAN ALLIANCE FOR HEALTH, PHYSICAL EDUCATION, RECREATION AND DANCE (AAHPERD)
1900 Association Dr., Reston VA 22091. (703)476-3488. Contact Person: Director of Public Information and Special Projects. **Description:** "AAHPERD is an alliance of voluntary professional associations totaling 50,000 individual members. Members share a common mission of educating and promoting the related areas of health education, safety, physical education, dance, sport, recreation and leisure services. Through its local, state, district and national membership networks, the alliance reaches into more than 16,000 school districts, more than 2,000 colleges and universities and over 10,000 community recreation units." **Services:** Provides advisory, interpretative and referral information on health, physical education, sports, athletics, recreation, dance, safety, leisure activities, physical activity for handicapped and senior citizens, *Jump Rope For Heart* (rope jumping), and youth fitness. Offers aid in arranging interviews, bibliographies, biographies, brochures/pamphlets, information searches, placement on mailing list and information service dealing with physical education and recreation for the handicapped. **How to Contact:** Write or call. Responds to most inquiries within a week. **Tips:** "Contact us far in advance of your deadlines because we have a small staff and limited resources." Recent information request: "What is 'Jump Rope For Heart' and its value as exercise?"

1365• AMERICAN HOCKEY LEAGUE
31 Elm St., Springfield MA 01103. (413)781-2030. Contact Person: Director of Public Relations. **Description:** Professional ice hockey league. "We have 13 active franchises and two inactive in North America, Nova Scotia and Canada. Schedule runs from October through April in regular season; playoffs in April and May each year. We have working agreements with many NHL teams." **Services:** Publications include *Annual Guide*, which contains current and all-time records of the league; and *AHL Rule Book* (updated every year). **How to Contact:** Write. Responds to most inquiries within a week. Charges for *Annual Guide* ($5) and *AHL Rule Book* ($1).

1366• AMERICAN RUNNING AND FITNESS ASSOCIATION
2420 K St. NW, Washington DC 20037. (202)965-3430. Contact Person: Editor. **Description:** "We are a nonprofit, educational membership organization providing information about running, fitness and well-being." **Services:** Provides information on running, nutrition, diet, fitness, health, sports and exercise. Offers brochures/pamphlets, informational newsletter, photos, press kits, research assistance and reference services. Publications include *Running and Fitness*. **How to Contact:** Write. Responds to most inquiries within a week. **Tips:** "Ask us for publications guidelines."

1367• AMERICAN SOCCER LEAGUE
401 Lyell Ave., Rochester NY 14606. Contact Person: Public Relations Director. **Description:** The ASL is made up of 7 active teams and 5 inactive teams which compete professionally in the sport of soccer. **Services:** Offers placement on mailing list, statistics, press guides, media guides and press releases. **How to Contact:** Write. Responds to most inquiries within a week. An accredited writer may get information free; charges to general public. **Tips:** Recent information requests: Names of teams and their standing; who won previous year's championship.

1368• AMERICAN WHEELCHAIR BOWLING ASSOCIATION, INC.
6718 Pinehurst Dr., Evansville IN 47711. (812)867-6503. Contact Person: Executive Secretary. **Description:** AWBA is a recreational organization for individuals with permanent disabilities. "We promote and regulate wheelchair bowling." **Services:** Provides advisory, bibliographical, historical, how-to, interpretative, referral, technical and trade information on wheelchair bowling. Offers brochures/pamphlets and informational newsletters. Publications include *11th Frame* (newsletter). **How to Contact:** Write, call or visit. Responds to most inquiries within a week. To receive newsletter regularly must be AWBA member.

1369• BASEBALL COMMISSIONER'S OFFICE
75 Rockefeller Plaza, New York NY 10019. (212)586-7400. Contact Person: Director of Information. **Description:** The commissioner's office oversees the organization of the National and American Baseball Leagues (26 clubs). **Services:** Provides advisory, analytical, historical, how-to, interpretative, referral, technical and trade information related to baseball. Offers aid in arranging interviews, informational newsletters, placement on mailing lists, research assistance,

statistics and telephone reference services. **How to Contact:** Write or call. Responds to most inquiries within a month.

1370• BASKETBALL HALL OF FAME
Box 175, Highland Station, Springfield MA 01109. (413)781-6500. Contact Person: Librarian or Promotion Director. **Description:** "The Basketball Hall of Fame is a museum and shrine dedicated to America's native sport, basketball; we are attempting to develop a complete reference library on the subject." **Services:** Provides historical, technical and trade information on basketball research. Offers biographies, library facilities, photos and research assistance. **How to Contact:** Write. Responds to most inquiries within a month. Charges for services "only if it involves out-of-pocket expense to us. Appointments are necessary."

1371• BIKECENTENNIAL
Box 8308, Missoula MT 59807. (406)721-1776. Contact Person: Publications Director. **Description:** "We promote bicycle touring in the United States and worldwide. We provide a clearinghouse of bicycling information and offer trips on routes that we research and map. The organization is member supported (20,000 members)." **Services:** Provides advisory, historical, how-to, referral, technical and trade information on the sport of bicycle touring (some racing, fair amount of commuting information, but mostly touring). Offers aid in arranging interviews, brochures/pamphlets, informational newsletters, library facilities, photos and press kits. Publications include *Bike Report*, bimonthly news journal, available by issue upon request. **How to Contact:** Write or call. Responds to most inquiries within a week. **Tips:** Recent information request: Interviews with cyclists who had traveled across America by bicycle.

1372• THE BUFFERIN BRAND GROUP AT BRISTOL-MYERS
c/o Manning, Selvage & Lee, 99 Park Ave., New York NY 10016. (212)599-6989. Contact Person: Account Executive. **Description:** The Bufferin Brand Group is developing and executing a sports injuries education program. **Services:** Provides advisory, bibliographical, how-to and referral information on sports medicine; prevention and treatment of sports injuries; running and tennis. Offers aid in arranging interviews, brochures/pamphlets, placement on mailing lists, press kits and statistics. Publications include *Sports Injuries: An Aid to Prevention and Treatment* ($1). **How to Contact:** Write or call. Responds to most inquiries immediately.

1373• CHURCHILL DOWNS, INC.
Box 8427, Louisville KY 40208. (502)636-3541, 589-3561. Contact Person: Director of Media Relations. **Description:** "Best known as the home of the Kentucky Derby, Churchill Downs conducts two thoroughbred race meetings per year—one in the spring and one in the fall for a total of approximately 80 days. In existence since 1875, the track keeps historical and statistical information related to racing, specifically the Kentucky Derby." **Services:** Provides advisory, bibliographical and historical information on thoroughbred horse racing. Offers aid in arranging interviews, annual reports, bibliographies, biographies, statistics, placement on mailing list, newsletter, photos and press kits (Derby press kits go only to accredited press). Publications include a Kentucky Derby Press Guide; a Fall Meeting Press Guide; Kentucky Derby Museum brochure; a King of Sports informational racing brochure; Kentucky Derby ticket information; and a Churchill Downs Group Program brochure. **How to Contact:** Write or call. "Members of accredited news media desiring press credentials must write on letterhead at least four weeks prior to the opening of the racing season." Responds to most inquiries immediately. "Prices for photography publication depend on use. Other photographs are $7 per 8x10 b&w print; $15 per 8x10 color photo; other sizes are available on request. Permission to use must be granted on photos for publication or commerical use." **Tips:** "Sufficient time required for research."

1374• COACHING ASSOCIATION OF CANADA
333 River Rd., Vanier, Ottawa, Ontario, Canada K1L 8B9. (613)746-5693. Contact Person: Vice President. **Description:** "The Coaching Association of Canada is a national, nonprofit organization. Its major aims are to increase coaching effectiveness in all sports and to encourage the development of coaching by providing programs and services to coaches at all levels. We also operate the Sports Information Resourcc Center (SIRC). It is a unique sport library and documentation center, and its services are accessible to all CAC members as well as to the sports community at large." **Services:** Provides advisory, bibliographical, how-to, referral and technical information. Offers annual reports, brochures/pamphlets and information searches.

Publications include *Coaching Review* (bimonthly magazine) and *Sport and Recreation Index*. **How to Contact:** Write. Responds to most inquiries immediately. **Tips:** "Contact coaches in the sport you are writing about."

1375• FIRST INTERSTATE BANK ATHLETIC FOUNDATION SPORTS LIBRARY
2141 West Adams Blvd., Los Angeles CA 90018. Mailing address: Box 60310, Terminal Annex, Los Angeles CA 90060. Contact Person: Managing Director. **Description:** "The First Interstate Bank Athletic Foundation's sports library, covering all sports, is considered to be the most complete in existence. The Olympic Games library is unsurpassed. The athletic foundation also maintains an extensive sports film library, as well as photographic files. Some films are available for special showings, on loan basis." **Services:** Provides historical information on all sports. Offers bibliographies, biographies, statistics and information searches. Publications include press and media releases. **How to Contact:** "The sports library is open for special research by members of the media, sports historians and researchers, authors and students, Monday through Friday, 10 a.m.-4 p.m. All research must be conducted in the library; no book loans." Responds to most inquiries immediately. Charges for services. **Tips:** "Prepare an outline of information needed, and follow it."

1376• GRODY/TELLEM COMMUNICATIONS
9100 S. Sepulveda Blvd., # 200, Los Angeles CA 90045. (213)873-4399, 417-3038. Contact Person: Editor. **Description:** Communications agency providing "authoritative information on the prevention, treatment and rehabilitation of sports injuries." **Services:** Provides advisory, bibliographical, historical, how-to, interpretative, referral, technical and trade information on all aspects of sports medicine. Offers aid in arranging interviews, informational newsletters, library facilities and research assistance. Publications include *Sportsmedicine Digest* (issue available on request). **How to Contact:** Write or call. Responds to most inquiries within a week. Charges for subscriptions. **Tips:** Recent information requests: "How can I choose a running shoe?"; "Who can provide me with more information on scuba diving?"; "Where are sports medicine centers located in the US?"

1377• HARNESS TRACKS OF AMERICA, INC.
35 Airport Rd., Morristown NJ 07690. (201)285-9090. Contact Person: Executive Assistant. **Description:** "Harness Tracks of America is an association of North American harness racing tracks dedicated to the advancement and progress of the harness racing sport. Activities enter into all areas of the race track business, including economic information and statistics." Information covers business, economics, history, law, politics and sports. **Services:** Offers statistics, brochures/pamphlets and newsletters. **How to Contact:** Write or call. Responds to most inquiries within a week. Some information is available only to members.

1378• INTERNATIONAL BATON TWIRLING ASSOCIATION OF AMERICA AND ABROAD (IBTA)
Box 234, Waldwick NJ 07463. Contact Person: Director. **Description:** "We promote baton twirling-talent internationally in a display of clean sportsmanship, in contests, seminars, judged by well-qualified judges of distinction. We promote scholarships, present awards and provide instruction in all phases." **Services:** Provides advisory, historical, how-to and interpretative information on instruction/contests/seminars/shows. Offers aid in arranging interviews, biographies, brochures/pamphlets and photos. **How to Contact:** Write. Responds to most inquiries within a week. **Tips:** Recent information requests: "Where can we take baton lessons?"; "Where can we enter contests?"; "What colleges offer scholarships?"; "Send us a list of teachers."

1379• THE INTERNATIONAL CHEERLEADING FOUNDATION, INC.
4425 Indian Creek Pkwy., Shawnee-Mission KS 66207. (913)649-3666. Contact Person: President. **Description:** A national association for high school cheerleading and pep club programs. "We publish textbooks (through major New York publishers), issue a magazine, offer a variety of services and conduct training camps in 44 states." **Services:** Provides advisory, bibliographical, historical, how-to, interpretative and referral information on the 84-year-old field of cheerleading and school spirit activities as they relate to athletics in America. Offers aid in arranging interviews, biographies, brochures/pamphlets, informational newsletters, photos and research assistance. Publications include *The Official Cheerleaders Handbook*; *The Handbook of*

School Spirit; *The Official Cheerleaders Manual*; *The Official Pompon Girls Handbook*; and *Cheerleader* Magazine. **How to Contact:** Write or call. Responds to most inquiries within a week. **Tips:** "As a member of the National Collegiate Athletic Association, we receive all types of questions that relate to sports activities. We can assist anyone doing work on sports events in which cheerleaders are involved." Recent information request: "How important are cheerleaders in America's sports programs?"

1380• INTERNATIONAL COUNCIL OF ASSOCIATIONS OF SURFING (ICAS)
Box 1315, Beverly Hills CA 90213. Contact Person: President. **Description:** ICAS is an international sport federation whose purpose is to gain Olympic recognition for the amateur sport of surfing and to increase economic opportunities for professional surfers. **Services:** Provides advisory, analytical, bibliographical, historical, how-to and technical information on the sport of surfing. Offers aid in arranging interviews, biographies, informational newsletters, photos, placement on mailing lists, research assistance and statistics. Publications include *ICAS Code*; and *The International Surfer* (quarterly). **How to Contact:** Write. Responds to most inquiries immediately.

1381• INTERNATIONAL SWIMMING HALL OF FAME
One Hall of Fame Dr., Ft. Lauderdale FL 33316. (305)462-6536. Contact Person: Executive Director. **Description:** "Educational shrine for the sport of swimming. The Hall of Fame honors swimming immortals and includes displays, trophies, films, souvenirs and aquatic books." **Services:** Provides advisory, historical, how-to and referral information on everything aquatic. Offers biographies, brochures/pamphlets, informational newsletters, library facilities and research assistance. Publications include aquatic books sold through Hall of Fame bookstore (mail order also). **How to Contact:** Write, call or visit. Responds to most inquiries within a week. Charges for photos and photocopies. "Books cannot be taken from the library."

1382• INTERNATIONAL TENNIS HALL OF FAME
194 Bellevue Ave., Newport RI 02840. (401)849-3990. Contact Person: Curator. **Description:** "We maintain a depository of tennis memorabilia." **Services:** Provides bibliographical and historical information on tennis. Offers aid in arranging interviews, biographies, brochures/pamphlets, informational newsletters, library facilities, photos, research assistance, statistics and telephone reference services. **How to Contact:** Write, call or visit. Responds to most inquiries within a week. "Appointments must be made before visiting."

1383• LITTLE LEAGUE BASEBALL, INC.
Box 3485, Williamsport PA 17701. (717)326-1921. Contact Person: Public Relations Director. **Description:** "Little League Baseball, Inc., is a youth sports organization." **Services:** Provides advisory, historical, how-to and referral information on youth baseball. Offers aid in arranging interviews, bibliographies, statistics, brochures/pamphlets, information searches, placement on mailing list, photos, press kits and an organizational profile. Publications include *Where Little League Stands in Service to Youth* and *Little League Today: The Total Community Program*. **How to Contact:** Write or call. Responds to most inquiries immediately. Give appropriate credit for copyrighted material.

1384• MARINA SPORTS MEDICINE AND HEALTH PROMOTION CENTER
4640 Admiralty Way, Suite 102, Marina del Rey CA 90291. (213)823-6036. Contact Person: Executive Director. **Description:** "Medically-based alternative to health clubs or spas. The center emphasizes the concept of 'wellness' through medically-supervised programs in exercise, nutrition, weight loss and stress management, as well as extensive rehabilitation programs for individuals with acute and chronic musculoskeletal injuries, hypertension, diabetes and chronic pain." **Services:** Provides advisory, how-to, referral, technical and trade information on all aspects of fitness, nutrition, biofeedback, health promotion, pain management, exercise physiology, health education. Offers aid in arranging interviews, brochures/pamphlets, photos, placement on mailing lists, press kits, research assistance and statistics. **How to Contact:** Write, call or visit. Responds to most inquiries immediately. **Tips:** Recent information requests: "What is the best way to prevent summer sports injuries?"; "What's new in nutrition?"; "What are the components of an executive fitness program?"; "How can I avoid tennis elbow and maintain my health in middle age?"

1385• NATIONAL ARCHERY ASSOCIATION
1750 East Boulder St., Colorado Springs CO 80909. (303)578-4576. Contact Person: Executive Secretary. **Description:** "The purpose of our organization is educational and charitable, to foster and direct the practice of the sport of amateur archery in the United States." **Services:** Provides referral and technical information: named competitors, list of tournaments throughout the country as well as international competitions. Offers aid in arranging interviews, biographies, informational newsletters, placement on mailing lists, press kits and statistics. Publications include rule books, instructional manuals and general information. **How to Contact:** Write. Responds to most inquiries within a week. Charges for some publications. "We have a limited staff and cannot provide individual research." **Tips:** Recommends "initial research either through publications available on the newsstand or in the public library, so that the person requesting information does have some background to bring to the specific questions being asked. We welcome the opportunity to verify specifics about competitors, records or results of competitions." Recent information request: "Please send me the listing of winners in national competition over the past ten years with their hometowns in all age groups."

1386• NATIONAL ASSOCIATION FOR STOCK CAR AUTO RACING (NASCAR)
Box K, Daytona Beach FL 32015. (904)253-0611. Contact: Public Relations Department. **Description:** "NASCAR's purpose is the sanctioning of automobile races." **Services:** Provides advisory, historical, interpretative and referral information on automobile races sanctioned by NASCAR. Offers aid in arranging interviews, biographies, brochures/pamphlets, informational newsletters, placement on mailing lists, press kits, research assistance and statistics. Publications include *NASCAR Record Book & Press Guide*; and *NASCAR Newsletter*. **How to Contact:** Write. Responds to most inquiries within a week.

1387• NATIONAL ASSOCIATION OF INTERCOLLEGIATE ATHLETICS
1221 Baltimore St., Kansas City MO 64105. (816)842-5050. Contact Person: Director of Communications. **Description:** "The purpose of the NAIA is to promote interests of the colleges of moderate enrollment." **Services:** Provides historical information about the association and its related championship events. Offers statistics, brochures/pamphlets and newsletter. **How to Contact:** Write or call. Responds to most inquiries within a week. Charges for photocopying. Give credit to NAIA for information.

1388• NATIONAL ASSOCIATION OF PROFESSIONAL BASEBALL LEAGUES
Box A, St. Petersburg FL 33731. (813)822-6937. Contact Person: Director of Promotion. **Description:** "We are the main governing body of minor league baseball and the central clearinghouse for all its paperwork and records." **Services:** Offers statistics, information searches and newsletter. Publications include a monthly newsletter and *Baseball* (annual magazine). **How to Contact:** Write; include SASE. Responds to most inquiries within a week. No personal information on players. **Tips:** Recent information request: Attendance figures for various clubs.

1389• NATIONAL BASEBALL HALL OF FAME AND MUSEUM, INC.
Box 590, Cooperstown NY 13326. (607)547-9988. Contact Person: Historian. **Description:** Baseball museum and library. Features memorabilia displays, films and library which is open only for serious baseball research. Information covers history, recreation and sports (baseball). **Services:** Provides bibliographical, historical and technical information on professional baseball. Offers bibliographies, biographies, statistics, brochures/pamphlets, information searches and photos. Publications include hall of fame booklet and brochure. **How to Contact:** Write or call; describe needed subject matter. Responds to most inquiries within a week. Library is open 9 a.m. to 5 p.m. on weekdays by appointment. **Tips:** "Be prepared to look through a considerable amount of material." Recent information request: "Provide a list of major and minor league teams for which a certain baseball star played."

1390• NATIONAL BASKETBALL ASSOCIATION
Olympic Tower, 645 5th Ave., New York NY 10022. (212)826-7000. Contact person: Director of Public Relations or Director of Information. **Description:** The NBA coordinates the activities of 23 professional teams and various league officials. **Services:** Provides advisory, analytical, historical, how-to, interpretative, referral and technical information covering marketing, promotion, rules, staffing, broadcasting of games and basketball statistics. Offers aid in arranging

interviews, biographies, brochures/pamphlets, clipping services, computerized information searches, informational newsletters, placement on mailing lists, press kits, research assistance and telephone reference services. Publications include *NBA Guide*; *NBA Register*; *NBA Today*. **How to Contact:** Write or call. Responds to most inquiries within a week. **Tips:** Recent information request: Biographical material on a particular basketball player.

1391• NATIONAL BOWLING COUNCIL
1919 Pennsylvania Ave. NW, Washington DC 20006. (202)659-9070. Contact Person: Public Relations Director. **Description:** "The National Bowling Council is the education and promotion arm of the sport, with a membership representing all facets of the game." **Services:** Provides information on business, celebrities, entertainment, history, how-to, industry, recreation, sport and technical data. Offers aid in arranging interviews, annual reports, bibliographies, statistics, brochures/pamphlets, information searches, placement on mailing list, photos and press kits. "We can supply or direct a writer to every aspect of the sport, thereby cutting down on the number of calls which must be made." Publications include *Bowling Factbook* (demographics on the sport). **How to Contact:** Write or call. Responds to most inquiries within a week.

1392• NATIONAL COLLEGIATE ATHLETIC ASSOCIATION
Box 1906, Mission KS 66201. (913)384-3220. Contact Person: Director of Public Relations. **Description:** The NCAA is a voluntary association of more than 900 institutions, conferences and organizations devoted to the sound administration of intercollegiate athletics in all phases. **Services:** Offers aid in arranging interviews, brochures/pamphlets, information searches, placement on mailing list, statistics, newsletter and press kits. **How to Contact:** Write or call. Responds to most inquiries within a week.

1393• NATIONAL HOCKEY LEAGUE
960 Sunlife Building, 1155 Metcalfe St., Montreal, Quebec, Canada H3B 2W2. (514)871-9220; 14th Floor, 1221 Avenue of the Americas, New York NY 10020. (212)398-1100. Contact Person: Montreal, Director of Information, Campbell Conference; New York, Director of Information, Wales Conference. **Description:** "We are a 21-team major professional sports league which has provided entertainment to fans in North America since 1917." **Services:** Provides advisory, bibliographical, historical, how-to, interpretative, referral and technical information on all matters pertaining to the present and past of the National Hockey League. Offers aid in arranging interviews, annual reports, biographies, brochures/pamphlets, computerized information searches, informational newsletters, library facilities, placement on mailing lists, research assistance and statistics. Publications include *NHL Guide*; *NHL Official Record Book*; *Goal Magazine*; *NHL Rule Book*; *NHL Schedule* and *NHL Media Directory*. **How to Contact:** Write, call or visit. Responds to most inquiries within a week. Publications price list available. **Tips:** "We deal with writers from major media outlets in terms of supplying printed matter, but comply readily to all information requests. Try to deal with the NHL team located nearby, since this generally helps develop regional exposure."

1394• NATIONAL JUNIOR COLLEGE ATHLETIC ASSOCIATION
12 E. 2nd St., Hutchinson KS 67501. (316)633-5445. Contact Person: Executive Director. **Description:** "We promote and foster junior college athletics on intersectional and national levels, so that results will be consisent with the total educational program of association members." **Services:** Provides advisory information on athletics, athletic administration and sports. Offers aid in arranging interviews, brochures/pamphlets, information searches and statistics (on national tournaments). Publications available. **How to Contact:** Write. Responds to most inquiries immediately. Charges for publications.

1395• NATIONAL MARINE MANUFACTURERS ASSOCIATION (NMMA)
353 Lexington Ave., New York NY 10016. (212)684-6622. Contact Person: Sales Promotion Manager. **Description:** "A trade association of the recreational boating industry, devoting energies and resources toward improving the lot of the recreational boater. The NMMA supports boating safety through education and standards." **Services:** Offers statistics, brochures/pamphlets, newsletter and photos. Publications include annual boating information guide; *Sailing Is Fun*; *Boating Speakers Bureau* and *Where to Learn to Sail*. **How to Contact:** "Boating writers may request to be put on news release mailing list free by writing to NMMA." Charges for some publications.

1396• NATIONAL MUSEUM OF RACING, INC.
Union Ave., Saratoga Springs NY 12866. (518)584-0400. Contact Person: Director. **Description:** "The purpose for which such a corporation is formed is to establish a museum for the collection and preservation of all materials and articles associated with the origin, history and development of horse racing and the breeding of the thoroughbred horse." **Services:** Provides bibliographical, historical and referral information on thoroughbred horses and horse racing. Offers some biographies, brochures/pamphlets, library facilities (limited) and photos. Publications include set of *Hall of Fame* books (one listing horses; the other trainers and jockeys); *Racing in America.* **How to Contact:** Write or call. Responds to most inquiries "depending upon the season." Charges for photos and publications, also for photocopying. **Tips:** "Due to staff limitations, questions should be reasonably specific. We do not offer individual research. Library service by appointment *only* (not available July 15-September 1)."

1397• NATIONAL RIFLE ASSOCIATION OF AMERICA
1600 Rhode Island Ave. NW, Washington DC 20036. (202)828-6000. Contact Person: Editor, *American Marksman.* **Description:** "We are the national governing body of the shooting sports, the largest organization of shooting sportsmen in the nation and a recognized authority on all firearms topics. We sponsor US Olympic and world championship teams and represent the interests of shooters, hunters and firearms collectors at all levels of government." **Services:** Offers aid in arranging interviews, annual reports, statistics, brochures/pamphlets, placement on mailing list, photos and press kits. Publications include 3 magazines: *The American Rifleman* ($15/year); *The American Hunter* ($15/year); *The American Marksman* ($6/year); and a newspaper *Report from Washington* ($6/year). **How to Contact:** Write or call. Responds to most inquiries within a week. For sports and general information, contact the NRA Office of Public Affairs. For political information, contact the NRA Institute for Legislative Action, Communications Division. **Tips:** Recent information request: Shooting sports in the Olympics.

1398• NATIONAL RUNNING DATA CENTER
Box 42888, Tucson AZ 85733. (602)323-2223, 326-6416. Contact Person: Director. **Description:** The NRDC is a nonprofit, independent organization serving as a basic source of information about long distance running. **Services:** Provides analytical, historical, interpretative and referral information on long distance running, race results, individual performances, etc. Offers brochures/pamphlets, informational newsletters and library facilities. Publications include *Certified Road Running Courses*; *Running US Distance Rankings*; *In-Depth Masters Road Rankings*; *NRDC News* (newsletter). Publications list available. **How to Contact:** Write or call.

1399• NATIONAL SENIOR SPORTS ASSOCIATION
317 Cameron St., Alexandria VA 22314. (703)549-6711. Contact Person: Deputy Executive Director. **Description:** "Our purpose is to assist our members in maintaining and improving physical and emotional health through sports participation." **Services:** Provides advisory, interpretative and referral information on sports activities of the organization, with emphasis on golf, tennis, and bowling. Offers aid in arranging interviews, brochures/pamphlets, photos, placement on mailing lists and research assistance. Publications include *Senior Sports News*, monthly newsletter. **How to Contact:** Write, call or visit. Responds to most inquiries immediately.

1400• NORTH AMERICAN SOCCER LEAGUE
1133 Avenue of the Americas, New York NY 10036. (212)575-0066. Contact Person: Public Relations Director. **Description:** Professional soccer league in the US and Canada. **Services:** Offers aid in arranging interviews (will direct to commissioner of league and public relations director of individual teams); biographies (select); information searches (limited); placement on mailing list; newsletter, statistics and photos. Publications include media guide "available to all qualified writers." **How to Contact:** Write or call. Charges for photos if they are to be used in a commercial book.

1401• NORTH AMERICAN TIDDLYWINKS ASSOCIATION (NATwA)
2701 Woodedge Rd., Silver Spring MD 20906. (301)933-3840. Contact Person: Archivist. **Description:** "The NATwA Archives preserves and disseminates information on the unique sport of tiddlywinks, which has been played in organized tournaments by winkers since

1955 and by the general populace since 1888." **Services:** Provides historical, how-to and referral information on tiddlywinks: rules, tournaments, etc. Offers research assistance and statistics. **How to Contact:** Write. Responds to most inquiries within a month. Charges for significant amounts of photocopying. "We would appreciate receiving copies of articles referring to NATwA or tiddlywinks." **Tips:** Recent information request: "How is Tournament Tiddlywinks different from the game we all played as children?"

1402• NORTH AMERICAN TRAIL RIDE CONFERENCE
1505 E. San Martin Ave., San Martin CA 95046. (408)683-2810. Contact Person: Secretary. **Description:** "Our purpose is to stimulate greater interest in the breeding and use of good horses possessed of stamina and hardiness and qualified to make good mounts for trail use; to demonstrate the value of type and soundness in the proper selection of horses for competitive riding; to learn and demonstrate the proper methods of training and conditioning horses for a long ride; to encourage horsemanship in competitive trail riding; and to demonstrate the best methods of caring for horses during and after long rides without the aid of artificial methods or stimulants." **Services:** Provides how-to information on management, judging and riding of competitive rides. Offers informational newsletters and manuals. Publications include *Judges Manual*; *Riders Manual*; *Management Manual*; and newsletter. **How to Contact:** Write or call. Responds to most inquiries within a week. Charges for manuals: $2.50 each or $6.50 for all 3. California residents add 6% sales tax. "NATRC permission is necessary to reprint any part of manuals or any other NATRC materials (newsletter articles, etc.)."

1403• PRESIDENT'S COUNCIL ON PHYSICAL FITNESS AND SPORTS
450 5th St. NW, Washington DC 20015. (202)272-3430. Contact Person: Director of Information. **Description:** "The council promotes national fitness and health in every segment of the population, including schools, business and industry. It provides assistance to groups seeking to formulate health and fitness programs." **Services:** Provides advisory, bibliographical, how-to, referral and technical information: personal, school, community and corporate fitness programs. Offers aid in arranging interviews with professional staff, bibliographies, biographies, statistics, brochures/pamphlets and "limited publications." **How to Contact:** Write or call. Responds to most inquiries within a month. **Tips:** "Request information about the subject area you're interested in and we'll advise you if we have a publication or where publications may be obtained if we don't." Recent information request: Statistics on exercise and sports participation.

1404• PRO FOOTBALL HALL OF FAME
2121 Harrison Ave. NW, Canton OH 44708. (216)456-8207. Contact Person: Librarian. **Description:** "Historical repository and showplace of information on professional football greats of the past." **Services:** Provides bibliographical, historical, referral and technical information on professional football. Offers aid in arranging interviews, biographies, placement on mailing list, statistics, photos and press kits. **How to Contact:** Write or call. Responds to most inquiries within 2 weeks. A $2 fee is charged for photos of enshrinees. If quantity of material is to be reproduced, a photocopying fee of 10¢/piece is charged. An appointment is necessary for the use of the research library. "Call one to two weeks in advance for an appointment. Library is open Monday—Friday 9 a.m.-5 p.m. There is no loaning of books." **Tips:** Recent information request: Basic biographical material on certain enshrinee, playing years, team played for, height, weight, career highlights.

1405• PROFESSIONAL ASSOCIATION OF DIVING INSTRUCTORS.
1234 E. Warner Ave., Santa Ana CA 92705. (714)540-7234. Contact Person: Vice President, Education and Public Affairs. **Description:** "The association is involved in the training and certification of underwater scuba instructors as well as the education of the general public in the safety aspects of skin and scuba diving." **Services:** Provides advisory, analytical, historical, how-to, interpretative, referral, technical and trade information on scuba diving, dive travel and dive retailing. Offers brochures/pamphlets and newsletters. Publications include *Diving Ventures* magazine; *Undersea Journal* ($12/year); *Dive Manual and Dive Tabler* ($9.95); *Instructors Manual* ($20); and information bulletins ($1). **How to Contact:** Write. Responds to most inquiries within a week. **Tips:** Recent information requests: Description of the popularity of dive travel; demographic and distribution information concerning scuba divers.

BEHIND THE BYLINE

Joe Falls
Sportswriter

He's covered all the major professional sports as well as the Kentucky Derby, the Indy 500 and the Olympics. He's written a book about the Boston Marathon. But veteran *Detroit News* sportswriter Joe Falls still likes writing about baseball best. "I'd have to say my favorite is a Sunday afternoon baseball game with the sun shining; the national anthem being sung; and mothers, dads and their kids watching in the stands. For awhile we are all involved."

Involvement is Joe Falls's watchword. He's been covering Detroit's teams for thirty years and says he understands the city and its teams. And he knows his audience. "People ask me why I don't leave this town. I don't think I could move to Dallas or LA or New York and have the same perception. I know the Tiger second baseman in 1924 was Del Pratt and the Tiger second baseman in 1982 was Lou Whitaker. That's why I stay." Falls brings continuity to the sports pages and gets respect in return. "When I say something about Sparky Anderson, the fans may not like what I say, but there's a feeling that somehow I've earned the right to say it."

He also continues to be a regular columnist for the *Sporting News*, which he calls his business's "paper of record" because it reports on all the games in all the major sports. How does he keep on top of it all? "I regularly read the *LA Times* and the *Boston Globe*, and I generally subscribe to different newspapers around the country for three-six months at a time. I rotate them; maybe I'll read a Montreal paper or a Chicago paper for awhile." He says this helps him get a feeling for what's going on in America's sports pages. Then there are record books. "Much of the research in writing sports has to do with records. There are more records in sportswriting than in any other business. Take baseball. There's the *Baseball Encyclopedia* (New York: Macmillan). It's probably the greatest sports reference book ever published. It goes back to day one of the game. Baseball is a numbers game; maybe a big part of its popularity is the numbers."

Statistics are important to both sportswriters and fans. But knowing statistics isn't the only requisite for being a good sportswriter. You have to be entertaining as well as informative, says Falls. (He should know, having been selected five times by the National Sportswriters and Sportscasters Association as one of the Top Three Sportswriters in the country.) "It's our job to go beyond the game a little. We need a balance in sportswriting. We have to bring both truth and joy to people. And that's a difficult task sometimes. The sports pages are different from the rest of the paper. People turn to them as an outlet—a way to get away from their own worries. And they want to hear only good things about their heroes. But sometimes you have to make them feel bad because the truth is their heroes aren't quite the heroes they'd imagined. Fans can resent you for that. But when you're writing for hundreds of thousands of people, there's no way you're going to please them all. I usually just write what's in my mind and in my heart.

"You can't just theorize about writing sports, though. You have to 'go where the cabbage is,' as Red Smith used to say. You have to be there and experience the town. There's a good story everywhere; not just at the Rose Bowl. It happens at every level. But to write about it, you've got to be there; you've got to care about sports and care about writing."

1406• PROFESSIONAL BOWLERS ASSOCIATION
1720 Merriman Rd., Akron OH 44313. (216)836-5568. Contact Person: Public Relations Director. **Description:** The PBA promotes the sport of professional bowling and conducts professional tournaments across the country. **Services:** Provides advisory, historical and referral information on professional bowling, outstanding performers on tour, tournament results. Offers aid in arranging interviews, brochures/pamphlets, clipping services, computerized information searches, informational newsletters, photos, placement on mailing lists, press kits, research assistance and statistics. Publications include books; annual *Press-Radio-Television Guide* and a *Tournament Tour Program.* **How to Contact:** Write. Responds to most inquiries within a week. **Tips:** Recent information request: "Why does the professional bowling tour on TV have a better rating than its competition?"

1407• PROFESSIONAL GOLFERS' ASSOCIATION OF AMERICA (PGA)
Box 12458, Palm Beach Gardens FL 33403. (305)626-3600. Contact Person: Communications Director or News Director. **Description:** "The Professional Golfers' Association of America is an association of 16,000 members and apprentices. The organization carries out various administrative functions for members, including education; operation of various activities such as professional golf tournaments; a credit union; membership processing; and annual business and executive meetings." **Services:** Provides advisory, bibliographical, historical and referral information on PGA of America programs, activities. Offers aid in arranging interviews, annual reports, bibliographies, biographies, statistics, brochures/pamphlets, information searches, placement on mailing list, newsletter, photos, press kits and films. Publications include *PGA Media Reference Guide* and *PGA Apprentice Program.* **How to Contact:** Write or call. Responds to most inquiries within a week. Charges $10/film, plus shipping costs. **Tips:** Recent information request: "How many women are enrolled in PGA Apprentice Program?"

1408• PROFESSIONAL RODEO COWBOYS ASSOCIATION
101 Pro Rodeo Dr., Colorado Springs CO 80919. (303)593-8840. Contact Person: Director, Media Relations. **Description:** "Operated and governed by members, the PRCA makes and enforces rules pertaining to its 650 rodeos and thousands of members. The PRCA approves its rodeos and works to insure adequate prize money for its contestants, as well as safety, sponsorship, publicity, etc." **Services:** Provides analytical, bibliographical, historical and referral information on top PRCA cowboys and other members (past and present); statistics about championships, top stock, etc.; information on all PRCA events, rodeos, board of directors, humane issues, putting on rodeos, careers in rodeo, Prorodeo Hall of Champions, etc. Offers aid in arranging interviews, biographies, brochures/pamphlets, clipping services, computerized information searches, descriptions of events, photos, placement on mailing lists, press kits, research assistance, statistics and films and video cassettes (deposit required). Publications include *Annual PRCA Media Guide*; humane brochure, *The Cowboy Sport* (event descriptions, etc.); *Prorodeo Sports News*; biographies of world champion cowboys, PRCA rule book. **How to Contact:** Write, call or visit. Responds to most inquiries immediately. Charges for certain publications (rule book, $1.25), or for work which involves extra time, etc. "We appreciate return of photos and transparencies." **Tips:** "Don't worry if you don't know anything about rodeo. We have basic information for the newcomer as well as facts for the long-time rodeo fan." Recent information requests: "How many PRCA members are there?"; "How many spectators at PRCA rodeos?"; "How much prize money is paid annually?"; "How can I contact a world champion cowboy for an interview?"

1409• ROCKWELL AND NEWELL, INC.
12 E. 41st St., New York NY 10017. (212)725-0420. Contact Person: President. **Description:** Public relations firm. **Services:** Provides advisory, historical, how-to, referral, technical and trade information on boating, canoeing and bicycles/mopeds, as well as gun storage/protection. Offers brochures/pamphlets, informational newsletters, photos, press kits and research assistance. **How to Contact:** Write, call or visit. Responds to most inquiries within a week.

1410• THE SOUTHLAND CORPORATION
c/o Carlson, Rockey & Associates, 360 Lexington Ave., New York NY 10017. (212)599-2670. Contact Person: Account Executive or Director, Southland Olympic News Bureau. **Description:** "The Southland Corporation is owner and franchiser of more than 7,000 7-Eleven convenience stores in the US and a major sponsor of the 1984 Olympic Games in Los Angeles; sponsor of ama-

teur cycling teams preparing for Olympics and contributor of the $3 million velodrome for Olympic cycling events in Los Angeles.'' **Services:** Provides advisory, bibliographical, historical, how-to, interpretative, referral and trade information covering corporate background, as well as all information on cycling as a sport and an Olympic event; US cycling team development; relationship with USOC and the Los Angeles Olympic Committee and cycling federations. Offers aid in arranging interviews, annual reports, biographies, brochures/pamphlets, clipping services, informational newsletters, library facilities, photos, placement on mailing lists, press kits, research assistance, statistics and telephone reference services. Publications available. **How to Contact:** Write or call. Responds to most inquiries within week. Give proper identification of the Southland Corporation and 7-Eleven. **Tips:** ''Simply telephone or write for needed information. Alternative telephone number (toll-free) is 800-221-1984 at The Southland Olympic News Bureau. Recent information request: ''Why is The Southland Corporation committing itself substantially to a sports program, and cycling specifically?''

1411• SPORT INFORMATION RESOURCE CENTER (SIRC)
Coaching Association of Canada (CAC), 333 River Rd., Vanier, Ottawa, Canada K1L 8B9. (613)746-5693. Contact Person: SIRC Manager. **Description:** ''The Coaching Association of Canada is a national, nonprofit organization. Its major aims are to increase coaching effectiveness in all sports and to encourage the development of coaching by providing programs and services to coaches at all levels. SIRC is a unique sport library and documentation center, and its services are accessible to all CAC members as well as the sports community at large.'' **Services:** Provides bibliographical and referral information on sport, physical education, recreation and sports medicine. Offers annual reports, brochures/pamphlets and information searches. Publications include pamphlets on the CAC and SIRC in English and French. **How to Contact:** Write or call. Responds to most inquiries within a week. Charges for photocopies: $2/article; computer searches: $7.50 minimum. ''Our library doesn't lend books.''

1412• SPORTS CAR CLUB OF AMERICA
6750 S. Emporia, Englewood CO 80112. (303)770-1044. Contact Person: News Department Manager. **Description:** ''We operate, administrate and organize automobile competitions—races, rallies, hillclimbs.'' **Services:** Provides advisory, analytical, historical, how-to, interpretative and technical information on SCCA Professional Racing Series (Can-Am, Trans-Am, Super Vee, Rabbit); SCCA Club Racing (250 events nationwide, how to become a driver, etc.); Rallies, Solo, and others. Offers aid in arranging interviews, biographies, library facilities, photos, placement on mailing lists, press kits and statistics. Publications include *SCCA Professional Racing News Guide and Record Book*; and *Sports Car Magazine*. **How to Contact:** Write or call. Responds to most inquiries within a week. **Tips:** Recent information requests: ''How do you become a race driver?''; accident rates in road racing; history of top drivers.

1413• UNITED STATES AMATEUR CONFEDERATION OF ROLLER SKATING
Box 83067, Lincoln NE 68501. (402)483-7551. Contact Person: Administrator. **Description:** ''We organize competitive roller skating in the US; select artistic, speed and hockey teams to compete in world championships.'' **Services:** Provides advisory, historical and referral information on artistic and speed skating, roller hockey and judging and refereeing roller skating. Offers aid in arranging interviews, biographies, brochures/pamphlets, informational newsletters and press kits. Publications include *Roller News* (monthly newsletter); and *Skate* (quarterly magazine). **How to Contact:** Write. Responds to most inquiries within a month. **Tips:** ''Contact *Skate* Magazine for feature information. Contact administrator for specifics on rules, competitions.'' Recent information requests: ''How many people in the US roller skate competitively?''; ''Who have won Roller Speed World Championships in 1970-1980?''

1414• UNITED STATES CROQUET ASSOCIATION
635 Madison Ave., New York NY 10010. (212)688-5495. Contact Person: President. **Description:** ''Our purpose is the development and promotion of association croquet. We sanction local, regional, national and international championship tournaments and sponsor US National Croquet Team.'' **Services:** Provides advisory, analytical, historical, how-to and technical information on croquet: growth of the sport in the USA, USCA rules of the American game, and historic and projected events. Offers aid in arranging interviews, informational newsletters, library facilities, photos, placement on mailing lists, photos, press kits and statistics. The Croquet Foundation of America, Inc. (at the same address) produces educational materials

including films and videotapes with instructional/how to play content. Publications include *US Croquet Gazette* (biannual); newsletters; and *Croquet—The Complete Guide to History, Strategy, Rules & Records* (Scribner, 1977). **How to Contact:** Write, call or visit. Responds to most inquiries immediately. Give credit/address of US Croquet Association in New York City. **Tips:** ''Be sure to distinguish between serious USCA croquet and the backyard version most people associate with the word 'croquet.' '' Recent information requests: ''What do you credit for the growth of serious/association croquet in America?''; ''What are the differences between the backyard and association games?''

1415• UNITED STATES GOLF ASSOCIATION
Liberty Corner Rd., Far Hills NJ 07931. (201)234-2300. Contact Person: Manager, Press Relations. **Description:** ''An association of 5,100 member golf clubs and courses. The governing body of golf in the US, the United States Golf Association (USGA) writes and interprets the rules of golf; conducts the 12 national championships of golf, including the US Open; tests balls and equipment so that they conform to rules; maintains golf house library and museum; offers USGA green section and turfgrass advisory service to member clubs; and supports turfgrass research at universities.'' **Services:** Provides historical, interpretative, referral and technical information on golf history and all aspects of golf, both modern-day and past. Offers aid in arranging interviews, annual reports, bibliographies, biographies, statistics, brochures/pamphlets, placement on mailing list, photos and press kits. Publications include material on golf rules, golf course maintenance, handicapping and course ratings, competitions and general golf literature. **How to Contact:** Written requests preferred. ''Quick questions may be taken over the phone.'' Charges for publications. ''USGA must be given proper credit when copyrighted material is used.'' **Tips:** ''Inquiries are handled more promptly during winter months due to heavy summer schedule. The USGA is a service organization, and, as such, can and will help researchers/writers with any project they might have.'' Recent information request: Background on JoAnne Carner.

1416• UNITED STATES HOCKEY HALL OF FAME
Box 657, Eveleth MN 55734. (218)744-5167. Contact Person: Executive Director. **Description:** Sports hall of fame. **Services:** Provides information on hockey. Offers 225 b&w and 25 color photos of players and teams, primarily of US origin. **How to Contact:** Write or call. Offers one-time rights. Charges $5/print.

1417• UNITED STATES ICAS COMMITTEE
Box 1315, Beverly Hills CA 90213. Contact Person: President. **Description:** ''The USIC is the American arm of the Council of Associations of Surfing (ICAS) and is a whole composed of two parts: the amateur American Surfing Association (ASA) and the American Professional Surfing Association (APSA), which governs surfing in the USA, provides competitive opportunities to amateur and professional surfers in ten events and works for Olympic recognition.'' **Services:** Provides advisory, analytical, bibliographical, historical, how-to, interpretative, referral, technical and trade information on the sport of surfing and its ten events: boat surfing, bodyboarding, bodysurfing, kayack surfing, kneeboarding, paddleboarding, standup surfing, surfboard sailing, and tandem surfing. Offers aid in arranging interviews, biographies, brochures/pamphlets, informational newsletters, photos, placement on mailing lists, press kits, research assistance and statistics. Publications include *All American Surfer* (quarterly); and *The ICAS Code.* **How to Contact:** Write. Responds to most inquiries immediately.

1418• UNITED STATES OLYMPIC COMMITTEE
1750 E. Boulder St., Colorado Springs CO 80909. (303)632-5551. Contact Person: Director of Public Information. **Description:** ''We are in charge of organizing the athletes for the Pan American games and the Olympic games.'' **Services:** Provides historical and referral information on the Olympic games. Offers biographies, photos (for sale), placement on mailing lists, research assistance, statistics and telephone reference services. Publications include *The Olympic Games.* **How to Contact:** Write or call. Responds to most inquiries within a week ''if possible.'' Charges $25/hour research fee. **Tips:** Recent information request: ''Who-what-when-where-why-how in the Olympics?''

1419• UNITED STATES SOCCER FEDERATION
350 Fifth Ave., Suite 4010, New York NY 10118. (212)736-0915. **Description:** National governing body for soccer. **Services:** Provides advisory, analytical, bibliographical, historical,

how-to, interpretative, referral and technical information on soccer. Offers brochures/pamphlets, clipping services, informational newsletters, photos, placement on mailing lists, press kits, statistics and telephone reference services. Publications include *Soccer: The World Game*; rule book. **How to Contact:** Call or visit. Responds to most inquiries immediately.

1420• UNITED STATES SPORTS ACADEMY
Box 8650, 124 University Blvd., Mobile AL 36608. (205)343-7700. Contact Person: Director of Public Relations. **Description:** "The United States Sports Academy is a nonprofit organization dedicated to upgrading sport and sport education through graduate education, research and service. We have or know of the best source for information on almost all phases of sport and sport-related information. We also offer a sport facilities consulting service. We are active both nationally and internationally. We have several sport and sport-related contracts with foreign nations, especially in the Middle East." **Services:** Offers newsletter and information on sport medicine, graduate sport education, and sources of best information on all aspects of sport and sport-related activities. **How to Contact:** Write or call. "We would prefer to work with known publications and writers with experience in the sports and sports-related field." **Tips:** "Get plenty of views on controversial subjects, pro and con; don't go only to the well-known sources on a topic. Don't take all information at face value; separate facts and statistics from opinion; and keep all promises made; you might have to use a source many times."

1421• UNITED STATES TROTTING ASSOCIATION
Publicity Dept., 750 Michigan Ave., Columbus OH 43215. (614)224-2291. Contact Person: Executive Editor of *Hoof Beats* and Racing Information Manager. **Description:** "US Trotting Association (USTA) is a breed organization for standardbred horses. It is the rulesmaking and recordkeeping body for the sport of harness racing in the US and Canadian maritimes. The publicity department coordinates all national press and generally anything and everything connected with the sulky sport." **Services:** Offers aid in arranging interviews, bibliographies, biographies, statistics, brochures/pamphlets, addresses and phone numbers for racing commissions in each state or any horsemen organization, placement on mailing list, regular informational newsletter, photos and press kits. Publications include *Trotting and Pacing Guide*, a statistical publication designed for sportswriters and sportscasters to assist their reporting, *Harness Handbook*, biographies and statistics on the sport's leading horses and horsemen; *Hoof Beats*, a monthly magazine of USTA featuring information pieces to industry and feature ideas for writers; *Year Book: Sires and Dams Book*; and *Microfiche Stats*, industry publications listing racing and breeding performances. **How to Contact:** Write or call. Responds to most inquiries within a week. If ordering publications or other materials, prefers written request.

1422• WALKING ASSOCIATION
4113 Lee Hwy., Arlington VA 22207. (703)527-5374. Contact Person: Executive Director. **Description:** "We promote walking for exercise, transportation and pleasure." **Services:** Provides advisory, bibliographical, how-to and technical information on walking. Offers aid in arranging interviews, brochures/pamphlets, informational newsletters, library facilities, photos, research assistance, statistics, telephone reference services and speakers bureau. **How to Contact:** Write, call or visit by appointment. Responds to most inquiries within a week. Give credit to association for aid and/or give referrals. **Tips:** "Read general books on walking first, and representative articles also." Recent information request: "What kind of shoes are good for walking; what are trends?"

1423• WILT'S ATHLETIC CLUB
1821 Wilshire Blvd., Suite 400, Santa Monica CA 90403. (213)829-1840. Contact Person: Account Executive. **Description:** "WAC currently trains some of the best track and field athletes in the United States. WAC provides the best in coaching, facilities and sports medicine." **Services:** Provides advisory, analytical, bibliographical, historical, how-to, interpretative, referral and technical information on "anything pertinent to track and field or athletics in general. The club is sponsored by sports personality, Wilt Chamberlain." Offers aid in arranging interviews, biographies, library facilities, photos and statistics. Publications available. **How to Contact:** Write or call. Responds to most inquiries within a month. "Wilt Chamberlain is available for interviews only pertaining to his track and field club. He will not talk about basketball." **Tips:** "Utilize the athletes' own personal stories. There are so many outstanding athletes in this club that a writer has a choice as to a number of different story angles. Just writing about Wilt and the club can be

rather one-dimensional.'' Recent information request: ''Should the government be involved with underwriting national sports programs?''

1424• WORLD CHAMPIONSHIP TENNIS, INC.
1990 1st National Bank Bldg., Dallas TX 75202. (214)748-5828. Contact Person: Public Relations Director. **Description:** Organization promoting professional tennis. **Services:** Provides advisory, historical, interpretative and referral information on tennis-related information including players, history and tradition of the game. Offers aid in arranging interviews, biographies, clipping services and information searches. **How to Contact:** Write or call. Responds to most inquiries within a week. **Tips:** Recent information request: Background on a player and pictures.

SECTION·TWENTY-SEVEN

TOURISM AND TRAVEL

The use of travelling is to regulate imagination by reality, and instead of thinking how things may be, to see them as they are.
—Samuel Johnson

The resources listed herein are those offering information on vacations, travel options, accommodations, tours, cruises, resorts and state tourism.

Additional travel information may be found in the Transportation category.

Bibliography

Fodor's Modern Guides. Annual. New York: David McKay. (Travel guide series for the world)

Heise, Jon O., ed. *The Travel Book: Guide to the Travel Guides*. New York: Bowker, 1981.

Milne, Robert Scott, ed. *Travelwriter Marketletter*. Monthly newsletter. Room 1745, The Plaza Hotel, New York NY 10019.

Mobil Travel Guides. Annual. Chicago: Rand McNally. (Evaluates points of interest, restaurants, etc. by regions of the US)

Post, Joyce A. and Jeremiah B., eds. *Travel in the United States: A Guide to Information Sources*. Detroit: Gale Research Co., 1981.

Simony, Maggy, ed. *Traveler's Reading Guides: Background Books, Novels, Travel Literature and Articles*. 3 vols. Bayport, NY: Freelance Publications, 1981.

Tours and Visits Directory. 2d ed. Detroit: Gale Research Co., 1981. (Directory of facility tours and on-site visits to business, cultural and educational firms)

Travel Weekly's World Travel Directory. Annual. New York: Ziff-Davis Publishing Co.

1425• AMERICAN RIVER TOURING ASSOCIATION
445 High St., Oakland CA 94601. (415)465-9355. Contact Person: President. **Description:**"We promote river touring and watersport trips and conduct educational programs." **Services:** Provides advisory, bibliographical, historical, how-to, and trade information. Offers brochures/pamphlets, photos and informational interviews. **How to Contact:** Write or call. Responds to most inquiries within a week. Give photo credits to American River Touring Association. **Tips:** "We can suggest published materials, government sources and people with whom to talk for information." Recent information request: "How was river rafting started and how did it grow as a vacation sport in the US?"

1426• AMERICAN WILDERNESS EXPERIENCE, INC.
Box 1486, Boulder CO 80306. (303)444-2632. Contact Person: President. **Description:** "We promote wilderness vacations and learning adventures throughout the American West." **Services:** Provides advisory, historical and interpretative information on horsepacking, backpacking, hot air ballooning, whitewater rafting, houseboating. Offers aid in arranging interviews, brochures/pamphlets, photos, placement on mailing lists and press kits. Publications include annual trip brochure and adventure guide. **How to Contact:** Write. Responds to most inquiries within a week. "Trip trade-offs are available, but we ask that a writer can give us some guarantee that an article will be published."

1427• AMERICAN YOUTH HOSTELS
1332 I St. NW, 8th Floor, Washington DC 20005. (202)783-6161. Contact Person: Director of Marketing. **Description:** Nonprofit organization and low cost travel information center for outdoor recreation. **Services:** Provides advisory, analytical, historical, how-to, interpretative, referral and technical information on low cost travel and various kinds of outdoor recreation, such as bicycling trips. Offers brochures/pamphlets, informational newsletters, library facilities, placement on mailing lists, press kits and statistics. Publications include *Hosteling U.S.A.*;

American Bicycle Atlas. **How to Contact:** Write or call. Responds to most inquiries within a week. Request clip of article if information supplied has been used. **Tips:** Recent information request: "How many hostels are there in the US?"

1428• AVENTOURS TRAVEL, LTD.
801 Second Ave., New York NY 10017. (212)867-8770. Contact Person: Vice President, Marketing. **Description:** "Aventours is a leading American tour operator with a unique series of cross-country camping and motel tours in which a specially-built portable kitchen is carried on board each motorcoach. Aventours also offers a series of luxury hotel tours in which the interior of a deluxe motorcoach has been custom-built to provide greater comfort for passengers. Finally, Aventours operates a series of camping tours in Europe and a deluxe barge cruise on the inland waterways of Holland." **Services:** Provides advisory, analytical, bibliographical and trade information. Offers aid in arranging interviews, biographies, brochures/pamphlets, informational newsletters, photos, placement on mailing lists, press kits, research assistance and statistics. Publications include tour brochures. **How to Contact:** Write, call or visit. Responds to most inquiries immediately. "Writers participating in a trip must be on assignment." **Tips:** Recent information request: "Send me the latest information on student travel."

1429• THE BED AND BREAKFAST LEAGUE, LTD.
2855 29th St. NW, Washington DC 20008. (202)232-8718. Contact Person: Director. **Description:** Private homeowners who offer accommodations for travelers. **Services:** Provides reservation service in 250 locations and advisory, how-to and referral information on bed and breakfast in America and England. Offers brochures/pamphlets, computerized information searches, informational newsletters, photos and telephone reference services. Publications include newsletter and bulletin. **How to Contact:** Write or call. Responds to most inquiries immediately. Recent information request: "How is Bed & Breafast growing in America as an alternative style of travel?"

1430• CRUISE LINES INTERNATIONAL ASSOCIATION
c/o Diana M. Orban Associates, Inc., 60 E. 42nd St., New York NY 10165. **Description:** The association promotes cruise vacations on behalf of 28 major cruise lines serving the North American marketplace. **Services:** Provides analytical, historical, how-to, referral and trade information on the history of cruising; cruise lines and their products; how to select a cruise; how travel agents can sell cruises. Offers aid in arranging interviews, brochures/pamphlets, photos, placement on mailing lists, press kits and statistics. Publications include news releases, tips brochures, film, speeches. **How to Contact:** Write. Responds to most inquiries within a week. **Tips:** "Please don't ask us to handle individual cruise arrangements unless you have a definite assignment from a legitimate publication. Also do not call for information on particular cruises, rates, dates—contact the line directly for that. Give credit to Cruise Lines International Association for information." Recent information request: "What kind of clothes should people take on cruises?"

1431• DELTA HOUSEBOAT RENTAL ASSOCIATION
Box 9140, Stockton CA 95208. (209)951-7821. Contact Person: Public Relations Manager. **Description:** "We publicize the joys of houseboating the fabulous waters of the 1,000-mile California Delta. The Delta is a labyrinthine network of over 1,000 miles of navigable waterways, set in about 700,000 acres of some of the richest agricultural land in the world." **Services:** Provides advisory, historical and interpretative information on sightseeing, swimming and waterskiing the waters of the 1,000-mile California Delta. Offers aid in arranging interviews, brochures/pamphlets, informational newsletters, photos, research assistance and telephone reference services. Publications include *Houseboating* (newsletter on houseboating the Delta); brochures from various rental firms; a map of the Delta waterway with the marinas shown. **How to Contact:** Write or call. Responds to most inquiries within a week. **Tips:** "We will give all help needed to any writer on legitimate assignment. We can even provide complimentary houseboats if the situation warrants it. There are some good books on the Delta available in libraries. They would answer most of a writer's questions. Know the difference between a houseboat and a floating home." Recent information request: "When is the best time to come to the Delta houseboating to catch striped bass?"

1432• THE DUDE RANCHERS' ASSOCIATION
Box 471, LaPorte CO 80535. (303)881-2117. Contact Person: Executive Director. **Description:** The organization promotes the western ranch way of life, through real ranch vacations. **Services:** Provides advisory, historical, how-to and trade information on how to choose a ranch for vacation purposes; how to purchase a ranch; how to operate a dude ranch; how to contact ranch owners for information. Offers aid in arranging interviews and brochures/pamphlets. Publications include *The Dude Rancher Magazine*; *The Directory of Authentic Western Ranches*. **How to Contact:** Write, call or visit. Responds to most inquiries immediately.

1433• EUROPEAN TRAVEL COMMISSION
630 Fifth Ave., Room 610, New York NY 10111. (212)307-1200. Contact Person: Manager of Press Relations. **Description:** The travel commission promotes travel to 23 countries in Europe. **Services:** Provides advisory, analytical, how-to, interpretative, referral and trade information on travel, lodging, statistics, restaurants, trends, travel packages. Offers aid in arranging interviews, clipping services, photos, placement on mailing lists, press kits, research assistance, statistics and telephone reference services. **How to Contact:** Call. Responds to most inquiries immediately. **Tips:** Allow plenty of time to fill a request. Recent information request: "What special events are scheduled in Europe next year?"

1434• GUNFLINT NORTHWOODS OUTFITTERS
Box 100 G.T., Grand Marais MN 55604. (218)388-2296. Contact Person: President. **Description:** "We educate and equip canoeists in preparation for wilderness canoe trips in the Boundary Waters Canoe Area." **Services:** Provides advisory, historical, how-to, interpretative, technical and trade information on wilderness camping, canoe skills and education, safety in the wilderness, user education, low impact camping. Offers aid in arranging interviews, brochures/pamphlets, photos, research assistance and statistics. **How to Contact:** Write. Responds to most inquiries within a week. Requests to review for accuracy the information writers obtain. **Tips:** "There are two sides to most issues in our wilderness management. Come and experience this wilderness if you are going to write about it."

1435• HANDY-CAP HORIZONS, INC.
3250 E. Loretta Dr., Indianapolis IN 46227. Contact Person: President/Editor/Tour Sponsor. **Description:** "Handy-Cap Horizons, Inc., is an organization which strives to bring the world to the door of handicapped and elderly, either by actual travel through the USA and other parts of the world—or by articles in its quarterly magazine of the same name. Nonhandicapped people also seem to enjoy the magazine (and libraries all over the country subscribe). All who become members are eligible for discounted tours, tours planned to fit the disabled and the older person who wishes a slower pace. For more along this line, read the history written by our quadriplegic vice president and associate editor. We are a nonprofit organization, chartered in Indiana with tax-exempt status. We are completely volunteer. We're people-to-people, too! We visit with our own government officials in foreign countries, as well as the VIPs of the country visited, handicapped groups, families, etc. (being international, we have members in so many places to help with the planning). Our tours are group tours only; several have asked us to plan independent travel. We are not a travel agent, rather a travel club and we cannot plan independent touring for many reasons." **Services:** Provides advisory, bibliographical, historical, how-to, referral, and some technical and trade information. Offers aid in arranging interviews, annual reports (to members), brochures/pamphlets, regular informational magazine and press kits for members. Publications include *Horizons Handy-Cap* magazine (quarterly) as well as *HCH History.* **How to Contact:** Write or call. Responds as soon as possible, depending on work load and urgency of inquiry. "We will help with information and articles only pertaining to handicapped activities and travel." **Tips:** "Read our literature (especially the magazine articles written by the handicapped travelers themselves) . . . or take one of our tours to observe how they are handled and what they mean to handicapped and elderly who must take slow-action travels, etc." Recent information requests: "What tours do you have to offer handicapped or elderly?"; "How handicapped can one be and yet become a member of any tour?"

1436• INTERNATIONAL ASSOCIATION FOR MEDICAL ASSISTANCE TO TRAVELERS
736 Center St., Lewiston NY 14092. (716)754-4883. Contact Person: President. **Description:** Organization which "gathers and disseminates health and sanitary information worldwide for the

benefit of travelers, and advises them of qualified medical care available when traveling outside their country of residence.'' **Services:** Provides advisory, how-to, interpretative, referral and technical information on medical aspects of travel, sanitation, health, prevention of diseases, climate. Offers brochures/pamphlets and telephone reference services. Publications include world climate charts and brochures on various health concerns (e.g., immunizations) for travelers around the world. **How to Contact:** Write or call. Responds to most inquiries within a month. Give credit to IAMAT.

1437• THE LEADING HOTELS OF THE WORLD

770 Lexington Ave., New York NY 10021. (212)838-7874. Contact Person: Public Relations Manager. **Description:** "We are an association of 167 deluxe hotels worldwide. As representatives of these hotels, we provide a reservation system for both trade and consumer users—plus marketing (sales, advertising, public relations).'' **Services:** Provides advisory, historical and trade information on hotel accommodations, availability, background, rates, "all types of media information.'' Offers aid in arranging interviews, brochures/pamphlets, photos, placement on mailing lists, press kits and research assistance. Publications include *Corporate Profile of HRI/The Leading Hotels of the World*; *Directory of the Leading Hotels of the World*. **How to Contact:** Write or call. Responds to most inquiries within a week. **Tips:** "Writers should be aware that these hotels are all deluxe and are members of the association. They are *not* chain hotels.'' Recent information request: Background on the introduction of caviar into Western Europe—particularly through the Ritz Hotel in Paris.

1438• THE MTA TRAVELERS-WHEELERS RV CLUB

Box 6279, Pensacola FL 32503. (904)434-0481. Contact: Public Relations. **Description:** MTA promotes RV camping and the exchange of ideas relative to RV camping and travel. **Services:** Provides advisory, how-to, interpretative, technical and trade information covering recreational vehicle usage, travel, camping, caravans, rallies, outings, maintenance and repair. Offers informational newsletters, photos, placement on mailing lists and press kits. **How to Contact:** Write. Responds to most inquiries within a week. **Tips:** "We prefer that freelance writers tell us where story and/or information is going to be published.''

1439• NATIONAL CAMPERS AND HIKERS ASSOCIATION

7172 Transit Rd., Buffalo NY 14221. (716)634-5433. Contact Person: Office Manager. **Description:** An organization of campers and hikers interested in outdoor activities and conservation. **Services:** Provides advisory, how-to and referral information on camping, hiking, carnets in Europe and information on wildlife and conservation. Offers annual reports, brochures/pamphlets, informational newsletters, photos, placement on mailing lists and press kits. Publications include *Camping Hotline*. **How to Contact:** Write, call or visit. Responds to most inquiries within a week. **Tips:** Recent information request: Best places to hike in a particular state.

1440• NATIONAL PARK SERVICE

Office of Public Affairs, Room 3043, Interior Bldg., Washington DC 20240. (202)343-6843. Contact Person: Public Affairs Officer. **Description:** "The National Park Service manages a system of 333 parks, historic sites and recreation areas throughout the US, including Puerto Rico, the Virgin Islands, Guam and Saipan. In addition, we administer a series of programs designed to provide advice and counsel to state and local governments and private organizations on historic preservation and public recreation.'' **Services:** Provides advisory, bibliographical, historical, interpretative, referral and technical information on areas of the national park system which the service administers. Offers attendance statistics and data on camping, swimming, boating, mountain climbing, hiking, fishing, winter activities, wildlife research and management, history, archaeology, nature walks and scenic features. **How to Contact:** Write. Responds to most inquiries within a week. **Tips:** "Plan a trip to Washington or Regional Office Headquarters and/or the NPS facility about which you are interested; especially for any in-depth or protracted piece of work. Generally, if requesters can limit their inquiries to those that can be satisfied with relatively little research—and I mean a few hours, not just a few minutes—we'll do our best to help. Our limited staff simply does not have the time to commit to doing someone's doctoral research for them. Regrettably, we get such requests often. Similarly, there must be an understanding that the complexity of an inquiry will relate to the speed of the response.''

1441• NATIONAL TOUR BROKERS ASSOCIATION
120 Kentucky Ave., Lexington KY 40502. (606)253-1036. Contact Person: NTBA News Bureau
Director. **Description:** The association "promotes public awareness of, and assures standards of
quality in the group/motorcoach tour industry throughout North America. We assist members with
marketing, education and governmental representation." **Services:** Provides advisory, analytical,
bibliographical, historical and how-to information on the motorcoach tour industry; allied
industries, i.e., hotel, attraction, sightseeing, etc.; governmental proceedings that affect travel
industry; association leadership. Offers aid in arranging interviews, annual reports, biographies,
brochures/pamphlets, clipping services, computerized information searches, photos, placement
on mailing lists, press kits, research assistance and statistics. "We can assist in arranging
familiarization tours for appropriate writers. These are trips in which the writer travels on an actual
tour and recounts his experiences." Publications include *Courier* (monthly); *Tuesday* (newsletter);
NTBA Story (historical); assorted brochures. **How to Contact:** Write or call. Responds to most
inquiries within a week. Charges for some membership directories. **Tips:** "Requests that are
accompanied by tear sheets, clips, samples, etc. are more likely to receive priority treatment."
Recent information request: Trends in the motorcoach tour industry.

1442• RECREATION VEHICLE INDUSTRY ASSOCIATION
Box 204, Chantilly VA 22021. (703)968-7722. Contact Person: Director of Public
Relations. **Description:** "We represent the interests of the recreation vehicle industry before
state, local and federal governments and the news media and generally promote the use of
recreation vehicles in outdoor recreation and travel. Our membership totals more than 200
manufacturers and suppliers. Our manufacturer members produce motor homes, travel trailers,
van conversions, truck campers and fold-down camping trailers (not mobile homes)." **Services:**
Provides advisory, analytical, bibliographical, historical, how-to, referral, technical and trade information on RV market and industry conditions; RV consumer demographics and trends; RV lifestyle; buying, using and maintaining RVs; RV safety; RV business opportunities; campground
information; RV types; RV construction standards. Offers aid in arranging interviews, brochures/
pamphlets, placement on mailing list, statistics, press kits and vehicle loans to writers with specific
assignments from editors of reputable consumer publications. Publications available. **How to
Contact:** Write or call. Responds to most inquiries immediately. "We provide free information
and press kits to writers." **Tips:** "Since there are limitless possibilities for RV articles—ranging
from business-type stories like how the industry is doing to human-interest stories like where to vacation in an RV—a good imagination can help you turn one research effort into several good stories. Never hesitate to contact us when you're researching an RV story; if we don't have what you
want, we know who does." Recent information request: "How popular are RVs and what do they
offer Americans?"

1443• RESORT CONDOMINIUMS INTERNATIONAL
9333 N. Meridian St., Indianapolis IN 46260. (317)846-4724. Contact: Public Relations
Department. **Description:** "Resort Condominiums International (RCI) is a reciprocal exchange
program. It is used primarily by owners of timeshares in condominiums in vacation resorts. Our
members 'spacebank' their timeshare and exchange it for another time and place. It is an exchange
service, not a direct barter. The resorts are in the US, Canada, Japan, Mexico, the Caribbean,
Europe and Australia." **Services:** Offers press kits. Publications include *Exchange Listing*; the
magazine *The Endless Vacation*; and article reprints. **How to Contact:** "Call or write RCI Public
Relations Department and explain the purpose of the information desired." Responds to most
inquiries within a week.

1444• SKI THE SUMMIT
c/o Blumenfeld and Associates Public Relations, 350 Fifth Ave., Suite 6617, New York NY
10118. (212)279-9220. Contact Person: Account Executive. **Description:** Resort association
representing the major ski resorts near Denver—Breckenridge, Copper Mountain and
Keystone/Arapahoe Basin. **Services:** Provides historical, how-to, referral and trade information
on lodging, rates, mountain statistics, learning to ski reservations, profiles on people and places.
Offers aid in arranging interviews, biographies, brochures/pamphlets, informational newsletters,
library facilities, photos, placement on mailing lists, press kits, research assistance, statistics and
telephone reference services. Publications include press kits on member resorts; brochures;
pamphlets; b&w and color illustrations; association newsletters. **How to Contact:** Write or call.
Responds to most inquiries immediately. **Tips:** "We are ready at a moment's notice to provide the

kind of information writers/researchers can use when developing stories about skiing in Colorado. We are well-connected in the ski industry. If we haven't got the answer, we can find out who does and refer that person/organization to the inquiring writer.'' Recent information request: Materials on child ski education.

1445• THE SOCIETY FOR THE ADVANCEMENT OF TRAVEL FOR THE HANDICAPPED
26 Court St., Brooklyn NY 11242. (212)858-5488. Contact Person: Administrator. **Description:** Individuals interested in promoting knowledge and awareness of the travel needs and abilities of handicapped persons. **Services:** Provides advisory and trade information on travel facilities, data and resources for handicapped travel. Offers brochures/pamphlets, informational newsletters and library facilities. **How to Contact:** Write or call. Responds to most inquiries within a week. Include SASE. Charges for some services. Library materials are not available for borrowing.

1446• STATE TOURISM OFFICES
Though they have many names—Office of Tourism and Travel, Agency of Development and Community Affairs, Department of Parks and Tourism, Department of Economic Development, Bureau of Publicity Information, State Travel Service, Department of Industry and Trade, etc.—designated offices in all 50 states promote travel within their boundaries. (See entry for Tourmobile Sightseeing for tourist information on Washington DC.) The state tourism offices provide writers and the general public with tourist-related information. Though pamphlet distribution policies and specific travel aids vary among the states, it is likely that any office will have ready information on the cultural, historical and natural attractions and events in the state, along with material on vacation packages, lodging, camping and recreation facilities. Many offices provide state and community maps, photos, newsletters and travel statistics. Some offer research assistance according to time and staff availability.

Contact the tourist information officer at the telephone numbers listed below for details on the materials and services provided by individual tourism offices.

ALABAMA
(205)832-5510

ALASKA
(907)465-2010

ARIZONA
(602)255-3618

ARKANSAS
(800)643-8383
(800)482-8999 (in AR)

CALIFORNIA
(916)322-2881

COLORADO
(303)866-2205

CONNECTICUT
(203)566-3385

DELAWARE
(800)441-8846
(800)282-8667 (in DE)

FLORIDA
(904)488-5606

GEORGIA
(404)656-3553

HAWAII
(808)548-7199

IDAHO
(208)334-2470

ILLINOIS
(217)785-4326

INDIANA
(317)232-8860

IOWA
(515)281-3401

KANSAS
(913)296-2009

KENTUCKY
(502)564-4930

LOUISIANA
(504)925-3850

MAINE
(207)289-2656

MARYLAND
(301)269-3517

MASSACHUSETTS
(617)727-3232

MICHIGAN
(800)248-5456
(517)373-0670 (in MI)

MINNESOTA
(800)328-1461
(800)652-9747 (in MN)

MISSISSIPPI
(601)354-6715

MISSOURI
(314)751-4133

MONTANA
(406)442-2405

NEBRASKA
(402)471-3111

NEVADA
(702)885-4322

NEW HAMPSHIRE
(603)271-2666

NEW JERSEY
(609)292-2470

NEW MEXICO (800)545-2040	PENNSYLVANIA (717)787-5453	VERMONT (801)828-3236
NEW YORK (518)474-4116	RHODE ISLAND (401)277-2601	VIRGINIA (804)786-2051
NORTH CAROLINA (919)733-4171	SOUTH CAROLINA (803)758-8735	WASHINGTON (206)753-5607
NORTH DAKOTA (701)224-2525	SOUTH DAKOTA (605)773-3301	WEST VIRGINIA (304)348-2286
OHIO (614)466-8844	TENNESSEE (615)741-7994	WISCONSIN (608)266-8773
OKLAHOMA (405)521-2406	TEXAS (512)475-4326	WYOMING (307)777-7777
OREGON (800)547-4901 (503)378-6309 (in OR)	UTAH (801)533-5681	

1447• SUGARLOAF/USA
Sugarloaf Mountain, Carrabassett Valley ME 04947. (207)237-2000. Contact Person: Director of Communications. **Description:** ''We specialize in ski vacations, ski instructions and vacation real estate.'' **Services:** Provides bibliographical, historical, how-to, referral and trade information on recreation and ski industry. Offers aid in arranging interviews, annual reports, brochures/pamphlets, clipping services, placement on mailing list, newsletters, photos and press kits. Publications include lodging guides, area brochures and material about special deals and offers. **How to Contact:** Write or call. Responds to most inquiries within a week. Give credit for photos to Sugarloaf. **Tips:** ''Lead time is as important to us as it is to publishers. We would suggest that the writer recontact the person from whom they get information to make sure writer's interpretations are correct.''

1448• TOURIST HOUSE ASSOCIATES
Rd 2, Box 355A, Greentown PA 18426. Contact Person: Director. **Description:** ''We promote tourist homes, guest houses and B&Bs in the US.'' **Services:** Provides advisory, bibliographical and how-to information on where the houses are located; what they are like; what the rates are; who the owners are; what their area offers, etc. Publications include *Bed & Breakfast, U.S.A.* (a guide to tourist homes and guest houses). **How to Contact:** Write. Responds to most inquiries within a week. **Tips:** ''The subject of B&Bs is currently the rage. Travelers are fed up with the impersonal plastic ambience of motels. Even 'budget' motels are pricey.'' Recent information requests: ''What is a B&B?''; ''How does one become a B&B host?''

1449• TOURMOBILE SIGHTSEEING
1000 Ohio Dr. SW, Washington DC 20024. (202)554-5100. Contact Person: Vice President, Marketing & Public Relations. **Description:** ''We provide interpretative shuttle tours for the public to historic sites, monuments, memorials and museums on the Federal Mall, in Arlington National Cemetery and to Mount Vernon, Virginia.'' **Services:** Provides advisory, historical, interpretative and trade information on Washington DC, Arlington National Cemetery and Mount Vernon ''from an historical and advisory perspective for visitors to the nation's capital.'' Offers brochures/pamphlets and press kits. **How to Contact:** Write or call. Responds to most inquiries within a week. ''No photos prior to clearance from our office. Contact us in writing in advance for complimentary tours, press kits, etc.''

1450• TRAVEL INDUSTRY ASSOCIATION OF AMERICA
1899 L St., Suite 600, Washington DC 20036. (202)293-1433. Contact Person: Manager of Information Services or Director of Communications. **Description:** The association represents the

US travel industry and promotes and develops travel and tourism within and to the US. **Services:** Provides analytical, historical, how-to, interpretative, referral and trade information on government travel, marketing, travel trends and patterns. Offers aid in arranging interviews, annual reports, biographies, brochures/pamphlets, clipping services, informational newsletters, library facilities, placement on mailing lists, press kits, research assistance, statistics and telephone reference services. Publications include *US Travel Roundup*. **How to Contact:** Write, call or visit. Responds to most inquiries within a week. **Tips:** "Allow us enough time to answer and research questions." Recent information request: "How has the state of the economy affected international travel to the US?"

1451• TRAVEL INFORMATION CENTER
Cox Rd., Woodstock VT 05091. (802)457-3838. Contact Person: Director or Managing Editor. **Description:** TIC gathers and distributes information on the travel and leisure industry. **Services:** Provides advisory, analytical, bibliographical, historical, how-to, interpretative, referral, technical and trade information on all aspects of the travel and leisure industry. Offers brochures/pamphlets, computerized information searches, informational newsletters, photos, placement on mailing lists, press kits, research assistance, statistics and telephone reference services. Publications include *Directions* (biweekly newsletter). **How to Contact:** Write or call. Responds to most inquiries within a week. **Tips:** "Call or write about our services. We have a questionnaire which we keep on our computer to help channel information to individuals." Recent information request: "Where would I go to get information on travel events in Michigan?"

1452• TRAVELER'S INFORMATION EXCHANGE (FORMERLY WOMEN'S REST TOUR ASSOCIATION)
356 Boylston St., Boston MA 02116. (617)536-5651, ext. 46. Contact Person: Editor/Director. **Description:** "Members of the Traveler's Information Exchange, established in 1891 as the Women's Rest Tour Association, share their travel experiences and practical advice through an annual magazine, newsletters, and foreign and American lodging lists. TIE also offers a Bed and Breakfast exchange for its members." **Services:** Provides advisory, historical and how-to information. "The TIE library contains a variety of travel resources, including vintage Baedeker, Cook, Muirhead and Hare guidebooks, plus 91 years of TIE history. As the organization was originally founded to provide practical information for women travelers, TIE can furnish background on notable women members over the years, including Alice Brown and Maria Reed (the founders) and Julia Ward Howe (TIE's first president). As a number of the documents are quite old, library use is restricted to office hours." Offers informational newsletters, library facilities and research assistance. Publications include *The Pilgrim Scrip* (magazine of travel articles); newsletters (3/year); *American and Foreign Lodging Lists* (for members only; restricted use for others). **How to Contact:** Write or call. Responds to most inquiries within a week. Charges for "research that expands the hours of the sole staff member of TIE." **Tips:** "TIE's founding and early days have deep roots in a feminist philosophy: helping women learn to travel alone, independently and intelligently. Those interested in feminism, background of notable women members or travel in general will find a wealth of information."

1453• UNITED STATES TRAVEL AND TOURISM ADMINISTRATION
Department of Commerce, 14th St. and Constitution Ave. NW, Room 1852, Washington DC 20230. (202)377-5211. Contact Person: Director of Policy and Planning. **Description:** The travel administration promotes tourism to the US. **Services:** Provides advisory, analytical, how-to, interpretative, referral, technical and trade information on travel to the US; tourism as an American export commodity; the world market place. Offers annual reports, brochures/pamphlets, research assistance and statistics. **How to Contact:** Write. Responds to most inquiries within a month. "Statistics are released when available."

1454• UNITED STATES TRAVEL DATA CENTER
1899 L St. NW, Washington DC 20036. (202)293-1040. Contact Person: Manager of Communications. **Description:** The center works "to advance the common interests of the travel industry and the public it serves by encouraging, sponsoring and conducting statistical, economic and scientific research concerning travel, the travel industry and travel-related industries; by gathering, analyzing, publishing and disseminating the results of such research; and by cooperating with all federal, state, and other government agencies and all organizations with

similar purposes in pursuit of its objectives.'' **Services:** Provides trade information on travel and tourism research; travel marketing studies. Offers statistics. Publications include quarterly and annual statistical reports. **How to Contact:** Write or call. Responds to most inquiries within a month. Charges for published and unpublished data. ''We expect to be credited as the source.'' **Tips:** ''Have a working knowledge of statistical research and interpretation. Be specific in asking for data, i.e., region of the country, time period to be covered.'' Recent information request: ''How many Americans traveled to the South in the first quarter of a certain year?''

1455• VACATION EXCHANGE CLUB
350 Broadway, New York NY 10013. (212)966-2576. Contact Person: Manager. **Description:** ''We compile and distribute a home exchange directory.'' **Services:** Provides advisory and how-to information on the home exchange program. Offers annual reports, brochures/pamphlets, computerized information searches, photos, placement on mailing lists, press kits and research assistance. **How to Contact:** Write, call or visit. Responds to most inquiries immediately.

1456• WAGONS WEST
RFD, Afton WY 83110. (307)886-5240. Contact Person: Owner. **Description:** ''We conduct covered wagon treks and wilderness pack trips in the Jackson Hole-Grand Teton National Park areas of Wyoming.'' **Services:** Provides advisory, historical, how-to and trade information on covered wagons treks, wilderness pack trips, general information on outdoor-related activity in the area. Offers informational newsletters, photos and placement on mailing lists. Publications include brochure and maps. **How to Contact:** Write or call. Responds to most inquiries immediately.

1457• WINDJAMMER ''BAREFOOT'' CRUISES
Box 120, Miami Beach FL 33139. (305)373-2466. Contact Person: Public Relations Director/Advertising Director. **Description:** ''We provide six-day, adventure cruises aboard famous schooners in the Caribbean to over 400,000 passengers who help sail, learn seamanship, learn to scuba dive, snorkel and explore islands.'' **Services:** Provides trade information. Offers brochures/pamphlets, placement on mailing list, photos and press kits. Publications include *Great Adventure Book* and *Round-the-World Cruise*. **How to Contact:** Write or call. ''Supply a list of credentials.'' Responds to most inquiries within a week.

TRANSPORTATION

Consider the wheelbarrow. It may lack the grace of an airplane, the speed of an automobile, the initial capacity of a freight car, but its humble wheel marked out the path of what civilization we still have.

—*Hal Borland*

This category includes information sources in the area of land (cars, trains, motorcycles, buses, etc.); sea (ships, boats, etc.) and air (planes, helicopters) transport and travel.

Space transportation resources are listed in the Science, Engineering and Technology section. Additional transportation references may be found in the Tourism and Travel category. Submarines are covered in the Government and Military section.

Bibliography

Blackburn, Graham. *The Illustrated Encyclopedia of Ships, Boats and Vessels*. Woodstock, NY: Overlook Press, 1978.

Blackburn, Graham. *The Overlook Illustrated Dictionary of Nautical Terms*. Woodstock, NY: Overlook Press, 1981.

Jane's Aerospace Dictionary; *Jane's All the World's Aircraft*; *Jane's Fighting Ships*; *Jane's Ocean Technology*, etc. Bridgeport, CT: Key Book Services.

Metcalf, Kenneth N., ed. *Transportation Information Sources*. Management Information Guide # 8. Detroit: Gale Research Co., 1965.

Norback, Craig T., ed. *Chilton's Complete Book of Automotive Facts*. Radnor, PA: Chilton Book Co., 1981.

Stark, Harry A., ed. *Ward's Automotive Yearbook*. Annual. Detroit: Ward's Communications.

Ward, Ian and Brian Innes, eds. *World of Automobiles: An Illustrated Encyclopedia of the Motor Car*. 22 vols. Reprint of 1974 ed. Milwaukee: Purnell Reference Books, 1977.

1458• AIRCHIVE
326 S. MacArthur Blvd., Springfield IL 62704. (217)789-9754. Contact Person: Founder/Executive Director. **Description:** AIRCHIVE "educates the public regarding the non-engineering aspects of aviation by acting as a central repository of data, a model aircraft museum and producer of slide presentations and model displays." **Services:** Provides bibliographical, historical, how-to and referral information on "all aspects of contemporary and historical aviation that are non-engineering related, including biographical data, photographs, published articles, an oral history collection and current/historical information regarding the evolution of model aircraft." Offers biographies, informational newsletters, library facilities, photos, research assistance and telephone reference services. Publications include *AIRChatter* (newsletter with data and reviews of current products); *AIRCHIVE Information Directory*, listing members, specialists and explanation of data retrieval system. **How to Contact:** Write, call or visit. Responds to most inquiries within a week. Charges for photocopying and postage. Give credit for photos and information to AIRCHIVE and original photographers, if known. **Tips:** "Confine requests to one subject at a time; don't send lists. Be specific." Recent information requests: "Do you have markings data for a/c flying from the U.S.S. Bennington in World War II, circa 1945?"; "Any cockpit photos of the F-4C?"; "Can you copy the article on Lindbergh that appeared in the July, 1949 issue of *Flying*?"

1459• AIRCRAFT OWNERS AND PILOTS ASSOCIATION (AOPA)
7315 Wisconsin Ave., Bethesda MD 20814. (301)654-0500. Contact Person: Senior Vice President, Public Relations. **Description:** "AOPA serves the interest of individuals who own and fly general aviation (nonairline, nonmilitary) aircraft. It offers services to members, plus representation of interests with the Federal Aviation Administration and Congress." **Services:**

Provides advisory, interpretative, referral, technical and trade information on industry and technical data. Offers aid in arranging interviews, statistics, brochures/pamphlets, placement on mailing list and press kits. Publications include aviation fact cards, safety fact sheets and reference articles. **How to Contact:** Write or call. Responds to most inquiries within a week. "Reasonable assistance can be given, but detailed research cannot be provided." Hourly charge if library research or technical evaluation requested. **Tips:** Recent information request: "What has been the effect of air controllers' strike on private flying?"; "What is safety rate for general aviation?"

1460• ALCO HISTORIC PHOTOS, AMERICAN LOCOMOTIVE COMPANY
B0x 655, Schenectady NY 12301. (518)374-0153. Contact Person: Chairman, Board of Trustees.
Description: "Alco Historic Photos is the curator/custodian of photographic negatives of railroad locomotives built by Alco Products (American Locomotive Co.) and its predecessors. These are the so-called builder's photos taken by the company photographer. Our organization has published a catalog of the negatives and supplies prints to order (a mail order activity)." **Services:** Provides historical, technical and trade information on products of American Locomotive Co. (ALCO)—primarily railroad locomotives. Offers information searches, photos, catalogs, photocopies of data and prints of engineering drawings. A publications and price list is available. **How to Contact:** Write. Responds to most inquiries within a week. Visits to research the photo collection are by appointment only. No charge for minor research; extensive research is by negotiation, subject to manpower limitations. Charges $4 postpaid/8x10 photo; prices for larger sizes on request. Charges $5/print published. Credit line and a copy of the publication required.

1461• AMERICAN ASSOCIATION OF PORT AUTHORITIES
1612 K St. NW, #900, Washington DC 20006. (202)331-1263. Contact Person: Director, Research and Publications. **Description:** "We are an information exchange for the port industry. Membership is basically port authorities in the Western Hemisphere with other classes for members also with an interest in the port industry." **Services:** Provides advisory, historical, how-to, interpretative, referral, technical and trade information on ports. Offers "for our *own* membership": annual reports, statistics, brochures/pamphlets and newsletter. "Outside sources are not usually placed on our mailing lists." **How to Contact:** Write. Responds to most inquiries immediately. **Tips:** Recent information request: AAPA's stand on user fees.

1462• AMERICAN AUTOMOBILE ASSOCIATION
8111 Gatehouse Rd., Falls Church VA 22047. (703)222-6334. Contact Person: Director of Public Relations. **Description:** Automobile clubs which provide travel, road and insurance services and promote the interests of motorists in general. **Services:** Provides advisory, analytical, historical, how-to, interpretative, referral, technical and trade information on automotive travel, mechanics, repairs, legislative policy, international travel and consumer information on traffic and safety. Offers aid in arranging interviews, biographies, brochures/pamphlets, informational newsletters, library facilities, photos, placement on mailing lists, press kits, research assistance, statistics and telephone reference services. Publications available. **How to Contact:** Write, call or visit. Responds to most inquiries within a week.

1463• AMERICAN BOAT AND YACHT COUNCIL, INC.
Box 806, 190 Ketcham Ave., Amityville NY 11701. (516)598-0550. Contact Person: Executive Director. **Description:** "The American Boat & Yacht Council, a nonprofit membership organization, is primarily an engineering and technical society devoted to the development and publication of safety standards and recommended practices covering the design and construction of boats and their equipment." **Services:** Provides advisory and technical information on recreational boats and related technical data. Offers brochures/pamphlets and information searches. Publications include *ABYC Is for Safer Boating* (descriptive brochure) and *Safety Standards for Small Craft* (a compendium of standards and practices). **How to Contact:** Write. Responds to most inquiries within a week. Charges $45/copy for *Safety Standards*. "All material is copyrighted and specific permission for its use is required. Assurance is needed that ABYC material will be presented in proper context, either by pre-publication review or full disclosure of intent and layout. Suitable acknowledgement of source is appreciated."

1464• AMERICAN MOTORS CORPORATION
27777 Franklin Rd., Southfield MI 48034. Contact Person: Director of Corporate Communication, (303)827-1830; Director of Product Communication,

(303)827-1850. **Description:** "We manufacture American Motor and Renault passenger cars and jeep vehicles." **Services:** Offers aid in arranging interviews, annual reports, biographies, brochures/pamphlets, information searches, placement on mailing list, photos and press kits. **How to Contact:** Write. Responds to most inquiries within a week.

1465• AMERICAN PEDESTRIAN ASSOCIATION
Box 624, Forest Hills NY 11375. Contact Person: Editor, Vice President. **Description:** The association works to "protect, advance and project the image of urban American pedestrians; their needs, welfare and interests." **Services:** Provides advisory, analytical, interpretive and technical information on pedestrian systems, environments, encroachments and methodologies. Offers informational newsletter and library facilities "for scholars." Publications include *Pedestrian Research Quarterly*, "America's only pedestrian-environment publication." **How to Contact:** Write. Include SASE. Responds to most inquiries within a month. Charges for services.

1466• AMERICAN TRUCK HISTORICAL SOCIETY
201 Office Park Dr., Birmingham AL 35223. (205)879-2131. Contact Person: Executive Director. **Description:** Individuals interested in collecting and preserving the history of trucks, the trucking industry and its pioneers. **Services:** Provides trade information and historical facts about the trucking industry. Offers biographies, informational newsletters, library facilities, photos and research assistance. Publications include *Wheels of Time* (bimonthly magazine). **How to Contact:** Write, call or visit. Responds to most inquiries within a week. **Tips:** "We welcome writers/researchers to spend as much time as they wish going through our library and archives. We do not have the manpower to search our records for detailed and extensive information. Tell us what you want and if it is merely a date or a name, we may be able to help you without research. Otherwise, plan to visit us. Research materials do not leave the premises. Copies may be made of any of our information." Recent information requests: "Who founded the Mack Trucks, Inc.?"; "What year did Cummins Engine first introduce the diesel engine?"

1467• ANTIQUE AIRPLANE ASSOCIATION
Box 172, Ottumwa IA 52501. (515)938-2773. Contact Person: President. **Description:** "The association was formed in 1953 to save, restore and fly classic airplanes. We publish three quarterly magazines. We have 40 chapters and hold numerous fly-ins, meetings and dinners." **Services:** Offers brochures/pamphlets, placement on mailing lists, photos and press kits. "We also provide consulting services to TV and the movie industry, air museums and writers and publishers dealing in historical aviation subjects." **How to Contact:** Write, indicating specific information required. Responds to most inquiries within a week. "Historical aviation research is a time-consuming subject and fees depend on commercial applications by those requesting such data."

1468• ASSOCIATION OF AVIATION AND SPACE MUSEUMS
6203 Yellowstone Dr., Alexandria VA 22312. (703)941-4724. Contact Person: Director. **Description:** "We collect and disseminate information on the more than 500 air and space museums and the more than 11,000 static display aircraft located throughout the world." **Services:** Provides historical, interpretive and referral information on air and space museums. Offers research assistance in arranging interviews and informational newsletters. **How to Contact:** Write. Responds to most inquiries within a week. Charges for services. **Tips:** Recent information requests: "Can you tell me where any F-4 Phantoms are on static display?"; "Please send me information on B-25s on display."

1469• AUTOMOTIVE INFORMATION COUNCIL
18850 Telegraph Rd., Southfield MI 48034. (313)358-0290. Contact Person: Information Coordinator. **Description:** "The Automotive Information Council is a voice for the motor vehicle industry. Its business is information—both to collect pertinent information from other sources and more importantly to digest, analyze and disseminate this information in useful form. It is our purpose to provide useful information that will help people in government, all forms of media and education. Our purpose, simply, is to create and sustain an image of honesty, reliability, quality and fair play where automotive products and services are concerned." **Services:** Provides bibliographical, referral and trade information on automotive products and services. Offers aid in arranging interviews, bibliographies and statistics. Publications include *The Automotive Information Council*. **How to Contact:** "Write or, if a simple question, call." Responds to most

inquiries within a week. Appointments can be made to use the reference center. Charges 20¢/page for copies and mailing costs and additional fees "if request requires that we bring in an outside researcher." **Tips:** "The public library is always a good place to start. After a writer has a good idea of scope of his or her subject matter, we can provide the details. Ask for specific information." Recent information requests: "How many cars were sold in 1981?"; "What is the size of the automotive aftermarket?"; "Who can I contact at GM for information on engineering?"; "What does it cost to own a car?"

1470• AVIATION SAFETY INSTITUTE
Box 304, Worthington OH 43085. (614)885-4242. Contact Person: President. **Description:** The institute's purpose is aggressive aviation accident prevention. It operates an anonymous hazard reporting system—over 44,000 reports since 1973. **Services:** Provides advisory, analytical, how-to, interpretative, referral and technical information on air traffic control accidents, aircraft performance, human factors, hazards, etc. Offers computerized information searches, informational newsletters and research assistance. "We will run seminars to train writers in aviation subjects." Publications include *Monitor* (biweekly newsletter). ASI offers 24-hour, toll-free (800)848-7386 telephone services for members who can call for "up-to-the-minute information on weather conditions at both ends of a planned trip, significant weather problems enroute, runway and airport conditions, verified ATC delays and other vital data." **How to Contact:** Write or call. Responds to most inquiries immediately. Charges for services "depending on the request." Give credit to Aviation Safety Institute. **Tips:** Recent information request: "What is status of air traffic system after PATCO strike?"

1471• CANADIAN SHIPBUILDING AND SHIP REPAIRING ASSOCIATION
Suite 801, 100 Sparks St., Ottawa, Ontario Canada K1P 5B7. (613)232-7127. Contact Person: President. **Description:** "The objectives of the association are the preservation, maintenance and development of the Canadian shipbuilding, ship repairing and allied industries for the advancement of the industrial, technological, economic, social, defense and sovereign interests of Canada. Our association consists of 25 shipbuilding and ship repairing companies and 50 allied manufacturing and consulting organizations." **Services:** Provides trade information on Canadian shipbuilding industry. Offers aid in arranging interviews, annual reports, statistics, publications list and newsletter. Publications include annual and quarterly reports, *Canadian Shipbuilding—Services, Products, Facilities*; papers presented at Annual Technical Conference and several periodical statistical reports. **How to Contact:** Write. Responds to most inquiries within a week. "Our staff is very limited; therefore, detailed inquiries cannot normally be answered." Charges for publications. **Tips:** Recent information request: "What size tankers can be built in Canadian shipyards?"

1472• CANAL MUSEUM
Weighlock Bldg., Erie Blvd. E, Syracuse NY 13202. (315)471-0593. Contact Person: Librarian. **Description:** "Our museum and library seek to inform and educate the public through exhibits, tours, lectures and the dissemination of information on the history of canals in America and abroad. We cover information on all canals, but the real strength of our collections is on the construction and finance of the New York state canal system." **Services:** Provides bibliographical, historical and technical information on canal history (American and foreign) in all of its aspects: economic, engineering, social history, etc. Offers bibliographies, newsletter, photos and reference center. Publications include a general descriptive brochure on the museum. **How to Contact:** "Call or write to ask questions about canals; the more specific the questions, the better." Responds to most inquiries within a week. Charges cost plus postage for duplication of maps and plans; 10¢/photocopy of documents or book pages; $5-10 for 8x10 b&w photo (charges subject to change). "We require a credit for any photos or illustrations we provide." **Tips:** "Do your basic research at the local library, consulting general works to get a background first. When you have specific questions, consult institutions that specialize in your subject. Call ahead before you visit a library out of town."

1473• CARRIAGE ASSOCIATION OF AMERICA, INC.
Box 3788, Portland ME 04104. (207)781-4020. Contact Person: Executive Vice President. **Description:** Nonprofit organization which collects and disseminates historical and technical information about carriages and horse-drawn vehicles generally and encourages their preservation and use. **Services:** Provides historical, how-to and technical information on

horse-drawn vehicles; breeds of harness horses; training and driving of harness horses; research, restoration and styles of vehicles. Offers brochures/pamphlets and research assistance. Publications include quarterly journal. **How to Contact:** Write. Responds to most inquiries within a week. Charges for membership, photocopying, photos and some carriage research. "Only in special cases would we allow a writer to use our library and picture collection. We have no special research staff so the number of inquiries we can deal with is limited." **Tips:** Recent information requests: Frequent questions about carriage building firms.

1474• CHESAPEAKE & OHIO HISTORICAL SOCIETY, INC.
Box 417, Alderson WV 24910. Contact Person: Archivist. **Description:** "We gather information on the Chesapeake & Ohio (C&O) Railway and its predecessors and disseminate this information and data through publications, displays, etc. We collect negatives and printed matter as well for reproduction and distribution, including engineering drawings and material associated with production of scale models." **Services:** Provides historical information on Chesapeake & Ohio Railway and its predecessors and successors; primarily technological history, but also economic, business, and social historical aspects. "Our subject is very specialized, but we do have materials that relate to the C&O in Virginia, West Virginia, Kentucky, Ohio, Indiana, Michigan and Ontario in which states it made considerable social and economic impact over the years. Some data we have on C&O may be applicable to larger considerations in economic social histories of these areas." Offers newsletter and photos. "We publish a fully illustrated monthly magazine, which provides current news, history and modeling information on the C&O Railway and its predecessors. We also publish special pamphlets and other material. We offer over 4,000 different prints from our negative files of photos dating from the 1890s through the 1970s. Our archival facility was opened in the spring of 1982 and is available by advanced appointment for researchers. It is located in the Captain John Smith Library at Christopher Newport College, 50 Shoe Lane, Newport News VA. Appointments may be arranged by contacting the Assistant Archivist, 207 Brigade Dr., Yorktown VA 23692 (804)898-5214." **How to Contact:** Write. Responds to most inquiries within a month. "We respond as soon as possible but we are all-volunteer and our staff is spread widely geographically. It takes time for the request to be assigned to an action officer and for him to prepare the response. If the question is general or specific and we can research it with minimum difficulty, there is no charge. We charge for photocopying, microfilm blowbacks, photographic prints, etc. as well as extensive research. There may be restrictions on specific uses for certain materials; this can be explained to the researcher directly if any exist. We try to keep restrictions to a minimum." **Tips:** "Write first with specific questions. We'll do the research for you if possible or let you know if the material is available to us and if it would be worthwhile for you to do research on site." Recent information request: "Give background on construction of C&O roundhouses in Canada."

1475• CHRYSLER CORPORATION
Box 1919, Detroit MI 48288. Contact: Corporate and Division Public Relations, (313)956-2894, 956-1909; Dodge Public Relations, (313)956-5346; Chrysler Plymouth Public Relations, (313)956-5344; Truck Public Relations, (313)956-3667. **Description:** "We develop, produce and market passenger cars, trucks and outboards and are the largest Chrysler job-training program under government contract." **Services:** Offers aid in arranging interviews, annual reports, biographies, brochures/pamphlets, information searches, placement on mailing list, statistics, photos and press kits. **How to Contact:** Write. Responds to most inquiries within a week. Mailing list is for media only. "We will try to answer anything related to Chrysler Corporation."

1476• COMMITTEE FOR BETTER TRANSIT, INC.
Box 3106, Long Island City, NY 11103. (212)728-0091. Contact Person: President. **Description:** CBT promotes improved public transportation. **Services:** Provides analytical, historical, interpretative, referral and technical information on urban and suburban transportation and related areas of city planning. Offers brochures/pamphlets, informational newsletters and research assistance. Publications include *Notes from Underground.* **How to Contact:** Write. Responds to most inquiries within a month. Charges for services "only if extensive work is involved."

1477• CONNEAUT RAILROAD MUSEUM
324 Depot St., Box 643, Conneaut OH 44030. (216)599-7878. Contact Person: President. **Description:** "An educational organization featuring historic artifacts and equipment of the steam railroad era as it relates to the development of the US. A haven for historic items dating

back to the mid-19th century, including authentic railroad artifacts. This is considered by most railroad buffs to be the most complete steam railroad museum in the country. It features the # 755 Berkshire engine that can be boarded.'' **Services:** Provides historical information. Offers brochures/pamphlets and newsletter. Publications include *Conneaut Railroad Museum*; *Semaphore*(monthly) and a book on the founding of the museum. **How to Contact:** Write. Enclose SASE. Responds to most inquiries within a week. ''This is a free museum, open Decoration Day through Labor Day, 12 noon—5 p.m. It is all volunteer.''

1478• ELECTRIC VEHICLE COUNCIL
1111 19th St. NW, Washington DC 20036. (202)828-7516. Contact Person: Executive Director. **Description:** Companies interested in promoting the use and acceptance of on-road electric vehicles. **Services:** Provides advisory, analytical, how-to, interpretative, referral, technical and trade information about on-road electric vehicles. Offers brochures/pamphlets, informational newsletters, placement on mailing lists, research assistance, statistics and telephone reference services. Publications include *Mini-Guide to EVs*; newsletter. **How to Contact:** Write. Responds to most inquiries within a week. **Tips:** ''Learn something about the area and pertinent issues. Get annual reports from public companies; use local libraries and search for previous articles on electrics.'' Recent information requests: Types of EVs available; cost range; overseas development of EVs; major manufacturers.

1479• FEDERAL AVIATION ADMINISTRATION
Public Inquiry Center, APA-430, Deptartment of Transportation, 800 Independence Ave. SW, Washington DC 20591. (202)426-8058. Contact Person: Public Information Specialist. **Description:** ''We provide the public with publication and inquiry service, a documents copying service, and a document inspection facility. We provide basic informational publications and other nontechnical directives, plans, studies and reports. We refer requests for all statistical, forecast or planning publications to the originating offices.'' **Services:** Provides advisory, interpretative and referral information on regulatory, technical and support functions of the FAA as well as such topics as safety and economics and the history of the aviation administration. Offers statistics, brochures/pamphlets and placement on mailing list. Publications include *Federal Aviation Administration*, a brochure explaining the workings of the agency and *Guide to FAA Publications*, listings and descriptions of agency publications. **How to Contact:** Write or call. Responds to most inquiries immediately. ''Writers should contact the news division, APA-300, (202)426-8521, for assistance on aviation matters currently in the news. Orders and handbooks of a technical nature are quoted on an individual basis by APA-420, Document Inspection Section, (202)426-8367. Write for a list of regional headquarters offices; public affairs offices in each region can assist writers wanting help in their local area.'' **Tips:** ''We are not set up to provide much in the way of photos.''

1480• FEDERAL HIGHWAY ADMINISTRATION
400 7th St. SW, Room 4208, Washington DC 20590. (202)426-0660. Contact Person: Assistant to the Administrator. **Description:** Government agency administering the federal aid highway program; appropriates funds for interstate, primary, secondary and urban system roads and bridges. **Services:** Provides advisory, analytical, historical, interpretative, referral, technical and trade information on federal-aid highway-related legislation; funding; programs and activities; research, technology and development; highway facility and motor carrier driver and vehicle safety; traffic operations; highway engineering, planning, design, construction and maintenance; beautification; environmental protection. Offers aid in arranging interviews, annual reports, biographies, brochures/pamphlets, clipping services, computerized information searches (limited), informational newsletters, photos (limited), placement on mailing lists, press kits, research assistance, statistics and telephone reference services. Publications include *America on the Move*; *Cost of Owning and Operating a Car and Van* (annual); *Drivers License Requirements and Fees*; *License Plates* (annual); *Highway Statistics* (annual). **How to Contact:** Call. Responds to most inquiries within a week. ''There might be a nominal charge for exceptionally extensive information if it requires a good deal of computer time. Define your needs explicitly.'' **Tips:** Recent information request: Overview of the legislative history of the Interstate Highway Program from inception to date.

1481• FORD MOTOR COMPANY
The American Road, Dearborn MI 48121. (313)322-9600. Contact Person: Manager, Corporate

News Department. **Description:** ''Ford Motor Company and its affiliated companies conduct a diversified international business, maintaining manufacturing, assembly or sales facilities in 29 countries and doing business on 6 continents. In addition to its production of cars, trucks and tractors, Ford's other products range from glass and steel to communciations base satellites.'' **Services:** Provides information on financial matters, executive changes, speeches, corporate (not product) legal matters, energy management and personnel and labor issues. Offers aid in arranging interviews, annual reports, biographies, brochures/pamphlets, statistics and photos. Publications available. **How to Contact:** Write or call. Responds to most inquiries within a week. ''We are not a research agency and can offer only what we have in stock or is available by interview. Photos are limited to our files, but we will occasionally fill special requests. We welcome the opportunity to explain our businesses. Give us your telephone number, the use for which the information is being sought and a reasonable time to respond. Also, we do not have time or staff to write term papers, but will send brochures or pamphlets.'' **Tips:** Recent information requests: History of company; ''What year was Model T introduced?''; ''Which came first Model A or T car?''

1482• FRERES CONSULTING
Box 510, N. Bellmore NY 11710. (516)781-6230. Contact Person: Vice President. **Description:** Freres Consulting provides historical aviation data, especially in the early period of aviation (1920-1935). **Services:** Provides advisory, historical, how-to, referral, technical and trade information covering early aviation inventors and airplane manufacturers; early aviation: types and construction of aircraft; early aviation: pioneer men and women in all parts of the world. Offers aid in arranging interviews, biographies, photos, research assistance, statistics and ''I was there'' knowledge of the leading people and aircraft of the era. **How to Contact:** Write or call. Responds to most inquiries within a week. Charges for time involved and material(s) required to answer inquiry. Requests editorial approval of material's use. **Tips:** ''Write first, outlining project, information desired and use to which information will be put. Do not depend on newspaper accounts or accounts prepared by 'armchair generals' in this field. Go to the people who were actually a part of the Golden Age in Aviation.'' Recent information requests: ''Who was the first woman pilot licensed in the United States and are photographs available?''; ''How would I get the blueprints for the Bellanca airplane flown in 1929?''

1483• GENERAL AVIATION MANUFACTURERS ASSOCIATION
1025 Connecticut Ave. NW, Suite 517, Washington DC 20036. (202)296-6540. Contact Person: Director of Communications. **Description:** ''The General Aviation Manufacturers Association (GAMA) represents US manufacturers of general aviation aircraft, avionics and accessories. It provides the general aviation industry with a Washington base and operations staff for dealing in international and national regulatory affairs, technical affairs and public affairs.'' **Services:** Provides advisory, analytical, historical, how-to, interpretative, referral, technical and trade information on general aviation. Offers aid in arranging interviews, annual reports, statistics, brochures/pamphlets, placement on mailing list, photos, and press kits; also, motion pictures, slide and tape material. Publications include *The General Aviation Story*. **How to Contact:** Write. Responds to most inquiries immediately. **Tips:** ''Just write our organization with requests and questions and if we cannot supply you with the correct information, we will refer you to someone who can.'' Recent information requests: ''Most are for the various GAMA and FAA publications. We receive requests for educational materials as well as questions on learning how to fly.''

1484• GENERAL MOTORS CORPORATION
3044 W. Grand Blvd., Detroit MI 48202. (313)556-2027. Contact Person: Director of News Relations. **Description:** ''We are engaged in the manufacture, assembly and distribution of various motor-driven products. Automotive products include passenger cars, trucks, coaches, major automotive components and parts and accessories. Nonautomotive products include diesel engines and locomotives.'' **Services:** Provides information about company and products, technology, etc. Offers aid in arranging interviews, annual reports, biographies, statistics, brochures/pamphlets, placement on mailing list, photos and press kits. **How to Contact:** Write or call. Responds to most inquiries within a week.

1485• THE GREYHOUND CORPORATION
111 W. Clarendon Ave., Phoenix AZ 85077. (602)248-5276. Contact Person: Director, Public Relations. **Description:** ''Greyhound Lines, Inc., is the nation's largest passenger transportation company. We have regular route services, charter service and group travel, with approximately

4,200 buses serving 15,000 locations nationwide.'' **Services:** Offers aid in arranging interviews, annual reports, bibliographies, biographies, statistics, brochures/pamphlets, placement on mailing list, photos and press kits. **How to Contact:** Write or call local Greyhound office. Responds to most inquiries within a week. **Tips:** Recent information request: History of company.

1486• GRUMMAN CORPORATION
1111 Stewart Ave., Bethpage NY 11714. (516)575-4938. Contact Person: Director of Advertising or Director of News Services. **Description:** "Grumman Corporation is a diversified aerospace company—primarily a manufacturer of military aircraft—that also makes solar and wind energy systems, fire trucks, ambulances, buses, truck bodies, canoes, boats and yachts. **Services:** Offers aid in arranging interviews, annual reports, biographies, brochures/pamphlets, placement on mailing list, photos and press kits. Publications include brochures on products and activities. **How to Contact:** Write or call. Responds to most inquiries within a week. "We prefer that requests be written, specific and reasonable.'' **Tips:** "Certain information on military aircraft may be classified and not available to the general public.'' Recent information request: Photo of a particular plane.

1487• INTERNATIONAL AIRLINE PASSENGERS ASSOCIATION, INC.
Box 220074, Dallas TX 75222. (214)438-8100. Contact Person: Manager, Public Relations. **Description:** "IAPA is a membership organization composed of 110,000 frequent airline passengers residing around the world. IAPA provides these individuals a package of travel-related services.'' **Services:** Provides referral and trade information on aviation (commercial), airports, passenger likes/dislikes and statistics. Offers brochures pamphlets, informational newsletters, placement on mailing lists, statistics and telephone reference services. Publications include *IAPA Membership Survey; APACE Newsletter*, various press releases. **How to Contact:** Write. Responds to most inquiries within a week. "Helping our members comes first; other requests are treated as secondary.'' **Tips:** Recent information requests: "How do airline passengers perceive deregulation?''; "Why is business class faring so well?''

1488• INTERNATIONAL CIVIL AVIATION ORGANIZATION (ICAO)
1000 Sherbrooke St. W, Montreal, Quebec Canada H3A 2R2. (514)285-8219. Contact Person: Public Information Office. **Description:** "An intergovernmental regulatory agency existing to foster the development of international air transport by establishing international standards and procedures and to promote safety, uniformity and efficiency in all technical aspects of civil aviation throughout the world. This organization provides the machinery for the achievement of international cooperation in the air.'' **Services:** Provides technical and trade information on international civil aviation and air transport. Offers brochures/pamphlets. Publications include *Facts about ICAO*. **How to Contact:** Write. Responds to most inquiries immediately.

1489• INTERNATIONAL UNION OF PUBLIC TRANSPORT
Avenue de l'Uruguay 19, 1050 Bruxelles Belgium. Tel. (02)673 33 25. Contact Person: Secretary General. **Description:** International organization "concerned with the study of all problems connected with the public transport industry.'' **Services:** Provides analytical, bibliographical, referral and technical information on urban public transport (operational, technical, economic aspects). Offers aid in arranging interviews, brochures/pamphlets, informational newsletters, library facilities, placement on mailing lists, research assistance and statistics. Publications include reports of the organization's International Congresses. **How to Contact:** Write. Responds to most inquiries immediately. Charges for research services.

1490• INTERSTATE COMMERCE COMMISSION
12th St. and Constitution Ave., Washington DC 20423. (202)275-7252. Contact: Public Affairs Office. **Description:** The Interstate Commerce Commission (ICC) has regulatory responsibility for interstate surface transportation by railroads, trucks, buses, barges, coastal shipping, express companies, freight forwarders and transportation brokers. Jurisdiction includes rates, mergers and operating rights. **Services:** Provides information on household moving, how to apply for a license authorizing interstate transfer of people or goods, statistics and material on ICC studies that have been conducted. **How to Contact:** Write for free list of publications.

1491• LIBRARY OF VEHICLES
12172 Sheridan Lane, Garden Grove CA 92640. (714)636-9517. Contact Person: Automotive

Engineer. **Description:** A facility of Wellington Everett Miller, Automotive Engineer. **Services:** Provides advisory, analytical, bibliographical, historical, how-to, interpretative, referral, technical and trade information on automobiles, trucks, buses, motorcycles, bicycles, wagons, carriages, buggies, coaches and sleighs. Offers annual reports, biographies, brochures/pamphlets, clipping services, library facilities, photos, research assistance, statistics, engineering, design and styling. **How to Contact:** Write, call or visit. Charges for research assistance and photocopying. Call for an appointment. **Tips:** "Be specific about subject time frame, locale, description and specifications. Copies of material past copyright can be supplied, but loans are sharply restricted."

1492• LYKES BROS. STEAMSHIP CO., INC.
Lykes Center, New Orleans LA 70130. (504)523-6611. Contact Person: Director, Public Affairs. **Description:** Global ocean freight transportation. **Services:** Provides bibliographical, historical, referral, technical and trade information on shipping industry, merchant marine. Offers aid in arranging interviews, biographies, brochures/pamphlets and photos. **How to Contact:** Write or call. Responds to most inquiries within a week. **Tips:** Recent information request: Names and photos of Lykes ships lost during World War II.

1493• MID-CONTINENT RAILWAY MUSEUM
Box 55, N. Freedom WI 53951. (608)522-4261. Contact Person: General Manager. **Description:** Educational and historical museum reflecting the Golden Era of Railroading by "displaying artifacts which relate to the history, skills, equipment and lore of the railroad industry." **Services:** Provides historical information on the railroad industry. Offers informational newsletters, library facilities, photos, press kits and research assistance. Publications include *Railway Gazette* (bimonthly). **How to Contact:** Write. Responds to most inquiries within a week. Charges "only when costs are incurred by us—such as copies of photos, etc. Give credit to museum for photos, information, etc." **Tips:** "Contact us in advance for access to library and archives."

1494• MOTOR BUS SOCIETY, INC.
Box 7058, W. Trenton NJ 08628. Contact Person: Vice President, Library and Research. **Description:** Individuals interested in preserving historical documents of the motor bus transportation industry. **Services:** Provides historical and trade information on motor bus transportation. Offers library facilities, photos and research assistance. **How to Contact:** Write.

1495• MOTORCYCLE SAFETY FOUNDATION
Box 120, Chadds Ford PA 19317. Contact Person: Director, Public Affairs. **Description:** "A national, private, nonprofit organization, MSF is sponsored by the five leading motorcycle manufacturers: Honda, Yamaha, Kawasaki, Suzuki and Harley-Davidson. Its purpose is to improve the safety of motorcyclists on the nation's streets and highways. To reduce motorcycle accidents and injuries, the foundation has programs in rider education, licensing improvement, public information, and research. These programs are designed for both motorcyclists and motorists." **Services:** Provides advisory, analytical, bibliographical, how-to, referral and technical information on motorcycle safety, licensing, rider education, public information and research. Offers annual reports, brochures/pamphlets, informational newsletters, library facilities, photos, press kits, research assistance and statistics. Publications include statistics and information sheets on various aspects of motorcycle safety. **How to Contact:** Write. Responds to most inquiries within a week. **Tips:** "MSF is concerned with information specific to the motorcycle operator, not the motorcycles themselves." Recent information request: Material on rider education courses.

1496• NATIONAL AERONAUTICS ASSOCIATION
821 15th St. NW, Suite 430, Washington DC 20005. (202)347-2808. Contact Person: Secretary, Contest and Records Board. **Description:** "We sanction, document and register all civilian and military aviation record attempts (including space) in the US and represent the US in the Federation Aeronautique Internationale (FAI), the world governing body for sporting aviation." Records national and world records in all sporting aviation activities including model aircraft flying, ballooning, soaring, hang gliding, aerobatic flying, general aviation, parachuting and helicopter flying. **Services:** Provides historical information and complete, current listings of all aviation-related US and world records. The publication *World and USA National Aviation & Space Records* offers complete listings of all current US and world aviation records. Revised quarterly; $35 for initial issue with revisions for 1 year. Revisions only $15 annually. **How to Contact:**

Write, call or visit. Responds to most inquiries immediately. "Credit must be given the National Aeronautics Association for material used from record book." **Tips:** Recent information request: Existing record data and margin to exceed in order to establish a new record.

1497•   NATIONAL AIR AND SPACE MUSEUM
6th St. and Independence Ave. SW, Washington DC 20560. (202)357-1552. Contact: Public Affairs. **Description:** "The museum is a national center for the collection, preservation, exhibition and study of the history of flight." **Services:** Provides advisory, bibliographical, historical, how-to and referral information. Offers aid in arranging interviews, bibliographies, biographies, brochures/pamphlets, placement on mailing list, statistics, photos and press kits. Publications available. **How to Contact:** Write or call. Responds to most inquiries within a week. Information "must be solely for educational, newsworthy or scholarly purposes. Cannot be promotional or commercial in intent." **Tips:** Recent information requests: Photos and description of the museum; archival photos on a particular aviation personality. (See entry 1258.)

1498•   NATIONAL ASSOCIATION OF RAILROAD PASSENGERS
417 New Jersey Ave. SE, Washington DC 20003. (202)546-1550. Contact Person: Executive Director. **Description:** Organization working for the improvement and expansion of rail passenger service. **Services:** Provides analytical, historical, interpretative and referral information primarily on intercity rail passenger service, but also commuter and urban transit. Offers brochures/pamphlets, informational newsletters, press releases and statistics. Publications include *NARP News* (newsletter) and *Getting There by Train Transit, Boat and Bus* (travel magazine). **How to Contact:** Write or call. Responds to most inquiries witin a month. Charges for certain reports. "We request acknowledgment of the source when reprinting from our newsletter." **Tips:** Recent information request: "How do the different travel modes (cars, planes, trains and buses) compare in energy-efficiency?"

1499•   NATIONAL HIGHWAY TRAFFIC SAFETY ADMINISTRATION
400 7th St. SW, Washington DC 20590. (202)426-9550. Contact Person: Chief of Public Affairs. **Description:** "We are a regulatory agency charged by Congress with reducing the number of fatalities and injuries on US highways occurring because of motor vehicle accidents." This is done through improving the safety characteristics of motor vehicles; the easy and safe movement of traffic; and the skill and awareness of drivers. The National Highway Traffic Safety effort is carried out in cooperation with state and local government, industries and other private organizations. **Services:** Offers aid in arranging interviews, annual reports, statistics, brochures/pamphlets, placement on mailing list and press kits. Publications available. **How to Contact:** Write. Responds to most inquiries within a week. **Tips:** Recent information request: "How many deaths were there on highways last year?"

1500•   NATIONAL MARITIME MUSEUM
Foot of Polk St., San Francisco CA 94109. (415)556-8177. Contact Person: Librarian. **Description:** Preservation of West Coast maritime history: collection of all forms of information including objects, vessels, photographs, documents, ship plans, published research on the subject, exhibits. **Services:** Provides bibliographical, historical, referral and technical information from gold-rush period to approximately 1940; sailing ship history; steamboat history; fisheries, series on San Francisco Bay and western rivers, shipbuilders; art (scrimshaw, paintings, drawings, prints). Offers library facilities, photos, research assistance and telephone reference services. **How to Contact:** Write or visit. Responds to most inquiries within a month. **Tips:** "Contact us a few days ahead of your visit and tell us what you are looking for. Be specific in describing your project: e.g., time frame, name of person(s), vessel(s), purpose of research." Recent information requests: History of early Sacramento River transportation; wreck of gold-rush vessel *Tennessee.*

1501•   NATIONAL MARITIME UNION OF AMERICA
346 W. 17th St., New York NY 10011. (212)620-5700. Contact Person: Editor. **Description:** The National Maritime Union of America is a "labor union for unlicensed seamen." **Services:** Offers statistics, placement on mailing list and newspaper. **How to Contact:** Write. Responds to most inquiries within a week. Requires written request from the publication a writer is working for. Charges for newspaper.

1502• NATIONAL MOTORCYCLE COMMUTER ASSOCIATION
1377 K St. # 107, Washington DC 20005, (703)437-6308. Contact Person: Chairman of the Board. **Description:** The association "promotes motorcycles as a fuel-efficient, convenient form of personal transportation and represents the rights of cyclists." **Services:** Provides advisory information on motorcycle commuting and motorcycles as a transportation option. **How to Contact:** Write. Responds to most inquiries within a month.

1503• NATIONAL SCHOOL TRANSPORTATION ASSOCIATION
Box 2639, Springfield VA 22152. (703)644-0700. Contact Person: Executive Director. **Description:** "The purpose of the NSTA is to provide school bus contractors from across the country with a unified and positive voice to work with federal and state legislatures, federal agencies and the public sector on matters regarding adequate driver training, tax issues, vehicle inspections, energy, pupil passenger safety and issues for total industry-wide improvements in all areas of public transportation. NSTA works with students, parents and school officials to foster safe and efficient pupil transportation in yellow school buses." **Services:** Provides analytical, historical, how-to, referral, technical and trade information on various aspects of school transportation in general and specifically contract operators. Offers aid in arranging interviews, informational newsletters, photos, research assistance, statistics and telephone reference services. Publications include *National School Bus Report* (quarterly magazine); newsletter (monthly). **How to Contact:** Write or call. Responds to most inquiries within a week. Charges for some services. Give credit to NSTA where appropriate. **Tips:** "Questions should be reasonably specific. Tell us where and how the information will be used. We have many leads and information on most aspects of school transportation." Recent information requests: Statistics on number of school buses in US; accidents involving such; times of occurrence.

1504• NATIONAL TRAILWAYS BUS SYSTEMS
Box 3343, Harrisburg PA 17105. (717)233-7673. Contact Person: Vice President, Traffic Manager. **Description:** "We are an intercity bus system and our activities include regular line passenger service and package express, charter buses for groups and tour buses." **Services:** Offers aid in arranging interviews, annual reports, brochures/pamphlets, information searches, placement on mailing list, photos and press kits. **How to Contact:** Write. Responds to most inquiries within a week. **Tips:** Recent information request: Total number of passengers per year.

1505• NATIONAL TRANSPORTATION SAFETY BOARD
800 Independence Ave. SW, Washington DC 20594. (202)382-6600. Contact: Public Information Office. **Description:** The board is responsible for the investigation and cause determination of transportation accidents and the initiation of corrective measures. "Work is about 80% in the field of aviation; balance is in selected cases involving highways, railroad, pipeline and marine accidents." **Services:** Offers accident reports and special studies involving transportation safety. **How to Contact:** Write or call. Responds to most inquiries within a week. Case history details of all cases available for review are in the public inquiry section of the safety board, (202)382-6735. Contact public inquiry section also for accident reports, special studies, safety recommendations.

1506• SOCIETY OF AUTOMOTIVE ENGINEERS, INC.
400 Commonwealth Dr., Warrendale PA 15096. (412)766-4841. Contact Person: Manager of Communications. **Description:** "SAE is a not-for-profit, educational and scientific organization dedicated to the advancement of automotive technology." **Services:** Provides technical information covering every facet of the technology of self-propelled vehicles; cars, trucks, aircraft and off-highway vehicles. Offers computerized information searches, library facilities and press kits. Publications include 1,000 technical papers/year; 30 books; automotive standards. **How to Contact:** Write or call. Responds to most inquiries within a week. Charges for research and online information searches $60/minimum. **Tips:** "Technical papers are gratis to press at the meeting where they are presented. SAE is the information resource for automotive technology. On-line data base goes back to 1965."

1507• THE SOCIETY OF AUTOMOTIVE HISTORIANS, INC.
National Automotive History Collection, Detroit Public Library, 5201 Woodward Ave., Detroit MI 48202. Contact Person: Secretary. **Description:** Nonprofit organization whose purpose is to preserve and record historical facts concerning the development and use of the automobile

worldwide from its inception to the present. **Services:** Provides advisory and referral information on the history of auto racing, including racing cars and drivers; the history of automobile manufacturers; biographical sketches of automotive pioneers. Offers informational newsletters and research assistance. Publications include *Automotive History Review.* **How to Contact:** Write. Responds to most inquiries within a month. **Tips:** Recent information request: Background on the actual racing activities of E.L. Cord before he became an automobile manufacturer.

1508• STEAMSHIP HISTORICAL SOCIETY OF AMERICA, INC.
414 Pelton Ave., Staten Island NY 10310. (212)727-9583. Contact Person: Secretary and Librarian. **Description:** Nonprofit organization dedicated to preserving the history of navigation by powered vessels. **Services:** Provides bibliographical, historical and referral information on ships, engines, charts and routes, history of companies, plans, menus and postcards. Offers brochures/pamphlets, library facilities, photos and research assistance. Library facilities are at University of Baltimore, 1420 Maryland Ave., Baltimore MD 21201. Publications include *Steamboat Bill* (quarterly magazine); *Canadian Coastal and Inland Steam Vessels—1809-1930*; *Merchant Vessels of the US 1760-1868 (Lytle-Holdcamper List).* **How to Contact:** Write or call. Responds to most inquiries within a week. Charges $10/hour for extensive research; 25¢/page for photocopying. **Tips:** "Try your local library first. Many questions sent to us can be answered in standard reference books widely distributed." Recent information request: Background on Mississippi steamboats.

1509• UNION PACIFIC RAILROAD
1416 Dodge St., Omaha NE 68179. (402)281-5822. Contact Person: Director of Audio Visual Services. **Description:** "Begun in 1865, The Union Pacific Railroad is one of the top railroads in the nation. We promote the Union Pacific Railroad and railroads in general." **Services:** Provides historical, referral and trade information on railroad equipment and operations, western states scenery and agriculture and other industry. Offers 15,000 color transparencies and many b&w prints of national parks and monuments, cities and regions covered by the railroad. Also photos of railroad equipment and operations, and western agriculture and industry. **How to Contact:** Write or call. Responds to most inquiries within a month. Credit line for photos required.

1510• URBAN MASS TRANSPORTATION ADMINISTRATION
400 7th St. SW, Washington DC 20590. (202)426-4043. Contact Person: Director of Public Affairs. **Description:** Government agency "providing technical and financial assistance to states and local governments and other public bodies to improve, develop and plan for public transportation systems." **Services:** Provides advisory, historical, how-to and referral information on urban mass transit. Offers aid in arranging interviews, biographies, brochures/pamphlets, computerized information searches, placement on mailing lists and press kits. Publications include agency-funded reports (limited quantities). **How to Contact:** Write, call or visit. Responds to most inquiries as soon as possible. **Tips:** Recent information request: "What is the cost of a standard 40-foot bus?"

SECTION·TWENTY-NINE

THE WORKPLACE

Far and away the best prize that life offers is the chance to work hard at work worth doing.
—*Theodore Roosevelt*

These information sources reflect on-the-job concerns. They include labor-management relations, unions, discrimination, personnel administration, quality control, career planning and training, labor reform, occupational safety and work options.

Bibliography

Bolles, Richard. *What Color Is Your Parachute?*. rev. ed. Berkeley, CA: Ten Speed Press, 1982. (Guide to career planning, résumés, job interviews)

Buckley, Joseph C. *Retirement Handbook*. 6th ed. Edited by Henry Schmidt. New York: Harper & Row Publishers, 1977.

Colgate, Craig, ed. *Directory of National Trade & Professional Associations and Labor Unions of the US and Canada*. Annual. Washington DC: Columbia Books.

College Placement Annual. Bethlehem, PA: College Placement Council. (Employment opportunities; job hunting contacts)

Fink, Gary M., ed. *Biographical Dictionary of American Labor Leaders*. Westport, CT: Greenwood Press, 1974.

US Department of Labor. *Dictionary of Occupational Titles*. 4th ed. Washington DC: Government Printing Office, 1977. (Also, *Selected Characteristics of Occupations Defined in the Dictionary of Occupational Titles*, 1981)

US Department of Labor. Bureau of Labor Statistics. *Employment and Earnings*. Monthly. Washington DC: Government Printing Office.

US Department of Labor. *Occupational Outlook Handbook*. Biennial. Washington DC: Government Printing Office. (Profiles of occupations: advancement, earnings, working conditions, trends, etc.)

1511• AFL-CIO
815 16th St. NW, Washington DC 20006. (202)637-5010. Contact Person: Director of Information. **Description:** "We are a labor organization." **Services:** Provides advisory, analytical, historical, interpretative and referral information on history, function, positions of organized labor and trade unions; operations of nation's oldest, largest labor federation. Offers aid in arranging interviews, annual reports, bibliographies, biographies, statistics, brochures/pamphlets, clipping services, placement on mailing list, newsletter and photos (limited). **How to Contact:** Write or call. Responds to most inquiries immediately. "Written requests preferred, but we will answer simple questions on the phone. Placement on free mailing list depends on Director's decision." **Tips:** Recent information request: View of AFL-CIO on current unemployment statistics.

1512• ALLIANCE AGAINST SEXUAL COERCION
Box 1, Cambridge MA 02139. (617)547-1176. **Description:** Organization fighting sexual harassment through services to those who are harassed; public education, speeches, and workplace trainings; and publications. **Services:** Provides advisory, analytical, bibliographical, historical, how-to, referral and issue-related information on sexual harassment. Offers aid in arranging interviews (occasionally), brochures/pamphlets, placement on mailing lists, research assistance and statistics. Publications include bibliographies. Publications list available. **How to Contact:** Write or call. "We return calls collect." Responds to most inquiries within a month. Charges for photocopying and publications; negotiates fees for consultation on case by case basis. **Tips:** Recent information requests: "What are some success stories dealing with the issue?"; "What should a good training program include?"

1513• AMERICAN OCCUPATIONAL MEDICAL ASSOCIATION (AOMA)
2340 S. Arlington Heights Rd., Arlington Heights IL 60005. (312)228-6850. Contact Person: Director of Public Relations. **Description:** "American Occupational Medical Association (AOMA) is the nation's largest professional society of physicians who provide employee health care. Approximately 4,000 members are engaged in the specialty of occupational medicine, both in the US and abroad. Most members work with business and industry, and others are affiliated with academic institutions or governmental agencies. The *Journal of Occupational Medicine*, internationally recognized as the foremost publication in the field, is AOMA's official scientific publication. The American Occupational Health Conference, one of the largest annual meetings dealing with occupational health issues, combines the annual scientific meetings of AOMA and the American Associaton of Occupational Health Nurses." **Services:** Provides information on promoting the health of workers through clinical practice, research and education. Offers aid in arranging interviews, placement on mailing list, newsletter, photos and press kits; also list of reprints from *Journal of Occupational Medicine*. Publications also include *AOMA Report*, usually made available to members only, but which "can be sent to members of the press in some cases." **How to Contact:** Write or call; prefers written requests. Responds to most inquiries immediately, "depending on the material needed." **Tips:** "Know your subject. Use of some material may require copyright permission." Recent information request: "How long do employers keep employees' medical records?"

1514• AMERICAN SOCIETY FOR PERSONNEL ADMINISTRATION
30 Park Dr., Berea OH 44017. (216)826-4790. Contact Person: Director, Communications. **Description:** "The purpose of the society is to provide international leadership in establishing and supporting standards of excellence in the personnel administration/industrial relations profession. Through publications, professional development seminars, problem-solving channels, conferences, Washington representation and sponsored research, the society works with its members to improve the quality of human resource management." **Services:** Provides advisory, bibliographical, how-to, referral and trade information on all aspects of the management of people at work. Offers aid in arranging interviews, bibliographies, statistics and placement on mailing list. Publications available. **How to Contact:** "Write or call the office with reference to a specific area of interest, and appropriate direction will be provided." Responds to most inquiries within a week. Charges for some materials; duplication of materials at cost. **Tips:** Recent information request: "What impact does Japanese management really have for and on American companies?"

1515• AMERICAN SOCIETY FOR QUALITY CONTROL
230 W. Wells St., Milwaukee WI 53203. (414)272-8575. Contact Person: Manager, Public Relations or Executive Director. **Description:** "The ASQC is dedicated to the advancement of quality. It provides business and industry with information and guidance in the pursuit of improved quality in American goods and services. The society serves approximately 40,000 members of the quality control, assurance and reliability profession. Over 250 corporations are sustaining members." **Services:** Provides advisory, analytical, bibliographical, historical, how-to, interpretative, referral, technical and trade information on quality control and quality assurance (both management of and actual activity). Offers interviews, research sources, biographies, and other information on the quality fields including education and training, career counseling and planning, conferences and exhibitions. Information on specific quality fields is also available in any of the following areas: banking, biomedical applications, computer-aided quality, environment, energy, government services, graphic arts, home appliances, home furnishings, human resources, insurance, metals, metrology, nondestructive testing, product safety and liability, quality auditing, quality circles, quality costs, software, special research and development, systems engineering, systems and program analysis, standards, vendor-vendee relations, automotive, aerospace and defense, chemical, food-drug and cosmetics, inspection, reliability, statistics, textile and needle trades. **How to Contact:** Call. Responds to most inquiries within a week. **Tips:** "We have volumes of both general and technical resources." Recent information request: Overview of what the quality issues are and who are the experts.

1516• AMERICAN SOCIETY FOR TRAINING AND DEVELOPMENT
600 Maryland Ave. SW, # 305, Washington DC 20024. (202)484-2390. Contact Person: Public Relations Manager. **Description:** "The American Society for Training and Development is a nonprofit educational society dedicated to the better use of human resource potential in the workplace. It is composed of nearly 50,000 members in 132 chapters who are responsible for

employee training and development in the private and public sectors.'' **Services:** Provides advisory, referral and trade information on human resource development; training and education in business and industry; education/work relations. Offers annual reports, brochures/pamphlets, computerized information searches, informational newsletters, library facilities, placement on mailing lists and press kits. **How to Contact:** Write or call. Responds to most inquiries within a week. **Tips:** Recent information request: ''What does American business and industry spend each year on training employees?''

1517• ASSOCIATION FOR WORKPLACE DEMOCRACY
1747 Connecticut Ave. NW, Washington DC 20009. (202)265-7727. Contact: Person: Office Manager. **Description:** The association works ''to bring individuals and organizations into a network to share insights, plans and projects which enhance democracy at work; to provide a forum of discussion of current news and vital issues affecting the workplace.'' **Services:** Provides analytical, historical and trade information on workplace democracy: worker-ownership, worker participation in management, quality of working-life programs, quality circles, worker buyouts, worker cooperatives, employee stock ownership plans, etc. Offers informational newsletters, research assistance and telephone reference services. Publications include *Workplace Democracy* (quarterly journal). Publications list available. **How to Contact:** Write. Responds to most inquiries within a month. Charges for membership. ''Contact publisher for permission to excerpt from our journal.'' **Tips:** ''Make questions specific; we mainly make referrals.''

1518• ASSOCIATION OF EXECUTIVE SEARCH CONSULTANTS
30 Rockefeller Plaza, New York NY 10112. (212)541-7580. Contact: Communications Committee. **Description:** ''We are the only association of the kind in the world comprising the leading executive search firms, large and small. Members work solely for client companies to locate executives in the $35,000 and higher salary range. Resumés from individuals seeking executive employment are accepted by Association of Executive Search Consultants (AESC) members, but there is no guarantee of employment as the firms never work for individuals seeking employment. AESC provides a list ($3), brochure and code of ethics to anyone.'' **Services:** Provides referral and trade information on executive demand and how to use an executive search consultant. Offers statistics, brochures/pamphlets and a list of member firms. Publications include *A Company's Guide to Executive Recruiting*, the AESC code of ethics and professional practice guidelines. **How to Contact:** Write or call. Responds to most inquiries immediately.

1519• ASSOCIATION OF PART-TIME PROFESSIONALS, INC.
Box 3419, Alexandria VA 22302. (703)370-6206. **Description:** Nonprofit organization promoting part-time professional employment with pro-rated benefits. **Services:** Provides bibliographical, how-to, interpretative, technical and trade information on part-time employment. Offers brochures/pamphlets, informational newsletters and press kits. Publications include quarterly newsletter; bibliography on part-time work; *Part-Timer's Guide to Federal Part-Time Employment*. **How to Contact:** Write or call. Responds to most inquiries within a month. ''Give credit to the association and list our name, address and phone number in articles, etc. Don't expect us to write the article.'' **Tips:** Recent information request: Trends in part-time employment.

1520• AUTOMOBILE, AEROSPACE AND AGRICULTURAL IMPLEMENT WORKERS OF AMERICA, INTERNATIONAL UNION/UNITED AUTO WORKERS
8000 E. Jefferson Ave., Detroit MI 48214. (313)926-5291. Contact: Public Relations Department. **Description:** ''We are a labor union.'' **Services:** Offers aid in arranging interviews, biographies, brochures/pamphlets, statistics, information searches, placement on mailing list and newsletter. Publications available. **How to Contact:** Write or call. Responds to most inquiries within a week. ''Written requests preferred, but we will answer brief questions on the phone.'' **Tips:** Recent information request: History of the union.

1521• BUREAU OF LABOR STATISTICS
1515 Broadway, New York NY 10036. (212)944-3121. Contact Person: Chief, Branch of Information and Advisory Services. **Description:** Statistics gathering agency of the Department of Labor. ''We disseminate information and advise the public on the use of our statistics. We have information on consumer and producer prices, employment and unemployment, productivity, occupational outlook, wages and industrial relations.'' **Services:** Provides advisory, analytical, bibliographical, historical, how-to, referral and technical information. ''We have 24-hour

recordings: Consumer price index (212)944-3125; Unemployment data (212)944-2923; and BLS update on research findings (212)944-3149." Offers bibliographies, statistics, brochures/pamphlets, microfiche, placement on mailing list, and newsletter. Brochures/pamphlets include *Handbook of Labor Statistics*; *Monthly Labor Review*; *Occupational Outlook Quarterly*; *BLS Handbook of Methods* and *Employment and Earnings*. **How to Contact:** Write, call or visit. Responds to most inquiries within a week. Charges 10¢/photocopy. Government Printing Office publications are for sale. **Tips:** "Use as many sources as possible. Check accuracy of data received."

1522• BUSINESS AND PROFESSIONAL WOMEN'S FOUNDATION
Marguerite Rawalt Resource Center, 2012 Massachusetts Ave. NW, Washington DC 20036. (202)293-1200, ext. 39. Contact Person: Librarian. **Description:** "An educational nonprofit organization that conducts research, administers scholarships and educational loans, funds research and provides a resource center. We provide reference and referral services to the public on issues involving women and work—including jobs, careers, occupational segregation, comparable worth, women's legal status." **Services:** Provides bibliographical, historical, interpretative and referral information on women and work; careers; jobs; occupational segregation; comparable worth; displaced homemakers; sexual harassment; pay equity; feminist theory; women's movement; education. Offers annual reports, computerized information searches, statistics and telephone reference services. Publications include *Foundation Publications List*; *Resource Center Selected Acquisitions* (bimonthly); *Information Digests* (occasional publications on special topics). **How to Contact:** Write, call or visit. Responds to most inquiries within a week. Charges for photocopying and computerized data base searches. Library collection does not circulate.

1523• CAREER WATCHERS, INC.
3857 N. High St., Suite 204, Columbus OH 43214. (614)267-0958. Contact Person: Business Manager. **Description:** "Because of the economic trends affecting employment, Career Watchers, Inc., was established for the purpose of career advancement. Career Watchers, Inc., offers the compilation of information into, and design of personal resumé portfolios. The service also provides clients with job search counseling, career assessment testing, outplacement seminars and conducts 'how-to' resumé workshops." **Services:** Provides analytical, how-to, technical and trade information on resumé writing, cover letters, job search, career advancement, phototypesetting/layout/design of resumé formats. Offers brochures/pamphlets and press kits. **How to Contact:** Write, call or visit. Responds to most inquiries immediately. "No fee to writers inquiring about information regarding services; fees charged for services rendered (resumé preparation, workshops, etc.). All material is copyrighted and should be reproduced only at our approval. Writers must inform us of publication usage."

1524• CENTER FOR OCCUPATIONAL HAZARDS
5 Beekman St., New York NY 10038. (212)227-6220. Contact Person: Director, Information Center. **Description:** National nonprofit clearinghouse for research and information on health hazards in the arts. **Services:** Provides advisory, bibliographical, interpretative, referral, technical and trade information on health and safety in arts, crafts, schools, universities, theatre, dance, museums, art conservation labs, etc. Offers informational newsletters, library facilities, research assistance, statistics and telephone reference services. Publications include *Art Hazards News*; *Data Sheets and Articles*. Publications list available. **How to Contact:** Write or call. Responds to most inquiries immediately. "Give proper credits and our address in your article for further information. Let us or our experts check your copy. Errors in health and safety articles can result in illness, injury to readers, and liability for writers." **Tips:** Recent information request: Accuracy of statements made about hazards of chemicals found in children's art materials.

1525• COUNCIL FOR CAREER PLANNING, INC.
310 Madison Ave., New York NY 10017. (212)687-9490. Contact Person: Executive Director. **Description:** "The council works to bring a high level of professional service to the career counseling field; to assure strong, creative approaches to the problems that beset people as they pursue satisfying jobs and careers; to provide a special access to resources and opportunities in the job market." **Services:** Provides career counseling, placement, career development programs and job opportunity resources. Offers brochures/pamphlets, newsletters, research assistance, and other information on careers and the job market. Publications include *Job Fact Sheets* on over 200 individ-

ual careers; booklets and cassettes on job-hunting techniques. **How to Contact:** Write or call. Responds to most inquiries within a week. Charges for career counseling services. **Tips:** Recent information request: "How can I change my job in the current tight job market?"

1526• EQUAL EMPLOYMENT OPPORTUNITY COMMISSION
Office of Public Affairs, 2401 E St. NW, Washington DC 20506. (202)634-6930. Contact Person: Director, Office of Public Affairs. **Description:** "The commission enforces Title 7 of the 1964 Civil Rights Act, which prohibits employment discrimination in the federal and private sector on the basis of race, color, sex, religion and national origin. The commission also enforces the Age Discrimination and Employment Act and the Equal Pay Act." **Services:** Offers aid in arranging interviews, annual reports, bibliographies, biographies, brochures/pamphlets, placement on mailing list, newsletter, photos and speakers' bureau. Publications list available. **How to Contact:** Write or call. Responds to most inquiries within a week. "Some information must be requested in writing. No information is given on individual companies or complainants." **Tips:** Recent information request: "How many charges of sex discrimination have been filed since 1981?"

1527• FEDERAL MEDIATION AND CONCILIATION SERVICE
2100 K St. NW, Washington DC 20427. (202)653-5290. Contact Person: Information Officer. **Description:** "The FM&CS represents the public interest by promoting the development of sound and stable labor-management relationships; preventing or minimizing work stoppages by assisting labor and management to settle their disputes through mediation; advocating collective bargaining, mediation,and voluntary arbitration as the preferred processes for settling issues between employers and representatives of employees. The FM&CS offers its services in labor-management disputes in any industries affecting interstate commerce, either upon its own motion or at the request of one or more of the parties in the dispute." **Services:** Offers brochures and annual reports. **How to Contact:** Write or call.

1528• INDEPENDENT PROFESSIONAL TYPISTS NETWORK (IPTN)
924 Main St., Huntington Beach CA 92648. (714)536-4926. Contact Person: National Coordinator. **Description:** IPTN works "to alleviate the public's opinion of the person who types at home as a business in addition to the person who works in an office at a 'real job.' " **Services:** Provides advisory, historical, how-to, referral, technical and trade information on how to set up a home-based typing/word processing business (equipment, advertising, doing the work, etc.); what qualifications a home-based typist must have and probably has; why the work isn't done 'cheap' but is charged at professional rates. Offers aid in arranging interviews, brochures/pamphlets, informational newsletters, photos, press kits, research assistance and telephone reference services. Publications include an overview of IPTN and "what is a professional home-based typist." **How to Contact:** Write. Include SASE and "preferably 2 stamps." Responds to most inquiries within a week. Charges only occasionally for long-distance calls or extensive photocopying. **Tips:** "Be very specific with the information you need. Give us time to answer or refer it elsewhere. And quote us accurately!" Recent information request: "I'm doing a story for a magazine about the 'state of today's secretary.' Where does the home-based businesswoman fit into this?"

1529• INSTITUTE FOR LABOR AND MENTAL HEALTH
3137 Telegraph Ave., Oakland CA 94609. (415)653-6166. Contact Person: Administrator or Program Coordinator. **Description:** "We were created to serve the needs of working people in the area of occupational stress. We have counseling services, consultation and documentation, as well as a national Occupational Stress Resource Center." **Services:** Provides bibliographical and referral information on occupational stress and the areas which relate to it, such as the economy and mental health, physical health hazards at work, family life, research, available resources, etc. Offers brochures/pamphlets, informational newsletters, library facilities, photos, placement on mailing lists, research assistance and statistics. Publications include *Occupational Stress Reporter*. **How to Contact:** Write or call. Responds to most inquiries within a week. Charges for consultations, counseling and newsletter.

1530• INTERAGENCY COMMITTEE ON HANDICAPPED EMPLOYEES
Equal Employment Opportunity Commission, 2401 E St. NW, Washington DC 20506. (202)755-6040. Contact Person: Program Manager. **Description:** "Our purpose is to provide a focus for federal and other employment of handicapped individuals and to review in cooperation with the Equal Employment Opportunity Commission the adequacy of hiring, placement and

BEHIND THE BYLINE

Walter Williams
Writer and professor

Economics is his specialty. And it is the economic perspective of a free society that Walter Williams brings to his students at George Mason University and the readers of his books, articles and nationally-syndicated newspaper column.

"My interest in economics began at California State at Los Angeles in 1962 when (as a sociology major) I read W.E.B. Dubois's book, *Black Reconstruction*. The book said that black people would never reach ultimate freedom until they understood the economic system." Ten years later, he had his Ph.D. in economics. Today, he calls himself a radical with a well-defined journalistic goal: "to sell Americans on individual freedom."

To do that, he studies labor economics, public finance and public policy analysis. His research consists of testing hypotheses—looking for empirical evidence, actual data to affirm or refute something. He talks about his recent book, *The State Against Blacks*, as an economic treatment of the hypothesis that racial discrimination is not the whole explanation for why some people find themselves locked into unfavorable socio-economic slots.

"Most of my research and writing is directed toward the intelligent layman," he says, "—that person who has an interest in economics and the economic approach to looking at society."

Williams recognizes the challenges connected with selling economics to a readership whose economic interests are as varied as they are. "One of my mentors said once that a person doesn't really understand economics unless he can explain it to someone having an alien or hostile mind toward it."

Williams's ability to explain economic complexities in lay terms is a conscious effort. "I believe one important part of communicating with people is being able to use examples to get your message across. I also respect the intelligence of people and don't talk down to them. I don't use a lot of jargon, except in class."

Williams gets the ideas for his columns from his research, from talking with students and from reading the newspaper. "Media coverage of economics has improved in recent years, as evidenced by people's understanding of the subject and the way inflation affects their pocketbooks." But Williams sees a need for more economic discussion in the media. He recognizes that the economic consideration is not a popular one among journalists. "In general they have an inadequate understanding of economics; they don't have an appreciation of it. As a result, they report both misinformation and incomplete information."

He recalls reading the Miami newspapers during a drought in that city. None of the newspapers addressed what effect raising the price of water would have on the situation— that it would get people to use less water for low-value uses (such as lawn sprinkling). Williams cites the absence of this economic consideration of the drought as an example of the public getting an incomplete picture of the situation.

"Economics is learned. It can be self-taught through books or studied formally. But journalists can't learn it only by reading each other's columns." Williams recommends Armen Alchian and William Allen's *Exchange and Production: Theory in Use*, Milton Friedman's *Free to Choose* and William Allen's *The Midnight Economist* as basics for understanding the economic discipline. "Writers could learn from them," he says, and then suggests that bureaucrats in Washington could, too.

advancement practices with respect to handicapped individuals in the federal service.'' **Services:** Offers aid in arranging interviews, annual reports, statistics, brochures/pamphlets and placement on mailing list. Publications include ''government publications concerning employment of handicapped individuals, and annual reports and statistics on the employment of handicapped individuals.'' **How to Contact:** Write or call. Responds to most inquiries within a week. ''The Interagency Committee addresses policy and program issues concerning nondiscrimination and affirmative action. Persons interested in how the federal government implements section 501 of the Rehabilitation Act of 1973 should get in touch with the Interagency Committee.''

1531• INTERNATIONAL BROTHERHOOD OF TEAMSTERS, CHAUFFEURS, WAREHOUSEMEN AND HELPERS OF AMERICA
25 Louisiana Ave. NW, Washington DC 20001. (202)624-6911. Contact Person: Press Secretary. **Description:** ''The International Brotherhood of Teamsters represents members in matters regarding wages, working conditions and fringe benefits. We are the largest union in the world.'' **Services:** Offers aid in arranging interviews, annual reports, bibliographies, biographies, statistics, brochures/pamphlets, information searches, placement on mailing list, newsletter, photos, press kits, library research department and audiovisual aids. Publications include *The International Teamster* (quarterly) and *The Teamster News Service*. **How to Contact:** Write. Responds to most inquiries within a week. Information cannot be used for advertising purposes.

1532• NATIONAL ASSOCIATION OF TEMPORARY SERVICES
119 S. Saint Asaph St., Alexandria VA 22314. (703)549-6287. Contact Person: Director of Public Relations. **Description:** The association promotes the temporary help service industry. **Services:** Provides advisory, analytical, referral and trade information. Offers brochures/pamphlets, informational newsletters, research assistance and statistics. Publications include *The Temporary Help Industry . . . The Issues and the Answers*. **How to Contact:** Write or call. Responds to most inquiries within a week. **Tips:** Recent information requests: ''How many temporary help workers were there last year?''; ''How big is the temporary help industry?''

1533• NATIONAL CENTER FOR EMPLOYEE OWNERSHIP
1611 S. Walter Reed, # 109, Arlington VA 22204. (703)979-2375. Contact Person: Executive Director. **Description:** Center promoting employee ownership. **Services:** Provides information, initial consultation on employee ownership to members. Offers clipping service, informational newsletter, referral service, conferences. Publications include newsletter; topical publications; ESOP model; *Annual Resource Guide*. **How to Contact:** Write or call. Responds to most inquiries within a week. Charges for publications and information.

1534• NATIONAL CHILD LABOR COMMITTEE
1501 Broadway, Suite 1111, New York NY 10036. (212)840-1801. Contact Person: Editor. **Description:** ''The National Child Labor Committee is a nonprofit organization promoting the education, health, safety, and well-being of children and youth. NCLC offers technical assistance and does research in these areas: youth employment, job training for teens, teen parents, education of migrant farmworkers' children and child labor legislation.'' **Services:** Provides advisory, analytical, bibliographical (limited), historical, interpretative, referral and technical information on youth employment, job training for teenagers (including cooperative education, summer job programs, and training for supervisors of youth); vocational and employment problems of teen parents; education of migrant farmworkers' children; child labor legislation (including state provisions, model legislation, health and safety regulations and history). Offers annual reports, brochures/pamphlets, informational newsletters, photos (limited historical photos), placement on mailing lists, press kits, research assistance, statistics and telephone reference services. Publications list available. ''In addition, a compendium of all national and state child labor laws and a massive study of US Hazardous Occupations orders are available; but these are highly specialized and distributed separately from other publications. Researchers should inquire directly about them.'' **How to Contact:** Write or call. Responds to most inquiries within a week. Charges for photocopying and some publications. Restrictions on use of some materials: ''photos have limited repro rights, for example. We prefer to know where material will be published.'' **Tips:** ''If a researcher can tell us what he or she is working toward, we can steer him or her to the right resources—but we don't have the staff to focus the story for a researcher.'' Recent information requests: ''What was the text of the proposed child labor constitutional amendment of 1927?''; ''Is

truck driving a prohibited occupation for 16-year-olds?''; ''How well is the federal migrant education program working?''

1535• NATIONAL COUNCIL FOR LABOR REFORM
406 S. Plymouth Court, Chicago IL 60605. (312)427-0207. Contact Person: Executive Vice President. **Description:** An organization which ''promotes peaceful, productive labor-management relations and the re-establishment of the rights of the individual employer and employee—especially the right to work, regardless of union or non-union membership.'' **Services:** Provides advisory, analytical, bibliographical, historical, how-to, interpretative, referral, technical and trade information on labor legislation in Congress, labor laws and practices. Offers aid in arranging interviews, biographies, brochures/pamphlets, clipping services, library facilities, placement on mailing lists, press kits, research assistance, statistics and telephone reference services. Publications include *Compulsory Unionism: The New Slavery*; *My Job: The Economics and Politics of Wages, Unemployment and Inflation*; *Industry-Wide Bargaining—A Threat to US Competition in the World* and others. **How to Contact:** Write or call. Responds to most inquiries immediately. **Tips:** ''Call us when you start your research or for topics about which you might write. We would like to have a copy of the final article, column or speech.'' Recent information request: ''How do union organizers sign up an employer without his or her employees being allowed to vote against compulsory membership in the union selected for them to join?''

1536• NATIONAL EMPLOYEE SERVICES AND RECREATION ASSOCIATION
20 N. Wacker Dr., Chicago IL 60606. (312)346-7575. Contact Person: Editor. **Description:** ''NESRA is a nonprofit organization dedicated to the principle that employee recreation, fitness and services programs are essential to effective personnel management. Our members are the directors and suppliers of such programs in business, industry and government. NESRA assists member organizations in developing and promoting employee programs.'' **Services:** Provides advisory, analytical, historical, how-to, interpretative, referral and trade information on management, sports, employee services, fitness, travel, hobbies, cultural/social activities, and studies on the leisure ethic. Offers aid in arranging interviews, brochures/pamphlets, informational newsletters, placement on mailing lists, press kits, research assistance and statistics. Publications include *Employee Services Management* (magazine); *Keynotes* (newsletter); numerous special topic brochures. **How to Contact:** Write or call. Responds to most inquiries within a week. **Tips:** ''Contact our organization one month or more before your deadline to allow us ample time to assist you. We request to approve any final manuscripts.'' Recent information requests: ''What is the future of employee services and recreation—do you foresee growth or decline?''; ''Where do employee services fit in the corporate plan?''

1537• NATIONAL INSTITUTE FOR OCCUPATIONAL SAFETY AND HEALTH
Clearinghouse for Occupational Safety and Health Information, US Public Health Service, 4676 Columbia Pkwy., Cincinnati OH 45226. (513)684-8326. Contact Person: Chief. **Description:** ''The Clearinghouse for Occupational Safety and Health Information provides the technical information support for NIOSH research programs. It also provides technical information upon request to other government agencies, researchers in occupational safety and health, and the public at large. The clearinghouse collects, organizes and retrieves published and unpublished technical information related to the field of occupational safety and health. This includes adverse effects of chemical substances, physical agents, psychological stress, samplings and analysis techniques, engineering controls, personal protective equipment, and recommended standards.'' **Services:** Provides bibliographical and referral information on ''all aspects of occupational health, including industrial hygiene, medicine, toxicology, pathology, engineering, nursing and chemistry.'' Offers computerized information searches, library facilities and interlibrary loan. Cumulative catalog of publications and periodic new publications lists available. **How to Contact:** Write or call. ''Services are limited only by availability of staff and time. In-house requests receive priority.''

1538• NATIONAL LABOR RELATIONS BOARD
1717 Pennsylvania Ave. NW, Washington DC 20570. (202)632-4950. Contact Person: Director of Information. **Description:** ''The NLRB is an independent federal agency established in 1935 to administer the nation's principal labor-relations law which generally applies to all interstate commerce, except railroad and airline. The purpose of the NLRB is to serve the public interest by reducing interruption in commerce caused by industrial strife. It provides orderly processes for protecting and implementing the respective rights of workers, employers and unions in their

relationships with one another. The NLRB has 2 primary functions: to determine and implement through secret ballot elections, the free democratic choice by employees as to whether they wish to be represented by a union, and if so, by which one; to prevent and remedy unlawful acts (unlawful labor practices) by either the employers or unions. The NLRB does not act on its own motion—rather it processes only those charges of unlawful labor practices and petitions for employee elections which are filed with it at NLRB offices throughout the nation." **Services:** Provides historical, interpretative and referral information on labor law, NLRB operations, board decisions, court reviews, labor election results. Offers aid in arranging interviews, annual reports, biographies, library facilities, news releases, research assistance, statistics and telephone reference services. Publications include *Weekly Summary of NLRB Cases* (by subscription). **How to Contact:** Write or call. Responds to most inquiries within a week. **Tips:** Recent information request: "What are the trends/statistics related to de-certification elections where workers file petitions to determine their preference in either ending their representation by an incumbent union or continuing their certification?"

1539• NEW WAYS TO WORK
149 9th St., San Francisco CA 94103. (415)552-1000. Contact Person: Writer/Editor. **Description:** "New Ways to Work is a national, nonprofit organization that conducts research and provides information and training on work-time options and other workplace issues. Established in 1972, the organizational goal is to encourage constructive and fulfilling work while improving the quality of work life for all." **Services:** Provides advisory, analytical, bibliographical, historical, how-to, interpretative, referral, technical and trade information covering "a variety of work issues but primarily focusing on work-time options: job sharing, work sharing, flexitime, permanent part-time employment, compressed work, time-income tradeoffs and sabbatical leaves." Offers aid in arranging interviews, annual reports, brochures/pamphlets, informational newsletters, library facilities, placement on mailing lists, press kits, research assistance and statistics. Publications include *New Ways to Work Newsletter; Work Times*, an international information exchange on alternative work time (sample copy only); various booklet giveaways "determined on a case-by-case basis." **How to Contact:** Write, call or visit. Responds to most inquiries immediately. Charges for "extensive photocopying." **Tips:** "It's usually a good idea to read our background materials first in order to ask more specific questions. There are basic differences between terms such as job sharing and work sharing that many people don't know." Recent information request: "How might work-time options be used to alleviate layoffs?"

1540• 9 TO 5, NATIONAL ASSOCIATION OF WORKING WOMEN
1224 Huron Rd., Cleveland OH 44115. Contact Person: Executive Officer. **Description:** Office worker organizations which fight sex and race discrimination on the job. Promotes programs such as monitoring Equal Employment Opportunity Commission and anti-discrimination agencies. **Services:** Provides advisory, resource and technical information. Offers training and assistance in job-related problems. Publications include *9 to 5 Newsletter*; resource list. **How to Contact:** Write.

1541• OCCUPATIONAL SAFETY AND HEALTH REVIEW COMMISSION
1825 K St. NW, Washington DC 20006. (202)634-7943. Contact Person: Public Information Specialist. **Description:** An independent agency of the executive branch of the government. Functions as a court by adjudicating contested cases under the Occupational Safety and Health Act (OSHA) of 1970. Operates under the mandates of the Freedom of Information Act. **Services:** Files are open to anyone who wishes to inspect them. Publications include press releases, *Rules of Procedure* and *Guide to the Procedures of OSHRC*. **How to Contact:** Write or call. Responds to most inquiries immediately. **Tips:** Recent information requests: Inquiries about companies that violate safety and health standards for employees and outcome of cases.

1542• OFFICE TECHNOLOGY RESEARCH GROUP
c/o Simon Public Relations, 11661 San Vicente, Suite 903, Los Angeles CA 90049. (213)820-2606. Contact Person: Executive Director. **Description:** "Office Technology Research Group (OTRG) is a national association of corporate executives interested in staying abreast of, understanding the ramifications of, and implementing 'office of the future' developments into their company's operations. The office of the future concept, also known as office automation, is an area of growing concern for executives, especially in the light of developing office technologies/systems." **Services:** Provides advisory, interpretative and trade information on the

implementation of future office technologies/Office of the Future. Offers aid in arranging interviews, biographies, statistics, placement on mailing list, newsletter, photos and press kits. "Our material covers an executive's view on future office operations from an overview perspective, not as a how-to approach." Publications include brochure on capabilities. **How to Contact:** Write or call. Responds to most inquiries within a week. Charge for service depends on scope of project/speech, etc. **Tips:** Recent information requests: "How is white collar productivity affected by installation of office automation/word processing/data processing equipment?"; "How is executive productivity measured?"

1543• THE PROFESSIONAL DEVELOPMENT GROUP, INC.
Box 137, 1850 Union St., San Francisco CA 94123. (415)543-5419. Contact Person: General Manager. **Description:** "PDG, Inc. is a management training/consultant firm specializing in interpersonal communications problems. We present two public seminars across the country (*Managing Conflict Productively* and *Anger at Work*) for companies that range in size from small to large. We also present 'in-house.' " **Services:** Provides advisory, how-to, interpretative, referral and trade information on topics such as Powers of Persuasion; Productive Reading and Writing; Management for the '80s—The Best in Japanese Management. Offers brochures/pamphlets, placement on mailing lists and research assistance. Offers audio tape series: *Managing Conflict Productively* and *Anger at Work*; and video tape series: *Managing Conflict Productively.* **How to Contact:** Write, call or visit. Responds to most inquiries within a week. Charges for services; consultation fees on individual basis. **Tips:** Recent information request: Effectiveness of direct mail services.

1544• PUBLIC SERVICE RESEARCH COUNCIL
8330 Old Courthouse Rd., # 600, Vienna VA 22180. (703)790-0700. Contact Person: Director, Public Relations. **Description:** "The Public Service Research Council is the nation's largest citizens' lobby concerned exclusively with curbing the abuses of public sector unions in the US." **Services:** Provides information on politics, union negotiations, trends and elections, labor legislation. Offers annual reports, statistics, brochures/pamphlets and newsletter. Publications include biweekly newsletter; *The Government Union Critique* (published 26 times/year); *The Effect of Collective Bargaining on Teacher Salaries*; *Compulsory Unionism in Government Employees*, *The Government Union Review* (quarterly journal); *Public Sector Bargaining and Strikes*. **How to Contact:** Write (preferred) or call. Responds to most inquiries within 3 weeks. Charges for newsletter and journal. "You can reprint, but give us credit."

1545• STEELCASE, INC.
c/o Carl Byoir & Associates, 380 Madison Ave., New York NY 10017. (212)986-6100. Contact Person: Account Executive. **Description:** "Steelcase is the world's largest designer and manufacturer of office furniture." **Services:** Provides analytical, referral, technical and trade information on attitudes of office workers; office design trends; human factors and employee relations, as they relate to office productivity and office technology. Offers aid in arranging interviews, brochures/pamphlets, photos, placement on mailing lists, press kits and statistics. Publications include *The Steelcase National Survey of Office Environments II* (conducted by Louis Harris & Associates); *The White Collar Productivity Study* (conducted by the American Productivity Center). **How to Contact:** Write or call Steelcase, Inc., 1120 36th St. SE, Grand Rapids MI 49501. (616)247-2287. Responds to most inquiries immediately. **Tips:** "Because more than 35 million Americans work in offices, developments within that environment have built-in interest. Writers seeking to report on trends should assume a broad perspective rather than concentrating solely on technological developments." Recent information requests: "What effect is the growing use of computers and other electronic equipment having on office design?"; "How are companies accommodating the new equipment being installed?"; "What are the office environment needs most commonly expressed by office employees?"

1546• UNITED MINE WORKERS OF AMERICA
900 15th St. NW, Washington DC 20005. (202)842-7240. Contact Person: Director, Office of Public Information. **Description:** Labor union. **Services:** Provides advisory, analytical, historical, how-to, interpretative, referral and trade information on the coal industry, labor unions and government. Offers aid in arranging interviews, brochures/pamphlets, placement on mailing list and press kits (for specific occasions). **How to Contact:** Write or call. Responds to most inquiries immediately. "We prefer written requests, but will answer simple questions on the

phone.'' **Tips:** Recent information requests: Questions relating to the policy, procedures and operations of the United Mine Workers of America within the industry and with government.

1547• UNITED STEEL WORKERS OF AMERICA
5 Gateway Center, Pittsburgh PA 15222. (412)562-2666. Contact Person: Director of Public Relations. **Description:** ''We represent our members who are in the steel, aluminum, nonferrous metals, can, fabricating and chemical industries.'' **Services:** Provides advisory, analytical, bibliographical, historical and interpretative information on industrial unions in the basic metals industry of North America. Offers aid in arranging interviews, statistics, brochures/pamphlets, information searches, placement on mailing list, newsletter, photos and occasional press kits. Publications include *Steelabor* (monthly). **How to Contact:** Write. Responds to most inquiries within a week. Give credit to United Steel Workers of America. **Tips:** Recent information request: Background data on collective bargaining in the basic steel industry.

1548• WIDER OPPORTUNITIES FOR WOMEN
1511 K St. SW, Suite 345, Washington DC 20005. (202)638-3065. Contact Person: Public Relations Coordinator. **Description:** ''We provide job development and training for women (blue-collar work), job referral and support system for women re-entering job market and information on career changing or upward mobility. We press for policy and social changes for equal employment.'' Women's Work Force Network—employment groups nationwide—provides technical assistance, public education and information related to women's employment. **Services:** Offers aid in arranging interviews, biographies, statistics, brochures/pamphlets, placement on mailing list and press kits. **How to Contact:** Write. Responds to most inquiries within a week.

1549• WOMEN'S BUREAU
Department of Labor, 200 Constitution Ave., Washington DC 20210. (202)523-6652. Contact Person: Public Information Officer. **Description:** ''We foster and promote women in the work force.'' Program development is on employment and training. **Services:** Offers statistics, brochures/pamphlets, publications list and technical assistance to organizations. **How to Contact:** Write or call. Responds to most inquiries within a week. **Tips:** Recent information requests: Data on legal rights, child care program, working relations and job sharing.

1550• WORKING WOMEN'S INSTITUTE
593 Park Ave., New York NY 10021. (212)838-4420. Contact Person: Executive Director. **Description:** A national, independent resource/research/action center and clearinghouse of information devoted to the elimination of sexual harassment on the job. **Services:** Provides advisory, analytical, bibliographical, interpretative and referral information on sexual harassment on the job and in education. Offers annual reports, brochures/pamphlets, informational newsletters, library facilities, placement on mailing lists, press kits, research assistance, statistics and telephone reference services. Publications include research reports; brief bank of legal cases; legal publications; reprint service checklist; bibliography; research clearinghouse legislative checklist. **How to Contact:** Write or call. Responds to most inquiries within a week. Charges for reproduction costs; some publications by subscription; fee for library use. **Tips:** ''Call for an appointment. Observe copyright laws.''

WORLD SCOPE

There can be hope only for a society which acts as one big family, and not as many separate ones.

—Anwar el-Sadat

World Scope information sources reflect global interests such as hunger, the United Nations and world peace. In addition, resources on Third World countries and other nations are included, along with a section on foreign embassies in the United States.

Nuclear arms resources are listed in the Public Affairs category; human rights organizations are covered further in the Society and Culture section; conservation organizations are found in the Environment/The Earth section.

Bibliography

Cartledge, T.M. and W.L. Reed, eds. *National Anthems of the World.* 5th ed. New York: Arco Publishing, 1979.

Countries of the World and Their Leaders Yearbook. 2 vols. Detroit: Gale Research Co., 1982.

Europa Yearbook. Annual. Europa Publications. Detroit: Dist. by Gale Research Co.

International Yearbook and Statesman's Who's Who. Annual. Kelly's Directories. Detroit: Dist. by Gale Research Co.

Kurian, George. *Encyclopedia of the Third World.* 3 vols. rev. ed. New York: Facts on Files, 1981.

Political Handbook of the World. New York: McGraw-Hill, 1981.

United Nations Publications in Print. Annual. New York: United Nations. (Catalog—including order number and price—of available publications)

1551• AMERICAN ASSOCIATION FOR STUDY OF THE UNITED STATES IN WORLD AFFAIRS
3813 Annandale Rd., Annandale VA 22003. (703)256-8761. Contact Person: Executive Director. **Description:** Nonprofit educational association, independent of government, party, lobby, sect, or foreign group. "USWA puts a mirror on the position of the United States in world affairs to let those American professionals who finance US operations abroad know how their tax-supported projects are received, and whether their purposes are accomplished. USWA monitors foreign press and shortwave radio, receives foreign embassy speakers, provides honoraria lectures and contracted media articles on foreign affairs in domestic and foreign news analysis." **Services:** Provides advisory, analytical and interpretative information on the underlying causes for change in international relations, primarily as it affects the US. "Change analysis includes economic, social, religious, intellectual and political trends to estimate and even forecast trends in the direction of the consequences of international activities." Offers annual reports and photos. "We are considered primary sources as consultants both in writings and lectures under contract and honoraria." **How to Contact:** Write. Responds to most inquiries within a month. Charges for services such as seminars, lectures, consortia and The Institute of the Position of the United States in World Affairs (6-week summer session).

1552• BUREAU OF ECONOMICS AND BUSINESS AFFAIRS
Department of State, 2201 C St. NW, Washington DC 20520. (202)632-1682. Contact Person: Special Assistant for Legislative and Public Affairs. **Description:** "The purpose of the bureau is to formulate and implement policy on international economic affairs in relation to domestic economic affairs." **Services:** Provides referral information on agriculture, business, economics, food, industry, energy, transportation, international finances and international trade with emphasis on international aspects. Offers aid in arranging interviews and brochures/pamphlets. **How to Contact:** Write or call. Responds to most inquiries

immediately. **Tips:** "Try to be specific in respect to interests." Recent information request: Description of US policy on the Soviet-European gas pipeline; copies of formal statements.

1553• CANADA—NATIONAL FILM BOARD PHOTOTHEQUE
Tunney's Pasture, Ottawa, Ontario, Canada K1A 0M9. (613)593-5826. Contact Person: Photo Librarian. **Description:** Photo library within a government agency. Serves to illustrate with still photography Canada to Canadians and people abroad. **Services:** Provides advisory, how-to, interpretative, referral and technical information and photo research. Offers photos, research assistance and telephone reference services. Publications include *Photos Canada* (catalog). **How to Contact:** Write, call or visit. Responds to most inquiries within a week. Charges fees for selected prints according to the intended use. "All our photo material is under copyright. Copyright laws must be respected." **Tips:** "Specify any requirement that might be needed for the photo (e.g., location, format, type of shot—aerial, low angle, etc.)." Recent information request: "Provide us with 10 color slides typical of primary industries in the province of Ontario."

1554• CENTER FOR INTER-AMERICAN RELATIONS
680 Park Ave., New York NY 10021. (202)249-8950. Contact Person: Director, Public Information or Director, Literature. **Description:** "We promote and encourage better understanding within the US of our neighbors to the north and south." **Services:** Provides advisory, bibliographical and referral information on Latin American literature and arts. Offers aid in arranging interviews, placement on mailing list and newsletter. **How to Contact:** Call. Responds to most inquiries immediately. **Tips:** "Before traveling to Latin America on a writing assignment, check in with us." Recent information request: "I would like to learn of authors interested in translating their work from Spanish into English."

1555• CENTER FOR RESEARCH ON ECONOMIC DEVELOPMENT (CRED)
307 Lorch Hall, University of Michigan, Ann Arbor MI 48109. (313)763-6609, 764-9490. Contact Person: Information & Resources Coordinator. **Description:** University research center which conducts research on development problems; provides training programs in development economics; provides short-term consulting services. **Services:** Provides advisory, analytical, bibliographical, interpretative, referral and technical information on economics, business, public health, development economics, agricultural economics, energy resources. Offers annual reports, brochures/pamphlets, informational newsletters, library facilities, placement on mailing lists, research assistance, statistics and telephone reference services. Publications include *CRED Discussion Papers*; *CRED Project Reports*; *Credits* (newsletter). **How to Contact:** Write. Responds to most inquiries within a week. Charges for photocopying and specific publications. "Materials must be used within our library facilities unless special permission is received." **Tips:** Recent information requests: "Do you receive the World Bank Staff Working Papers and do you have such-and-such by so-and-so, in that series?"; "What is the currency used in Ghana and what is the current exchange rate (US $)?"

1556• COORDINATION COUNCIL FOR NORTH AMERICAN AFFAIRS
Information and Communication Division, 159 Lexington Ave., New York NY 10016. (212)725-4950. Contact Person: Director. **Description:** "We disseminate information on the Republic of China (Taiwan)." **Services:** Provides advisory, analytical, historical, how-to and interpretative information on general topics, political, economic, cultural, social activities and tourism. Offers brochures/pamphlets. **How to Contact:** Write or call. Responds to most inquiries within a week. **Tips:** Recent information request: Photos to illustrate an article.

1557• COUNCIL ON HEMISPHERIC AFFAIRS (COHA)
1900 L St. NW, Suite 201, Washington DC 20036, (202)775-0216. Contact Person: Director. **Description:** "The Council on Hemispheric Affairs (COHA) monitors the full spectrum of the economic, political and social aspects of US-Latin and Canadian-Latin American relations, including the human rights performance of nations in the hemisphere. COHA publishes an 8-page biweekly newsletter, *The Washington Report on the Hemisphere*. The report covers Latin America from a Washington perspective and includes news stories and features on Latin American policy makers and a summary of congressional actions on issues affecting Latin America. COHA publishes an average of three research memoranda weekly on a variety of inter-American topics, as well as periodic in-depth analyses on current topics. It has been particularly active in encouraging and assisting research of newspaper, magazine and journal articles on regional topics and in aiding

authors of hemispheric studies." **Services:** Offers aid in arranging interviews, bibliographies, statistics, clipping services, information searches and newsletter. Publications include descriptive brochures on COHA, "regular human rights reports on Latin American human rights violators, and updates on current developments in specific Latin American nations and in US-Latin relations. Also, economic reports, diplomatic analyses and newsletters to Congress and Latin American specialists." **How to Contact:** Write or call. "Specific requests will, in general, be handled free of charge. We will be pleased to work with any writer doing serious work on some inter-American theme." Charges $30/year for subscription to weekly COHA research memoranda; $35/year for newsletter. **Tips:** Recent information request: An evaluation of the human rights records of countries in the hemisphere.

1558• THE EAST-WEST CENTER

1777 East-West Rd., Honolulu HI 96848. (808)944-7204. Contact Person: Public Information Officer. **Description:** "International educational institution established in 1960 by US Congress with mandate to promote better relations and understanding among the nations of Asia, the Pacific and US through cooperative study, training and research." **Services:** Provides analytical, interpretive and referral information on major Asia-Pacific-US problems in the areas of communication, cultural contact, population, environment, and resource systems (food, energy, raw materials); Pacific Islands development; general information on Asia and the Pacific. Offers aid in arranging interviews, brochures/pamphlets, informational newsletters, placement on mailing lists, press kits and statistics. Publications include *East-West Perspectives* (quarterly magazine); research reports; program booklet listing research institutes, current programs, staff. **How to Contact:** Write, call or visit. Responds to most inquiries immediately. **Tips:** "Contact us if you need information about Asia and the Pacific. Chances are that a staff member or a visiting expert can help you." Recent information request: "What impact will the increasing use of coal have on the environment and what can be done to meet energy needs while protecting the environment?"

1559• FOOD AND AGRICULTURE ORGANIZATION OF THE UNITED NATIONS

Liaison Office for North America, 1776 F St. NW, Washington DC 20437. (202)634-6215. Contact Person: Regional Information Advisor. **Description:** "The Food and Agriculture Organization (FAO) of the UN works to raise levels of nutrition and standards of living of rural people. It also attempts to improve the efficiency of production and distribution of all food and agricultural products. The FAO is headquartered in Rome, Italy, and has a membership of 152 nations. Field project activities involve specialists in 141 countries working in various aspects of agriculture, forestry and fisheries. FAO also serves as a forum for world exchange of various agricultural questions and gathers global statistics. In addition, it sponsors major events such as the World Conference in Agrarian Reform and Rural Development (WCARRD); and World Food Day, which is observed each October 16." **Services:** Provides analytical and technical information on world food and agricultural issues, forestry and fisheries. Offers aid in arranging interviews, annual reports, bibliographies, statistics, brochures/pamphlets, placement on mailing list, newsletter and photos. "Basic brochures on the work of FAO are available—e.g., *The FAO, What It Is, What It Does, How It Works*; *Seeds of Progress*; summary sheets on various aspects of FAO's work in forestries, fisheries and agriculture; and the FAO catalog, *Books in Print.* **How to Contact:** "Contact the information section of the FAO Liaison Office for North America. Responds to most inquiries immediately. No fees are charged for any material furnished by *this* office. If it's necessary to request either black and white prints or color slides from FAO headquarters, however, a charge of $5/item, plus a $25 flat research fee, is made." Credit line must be given. **Tips:** Recent information request: "What is the extent of starvation in the world?"

1560• GREATER NEW YORK CONFERENCE ON SOVIET JEWRY

8 W. 40th St., Suite 602, New York NY 10018. (212)354-1316. Contact Person: Director of Media and Publications. **Description:** "The GNYCSJ is a nonprofit human rights organization which works to secure free emigration and cultural and religious freedom for Jews in the Soviet Union. As the largest umbrella organization of its kind in the world, the GNYCSJ disseminates information and coordinates Soviet Jewry activities for 85 Jewish organizations in the greater New York area. The GNYCSJ works closely with elected leaders, professionals and other community leaders." **Services:** Provides advisory, analytical, bibliographical, historical, how-to, interpretive and referral information on cases of individual Soviet Jews (activists and prisoners); Jewish culture in the USSR; US human rights policies; the Soviet Jewish emigration movement;

Soviet and international laws regarding human rights; Soviet anti-Semitism; emigration trends, statistics, analysis; Soviet-American relations. Offers aid in arranging interviews, annual reports, biographies, brochures/pamphlets, clipping services, informational newsletters, library facilities (limited), photos, placement on mailing lists, press kits, research assistance and statistics. Publications include *Soviet Jewry Update* (monthly); *Currents* and *Action Pak* (bimonthly); biographies and analytical papers. **How to Contact:** Write, call or visit. Responds to most inquiries within a week. Charges for some materials (prisoner posters, greeting cards, etc.). **Tips:** Recent information requests: "What can people do to help Soviet Jews gain religious and cultural freedom?"; "Which international laws and agreements apply to Soviet Jews?"; "Why have the Soviets curtailed Jewish emigration?"

1561• INFORMATION CENTER ON CHILDREN'S CULTURES (UNITED STATES COMMITTEE FOR UNICEF)
331 E. 38th St., New York NY 10016. (212)686-5522, ext. 470. Contact Person: Chief Librarian. **Description:** A special library funded by a nonprofit organization to disseminate information about the lives of children in the developing countries. **Services:** Provides advisory, bibliographical, interpretative and referral information on the lives of children in Africa, Asia, Middle East, Latin America, Caribbean, Pacific; as well as games, songs, crafts, festivals and holidays and children's literature in these areas. Offers library facilities, photos, research assistance and telephone reference services. "Photos are slides and b&w glossies of children taken in many developing countries and color slides and transparencies of children's paintings from all parts of the world." Publications include bibliographies and other educational materials. Publications list available. **How to Contact:** Write, call or visit. Responds to most inquiries within a month. Charges for photos and extensive research projects. "The library and our reference services are open to anyone. Our photos cannot be used for fund raising by other organizations. Indicate use of material; appointments are helpful." **Tips:** "Our collection is a unique resource in that it contains materials from the US and countries around the world. Our emphasis on the cultural aspects of child life in other countries cannot really be matched anywhere else. I would encourage writers to *visit* if they can." Recent information requests: "How is Christmas celebrated in various African countries?"; "Can you give me information on children's literature in Pakistan?"; information on Mexican children's daily life and school schedule.

1562• INFORMATION SERVICES ON LATIN AMERICA (ISLA)
464 19th St., Oakland CA 94612. (415)835-0678. Contact Person: Coordinator. **Description:** Clipping service providing organized information from the English language press on events in Latin America. **Services:** Provides analytical, historical, interpretative and trade information on press coverage of all countries in Latin America as published in the major English language newspapers. **How to Contact:** Write, call or visit. Responds to most inquiries within a week. Charges for services.

1563• INSTITUTE FOR WORLD ORDER
777 United Nations Plaza, New York NY 10017. (212)490-0010. Contact Person: Director, Communications. **Description:** Nonprofit organization which serves "both as a scholarly research center and a communications network. Through its research, it produces studies of world politics and the development of policy recommendations emphasizing linkages with the humane goals of peace, economic well-being, social justice and ecological balance." **Services:** Provides advisory, analytical, bibliographical, historical, how-to and interpretative publications and information on world security/peace, economic policies, ecological issues, human rights, demilitarization, international politics. Offers aid in arranging speakers/interviews, brochures/pamphlets, informational newsletters, placement on mailing lists, press kits, research assistance, statistics and telephone reference services. Publications catalog available. **How to Contact:** Write, call or visit. Responds to most inquiries immediately. Charges for publications and handling. Give credit to the Institute for World Order where appropriate. **Tips:** "Our current research work includes three principal areas: building systems to resolve global disagreements peacefully and fairly; redirecting nations away from reliance upon and use of nuclear and conventional weapons to resolve international conflicts; and developing an equitable and socially just world economy to underpin a peaceful world." Recent information requests: Examples of negotiations pushed forward by public opinion; examples of new peace-related activities in mainstream religion.

1564• INTERNATIONAL ASSOCIATION OF EDUCATORS FOR WORLD PEACE
Box 3282, Blue Springs Station, Huntsville AL 35810-0282. (205)539-7205. Contact Person: Executive Vice President. **Description:** Nongovernmental organization of the Economic and Social Council of the United Nations and the UN Educational, Scientific and Cultural Organization. The association is composed of individuals working "to promote international understanding and world peace through education; to implement everywhere the universal declaration of human rights; to conduct seminars on personality development, human relations and administrative skills." **Services:** Provides advisory, historical, interpretative, technical and trade information. Offers annual reports, biographies, brochures/pamphlets, informational newsletters, placement on mailing lists and research assistance. **How to Contact:** Write. Responds to most inquiries within a week.

1565• INTERNATIONAL CENTER FOR RESEARCH ON WOMEN
1010 16th St. NW, 3rd Floor, Washington DC 20036. (202)293-3154. Contact Person: Research Center Coordinator. **Description:** Women's councils interested in "research and policymaking in the field of women in development, focusing on income-generating activities for poor Third World women." **Services:** Provides advisory, analytical, bibliographical and interpretative information on women in development; socioeconomic profiles of developing countries. Offers brochures/pamphlets, library facilities, research assistance and telephone reference services. Publications list available. **How to Contact:** Write or call. Responds to most inquiries within a month. Charges 10¢/page for publications. "Call in advance to make an appointment." **Tips:** "Make questions as specific as possible, by region and subject." Recent information requests: "What information do you have on women in Haiti?"; "What is women's role in food production in Africa?"

1566• HELEN KELLER INTERNATIONAL, INC.
22 W. 17th St., New York NY 10011. (212)620-2100. Contact Person: Public Information Officer. **Description:** "Helen Keller International, Inc., is the oldest agency in the United States devoted to alleviating the problems of blindness in the developing countries. The organization works in the fields of prevention of blindness, education of blind children, and rehabilitation of blind adults. Helen Keller was a founder, staff member and trustee of the organization from 1915 until her death in 1968." **Services:** Provides advisory, bibliographical, historical, interpretative and referral information on blindness prevention in Third World countries; eye disease in Third World countries; rehabilitation of the rural blind; Helen Keller. Offers aid in arranging interviews, annual reports, statistics, brochures/pamphlets, placement on mailing list and newsletter. Publications include *The Right to See* (brochure describing prevention program) and *Nutritional Blindness*. **How to Contact:** Write. Responds to most inquiries within a month.

1567• LIBRARY OF CONGRESS, ASIAN DIVISION
Washington DC 20540. (202)287-5420. Contact Person: Acting Chief, Asian Division. **Description:** The Asian Division "develops, maintains, and services the Asian language collections in the Library of Congress; provides bibliographic, reference, research, and consultative services relating to the countries of Asia to the Congress, government agencies, scholars, and the general public." **Services:** Provides bibliographical, historical and referral information on China, Japan, Korea, Mongolia, Tibet, India, Pakistan, Sri Lanka, Bangladesh, Nepal, Burma, Thailand, Vietnam, Cambodia, Laos, Malaysia, Singapore, Indonesia, the Philippines. Offers library facilities, research assistance and telephone reference services. Publications include *Chinese Periodicals in the Library of Congress* (1978); *Japanese National Government Publications in the Library of Congress* (1981); *Vietnamese Holdings in the Library of Congress* (1982). **How to Contact:** Write, call or visit. Responds to most inquiries within a week. "Materials in the collection must be used in the Library of Congress, but most are also available for loan through other research libraries." **Tips:** Recent information request: Statistical data relating to the Japanese production and export of steel (and other manufactured products).

1568• LIBRARY OF CONGRESS, EUROPEAN DIVISION
LA 5244, Washington DC 20540. (202)287-6520. Contact Person: Chief, European Division. **Description:** The European Division provides assistance to researchers and the general public on all topics pertaining to European countries, except Spain and Portugal. **Services:** Provides advisory, bibliographical and historical information on all topics, "but especially the humanities and social science fields." Offers computerized information searches, library facilities

and research assistance. Publications include several bibliographies and other research tools on European topics. **How to Contact:** Write or visit. Responds to most inquiries within a week. **Tips:** "We assist writers/researchers in finding suitable sources of information. We do *not* do the actual research for them. Call the Chief or the Assistant Chief and chat with them before you plan a long visit or research trip." Recent information requests: Bibliography on the Czech system of higher education; references and explanations concerning folk festivals in France.

1569• LIBRARY OF CONGRESS, HISPANIC DIVISION
Thomas Jefferson Building, Room 239E, Washington DC 20540. (202)287-5400. Contact Person: Chief, Hispanic Division. **Description:** The Hispanic Division "serves as a center for the pursuit of studies in Spanish, Portuguese, Brazilian, Spanish-American, and Caribbean cultures in the Library of Congress. Activities include the development of the library's Hispanic collections, reference assistance to researchers, and the preparation of research tools." **Services:** Provides advisory, analytical, bibliographical, historical, interpretative, referral and trade information on "most major subject areas in all time periods for the study of Spanish, Portuguese, Brazilian, Spanish-American, and Caribbean culture. Materials on clinical medicine and scientific agriculture are found in other libraries in Washington; legal materials in the field can be found in the Hispanic Law Division, Library of Congress." Offers computerized information searches, library facilities and telephone reference services. Publications include *Handbook of Latin American Studies*; *The Archive of Hispanic Literature on Tape: A Descriptive Guide*. **How to Contact:** Write, call or visit. Responds to most inquiries within a week. **Tips:** "Writers should contact the division in advance if contemplating long term research in the library in order to facilitate study; writers should think through their project before coming to the library."

1570• LIBRARY OF INTERNATIONAL RELATIONS
666 Lake Shore Dr., Chicago IL 60611. (312)787-7928. Contact Person: Director. **Description:** The library maintains an important collection of twentieth century materials which offers economic, political and social information for all countries. **Services:** Provides bibliographical and referral information on international trade, population figures, questions on the UN, the FAO, the South Pacific Commission, etc. Offers library facilities. "Our staff is limited and therefore our services must also be." Publications include bank reports; foreign affairs ministries; periodical material from foreign countries; documents of official international organizations. **How to Contact:** Call. Responds to most inquiries as soon as possible. Charges for photocopying. "If time needed is excessive, that will be discussed." Materials are for reference only and cannot be loaned.

1571• PAN AMERICAN INSTITUTE OF GEOGRAPHY AND HISTORY
Ex-arzobispado 29 Col. Observatorio, México, 11860 D.F. Tel. 2-77-58-88. Contact Person: Secretary General. **Description:** International organization promoting geographical, cartographical, historical and geophysical studies. **Services:** Provides bibliographical information and offers library facilities. Publications include *Revista de Historia de América*; *Boletin de Antropologia Americana; Revista Cartográfica; Folklore Americano; Revista Geográfica; Revista Geofisica*. **How to Contact:** Write, call or visit. Responds to most inquiries within a week. Charges for publications.

1572• PEACE CORPS
806 Connecticut Ave. NW, Washington DC 20526. (800)424-8580. In Washington DC (202)254-5010. Contact Person: Director, Office of Communications. **Description:** US government agency. The Peace Corps sends US citizens as volunteers to developing countries to assist in economic self-sufficiency; to promote world peace and friendship; to sensitize Americans about the Third World. **Services:** Provides historical, how-to, referral, technical and trade information on the Peace Corps and related subjects. Offers annual reports, bibliographies, biographies, statistics, brochures/pamphlets, regular informational newsletter, photos and press kits. Publications include "pamphlets on the Peace Corps, describing programs, requirements, how to apply and benefits." **How to Contact:** Write or call. Responds to most inquiries within a week. **Tips:** "Write in advance requesting information; draw up a list of research questions with your initial correspondence. The Privacy Act prohibits access to volunteers files, names/addresses, etc." Recent information requests: "What percentage of full-time staff are returned Peace Corps volunteers?"; "How has Peace Corps changed since Kennedy's era?"; "Is Peace Corps still around?"; "Is Peace Corps growing or declining in volunteer strength?"

1573• PEOPLES TRANSLATION SERVICE
4228 Telegraph Ave., Oakland CA 94609. (415)654-6725. Contact Person: Secretary. **Description:** Individuals who provide international information from the overseas press—news not easily available in the US. **Services:** Provides advisory, bibliographical, historical, how-to and referral information on international politics. Offers brochures/pamphlets, informational newsletters, library facilities, photos and research assistance. **How to Contact:** Write, call or visit. Responds to most inquiries immediately. Charges for services. **Tips:** "Call for an appointment." Recent information request: Background on the peace movement in East Germany.

1574• PUBLIC ARCHIVES OF CANADA
National Photography Collection, 395 Wellington St., Ottawa, Canada K1A 0N3. (613)992-3884. Contact Person: Head of Reference. **Description:** "The collection provides a photographic record of Canadian history and culture. It consists of 8.5 million items and is growing." **Services:** Provides advisory and historical information on Canadian history 1850-present, all areas; history and development of Canadian photography. Offers b&w prints and 35mm color transparencies of Canada: historical views, events, portraits. Material is in the public domain. "We have photos of all Canadian subjects, documenting the political, economic, industrial, military, social and cultural life of Canada from 1850 to the present." **How to Contact:** Write. Responds to most inquiries within a month. "On unrestricted or noncopyright material, reproduction rights are normally granted upon request after examination of a statement of purpose, use legitimate use in publication, film or television production, exhibition or research." Charges $5.50/8x10 b&w print (subject to change without notice). Charges for copy prints.

1575• SURVIVAL INTERNATIONAL (USA)
2121 Decatur Place, NW, Washington DC 20008. (202)265-1077. Contact Person: Administrative Assistant for Membership Development. **Description:** Nonprofit organization working "to advance the rights of indigenous tribal peoples and helping them to exercise their right to survival and self-determination. SIUSA represents indigenous peoples in international organizations such as the UN and the OAS; informs network of supporters about rights violations through Information Action Packs." **Services:** Provides bibliographical, historical and referral information covering anthropology, international law, human rights—as they relate to indigenous peoples. Offers brochures/pamphlets, informational newsletters, placement on mailing lists and press releases. Publications include *SIUSA News* (quarterly newsletter); *Survival International Review* (quarterly journal). **How to Contact:** Write or call. Responds to most inquiries within a week. Charges for publications, photocopying and postage. "We prefer to know in what publications articles including SIUSA will be published. We cannot handle large-scale research requests as our staff is small, so please be specific."

1576• UNITED NATIONS CENTRE AGAINST APARTHEID
Room 2775, United Nations, New York NY 10017. (212)754-6674. Contact Person: Chief of Branch for Publicity Assistance and Promotion of International Action. **Description:** "The purpose of the centre is to administer the UN Trust Fund for South Africa, the UN Educational Training Programme for Southern Africa and the UN Trust Fund for Publicity Against Apartheid; to service the General Assembly's Special Committee against Apartheid, the Advisory Committee on the United Nations Educational and Training Programme for Southern Africa and the Committee of Trustees of the United Nations Trust Fund for South Africa." **Services:** Provides analytical, bibliographical, historical and technical information on all aspects of apartheid in South Africa and UN efforts at eliminating apartheid. Offers aid in arranging interviews, statistics, brochures/pamphlets, placement on mailing list, newsletter and photos. Publications include pamphlets, posters and *Notes and Documents* (occasional). **How to Contact:** Write. Responds to most inquiries within a week. Acknowledge centre as source and send one copy of the publication reproducing centre's material. **Tips:** Recent information request: "Provide information on what apartheid is about and what the United Nations is doing about it."

1577• UNITED NATIONS DEVELOPMENT PROGRAM
1 United Nations Plaza, New York NY 10017. (212)754-4690. Contact Person: Director, Special Services. **Description:** "We provide assistance to the development projects of developing countries, at their request, in the form of experts' services, equipment, consultations and fellowships. Projects assisted are in all economic and social areas (agriculture, industry,

education, health, planning, transportation, communication, etc.).'' **Services:** Provides analytical, historical, interpretative, referral and trade information. Offers annual reports and brochures/pamphlets. Publications include basic information brochures on activities; background briefs on development issues; descriptions of technical cooperation among developing countries and fact sheets on various sectors of activity. **How to Contact:** Write or call. Responds to most inquiries immediately. ''We can provide information only on development activities with which the UN Development Program is concerned. We do not have basic information on individual countries.''

1578• UNITED NATIONS ECONOMIC COMMISSION FOR EUROPE
Palais des Nations, CH-1211, Geneva 10, Switzerland. (022)34-60-11. Contact Person: Information Officer. **Description:** ''All UN member countries in Europe and the US and Canada (34 countries) are members of the Economic Commission for Europe (ECE), which provides a permanent means of intergovernmental consultation and action on a wide variety of economic, scientific and technological subjects. Priorities are in the fields of promoting trade (particularly East-West trade), scientific and technological exchange, protection of the environment, and long-term projections and programming.'' **Services:** Provides advisory, bibliographical, historical and referral information on agriculture, economics, energy, environment, industry, technical data, inland transport, timber, trade and technology. Offers aid in arranging interviews, statistics and placement on mailing list. Publications include *Economic Bulletin for Europe*. **How to Contact:** Write. Responds to most inquiries within a week. ''Most ECE documents (as distinct from publications) are for restricted circulations only. An enquiry to the Information Officer will determine whether a particular item may be available. Also, most ECE meetings are open only to governments and other accredited organizations.'' **Tips:** Recent information requests: ''Typical query would be someone writing to find out what ECE was doing toward protection of the environment or with regard to developing countries.''

1579• UNITED STATES ASSOCIATION FOR THE CLUB OF ROME
1525 New Hampshire Ave. NW, Washington DC 20036. (202)745-7715. Contact Person: Executive Administrator. **Description:** Individuals interested in ''disseminating information about the interlinkage of complex global problems, and the role and responsibility of the United States in these problems.'' **Services:** Provides analytical and how-to information on population, economics, environment and social systems. Offers brochures/pamphlets, informational newsletters and placement on mailing lists. Publications include *Making It Happen: A Positive Guide to the Future*. **How to Contact:** Write or call. Responds to most inquiries within a week. Charges for publications.

1580• UNITED STATES COMMITTEE FOR REFUGEES
20 W. 40th St., New York NY 10018. (212)398-9142. Contact Person: Staff Assistant. **Description:** ''The US Committee for Refugees, a program of the American Council for Nationalities Service, is a citizen-sponsored program that has been concerned since 1958 with public information and advocacy regarding worldwide refugee issues. USCR's primary tasks are to provide information and to focus the attention of the American public on national and international refugee situations, the needs of refugees, the responses of the private and public sectors to these needs, and the comparative participation of the US and other nations in programs addressing these needs. USCR participates actively as a refugee advocate in the development of US public policy with respect to refugees here and abroad.'' **Services:** Provides analytical, bibliographical and referral information. Offers brochures/pamphlets, informational newsletters, photos, placement on mailing lists, research assistance and statistics. ''The Committee participates in media presentations and other public forums, assists others in planning public information efforts regarding refugees, provides background information and photographs, and operates a referral service for the media and general public.'' Publications include *World Refugee Survey* (annual), covering worldwide issues and providing statistical information; a series of issue papers on the most vulnerable refugees: the Poles, Afghans, Ethiopians, Cambodians and Salvadorans. **How to Contact:** Write or call. Responds to most inquiries immediately. **Tips:** Recent information requests: ''How many Salvadoran refugees are in various Latin American countries?''; ''What are the ceilings for this fiscal year established by the federal government, regarding admission of refugees from specific regions of the world?''

1581• VON KLEINSMID LIBRARY (WORLD AFFAIRS)
M-0182, University of Southern California, University Park, Los Angeles CA 90089. (213)741-7347. Contact Person: Reference Librarian. **Description:** Library of over 150,000 volumes housing the university's major collections in international relations; political science; public administration; and urban and regional planning. This library attempts to collect all publications of the United Nations: the Organization for Economic Cooperation and Development; the International Labor Organization, UNESCO; the Council of Europe; the Food and Agriculture Organization of the UN; the various international financial agencies; and is a depository of documents of the European Communities and the Organization of American States. The separately cataloged *Planning Documents Collection* contains over 2,000 planning documents and reports from local, regional, and state planning agencies. **Services:** Provides bibliographical and historical information on political science, international relations, public administration and urban and regional planning. **How to Contact:** Call for appointment to use services. Responds to most inquiries within a week. Nonstudents may not take material from library. Student demand comes first.

1582• WASHINGTON OFFICE ON LATIN AMERICA
110 Maryland Ave. NE, Washington DC 20002. Contact Person: Administrative Assistant. **Description:** "Washington Office on Latin America (WOLA) was created by a board coalition of churchpersons and scholars to monitor events in Latin America and Washington (as they relate to Latin America) with emphasis on human rights and efforts to promote participation in government." **Services:** Provides analytical, interpretative and referral information on human rights issues in Latin America. Offers brochures/pamphlets, placement on mailing list and newsletter. "We are willing to do occasional briefings on current developments in US/Latin America for interested journalists." Publications include *Update*. **How to Contact:** Write or call. "We respond better to phone calls; writing letters in response to inquiries requires too much time. Be as specific as possible about issues and countries of concern." Responds to most inquiries within a week. Donations appreciated. Charges 10¢/photocopy, plus postage; $1 for individual updates or cost of annual subscription. "We are not a research organization, so we don't furnish a variety of materials; only our *Update*, brochures and occasional papers."

1583• WORLD BANK, INTERNATIONAL DEVELOPMENT ASSOCIATION
1818 H St. NW, Washington DC 20433. (202)477-2403. Contact: Publications Department. **Description:** "The International Bank for Reconstruction and Development (IBRD), founded in 1945, has 144 countries as members. The purpose of the World Bank, as it is known today, is to help raise the standard of living in its developing member countries by financing high priority development projects, by providing technical assistance, and by conducting an economic policy dialogue with borrower governments. The bank raises its funds mainly in the world's capital markets. Its affiliate, the International Development Association (IDA), is funded by government contributions; IDA's purpose is to lend for development projects in the poorest countries at concessional terms. Another affiliate, the International Finance Corporation (IFC) promotes private enterprises in developing countries through equity participation and loans." **Services:** Provides analytical, technical and trade information covering agriculture, economics, education, population and public health, trade, regional integration, environment, industry, transportation and many other subjects relating to development aid and economics. Offers annual reports, statistics, brochures/pamphlets and placement on mailing list. "The World Bank studies and analyzes a wealth of economic and social data that it is in a unique position to collect. *The World Bank Catalog of Publications* lists available materials, including a descriptive brochure, *The World Bank*; annual reports; *World Bank Atlas*; and country studies." **How to Contact:** Write. Responds to most inquiries within a month. "All World Bank publications, free or for sale, are listed in the catalog which is provided without charge. All orders must be prepaid." **Tips:** Recent information requests: Background on Third World debt; bank borrowing on international capital markets; agricultural development; lending to the health sector.

1584• WORLD CITIZEN ASSEMBLY
312 Sutter St., Room 608, San Francisco CA 94108. (415)421-0836. Contact Person: Secretary General. **Description:** "The purpose of the World Citizen Assembly is to organize people and organizations into an effective global movement for controlled disarmament and world peace, and to build a representative UN able to settle disputes between nations through the framework of world law. We hold a large World Citizen Assembly every two years, which is attended by people

and organizations from many countries." **Services:** Provides how-to and interpretative information on disarmament, environmental issues, global education, world organization, government, UN, etc. Offers statistics, brochures/pamphlets and newsletter. **How to Contact:** Write or call. Responds to most inquiries within a week. **Tips:** Recent information request: "What were the results of the UN Special Session on Disarmament in 1982?"

1585• WORLD ENVIRONMENT CENTER
605 Third Ave., 17th Floor, New York NY 10158. (212)986-7200. Contact Person: President. **Description:** The center works to "increase public understanding of international environment issues; to provide information on these issues to industry, government agencies, news media, educational and research institutions." **Services:** Provides interpretative and referral information on energy technologies, toxic substances, environmental policies of foreign countries, UN agencies, trends in a wide range of environmental areas such as industrial pollution, forestry, wildlife, resource management, and training. Offers aid in arranging interviews and informational newsletters. Publications include *World Environment Report* (twice monthly newsletter); *World Environment Handbook*. **How to Contact:** Call. Responds to most inquiries immediately. Charges for publications. Give credit to World Environment Center. **Tips:** "The center is primarily a referral service; consequently writers should not expect definitive information from us unless this happens to be available." Recent information request: "What are the programs of the UN Environment Program regarding marine pollution?"

1586• WORLD HUNGER EDUCATION SERVICE
1317 G St. NW, Washington DC 20005. (202)347-4441. Contact Person: Executive Director. **Description:** Nonprofit organization making connections "to build support for more effective actions and policies on behalf of hungry people everywhere." **Services:** Provides analytical, bibliographical, referral and technical information on food and hunger issues, Third World development, agriculture, nutrition, public health, economic justice, poverty/social issues, career counseling. Offers brochures/pamphlets, clipping services, informational newsletters, library facilities, research assistance, statistics and telephone reference services. Publications include *Hunger Notes* (10/year); *Who's Involved with Hunger* (directory); *AV Guide to Politics of Hunger*. **How to Contact:** Write, call or visit. Responds to most inquiries within a week. Appointments are preferred. Charges for publications. **Tips:** "We are a good starting point for writers beginning research on hunger issues. We are happy to recommend resources, organizations, experts. We have a number of reports and documents that are no longer available except through the Government Printing Office (i.e., *Presidential Commission Reports on World Hunger*)." Recent information requests: Forecasts of future famines in Africa; the number of malnourished people in the world.

Embassies

An embassy is the official headquarters of an ambassador and his staff. It represents a home government in a foreign country. In addition, an embassy promotes the interests of its home country and works to enhance diplomatic relations between its country and the place where the ambassadors, ministers and other officials perform their duties. Toward these ends, an embassy generally provides visa and port-of-entry guidelines, as well as general information on the home country.

A complete list of foreign embassies can be found in the *Diplomatic List*, a quarterly publication of the US State Department. (The directory is often available in large public and academic libraries.) It may be purchased from the Superintendent of Government Documents,

US Government Printing Office, Washington DC 20402. Single copies $4.75; yearly subscription $12. The *Diplomatic List* includes the chancery addresses and telephone numbers and the names of the ambassadors and other embassy officials. National holidays of the countries are also included.

Staff size and embassy budgets vary, but many embassies maintain an information/press office equipped to answer questions, make referrals and supply materials on the history, culture and current affairs of their home country. The embassies listed on the following pages have completed questionnaires indicating the scope and range of the various information services they provide to writers and the general public.

1587• EMBASSY OF AUSTRALIA
1601 Massachusetts Ave. NW, Washington DC 20036. (202)797-3000. Contact Person: Information Assistant. **Description:** The embassy "represents Australia's interests in the US and provides a factual and accurate portrayal of Australia and its people designed to increase knowledge and understanding to foster favorable conditions for achieving Australia's objectives." **Services:** Provides advisory, bibliographical, historical, referral, technical and trade information covering a wide range of material relating to Australia in general and a collection of frequently updated fact sheets, reference papers and current reports on specific subjects. "Our reference library has many reference books which can be used." Offers possible aid in arranging interviews, biographies, brochures/pamphlets, informational newsletters, library facilities, placement on mailing lists, press kits, research assistance and statistics. Publications include Australian government publications; *Australia Handbook*, etc. **How to Contact:** Write, call or visit. Response time "depends on how detailed a response is needed, and whether we have to refer to Canberra." **Tips:** "The amount of assistance given depends on our assessment of how important the inquiry is to Australia. For instance, we would go to great lengths to supply material for, say, an article in *Barrons* on Australia's trade prospects. If the matter is not urgent, write in the first instance. Include a phone number." Recent information requests: "What is Australia's inflation rate? unemployment rate?"; "How much did wages rise between 1973 and 1975?"

1588• EMBASSY OF THE PEOPLE'S REPUBLIC OF BANGLADESH
3421 Massachusetts Ave., Washington DC 20007. (202)337-6644. Contact Person: Education Attaché. **Description:** Embassy representing Bangladesh and its interests in the US. **Services:** Provides bibliographical and referral information on all aspects of Bangladesh (life, history, culture, etc.). Offers aid in arranging interviews, informational newsletters, placement on mailing lists, press kits, research assistance and statistics. Publications include *Embassy Newsletter*. **How to Contact:** Write, call or visit. Responds to most inquiries immediately.

1589• BRITISH EMBASSY
3100 Massachusetts Ave. NW, Washington DC 20008. (202)462-1340. Contact Person: Counselor (Information). **Desription:** Embassy representing Great Britain and its interests in the US. **Services:** Provides information on the British government and its policies. **How to Contact:** Write or call. Responds to most inquiries as soon as possible. **Tips:** "The British Information Services in New York, 845 Third Ave., New York NY 10022, (212)752-8400, has a rather more extensive reference library, and can frequently provide background information on British Parliament, British institutions, British regulations and British publications. Contact the Reference Section."

1590• EMBASSY OF CAMEROON
2349 Massachusetts Ave. NW, Washington DC 20008. (202)265-8790. Contact Person: Chief of Press and Information. **Description:** Embassy serving as diplomatic, economic and trade mission and as press and information center. **Services:** Provides historical, referral and trade information on the historical, economic, social, cultural and educational activities of Cameroon. Offers brochures/pamphlets and informational newsletters. Publications include newsletter (monthly) and information brochures (if available). **How to Contact:** Write, call or visit. Responds to most inquiries within a month.

1591• CANADIAN EMBASSY LIBRARY
1771 N St. NW, Washington DC 20036. (202)785-1400. Contact Person: Reference Librarian. **Description:** "The Embassy Library is a collection of about 5,000 volumes of books, periodicals, and government documents devoted to Canada—especially contemporary issues." **Services:** Provides bibliographical, historical and referral information on Canada in the fields of political science/government, history, economics, law, literature, art, music, etc. Offers brochures/pamphlets, library facilities, research assistance, statistics and telephone reference services. **How to Contact:** Call or visit. Responds to most inquiries within a week. **Tips:** "Ready reference questions can be answered by telephone. For research we suggest that the writer visit the library (Mon.-Fri. 12:30-4:30 p.m.). Photocopying limited to five pages. Much of the collection must be used in the library."

1592• EGYPTIAN EMBASSY
Press and Information Bureau, 1825 Connecticut Ave. NW, Suite 216, Washington DC 20009.

Contact Person: Head of Press & Information Bureau. **Description:** The embassy represents Egypt and Egyptian interests in the United States. **Services:** Provides advisory, bibliographical (limited), historical, referral and trade (limited) information on cultural, travel, political, social and economic aspects of Egypt. Offers aid in arranging interviews, biographies, brochures/pamphlets and photos. Publications include *School Address (Pen Pals); Islam; Coptic Churches in the US and Canada; What to see in Egypt; Anwar El Sadat; Hosni Mubarak . . . Egypt: The Quest for Peace and Prosperity Continues.* **How to Contact:** Write. Responds to simple inquiries within a week; others, up to a month. "Specific requests involving credit to the Egyptian government should be cleared first. Put requests in writing—they are not handled any other way." **Tips:** "Ask well in advance because the Egyptian Embassy receives a very high volume of requests; though we have an excellent system for responding and tracking requests, we are always (with the exception of the summer months) working under a heavy workload. Also, don't write to the Ambassador—this delays the Press Office getting the request as his office is in another building. Because we receive so many requests for information, we have to limit the number of copies we send (only one) to any one request. We also have to limit the variety of materials as well as the different kinds of information requests from one individual." Recent information requests: "What's the weather like in Egypt at a specific time of year?"; "What about Nile cruises?"; questions on posters, coins, stamps; specific historical questions; information for children's school reports.

1593•   EMBASSY OF THE FEDERAL REPUBLIC OF GERMANY
4645 Reservoir Rd. NW, Washington DC 20007. (202)298-4000. Contact Person: Counselor, Press and Public Affairs. **Description:** Embassy representing West Germany and its interests in the US. "We maintain contact with the American press and media and cooperation with the German press in America; we schedule briefings and press conferences for political visitors/ministers; we provide general information about Germany to the public." **Services:** Provides information about Germany on anything except tourism questions and those dealing with economic/commercial concerns. "In the case of the latter two instances and any other requests we cannot answer, we will refer you to someone who will provide the needed information." Offers biographies, brochures/pamphlets, photos, press releases, research assistance (involving not too much time), statistics and telephone reference services. **How to Contact:** Write or call. Prefers phone calls for questions that can be answered quickly. Responds to most inquiries within 2 weeks. **Tips:** Recent information requests: "How does the constitutional system in Germany work?"; "What is the procedure to dissolve the German parliament?"; "What is the best German wine?"

1594•   EMBASSY OF FINLAND
3216 New Mexico Ave. NW, Washington DC 20016. (202)363-2430. Contact Person: Press Attaché or Information Secretary. **Description:** Embassy representing Finland and its interests in the US. **Services:** Provides general and tourist information on Finland. Offers aid in arranging interviews, brochures/pamphlets and statistics. **How to Contact:** Write. Responds to most inquiries within a week.

1595•   EMBASSY OF THE GERMAN DEMOCRATIC REPUBLIC
1717 Massachusetts Ave. NW, Washington DC 20036. (202)232-3134. Contact Person: Cultural Attaché. **Description:** Embassy representing the German Democratic Republic and its interests in the US. **Services:** Provides advisory, how-to and referral information about life, politics, culture, economy, etc. in the G.D.R. Offers brochures/pamphlets, photos, placement on mailing lists and statistics. **How to Contact:** Write, call or visit. Responds to most inquiries within a week. Respect copyright on photos.

1596•   GHANA NEWS
2460 16th St. NW, Washington DC 20009. (202)462-0761. Contact Person: Minister Counselor, Information. **Description:** Government agency which seeks "to enlighten the American public on activities in Ghana and attract prospective investors to the enormous mineral resources in Ghana." **Services:** Provides bibliographical and trade information on Ghana. Offers placement on mailing lists. **How to Contact:** Write, call or visit. Responds to most inquiries immediately.

1597•   EMBASSY OF GREECE
Press & Information Office, 2211 Massachusetts Ave. NW, Washington DC 20008. (202)332-2727. Contact Person: Press Counselor. **Description:** Embassy representing Greece and its interests in the US. **Services:** Provides advisory, historical and referral information on

Greece. Offers aid in arranging interviews, library facilities, photos, placement on mailing lists, press kits and statistics. Publications include embassy bulletin. **How to Contact:** Write. Responds to most inquiries within a week. Give credit to the embassy for information received.

1598• EMBASSY OF INDIA
2107 Massachusetts Ave. NW, Washington DC 20008. (202)265-5050, ext. 273. Contact Person: First Secretary (Press) or First Secretary (Information). **Description:** The embassy represents India and Indian affairs in the US. **Services:** Provides information on all aspects of Indian life, history, art, culture, science. Offers aid in arranging interviews, biographies, brochures/pamphlets, informational newsletters, library facilities (reference), photos, placement on mailing lists, press kits, research assistance, statistics, telephone reference services and collection of films on India, and records and tapes of Indian music. Publications include *India News* (weekly). **How to Contact:** Write or call. Responds to most inquiries as soon as possible. **Tips:** "We receive requests from students, professionals and businesses interested in India. We are happy to provide an information service."

1599• EMBASSY OF ISRAEL
3514 International Dr., Washington DC 20008. (202)364-5500. Contact: Information Department. **Description:** The embassy represents the state of Israel in the capital of the United States. **Services:** Provides analytical, bibliographical, historical, interpretative and referral information covering historical, political, cultural and social aspects relating to the state of Israel. Offers biographies, brochures/pamphlets, informational newsletters, photos, placement on mailing lists, press kits and research assistance. Publications vary with availability. **How to Contact:** Write or call. Responds to most inquiries within a week. "Photographs must be returned. The embassy should be credited in photo reproductions."

1600• EMBASSY OF ITALY
1601 Fuller St. NW, Washington DC 20009. (202)328-5500. Contact Person: First Secretary or Cultural Attaché. **Description:** Embassy represents Italy and Italian interests in the US. **Services:** Provides information "on the official Italian position on certain political issues, plus cultural information." **How to Contact:** Write or call. Responds to most inquiries within a month.

1601• EMBASSY OF JAPAN
2520 Massachusetts Ave. NW, Washington DC 20008. (202)234-2266. Contact Person: Information Officer. **Description:** Foreign embassy representing Japan and Japan .e interests in the US. **Services:** Provides bibliographical, historical and trade information on Japan. Offers brochures/pamphlets, library, press kits, research assistance, statistics and various publications. **How to Contact:** Write, call or visit. Responds to most inquiries within a month. "Library books do not circulate; on-site perusal only."

1602• JORDAN INFORMATION BUREAU
1701 K St. NW, 11th Floor, Washington DC 20006. (202)659-3322. Contact Person: Director. **Description:** Press and Information office for the Embassy of the Hashemite Kingdom of Jordan. **Services:** Provides advisory, bibliographical, historical, referral and trade information on economy, trade and industry, tourism, narration slide sets, films, speakers, and "almost any other information on the country of Jordan." Offers aid in arranging interviews, biographies, brochures/pamphlets, clipping services, informational newsletters, library facilities, photos, films, video cassettes, placement on mailing lists, press kits, research assistance, statistics and telephone reference services. Publications include *Jordan*, a quarterly tourist magazine; *Al-Urdun*, a bimonthly newsletter. **How to Contact:** Write. Responds to most inquiries within a week.

1603• KOREAN INFORMATION SERVICE/EMBASSY OF KOREA
1414 22nd St. NW, Suite 101, Washington DC 20037. (202)296-4256. Contact Person: Press Attaché or Director. **Description:** Embassy "promoting understanding and friendship toward Korea among American people." **Services:** Provides analytical, bibliographical, historical and referral information on the history and culture of Korea. Offers brochures/pamphlets, informational newsletters, photos, films, video cassettes, placement on mailing lists, press kits and research assistance. Publications include *Korean News/Views* (bulletin); *Korean Newsletter* (monthly). **How to Contact:** Write. Responds to most inquiries within a month.

1604• EMBASSY OF MEXICO
2829 16th St. NW, Washington DC 20009. (202)234-6000. Contact: Office of Cultural Affairs. **Description:** The embassy carries out a diplomatic mission and represents Mexican interests in America. **Services:** Provides bibliographical and general information on Mexico. Offers brochures/pamphlets. **How to Contact:** Write. Responds to most inquiries within a month. **Tips:** "Our library is no longer available for public use. All inquiries must be made in writing."

1605• ROYAL NETHERLANDS EMBASSY
4200 Linnean Ave. NW, Washington DC 20008. (202)244-5300. Contact: Press Office. **Description:** Diplomatic representation of the Netherlands in the US. **Services:** Provides advisory, analytical, bibliographical, historical, how-to, referral, technical and trade information covering all aspects of the Netherlands: political, historical, defense, agricultural, business and trade, economics, cultural, etc. Offers aid in arranging interviews, biographies, brochures/pamphlets, photos, placement on mailing lists, press kits, research assistance, statistics and telephone reference services. Publications include pamphlet series, *The Kingdom of the Netherlands* and other topic-related publications on all subjects. **How to Contact:** Write or call. Responds to most inquiries within a week. **Tips:** "Please exhaust readily available resources and define your subject before contacting embassy so that we will be able to provide well-focused help. We are a small office, and cannot take people through the basic, preliminary process."

1606• EMBASSY OF NEW ZEALAND
37 Observatory Circle NW, Washington DC 20008. (202)328-4800. Contact Person: Information Officer. **Description:** Embassy representing New Zealand and its interests in the US. **Services:** Provides bibliographical, historical, referral, technical and trade information on New Zealand including business, trade, investment, geographical, historical, cultural and tourist information. Offers biographies, brochures/pamphlets, informational newsletters, library facilities (interlibrary loan), photos, research assistance and statistics. Publications include *New Zealand Update*, monthly newsletter on events in New Zealand. **How to Contact:** Write or call. Responds to most inquiries within a week.

1607• NIGERIA INFORMATION SERVICE CENTRE
2215 M St. NW, Washington DC 20037. (202)822-1650 through 1655. Contact Person: Minister, Information. **Description:** Government agency offering publicity and information about Nigeria. **Services:** Provides advisory, analytical, bibliographical, historical and trade information on all aspects of Nigeria. Offers biographies, brochures/pamphlets, informational newsletters, photos, placement on mailing lists, research assistance, statistics and telephone reference services. Publications available. **How to Contact:** Write, call or visit. Responds to most inquiries immediately. Give credit to the Information Service Centre. **Tips:** "Give us a call to make sure the material requested is available." Recent information request: Agriculture (Green Revolution) vs. population growth in Nigeria.

1608• EMBASSY OF PANAMA
Commercial Office, 2862 McGill Terrace NW, Washington DC 20008. (202)483-1407. Contact Person: Commercial Counselor. **Description:** Government agency promoting exports from Panama and investment to Panama and providing business information and general public relations for Panama. **Services:** Provides advisory, bibliographical, how-to, referral and trade information such as "general information about the country; specific information to do business in Panama; incentives for investment and how to incorporate in Panama; legislation and advantages of Panama banking/commerce/industry, etc." Offers aid in arranging interviews, brochures/pamphlets, library facilities, statistics, telephone reference services and information kit for investment. **How to Contact:** Write or call. Responds to most inquiries within a week. No political publications. "Contact us for an appointment." **Tips:** "We can offer personal names and addresses of key people to contact in Panama's public and private sector." Recent information request: "What advantages are there in using the Colon Free Zone?"

1609• EMBASSY OF PERU
1700 Massachusetts Ave. NW, Washington DC 20036. (202)833-9860. Contact Person: Minister in Charge of Cultural Affairs. **Description:** "Embassy promoting the image of Peru through good relations with other countries." **Services:** Provides advisory, bibliographical, historical,

interpretative, referral and trade information covering culture, finance, commerce, politics and tourism of Peru. Offers aid in arranging interviews, brochures/pamphlets, informational newsletters (in Spanish), library facilities, photos, statistics and telephone reference services. Publications include Peruvian newspapers. **How to Contact:** Write, call or visit. Responds to most inquiries within a week. **Tips:** ''Make an appointment in advance.'' Recent information request: Inquiries on colonial art.

1610• EMBASSY OF POLAND
2640 16th St. NW, Washington DC 20009. (202)234-3800. Contact Person: Information Officer. **Description:** Embassy representing the Polish government in the USA. **Services:** Provides advisory, historical and referral information on Poland. Offers aid in arranging interviews, biographies, brochures/pamphlets, informational newsletters, placement on mailing lists and statistics. **How to Contact:** Write or call. Responds to most inquiries within a month.

1611• SAINT LUCIA MISSION TO THE UNITED NATIONS
41 E. 42nd St., Suite 315, New York NY 10017. (212)697-9360, 9361. Contact Person: Counselor. **Description:** Diplomatic representation to the United Nations; promotes investment and tourism in Saint Lucia. **Services:** Provides advisory, historical and trade information on Saint Lucia. Offers aid in arranging interviews, brochures/pamphlets, informational newsletters, photos, placement on mailing lists and statistics. Publications include information pamphlets on Saint Lucia. **How to Contact:** Write, call or visit. Responds to most inquiries immediately. **Tips:** ''Make initial contact in writing.'' Recent information request: Relevant data on Saint Lucia's involvement in settlement of international claims by lump sum agreements.

1612• SOUTH AFRICAN EMBASSY
3051 Massachusetts Ave. NW, Washington DC 20008. (202)232-4400. Contact Person: Minister, Information. **Description:** Embassy representing South Africa in the US and distributing information on South Africa. **Services:** Provides historical, interpretative, technical and trade information covering all aspects related to South Africa. Offers aid in arranging interviews, brochures/pamphlets, informational newsletters, photos, placement on mailing lists, statistics and telephone reference services. Publications on South Africa available. **How to Contact:** Write. Responds to most inquiries within a week. **Tips:** Recent information request: The question of political freedom in Africa.

1613• EMBASSY OF SPAIN
Information Office, 2700 15th St. NW, Washington DC 20009. (202)265-1084. Contact Person: Information Counselor, or Information Attaché. **Description:** Government agency of a foreign government providing US public with information about Spain; and providing Spanish government with information about US. **Services:** Provides bibliographical, historical and referral information on Spain. Offers aid in arranging interviews, annual reports, biographies, brochures/pamphlets, clipping services, informational newsletters, limited library facilities, photos, research assistance and statistics. **How to Contact:** Write. Responds to most inquiries within a week. ''Photos must be returned for our files; credit should be given to embassy if photos used.'' **Tips:** ''Write a specific query well in advance of deadline.'' Recent information request: Spelling of names and titles of various members of Spanish royal household.

TITLE INDEX

B

C

Country Music Hall of Fame 83
Crayon, Water Color and Craft Institute, Inc. 84
Creation Research Society 1068
Creative Education Foundation 292
Credit Union National Association 176
Criminal Justice Statistics Association 1012
Crochet Association International 85

Cruise Lines International Association 1430
CSA Fraternal Life 429
Custody Action for Lesbian Mothers (CALM) 466
Customs Service 1013
Cystic Fibrosis Foundation 681

D

Dali Foundation, Inc., The Salvador 86
Daly Associates, Inc. 234
Dance Critics Association 87
Dance Notation Bureau, Inc. 88
Danish Brotherhood in America, The 430
Data Center, The 945
Data Courier, Inc. 946
Day Care & Child Development Council of America 467
Deer Unlimited of America, Inc. 19
Defense Logistics Agency 607
Delta Houseboat Rental Association 1431
Deltiologists of America 790
Democratic National Committee 1170
Democratic Socialists of America 1171
Dental Library 682
Department of Agriculture 518
Department of Agriculture (USDA)/National Agricultural Library 519
Department of Commerce 177
Department of Defense 608
Department of Defense, Audio-Visual Division 609
Department of Energy 359
Department of Justice 1014
Department of State 610

Department of the Army 611
Department of the Interior 360
Department of the Navy, Office of Information 612
Department of the Navy, Office of Naval Research 613
Department of the Treasury 178
Desert Botanical Garden 20
DIALOG Information Services, Inc. 947
Dickens House Museum, The 981
Direct Marketing Association 179
Direct Selling Association 180
Discount America 181
Disney World, Walt 791
Disneyland 792
Dividends from Space 1235
Doctors Ought to Care (DOC) 683
Do-It-Yourself Research Institute 1320
Doll Collectors of America, Inc. 793
Dow Chemical Company, The 1236
Dow Jones News/Retrieval Service 948
Drum Corps International, Inc. 89
Dude Ranchers' Association, The 1432
Dull Men's Club, The 1321
Dupont de Nemours and Company, E.I. 1237

E

E.C.R.I. 684
Earthscan/International Institute of Environment and Development 361
Earthwatch: Field Research Corps 362
East Germany (see German Democratic Republic, Embassy of the)
Easter Seal Research Foundation 685
East-West Center, The 1558
Eckrich and Sons, Inc., Peter 520
Economic Research Service Reference Center 521
Edgewater Community Council 1172

Edison Electric Institute 1238
Educational Film Library Association 235
Educational Foundation for Nuclear Science 1239
Edward-Dean Museum of Decorative Arts 90
Egyptian Embassy 1592
Eighteen Nineties Society, The (incorporating the Francis Thompson Society) 982
Eisenhower Library, Dwight D. 737
Electric Vehicle Council 1478
Electronic Industries Association 1240
Electronic Realty Associates (ERA) 850

F

G

Grody/Tellem Communications 1376
Grumman Corporation 1486
Guild of Professional Drycleaners 578
Gunflint Northwoods Outfitters 1434

Guttmacher Institute, The Alan 472
Guyon Society, Rene 1328
Gypsy Lore Society 436

H

Hackley Collection, E. Azalia 97
Hair Science Institute 579
Hakluyt Society, The 744
Halt—An Organization of Americans for Legal Reform 1020
Handwriting Analysis Research Library 242
Handy-Cap Horizons, Inc. 1435
Hanna-Barbera Productions 243
Hardwood Plywood Manufacturers Association 1120
Harness Tracks of America, Inc. 1377
Harris and Associates, Louis 1296
Hastings Center, The 1297
Haunt Hunters, The 1329
Hayden Planetarium (American Museum) 1220
Hayes Presidential Center, Rutherford B. 745
Hazelden Foundation 905
Headwear Institute of America 580
Health Insurance Association of America 184
HEATH Resource Center 307
Hemlock Society 1330
Hershey Museum of American Life 746
Higgins Library of Agricultural Technology 530

Hirshhorn Museum and Sculpture Garden 98
Hohner, Inc., M. 99
Hollywood Studio Collector's Club 799
Holt International Children's Services 473
Holt-Atherton Pacific Center for Western Studies 747
Home Box Office, Inc. 244
Home Economics Reading Service, Inc. 858
Homemakers' Equal Rights Association (HERA) 859
Homosexual Information Center, Inc. 1331
Honeywell 1244
Hoose Philosophy Library 1077
Hoover Presidential Library, Herbert 748
Horticultural Society of New York, The 25
Household International 185
Hoya Society International, The 26
HUD User 860
Human Rights Internet 1298
Humane Society of the United States, The 27
Humanities Research Center (HRC) 1299
Hymn Society of America, Inc., The 1078

I

IMC Needlecraft 100
Immigration History Society 437
Impact 1175
Imperial Knife 861
INA Archives 186
Independent Petroleum Association of America 375
Independent Professional Typists Network 1528
India, Embassy of 1598
Indian and Colonial Research Center 749
Indian Arts and Crafts Board 101
Industrial Fabrics Association International 1121
In-Fact, Research and Information Service 951

Info-Mart 952
Informatics General Corporation 1245
Information Access Company 953
Information Center on Children's Cultures (United States Committee for UNICEF) 1561
Information Documentation 954
Information Futures 955
Information Industry Association 956
Information on Demand 957
Information Services on Latin America (ISLA) 1562
Informed Homebirth 474
Institute for Burn Medicine 687
Institute for Child Behavior Research 688

J

K

L

Lockheed Missiles and Space Company 1252
London Club 1025
London Research Center, Jack 991
Loners on Wheels, Inc. 1338
Longwood Gardens 31

Los Angeles Public Library 967
Luce Press Clippings, Inc. 935
Lutheran Church—Missouri Synod 1082
Lykes Bros. Steamship Co., Inc. 1492

M

Magic Lantern Society of the US and Canada 809
Make Today Count, Inc. 908
Man Watchers, Inc. 1339
Mandala Holistic Health 693
Manufacturers Hanover Corporation 192
Maple Research Laboratory 538
Marble Collectors Society of America 810
March of Dimes Birth Defect Foundation 694
Marina Sports Medicine and Health Promotion Center 1384
Marine Corps 619
Marine Corps Aviation Museum 620
Marine Land of Florida 32
Marine Technology Society 379
Marquandia Society for Studies in History and Literature 1303
Marquetry Society of America 114
Marriott's Great America 811
Mayer Library, Louis B., The American Film Institute 252
Maytag Company, The 866
Media Alliance 253
Media Center for Children 254
Medline Data Base 695
Mennonite Library and Archives 1083
Men's Fashion Association of America 585
Men's Garden Clubs of America, Inc. 33
Men's Rights, Inc. (MR, Inc.) 1340
Metascience Foundation 1253
Metro-Help/National Runaway Switchboard 479
Metropolitan Museum of Art, The 115
Metropolitan Organization to Counter Sexual Assault 909

Mexico, Embassy of 1604
Mid-Continent Railway Museum 1493
Migrant Legal Action Program 539
Mobil Corporation 380
Monsanto Company 1254
Moore & Associates, Julie 34
Moorland-Spingarn Research Center 442
Mormon History Association 1084
Morris Society, United States Branch, The William 992
Morrison Planetarium 1255
Morton Library, Sterling (The Morton Arboretum) 35
Motor Bus Society, Inc. 1494
Motorcyle Safety Foundation 1495
Movie Star News 255
MTA Travelers-Wheelers RV Club, The 1438
Muscular Dystrophy Association 696
Museum of Afro American History 443
Museum of Cartoon Art 116
Museum of Geology 381
Museum of Independent Telephony 256
Museum of Modern Art 117
Museum of Modern Art (Film Stills Archive) 257
Museum of Modern Art of Latin America 118
Museum of Repertoire Americana 119
Museum of the Confederacy, The 753
Museum of the Fur Trade 754
Musical Museum, The 120
Mutual of Omaha 193
Mystic Marinelife Aquarium 36
Mythopoeic Society, The 993

N

N.A.P. Consumer Electronics Corporation 1256
National Abortion Rights Action League 1181
National Academy of Design 121
National Academy of Television Arts & Sciences, Inc. 258

National Action Forum for Midlife and Older Women 1341
National Action/Research on the Military Industrial Complex (NARMIC) 1182

O

P

T

Tippers International 1353
Titanic Historical Society, Inc. 768
Toastmasters International 274
Tobacco Growers Information Committee 559
Tobacco Institute, The 719
Tourist House Associates 1448
Tourmobile Sightseeing 1449
Toy Manufacturers of America 835

Tranet (Transnational Network) 1354
Transit Advertising Association, Inc. 210
Travel Industry Association of America 1450
Travel Information Center 1451
Traveler's Information Exchange 1452
Twain Memorial, The Mark 1003
Twinings Tea 560

U

Unicorns Unanimous 836
Union Camp Corporation 408
Union for Radical Political Economics 1206
Union Pacific Railroad 1509
United Church of Christ 1094
United Farm Agency, Inc. 879
United Fresh Fruit and Vegetable Association
    561
United Humanitarians 49
United Mine Workers of America 1546
United Nations Center against Apartheid 1576
United Nations Development Program 1577
United Nations Economic Commission for
    Europe 1578
United Presbyterian Church, United States of
    America 1095
United States Air Force Museum 630
United States Amateur Confederation of Roller
    Skating 1413
United States Army Air Defense Artillery Mu-
    seum 631
United States Army Military History Institute
    632
United States Association for the Club of
    Rome 1579
United States Capitol Historical Society 769
United States Chamber of Commerce 211
United States Choice in Currency Commission
    212
United States Civil Defense Council 1207
United States Commission on Civil Rights 633
United States Committee for Refugees 1580
United States Croquet Association 1414

United States Golf Association 1415
United States Hockey Hall of Fame 1416
United States ICAS Committee 1417
United States Jaycees, The 1208
United States Marshals Service 1042
United States Metric Association 1276
United States Military Academy 634
United States Naval Academy Museum 635
United States Olympic Committee 1418
United States Postal Service 1143
United States Soccer Federation 1419
United States Space Education Association
    1277
United States Sports Academy 1420
United States Student Association 329
United States Tobacco Museum 562
United States Travel and Tourism Administra-
    tion 1453
United States Travel Data Center 1454
United States Trivia Association, Ltd. 837
United States Trotting Association 1421
United Steel Workers of America 1547
United Way of America 925
University of Tennessee Space Institute
    (UTSI) 1278
Upholstered Furniture Action Council (UFAC)
    880
Urban Land Institute 409
Urban Mass Transportation Administration
    1510
Urban Wildlife Research Center, Inc. 50
Utah Field House of Natural History and Di-
    nosaur Gardens 410

V

Vacation Exchange Club 1455
Vampire Research Center 1355
Vanderbilt Television News Archive 275
Vascular Diagnostic Services, Inc. (VDS) 720
Vegetarian Information Service, Inc. 1356

Veterans Administration 636
Veterans of Foreign Wars of the United States
    637
Vinyl Siding Institute 881

W

Y

Z

SUBJECT INDEX

Please Note: The numbers in this index correspond to entry numbers in Writer's Resource Guide.

A

B

C

D

E

F

G

H

I

J

K

L

M

N

O

P

T

U

V

W

Y

Z

Other Writer's Digest Books

General Writing Books
  Beginning Writer's Answer Book, edited by Polking, et al $9.95
  How to Get Started in Writing, by Peggy Teeters $10.95
  Law and the Writer, edited by Polking and Meranus (paper) $7.95
  Make Every Word Count, by Gary Provost (paper) $6.95
  Teach Yourself to Write, by Evelyn Stenbock $12.95
  Treasury of Tips for Writers, edited by Marvin Weisbord (paper) $6.95
  Writer's Encyclopedia, edited by Kirk Polking $19.95
  Writer's Market, $18.95
  Writer's Resource Guide, edited by Bernadine Clark $16.95
  Writing for the Joy of It, by Leonard Knott $11.95
Magazine/News Writing
  Craft of Interviewing, by John Brady $9.95
  Magazine Writing: The Inside Angle, by Art Spikol $12.95
  Newsthinking: The Secret of Great Newswriting, by Bob Baker $11.95
  Stalking the Feature Story, by William Ruehlmann $9.95
  Write On Target, by Connie Emerson $12.95
  Writing and Selling Non-Fiction, by Hayes B. Jacobs $12.95
Fiction Writing
  Fiction Writer's Help Book, by Maxine Rock $12.95
  Fiction Writer's Market, edited by Jean Fredette $17.95
  Handbook of Short Story Writing, edited by Dickson and Smythe (paper) $6.95
  How to Write Best-Selling Fiction, by Dean R. Koontz $13.95
  How to Write Short Stories that Sell, by Louise Boggess $9.95
  One Way to Write Your Novel, by Dick Perry (paper) $6.95
  Writing Romance Fiction—For Love and Money, by Helene Schellenberg Barnhart $14.95
  Writing the Novel: From Plot to Print, by Lawrence Block $10.95
Special Interest Writing Books
  Children's Picture Book: How to Write It, How to Sell It, by Ellen E.M. Roberts $17.95
  Complete Book of Scriptwriting, by J. Michael Straczynski $14.95
  How to Make Money Writing . . . Fillers, by Connie Emerson $12.95
  How to Write and Sell Your Personal Experiences, by Lois Duncan $10.95
  How to Write & Sell (Your Sense of) Humor, by Gene Perret $12.95
  How to Write "How-To" Books and Articles, by Raymond Hull (paper) $8.95
  Mystery Writer's Handbook, edited by Lawrence Treat (paper) $8.95
  Poet's Handbook, by Judson Jerome $11.95
  TV Scriptwriter's Handbook, by Alfred Brenner $12.95
  Travel Writer's Handbook, by Louise Purwin Zobel $13.95
  Writing and Selling Science Fiction, Compiled by The Science Fiction Writers of America (paper) $7.95
  Writing for Children & Teenagers, by Wyndham/Madison $10.95
  Writing to Inspire, by Gentz, Roddy, et al $14.95
The Writing Business
  Complete Handbook for Freelance Writers, by Kay Cassill $14.95
  How You Can Make $20,000 a Year Writing, by Nancy Edmonds Hanson (paper) $6.95
  Jobs for Writers, edited by Kirk Polking $11.95
  Writer's Survival Guide: How to Cope with Rejection, Success, and 99 Other Hang-Ups of the Writing Life, by Jean and Veryl Rosenbaum $12.95

To order directly from the publisher, include $1.50 postage and handling for 1 book and 50¢ for each additional book. Allow 30 days for delivery.

Writer's Digest Books, Department B
9933 Alliance Road, Cincinnati OH 45242
Prices subject to change without notice.